CONTEMPORARY
PSYCHOLOGY

A Series of Books in Psychology

Editors:
Richard C. Atkinson
Jonathan Freedman
Gardner Lindzey
Richard F. Thompson

INTRODUCTION TO

CONTEMPORARY PSYCHOLOGY

EDMUND FANTINO
GEORGE S. REYNOLDS

UNIVERSITY OF CALIFORNIA, SAN DIEGO

 W. H. FREEMAN AND COMPANY
SAN FRANCISCO

Library of Congress Cataloging in Publication Data

Fantino, Edmund J
    Introduction to contemporary psychology.

    Includes bibliographies and index.
    1. Psychology. I. Reynolds, George Stanley,
1936-   joint author. II. Title. [DNLM: 1.
Psychology. BF121 F216i]
BF121.F25   150   74–23201
ISBN 0–7167–0761–6

9 8 7 6 5 4 3 2

GENERAL PLAN OF THIS VOLUME

CONTENTS

MAJOR AREAS OF CONTEMPORARY PSYCHOLOGY

Photographs Accompanying Unit Introductions

UNIT ONE
Learning and Memory

Japanese children playing violins. [United Press International Photo]

UNIT TWO
Motivation and Emotion

Russian gymnast Olga Korbut working on the balance beam. [V. Un Da-sin. TASS from Sovfoto]

UNIT THREE
Thought and Language

Lana the chimpanzee selecting a sequence of symbols in a study of symbol manipulation by primates. [Courtesy of the Yerkes Regional Primate Research Center, Emory University, Atlanta, Georgia]

UNIT FOUR
Sensation and Perception

Indian Yogi L. S. Rao holds a burning rag in his hand as he walks on burning coals. [United Press International Photo]

UNIT FIVE
Instinct and Heredity

A young monkey clinging to a large dog. [Courtesy of William A. Mason, University of California, Davis]

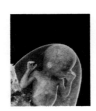

UNIT SIX
Developmental Psychology

A human fetus eighteen weeks from conception. [Photo by Lennart Nilsson, from *A Child is Born*]

UNIT SEVEN
Social Psychology

"People in love." [David Powers/Jeroboam Inc.]

UNIT EIGHT
The Study of Personality

Sigmund Freud in his study. [Historical Pictures Service, Chicago]

UNIT NINE
The Study of Abnormal Personality

"Ohio Insane Asylum." [Jerry Cooke © 1964]

UNIT TEN
Psychotherapy

Ivar Lovaas with two autistic boys. [Photo by Allan Grant]

PREFACE

We have attempted to present the vast panorama of contemporary psychology, with its wide range of interests, view points, methods, and theories, between the covers of this single volume. As psychologists, we naturally have our own personal prejudices and points of view. In writing this book, we have resolved to lay them aside, temporarily, and to present each area of contemporary psychology from the point of view that prevails among those specializing in that area. At the same time, we have indicated where apparently conflicting points of view in fact agree and where further agreement is likely in the future.

In the first half of the book, we are concerned with the basic psychological processes that underlie human behavior. We look at the principles of learning, remembering, thinking, motivation, and instinct; at the workings of our senses and the rules of perception; and at how the human mind learns about and understands the world.

In the second half of the book, we turn our attention to psychological knowledge divided, not by processes, but by areas. In a sense, our study of basic processes lays the groundwork for an appreciation of these areas. We examine the development of individuals; the human personality; social psychology; abnormal personality; and various methods of psychotherapy. These areas of study cut across all of the psychological processes.

Writing an eclectic account of contemporary psychology has been stimulating and —dare we say it?—fun. We hope that the reader will share both the stimulation and the fun.

Throughout the volume, the reader will find that glossary items are indicated by brown underscores where they first appear in the text. The glossary begins on page 565.

We extend our gratitude to our teachers, colleagues, students, and staff (especially Karen Fiegener and Rosemary Painter, who helped prepare the manuscript).

December 1974   E.J.F.
                                                                                G.S.R.

CONTEMPORARY PSYCHOLOGY

CHAPTER ONE

Origins, Issues, Methods, and Theories

In the beginning was philosophy. At the dawn of the modern era, thinkers who studied and discussed the world and its phenomena were called philosophers. Gradually, over the centuries, specialized fields of study appeared within philosophy. As knowledge accumulated about particular types of natural phenomena, separate sciences emerged— astronomy, the study of the universe beyond the earth; chemistry, the study of substances and their interactions; biology, the study of living organisms. The study of matter and energy became physics only after centuries of being "natural philosophy." A similar story can be sketched for all of the fields that compose modern science.

Psychology, the study of all forms of animate behavior, is one of the youngest of the sciences, not having gained recognized independent status as a field of study until well into the twentieth century. The word *psychology* predates the science by at least two centuries, having originally meant the study of the soul, or psyche. *Psyche,* which referred to "the animating principle" in men and other living creatures, can be traced back to an ancient Greek word meaning simply "to breathe." The foundations of the modern science of psychology were laid by psychologists, philosophers, physicists, physicians, biologists, and naturalists, among others.

In part, psychology's independence from philosophy was delayed by the complexity of its subject matter—creatures that breathe do a great variety of different things! Even today, one might well ask: how can the study of hearing and the treatment of mental illness both be part of psychology? Or, what is it that students of instinct, of thinking, of development, and of personality have in common? In answer to these questions, we can say that there *is* a common thread running through all of psychology: *an interest in gaining knowledge, by close and systematic observation, about everything that people and animals do.*

We have divided our *Introduction to Contemporary Psychology* into two parts. One deals with the basic psychological processes:

Learning and Memory
Motivation and Emotion
Thought and Language
Sensation and Perception
Instinct and Heredity

The second deals with the major areas of contemporary psychology, each of which is concerned with all of the psychological processes from its own particular point of view:

Developmental Psychology
Social Psychology
The Study of Personality
The Study of Abnormal Personality
Psychotherapy

POINTS OF VIEW

As the book unfolds, the reader will discover not only many recurrent themes but also continuities and discontinuities, harmonious views and conflicting views. Although differences among psychologists derive mainly from the diversity of their areas of interest and points of view, there are basic, important differences in method and theory as well. For example, a persistently recurrent theme in contemporary psychology is the difference between *mentalists* and *behaviorists*. Although there are many other differences among psychologists, this is one of the most important. Behaviorists limit their study to overt, observable behavior, although some maintain that covert, invisible thoughts and emotions are also behavior. Behaviorists construct their theories only in terms of observable and repeatable *functional* relationships between behavior and its environmental causes: what specific environmental events function to bring about what specific behavior? Mentalists are concerned with the workings of the human mind. Mentalists theorize about the way the mind must be constructed in order to perform its functions, and frequently they make use of mathematical and computer *models* of the mind's functioning. Chapter 2 contains a representative sample of contemporary mentalistic views; Chapter 4 introduces contemporary behaviorism. We shall see that both groups have had and continue to have great impact on the

progress of contemporary psychology.

This book is intentionally eclectic. Instead of adopting a single personal point of view—or none at all—we try to present each different approach to contemporary psychology from the point of view of those psychologists who practice it: when we write about development, we try to give the point of view of developmental psychologists; when we write about behavior, we try to give the point of view of behavioral psychologists; when we describe Freud's theories and psychoanalysis, we try to give the point of view of Freudians. And so on, through all of contemporary psychology. This method has the disadvantage of producing a segmented book, but today's psychology *is* segmented. We know that students profit most from multiple viewpoints and that it is neither proper nor realistic to attempt to force all of psychology into a single, arbitrary mold. At the same time, we present multiple viewpoints within areas of psychology where they exist. To take one example: in presenting social psychology, we find it possible to include both the mentalistic and the behavioristic points of view. Although we feel that there is not necessarily any incompatibility among prevailing psychological points of view, we also feel that the introductory student deserves a fair look at, and a sure feel for, all of them. We have included ample opportunities for, and examples of, comparison and even reconciliation.

Before we proceed further with our outline of this book, we should explain the way we intend to treat the relation of physiology and psychology. Behaviors are correlated with physiological events in much the same way that physiological events are correlated with electrochemical events. Considerable progress has been made in finding specific correlations between the physiological and the behavioral. For example, the general electrical activity of our brains changes in predictable ways when we go to sleep or when we become truly interested in someone or something (Chapter 10). The removal of parts of the brain can produce changes in a person's appetite (Chapter 5) and his personality (Chapter 29). Perhaps the best-explored physiological-behavioral correlations are in the sensory area (Chapter 12). In this book we have chosen to bring in the physiological correlates of behaviors whenever they are useful in understanding the behaviors. Thus, for example, we look at how the sensory nervous system works in Unit IV, Sensation and Perception, and we look at the effects of brain damage on needs and drives in Unit II, Motivation and Emotion.

BASIC PSYCHOLOGICAL PROCESSES

Keeping in mind the common goal of psychologists as well as the fact that we shall encounter a multiplicity of topics and viewpoints, let us begin our study of contemporary psychology with a brief sampling of the basic psychological processes we shall discuss in the first part of this book.

Unit I. Learning and Memory   How does a child *learn* to play the violin? How do you *train* a lion to do backflips? Why do we *forget* things that we once knew very well? What is the best way to commit a list of irregular French verbs to *memory*? The various meanings of "learning" and "memory" that are implicit in these questions are partly the result of the structure of the English language, which leads us to categorize many different events we observe as either "learned" or "memorized." The prevailing trend in contemporary psychology is to trace instances of learning and memory to one common core: a special type of event, called "reinforcement" by most theorists. Thus, the circus lion is said to turn backflips because that is the behavior that results in its daily ration of food; a person is said to remember some things and forget others because those things that are recalled result,

or once resulted, in specially meaningful, and therefore reinforcing, associations. But is this the whole story? In Unit I, we shall explore this topic further.

Unit II. Motivation and Emotion   *Why* is a young man going to a party? *Why* is a politician praising his country? *Why* is Mrs. Smith eating at the Bur-Gur Pit Restaurant at 12:45 PM? Such questions may be trivial or important, depending on circumstances; they may be answered well or badly, depending on one's knowledge and judgment; and the answers may be simple or complex. In any case, such questions are relatively inaccessible to close and systematic study and thus serve to illustrate the problem faced by those who attempt to explain the behaviors of everyday life. Furthermore, questions of causation are hard to answer because one can always ask why the answer works. ("The young man is going to the party to meet his friends." Why? "Because he has an affiliative need." Why? "Because that is a characteristic of young men." Why? Because . . . ," etc.) Nevertheless, such questions have absorbed enormous amounts of innovative psychological work, and some points are fairly certain: for example, animals, and people too, will rarely work hard for things that they already have in sufficient quantity. But motivational psychologists have not yet provided definitive answers to such questions as why some people are hard-working and others are lazy, or why some go to parties while others study—but they continue to try. We shall examine the scope of motivational research in Unit II and shall also discuss a closely related field, the study of emotion.

Unit III. Thought and Language   Suppose a friend of yours writes you a letter in which she says, "They are sailing ships." The meaning of the sentence is different depending on whether she has just mentioned sailors or ships. If the topic is sailors, then the ambiguous word, "sailing," is probably part of the verb "are sailing." But if the topic is the ships, then "sailing" is probably an adjective in the phrase "sailing ships." Such contextual determinants of meaning are only part of the story according to contemporary psycholinguists, as we shall discover in Unit III.

Unit IV. Sensation and Perception Many people who live near an airport complain about the noise of jets. Assuming that most of them would be satisfied if the planes were only half as loud, how many engines must be removed from a four-engine plane in order for it to sound half as loud? Two of them? How can we make sure? This brings up a central problem in the study of the sensory processes: how is the magnitude of sensation (for example, the loudness of the engines) related to the magnitude of the stimulus (for example, the number of engines). To answer our question, suppose we simply poll people about the loudness of a plane's engines. For the sake of safety, we will keep the plane on the ground. Experiments have shown that people will report that stopping two or even three of the four engines does not make the plane sound half as loud. In fact, if we put two four-engine planes together and start up all eight engines, we will have to stop *seven* of the engines in order to reduce the total loudness by half! We shall discuss the surprising relations of stimulus magnitude to the magnitude of sensation in Unit IV, along with a variety of other phenomena related to the way we perceive the world around us.

Unit V. Instinct and Heredity Suppose that we raise several generations of ferrets (weasel-like creatures who kill rats) in a laboratory environment and generations of rats in the same way, so that it is impossible that either the ferrets or the rats could have learned anything at all about each other either from their own experience or from that of their parents or their grandparents. Then suppose that we put a ferret and a rat together in a bare room. We would typically find that both rat and ferret behave like their wild ancestors: the rat lies on its back and bares its teeth as the ferret approaches; the ferret grabs the rat by the hind foot, violently turns it over, and then kills it by crushing its neckbones between its teeth. Both animals exhibit stereotyped behavior that must be instinctive (part of their inherited nature), since they have had no chance at all to learn it, either by themselves or from any living ancestor. An interesting modification of this demonstration might take place if the ferret and the rat were raised together from birth. There is good reason to expect (as we shall see in Chapter 15) that they would grow up as friends. In Unit V, we shall discuss species-specific behaviors as well as the influence of genetic inheritance on individual differences.

MAJOR AREAS OF CONTEMPORARY PSYCHOLOGY

In the second half of the book, we shall discuss five major areas of research in contemporary psychology.

Unit VI. Developmental Psychology What was once called "child psychology" has grown up: contemporary developmental psychology deals with the whole span of growth, maturity, and aging. But the emphasis of the field is still on the formative years of childhood. It is easy for adults to forget the perspectives of childhood. For children, the dining-room table may be at eye level; a tennis ball may be as relatively large as a basketball is for an adult; things may no longer seem to exist if you cannot see them; and the same number of objects may seem to be larger if they are spaced out than if they are bunched together. The world of the child —vastly different from ours physically, perceptually, intellectually, and behaviorally—is the main subject of Unit VI.

Unit VII. Social Psychology   There are obvious behavioral differences among human groups —cultural differences, social differences, regional differences, and so forth. In our culture, for example, some people are regarded as highly attractive, and others are regarded as definitely not attractive. Why should this be so? And why do two particular people find each other mutually attractive? In regard to the latter question, the answer that has emerged from social psychological research is surprisingly simple, as we shall see in Unit VII. It points to the very chancy nature of attractions, some of which may change our lives profoundly.

Unit VIII. The Study of Personality   The American psychologist William James (1842–1910) quoted a carpenter of his acquaintance as having said, "There is very little difference between one man and another; but what little there is, is very important." James observed, "This distinction seems to me to go to the root of the matter." In Unit VIII, we shall discuss some of the reasons for the individual differences that are studied by contemporary psychology.

Because people differ in their abilities and skills, there arises the practical task of assessing differences among individuals. Who will go to college or medical school? work in a bank? sell stocks and bonds? be an astronaut? Psychologists have often been asked to help select the people who will be most happy, successful, and effective at a particular job. The methods for constructing, using, and evaluating the *psychological tests* by which people are judged are described and criticized in Unit VIII.

Unit IX. The Study of Abnormal Personality   In the normal course of events, we all have our own worries, and we sometimes encounter people who are truly shackled by anxiety over some hang-up or other—but we rarely encounter anyone who is so little in touch with reality as a schizophrenic, who might address us in this manner:

> I have been now on this property on and off for a long time. I cannot say the exact time because we are absorbed by the air at night, and they bring back people. . . .

In our society, people who talk in this way are generally judged to be ill and are confined in mental hospitals. Why does a person talk this way? Is it a disorder of language? the result of brain damage? an intentional escape from responsibility? or none or all of these? This is one of the topics we shall discuss in Unit IX.

Unit X. Psychotherapy   A psychotherapist of the behaviorist school, who practices what is known as behavior modification, once encountered an adult woman who weighed only forty-seven pounds and was progressively losing weight because she would not eat. In most ways, the woman was quite normal: she enjoyed social contact with people and especially liked TV shows. Before treatment with behavior modification, however, she had been treated unsuccessfully with several therapeutic techniques and was on the verge of starvation. Yet behavior modification had her eating again—and ultimately enjoying it—in a few days. How it was done is explained in Unit X.

THE PSYCHOLOGICAL POINT OF VIEW

It is apparent that a great many interesting and
diverse topics are explored by contemporary psychology. But in spite of the broad range of attitudes,
interests, approaches, and techniques, there is also
a common core: a psychological point of view that
sets off psychology from other sciences and from
other disciplines. Consider the following illustrations. A person may study the electrical activity
of the nerves that run from the eye to the brain.
He is a psychologist—not a physiologist—if his
focus is on how people see, not how the nerves
work. A person may study an animal's instinctive
behavior. He is a psychologist—not a biologist—if
his focus is on the behavior itself, not how the
instincts evolved. A person may simulate human
thinking with an elegant computer and its programs.
He is a psychologist—not an electrical engineer—if
his focus is on how people think, not how the
computer works. A person may monitor the changes
in heart rate and breathing that accompany an
emotion. He is a psychologist—not a physician—if
his focus is on the emotion, not the physical
health of the subject. A person may write a fictional
biography in an attempt to describe the world of
the mentally ill. He is a psychologist—not a fiction
writer—if what interests him is the study of mental
illness, not the artistic interpretation of mental
illness. What these people have in common is the
psychological point of view—an interest in what
living organisms do.

EXPERIMENTAL SUBJECTS

The diversity of interests among psychologists is
mirrored in the diversity of the organisms they
observe. In the laboratory, psychologists have studied
the behaviors of worms, cockroaches, sea anemones,
mice, rats, pigeons, monkeys, other animals, and,

of course, human subjects. For obvious reasons,
psychologists leave their laboratories to study such
animals as wild baboons, giraffes, and elephants.

In regard to their treatment of humans and
animals, psychologists are bound by the same ethical
and legal restraints that bind all members of society.
In addition, they have a rigid code of professional
ethics, which prescribes standards for the treatment
of experimental subjects. Psychologists must avoid
physical harm to their animal subjects whenever
possible and must not inflict pain on them except
as a necessary and integral part of a fully justified
experiment. Physical and psychological harm and
pain are normally out of the question with regard
to humans; when it is necessary to mislead or
misinform a human subject in the course of an
experiment or to cause pain, the experimenter must
obtain the subject's permission and fully explain
the experiment to the subject after, and sometimes
even before, the person participates.

THE METHODS OF PSYCHOLOGY

As scientists in pursuit of knowledge, psychologists
respect and practice what is called the *scientific method.*
There is nothing mysterious about the scientific
method. Indeed, it is easily summarized by listing its
three essential ingredients: (1) reasonable certainty,
(2) repeatability, and (3) communicability.

  1. *Reasonable certainty.* When we say that doing A
results in or causes B or that D only results from
doing C, we want to be as sure as we can be that it
is A and not something else that causes B and that
D will not occur without the prior occurrence of C.
Later in this chapter we shall discuss two key
concepts that are related to reasonable certainty in
experimental results: they are (a) *control groups,* which
assure that extraneous causes are not operating, and

(b) the relatively easy distinction between *necessary causes* and *sufficient causes.*

2. *Repeatability.* No scientific statement retains its credibility if it is based on a demonstration or experiment that is not repeatable. For example, before we and our colleagues can believe a friend of ours who says that his work has established a certain relationship—say, that pain causes aggression—we want to see his work repeated by other trustworthy investigators, if not repeated by ourselves personally.

3. *Communicability.* In order to assure repeatability, which is a necessary adjunct to reasonable certainty, we have to be able to communicate to other people exactly what we have done and exactly what we think we have discovered. Communication requires accurate (usually *operational*) *definitions* and *measurements* that allow us to employ *numbers*, which are more precise than words.

To summarize: *the scientific method enables us to know, with reasonable certainty, relationships between causes and effects and to communicate them accurately to other people so that they can demonstrate the relationships themselves at first hand.* This, in a few words, is the essence of science—the struggle to know and to understand causes and effects and eventually to predict future events and thus to gain control over previously uncontrollable events.

Science thrives on experiment, but it also benefits from *introspection* (thoughtful self-examination) and simple observation. We shall examine these approaches to knowledge before discussing the advantages of experimentation as a route to knowledge.

Introspection   Once upon a time, the study of psychology consisted entirely of descriptions of what people sensed and felt; these descriptions were based on self-examination. Today, introspection remains important, because some psychological phenomena, such as thinking, can be observed directly only by self-examination. But introspection is no longer enough; scientific data must be accessible and repeatable. Using introspection alone, there is no way that one investigator can be sure that what he feels or senses is the same as what another investigator does. For example, one goal of introspection was to establish *unitary sensations* that could not be broken down into more elementary components of sensation. For example, the sensation of "wet" on the fingers can be simulated by the sensations of "smooth" and "cold." This can be demonstrated by having experimental subjects touch smooth and cold plastic wrapping tape in the dark: it will feel wet. Such a demonstration supports the results of one's own careful introspection, which suggests that "wet" can be produced by "cold" and "smooth." But there are sensations that cannot be agreed upon so easily. A famous debate centered on the nature of the sensation of "green." Is one's experience of green unitary, or can it be broken down into other sensations? Psychologists could not agree. Some insisted that green was a unitary sensation, but others insisted that green was a combined sensation that was just as yellow as it was blue. Because of the introspective nature of the data, there was no argument or demonstration or experiment that one side could perform to convince the other unequivocally that it was wrong in its analysis of the sensation of green. Lacking reliable communicability and repeatability, and so certainty, introspection failed as the single method of study in psychology.

Observation   A great deal can be learned about behaviors simply by observing them. Regularities, recurring activities, and sequences of events may be noted. The science of animal behavior, *ethology*

(Chapter 15), is largely based on simple but intensive and thorough observations of what animals do in their natural habitat, and social psychology (Unit VII) has derived many ideas from observing what people do in everyday situations.

But there are difficulties with pure observation. First, one's personal perspective may contribute *bias*, as in the old story of the six blind men who each examined a different part of an elephant and came away with very different impressions. Distortions can also be contributed by the observer's degree of care in watching and his expectations. Good observation avoids these pitfalls by having more than one observer of the same phenomenon so that reports may be compared. (In other words, not only do we have six observers but we also make sure they examine the same part or parts of the elephant.)

A more important limitation of observation as a method is that observation alone cannot establish cause; it can only uncover sequences and correlation. Suppose for example, that we observe that A and B invariably occur together. Although it is tempting to think that A causes B or B causes A, it may be that a third factor causes A and B to occur together. Even in cases where the occurrence of A is invariably followed by B, it is risky to conclude from observation alone that A causes B. It could be that A is necessary for B to occur, but, because other conditions are also necessary, A is not a *sufficient cause* of B. Or, A can be a sufficient cause of B, in the sense that A is always followed by B, but not be a *necessary cause*, because other factors besides A can cause B if A does not occur. Establishing causal relationships requires experiments in which we, as scientists, systematically manipulate the factors and deduce from the results of the manipulation how the causal relations actually work. Experimentation is, in fact, the most used and most useful and productive method in contemporary psychology.

Experimentation   Our word *experiment* comes from a Latin word meaning "to try, put to the test." Children are active experimenters: they squeeze things just to see what comes out, they tinker with mechanical toys to see what will happen when they push or pull this or that, and they work at getting other people to do things for them. Such experimenting can bring children enjoyment and satisfaction as they gain knowledge about the world.

As experimenters, we like to be able to change something in a situation and then observe what else changes as a result of our change. Of course, there are many things, like the age or height of a child, that we cannot change; however, we can observe a given child growing older or taller, or select among children of varying ages or heights. In either case—whether we actually manipulate something or merely select it—we call it an *independent variable* (we have independently established or selected its value). What changes as a result of our change in an independent variable is called a *dependent variable* (its value depends on the value we have independently established or selected).

An experiment seeks to establish the truth about some particular hypothesized cause-and-effect relationship. For example, in studying an animal's hunger we may relate increases in food deprivation (our independent variable might be the time since the animal last ate) to the amount of hunger (our dependent variable might be how large a weight the animal will move in order to get some food). In studying human motivation, we may relate the strength of a person's desire to succeed to his actual success. Or, in studying why people like each other, we may relate the similarity of their interests (*independent variable*) to the strength of the attachment (*dependent variable*) between the two people.

Two problems are immediately apparent. First, how do we measure these variables, and, indeed, what does it mean to measure them? Second, how do we know for sure that changes in the independent variable actually cause the changes we observe in the dependent variable? To answer the first question we must refer to the theory and practice of measurement; to answer the second question we must discuss (1) the art of *controlled experimentation,* (2) the evaluation of *statistical evidence* of change, and (3) techniques in the *experimental analysis of behavior.* We shall take up each of these topics in turn.

MEASUREMENT

It is convenient to show the relation between an independent and a dependent variable in a graph (such as Figures 1.1 and 1.2). Each point on a graph is determined by two values: (1) the value of the independent variable (on the horizontal scale) and (2) the value of the dependent variable (on the vertical scale).

Numerical scales vary greatly in meaning. Some do not result from measurements at all. For example, consider a roster of baseball players. When we identify baseball players by numbered jerseys, we are using numbers simply as names not as values. We could just as easily use letters. The numbers do have meaning to a baseball fan—Number 9 on the Oakland Athletics is identifiable, as was Number 44 on the Atlanta Braves—but the numbers are not assigned with regard to the amount of anything. Number 10 need not be bigger or better than Number 9; Number 9 need not be bigger or better than Number 4, and so on. Numbers in such a system are just names; they form a *nominal scale.*

Of course, it is more common to assign numbers according to the value or amount of some variable that is displayed. Suppose we numbered baseball players according to their weight or intelligence. These numbers would be more informative than

those in a nominal scale. We would know from their jerseys that Number 89 was heavier than Number 10 or that Number 4 was not so smart as Number 23. We would have what is called an *ordinal scale;* the numbers would tell us something about the order in which the players exhibited a characteristic. Psychologists use numbers in this way whenever they "rank-order" a set of items.

Numbers are even more informative when they have been assigned according to the rules of an *interval scale.* On such a scale, each increase from one number to the next represents an *equal* increase in the variable being numbered. We have an interval scale when we count objects, say oranges. The difference between 4 and 5 oranges is exactly the same (1 orange) as the difference between 1,004 and 1,005 oranges. Thus we can *meaningfully* add and subtract numbers from an interval scale, which we cannot do with numbers from an ordinal or nominal scale. It is *possible,* but *meaningless,* to add Number 5 (a pitcher) and Number 7 (a catcher) to get Number 12 (a shortstop).

A *ratio scale* permits us to multiply and to divide values as well as to add and to subtract them. On a ratio scale, such as a ruler, four units is *twice* as much as two units, and *half* as much as eight units. When we simply count oranges, we have a ratio scale as well as an interval scale, since 4 oranges is twice 2 oranges and half as many as 8 oranges. But if we talk about the *edibility* of oranges, we do not have a ratio scale: 4 oranges may not be twice as edible as 2, and 8 are certainly less than twice as edible as 4—few people would eat 8 oranges at a sitting. A common example of an interval scale that is not also a ratio scale can be found on thermometers. A temperature of 80° is twenty degrees higher than a temperature of 60°, and 60° is twenty degrees higher than 40°. But it is meaningless to say that the 80° temperature is *twice as warm* as the 40°

temperature. Once again, it is the rules by which numbers are assigned—measurement—that limit what we can meaningfully do with them.

An understanding of the *logic of measurement* is very important in contemporary psychology. For example, an interval scale is sometimes assumed to exist when there is really only an ordinal scale, and researchers, instead of limiting themselves to the claim that a score of 10 on a test is higher than a score of 5, mistakenly claim that a 10 is as much greater than a 5 as it is less than a 15. Psychologists must always ask what the numbers mean and how they were assigned.

DESIGNING CONTROLLED EXPERIMENTS

As we have said before, when we relate a dependent variable to an independent variable in an experiment, we want to be sure that no other variables have changed in a way that could misleadingly have caused the change in the dependent variable. For example, suppose we want to examine the effect of age on weight in children of ages two through six. We could select a group of children, weigh them, and make a graph of the total weight of children of each age against that age. Obviously, we would select the same number of children of each age, since it would be illogical to compare the total weight of six three-year-olds with that of eight four-year-olds. But other factors may not be so obvious: we would want to be sure that all the children are of normal height for their age, have normal (if not identical) diets, and are weighed on the same machine. Non-uniformity of these factors could introduce variations in our measurements; they could *confound* the relationship we want to establish. This is why we would want to *control* them—in this instance, to make them uniform.

A number of procedures have been worked out for controlling such potentially confounding variables.

Table 1.1
Control Groups for Our Study

GROUP	STUDIES IN JANUARY	STUDIES IN FEBRUARY
A	French	Spanish
B	Nothing	Spanish
C	Any Subject (physics for example)	Spanish
D	Chinese	Spanish

The following fictitious example will serve to introduce the notion of experimental control. Suppose that we want to assess the effect of having learned French on the speed with which people subsequently learn Spanish. We decide to teach French to a group of people and then see whether they learn Spanish more easily. But, more easily than whom? We need another group—or groups—for comparison. In Table 1.1, Group A is the one we have just mentioned. Group B provides a comparison group, since they did not study French earlier. If Group A learns Spanish faster than Group B, can we attribute the difference in speed to studying French earlier? Not with certainty. Perhaps studying anything at all will enhance the learning of Spanish; hence we add Group C. Or, perhaps studying any language will have an effect; hence we add Group D, which studies Chinese in January before attacking Spanish in February. What we have been doing is systematically adding *control groups* to rule out other possible causes. If we find that Group A shows a clear superiority over the other three Groups, then we can conclude with some confidence that learning French facilitates learning Spanish. (We shall refine the notion of *confidence* in the next section).

Since we are proposing to compare groups of people with respect to their speed of learning, we need to define how we are going to measure it. One way is to define speed of learning arbitrarily as the number of points earned on a final examination taken at the end of study. So, in comparing Group A with Group B, we might have the results shown in Table 1.2. The scores for Group A range from 72

Table 1.2
Scores on Spanish Exam (One Possibility)

Group A		Group B	
Student	Score	Student	Score
1	85	1	56
2	72	2	65
3	93	3	71
4	96	4	42
5	82	5	66
6	78	6	52
7	88	7	61
8	90	8	63
9	95	9	31
10	83	10	57
Average = 86.2		Average = 55.4	
Range = 72–96		Range = 31–71	

Table 1.3
Scores on Spanish Exam (Another Possibility)

Group A		Group B	
Student	Score	Student	Score
1	50	1	25
2	75	2	52
3	55	3	30
4	80	4	55
5	60	5	35
6	85	6	60
7	65	7	40
8	90	8	65
9	70	9	45
10	95	10	70
Average = 72.5		Average = 47.5	
Range = 50–95		Range = 25–70	

through 96 and average 86.2. The scores for Group B range from 31 through 71 and average 55.4. Moreover, no person in Group B did as well as anyone in Group A. We can conclude that Group A is clearly superior. (Notice, though, that the scores of our control groups have to be studied before we can be sure what this clear superiority means).

STATISTICAL INFERENCE

Unfortunately, experimental results are usually not as clear as those we have just seen. Usually there is an overlap in the scores of the two groups, and often there is a question about the confidence we can have in the superiority of the higher scoring group. Maybe they scored higher just by chance. *Statistical inference* is a set of techniques that allows us to judge how confident we should be that a given difference between two groups arises because of nonchance factors. Consider the sets of scores shown in Table

1.3. Quite a different story from that shown by Table 1.2! Are the groups different? To find out, we shall apply statistical inference.

We begin with the assumption that the groups are the *same,* that is to say, that they are no more different than two random samples of a single large group. Starting with that assumption, we then try to show that there are grounds for believing that they are in fact different.

To see how this works, suppose that Groups A and B were selected at random from the roster of an introductory class of 1,000 students whose scores on the Spanish exam are distributed as shown in Figure 1.1. It is obvious that we might draw two groups identical to Group A and Group B from this pool if we have the bad luck to pick ten relatively high scorers for Group A and ten relatively low scorers for Group B. In fact, it is possible to draw a group of ten students whose scores could average to almost any given value. Indeed, if we continued

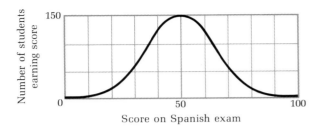

Figure 1.1
The Spanish-exam scores in our example form a symmetrical, bell-shaped distribution (called a _normal
distribution_).

to draw groups of ten names and to replace them
in the list of 1,000 between draws, sometimes we
would draw two groups whose averages were widely
separated, and sometimes we would draw two groups
whose averages were essentially identical. The key
question, which statistics can answer, is how often
would we randomly draw two groups whose averages
differed by a given amount?

In our example, the averages of 72.5 and 47.5
differ by twenty-five points. Now, if statistics tells
us that the chances are that we will randomly draw
two groups whose averages differ by twenty-five
points half the time, then we cannot have much
confidence that the difference between our groups
is not accidental. However, if statistics tells us that
our difference would arise by chance in a random
drawing only once in every thousand pairs of groups,
then we would be quite willing to believe that the
difference was caused by nonchance factors—in this
case, studying French. Psychologists generally agree
that any difference that would arise by chance only
five or fewer times in a hundred can reliably be
assumed to be not due simply to chance. This 5
percent _level of significance_ runs a certain risk: namely,
5 percent of the findings that are considered
significant (not due to chance) will, in fact, be due
to nothing but chance. But that is a risk that must
sometimes be taken. It can be lessened if we agree
instead on the 1 percent level of significance; then
we have confidence in differences only when they
are so big that they can be expected to occur by
chance only once in a hundred times.

Although the computations themselves are beyond
the scope of this discussion, statistics tells us that
the difference we found between Groups A and B
would arise very rarely by chance, and so we can
have confidence that it is not due to chance. (For a
further discussion of confidence, chance, and probability, the reader should consult an elementary text
on statistics).

Correlation   It often happens that we cannot
manipulate the variables we want to study. Teaching
French before Spanish changes our group's previous
experience with language, and we can study the
effects of the change. But if we wish to study the
effects of amount of annual income, of height, or
of racial background, we cannot directly change
these variables. But we can study the effects of
different values of each in terms of its _association_
or _correlation_ with other variables such as political
preferences or closeness to the family.

The simplest expression of an _association_ between
two variables is seen in a two-by-two table. Suppose
we want to see if annual income—under or over
$25,000 a year—is associated with political preference
—Democratic or Republican. We find a group of 100
people making under $25,000 per year and a group,
ideally of the same size, making over $25,000. Then
we inquire of each person whether he or she is
registered as a Democrat or a Republican. Our
results might be the hypothetical ones shown in
the following two-by-two table:

	Democrat	Republican	Total
"Rich"	25	75	100
"Poor"	60	40	100

The results indicate a strong association between
income and political preference: 75 percent of the
"rich" people are Republicans, and 60 percent of
the "poor" are Democrats.

There is no reason to limit such association tables

Table 1.4
Relation of Income to Political Affiliation

INCOME ($ PER YEAR)	DEMOCRAT	REPUBLICAN	DON'T CARE	TOTAL
Over 25,000	25	75	0	100
20–25,000	10	90	0	100
15–20,000	20	80	0	100
10–15,000	70	30	0	100
5–10,000	80	0	20	100
0–5,000	50	0	50	100

to two dimensions. We might uncover an even stronger association if we break down our two variables further. For example, consider six groups of 100 people assorted by income as indicated in Table 1.4. We see that the original 40 percent of Republicans among the "poor" (under $25,000) is accounted for solely by people with incomes over $10,000. And by adding the "Don't Care" category, we pick up an association of political apathy with lower income.

In some cases, an even finer breakdown is possible; if so, we turn to graphs instead of tables for presenting the data, and to *correlation* instead of association as a means of expressing the relationship. Take the correlation between the amount of time (from 0 to 100 hours) spent studying psychology over a ten-week period and the score earned on the final exam (from 0 to 100 points). We typically obtain results like those shown in Figure 1.2, where the hours (horizontal scale) and score (vertical scale) of each student each determine one point on the graph. We immediately see a strong correlation between the amount of study and score, although it is not perfect. Students who spend no time still get some points from the knowledge they had before the course, and even 100 hours is not enough to master all the material covered on the final. And, for any given number of hours, there is variation in the scores earned. This is because the score is influenced by factors other than hours of study.

A final word of caution about association and correlation. Although it appears in our examples that hours of study were responsible for—caused— higher scores and that it was income that influenced political preference, it is usually not possible to

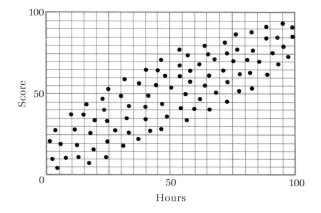

Figure 1.2
A graph expressing the correlation between final-exam scores and the number of hours spent studying in the course. Each point on the graph represents a student's score (vertical value) and the number of hours that student studied for the exam (horizontal value).

attribute cause on the basis of correlation alone. Only careful experimentation can establish cause with certainty. Often, apparent causes are not true causes, and correlations often turn out to exist because the changes in the two variables are both caused by a third variable. There is, for example, a correlation between the miles of road that need repairs in New York State in any given year and the number of deaths in India for the same year. However, better roads in New York will not save lives in India nor will saving lives in India improve the roads in New York, for both road damage in New York and deaths in India are caused by climatic variations. Correlation can be a trap for the causally unwary.

EXPERIMENTAL ANALYSIS

When psychologists have more or less complete control over their independent variables and can measure changes in the dependent variable with considerable accuracy, as in some studies of learning and motivation, they can apply the method called the *experimental analysis of behavior*. This method will be explored in depth in Chapters 4 and 32; two examples will suffice here. (1) If we want to know whether the tendency of an animal we are studying in the laboratory to seek food depends on how long it has been deprived of food, we can—because we have complete control over deprivation—establish that relationship unequivocally; we can increase it or decrease it as we wish; we can accurately measure how much the animal eats under each condition of deprivation. (2) If we want to know if a schoolboy misbehaves in a class to get attention from the teacher or from fellow pupils, we can alternately allow misbehavior to attract (*a*) no attention, (*b*) only the teacher's attention, (*c*) only that of peers, or (*d*) that of both peers and teacher. In this way, we can actually watch the misbehavior become more frequent or less frequent depending on whether it has one or another consequence.

THEORY IN PSYCHOLOGY

A theory is a set of statements about why or under what conditions specified events take place. We shall encounter several scores of theories in this book. Some theorizers refer to nonpsychological fields, such as physiology or biology, to explain psychological phenomena. Others try to account for human behaviors in terms of their correlation with other measurable human characteristics, such as degree of motivation. Others set up assumptions about psychological events, deduce precise propositions

or predictions from the assumptions, and then try to test the predictions with experiments, whose results determine changes and refinements in the theory. And still others draw detailed analogies between how people function and how other complex systems, such as computers, function. The goal in all cases is to understand, explain, or account for what people and other living organisms do.

Suggested Readings

THE HISTORICAL DEVELOPMENT OF
CONTEMPORARY PSYCHOLOGY

Boring, E. G. (1950) *A history of experimental psychology.* (2nd ed.) New York: Appleton-Century-Crofts. [A detailed treatment.]

Herrnstein, R. J., & Boring, E. G. (1965) *A source book in the history of psychology.* Cambridge, Mass.: Harvard University Press. [A somewhat more detailed look at some highlights.]

Murphy, G. (1949) *Historical introduction to modern psychology.* New York: Harcourt Brace Jovanovich. [Another detailed treatment.]

Nordby, V. J., & Hall, C. S. (1974) *A guide to psychologists and their concepts.* San Francisco: W. H. Freeman and Company. [Brief biographies and outlines of the contribution of the three dozen or so best known psychologists of the twentieth century.]

POINTS OF VIEW IN PSYCHOLOGY

Mandler, G., & Kessen, W. (1959) *The language of psychology.* New York: Wiley.

Wann, T. W., ed. (1964) *Behaviorism and phenomenology: contrasting bases for modern psychology.* Chicago: University of Chicago Press. [A particularly pointed, often personal exchange of views.]

STATISTICAL AND TRADITIONAL RESEARCH METHODS

Senter, R. J. (1969) *Analysis of data.* Glenview, Illinois: Scott Foresman. [A very easy and clear presentation.]

SCIENTIFIC RESEARCH

Bernard, C. (1961) *An introduction to experimental medicine.* (Translated by H. C. Greene.) New York: Macmillan. [A concise introduction to scientific method and thought, although the subject is physiology rather than psychology. A classic.]

Sidman, M. (1960) *Tactics of scientific research.* New York: Basic Books. [Numerous examples of the experimental analysis of behavior.]

Wilson, E. B., Jr. (1952) *An introduction to scientific research.* New York: McGraw-Hill. [Brilliant and thorough.]

MENTALISM

Miller, G. (1962) *Psychology: the science of mental life.* New York: Harper and Row. [A good introduction.]

BEHAVIORISM

Skinner, B. F., (1974) *About behaviorism.* New York: Alfred Knopf. [A recent statement of behaviorism.]

BASIC PSYCHOLOGICAL PROCESSES

UNIT ONE

Learning and Memory

Shinichi Suzuki, a Japanese educator, asserts that any child who has learned to speak his or her own native language can learn to play the violin. To prove his point, thousands of children ranging in age from three to fifteen are brought together every year to perform the works of Bach, Mozart, and other great composers in a mass concert. These children, who have not been selected on the basis of special ability, have been taught to play the violin by Suzuki's easygoing but careful method of instruction—a method that makes use of positive reinforcement (which we shall discuss in Chapter 4) as well as imitation of adult violinists. Two broad questions that could be asked about these children or about any behaving organisms express perhaps the most important issues in psychology: how do they learn? how do they remember what they have learned?

In this unit, we will attempt to sketch the best answers to these questions that contemporary psychology can provide. We will examine the fundamental principles of learning, remembering, and forgetting that have been clearly identified in the course of the past century. We will also examine the current frontiers of psychological theory and research regarding these subjects, where the answers necessarily become more speculative and less certain.

One of our topics, memory, is something most of us take for granted most of the time—except perhaps when we are struggling to remember a word, a telephone number, or the answer to a question on a test. By contrast, Henry M. is a person who cannot take his memory for granted at all.

If you were to visit Henry M., you might be impressed by his intelligence, which is above average. You might have a pleasant chat with him. He might tell you something about his early life. You might tell him a joke and make him laugh. When you said goodbye to Henry M., you might well conclude that you had just met a "normal person." However, suppose you returned to visit Henry M. five minutes later. Henry M. would not remember the joke you told him. If you told the same joke to him again, it would probably get the same response from him that it got the first time. Indeed, if you came back every five minutes and told Henry M. that same joke, he would never remember having heard it before. Of course, every time you visited Henry M., you'd have to introduce yourself, because to him you would be a complete stranger.

In Chapter 2, we will see how Henry M.'s bizarre behavior tells us something important about the nature of memory.

Our second main topic in this unit is learning. In our discussion of learning in Chapters 3 and 4, we will spend most of our time on conditioning procedures that are used in laboratories to modify the behavior of pigeons, rats, and other animals in very simple environments. Although the behavior of such animals is not without its own inherent interest, the ultimate objective of many behaviorists who conduct such conditioning experiments is nothing less than an understanding of human behavior in all its rich variety and complexity.

Although our current understanding of the way organisms learn behaviors is rather like a half-finished jigsaw puzzle, certain principles that apply equally well to laboratory pigeons and rats and to people have been clearly established. These principles account for many human behaviors we observe every day. Furthermore, some techniques for modifying human behavior make use of these principles. For example, take the case of a twenty-one-year-old man we shall call John D.

John D. was referred to a behavioral therapist after he tried to kill himself. He told the therapist that he has been severely depressed for some time because of his sexual behavior. For six years, John D. had experienced "feelings of discomfort" around young women and had been sexually aroused and gratified only by other young men.

Homosexuality is a type of behavior that has long been observed among humans and other higher mammals, particularly where members of one sex are confined together for long periods of time. Thus, from a scientific point of view, it would be hard to make the case that homosexuality in itself is "unnatural" or intrinsically harmful, although it is a form of behavior that is looked on with disfavor in most societies.

Regardless of the causes, this behavior had become a source of suicidal despair for John D. It is for this reason that the therapist suggested to John D. that it might be possible to replace his homosexual behavior with heterosexual behavior through the use of certain simple conditioning principles. John D. liked this idea. As it developed, it took only four half-hour sessions to shift John D.'s sexual interest from males to females.

What the therapist did was to obtain two sets of colored slides, one that showed attractive nude males and one that showed attractive nude females. Using what is called a fading technique, the therapist would show John D. the nude males until John D. felt sexually aroused. At this point, the therapist gradually faded out a nude male and faded in a nude female. During this gradual change in the stimulus, John D. was instructed to see how long he could sustain his sexual arousal. After this process had been repeated a number of times, John D. found the nude females by themselves to be sexually arousing. By the end of the four training sessions, his responses to the nude females were those of a typical heterosexual man.

John D. lost his feelings of discomfort around young women and began to enjoy their company. Soon he was dating young women and was free of the depression that had apparently been specifically linked to his prior behavior.

Similar techniques have been applied to other behaviors that people wish to change, including smoking, stuttering, irrational fears (phobias), bed-wetting, and exhibitionism. Success in this field can be attributed largely to the intelligent and systematic application of conditioning procedures to human behavior.

At the end of this book, we devote an entire chapter to a discussion of the modification of human behavior with conditioning procedures, and, as we have mentioned, Chapters 3 and 4 discuss various conditioning techniques that are studied in the laboratory. Moreover, throughout this volume, it will become clear that learning and memory are recurrent themes in psychology—themes that emerge whether the topic under discussion is motivation, perception, the development of behavior, social behavior, personality, or behavioral disorders. Indeed, the central importance of learning and memory is acknowledged by all psychologists, no matter how much they differ on various theoretical issues. Psychologists agree that if they wish to understand behavior, they must understand learning and memory.

CHAPTER TWO

Memory

Why do we remember some things and forget others? Why is some material easy to memorize and other material difficult or impossible? What, in short, are the psychological factors that influence remembering and forgetting? How do they operate? In this chapter, we will see that many of these factors have been identified but that we do not yet fully understand how they operate. Fortunately, there are several hypotheses and theories that are consistent with most of what is known about memory. Besides providing hints as to how we might improve our memories, they also provide good questions for future psychological research to answer.

THE IMPORTANCE OF ORGANIZATION

An appropriate beginning for this chapter is a simple psychological experiment the reader can undertake on his or her own memory. First, look at the digits in Figure 2.1 for ten seconds or so and then cover them up. Immediately try to say the digits aloud in sequence. Next, do the same thing with Figures 2.3 and 2.5. (Don't read the next paragraph until you have finished this experiment.)

You probably had little success in memorizing the sixteen digits in Figure 2.1. Indeed, if you were able to recall the first six or seven digits, you were doing unusually well. Chances are you did only slightly better with the numbers in Figure 2.3. The commas separating each three digits probably prevented you from seeing that the digits form meaningful units in groups of four. Nonetheless, you may have done better than you did with Figure 2.1 because you may have tried to memorize the digits as three-digit numbers (like "492") rather than as separate items (4 9 2). If you did this, you used the technique known as *chunking*, which, as we shall see below, permits remarkable feats of memory.

Finally, you probably will not have much trouble remembering the digits in Figure 2.5, because they are grouped into familiar four-digit units, each of which is a familiar historical date; if you recognize the four dates, you have to remember only four familiar "chunks" of information rather than sixteen unfamiliar "chunks." (By now you may have noticed that the digits that appear in Figure 2.5 are the same digits that appear in the same sequence in Figure 2.3. They also appear, in reverse

Figure 2.1

sequence, in Figure 2.1.)

The preceding experiment has several implications for our study of human memory. One implication is that, in order to memorize a large set of items, it is wise to group the items into familiar chunks if possible. Even more significant is the implication that although we can reproduce only a small *number of items* immediately after they are presented to us, the *complexity* of each item can vary greatly (from "2" to "1492" to "0123456789" to "abcdefghijklmnopqrstuvwxyz" and so on).

A fascinating observation has been made in many experimental studies of memory: the number of chunks we can remember (our *memory span*) seems to be fairly constant whether the chunks are long or short, complex or simple. In general, people can easily recall five familiar chunks, have some difficulty with seven, and seldom recall more than nine. Thus the human memory span—which is a span of items not of time—is often said to be "seven plus or minus two."

The psychologist George Miller was among the first to view the human being as an "information processor" whose work could be made easier and more efficient by the proper organization of material, for instance, by recoding material into fewer units. An example that Miller has given concerns a code used by engineers to help them remember the setups of the complex electrical circuits of digital computing machines that have long rows of lights that indicate which relays are closed. In order to remember which of fifteen or twenty relays are closed and which are open, the engineers made up the arbitrary code shown in Figure 2.2, grouping the lights into successive triplets and assigning a number to each of the eight possible patterns. Knowing this code, they could immediately translate the sequence "off, on, on, off, off, off, on, off, on, off, off, on, on, on, on" to "30517."

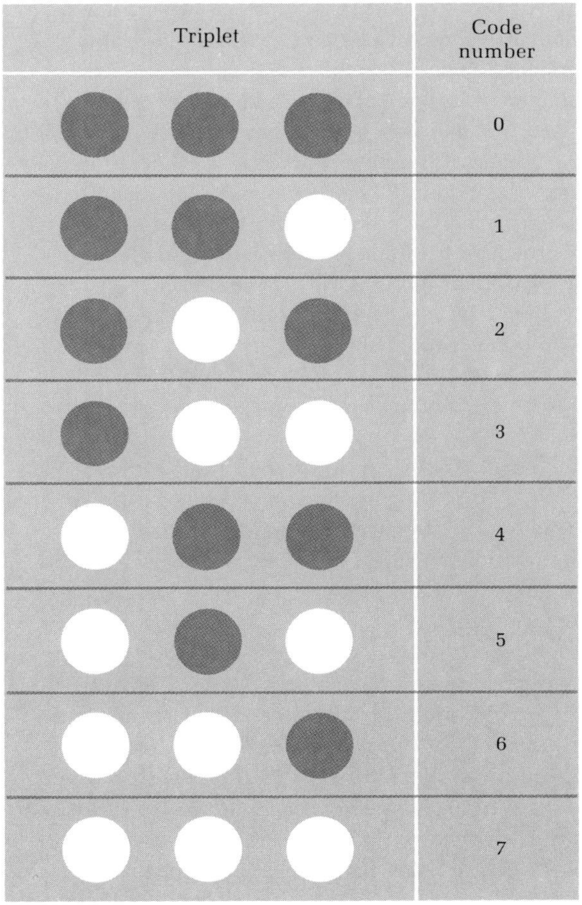

Triplet			Code number
●	●	●	0
●	●	○	1
●	○	●	2
●	○	○	3
○	●	●	4
○	●	○	5
○	○	●	6
○	○	○	7

Figure 2.2
Long rows of lights are quickly read by engineers using the code shown here. [Adapted from G. A. Miller, "Information and Memory," *Scientific American*, August 1956, 42–46. Copyright © 1956 by Scientific American, Inc. All rights reserved.]

1, 492, 177, 618, 121, 984

Figure 2.3

The work of Miller and his co-workers has shown recoding to be an immensely powerful tool for increasing the amount of information that humans can remember. Indeed, coding is probably used in some way or another in almost every phase of human "information processing." One example most of us recall from our own childhoods is memorizing the alphabet. The alphabet is often learned by breaking it down into manageable chunks (that is, "ABCD," "EFG," "HIJK," "LMNOP," and so on). If you don't remember chunking the alphabet in this manner, try reciting it backwards. The places at which you have the most difficulty are probably the boundaries between the chunks into which you originally organized the alphabet. Another example we can draw from childhood is learning to read. A child begins to read by looking at each letter sequentially until he is familiar with it and able to recognize more complex chunks (words), then still more complex chunks (phrases).

As adults, we are often called upon to memorize new phone numbers (and, at the same time, to forget old ones). Phone numbers are divided into two chunks: a three-digit chunk and a four-digit chunk. We tend to apply the same division when we are trying to memorize phone numbers (and even when we say them out loud). As a result, we memorize the two chunks more readily than we would a string of seven single digits. With practice, the individual digits within a chunk of three, four, or even seven numerals become grouped together; eventually we are able to process them as a single item. Items of such familiarity—for example, our own telephone number or date of the American Revolution—are stored in our long-term memory, a system of almost limitless capacity. Let us now examine this system as well as the others that are believed to exist.

THREE KINDS OF MEMORY

The evidence suggests that we have three kinds of memory: *immediate memory*, *short-term memory*, and *long-term memory*.

Immediate Memory   Immediate, or sensory, memory refers to the process by which we can recall something a split second after having perceived it. For example, look at the stimulus display in Figure 2.4. If this display were flashed in view for one-twentieth of a second, how many of the individual symbols could you accurately report? It is reasonable to assume that you might report six of the twelve, a number close to the normal memory span for recalling digits. Next, let us suppose that the conditions were changed. Instead of reporting the entire display, you were required to give only a "partial report"—to report one row of letters only. While the display was on, you would not know which row you would be asked to report, but one-fourth of a second after the display was terminated, a musical "instruction" tone would indicate which row to report. Now, surprising as it may seem, you would probably be able to report a much higher percentage of letters correctly.

In a series of experiments of this nature, George Sperling of the Bell Telephone Laboratories has demonstrated that all twelve items are available for recall for about a half-second after presentation, because a subject remains able to "see" the stimulus array for that length of time. This type of "seeing" recall is called immediate memory. After the half-second elapses, subjects report a decaying visual image, and tests of their recall ability support those reports. Consequently, since it takes time to recite the letters, subjects who are attempting to report all the letters are able to give only the first

```
Z  K  F  X

R  F  N  Y

S  J  B  J
```

Figure 2.4
Example of a stimulus display used by George Sperling
in his experiments on immediate memory. [Adapted
from L. R. Peterson, "Short-term Memory." *Scientific
American*, July 1966, 90–95. Copyright © 1966 by
Scientific American, Inc. All rights reserved.]

five or so before the others have "faded from
view." Apparently, the high degree of accuracy of
the partial reports is due to the "persistence of
sensation"—or to what can be read from the
lingering visual image of the turned-off stimulus
display before the image decays.

By requiring only partial reports of single
four-letter rows, the experimenter can determine
the amount of information available in the subject's
immediate memory. For example, if a subject is
consistently able to report correctly the four letters
of any one of three rows, selected at random after
he sees it, even when the display is different each
time, we can infer that *all twelve* items are available
for recall in immediate memory for at least a half
second. This means that the span of immediate
memory exceeds the short-term memory span
("seven plus or minus two").

Short-Term Memory   Items committed to
short-term memory (STM) also dissipate rapidly.
STM differs from immediate memory, however, in
the following important ways: (1) whereas the
sensory image decays regardless of the subjects'
action, rehearsal by the subject can keep material
in STM indefinitely; (2) whereas the sensory image
remaining in one's immediate memory decays in less
than one second, the information temporarily stored
in STM may endure as long as thirty seconds or
so, even if the material is not being rehearsed;
(3) despite these advantages, STM has severely
limited storage capacity.

You will be able to gain some understanding of
the operation of STM by performing another brief
experiment. In this one, you will be asked to look
at Figure 2.6, on the next page—but not until you
have read the following instructions. A set of
three alphabet letters appears in Figure 2.6. Look at
the letters for just a half-second or so. Then,
immediately close the book and begin to count
backward from 1,000 by three's (1,000, 997, 994,
and so on) until you reach 925. Proceed as rapidly
as you can, without losing count. You should get to
925 in about thirty seconds. Do not try to recall
the three letters: instead, concentrate on the task of
counting backward swiftly and accurately. When
you are finished, see if you can recall the three
letters correctly (check the letters in Figure 2.6).
When the experiment is done correctly, it is almost
impossible to remember the three letters!

If you wish, you can repeat the experiment using
the set of three letters in Figure 2.8. If you are not
convinced, or if the demonstration did not work
for some reason (perhaps you managed to recall the
three letters correctly—an unusual feat), try the
same demonstration on a friend. Give him the
instructions first, and then verbally present him with
three consonants (which you have written down
beforehand). See if he can recall them after
counting backward to 925.

If your friend is disturbed because he cannot
remember as few as three letters for a period as
short as thirty seconds, you will be able to offer
some reassurance based on the following analysis
of the experiment.

Normally, of course, we are capable of much
greater mnemonic feats; indeed, three items is
below the lower limit of the usual human memory
span of "seven plus or minus two." What the
foregoing demonstration shows is that items
generally do not remain in short-term memory if
they are not rehearsed. Under normal conditions,
when there is no competing requirement that
prevents rehearsals, you will have no trouble
recalling three letters after thirty seconds. But

(1492) (1776) (1812) (1984)

Figure 2.5

H

K

Z

Figure 2.6

you cannot rehearse (repeat) the letters while you are counting backward. To demonstrate the difference, try the same test with the three letters in Figure 2.13, but do not count backward. It will not even be necessary to try to rehearse the items. Do whatever you like in the thirty-second interval, such as looking at the clock or daydreaming. It is likely that you will recall the letters, probably because *some* rehearsal automatically took place during the thirty seconds, so that the letters were retained in STM. When rehearsal is prevented from occurring (by presenting the subject with an explicit and demanding competing task, such as that of counting backward rapidly), the rapid decay of STM becomes apparent.

Classic experiments similar to those you have just performed were originally carried out in the late 1950s by Lloyd Peterson and Margaret Peterson, who showed that retention of a three-consonant triad declined precipitously as the interval between presentation of the stimulus and the request for recall increased. After a period of only three seconds, for example, the stimulus item was recalled on 80 percent of the trials, but when the retention interval was increased to eighteen seconds, successful recall occurred on only 8 percent of the trials. Subsequent studies have shown that the result depends in part upon the *meaningfulness* of the material being retained. For example, retention of a single monosyllabic word for an eighteen-second interval is much less impaired under the same conditions of counting backward. Indeed, we have to ask the subject to retain a cluster of three monosyllabic words before his retention of them is as poor as his retention of three consonants. This finding is illustrated in Figure 2.7. Thus the Petersons' studies demonstrate that our retention of unfamiliar material is surprisingly short-lived without rehearsal. The capacity of STM is limited anyway; without rehearsal, our ability to remember material is even more limited.

An interesting aspect of STM is the *acoustic* nature of its storage system—at least in many individuals and under certain circumstances. When an item in immediate memory is transferred to STM, it is apparently transformed from a visual (or other sensory) image into an auditory one. The evidence for this is that most errors that are made in recalling items from STM tend to result from acoustic confusions rather than visual or semantic confusions. For example, an "E" is more likely to be incorrectly recalled as a "C" than as an "F". Sounds, not shapes, are confused with one another.

Long-Term Memory Since long-term memory (LTM) has been studied much more extensively than STM, we know considerably more about it—at least in terms of the number of empirical generalizations we can make about LTM. Unlike STM, LTM has a seemingly limitless capacity, undergoes little or no decay, and requires little if any rehearsal. Intriguingly, LTM storage appears to be semantic (rather than auditory), that is, items are somehow stored according to their meaning. Thus, errors in LTM are generally due to semantic confusions, rather than the acoustic confusions that occur in STM, although acoustic confusions may also occasionally occur in LTM. For example, "wish" is more likely to be inaccurately recalled from LTM as "hope" than as "wash" or fish."

It is not clear *how* items pass from the imagery of immediate memory into the auditory storage of STM and on into the semantic storage of LTM. We *do* know that rehearsal is important. Apparently,

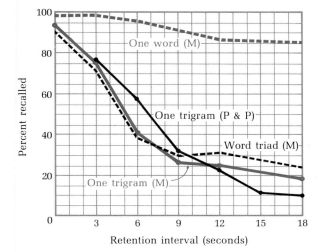

Figure 2.7
Results from two experiments investigating the short-term retention of verbal material. Each of the curves plots the percentage of words recalled against the duration of the retention interval. P & P: Lloyd Peterson and Margaret Peterson studied retention of three-consonant trigrams like HKZ. During the retention interval, subjects were required to count backward in order to prevent rehearsal. M: Bennet Murdock obtained comparable results with trigrams and word triads (sets of three monosyllabic words) but found enhanced retention when the test items were single words. [Adapted from L. Postman, "Transfer, Interference, and Forgetting," in J. W. Kling and L. A. Riggs, *Woodworth and Schlosberg's Experimental Psychology*. (3rd ed.) New York: Holt, Rinehart and Winston, 1971, Pp. 1019–1132. Data from L. R. Peterson and M. J. Peterson, "Short-term Retention of Individual Verbal Items," *Journal of Experimental Psychology*, 1959, *58*, 193–198, and B. B. Murdock, Jr., "The Retention of Individual Items," *Journal of Experimental Psychology*, 1961, *62*, 618–625.]

rehearsal not only permits an item to remain in STM, but also increases the likelihood that it will pass into LTM for more permanent storage. When we are not rehearsing material that has entered STM, we are almost always attending to something else. Consequently, it is quite probable that whatever else our attention focuses on will replace some of the material in STM, partly because it is difficult to do two things at once. Studies of STM suggest that items that succeed in gaining admission from immediate memory will soon exit unless attention is focused on them. If attention is

Figure 2.8

disrupted, items may pass out of STM and be unavailable for transfer into LTM; these items are forgotten. For example, in one experiment, subjects trying to memorize a seven-digit phone number were severely hampered by the apparently simple requirement of dialing "1" before the number. For many subjects the dialing of the number "1" diverted their attention enough to allow some of the digits to slip out of STM. The development of a model of the relation between STM, LTM, and rehearsal is depicted in Figures 2.9–2.12.

Although the distinction between STM and LTM has intuitive appeal, the possibility remains that it may be more a reflection of differences between STM research and LTM research than of the nature of memory. Perhaps the most convincing evidence suggesting that there are at least two distinct memory systems comes from the case of Henry M., which we described in the unit introduction. Both of the lower side-lobes (the "temporal lobes") of Henry M.'s brain had been removed in the medical treatment of an unusually severe case of epilepsy. These areas included the *hippocampus*, which is believed to function somehow in the transfer of information from STM to LTM. After the operation, Henry M.'s seizures disappeared. For some reason, his IQ increased from 104 to an above-average 118 after the operation. But, as we indicated, Henry M. was incapable of new learning. He could remember everything that had happened to him before the operation—indicating normal LTM—but could remember nothing that had occurred since. His STM was also unimpaired. For example, in tests of digit recall, he remembered seven digits—a normal number—and he could carry on a perfectly normal conversation. He could even appreciate a funny story whose punch line was based on semantic ambiguity. However, the story and the storyteller were forgotten five minutes later. What was apparently lacking,

Figure 2.9

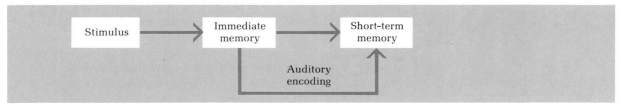

Figure 2.10

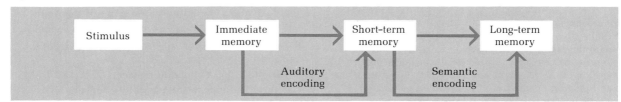

Figure 2.11

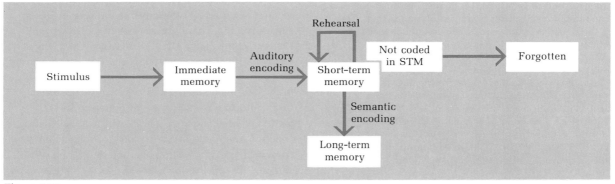

Figure 2.12

Figures 2.9–2.12
A process model for remembering and forgetting. If a stimulus is attended to, it enters immediate memory. Some items in immediate memory are encoded into short-term memory (STM), others are forgotten. Once an item is in STM, it remains there until it is passed into long-term memory (LTM) or is forgotten. The more material in STM is rehearsed, the longer it may remain in STM and the greater the likelihood it will be encoded into LTM. Without rehearsal, items in STM may be forgotten after several seconds. Once material is in LTM, it is likely to be remembered indefinitely providing retrieval from LTM is assisted by appropriate mnemonic (memory) cues. It is also likely, however, that some forgetting occurs from LTM (as well as from immediate memory and STM).

Q
M
J

Figure 2.13

then, was neither STM or LTM, but rather the transfer of information from STM to LTM.

THE STUDY OF MEMORY

Memory is a function (1) of the way in which the sensory system and the brain process and store sensory information, (2) of the capacities of the individual learner, and (3) of the individual's life history. In addition, what contemporary psychologists know about memory has been determined in large measure by the kinds of materials, apparatus, and measurements that have been used in its study. We must become acquainted with the latter factors before we can adequately understand what is known about human memory.

Materials   In most experiments on human memory, researchers have used simple verbal materials of some kind. Two common types of materials that have been used extensively in investigating the parameters of verbal learning are *serial lists* and *paired-associate lists.* A serial list is a series of verbal units that is presented to the subject for memorization and recall. A list may be composed of words (for example, TENT, BAKER, TULIP), or numbers (39, 71, 34, 26), or *nonsense syllables* (MIB, PAB, KAZ, JIV) or three-consonant *triads* (HKZ, WZP, SLJ, KDP). Nonsense syllables and triads are groups of letters used for retention tasks because they are presumed to have no meaning for most subjects; thus they are presumed to minimize the effects of a subject's familiarity or prior experience with verbal material on his retention. If the serial list consists of words, there is generally no meaningful relationship between them. If a goal of the study is to explore the effects of meaningful relationships upon retention, however, deliberate relations between items are built

into the list: DOVE, PEACE, DREAMS, GLORY, PASTURES, PLENTY. In this list, of course, each item appears in a common phrase with another (for example, "dove of peace"; "dreams of glory"; "pastures of plenty"). These relationships between the items provide structure to the list, making it easier to retain. A paired-associate list consists of a series of paired (but not necessarily related) words, digits, or nonsense syllables presented sequentially (CORN–MUSIC; BOX–DEER; WATER–BOOK). After the subject looks at each pair for a brief period of time (usually about three seconds), the first member of each pair (the stimulus) is presented alone, and the subject tries to recall the other member of the pair (the response).

In both paired-associate and serial learning, the subject's attempt to recall is usually followed by a presentation of the correct response: that is, *feedback* (the results of one's own performance) is provided. Examples of serial-list learning in nonexperimental settings include memorization of the alphabet and the list of U.S. Presidents in order. An example of paired-associate learning is the acquisition of foreign-language vocabulary items that are paired with their English equivalents.

Other types of materials used in studies of recall are excerpts of actual blocks of language, either written or spoken, rather than unrelated language items. These might be entire sentences, paragraphs, or longer passages. Since each item in ordinary verbal communication depends to some extent on those that precede and follow it, such material is called *connected discourse.*

Between these two extremes of isolated units and connected discourse is a wide range of verbal material, which George Miller has called "approximations to English." Miller devised passages that varied from what he called "zero-order approximations to English" (composed of words selected at

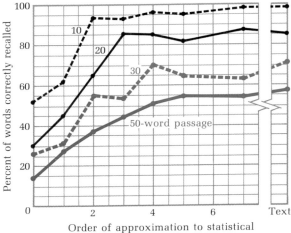

Figure 2.14
Percentage of words correctly recalled plotted against the order of approximation to the statistical structure of English. Examples of the approximations to English used in the experiment are given in the text. [Data from G. A. Miller and J. Selfridge, "Verbal Context and the Recall of Meaningful Material," *American Journal of Psychology*, 1950, 63, 176–185.]

random from an English dictionary) to "tenth-order approximations" (intact excerpts from works of English prose). Miller and J.A. Selfridge used the following approximations to English in a study they made in 1950:

Zero order: byway consequence handsomely financier bent flux cavalry swiftness weather-beaten extent
First order: abilities with that beside I for waltz you the sewing
Second order: was he went to the newspaper is in deep and
Third order: tall and thin boy is a biped is the beat
Fourth order: saw the football game will end at midnight on January
Fifth order: they saw the play Saturday and sat down beside him
Seventh order: recognize her abilities in music after he scolded him before
Text: the history of California is largely that of a railroad*

The intermediate-order approximations approach actual English by increasing the number of words that formed a sensible cluster. For example, in a *third*-order approximation, every string of *three* words could occur in ordinary English—"tall and thin," "and thin boy," "thin boy is," "boy is a," and so on; but a string of four words could not—"is a biped is." Higher-order approximations simply assure that longer sequences of words could occur in sensible English.

The results of such studies indicate that the more closely the material approximates English, the greater the number of words that can be recalled. In the higher-order approximations, groups of

*G. A. Miller and J. A. Selfridge, "Verbal Context and the Recall of Meaningful Material," *American Journal of Psychology*, **63** (1950), 176–185.

words that make sense as a unit (like "tall and thin boy") are remembered as a chunk. It is of interest that these studies supported the finding that the total number of chunks a person can remember is fairly constant. Note in Figure 2.14, however, that although recall increases from the zero-order sample to about the fourth-order sample, little increment occurs with higher-order approximations.

Apparatus In the studies illustrated in Figure 2.14, the experimenter simply read the word passages out loud and the subjects were required to write the words they remembered; in other experiments, tape recorders have been used for the same purpose. In most studies, however, the verbal material is presented visually. Traditionally, the most commonly employed apparatus for visual presentation, especially if the material constitutes serial or paired-associate lists, has been the *memory drum*. Components of the list are presented sequentially in the window of the drum. The subject sees each item (or pair of items) for a specified amount of time, and the time between items can be regulated automatically. Recently, reliance on the memory drum has declined sharply; electronic computers offer more flexibility in the presentation of items.

Measures and Criteria The amount of material a person retains (or remembers) equals the amount he has learned (or successfully memorized) minus the amount he has forgotten. Although the amount of forgetting must be inferred from the absence of retention, the amount of _retention_ may be measured directly if we know how much material was learned originally. Two common, direct measures of retention are _recognition_ and _recall._ In a recognition test, items that the subject has seen before are presented to him—usually along with new items—and he is asked to point out those that he has seen before. In a recall test, the subject must generate the items himself. There are several procedures for testing both recognition and recall, but we shall discuss only those most commonly used.

Two important procedures for measuring recognition are tests of _simple recognition_ and _multiple-alternative recognition_. In a simple-recognition test, the subject is presented with an item and must decide whether or not he has seen it before. For example, a typical question might be "Have you seen DOVES as an illustrative example in this chapter?" In a multiple-alternative recognition test, the subject is presented with several items and is asked to identify which of the items he has seen before. For example, "Which one of the following has appeared as an illustrative example in this chapter: SLEEP, GREATNESS, PASTORAL, PASTURES, QMF?"

In the measurement of recall, three common methods are _free recall_, _probed recall_, and _serial recall_. In free recall, subjects are asked to recall _in any order_ as many items as possible from the list they have seen. In probed recall, the subject is presented

with some cue that should suggest the appropriate item: if the item to be recalled is from a paired-associate list, the cue might be the first member of the pair (for example, what word appeared with CORN in a previous example?); if the item is from a serial list, the cue might be the location of the item in the list. Finally, in serial recall, the subject is asked to repeat the items in the same order in which they were presented during the experiment.

In the study of memory, a subject's degree of retention depends, in part, on whether a recognition test or a recall test is employed. Recognition is generally easier for the subject than recall, since stimuli are provided, and one has only to decide which were seen before. In recall, the subject must do much more: he must generate the stimuli himself and also decide which, if any, are correct. Thus multiple-choice examinations are easier than those without alternative answers. For example, consider the following questions.

1. What is the term for the total number of items that can be correctly reproduced immediately upon conclusion of a single presentation?

2. Barry M. Goldwater was the Republican candidate for President in 1964. Who was the Republican candidate for Vice President?

These recall questions are somewhat less likely to be answered correctly than corresponding simple or multiple-recognition questions on the same subjects:

1. Is the term for the total number of items that can be correctly reproduced after a single presentation a "chunk"?

2. In 1964, Barry M. Goldwater's running mate was:
   (a) Strom Thurmond
   (b) William E. Miller
   (c) Harold E. Stassen
   (d) Spiro T. Agnew

Note that a person who knew what a "chunk" was—but did not remember what a "memory span" was—would be able to give the correct answer "no" in the simple recognition task but would not have answered correctly in recall.

Of all the recall tests, serial recall demands the most of the subject, since he must recall not only all of the correct items but also the order in which they appear.

When we compare the results of studies in which different procedures for measuring retention have been employed, it is important to take into account the extent to which those procedures are comparable.

FACTORS INFLUENCING MEMORIZATION AND RETENTION

The ease with which material is memorized (learned) and retained depends on many factors, including the nature of the material, the method of memorizing, and a variety of characteristics of the individual subject. In addition, the subject's strategy may have a strong influence in facilitating memorization and retention. Examples of strategies that have already been discussed in this chapter are chunking and organization. Other strategies for memorizing are exhibited by the night club performer whose act consists of demonstrating dramatic feats of memory. These different types of variables—in materials, method, strategy, and individual memorizers—are the subjects of this section.

Influence of Materials We have already seen that the nature of the material will influence the ease with which it is memorized. Thus a meaningful three-letter word is much easier to memorize than a group of three meaningless letters. Sim-

Figure 2.15
Hermann Ebbinghaus. [Historical Pictures Service, Chicago]

ilarly, material that stands out in some way is also readily learned: most of us remember what we did on the night of the last presidential election, and on the day of our high school graduation. Both of these variables—the meaningfulness of materials and its emotional or perceptual impact—have been studied systematically in the laboratory.

The use of nonsense materials in the experimental study of human memory began with the German psychologist Hermann Ebbinghaus (1850–1909), who conducted studies of his own memory. In order to minimize the effects on the results of his studies of what he had already learned, he decided to memorize nonsense materials and then to determine how much he remembered after longer and longer periods of time without further practice. His very successful studies of retention established nonsense materials as useful in subsequent studies of human memory.

Nonsense syllables are usually more difficult to memorize than meaningful material. The relative

LIST A	LIST B
winged	beef
braise	spinach
flower	cheese
beer	veal
listen	beans
patio	custard
grief	goalie
tender	pork
splash	corn
waltz	steak

Figure 2.16
Two lists of words that may be used to illustrate the *von Restorff effect*: items clearly distinct from other (more homogeneous) items in a list tend to be retained more readily.

ease of memorizing nonsense syllables depends upon the extent to which they resemble or suggest known words. This has been demonstrated in studies that have measured the *association value* of items—the number of words that are associated with a particular word or nonsense syllable in a given amount of time—and then shown that items of higher association value are more easily memorized. One way of measuring the association value of a series of words or nonsense syllables is to present each, one at a time, to subjects and ask them to call out any words that come to mind during a sixty-second period following the presentation. In one study that used both words and nonsense items, the obtained *index of meaning* or the degree of *associability* for each word ranged from less than one for the word "gojey" to almost ten for the word "kitchen." Some nonsense items, such as "rompin" or "kuz," had a higher associability score than certain infrequently used words, such as "matrix." The conclusion that the more associable the material is, the more readily it will be committed to memory, holds true for a list of nonsense syllables, a selection of unrelated words, or a passage of connected discourse; it also holds true for a list of paired-associates or a serial list. Furthermore, it holds true whether the degree of retention is measured by a recall or a recognition test. Thus, the relationship between associability and ease of memorizing has considerable generality.

An item that is clearly distinct from other items tends to be more readily retained. This phenomenon is known as the *von Restorff effect*. It may be demonstrated by requiring a subject to memorize a list of ten words, nine of which are printed in black and the tenth in red. The distinguishable red word will be learned more readily than the others. Similarly, if a list contained nine words belonging to a particular category (such as types of food) and one word totally unrelated to the others, the exceptional word will be learned more quickly than it would if it were presented in the same position but in a list in which it belonged to the same category as the other nine words. Examples of word lists containing one sharply distinguishable item are shown in Figure 2.16.

Influence of Method   What is the best way to memorize a series of equations for a chemistry class? a list of formulas for physics? or a part in a play for a drama group? Given that you have ten hours to devote to the task, should you divide your time into several short practice sessions spaced as far apart as possible? or should you attempt to learn the subject matter in one long, concentrated effort? Should you divide the material into parts? or should you try to master it in its entirety?

The way in which the practice time is organized is important in memorizing. In general, spacing, or *distributed practice*, is superior to concentrated effort, or *massed practice*, even though the total amount of time spent (including the "spaces") is usually greater. However, if you have, for example, two hours to learn some equations for a quiz to be given later the same day, it obviously would be better to devote the entire two hours to the material than to alternate fifteen-minute periods of practice and rest. This is because the total amount of time spent studying is more important than the method of study. But, if the quiz is a few days away and you have decided to spend no more than two hours preparing for it, then it would be more productive if you were to employ the distribution procedure.

The advantage of distributed practice to massed practice is often more evident in motor tasks than in verbal tasks. Thus in learning to type or to play the piano, for example, massed practice can produce motor fatigue, which, in turn, causes inefficient learning. Besides facilitating acquisition, distributed practice results in superior retention of various types of acquired skills, as subsequent testing of subjects has shown. For example, a person who takes five daily one-hour driving lessons learns to drive more quickly and skillfully than he would after a single five-hour session, and furthermore, he will probably be more proficient when tested a month later after no further practice.

In verbal tasks, one advantage of distributed practice is the opportunity it gives the learner to rehearse the material. As we noted earlier in this chapter, rehearsal is often essential if the material is to pass into LTM storage. The rest period between trials may in part constitute an additional training period, during which some kind of conscious—or even unconscious—rehearsal takes place. Although distributed practice has not been shown to be superior to massed practice for *short-term* retention of verbal material, it does seem to be more valuable for long-term retention. Hence the advantage of distributed practice if you are preparing for an examination to be held the following week and of massed practice for tomorrow's exam. Another advantage of distributed practice, if there is time for it, is that you will retain the subject matter for a month or two longer, and thus be more proficient during subsequent examinations in the same course. If the material is worth retaining, distributed practice is usually preferable.

The way in which you arrange the material itself—whether you divide it into sections or approach it as a whole—is another important variable in method. For example, if you are practicing for the lead in a three-act play, you should probably rehearse the part in sections before attempting to recite all of it from memory. If, however, you are merely trying to memorize a single sentence, the preceding one for example, it may not be worthwhile to divide it into sections. Thus, the nature of the material is an important determiner of whether the *part method* or the *whole method* is more efficient for the learning and retention of verbal material. Generally, as the length of the material increases, the whole method becomes increasingly unwieldy and the part method correspondingly more efficient. The major drawback of the part method, of course, is that the learner must then put the parts together, or reconstruct the whole from the parts. For many tasks, such recombination constitutes about half the total learning time. The primary disadvantage of the whole-method is that portions of the material that have already been learned continue to receive unnecessary attention as the subject repeatedly works through the entire set of materials. Whether the whole method or the part method is more advantageous for a particular task also depends upon the nature of the material. If the material is highly integrated, that is, if the various parts are closely interrelated, the whole method may be more efficient; but if the material is easily divided into meaningful units (as is a series of equations or formulas, or a sequence of responses to cues in a play), then the part method tends to be more useful.

Feedback is another variable affecting the learning of a skill or a body of material. Whether the task is a motor task (such as typing or throwing darts) or a verbal task (such as memorizing material),

LIST A	LIST B
box	book
lumber	telephone
painting	vineyard
pencil	tennis
chair	building
lamp	basket
mirror	woman
insect	elastic
rock	paper
window	auto

Figure 2.17

progress is greatly facilitated if the subject receives immediate _feedback_ on the results of his performance. Thus if a novice dart thrower cannot see the target after he releases the dart, he will pick up the game less quickly than he would if the target were not blocked from view, and immediate feedback were thus available.

Another important variable is _overlearning_ (or overtraining); the more you continue to practice the material after perfect recall has been attained, the better you will retain it. If you learn the material well enough to produce one perfect recall, for example, you may not retain it as well a day later as you would if you had practiced until you had produced twenty consecutive correct recalls. In general, the greater the overtraining, the more accurate and durable the retention.

Influence of Strategy The effects of the various strategies that are employed in memorizing are of considerable interest to those of us who must memorize a great deal of material. For example, by rehearsing material and by organizing it into meaningful chunks (as illustrated in Figure 2.1, 2.3, and 2.5), people often are able to increase their memorizing capabilities far beyond the normal range. We recall that chunking increases the amount of information in each item. Since the human memory span is the _number_ of items (seven plus or minus two) a person can recall, and since this number is not greatly influenced by the _amount_ of information being processed, if we organize the material into information-laden chunks, we can maximize the amount we remember. As suggested in the first section of the chapter, it is possible to devise systems, utilizing chunking, that permit a person to recite a phone number of forty digits after hearing it only once.

Other kinds of strategies—called _mnemonics_ or

memory aids—also permit us to expand our powers of learning and retention. In one type of mnemonic, verbal material is paired in a meaningful way with an already overlearned sequence of material (such as the alphabet or ordinary numbers). Try the following scheme (developed by George Miller and his associates) on yourself or on a friend: After looking through List A in Figure 2.17 once, try repeating the words in order. Since the words have no particular relationship to one another, you will almost certainly be unable to do so.

Now learn the following _rhyming plan_ for memorizing a list:

One is a bun,
Two is a shoe,
Three is a tree,
Four is a door,
Five is a hive,
Six are sticks,
Seven is heaven,
Eight is a gate,
Nine is a line,
And ten is a hen.

Once this ditty is memorized thoroughly enough that you have no trouble remembering that "seven is heaven" or that "four is a door," you can proceed to the crucial portion of the demonstration. Read over List B in Figure 2.17. As you look at each word, make an association with the word on the rhyming list, preferably an association that is ludicrous or bizarre. Thus the first word "book" must be related to "bun" in some way: for example, you might picture a bun on one side of a toaster and a book on the other; or a bun as a bookend. It should take about five seconds to form each of the associations. Next, attempt to recall the words in List B. If you begin by saying to yourself, "One is a bun," you should immediately recall the association between "bun" and "book." Using this method, then, you should be able to recall all ten words in their exact order. Thus, the prior learning of the ditty gives you a mnemonic organization or structure that can be used to retain material that would normally strain your retentive capacity.

Other kinds of mnemonic strategies have been used profitably both by students and by mnemonicists (performers who make a living by demonstrating their extraordinary memories). Many mnemonicists employ a technique known as the *method of loci*, in which the items to be learned are mentally located in some familiar setting, such as one's living room or office. For example, it is surprisingly simple to recall a book that is mentally placed on top of a television set, or, better yet, hung from the ceiling at the end of a light cord. The principle is similar to that of the rhyming plan: by associating new items with familiar and structured items, the learner imposes a ready-made structure on the new material. When one is using the method of loci to learn ordered material, it is desirable to preserve cues for ordering. For example, the items to be learned should be mentally placed in the familiar room in a fixed sequence (perhaps from left to right around the room). A famous mnemonicist, studied by the Russian psychologist Luria, was able to perform amazing feats of retention by placing objects at specified places along a familiar road that he mentally traveled.

Other mnemonic systems exist as well, but in all of them the same types of organizational techniques —illustrated by the method of loci and the rhyming plan—are employed. In particular, most of them are systems for converting long and unrelated series of items into short and meaningfully related ones. The ideal strategy for memorizing is one that reduces the material into manageable chunks, integrates the chunks so that they have a cohesive internal organization (permitting easy combination later), and provides a meaningful association between what must be learned and some familiar material (so that easy access to the familiar generates access to the new).

Emotional and Motivational Variables
Memory may also be influenced by our emotions and motivation. If an experience has been intensely pleasurable, it is likely to be recalled. However, the effects of intensely unpleasant experiences on memory are unpredictable. Some are vividly remembered; others are repressed (Chapter 24). Material that we are strongly motivated to learn is more likely to be remembered than material to which we are indifferent. Thus you are probably better able to summarize a current newspaper article you were highly motivated to read than one you read with little interest. One reason for this variation, of course, is that you pay closer attention to material that interests you and are more inclined to "give it some thought" later; in effect, then, you are rehearsing the interesting material.

Individual Variables
A few people, including some of the great mnemonicists, possess an uncanny type of imagery called *eidetic imagery* (also known as "photographic memory"). An eidetic image is one that the subject can "project" onto external surfaces in much the same way as perceptual afterimages (Chapter 13). In Figure 2.18, for example, the eidetic person can project the image shown on the left onto the one in the center to see the combination picture of a face shown on the right.

Eidetic imagery is unusually clear and detailed and

Figure 2.18
When combined, the figures on the left and in the center form the face on face on the right. Children were shown the picture on the left. After it was replaced with the center picture, those children with eidetic imagery were able to describe the face without ever having seen it; this demonstration suggests that the eidetic children were "projecting" the left-hand picture onto the center picture. [Reprinted, by permission, from R. Haber, "Eidetic Images." *Scientific American*, April 1969, 36–44. Copyright © 1969 by Scientific American, Inc. All rights reserved.]

can be scrutinized as an actual picture might be. Certain eidetic children, for example, can be shown a picture that contains a cart. Later, upon examining their eidetic image, they can count the number of spokes on the wheel! Unlike conventional after-images, however, eidetic imagery does not shift its position as a result of eye movements. Eidetic imagery, then, is a unique and poorly understood phenomenon that is known to be different from normal memory and normal afterimages, and yet has much in common with both. We do not know whether eidetic imagery is primarily a visual process or a memory process. We do know that people capable of eidetic imagery can perform unusual retention feats. It is also known that approximately 5 percent of today's grade-school children can project eidetic images that remain vivid for a half-minute or more. Also, this imagery is extremely rare among adults. What causes eidetic imagery, what distinguishes those who possess it from those who do not, and what causes it to disappear with age, are all perplexing riddles at this time.

In recent years, Ralph Haber has conducted a number of experiments on eidetic imagery, and the following dialogue between a ten-year-old eidetic boy (*S*) and the experimenter (*E*) is taken from one

Figure 2.19
A test picture used by Ralph Haber in his study of eidetic imagery in elementary school children. After the picture was exposed for thirty seconds and removed, some subjects were able to provide unusually detailed reports of what they had seen, for example, the number of stripes on the cat's tail. [This illustration, by Marjorie Torrey, is from Josette Frank's abridged version of Lewis Carroll's *Alice in Wonderland* and is reproduced with the permission of Random House.]

of Haber's reports. The boy has just seen a colored version of the drawing shown in Figure 2.19 and is answering questions about his mental image of the drawing, which he is projecting onto a blank surface on an easel in front of him.

E. Do you see something there?
S. I see the tree, gray tree with three limbs. I see the cat with stripes around its tail.
E. Can you count those stripes:
S. Yes [*Pause*] There's about sixteen.
E. You're counting what? Black, white or both?
S. Both.
E. Tell me what else you see.

S.   And I see the flowers on the bottom. There's
     about three stems, but you can see two pairs
     of flowers. One on the right has green
     leaves, red flower on bottom with yellow
     top. And I see the girl with a green dress.
     She's got blonde hair and a red hair band
     and there are some leaves in the upper left-
     hand corner where the tree is.

E.   Can you tell me about the roots of the tree?

S.   Well, there's two of them going down here
     (*points*) and there's one that cuts off the left-
     hand side of the picture.

E.   What is the cat doing with its paw?

S.   Well, one of them he's holding out and the
     other one is on the tree.

E.   What color is the sky?

S.   Can't tell.

E.   Can't tell at all?

S.   No. I can see the yellowish ground, though.

E.   Tell me if any of the parts go away or
     change at all as I'm talking to you. What
     color is the girl's dress?

S.   Green. It has some white on it.

E.   How about her legs and feet?

                    (*The subject looks away from the easel
                     and then back again.*)

E.   Is the image gone?

S.   Yes, except for the tree.

E.   Tell me when it goes away.

S.   [*Pause*] It went away.*

Are there other differences among individuals, in
particular between adults and children, besides the
capacity for eidetic imagery? As might be expected,
adults generally do better than children on retention tasks. This superior performance reflects in
part the adult abilities to pay closer attention to the
task without being distracted and to follow instructions well, as well as a willingness to persevere. In

*Reprinted, by permission, from R. Haber, "Eidetic Images,"
Scientific American, April 1969. © 1969 by Scientific
American, Inc. All rights reserved.

addition, adults have probably developed better
strategies for learning and retention and also
possess greater retentive capacities than do young
children, at least for most tasks. We do know, for
example, that the child's STM tends to increase
with age.

Differences Among Species   Despite the maxim,
"elephants never forget," it is probably true that the
animal's retentive powers are no greater than our
own. What limited knowledge of animal memory
we have suggests that the lower primates have
short-term and long-term memory systems, and
that their memories are subject to the same types
of variables that affect human retention. Undoubtedly, significant differences in memory between
human beings and lower primates do exist, but
these are very difficult to assess, since much of
what is known about human memory comes from
subjective reports and responses to complex verbal
material, neither of which has been obtained from
animals.

FACTORS INFLUENCING FORGETTING

There is a story that is sometimes told about a
brilliant American mathematician who was for
many years a professor at the Massachusetts Institute
of Technology. According to the story, the professor
was strolling across the campus one sunny afternoon
when a student stopped him and asked him a
question about a difficult topic the student had
encountered in his studies. The professor patiently
answered the student's question. When he had
finished, the student thanked him and was turning
to go when the professor caught his arm. "By the
way," he said to the student, "can you tell me
which direction I was going when you stopped
me?" "Why yes," said the student pointing down

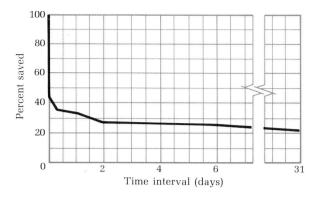

the path, "you were going that way." "Ah good," said the professor, "then I've already had my lunch. Thank you." And he headed back toward his office.

Apparently, mathematics had crowded lunch right out of the professor's mind. This seems like a good example of what some psychologists have called *interference* (that is, forgetting that is due to the interference produced by intervening activities). Other psychologists have stressed the importance of *decay* (that is, forgetting that is due mainly to the passage of time). Although it is hard to see how the professor's absentmindedness could be accounted for by the decay principle, there is strong evidence, dating back to Ebbinghaus's classic *forgetting curve* (Figure 2.20), that the passage of time is a significant factor in forgetting. Contemporary psychologists do not feel compelled to make an either-or choice between the interference principle and the decay principle but rather tend to see some truth in each.

In a number of experiments, the nature of the activity intervening between initial learning and attempted recall has been varied. The results of these experiments have suggested that most—but not all—forgetting is due to intervening activity. The findings of one study on the relationship between the recall of verbal material (nonsense syllables) and the nature of the intervening activity (being asleep or being awake) is shown in Figure 2.21, in which the performance of someone who slept between learning and recall is compared with the performance of someone who was awake between learning and recall. The results are consistent with both the interference principle and the decay principle; they also illustrate how difficult it is to separate the two factors. If we assume that sleep produces less interference than other activities, but that the same amount of decay occurs in both the sleeping and waking states, then the higher retention scores of the sleeping subjects supports the proposal that

Figure 2.20
Percent savings as a function of retention interval (in days). This is the classic *forgetting curve* first reported by Hermann Ebbinghaus. "Percent savings" refers to the amount of time—or number of trials—saved in relearning material, compared with the amount of time taken to learn the same material originally. Thus, a *savings score* of 100 percent signifies perfect retention (no relearning required); 0 percent signifies total lack of retention (the same amount of time needed to relearn as was needed to learn originally). [Data from H. Ebbinghaus, 1885.]

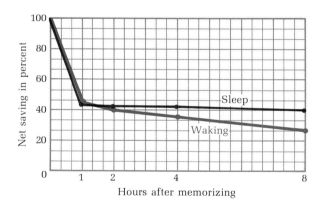

Figure 2.21
Retention—again measured in terms of a savings score—as a function of retention interval in subjects who spent the interval sleeping or waking. The material memorized consisted of nonsense syllables. [Data from E. B. van Ormer, "Retention after Intervals of Sleep and Waking," *Archives of Psychology*, 1932, No. 137.]

forgetting is caused by interference. However, since even the sleeping subjects forgot almost half the material, the results also suggest either that pure decay occurs or that dreaming interferes with retention.

Another factor that seems to influence forgetting is the intake of alcohol and other kinds of drugs. We know that certain drugs impair one's ability to recall and that experiences that occur while someone is under the influence of sufficient doses of these drugs may not be remembered well later. Perhaps the most common example is the failure to recall some of the things one has said and done while intoxicated. However, although there is no question that these substances may impair retention if taken in large quantities, not everything we forget that has occurred during intoxication can be attributed to the effects of alcohol. For example, it is true that a person who has drunk a substantial quantity of alcohol may have trouble remembering where he parked his car, but *every* car owner has probably forgotten where he left his car at one time or another, even without the influence of alcohol. Moreover, it is known that *state-dependent learning and retention* can occur—we supposedly remember events best when we are in the same state as when we experienced them. Thus, events occurring while we are intoxicated (or asleep, or hypnotized, or whatever) may be poorly remembered when we are alert but may be better recalled when we are again in the state in which the event occurred. Unfortunately, little is known about such state-dependent effects. The uncertainty about these effects notwithstanding, the following three conclusions would seem to be appropriate: (1) memories are fallible and retention is rarely certain; (2) retention may be impaired if a person has taken sufficient amounts of alcohol or certain other drugs at the time of learning or at the time of attempted recall;

(3) there is no compelling evidence that drugs *improve* retention.

FURTHER CONSIDERATIONS

TRANSFER OF TRAINING

In the preceding sections in this chapter, we have been concerned primarily with the learning and retention of single items or single lists of items, studied more or less in a vacuum. In the everyday world, however, what we learn and retain is influenced, to some extent, by what we have experienced in the past and by what we will experience in the future. The general name given to the influence of one learning experience on another is *transfer of training*.

If you have learned Task A—for example, if you have learned how to recite a certain list—will the effects of this experience *facilitate* or *interfere* with the subsequent learning of Task B? In order to answer this question, we must first distinguish between *general transfer* and *specific transfer*.

General transfer refers to the utilization of specific skills, strategies, and modes of operating that have been acquired in the learning of prior tasks. To the extent that these learned habits and styles can be applied to a new task, the performance of that task will be facilitated. Thus, virtually any kind of experience in memorizing verbal lists will facilitate the memorization of subsequent lists; learning to write computer programs in one computer language will aid in learning to write them in a second computer language; a third language is acquired more rapidly than a second. In general, the more the tasks resemble one another, the greater the amount of positive transfer that will occur. Thus, practice with paired-associate lists will facilitate subsequent paired-associate learning more than it will serial-list learning; it will facilitate list learning memorization

LIST A	LIST D
book–cream	steel–beef
chew–wharf	car–white
week–towel	voice–star
bear–yell	beer–long
crow–dish	pipe–night
fire–lend	peas–wind

LIST B	LIST E
chew–pier	corn–wind
crow–plate	speak–star
book–milk	iron–beef
fire–give	cigar–night
bear–roar	ale–long
week–cloth	auto–white

LIST C	LIST F
week–tire	tree–long
fire–tear	hand–night
chew–felt	wood–beef
book–door	game–wind
bear–radio	soup–white
crow–study	farm–star

Figure 2.22
Lists of words that could be used to demonstrate negative and positive specific transfer. When the stimuli are identical and the responses differ—as in Lists A, B, and C—*negative specific transfer* occurs. Thus, a subject who has memorized the paired-associates in List A will have more difficulty learning the pairs in List B than a subject who had not learned List A. When the response members are identical and the stimuli differ—as in Lists D, E, and F—*positive specific transfer* occurs. Under each set of conditions, the order of items common to the lists is changed so that the serial position of the words will not influence retention.

of another *kind* of list more than it will the memorization of a lengthy passage. (However, acquisition of a motor skill—for example, learning to ride a bicycle—will be unaffected by the list-learning experience.)

Another kind of general transfer is possible. *Negative general transfer* interferes with subsequent learning. For example, people who have learned particular solutions to a problem may persevere in using that approach when it is no longer the best one; thus, a previously learned approach can interfere with the solution of a new kind of problem. (In contrast, people without the prior problem-solving experience will be more apt to see the more appropriate solution.) Such negative transfer is said to result from the *set* the subject has learned in the prior problem-solving experience and from his subsequent rigidity (see the discussion of "functional fixedness" in Chapter 8).

Specific transfer refers to the transfer of specific information. It has been studied most thoroughly with paired-associate materials. When stimuli and responses are entirely different in two successive paired-associate lists, transfer is minimal. What little transfer does occur is general transfer (of an approach or mode of operation, for example). Subjects who have had a great deal of experience with paired-associate learning (and will therefore profit little from additional general transfer) show no *positive specific transfer* when the corresponding stimulus and response pairs of the two successive paired-associate lists are entirely dissimilar (for instance, if the first list consists of pairs of nonsense syllables and numbers, and the second of Greek letters and English words). When the stimuli are identical but the responses differ (as in the lists shown in Figure 2.22) *negative specific transfer* occurs. Thus if the pair BOOK-CREAM has been learned, learning to say MILK in response to BOOK will be

impeded, or interfered with, rather than facilitated. The more the response items differ, the greater the negative specific transfer will be. Thus, after learning BOOK-CREAM, learning the pair BOOK-DOOR (List C) will tend to be more difficult than learning BOOK-MILK. On the other hand, when the response members of the paired associate lists are identical, and the stimulus items are different, *positive specific transfer* occurs. Lists exhibiting positive specific transfer are illustrated in Lists D, E, and F in Figure 2.22. Again the magnitude of the transfer effect depends upon the degree of similarity between the stimulus items: the more related the stimulus members, the greater the positive transfer effect. Thus, if someone has learned the paired associates list in List D, a larger positive transfer effect would occur for List E than for List F.

These generalizations have implications for studying a language. When we are learning the vocabulary of a second language, it is easier to learn the English equivalent of the foreign word than to learn the foreign equivalent of the English word. Translation from the foreign language into English is facilitated by positive transfer, but translation from the English into the second language is subject to interference by negative transfer (since we already have numerous English associations for each English word).

Proactive and Retroactive Inhibition Interference, then, refers to the negative, inhibiting effects of one learning experience on another. It has been suggested that there are two kinds of interference—*retroactive inhibition* and *proactive inhibition*, which are diagrammed in Figure 2.23.

Retroactive inhibition occurs when the retention of previously learned material is impaired by the acquisition of new material, particularly if the second learning experience follows the first within a reasonably short period of time. For example, a second list of words or equations may hamper the retention of a first list. The more dissimilar the interpolated material is to the preceding items, the less the retroactive inhibition. One way of minimizing retroactive inhibition is simply to learn the new material in a different location, but if you want to maximize retention of a given body of items—for example, if you are studying for a particular examination—a good strategy is to study in the same room in which you will be tested. The reason is that the responses you learn will, in part, be conditioned by the cues in the room. Those responses will then have maximum strength when

RETROACTIVE INHIBITION

Experimental group	Learn A → Learn B → Test A
Control group	Learn A → [Do nothing] → Test A

PROACTIVE INHIBITION

Experimental group	Learn A → Learn B → Test B
Control group	[Do nothing] → Learn B → Test B

Figure 2.23
Diagram of procedures for studying retroactive inhibition (RI) and proactive inhibition (PI). In assessing RI, the experimental group learns the potentially interfering (or "inhibiting") material (here B) *after* learning A and before being tested for retention of A. In assessing PI, the potentially interfering material (here A) is learned by the experimental group before learning B and being tested for B. In neither case are subjects in the control group exposed to the interfering material.

tested in a situation as similar as possible to that which prevailed at the time they were initially learned.

Although it is true that the more similar the interpolated activity is to the prior experience, the greater the retroactive inhibition will be, there is one obvious qualification to this generalization: if the new materials are highly similar or identical to the preceding matter, the acquisition of the new material actually constitutes further practice rather than interference. The relationship of the degree of similarity between original material and interpolated material to the ease of retention is illustrated in Figure 2.24. This effect of the degree of similarity on efficiency of recall, as represented by the U-shaped curve in the figure, is known as the *Skaggs-Robinson hypothesis*.

Proactive inhibition is a more puzzling phenomenon, since the interfering material is actually learned *prior* to the material that it is interfering with. It turns out that little proactive interference occurs if the second material (List 2) is tested immediately after it is learned, when the recall of List 2 is high and that of the interfering material (List 1) is low (partly because List 1 has

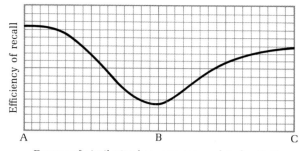

Degree of similarity between interpolated activity
and original memorization (decreasing from A to C)

Figure 2.24
Illustration of the Skaggs-Robinson hypothesis, which
relates efficiency of recall to the degree of similarity
between the material memorized and the activity interpolated between memorization and testing. As you look
from A to C, the degree of similarity decreases. Note
that interference produced by the interpolated activity
is greatest for intermediate degrees of similarity.
[Reprinted, by permission, from E. S. Robinson, "The
'Similarity' Factor in Retroaction," *The American
Journal of Psychology*, 1927, 39, 297–312.]

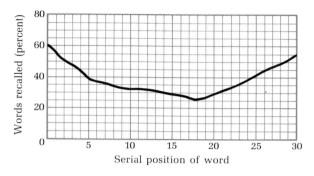

Figure 2.25
A typical serial-position curve relating the percentage
of words recalled to the serial position of the word
in a list.

just undergone retroactive interference by learning
List 2). However, if testing is carried out some time
after learning both lists, the retroactive interference
of List 2 on List 1 apparently declines. The strength
of the first list is therefore increased, as is its
proactive interference with the second list.

THE SERIAL-POSITION CURVE

In trying to recall a series of events, we tend to
remember most clearly what has happened first
and last. Thus, items that are presented at the
beginning and end of a classroom session or of an
argument are more likely to be retained by the
listener or reader than items presented in the
middle. Lists of words have been used as the
material in most of the studies of the influence of
the serial position of an item in a list on its recall.
In Figure 2.25, for example, the efficiency of
retention is plotted against the *serial position* of
each word in a list of thirty. Note that the highest
percentage of words recalled are those in the
beginning and end of the list. The enhanced
retention at the beginning of the list is called the
primacy effect (the first items to be presented are
more readily remembered) and the enhanced

retention at the end of this list is called the *recency
effect* (those items most recently presented are
more readily remembered). The terms for these
two "effects" are merely labels describing what
has been empirically observed. What causes the
shape of the curve? Some psychologists have
suggested that this effect can be explained by
proactive and retroactive inhibition: that those
items at the beginning of a list are more prominent
because they receive no proactive interference from
earlier items, and those at the end benefit from
receiving no retroactive interference from later
items. The items in the middle of the list, therefore,
are the most difficult to recall because substantial
amounts of both proactive inhibition (from earlier
items) and retroactive inhibition (from subsequent
items) work against their effective retention.
Although these types of interference may indeed
help to cause the serial-position curve, the recency
effect is also partly due to the operation of
short-term memory. Since the most recently
presented items are still stored in STM, they are
therefore more prominent than the preceding items,

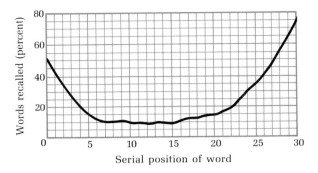

Figure 2.26
When retention is measured immediately after a list
is learned, the last items in the list are better retained.
Thus, the *recency effect*, but not the *primacy effect*,
shown in the serial-position curve of Figure 2.25, is
enhanced.

which will be recalled only if they have passed into
LTM. This function of STM is demonstrated by the
fact that the recency effect—but not the primacy
effect—is enhanced when retention tests are
conducted immediately after the list has been heard
(Figure 2.26).

AMNESIA

On occasion, a person may exhibit an unusual
degree of forgetting after some harshly unpleasant
event, such as an accident or psychological trauma.
The phrase *retrograde amnesia*—that is, forgetting
that moves backward in time—describes cases in
which everything or nearly everything that has
occurred for a period of time prior to the disturbing
event is forgotten. In many victims, retrograde
amnesia is actually a form of *motivated forgetting*—
forgetting that enables the person to avoid remembering the event itself or the preceding actions that
may have been responsible for it. Other cases of
retrograde amnesia, however, are definitely caused
by brain damage. When the material that is forgotten occurred *after* a certain event, the inability
to recall is labeled *anterograde amnesia*. One example
of anterograde amnesia is the deficiency observed
in Henry M. after his hippocampus had been
removed.

RETRIEVAL FROM LONG-TERM MEMORY

Any comprehensive theory of remembering must
explain why some and not other items are stored
in LTM, how and where they are stored, and to
what extent stored items may be *retrieved* for use.
We have already noted that most forgetting may be
attributed to interference caused by other material.
Decay, or the mere passage of time, may also be
the cause of some forgetting, but apparently only
of items in STM that have not passed into LTM.

If an item is stored in LTM, can we describe
exactly what is stored by the brain and how it is
retrieved? These questions—about the physiological
locus and process of storage and about the process
of retrieval—are obviously interrelated. Moreover,
the only direct evidence that storage has been
successful is a demonstration of successful retention. When an item cannot be retrieved, it is
impossible to be certain whether or not it is still
stored in LTM. One standard analogy is a book
that is missing from its place in a library: has it
been shelved in the wrong place, or stolen? If the
library is large, the answer may never be learned.
If the book is found, its retrieval is proof of
storage, but if retrieval does not occur, then it
remains uncertain whether or not the book is
stored anywhere in the library. If our LTM is
efficient, items should be stored according to a
particular system, as are books in a library. How
else would we be able to retrieve the appropriate
item from such an incredibly large number? We
shall see that LTM material is indeed organized.
Evidently, it is stored according to a system of
semantic organization, although there is some
evidence for an acoustic organization as well. We
shall see also that the originally stored item and
that which is retrieved are by no means always

identical—the retrieved item is often distorted by our prejudices, experiences, and expectations.

The Repression Theory We mentioned that one form of forgetting is motivated forgetting, such as that occurring in some retrograde-amnesia patients. Milder forms of amnesia occur as well, and some theorists assert that we all suffer from it to some extent. In fact, Sigmund Freud proposed that we often fail to retrieve information from LTM because of this kind of active process of defensive but automatic (rather than deliberate) forgetting, which is called *repression* (see Chapters 24 and 30 for further discussion).

The Tip-of-the-Tongue Phenomenon Whenever we cannot quite retrieve an item that we know is stored in our memory—for example, when we grope for the name of an old acquaintance, of a once-familiar street, or of the back-up quarterback on our favorite football team three years ago—we are experiencing the *tip-of-the-tongue phenomenon*. We may even be able to identify many characteristics of the item (for example, the number of syllables in a name, or the first letter). Indeed, we are certain that it is available to us, but we cannot gain complete access to it. The tip-of-the-tongue phenomenon (TOT) has been studied systematically by Roger Brown and David McNeill. In the late 1960s, they showed that recall of TOT items actually displays a serial-position curve similar to the one in Figure 2.25; this means that the beginning or the end of a word on the "tip of the tongue" is more likely to be recalled than the middle. In one experiment, Brown and McNeill gave subjects a definition of a fairly uncommon English word, *sextant,* and asked them what the word was. Subjects were told that the word stood for "a navigational instrument used in measuring angular distances, especially the altitude of sun, moon, and stars at sea." This particular definition created a TOT state in nine of Brown and McNeill's fifty-six subjects. (Of the other forty-seven subjects, some stated the word unhesitatingly, and the others produced no answer at all, suggesting that they were unacquainted with the word.) The words that the nine reported during the TOT state included some that were similar in *meaning* to the target word, such as "astrolabe," "compass," and "protractor," and some that were similar in *sound* to the target word, such as "secant," "sextet," and "sexton." Some subjects proposed more than one word, offering answers that were similar in meaning to the target word and others that were similar in sound. This would suggest that retrieval was progressing along both auditory and semantic routes. The TOT phenomenon, then, provides a dramatic illustration of the distinction between storage and retrieval; that the words are still in storage is demonstrated by the semantic and acoustic confusions, and by their ultimate retrieval, but, for a period of time at least, they are not retrievable.

Retrieval as Reconstruction Whether a person is on a therapist's couch trying to recall a repressed experience (Chapter 30) or groping for the name of a word that is on the tip of his tongue, it seems that much of what we call remembering is actually the retrieval of stored items by means of a process of *reconstruction*. One of the best examples of the reconstruction process was provided by the British psychologist Frederic Bartlett in his classic studies of remembering in the 1920s and 1930s. Bartlett's most interesting experimental technique was called the *method of repeated reproduction*, in which the subject was asked to look at a drawing or read some material and

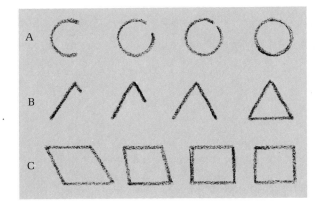

Figure 2.27
Successive reproduction of figures causes them to be distorted in the direction of more symmetrical and meaningful figures. Thus, the crescent figure might become a circle; the line figure, a triangle; the trapezoid, a rectangle or square.

then to reproduce it from memory on several subsequent occasions. Bartlett studied the errors of the typical subject and the trends that developed in the repeated attempts at recall.

Bartlett found that *precise recall or reproduction was the exception rather than the rule.* Moreover, the successive attempts at recall revealed a continuing revision of the material (1) toward fewer details and (2) toward the more familiar, recognizable, and meaningful. Occasionally, after repeated reproduction of a drawing had produced a simplified figure, elaboration of that simple figure would then occur; the resulting figure might bear only remote resemblance to the original. Or, in the reproduction of a story, many subjects omitted unfamiliar details or altered them to those to which they were more accustomed. (For example, culturally alien material was often altered to conform to the culturally familiar. Thus, the supernatural aspects of a story about ghosts—important in some cultures—were omitted by Bartlett's British subjects.) Certain items became stereotyped early in the reproduction sequence and remained stable in subsequent reproductions. Also, although striking details of a photograph or story were remembered quite well by many, even these might be forgotten by some if they did not conform to their preconceptions.

In discussing his remarkable findings, Bartlett concentrated on the organization subjects imposed on stored material as they tried to reconstruct it. Often, what a subject recalled was strongly determined by his own feelings and prejudices and not at all related to what he had actually seen or heard. Even more disturbing—especially if one considers the implications for, say, the validity of a witness's testimony before a jury or of a jury verdict or of eyewitness accounts—was the fact that Bartlett's subjects were generally unaware of how inventive their accounts actually were. Indeed,

the more coherent the reproduced recall, and the more it conformed to the subject's preconceptions, the more certain the subject tended to be that his recall was accurate.

Bartlett's work, then, showed that much of what we remember is grossly distorted at the time it is recalled, as we reconstruct events the way we would like them to have been, or the way they have usually been, rather than as they were in fact. His observations have been replicated by many other workers who have employed different stimulus materials. For example, Figure 2.27 illustrates the way in which successive reproductions of a sketch are distorted to produce a more symmetrical and meaningful figure: the crescent figure in Figure 2.27 gradually becomes a circle; the line figure, a triangle; and the trapezoid, a rectangle, and then a square. We shall now discuss three types of reconstruction: (1) the recall of ambiguous figures, (2) the experimental study of rumor, and (3) the study of sentence recognition.

Recall of Ambiguous Figures The stimulus figures in the center of Figure 2.28 are ambiguous because they could be schematic representations of more than one object. Thus, the top figure could be easily seen as either a "B" or a "13"; the second,

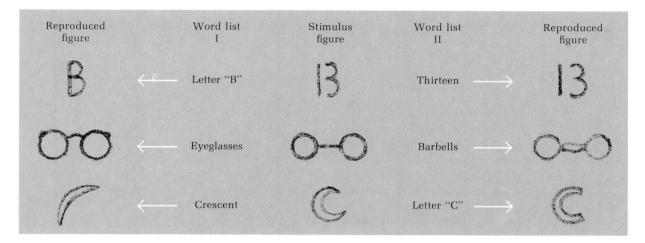

Reproduced figure	Word list I	Stimulus figure	Word list II	Reproduced figure

Figure 2.28
The stimulus figures in the center are ambiguous, since they could represent more than one object (for example, the top figure might be the letter B or the number 13). Subjects given a verbal label (for example, "the letter B" or "thirteen") are likely to distort the figure in the direction of the verbal label.

as either a pair of eyeglasses or barbells; the third as either a crescent or a "C." If one is given verbal labels for each of the figures, and then asked to reproduce these figures, his reproduction will be distorted in the direction of the verbal labels. For example, when subjects are asked to draw the middle object in the figure from memory, those who are given the label "eyeglasses" will reconstruct the figure to make it resemble more closely a pair of glasses; subjects who are given the label "barbells" will reconstruct the figure accordingly.

The Psychology of Rumor If one individual distorts remembered material to conform with his expectations and prejudices, imagine how much distortion must occur when material is passed from one person to another. This type of reconstruction has been measured in studies of *rumor*. The method is similar to Bartlett's method of repeated reproduction except that the successive reproductions are made by different subjects. The first of a series of ten people is asked to read a paragraph or look at a picture, in which some action or series of actions is portrayed, and then to tell the next person what he has read or seen. The sec-

ond person repeats the description to the third, and so on. As might be expected, by the time the message gets to the last person, it is greatly distorted. This technique has been used in the study of prejudice; if a picture shows a man picking someone's pocket in a subway, and if one or more of the people participating in the experiment hates or fears a certain ethnic group, chances are that the story will change so that the thief becomes a member of that ethnic group.

Sentence Recognition Another, more passive type of reconstruction is illustrated by a study of someone's *sentence recognition*. Have you ever read this sentence: "It is important to make a distinction between general and specific transfer."? If you remember the discussion of transfer of training earlier in the chapter, you have probably answered "yes." If, however, you refer to the second sentence in the second paragraph of that discussion, you will see that the sentence here is worded quite differently from the one you read. Nonetheless, the two sentences are similar enough in *meaning* that it is easy to confuse them. This phenomenon can be readily demonstrated in the laboratory; people will think they recognize sentences and paragraphs they have never seen, if the sentences and paragraphs are similar in meaning to what they have actually seen before. This failure to recognize a sentence as novel is actually adaptive, since what has been recognized is the important meaning. Since it is the meaning that is important, there is no need for separate retention of the various ways we may have heard the same meaning expressed.

The process of recall, then, is not so much the retrieval of a given item as it was originally stored in LTM according to systems of semantic and acoustic organization, but more the retrieval of an item that has undergone some kind of reconstruction, strongly influenced by past experience, expectations, and wishes. Just as these variables affect our perceptions of the immediate sensory world (see Chapter 14), they also alter recall—which is our current account of previous perceptions.

Suggested Readings

Bartlett, F. C. (1932) *Remembering: A study in experimental and social psychology.* New York: Cambridge. [Bartlett's classic is still one of the most interesting and lively books on memory.]

Crovitz, H. F. (1970) *Galton's walk.* New York: Harper and Row. [A fascinating treatment of thinking, intelligence, and creativity. Includes some interesting material on memory.]

Deese, J., & Hulse, S. H. (1967) *The psychology of learning,* (3rd ed.) New York: McGraw-Hill. [Chapters 8–11 constitute an excellent review of research in the areas of verbal learning (memorization), transfer of training, and forgetting.]

Haber, R. (1969) "Eidetic images." *Scientific American,* April, 36–44. Reprinted as Scientific American Offprint 522. [An interesting article on Ralph Haber's work with eidetic children.]

Lindsay, P. H., & Norman, D. A. (1972) *Human information processing.* New York: Academic Press. [The best and most complete treatment available of the modern human information-processing approach to memory is contained in Chapters 8–11].

Luria, A. R. (1968) *The mind of a mnemonist.* New York: Basic Books. [An engrossing report by the great Russian psychologist of a man with extraordinary powers of retention whom Luria studied over a period of years. A short, highly readable book.]

Neisser, U. (1967) *Cognitive psychology.* New York: Appleton-Century-Crofts. [Contains an interesting treatment of memory, including visual memory and echoic (or auditory) memory.]

Richardson, A. (1969) *Mental imagery.* New York: Springer. [An excellent study of mental imagery, including after-imagery, eidetic imagery, and imagination.]

CHAPTER THREE

Pavlovian Conditioning and Habituation

PAVLOVIAN CONDITIONING: BASIC CONCEPTS

When you hear a loud noise or receive an electric shock, you jump. When you eat, glands in your mouth and stomach secrete various fluids. In each of these instances, your body is reacting automatically to an external event—noise, shock, dinner. The fact that the reaction is automatic means that it will occur over and over again without any special training, learning experience, or conscious effort on your part. These innate, automatic reactions that occur in all organisms, both animal and human, are called *reflex actions,* or *respondent behavior,* and the events that invariably produce them are called *eliciting stimuli.*

The experimental procedure known as *Pavlovian conditioning* developed from a study of reflexes conducted in the early years of this century by the Russian physiologist, Ivan Pavlov (1849–1936). In studying digestion, Pavlov had developed a technique whereby he could measure the fluids secreted in a dog's mouth and stomach. He was thus in a position to investigate the precise relationship between a stimulus (food) and a response (salivation). As his work on digestion progressed, he encountered an unforeseen problem: the dogs were salivating pre-

Figure 3.1
Ivan Pavlov. [Historical Pictures Service, Chicago]

Figure 3.2
Pavlov watching a conditioning experiment in 1934.
[TASS from Sovfoto]

maturely, before they ate, before they even saw food; in fact, they salivated as soon as Pavlov walked into the room. Pavlov began to study this phenomenon, which he called "conditioning." The conditioning process has since been intensively investigated and applied experimentally to behavior other than reflex actions (as we shall see in Chapter 4, Operant Conditioning). Pavlov's work was the first done, however, and the process he discovered is a distinctive form of conditioning dealing mainly with reflexive be-

havior. For these reasons, it is sometimes called *"classical conditioning."*

Conditioning is a process in which an organism's responding is modified by environmental conditions. In Pavlov's laboratory, the dog's salivary glands began to react not just to food, the normal stimulus, but to the sight of Pavlov, a new stimulus that had originally been *neutral* (that is, had not caused salivation at all). Furthermore, it was found that the dog would also respond in the same manner to other originally

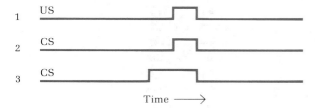

Figure 3.3
In simultaneous conditioning, the conditioned stimulus (CS) occurs at the same time as or just prior to the onset of the unconditioned stimulus (US). (Lines 2 and 3 show the two different cases.)

neutral stimuli—the sound from a tuning fork, a light, a ringing bell, even to circles painted on cards —provided that these stimuli were systematically paired with presentations of food.

Before the advent of biofeedback techniques, reflex actions—such as heartbeat, the dilation of blood vessels, salivation, and perspiration—could not easily be observed or measured. For this reason, little research was done on them before the beginning of the twentieth century. Indeed, Pavlov won the Nobel Prize in 1904 for his pioneering studies of digestion. One of his achievements was to devise a surgical method of observing the rate of digestive secretions in living dogs. He implanted tubes in the mouths and stomachs of the dogs; the tubes led out through the skin to receptacles. In this way, the rate and amount of the secretions could be measured separately and accurately. The application of an objective means of measurement to the hitherto invisible reflex actions enabled physiologists to study them scientifically.

Pavlov's fortuitous discovery of the _conditioned reflex_—which could be artificially created in the laboratory and then studied in just the same way as a natural, innate reflex—opened up a new way

of looking at behavior. Pavlov described his dogs' reflexes to experimental stimuli without speculating as to what the dogs were feeling or thinking. Other scientists began to accept the view that the behavior of organisms could be described and understood in terms of observable and measurable reflexes. Indeed, some held that all behaviors—whether learned or innate—could be analyzed into their component reflexes. Thus, the foundation was laid for modern _behaviorism_ (which we shall discuss in Chapter 4).

PAVLOVIAN CONDITIONING: BASIC PHENOMENA

Figure 3.3 illustrates the sequence of events in the experiments set up by Pavlov. A hungry dog was restrained in the apparatus shown in Figure 3.4. Great care was taken to isolate the animal as much as possible from distracting stimulation, such as people's voices, noise in the corridor, and so forth. The tube leading from the animal's mouth carried saliva directly from the salivary gland to a receptacle, where it could be measured. When food powder— the eliciting or _unconditioned stimulus (US)_—was placed in the dog's mouth, the animal salivated reflexively. Salivation was the _unconditioned response (UR)_ to food in the mouth. In continuing the experiment, Pavlov struck a tuning fork one-half second before each presentation of the food. After a number of such _pairings_ of tone and food, he would occasionally sound the tuning fork alone, without presenting any food. On these _test trials,_ in which the food _(US)_ was omitted, the tone by itself was sufficient to elicit salivation in almost the same amounts as when food was actually put in the dog's mouth! The originally neutral stimulus, the tone produced by the tuning fork, had become a _conditioned stimulus (CS),_ capable of eliciting a _conditioned response (CR),_ salivation, which it formerly did not elicit.

Figure 3.4
Experimental arrangement used by Pavlov for studying salivary conditioning. Soon after a tone (the CS) sounded, the dish containing dry powdered food (the US) was placed near the dog, who took some into his mouth. Salivation (the UR) was measured by collecting saliva in a small funnel that led to a measuring tube. Enroute to the measuring tube, the drops of salivia activated a moving recorder that graphed saliva flow on a continuous record. After a number of CS-US pairings, the dog salivated to the sound of the tuning fork: a conditioned reflex had been established.

Measurement There are several methods of measuring responses in such conditioning experiments. One is to record the *magnitude* of each successive response, for example, the amount of saliva that flows into the tube shown in Figure 3.4 on each trial.

When these amounts are plotted against trials on a graph, they show a function that has a specific shape. Differences in the characteristics of such functions illustrate the precise way in which conditioned responses are acquired under different experimental conditions. For example, in an experiment in which the CS precedes the US by one-half second, the function will be quite different from one in which the CS precedes the US by ten seconds.

Responses may also be measured in terms of *latency,* the time between the presentation of the stimulus and the appearance of the response. Still another measure is the *reliability* with which the CS elicits the CR: that is, the percentage of trials on which the response is elicited.

CR Versus UR The conditioned response and the unconditioned response in Pavlov's experiment seem to be the same, but they are not really identical. Classical conditioning is not a simple process of substitution in which one stimulus (the CS) merely replaces another stimulus (the US). Even when the CR and UR appear to be the same, they differ in several detectable ways: in latency, in magnitude, and in reliability. In other instances, the CR obviously bears no resemblance to the UR. For example, in one type of classical-conditioning experiment, a rat is confined in a dark cage with a grid floor. Periodically, a light (CS) is turned on in the cage for five seconds. It is followed by a moderately intense electric shock (US) delivered through the floor for two seconds. The rat's initial orienting response to the light is to look at it; his responses to the electric shock are likely to include jumping and running around the cage. After a few pairings of light and shock, however, he will begin to make conditioned responses to the light, responses that will probably include *freezing* (rigid immobility). In this instance, the conditioned response to the light is not only different from the unconditioned response to the shock; it is actually incompatible with it— rigid immobility precludes simultaneous jumping and running.

Types of Procedures In Pavlovian conditioning, the CS and the US both precede the response. It turns out that variation of the time interval between the CS and the US has a great effect on the progress of conditioning. In Pavlov's earliest experiments, the *simultaneous conditioning* procedure was the one most frequently used, and it remains the most common and effective method. It is known as simultaneous conditioning because the CS and US occur almost simultaneously (although, by tradition, the CS may begin as much as five seconds before the US). When

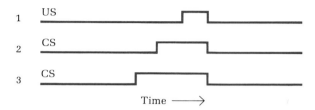

Figure 3.5
In delayed conditioning, the CS begins more than five seconds before the US. Otherwise, delayed conditioning is the same as simultaneous conditioning (Figure 3.3), in which the CS precedes the US by five seconds or less. (Line 2 shows a relatively short delay, say six seconds; Line 3 shows a longer delay.)

the onset of the CS precedes that of the US by more than five seconds, the procedure is conventionally called *delayed conditioning*. As Figure 3.5 shows, however, the CS and US continue to overlap in time, and they terminate together in both procedures. On test trials in either simultaneous or delayed conditioning, the CS elicits the CR at a time just before the US would normally appear. Delayed conditioning is thus qualitatively similar to simultaneous conditioning.

Three other conditioning procedures, in which the temporal relationships between the CS and US are quite different, are illustrated in Figures 3.6–3.8.

In *trace conditioning* the CS is presented alone for a short period of time and then terminated. Then, after a specified interval, the US is presented alone, as shown in Figure 3.6. If the interval is sufficiently long, it can be shown that the CR does not occur immediately when the CS is presented but tends to occur just before the US is presented.

In *temporal conditioning*, there is no specific external CS. Instead, the US is presented at regular intervals, as shown in Figure 3.7. In this procedure, the amount of time since the previous US presentation becomes in itself a CS. On test trials, the CR occurs slightly

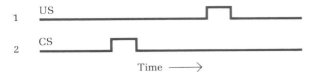

Figure 3.6
In trace conditioning, the CS terminates *before* the onset
of the US.

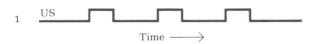

Figure 3.7
In temporal conditioning, there is no specific external
CS. Instead, the US is presented at regular intervals.

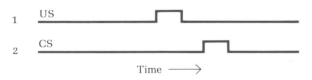

Figure 3.8
In backward conditioning, the CS is presented *after*,
rather than before, the US. This procedure is generally
ineffective in producing conditioning.

in advance of the time when the US would normally
occur. In the same way, people accustomed to regular
mealtimes begin to secrete stomach acids and to
grow hungry as mealtime approaches.

Finally, in *backward conditioning*, the CS is presented
after, rather than before, the US. The backward-
conditioning procedure, illustrated in Figure 3.8, is
generally ineffective in producing conditioning.
Apparently, the CS must precede and, in effect, predict the occurrence of the US for effective conditioning to occur.

Predictive Function of the CR Indeed, the CS
often functions as a warning, and the CR helps to
prepare the organism for the impending US. The
conditioned salivation response by Pavlov's dogs
prepared them for eating the food when it arrived,

and the rat's freezing response may have prepared
him for jumping when the shock arrived. This effect
occurs in everyday life as well as in the laboratory.
The sound of dishes rattling in the kitchen or the
smell of cooking food may become a CS that elicits
salivation in humans. The sound of an auto horn
while you are crossing a street may cause you to
freeze temporarily while you try to locate the source
of impending danger.

Experimental Extinction Pavlovian conditioning,
which can modify behavior considerably under
laboratory conditions, can be quite effective in everyday life as well. Its effects are not necessarily permanent, however—Pavlov's dogs did not spend the
rest of their lives salivating to tuning forks. When
a CS is presented several times *without being followed
by the US,* the magnitude of the CR begins to decrease, and so does the probability of its appearing
at all. This process is called *extinction;* during extinction, the CS eventually loses the power to elicit the
CR. In short, when Pavlov no longer fed the dog
after sounding the tuning fork, it salivated less and
less to the sound on successive trials, and on some
trials did not salivate at all. When a response no
longer occurs on several trials in a row, it is said to
have been extinguished.

As another example of extinction, consider a small
child who has been bitten by a puppy. The pain of
being bitten can be considered to be the US; the
puppy itself is the CS. The child is startled and
terrified (CR); he refuses to approach the puppy
again. His fear *generalizes* to other dogs (see the discussion of generalization below); for several months
afterward, he will not go near a dog. Then he is
introduced to another, more placid, puppy. A cautious approach to this animal (another CS) does not
result in being bitten; in fact, nothing the child does

will induce this puppy to bite. The child grows less fearful; the sight of the dog gradually ceases to elicit the former CR's of fear. His newfound confidence generalizes: he is no longer afraid of dogs.

Spontaneous Recovery Suppose, in an experiment like Pavlov's, a CS like the tuning fork has been presented to a dog every ten minutes, without the US, until no salivation occurs for five successive trials. The response is presumably extinguished. Yet, twenty-four hours later, when the tuning fork is again sounded, the dog salivates as it did before, even though there have been no further pairings of tuning fork and food. This phenomenon—the reappearance of an apparently extinguished CR after an interval in which the pairing of CS and US has not been repeated—is called *spontaneous recovery.* If the experimenter continues to omit the food, however, the CR extinguishes even more rapidly than it did before.

Many researchers agreed with Pavlov in attributing extinction to active process of *inhibition* that disappears over time, allowing spontaneous recovery. The best support for the inhibition hypothesis comes from the fact that a novel stimulus presented during extinction—such as a loud noise—may lead to the renewed occurrence of the CR. Such novel stimuli are thought to interfere with the inhibition, thus allowing the CR to recur. This interfering effect is called *disinhibition.*

Disinhibition also occurs during trace and temporal conditioning. In each instance, a novel stimulus presented prior to the usual occurrence of the US tends to produce the CR prematurely. It is speculated that the CR is normally inhibited until the appropriate time but that a novel stimulus causes disinhibition and hence the premature occurrence of the CR.

Generalization and Discrimination In a previous example, the small child who was bitten by a puppy displayed fear, not only of the puppy, but of all other dogs. This phenomenon is called *generalization*: in Pavlovian terms, a CR generated by one CS is also elicited by other stimuli that more or less resemble the original CS. In a conditioning experiment, a dog that has been conditioned to salivate to the tone of one turning fork may also salivate to other tones that are higher or lower. But the dog's response to tones other than the original CS is generally weaker and less reliable than the response to the original CS. This indicates that a certain amount of *discrimination* has also taken place. The amount of generalization decreases as the difference between the original CS and the other stimuli increases. In other words, the dog will tend to salivate quite a bit to a tone that is only one note higher or lower than the CS but less and less to tones that are increasingly higher or lower than the CS.

In order to measure generalization (and discrimination), experimenters map out a *generalization gradient.* A typical generalization gradient for a classically conditioned response in human subjects is shown in Figure 3.9.

In one experimental group, a pairing of vibration (CS) and electric shock (US) was applied to the subjects' shoulders. In another group, the stimuli were applied to their ankles. A galvanometer was used to measure the galvanic skin response (GSR) of the palms of the hands, which is part of the human body's reaction to electrical shock. (The GSR comprises changes in the skin's resistance to a weak external electric current and is related to the activity of the sweat glands.) After conditioning was established in each group, the vibratory stimulus was applied on test trials at points farther and farther away from the original point of application. The

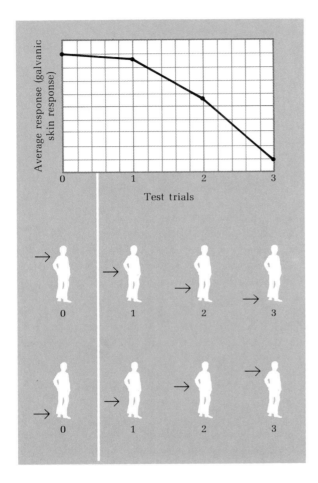

Figure 3.9
The graph (*top*) shows the amount of generalization of a conditioned response to vibratory stimulation as a function of distance from the point of shock application during conditioning. The CS is vibration, the US is electric shock, and the response is the galvanic skin response. Subjects in one group (*center*) had received vibration and shocks on the shoulder during training (the "O" point on the graph), subjects in the other group (*bottom*) on the ankle. In each case, the degree of generalization decreased the farther the location of stimulation on the test trial from the point of application during conditioning. [Adapted from H. L. Rachlin, *Introduction to Modern Behaviorism*, San Francisco: W. H. Freeman and Company, 1970. Data from M. J. Bass, and C. L. Hull, "The Irradiation of a Tactile Conditioned Reflex in Man," *Journal of Comparative Psychology*, 1934, *17*, 47–65].

farther the CS was moved from the point where the US was originally applied, the smaller was the GSR.

We may explicitly train an experimental subject in discrimination by presenting different stimuli during differing conditioning trials, and following one stimulus (the CS+) with the US and the other stimulus (the CS−) with no US. In this procedure, only the CS+ comes to elicit the CR.

THE RELATION OF CONDITIONING TO NEUROSIS, FEAR, AND ANXIETY

Experimental Neurosis One of Pavlov's students, Dr. Shenger-Krestovnikova, performed a discrimination experiment in which she conditioned dogs to salivate when they were presented with circles painted on cards. She established the fact that the dogs would also salivate to an ellipse—in other words, she established that generalization occurred. She then taught the dogs to discriminate between the circle and the ellipse; she presented the food powder (US) only with the circle, not with the ellipse. Thus, the circle became a CS+, and the ellipse became a CS−. Once the dogs had acquired the ability to discriminate between circle and ellipse, she began making the discrimination more difficult by presenting cards with ellipses that looked more and more like circles. The successive stages of the procedure are illustrated in Figure 3.10.

As the stimuli became more similar, the dog's discrimination between them grew worse and finally disappeared altogether. In addition, the way the dogs acted changed remarkably. In Pavlov's words:

The hitherto quiet dog began to squeal in its stand, kept wriggling about, tore off with its teeth the apparatus . . . , and bit through the tubes connecting the animal's room with the observer, a behavior which never happened before. On being taken into the experimental room the dog now

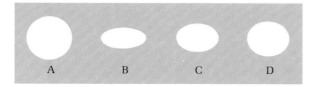

Figure 3.10
After dogs had learned a simple discrimination between the circle (the CS+) and the ellipse (the CS−) shown in A and B, the ellipse was replaced with progressively more circular stimuli (as in C and then D), until the discrimination became extremely difficult. This procedure was the first to produce neurosis in the laboratory (hence the term "experimental neurosis").

barked violently, which was also contrary to its usual custom; in short it presented all the symptoms of acute neurosis. On testing the cruder differentiations [easier discriminations] they were also found to be destroyed . . .*

In this early study, an *experimental neurosis* had been created in the laboratory by repeatedly presenting a subject with an extremely and increasingly difficult problem in discrimination. Such experimental neuroses have subsequently been produced in a number of laboratories with several different procedures and a number of different organisms: monkeys, sheep, cats, and rats. The procedures generally incorporate stressful situations—such as those produced by inescapable conflict, unusually difficult discriminations, or prolonged exposure to aversive stimulation. The resultant behavior is marked by anxiety and by unusual symptoms that serve as only a partial solution to the conflict. The behavior of the experimentally neurotic animal is thus very similar to that of the neurotic human (as we shall see in Chapter 28).

In Figure 3.11 we see the experimental setup used by J. H. Masserman to induce neurotic behavior in cats. After a cat had learned to get food from a covered box, it would occasionally get a blast of air instead and would retreat in fear. If the air blasts

*I. P. Pavlov, *Conditioned Reflexes*. New York: Dover, 1960, p. 291.

Figure 3.11
This is the apparatus used by Jules H. Masserman in the early 1940s when he produced experimental neurosis in cats. The relevant features of the apparatus are (1) a hinged food box at the left of the cage, (2) a rotary feeder wheel to the left of the cage, which would be set up to deliver food to the food box on variable schedules, and (3) a device to the lower left of the cage (not clearly visible) that delivered an airblast to the cat's face in lieu of food on some occasions. (The fan at right is for ventilation.) Cats that had been well trained to open the box for food began to receive blasts of air instead on some occasions. Some of the behaviors that ensued included indecision about approaching the food box, a lack of interest in mice, and a variety of actions and postures—one cat kept its head in the box, another tried to climb the walls of the cage, another walked into the walls. (Other features of the apparatus, including lights, bells, buzzers, and an electric-shock device, were used in other investigations.) [Photograph courtesy of J. H. Masserman. This photograph first appeared in Masserman's *Behavior and Neurosis*. Chicago: University of Chicago Press, 1943.]

were continued over a period of time, dysfunctional behaviors (restlessness, viciousness, or apathy) would appear and would persist even after the air blasts were discontinued.

Perhaps the most ambitious investigation of experimental neurosis was carried out with sheep by H. S. Liddell at Cornell University from the late 1920s to around 1960. In one experiment, a sheep was given a mild shock (US) on the leg after the presentation of a CS—the sixth beat of a metronome beating once per second. The sheep's unconditioned response to electric shock was to lift the shocked leg (leg flexion). This response was soon conditioned to the exact CS—the sheep was able to discriminate the sixth beat of the metronome (the one followed by shock) from the other five. After a series of sessions with only ten trials, the number of trials was doubled to twenty, so that the sheep received twice as many shocks per session. On the second day of the longer sessions, the normally calm sheep became agitated, struggling violently during the CS and the shock, and displaying other signs of agitation during the intervals between signals—defecation, bleating, jerking of the foreleg, repetitive movements of the head and ears, and labored breathing. The next day the sheep resisted entering the laboratory and continued its heightened agitation during the session. The agitation continued even when the signals and shocks were eliminated and the sheep merely stood undisturbed in the apparatus. In this case, the experimental neurosis was produced not by making the discrimination more difficult but by increasing the number of times the organism was exposed to a moderately difficult discrimination.

This particular neurosis was not confined to the sheep's experimental situation. The animals became incapable of dealing effectively with dangerous situations and were invariably the victims of dogs that periodically invaded the pasture where the flock of sheep were kept. In Liddell's words, "The animal's neurosis so damages its gregariousness that while the other members of the flock escape together in one direction the neurotic animal flees in panic by itself."*

In animals as well as humans, the neurotic symptoms produced by conditioning may persist for many

*Quoted from the article listed at the end of this chapter.

years unless therapeutic techniques are applied (to be discussed in Chapter 32). In one instance, an experimenter encountered a 400-pound neurotic sow that he had not seen in over a year. He was lured into a fence corner by the sow's "friendly overtures" and was then so viciously attacked that he required medical attention. Perhaps the sow was conducting its own investigation of experimental neurosis!

One of the most interesting factors affecting the occurrence of experimental neurosis in young sheep is the presence or absence of the mother sheep. In an experiment involving exposure to inescapable shock, conducted by Liddell in the 1950s, the subjects were a mother sheep and her twin lambs. Each twin occupied a separate room, as pictured in Figure 3.12, with the mother in one of the rooms. As the figure shows, the lambs were connected to recording equipment in the ceiling and had electrodes attached to their forelegs. Each lamb was free to move around the room during the test hour, and its movements were recorded on paper tape. Every two minutes, the room lights were dimmed for ten seconds (the CS), after which a brief shock (the US) was administered. There were twenty trials each day. The motherless lamb developed a characteristically neurotic pattern of behavior during the intervals between the CS's. First, it avoided the center of the room, and instead moved cautiously along the walls; then it restricted its movements along one wall; finally it cowered in one corner of the room. Other behavioral signs of neurosis were also evident —defecation, repetitive head movements, and so on. In contrast, the twin in the other room failed to show this pattern and moved freely around the room, as shown in the recordings in Figure 3.13. It seems as if the mother's presence prevented the development of neurosis, presumably by keeping the lamb relaxed. The importance of relaxation in overcoming neurotic behavior in humans will be discussed later

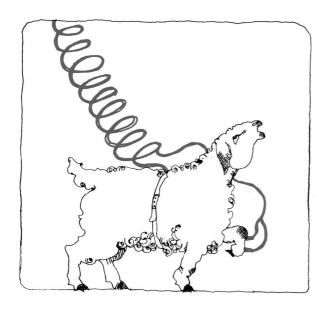

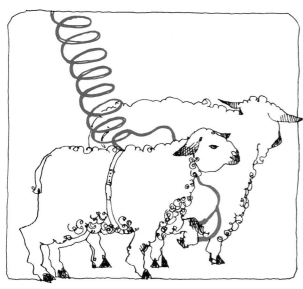

Figure 3.12
Behavior of twin lambs, one without its mother (*top*) and one with its mother (*bottom*). Each lamb received inescapable electric shocks but was free to move around the room; its movements were recorded on paper tape. Only the isolated lamb developed characteristically neurotic movement patterns and other neurotic behaviors. [Figures 3.12 and 3.13 are adapted from H. S. Liddell, "Conditioning and Emotions," *Scientific American*, January 1954, 48–57. Copyright © 1954 by Scientific American, Inc. All rights reserved.]

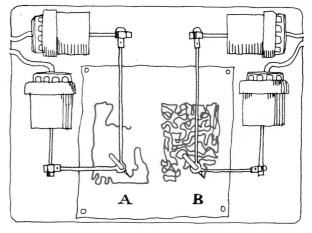

Figure 3.13
The recordings of movements depicted in Figure 3.12 by the motherless lamb (A) and the lamb with mother (B). Note that the movements of the motherless lamb are restricted and repetitive, whereas those of the lamb with its mother are freer. [Copyright © 1954 by Scientific American, Inc. All rights reserved.]

in this chapter and again, more fully, in Chapter 32.

The conditioning of emotional responses in humans was studied by the father of behaviorism, the American psychologist John B. Watson (1878–1958). For his US, Watson used a sudden loud noise, which elicits fear, crying, and trembling in young children. The CS was a white rat. Before conditioning, the experimenters demonstrated that the subject, a child named Albert, would try to play with the rat. Next, they paired touching the rat and the sight of the rat with the loud noise. After several pairings, a clear emotional reaction developed: young Albert would whimper and recoil at the sight of the rat he had once trusted as a playmate (see Figure 3.14).

Figure 3.14
Watson's early experiment on the conditioning of emotional responses used a little boy named Albert.

The conditioned fear response to the rat generalized to other furry objects, such as a rabbit, fur coats, dogs, and even a Santa Claus mask! That Albert's behavior was controlled by the "furry" aspect of the stimulus was evident from his failure to display fear of nonfurry objects that resembled rats in other respects.

Albert's fear was developed experimentally, but the pairing of conditioned with unconditioned stimuli in everyday life also produces conditioned emotional reactions. For example, most of us have emotional reactions to many of the stimuli sketched in Figure 3.15. Many of us who watched the televised 1968 Democratic convention in Chicago or similar scenes may have conditioned aversive reactions to the sight of gas-masked policemen or peace symbols, depending upon our points of view.

Conditioned Fear and Anxiety There are many additional examples of the role that conditioning plays in the development of human fears and anxieties. Some of these fears are highly functional or *adaptive,* that is, they increase the individual's chances for survival in his environment. For instance, when the child who has been burned by playing with fire comes to fear the sight of fire, he is much less likely to be burned.

On the other hand, certain fears and anxieties are dysfunctional, or *maladaptive*; that is, they decrease either the individual's chance of survival or his normal enjoyment of life. Examples are Liddell's sheep that failed to flee from attacking dogs, and humans with anxieties that prevent normal sexual relationships. In fact, many common behavioral disorders are derived from anxiety reactions that are conditioned responses to certain stimuli in the environment. As Mark Twain put it, "We should be careful to get out of an experience only the wisdom that is in it—and stop there; lest we be like the cat that sits

Figure 3.15
Pictures and symbols may elicit emotional reactions in many of us. Such reactions are called *conditioned emotional reactions*. (continued)

Figure 3.15 (continued)
More pictures and symbols that may elicit conditioned emotional responses.

down on a hot stove lid. She will never sit down on a hot stove lid again—and that is well; but also she will never sit down on a cold one any more.''

An extreme case of an irrational, persistent fear (or _phobia_) due to conditioning is a child who becomes so frightened of dogs after being bitten by one that he is reluctant to venture out alone. Although his conditioned fear of dogs may be natural and understandable, the _strength_ of his reaction—and the extent to which the reaction generalizes—is maladaptive.

Since dogs are frequently encountered in our society, the child becomes a shut-in or a recluse until his phobia is eliminated.

In a more complex case, a young man who has had several unfortunate encounters with attractive women may become so anxious in the presence of attractive women—who have become CS's for anxiety reactions—that he is unable to have normal social relations with such a woman, much less satisfactory sexual ones.

Consider an example of how such a sexual problem may be conditioned. Parents with Victorian attitudes may instill a full complement of conditioned anxieties related to sexual behavior into their daughter—for example, by berating her for the slightest hint of promiscuity or provocative dress. Although the parents' strict disapproval of sexuality may be effective in curbing promiscuity, it may also carry over disadvantageously into appropriate sexual relations. This carry-over, of course, may occur without any conscious effort on the part of the daughter: stimuli (the CS's) normally associated with sexual arousal may cause her anxiety (the CR)—owing to the previous pairing of the CS's with the parents' disapproval (the US). In such cases, normal sexual relations may develop only with difficulty. The girl may try to remove the sexually arousing stimuli, perhaps by avoiding them or by engaging in behavior incompatible with sex. Thus the girl's problem may be similar to that of the anxious male discussed above.

The phenomenon of extinction and the concept of inhibition have been used successfully in the treatment of neurotic anxieties and phobias. One method for extinguishing these anxiety reactions is the technique of *systematic desensitization.*

The objective of systematic desensitization is to condition the patient to *relax* in the presence of anxiety-arousing stimuli. Since relaxation and anxiety are incompatible, as the patient learns to relax, he simultaneously learns not to be anxious. In other words, relaxation is a *competing* response to the CS; relaxing comes to replace anxiety. Systematic desensitization can thus be thought of as a means of *counterconditioning*: relaxation is conditioned in the presence of a particular stimulus in order to counter, or oppose, the previously conditioned response of anxiety.

For example, sexual impotence that is owing to anxiety may be treated in the following manner. The patient and his female partner are instructed that he is *not* to attempt intercourse when they engage in sex play. As the patient learns to relax and enjoy sex play, he becomes more responsive sexually. As Malcolm Kushner notes, the patient who has complained of impotence

. . . is told that only when he has both a very strong erection and an overwhelming desire to have intercourse is he to do so and then he is to enter immediately and let himself go, disregarding efforts to prolong the act or to try to please his partner. If instructions are followed expressly, success is readily achieved (allowing) for a continued development of satisfactory coital expression. As can be recognized, this approach requires the full cooperation and understanding of the female partner.*

Systematic desensitization has proved an excellent technique for dealing with anxiety, which is at the root of most neuroses. Although the success rate of systematic desensitization varies with the specific neurosis, treatment is successful in about 90 percent of the cases in which it is attempted. This includes not only sexual disorders like impotence and frigidity but also a score of phobias (irrational fears of everyday activities like public speaking, flying, and driving).

PSEUDOCONDITIONING

Test trials during the Pavlovian conditioning procedure may show increases in the magnitude of response that are *not* due to Pavlovian conditioning itself. A common example is *pseudoconditioning*.

In pseudoconditioning, *any sudden stimulus* will elicit a response indistinguishable from the UR

*M. Kushner, "The Reduction of a Long-standing Fetish by Means of Aversive Conditioning." In Ullman, L. P. and Krasner, L., Eds., *Case Studies in Behavior Modification* (New York: Holt, Rinehart and Winston, 1965, Pp. 239–242).

after several presentations of the US alone, without pairing. For example, imagine a situation in which a subject is given a series of electric shocks (US's). Following this set of trials, he is presented with either a flash of light or vibratory stimulation. These stimuli by themselves elicit a startle response indistinguishable from the UR to shock. This pseudoconditioned startle response does not require previous CS–US pairings and is thus not an example of true Pavlovian conditioning.

How can the experimenter be sure that his procedure has achieved Pavlovian conditioning? One way is to set up a control group in which some subjects are exposed only to the US. Conditioning can be inferred if the CS–US pairing in the experimental group results in more CR's than does the presentation of only the US to the control group.

An elegant procedure that controls for pseudo-conditioning—as well as for other phenomena that resemble Pavlovian conditioning—has been called the *truly random control procedure*. In this situation a stimulus (say a tone) is presented to subjects in the control group completely independently of the US (say food). This independence is achieved by adding random presentations of the food to a regularly occurring sequence of tones. Chance pairings of tone and food may occur, but such occurrences are completely nonsystematic. The crucial aspect of the control procedure is that the occurrence of the tone gives the subject *no predictive information* whatsoever about future occurrences of the food (the US). By contrast, when the tone and food are paired in actual conditioning trials, the tone regularly precedes the food by a fixed amount of time and does give the subject the information that the food will soon follow. The random control procedure avoids this. Thus, systematic pairings—the basis of true conditioning—are eliminated in the control group, but

the control organisms receive the same total amount of stimulation—the same number of presentations of the stimuli—as do the experimental organisms. Any effects of repeated tone presentations or of repeated food presentations (independently of CS–US pairings) should be evident in both experimental and control groups, and any differences in response increments between the two groups must be those representing Pavlovian conditioning, that is, the results of the CS–US pairings. In order to be certain that Pavlovian conditioning has taken place, we have to be certain that it is the pairings—and nothing else—that are responsible for the elicitation of the CR.

HABITUATION

Many behaviors are modified simply as a result of repeated exposure to a particular stimulus. Such changes in *responsiveness* are of two basic types: *sensitization*, which refers to an *increase* in responsiveness with repeated stimulation, and *habituation*, which refers to a *decrease* in responsiveness with repeated stimulation. Sensitization and habituation are probably the most primitive types of changes in behavior. Habituation is an important behavioral adjustment and has been the object of more intensive study than sensitization in recent years.

An interesting example of habituation occurs in relation to the organism's ability to pay attention to a new or unexpected stimulus in its environment. This behavior, known as the *orienting reaction*, is important in that it helps the organism to detect and prepare for new and potentially dangerous situations. Jumping at a loud noise and surpise at finding a person in a supposedly empty room are examples of orienting reactions. It would be maladaptive—or at least inefficient—however, for the organism to show an orienting reaction to every occurrence of a once-novel stimulus. Thus, a dog that pricks up its ears

Figure 3.16
A dog will prick up its ears to a fairly novel sound
(such as that made by the lawn mower). This is an
example of an *orienting reaction*. After awhile, however,
the dog will cease to react to the continuing sound of
the mower. This loss of reaction to a repetitive stimulus
is an example of an important behavioral phenomenon,
habituation.

at a strange sound will cease to pay attention if the
noise continues for some time (Figure 3.16).
This loss of reaction is habituation: repetition of the
novel stimulus without any consequences for the
organism results in a *decrease* in the organism's
responsiveness to that stimulus. (Orientation and
attention will be discussed further in Chapter 10.)

Habituation is a gradual decrease in the amount
and frequency of response to a single unconditioned
stimulus that is presented repeatedly at regular
intervals. In some cases, the response may even
disappear completely. It is as if the animal has, with
repeated exposure, learned *not* to make the response.
This decline in response is, however, only temporary.
After a relatively long interval (anywhere from a few
hours to a few days), during which the habituating
stimulus is not encountered, the response returns.
With renewed stimulation, learning what not to do
must nearly begin all over again.

Habituation is a very common phenomenon that
occurs among organisms as deceptively simple as
primitive worms and as obviously complex as

humans. For example, very recent work has shown
that habituation occurs in the *sea anemone*, a primitive
organism that lacks a central nervous system. Sea
anemones close and retract their tentacles when
water strikes them from above. Contraction is probably a protective response that prevents intense
stimuli from harming the organism. But sea anemones also use their tentacles to gather food in the
form of other organisms living in the water. Now,
if anemones that live in tide pools contracted each
time they were struck by a wave or each time a
strong current of water passed over them, they would
lose the tremendous food-gathering advantage of
having their tentacles extended ready to capture any
food that might pass by. For this reason, then, it is
adaptive for such animals to habituate (cease
responding) to repeated presentations of water hitting
them from above. That they in fact do so has been
demonstrated in the laboratory: after a number of
repeated presentations of a stream of water from
above, the animals eventually cease contracting.
These extremely primitive animals have essentially
learned that the unconditioned water-stream stimulus
is not serious enough to justify continued response.
Instead, they habituate.

You could demonstrate habituation for yourself
by walking up behind a pet or an unsuspecting
friend (making sure it was a good friend) and clap-

ping your hands. Your subject would most likely emit a startle reaction, such as jumping or turning quickly around (see Figure 3.17). If you were to do this repeatedly, your clap would eventually cease to produce the startle reaction (although you might have an angry friend or pet on your hands). The habituated response would nonetheless return—the next day your clap would be as effective as ever. For the sea anemone too, *recovery* of the response occurs. If water is not presented for twenty-four hours, the next water-stimulus produces a response almost as intense as that originally elicited.

Allowing time to pass is one way to reinstate the original strength of an habituated response. An alternative method is that of *dishabituation*, in which a novel stimulus is presented. For example, suppose that on one occasion we stimulate the sea anemone that has habituated to the stream of water with a glass rod instead of a water stream. This results in an immediate loss of habituation: the next few times the water stream is presented alone, the sea anemone contracts. The renewed responding is short-lived, however; after only a few more water streams, the anemone again habituates.

An interesting characteristic of dishabituation is that it can itself become habituated. If poking were repeated at intervals along with the regular presentation of the water stream, the poke would produce gradually less and less dishabituation until finally it too would have no effect at all.

If habituation is to be considered a form of simple learning, it is important to distinguish between it and nonlearning phenomena that produce similar effects. For example, both fatigue and sensory adaptation represent decreases in responding that are thought not to involve learning.

In *fatigue*, a reduction of response may occur simply because the muscles that execute the response have become exhausted. This would not seem to indicate any kind of learning. And experiments have

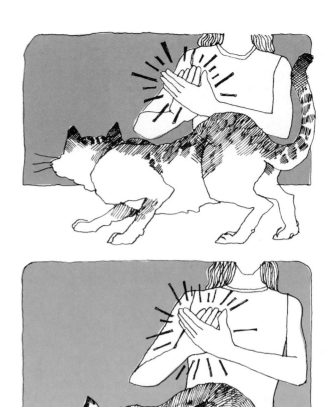

Figure 3.17
Although most animals—such as the cat above—will show a *startle reaction* to a sudden loud sound, this reaction quickly "habituates" upon repeated exposures to the same sound.

successfully distinguished between habituation and fatigue by showing that even after habituation has occurred to one stimulus (presentation of a water stream), the same response can still be elicited by a different stimulus (poking with a glass rod). Since this shows that the motor elements used in making the response are all in good working order, the original lack of response must have been an instance of habituation, not fatigue.

It is more difficult to distinguish between habituation and sensory adaptation. *Sensory adaptation* occurs when the sensitivity of physiological receptors receiving stimulation is altered for one reason or another. An example of sensory adaptation is the adaptation of the retina of the eye to changes in illumination. (This will be discussed in Chapter 13.) Unlike habituation, such purely sensory changes do not represent learning. Habituation and sensory adaptation can most often be distinguished by the relative speed of the recovery of responding. Adaptation effects generally dissipate much more quickly than habituation effects. For example, a loss of responding that required half a day to recover would more likely be a case of habituation than sensory adaptation.

In summary, if fatigue and sensory adaptation can be eliminated as the sources of a given decrease in responding as a result of repeated stimulation, the decrease may represent habituation.

Habituability Although we have characterized habituation as a very widely occurring phenomenon, only certain types of responses habituate readily, and those only under certain conditions. For example, habituation is generally assumed to apply only to innate responses. In the language of Pavlovian conditioning, these are unconditioned responses.

The degree to which an organism's response habituates may vary according to the circumstances. The number of stimulus presentations, their duration and intensity, the interval between them, and the idiosyncrasies of the particular organism under study are among the factors determining the amount of habituation. Although it initially appears to be quite simple, habituation displays much of the complexity characteristic of other, more familiar forms of learning. Careful study of this, the simplest case, may provide basic information applicable at all levels of learning.

We shall next turn from the experimental study of respondent behavior and habituation to the experimental study of operant behavior.

Suggested Readings

Denny, M. R., & Ratner, S. C. (1970) *Comparative psychology: Research in animal behavior.* Homewood, Illinois: Dorsey. [Chapter 10 contains an excellent treatment of habituation.]

Liddell, H. S. (1954) "Conditioning and emotions." *Scientific american,* January 1954, pp. 48–57. Reprinted as Scientific American offprint 418.

Masserman, J. H. (1950) "Experimental neuroses." *Scientific american*, March, pp. 38–43. Reprinted as Scientific American Offprint 443. [This and the preceding article summarize the highlights of Liddell's and Masserman's work on experimental neurosis.]

Pavlov, I. P. (1927) *Conditioned reflexes.* (Translated by G. V. Anrep.) London: Oxford. [The classic work on the subject.]

Rachlin, H. (1970) *Introduction to modern behaviorism.* San Francisco: W. H. Freeman and Company. [A good background to behaviorism and research in conditioning, especially in the first two chapters.]

Terrace, H. S. (1973) "Classical conditioning." In Nevin, J. A. & Reynolds, G. S., eds. *The study of behavior: Learning, motivation, emotion, and instinct.* Glenview, Illinois: Scott, Foresman, pp. 70–112. [A recent review of the current status of research and theory in Pavlovian conditioning.]

CHAPTER FOUR

Operant Conditioning

If a little girl enjoys her first ice cream cone, she is likely to ask for one in the future. If she is taken to the ocean and is tumbled by a wave, she is likely to refuse to enter the ocean again for a long time. These are everyday examples of the effects of *reinforcement* and *punishment*. In the vocabulary of experimental psychology, "reinforcement" means the occurrence of a *reinforcing stimulus*, or *reinforcer* (such as the taste of ice cream), that *increases* the probability that the action it follows (eating ice cream) will recur in an organism's future behavior. "Punishment" means the occurrence of an *aversive stimulus* or *punisher* (being knocked down by a wave) that *decreases* the probability that the action it follows (entering the water) will recur. According to many contemporary psychologists, a great deal of human and animal behavior can be explained by the presence, absence, and sequence of reinforcers and punishers.

BASIC CONCEPTS

It was the American psychologist B. F. Skinner (b. 1904) who suggested that much of an organism's observable behavior could be broken down into classes of actions that he called "operants" because they operated on the environment and changed it in some specific, definable way. *Operant*, or *instrumental*, *conditioning* is the process by which an organism's interactions with its environment modify its subsequent behavior—specifically, by the reinforcement and punishment of the organism's operant behavior.

Responses that are followed by reinforcement are more likely to recur. Rarely, however, do you insert a fork in your mouth unless there is food on it or stare at the television set unless it is turned on. Another term is needed, therefore, in addition to response and reinforcement, and the term commonly used is *discriminative stimuli* (SD)—that is, stimuli which precede and accompany operant responses. They are called "discriminative" because they tell the organism when responses may be effective in producing positive reinforcement or in avoiding or reducing punishment. In other words, they identify or *set the occasions* on which operant responses are reinforced. Thus, food on a fork might signal "bite me," and a lit-up picture tube might signal "watch me."

The Three-Term Contingency The relationship between these three events—discriminative stimulus, operant response, and reinforcer—is interdependent. It may be stated as a *"three-term contingency."* A *response that is emitted and reinforced in the presence of an S^D will become more probable in the future in the presence of the same S^D.* For instance, a man who inserts a dime into a machine dispensing a soft drink is more likely to try that machine in the future if he obtains the drink and enjoys it. In this instance, the S^D is the vending machine; the response is the insertion of the coin; the reinforcer is the presentation of the soft drink. What happens if he loses his coin in the machine, or if the drink is too sweet? If no drink is obtained, no reinforcement has occurred; he is less likely to insert a dime into that machine again. On the other hand, if the drink is not liked, it is not an effective reinforcer; again, there is less chance of the response being repeated.

The three-term contingency is the basis for the acquisition of new behavior—learning—by means of operant conditioning. In a typical experiment in operant conditioning, a pigeon is placed in a special cage (commonly called a "Skinner box") that has an illuminated plastic disk, called a "key," set into one wall. Beneath the key is a feeding tray and a hopper leading to a grain magazine. When the pigeon pecks the lighted key, the key becomes dark, and the hopper releases a small amount of grain into the tray. If the bird pecks anywhere else in the cage, he receives no grain. In this arrangement, the lighted key is the S^D, pecking it is the response, and the grain is the reinforcer.

Thus the pigeon acquires a new way of behaving when a particular behavior is reinforced. Pecking, of course, is normal for pigeons, but pecking a key in order to obtain grain is not (Figure 4.1). Each pigeon placed in the box learns this individually, in much

Figure 4.1
In this setup, pecking is the response, the key is the discriminative stimulus, and grain is the reinforcer. [Will Rapport]

the same way that each child in our culture learns to manipulate a knife and fork.

Pavlovian Versus Operant Conditioning Although operant conditioning and Pavlovian conditioning are both ways of modifying behavior, there is a significant difference in the kind of behavior they affect. Pavlovian conditioning deals with respondent behavior—specifically, it deals with responses that invariably follow a specific stimulus and are thus *elicited*—blinking at a bright light, jumping at an electric shock, salivating to the taste of food, and so forth. Operant conditioning deals with operant behavior—behavior that is *emitted* (rather than elicited)—the organism *seems* to initiate operant behavior on his own without a single, explicit, preceding stimulus. The following example may help the reader keep this difference in mind: it is almost impossible for someone *not* to blink his eyes when a sudden blast of air is directed at them (an elicited reflex action), but it is possible for him to refuse to insert a coin in a vending machine (an emitted act). A further example is shown in Figure 4.2: in a Pavlovian-conditioning setup, the dog simply learns that a tuning-fork sound (CS) precedes an electric shock (US); in an operant-conditioning setup, the dog can learn to avoid the electric shock by lifting its paw.

Another difference between the two kinds of conditioning is the order of events. In Pavlovian conditioning, the CS and US occur in a regular sequence arranged by the experimenter, regardless of the organism's responses. Thus, the sequence of events is: tuning-fork sound (CS) → shock (US) → leg movement (CR and UR). The critical relationship is between the two kinds of stimuli. In operant conditioning, the organism perceives the S^D, responds in its presence, and the response is reinforced. The sequence here is: lighted key (S^D) → key peck (operant response) → food (reinforcer). The critical relationship is between the response and the reinforcing stimulus that follows it.

Generalization and Discrimination in Operant Conditioning Responses that have been reinforced in the presence of one stimulus may tend to occur in the presence of similar stimuli. For example, a pigeon that has previously received reinforcement for pecking a key illuminated by a red light is presented with a key illuminated by a green light. If he pecks that one also, we say that the response to the red key has *generalized* to the green key. If he does not, we say that the bird has *discrim-*

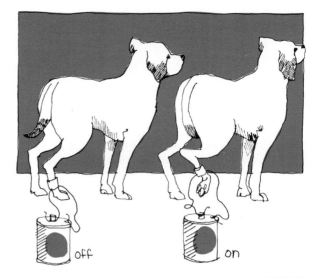

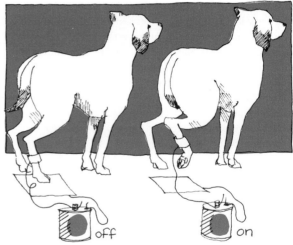

Figure 4.2
In classical conditioning (top), the response neither avoids nor escapes the US. In operant conditioning (bottom), the response does operate on (or affect) the occurrence of the US. Two types of operant conditioning are avoidance and escape. In avoidance conditioning, a response (here, lifting the paw) prevents the occurrence of the US (here, electric shock). In escape conditioning, the US may not be avoided but may be escaped by a response after the US begins. The bottom figure represents avoidance conditioning, since no shock will be experienced as long as the paw is lifted. [Adapted from H. Rachlin, *Introduction to Modern Behaviorism*. San Francisco: W. H. Freeman and Co. Copyright © 1970.]

inated between the two stimuli. A little boy is generalizing when he calls all four-footed animals "doggy." Later, he begins to discriminate between dogs, cats, horses, and cows.

If varying one property of an established S^D (for example, its color, shape, or location) has no effect at all on the organism's response, the experimenter assumes that the organism has not been *attending* to that particular property. In other words, if the pigeon does not favor either the red or the green light, his attention is directed to something other than the color of the light: perhaps to the shape of the key, or to light itself. If he does not peck at the green light, it seems plain that he had been attending to the color of the red light and hence noticed its change to green.

Deprivation How does an organism's physiological condition affect its responding? If a soft drink reinforces the act of dropping a coin in a vending machine, will a person always perform that action in the presence of a vending machine? Not necessarily. A person's state of *deprivation* greatly influences the probability of his making a certain response. If he has just finished five bottles of the drink, it is unlikely that he would use the vending machine to obtain a sixth, unless he were very thirsty indeed. For this reason, experiments using food as a reinforcer start with hungry animals; those using water start with thirsty ones; and so on. The influence of deprivation on responding is the basis for one of the oldest theories of reinforcement: the theory that reinforcers reduce primary physical "drives," such as hunger, thirst, fatigue, or sex—all of which increase with deprivation.

It is important to note that satiety—the absence of deprivation—does not permanently affect the ability of the S^D to produce a response. The individual has already learned how to obtain a drink when he wants one, and when he is thirsty again, he will

very likely insert a coin in the machine as soon as he sees it.

Learning Versus Performance Operant conditioning includes both the learning of new behavior and the performance of already learned behavior. The distinction between learning and performance has been clearly demonstrated by several experiments. In one of these, a rat is placed at the entrance to a complex maze. It can only reach the goal box at the end of the maze by making a particular sequence of left and right turns. Hungry rats that receive food reinforcement in the goal box learn to make the correct sequence of choices and traverse the maze rapidly after a number of trials. During the same number of trials, however, hungry rats that *do not* receive food in the goal box make many errors and take their time meandering through the maze. These unreinforced rats have apparently not learned the appropriate sequence of choices.

What happens when food is placed in the goal box for the previously unreinforced rats? One would predict that, since they have apparently not learned the correct sequence of choices, they should take about the same number of additional trials to learn the correct path as the rats that had food reinforcement from the beginning. The *learning curve* describing their rate of acquisition of the correct behavior over successive trials should show the same gradual reduction in errors as did the learning curve for the other rats. These predictions are illustrated in Part A of Figure 4.3.

Instead, after a single exposure to food in the goal box, the rat correctly performs the appropriate sequence of choices and runs the maze at about the same speed as the rats that have been rewarded all along. Part B of Figure 4.3 illustrates these dramatic improvements.

Obviously, the rats had learned more than their performance suggested during the trials preceding the

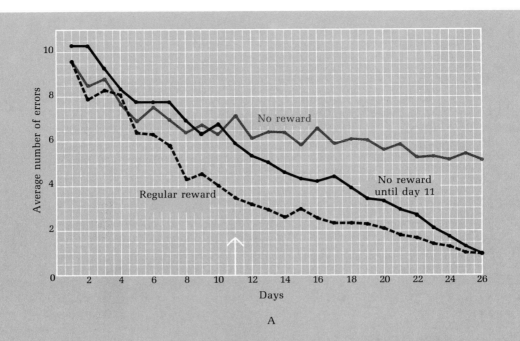

A

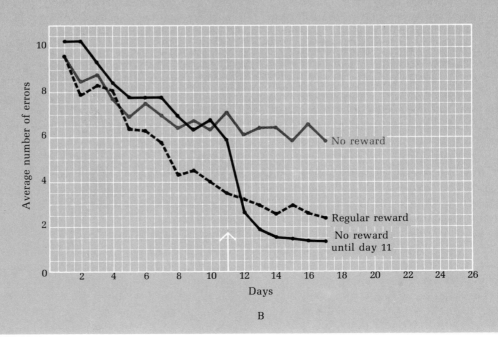

B

introduction of food. This phenomenon is called *latent learning*; the use of an appropriate reinforcer, food, was necessary to translate the unobserved learning into observable—and measurable—performance.

The learning–performance distinction is critical for appreciating human learning. The child in the classroom may actually have learned more and be able to perform his school work better than his performance indicates. His latent learning may be revealed in performance when effective reinforcers are made available. Recent work has suggested that the application of suitable reinforcement in the classroom enhances student performance, not only by accelerating the rate of learning but also by dramatically assisting the process whereby learning is translated into performance.

THE NATURE OF REINFORCEMENT

Reinforcement is an event that strengthens the behavior that it follows; presentation of a reinforcing

Figure 4.3 *(opposite)*
An experiment on latent learning. Two sets of results, one hypothetical and one real, are shown. In each graph, one line shows the average number of errors made by a group of rats *never* receiving food in the goal box, a second line shows the error scores for the group receiving food in the goal box on *every* trial, and a third line shows the error scores for a group receiving food in the goal box *beginning on the eleventh day*. If this last group had not learned about the maze in the first ten days, food reinforcement should have produced a gradual improvement in performance (fewer errors) after the eleventh day, as shown by the hypothetical data in A. Instead, a dramatic improvement occurs in performance, as shown by the actual data in B. [Adapted from E. C. Tolman and C. H. Honzik, "Introduction and Removal of Reward, and Maze Performance in Rats," *University of California Publications in Psychology*, 1930, 257–275.]

stimulus following a response in a given situation increases the probability that the response will recur in that situation. How many different reinforcers are there? Traditionally, it was thought that there was a limited number of reinforcing stimuli associated with vital or pleasurable activities, such as eating, drinking, and sex. Although physiological needs certainly do influence whether or not stimuli will serve as effective reinforcers, they are not essential. We now know that almost any event may be a reinforcer, provided that its scheduling and the reinforced response are chosen according to certain rather simple rules. Before dealing with those important rules, we shall briefly discuss the opposite position—that there are *no* reinforcers!—taken some years ago by the ingenious learning theorist Edwin R. Guthrie (1886–1959). If we can explain behavior without resorting to the concept of reinforcement—and without substituting one or more competing concepts—we would do well to get rid of it in the interest of simplicity.

Guthrie's Contiguous Conditioning   Guthrie believed that all conditioning could be explained *by the contiguous occurrence of stimuli and responses:* a stimulus–response pair is created whenever the stimulus and the response occur together. The response we give to a stimulus is the same response we gave to the stimulus the last time it occurred. This is because, according to Guthrie, a stimulus becomes firmly associated with the *last* response that occurs in its presence. If a particular response is followed by an abrupt change in the stimulus, then that response must recur the next time the stimulus is presented because that response was the last one made to the stimulus (before it changed). The sudden stimulus change prevents any *other* responses from being made in the presence of the stimulus, and so the original response continues to be elicited by the stimulus. Guthrie's theory is both ingenious and tricky; the following two examples will help the reader understand Guthrie's point.

1. Consider first the response of opening a door. You are heading out of a lecture hall to keep a coffee date with an intimate friend, but you can't get Door A to open. You turn the knob, kick the door, and finally turn away to find another door. When you turn the knob on Door B, it immediately swings open and you are facing the sunlit path to the Coffee Hut. In the future, you leave the lecture hall by way of Door B. Why? Reinforcement theory has an obvious answer: you were reinforced for turning the knob on Door B (by the opening of the door and the subsequent access to the outdoors and, ultimately, your date) but not for turning the knob on Door A, and so Door A is not an S^D. But are these necessary assumptions? Guthrie could have accounted for the same outcome without invoking reinforcement. The last response you made to Door A was to turn away from it; therefore you should do so in the future. On the other hand, the response of turning the knob on Door B was followed by an abrupt change in stimulation: from the closed door to an outdoor campus setting. Thus, the last response made to the door—the knob turning—should recur the next time you approach it.

2. When a hungry pigeon pecks at a key and obtains food in a cup several inches below the key, it immediately moves down to the cup and eats the food (Figure 4.4); if the key-peck has no consequence, however, behaviors other than pecking will occur in the presence of the key. These other behaviors will supplant pecking as the last response made to the key, and so they—not pecking—will occur the next time the bird sees a key. Thus, according to Guthrie, reinforcement appears to work only because it produces a marked *stimulus change*

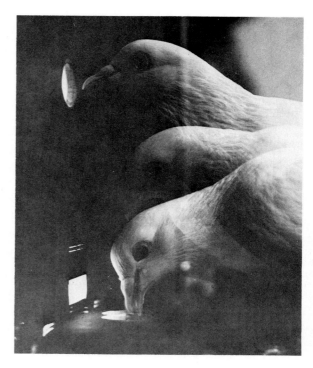

Figure 4.4
This multiple-exposure photograph shows a pigeon that pecks a key and then immediately lowers its head and eats the small amount of grain that has appeared in its food cup. [Courtesy Norman Guttman]

that prevents any subsequent responses' interfering with the particular stimulus–response association that preceded the stimulus change.

Guthrie himself was fond of citing puzzling cases which he could explain but which seemed implausible from the point of view of reinforcement. The best of these cases are situations in which people continually do things that cause them pain. The theory of punishment, of course, says that they should cease to do them. But we all do, and Guthrie had a good explanation in terms of his contiguity theory. Here is one of his examples:

Suppose a man walks up to a roll-up garage door, rolls it up, walks in, and bumps his head on a low beam—for the fifth or sixth time. Guthrie contended that reaching the door is the stimulus for immediately rolling up the door. The door going up is the stimulus for immediately going into the garage—and once the man starts in, he hits his head. Unless the man can interrupt this sequence (perhaps by putting a big sign on the door), the same old going-in response will continue to occur—despite punishment.

We have discussed Guthrie's theory because it is ingenious, parsimonious, and thought-provoking. Unfortunately, there are several phenomena that Guthrie's theory can explain only with such difficulty that his account becomes overly complex and cumbersome, undermining the very simplicity that made it so appealing in the first place. One finding that is troublesome for Guthrie is that simple and immediate punishment most often weakens the probability that a given behavior will recur (his garage door example notwithstanding). According to Guthrie's basic principle of contiguity, a response followed by punishment should be strengthened as much as one followed by reinforcement, provided that the degree of stimulus change (and therefore, protection of response) is equivalent. Instead, reinforcement strengthens behavior, whereas punishment weakens it, and a simple application of Guthrie's stimulus-response theory is not satisfactory.

Fortunately, adding reinforcement to the concepts of stimulus and response adds only a small degree of complexity, and, as we shall see, greatly enhances our ability to understand and control behavior. Properly applied, reinforcement theory and the three-term contingency are powerful tools for explaining behavior, and provide extremely potent tools for changing behavior.

Premack's Theory While B. F. Skinner has been primarily responsible for the development of operant conditioning and reinforcement theory, a recent and important breakthrough has been made by David Premack. He pointed out that the traditional conception of a limited number of reinforcing stimuli, each of which has an immutable status as a reinforcer, was oversimplified. Moreover, that conception stood in the way of a more powerful and more generally valid conception of reinforcement.

In the first place, Premack emphasized that it was more useful to discuss reinforcers in terms of responses rather than in terms of stimuli. Thus the reinforcer for the behavior of operating the vending machine may be thought of as drinking the soft drink (a response) rather than the soft drink itself (a stimulus), and the reinforcer for the hungry pigeon's key-pecking may be thought of as eating (a response) rather than food (a stimulus).

Premack showed experimentally that the same event that serves as a reinforcer for some responses may be ineffective as a reinforcer for other responses. Moreover, reinforcers can often change places with the activities that produce them: a thirsty rat will run to get water, but Premack showed that a long-idle rat would actually drink in order to get a chance to run. In the first case, drinking reinforces running; in the second case, running reinforces drinking. It turns out, in general, that any behavior that an organism performs can serve as a reinforcer for any other behavior that the organism performs less frequently. In other words, there is a *reinforcement hierarchy*—those at the top being behaviors we would perform with greatest likelihood, given the chance; those at the bottom being those we would rarely engage in even if the opportunity to do so were unlimited. In Premack's terms, *for a given organism, any response in the hierarchy may reinforce any response below it and may itself be reinforced by any response above it.*

Evidence for this *Premack principle* has been ably marshalled. Consider a situation in which children are given the choice of eating candy or operating a pinball machine. Premack found that children who preferred eating candy would increase their frequency of pinball playing if it were required to obtain candy. Similarly, children who preferred playing the pinball machine would increase their intake of candy if eating candy was required to get the opportunity to play the pinball machine. Moreover, these relations could be *reversed*. For example, when a child who preferred the pinball machine became sufficiently hungry, candy would come to reinforce pinball playing. In general, then, a shift in the relative probabilities of engaging in particular activities brings with it a shift in the reinforcing effectiveness of these activities.

The Premack principle has long been applied by laymen who are intuitively wise in the ways of behavior. When a parent requires a child to clean up his room before he can watch his favorite TV program, he is employing the principle. On the other hand, he is *not* doing so if he tells the child he can watch the program provided that he cleans his room afterwards. The Premack principle has had successful application in the classroom as well as the home. For example, pupils' writing abilities have been significantly increased by allowing the students the opportunity to play after successfully completing their assignments. In one study, the opportunity to engage in a highly preferred academic subject actually served to improve performance in a less-preferred subject.

Aversive Control   Up to this point, we have concentrated on the positive reinforcement of behavior. Behavior that is punished follows the same principles as behavior that is reinforced, except that the effects are reversed: reinforcement increases the tendency to respond, punishment weakens it. When responses are *punished* by aversive stimuli, such as electric shocks or verbal abuse, they are less likely to recur in the future.

Just as organisms will learn to make a certain response if the response is reinforced, they will learn *not* to make that response if it is punished.

Organisms will also learn to *make* a response in order to *escape* or *avoid* a punishing, aversive stimulus. This situation, in which every action but the one selected for conditioning is punished, is called *negative reinforcement*. In escape and avoidance, the removal or nonoccurrence of an aversive stimulus following a response reinforces that response. The term "negative reinforcement" is used because there is a negative correlation between the occurrence of the reinforced response and the aversive stimulus. For example, a dog will readily learn to jump over a hurdle to escape an electric shock delivered through the floor of his cage. After a number of trials, the escape response usually becomes an *avoidance* response: the dog leaps so quickly at the start of the trial that he is not shocked at all. Although some avoidance responses, like jumping, are relatively easy for most organisms to acquire, others are extremely difficult to learn. Some of these difficult responses will be discussed later in this chapter.

MEASURING AND STUDYING OPERANT BEHAVIOR

The principles that govern learning and performance have been discovered by experiments that have usually used animals, rather than humans, as subjects.

The advantages of studying lower organisms, such as rats and pigeons, are many: they are inexpensive and can be easily bred, housed, and maintained in a laboratory. They can be subjected to conditions of deprivation or discomfort that would be undesirable or impractical for human subjects. The experimenter's control over his laboratory-bred animal extends to its entire past experience, which can be observed and regulated from birth. Experiments on laboratory animals can be carefully controlled and tend to yield reliable, unambiguous results.

On the other hand, humans or nonlaboratory animals bring to the laboratory a rich and largely unknown behavioral past, which can interfere with the experimental variables under study and alter the results. Despite the heavy concentration on animal experimentation, however, all of the basic principles of operant conditioning have been successfully extended to, and confirmed with, human subjects.

Methods of Measurement Studying learning would be impossible without some means of measuring behavior. How long does it take a rat to learn to negotiate a maze successfully? How many times does a pigeon peck the key? How fast does a dog jump in order to escape a shock? How much faster to avoid it altogether?

Over the years psychologists have realized that in order to guarantee valid, unambiguous data, they have to measure behavior as precisely as possible. Many kinds of conditioning apparatus have been developed, ranging from the ingeniously simple to the extremely sophisticated; Figures 4.5 through 4.16 illustrate some of them. They all have one thing in common: they provide a means of recording and measuring responses accurately and efficiently.

There are a number of ways in which responses can be measured, depending on the kind of information the experimenter wants to obtain. One is *latency*, the length of time between the presentation of the S^D and the subject's response. For example, suppose the experimenter wants to study how cats learn to escape from a "puzzle box"—as Edward L. Thorndike (1874–1949) did in one of a series of conditioning experiments conducted early in this century. How long does it take the cat to get out of the box the

Figure 4.5
A maze similar to that devised by Willard Stanton Small in 1901. The rat begins at the start and must learn to reach the goal to obtain food. [Robert J. Smith, from Black Star]

Figure 4.6
The Hampton Court Gardens Maze in England from which Small patterned his maze. [Crown copyright reserved.]

first time? the fifth time? the twentieth time? In an experiment using an aversive stimulus, how long does it take a dog to leap off the floor after a buzzer signals that a shock is due? In experiments that measure latency, the response to be conditioned must be chosen and defined with great care, so that there is no doubt when it begins and ends.

Some responses must be repeated many times after the presentation of a single S^D before reinforcement occurs. For example, a pigeon may be required to peck a key ten or twenty times before a peck is reinforced with a small amount of grain. In this sort of conditioning experiment, one useful measure is the *rate of responding*—or the number of responses per unit of time. An increase in the number of responses in a given time is an indication of the strength of the response and the effectiveness of the reinforcer.

Another method of measurement commonly used in more complex experiments is *choice*. It is frequently used to measure the relative effectiveness of one or more reinforcers. An animal may be given an opportunity to respond to one of two S^{D}s, each of which results in a different kind or amount of reinforcement. The measure is usually the fraction of the total number of responses that occur to one of the two choices.

The *resistance to extinction* of responding may also indicate the strength of responding. When a learned response is no longer reinforced, the number of responses diminishes over time, and the response may eventually cease altogether. The behavior is then said to be extinguished. The slower the decline in responding, the greater its resistance to extinction, and presumably the greater its strength. The resistance to extinction depends in part on the degree of difference between the original experimental situation, in which responses were reinforced, and the new one, in which they are not. We shall return to this point later in the chapter, after discussing schedules of reinforcement.

Basic Apparatus The Skinner box, devised by B. F. Skinner for the study of operant conditioning (Figure 4.17), is a very simplified, isolated environment that insulates the organism from extraneous and potentially disturbing influences during an experiment. The box is often starkly simple—four walls, ceiling, floor grating, lights or sounds for S^{D}s, a lever

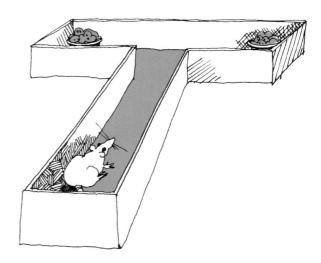

Figure 4.7
A simple T-maze. The rat (or other small animal) must learn whether to turn left or right.

Figure 4.8
A Lashley jumping stand. The rat must jump at the appropriate card, which will give way, allowing the rat to land behind it, where there is food. The other card will not move, and the rat will fall into the net below.

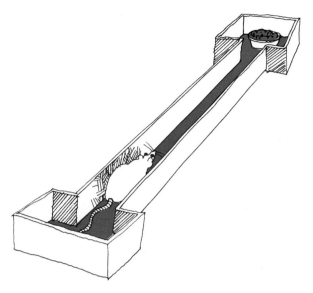

Figure 4.9
A runway. Unlike the T-maze and Lashley jumping stand, in which the subject must make the correct choice, the runway's dependent variable is the speed with which the subject reaches the goal box which contains food.

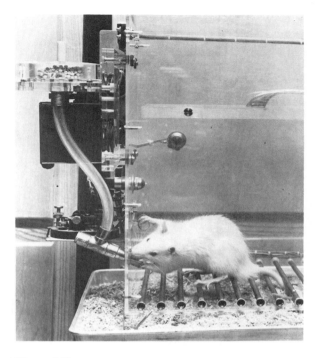

Figure 4.10
A rat responding in a Skinner box. Choice can be studied in such an apparatus if each of two levers have different consequences. The effects of these consequences on the subject's choice behavior—the number of presses on the lever relative to the number of presses on the other lever—is then assessed. [Courtesy Pfizer, Inc.]

Figure 4.11
A puzzle box, used by Thorndike, Guthrie, and others to study instrumental behavior in the cat.

Figure 4.12
A monkey at work on a mechanical puzzle. [From a photograph by Harry F. Harlow]

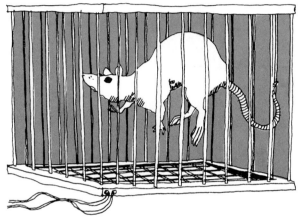

Figure 4.14
In some experiments, animals must respond to avoid or escape electric shock, delivered in this case through the grid floor of the chamber.

Figure 4.13
A cat responds to either of two distinctive stimuli. Food is found under only one of the stimuli.

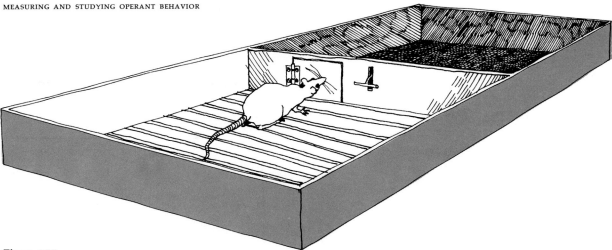

Figure 4.15
In a shuttle box, the subject must run from the left
compartment to the right compartment in order to avoid
or escape shock delivered through the grid floor of the
left compartment.

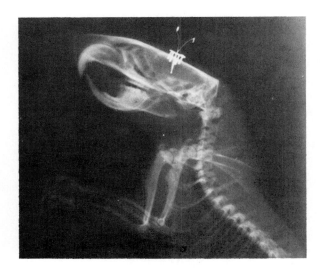

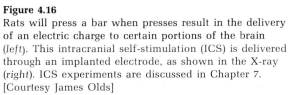

Figure 4.16
Rats will press a bar when presses result in the delivery
of an electric charge to certain portions of the brain
(*left*). This intracranial self-stimulation (ICS) is delivered
through an implanted electrode, as shown in the X-ray
(*right*). ICS experiments are discussed in Chapter 7.
[Courtesy James Olds]

or key defining the response, and provision for delivering the reinforcer. But the number of stimuli and responses available in a particular experiment can be increased and varied automatically at the will of the experimenter (Figure 4.18).

Typically, the entire apparatus is automated, so that a bar-press or key-peck will trip a switch that will deliver a food pellet or a few drops of water on a schedule determined in advance by the experimenter. Both the response and the reinforcement can be automatically recorded, by a device like that shown in Figure 4.19.

The Skinner box and its variants permit precise measurement of the organism's behavior, typically the rate of responding or the latency of each response. At the same time, the device clearly separates the three elements of the basic reinforcement contingency: the S^D, the response, and the reinforcer. This allows the experimenter complete control over the three most important elements in an experiment on operant conditioning: (1) occurrences of the S^D and of the reinforcer, (2) the definition and measurement of the response, and (3) the relationship between the S^D, the response, and the reinforcer.

Skinner's box evolved from earlier pieces of apparatus for studying learning. Experimental mazes have ranged from extremely simple to quite complex. One of the more complex ones was also one of the earliest, Willard Stanton Small's (1870–1943) maze, adapted in 1901 from the Hampton Court garden maze (Figures 4.5 and 4.6), a diversion for the English aristocracy. Later mazes have been simplified in efforts to study the effects of different reinforcers or specific discriminations. For example, the very simple T-maze (Figure 4.7) has two goal boxes (Small's had only one), so that it is possible to vary the consequences of choosing each arm of the T. Small's maze had many choice points; as the rats learned the maze, something about each choice point obviously signaled "right way" or "wrong way," but it would

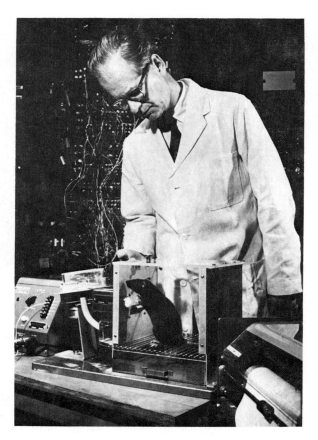

Figure 4.17
B. F. Skinner with the experimental device that bears his name. [Nina Leen, Time-Life Picture Agency]

have been nearly impossible to say exactly which stimuli controlled the rat's behavior at each choice. With the T-maze, however, there is only one choice point, which can be provided with different cues (a red and a green card, or a white and a black floor), which are S^Ds signaling the kind of reinforcement placed in the goal box at the end of the arm. This not only facilitates the learning process but also allows the experimenter to study subtle discriminations (between two nearly identical gray floors, for example).

One disadvantage of every maze is that it necessitates a *delay of reinforcement*. After the rat makes his choice, it takes him a certain amount of time to run down the arm to the reward in the goal box. Also, the experimenter must (usually manually) return the

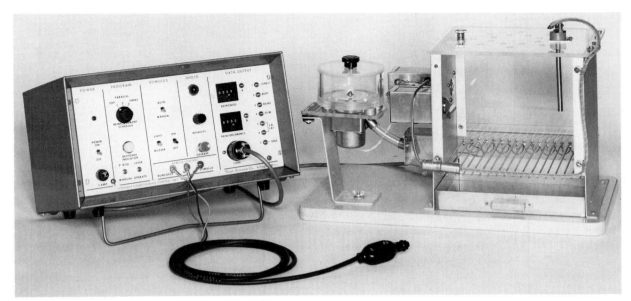

Figure 4.18
A Skinner box with an operant-conditioning control unit. [Pace Photo, Inc. Courtesy Ralph Gerbrands Co., Inc.]

rat to the start of the maze after each trial. This means that handling the rat, no matter how carefully, can influence the results; also, the experimenter must stay near the maze during the experiment. Skinner reasoned that the actual running by the rat is not necessary, so he eliminated the alleys, leaving only a goal box. In the goal box, he replaced running with bar-pressing, and arranged that presses cause the delivery of the reinforcer. Thus, reinforcement can be delivered immediately after a response, and the animal need not be touched or artifically moved during the experiment. This automation allows the experimenter to study his results while the rat is working rather than interrupting the experiment to carry the rat back to a starting point after each trial.

Many other kinds of apparatus have been designed to study learning. Each of them arranges an environment in which behavior has certain consequences under certain circumstances. They differ in the behavior, the consequences, the kinds of circumstances, and the ease with which the behavior can be measured and studied. The historically most important pieces of apparatus are shown in the figures in this chapter.

Figure 4.19
A cumulative recorder. As the motor-driven cylinder rotates at a constant speed, it moves the recorder paper and the pen writes on the moving paper. If no responses occurred, this would produce a horizontal line. Each response steps the pen upwards (to the left in the picture). The faster responding occurs, the less flat the line. In this way, a picture of cumulative responses graphed against time is generated. The "pips" or slash lines on the record denote reinforcement. [Pace Photo, Inc. Courtesy Ralph Gerbrands Co., Inc.]

LEARNING PHENOMENA

The reinforcement or punishment of responses that already exist in an organism's behavior repertoire will increase or decrease their rate of emission. But how can an organism's behavior be altered so that it will emit particular novel responses that it cannot now perform? For example, how can a rat be trained to press a lever or a chicken to play "Light My Fire" on a toy piano?

Acquisition and Shaping of New Behavior

New behaviors such as these may be easily taught through a process called *shaping*. The experimenter begins with responses that the organism already emits with some frequency and utilizes differential reinforcement to shape these responses into closer and closer approximations to the desired terminal behavior. For example, the experimenter may first provide the rat with reinforcement only when it happens to wander near the lever. This will increase the frequency of remaining near the lever and moving toward it when away. Next, the experimenter carefully reinforces only certain ways of moving toward the lever, ways that bring the rat closer and closer to touching it with its paw. Usually, any raise of the paw is reinforced. Then, only higher raises are reinforced, until the paw is above the lever. Ultimately, only pressing the lever is reinforced. At each stage in this process, the experimenter is aided by the variability that behavior exhibits when it is no longer reinforced: the rat who has been reinforced for touching the lever will perform a flurry of different behaviors when reinforcement no longer follows lever-touching. Such behavioral variability increases the likelihood that the rat will emit a lever-press, and thus be reinforced. Use of the *principle of successive approximations* has enabled experimenters to shape behaviors that do not resemble, even remotely, those that the organism normally emits. Such shaping is

Figure 4.20
Spectacular animal acts are developed by the process of shaping new behavior. [Photo by Mike Warren. Courtesy Marine World Africa U.S.A.]

the basis for a variety of animal-training demonstrations, such as chickens that play a toy piano, porpoises that jump through hoops (Figure 4.20), or pigeons that play a form of ping-pong. Shaping is so powerful a tool that it should never be assumed that an organism is incapable of learning anything of which it is physically and biologically capable.

Schedules of Reinforcement   Although in some situations reinforcers are provided each time an appropriate response occurs (as when we insert a coin in a well-maintained vending machine), most

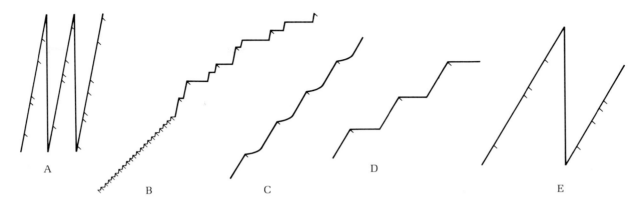

A   B   C   D   E

reinforcers—both those we encounter in our every-day lives and those in laboratory experiments—do not occur on schedules of _continuous reinforcement (crf)_. They are instead obtained on schedules of intermittent reinforcement. In everyday life, only some of our telephone calls are answered; we may have to drive around a block a few times before we find a parking space; we leave a class only after a fixed interval of time. There are many such intermittent schedules of reinforcement. We shall restrict our discussion here to the four most basic ones: _fixed interval (FI); fixed ratio (FR); variable interval (VI)_ and _variable ratio (VR)_. These capital-letter abbreviations (FI, FR, VI and VR) are important technical terms in operant conditioning.

An FI schedule provides reinforcement for the first response that occurs after a fixed interval of time has elapsed since the last reinforcement. Thus, in a fixed interval one-minute schedule, the schedule reinforces only the first response that occurs after one minute has elapsed since the previous reinforced response. Even though responses _during_ the interval are irrelevant, the organism may make many, as shown in the cumulative response record in Figure 4.21. Note that there is a pause following reinforcement, which is followed by a rapid acceleration of responding as the interval comes to an end.

Everyday examples of these simple schedules of reinforcement are not always easy to find or recognize. Much of human behavior is under the control of more complicated schedules that only recently

Figure 4.21
(A) A cumulative record of responding on a _variable-ratio schedule_, in which a certain number of responses is required for reinforcement. Unlike fixed-ratio schedules, the number of responses varies and responding is maintained at a steady rate. (B) A cumulative record of responding on a _fixed-ratio schedule_, in which reinforcement is first delivered after every twenty-fifth and later after every hundredth response. This record shows a "break and run" pattern. The "break" is known as an "FR pause." Breaks sometimes occur _during_ the performance, as when the ratio is abruptly increased from twenty-five to one hundred. (C, D) Typical cumulative records of responding on a _fixed interval schedule_ in which the first response after the interval has elapsed is reinforced. One record (C) shows the gradual acceleration of responding within the fixed interval that is known as a fixed-interval "scallop." The other record (D) shows a "break and run" pattern, more typical of behavior on well-practiced FI schedules. (E) A cumulative record of responding on a _variable-interval schedule_, in which the first response after each interval has elapsed is reinforced. Unlike fixed-interval schedules, however, the size of the interval varies and responding is maintained at a steady rate.

have begun to be studied in the laboratory. The laboratory study of simple schedules is scientifically valuable, however, because it provides a basis for the study of more complex schedules. And there are some fairly accurate approximations to simple schedules in everyday life. For the FI, consider how the behaviors preparatory to departing increase toward the end of a fixed interval of confinement of fifty minutes in a lecture or four to eight hours in an office.

An FR schedule stipulates that reinforcement will occur after the emission of a fixed number of responses. Figure 4.21 illustrates performance on an "FR-25" schedule of reinforcement. Note the pause after reinforcement followed by the rapid "ratio run" until the next reinforcement occurs after the twenty-fifth response. The larger the FR requirement, the longer the pause. With very short ratios, little or no pausing occurs. Wages that are paid on a *piecework* system provide a common example of an FR schedule. Workers often tend to take a break after completing each large block of work; while working, however, they do so at the fairly constant pace that characterizes behavior reinforced on FR schedules.

VI and VR schedules are analogous to FI and FR schedules, respectively, except that responses are reinforced after a variable amount of time has elapsed (VI) or a variable number of responses has been emitted (VR). A typical VI sequence might reinforce the first response after 90 seconds have elapsed since the last reinforcement, then after 30 seconds, then after 15 seconds, and so on, after 100, 70, 180, 5, 40, 20, and 50 seconds. After another interval of 90 seconds, the sequence would be repeated again and again until the experiment was concluded. This particular VI schedule is a "VI-60" schedule because 60 seconds is the *average* of the ten different intervals composing the VI sequence.

Both VI and VR schedules maintain fairly constant rates of responding, as shown in Figure 4.21, because responses may be reinforced at almost any time. Thus, the pauses characteristic of FI and FR schedules do not occur on variable schedules.

Rates of responding are much higher on VR schedules than on VI schedules. The faster the subject responds on a VR, the faster he collects reinforcements. On the VI, however, the subject does not appreciably affect his rate of reinforcement by

responding at a higher rate. Thus, VR schedules are extremely effective in generating high rates of uninterrupted responding. It is not surprising, therefore, that VR schedules are used by gambling houses in slot machines, such as the "one-armed bandit". The persistence of many gamblers in playing these machines is typical of behavior generated by VR schedules.

More complex reinforcement schedules may usually be reduced to variations or combinations of these four elementary schedules, that is, reinforcement is scheduled after a fixed or variable time interval or after a fixed or variable number of responses. In all cases, reinforcement schedules have predictable, orderly—and profound—effects upon the organism's pattern and rate of responding.

Extinction   We saw earlier that, without reinforcement, responding decreases in frequency and that the rate at which extinction takes place depends in part upon the reinforcement conditions in effect prior to extinction. The schedule of reinforcement that has been in effect prior to extinction influences this effect. Extinction after continuous reinforcement (when each response has been reinforced) is rapid because the organism has been shifted from a situation in which *all* of its responses are reinforced to a situation in which *none* of its responses is reinforced. The organism quickly discriminates between the former and the latter situations, and its responding extinguishes rapidly. On the other hand, extinction following intermittent schedules is slower because it is harder to discriminate between the new and the old situations, especially in the case of extremely variable schedules. For example, a VR-500 schedule will contain some very long sequences of unreinforced responses—indeed, several thousand responses may occur between reinforcements. Thus, it may take several hours of extinction before the new situ-

Figure 4.22
Since the one-armed bandit pays off infrequently, the gambler will have trouble telling when it is fixed or broken. Soft-drink machines pay off regularly, however, and a broken one will maintain only one or two responses (coin insertions) by any given person. These examples illustrate the point that *resistance-to-extinction* is greater after partial reinforcement than after continuous reinforcement.

ation (no reinforcement) is discernibly different from the old one. Thus, a broken slot machine may maintain thousands of unreinforced responses (coin insertions) by the gambler who has become accustomed to infrequent reinforcements and who has no way of knowing that the machine's schedule is now one of extinction. When a Coke machine fails to operate, however, it is unlikely that one will insert more than two dimes, because a vending machine should operate on a continuous-reinforcement schedule (Figure 4.22).

The greater *resistance to extinction* of responding following intermittent (or "partial") reinforcement— known as the *partial-reinforcement effect*—has far-reaching practical implications for behavior. A mother who *occasionally* reinforces her child's undesirable temper-tantrums by comforting the child is building stronger and more persistent tantrums than the mother who *always* comforts an unhappy child. The child with a history of intermittently reinforced

tantrums will emit them seemingly endlessly in the future, even when the parents attempt to extinguish them by ignoring them. Common sense indicates that what the parents *should* be doing is reinforcing the child when he is quiet or otherwise behaving appropriately.

Even after extinction has been carried out to its apparent completion, the tendency to emit the previously reinforced response readily surfaces under certain conditions. For example, if a day or so is allowed to elapse between the completion of extinc-

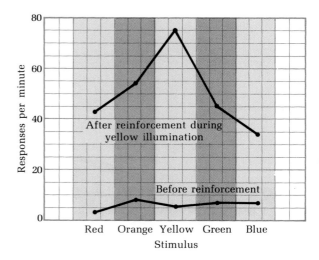

Figure 4.23

A typical *generalization gradient*. A pigeon whose key pecks have been reinforced when the key is yellow is presented with key lights of several different colors in a generalization test conducted "in extinction" (that is, under conditions of extinction—without further reinforcements). The generalization gradient has a peak at yellow (the stimulus to which pecks had been reinforced previously). The closer the color is to yellow, the more responding occurs in its presence. [Adapted from G. S. Reynolds, *A Primer of Operant Conditioning*, 2nd ed. Copyright © 1975 by Scott, Foresman and Co. Reprinted by permission.]

tion and the next opportunity to perform the response, we usually observe the phenomenon of spontaneous recovery—"spontaneous" because no further reinforcements have occurred. The response will once again be emitted at a rate reminiscent of that seen prior to extinction. Without further reinforcements, however, the spontaneously recovered response quickly extinguishes again. After additional experiences of this sort, spontaneous recovery gradually ceases to occur. Spontaneous recovery indicates that responding in the presence of a *new* opportunity for reinforcement has not yet been extinguished. For example, if you lost two dimes to a broken Coke machine on a Monday, responding to the machine extinguishes. Yet, you may hopefully insert another dime into the machine on Tuesday!

Discrimination, Generalization, and Attention   A pigeon whose responses have been reinforced in the presence of a red key-light is presented with lights of a variety of different colors. Will he respond? When he does, we say that the response to the red light has been *generalized* to the other lights. When he does not, we say that the pigeon *discriminates* the other colors from red. The processes of generalization and discrimination are matters of degree; they have been studied by measuring *generalization gradients* indicating the extent to which responses reinforced in the presence of one stimulus generalize to other stimuli. In a typical experiment, the organism is intermittently reinforced in the presence of one stimulus and is then shown a series of stimuli—including the original one—during extinction. The experimenters measure the rate of responding to the stimuli as a function of their value on a particular "stimulus dimension"—such as the color of a light or the pitch or loudness of a tone. A typical generalization gradient is shown in Figure 4.23. This gradient reveals both discrimination (to

a degree) and generalization (to a degree): discrimination because the subject responds differently in the presence of the different stimuli; generalization because the discrimination is not perfect, and the tendency to respond in the presence of the former S^D generalizes to other stimuli. The closer the stimuli are to the S^D, the greater the degree of generalization.

When an organism is exposed to a situation that alternates (*a*) an S^D—say a yellow light—for reinforced responding with (*b*) a stimulus that signifies extinction—say, an unlit key or a green light—it soon forms the appropriate discrimination and responds only to the S^D. The yellow light is an S^D for reinforced responding whereas the unlit key or the green light indicates *non*reinforcement. An interesting byproduct of discrimination-formation is the phenomenon of *behavioral contrast*: responses during the S^D are actually emitted at a higher rate than they are when there is no extinction stimulus alternating with the S^D.

It sometimes happens that reinforcement of a response in the presence of an S^D fails to bring all of the properties of the S^D (for example, its color, shape, location) into control over the response. In that case, variation or even complete elimination of the noncontrolling properties has no effect upon responding—the gradient of generalization is flat and horizontal. If this occurs, we say that the organism has not been *attending* to these stimulus properties. But variation of the properties that are in control, such as the color of the lights in Figure 4.23, has a significant effect upon responding. In this case we say that the organism's *attention* has been directed to this sensory property. Discrimination occurs because at least some aspect of the stimulus has been attended to.

What determines which properties of a stimulus attract an organism's attention? At least two are important: the biological characteristics of the organism and its previous behavioral history. Pigeons, for example, are apparently visual animals—they attend closely to visual stimuli and hardly at all (unless forced) to auditory stimuli. If an organism has learned that some stimuli are more important than others, the important ones will attract its attention and even *overshadow* other stimuli that are present. At a stop light, someone may so attend to the change from red to green that he does not notice (attend to) a dog crossing the street in front of him. In a common demonstration, people are asked to memorize the titles of some twenty magazines in a pile; then they are asked, not for the titles, but for the colors and the pictures on the covers. They certainly saw them, but most did not attend to and cannot recall them. Birds that have been trained to discriminate the brightness of lights may not attend to other stimulus properties that are subsequently introduced.

Conditioned Reinforcement and Chains of Behavior Stimuli that accompany reinforcers may themselves acquire *conditioned reinforcing* properties. Much of our behavior is believed to be controlled by conditioned reinforcement, although there is little general agreement on the necessary and sufficient conditions for establishing a stimulus as a conditioned reinforcer. Two assertions appear sound. (1) Stimuli that have served as S^Ds for reinforced responding will tend to acquire the status of conditioned reinforcers. As such, the S^Ds can control the rate and pattern of responding that produces them. (2) The strength of a conditioned reinforcer is a function of the length of time between its occurrence and the subsequent occurrence of the unconditioned reinforcer: the greater the reduction in the subjective "psychological distance to reward" signified by the onset of a stimulus, the greater its conditioned reinforcing strength.

By properly utilizing conditioned reinforcers, we can construct elaborate chains of behavior that culminate in only a single primary reinforcement. For example, grapes are a powerful reinforcer for a chimpanzee. If the chimp is given poker chips that can be traded in for grapes, the poker chips become conditioned reinforcers. This is demonstrated by the fact that poker chips can then reinforce the chimp's responses. The chimp will learn to operate a vending machine such as the one shown in Figure 4.24 (the "Chimp-O-Mat") which dispenses only poker chips. What we have here is a chain of behavior: the chimp operates the machine, obtains a poker chip, exchanges the chip for a grape, and eats the grape. Note that the poker chip is both a conditioned reinforcer for responding to obtain it and a discriminative stimulus (S^D) for responding to obtain a grape.

Far more complex behavioral chains are commonplace in animal training acts. For example, Barnabus the Rat of Brown University was trained to climb a

Figure 4.24
The "Chimp-O-Mat." Chimps learn to earn tokens when the tokens can be exchanged for a reinforcer such as grapes. In one study, some female chimps stopped working for the tokens; instead, they obtained them from male chimps in return for sexual favors. Some chimps hoard the tokens, just as some humans hoard money. [Yerkes Regional Primate Research Center, Emory University. Henry Nisser]

spiral staircase when a light (the first of several S^Ds) was illuminated. He would then push down a raised drawbridge and cross it to another platform from which he would ascend a ladder, pull a chain hand-over-hand (or paw-over-paw?) to summon an attached car, pedal the car over a bridge, mount another flight of stairs, run through a tube, enter an elevator at the end, and raise a Brown banner. When the flag was raised, the elevator descended to the ground floor. Here, when a buzzer sounded, Barnabus ran over to a lever, pressed it, and was at long last reinforced with a food pellet. When the

buzzer stopped, Barnabus turned back to the spiral staircase and waited for the light signaling the beginning of a new performance. Barnabus' flag-raising routine is illustrated in Figures 4.25 and 4.26.

Humans routinely perform behavior chains that are far more complex than that of Barnabus. Indeed, according to some behavioral psychologists, much of our behavior is controlled by conditioned reinforcers. Consider what the seemingly straightforward activity of going to the movies on a cold winter's day entails: selection of the movie, determination of the show times and theater location, dressing in warm clothes, walking to the bus stop, waiting for a bus, paying the fare, taking a seat, and so forth. All of which may, or may not, be reinforced by the particular movie. Much of human behavior seems to comprise such bits and pieces of complex response chains that are performed for reinforcers far more remote than the pellet that awaited the successful completion of Barnabus' routine.

In a chain of behavior, the conditioned reinforcer that is closest to the unconditioned reinforcer is the strongest. The response it follows is the first to be learned and the last to be extinguished. Behavioral chains are, in fact, taught backwards. Barnabus first learned to press the lever at the sound of the buzzer in order to receive a food pellet (the primary reinforcer). He was then required to ride the elevator in order to reach the box containing the buzzer and the lever, which had both become S^Ds for the pressing response and conditioned reinforcers for riding. Once the elevator ride had become an S^D, it could become a conditioned reinforcer for raising the flag, which, in turn, reinforced running through the tube and entering the elevator, and so on.

The extinction of conditioned responses in a complex chain reverses the learning order—those components learned last extinguish first. Thus, if delivery of the food pellet were discontinued, the whole chain would be extinguished, with the lever-

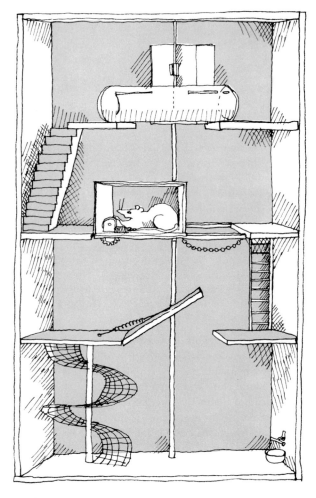

Figure 4.25
The apparatus used to demonstrate the rat Barnabus' mastery of a complex behavioral chain (described in the text).

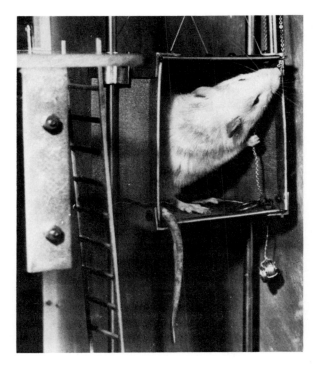

Figure 4.26
Barnabus riding his elevator. [New York Times]

press the last to go. Suppose, instead, that the chain were broken somewhere in the middle. For example, suppose that in Barnabus's chain the tube no longer led to the elevator but to a dead end. In that event, activities in the first part of the chain—such as running through the tube, climbing the stairs, and riding the car would extinguish. But those response components of the chain *following* the break would not be extinguished since there would be no opportunity for them to occur. Thus, if Barnabus were placed at the entrance to the elevator—following

complete extinction of the earlier responses—he would enter, raise the flag, and ride down to press the lever. Of course, if the food pellet no longer appears, these later response components of the chain would also extinguish.

Choice Most of our behaviors require a choice: left or right? Hamburger or chicken? Channel 2 or Channel 4? Work or rest? A root-beer float or a chocolate shake? And so on. A convenient method for studying choice is to present at least two schedules of reinforcement simultaneously; if this is done, the schedules are technically called *concurrent schedules*. If there are two schedules, the subject may respond on either or both. If the two schedules are variable-intervals, for example, the organism's responses on each of two response bars or keys are reinforced according to the VI schedule associated with that key. The consequences of responding on each of the two keys may be systematically varied, and the effects upon the animal's choice of response may be measured.

MORE COMPLEX PHENOMENA

The simple three-term contingency between stimuli, responses, and reinforcement has enormous power and range in the description and explanation of behavior, as we have seen in considering the acquisition and maintenance of behavior, including discrimination, attention, conditioned reinforcement, and response chains. But the three-term contingency is by no means the whole story. The phenomena to be discussed here illustrate how much reinforcement theory may have to be refined and perhaps amended before it can be considered complete.

Instinctive Drift   A pair of psychologists who became superb animal trainers, Keller and Marion Breland, have reported several cases of "misbehavior" in their animals. The Brelands utilized reinforcement to condition dramatic chains of unusual and entertaining animal behavior, but they also found that naturally occurring behaviors would sometimes interfere with the acquisition or performance of the behavior chain. For example, a turkey will readily acquire the response chain of obtaining a coin, carrying it over to a piggy bank, and depositing it in the bank, thereby obtaining food. After a few days of adequate performance, however, the Brelands noticed that they were being shortchanged. The turkeys had begun swallowing the coins, even those as large as quarters.

A similar occurrence was reported by Skinner in 1937, when he found that a rat that had learned to pick up a marble and deposit it down a chute (to obtain food) began holding on to the marble instead. This behavior, which occurs only after many associations of the conditioned reinforcer—coin or marble—with food, has also been observed in many other species, including pigs, raccoons, and porpoises. Indeed, one of Florida's Marineland

porpoises met an untimely death during a game of "catch" when it swallowed a baseball that had been associated with food.

In all of these cases, the "misbehavior" replaces or delays the previously reinforced response, and delays reinforcement as well. As the Brelands note:

> The problem here occurs, as we have noted, after manipulating the object in question has been followed with food reinforcement. The object becomes virtually a food surrogate to the animal; he becomes more and more reluctant to let it go but treats it like a piece of food.[*]

This phenomenon is called _instinctive drift_ or _instinctive breakthrough_ because the previously reinforced behavior has been replaced by one that is more natural or "instinctive" to the organism. Such instances of instinctive breakthrough emphasize the importance of an organism's natural behavior patterns, which may either interfere with or improve the performance of reinforced responses, but they do not necessarily call for a reinterpretation of reinforcement theory. We can speculate that, after being repeatedly paired with food, the objects become not only S^Ds for emitting the conditioned response but also S^Ds for emitting unconditioned food-related responses, such as eating. In cases of instinctive breakthrough, it is possible that the responses of manipulating, chewing, or swallowing the surrogate food are favored because they can be performed more rapidly than the conditioned responses that complete the response chain.

Autoshaping and Automaintenance   A hungry pigeon that has never before been an experimental subject is placed in a standard pigeon chamber. A key in the box is repeatedly illuminated once every

[*]K. Breland and M. Breland, _Animal Behavior_. New York: MacMillan, 1966, p. 68.

minute for six seconds. When it turns off, food is presented to the pigeon. The light stays off for fifty-four seconds and then turns on again. In this procedure, food is delivered *independently* of the pigeon's behavior toward the key—the food will appear even if the pigeon *never* pecks the key. Nonetheless, the pigeon soon begins to peck at the key as soon as it is illuminated. This procedure is called *autoshaping*, since the organism's key-pecking response is acquired without the usual shaping by differential reinforcement and successive approximations. All that is necessary is that lighting of the key be associated with food.

Autoshaping itself provides no great problem for reinforcement theory, since any pecks at the lit key that "accidentally" occur are in fact reinforced by the presentation of food. It is perhaps not surprising that the bird pecks the lit key, since it is a salient stimulus and the bird in its natural habitat does peck to eat its grain. Moreover—as we saw in the previous section, on *instinctive drift*—after repeated pairing with food, stimuli become S^Ds for food-related responses, in this case pecking. Since the "misbehavior" in autoshaping is actually reinforced, it is neither very puzzling nor maladaptive for the organism.

In a procedure called *automaintenance*, however, pecks at the lighted key actually prevent the next scheduled presentation of food. Here, when the pigeon pecks the lighted key, it blocks reinforcement for a period of time; when it fails to peck the lighted key, it does receive food. Nevertheless, some birds acquire the pecking response to such a degree that they rarely obtain food. The autoshaping and automaintenance procedures are illustrated in Figure 4.27.

The automaintenance phenomenon creates more serious problems for reinforcement theory than those considered earlier. Apparently, automaintenance depends in part upon instinctive drift and in part on

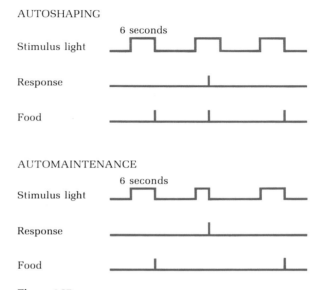

Figure 4.27
Diagram of the temporal relations in the autoshaping and automaintenance procedures. In *autoshaping*, a response in the presence of the light produces food immediately; in the absence of a response, food is presented automatically with the termination of the light. *Automaintenance* is identical with one crucial difference: a response during the light eliminates food presentation on that trial; instead, the response turns off the light and begins a new trial. Pigeons acquire pecking even under these conditions.

conditioned reinforcement. When discussing autoshaping, we have already indicated the role played by instinctive drift. To see how conditioned reinforcement may play a role, we should examine the fine details of the experimental procedure. As in autoshaping, pecking the key does have one effect—turning off the key light—although, unlike autoshaping, food is not presented. On trials when the subject does *not* peck for six seconds, the key light is turned off and food is simultaneously provided. Thus, primary reinforcement (the food) is always

preceded by the termination of the light. It could be
that the termination of the key light develops into a
conditioned reinforcer after repeated pairings of
light-termination and food. A related possibility is
that the immediate stimulus change resulting from
light-termination is more reinforcing than the food
reinforcement, which is delayed until several seconds
have gone by without responding. In other words,
the termination of the light may function as an
immediate conditioned reinforcer while the food
functions as a delayed primary reinforcer.

These contentions have been supported by several
studies that showed that automaintained pigeons
cease to respond when a delay of several seconds is
interposed between the peck and the termination of
the key light. It appears that the prompt termination
of the light is indeed reinforcing the automaintained
behavior. The importance of stimulus change will be
referred to again in the final section of this chapter.

Avoidance Learning and Species-Specific Defense Reactions

We mentioned earlier that
many avoidance responses are acquired with difficulty. Although a rat quickly learns to press a lever
to obtain food, it learns only very slowly to press a
lever to avoid electric shock. On the other hand, the
rat will very quickly learn other avoidance responses,
such as jumping on a platform or running in a
shuttle box. Indeed, if an animal must learn to press
a lever to avoid shock, its behavior will be greatly
facilitated if it is first required to run to the lever.
This surprising result is illustrated in Figure 4.28.
The rats whose data are represented by Curve A
have just five seconds to avoid the shock: in that
time the rats must run from one box to another
when a door drops open, and then press a lever in
the second box. The rats whose data are represented
by Curve B start the trial in the same box with

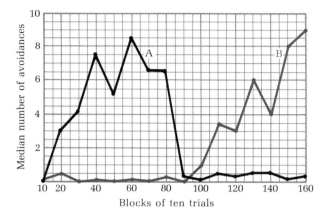

Figure 4.28
In the first eighty trials, rats in Group A learn to run
from one chamber to another and to press a bar, all
within five seconds in order to avoid shock, while rats
in Group B fail to avoid shock even though they need
only press the bar. When the conditions are reversed
for the two groups, the results reverse also. Interestingly,
rats in Group A that have been successfully avoiding
shock after running and pressing fail to avoid shock
when they need merely press. [Adapted from E. Fantino,
D. Sharp, and M. Cole, "Factors Facilitating Lever-Press
Avoidance," *Journal of Comparative and Physiological
Psychology*, 1966, 62, 214–217.]

the lever and have five seconds to press it: since
they generally stay near the lever at all times, the
requirement that they press the lever within five
seconds would appear to be trivial. The figure
illustrates just the opposite result: rats that must run
and then press learn rapidly, while those that need
merely press demonstrate virtually no learning.
After eighty trials, the requirements for the two
groups of rats were reversed. The group of rats that
was now required to run acquired the response
rapidly, as one would expect from the results of the
first part of the experiment. But the rats that had
learned to run and press no longer pressed when

the response was made apparently simpler by eliminating the running. Rats in this condition showed no trace of their earlier learning, indicating that they had in fact not learned to lever-press during the eighty-trial training period, but rather only to run-and-lever-press. These findings underscore the importance of detailed attention to the nature of the response that achieves reinforcement.

The importance of the response used in avoidance has also been underscored by Robert Bolles. In 1970, he pointed to (*a*) the slow learning of avoidance responses in the laboratory and (*b*) the premise that animals must enter their natural environments with defensive reactions already available in their behavioral repertoires. Bolles predicted that avoidance responses will be rapidly acquired in the laboratory only if they are part of the subject's *species-specific defense reactions (SSDR).* For the rat, the SSDR repertoire includes freezing, fleeing, and hiding. Thus, certain laboratory avoidance responses, such as running in the shuttle box or jumping out of a box, are readily acquired because they are compatible with the behaviors in the SSDR repertoire. On the other hand, responses such as bar-pressing, wheel-turning, and chain-pulling are not behaviors in the SSDR repertoire and are difficult to acquire in the avoidance situation.

This difficulty in learning avoidance responses shows that no single term in the three-term contingency should be considered in isolation from the other two. There are important interactions between (1) the effectiveness of a reinforcer and (2) the particular stimulus and (3) responses associated with the stimulus. For example, an organism may learn one response (lever-pressing) more readily than others when a particular reinforcer (food) is used, but may learn a different response (jumping) more readily when another reinforcer or punisher (shock)

Figure 4.29
Pigeons and rats will respond for food even in the presence of freely available food.

is used. (In Chapter 5 we will see that there are striking interactions between stimuli and reinforcers as well.)

Responding for Food When Food is Abundant
Pigeons and rats who have food continuously available (Figure 4.29) will nonetheless acquire key-pecking or lever-pressing to obtain access to a second source of the same food. This phenomenon of responding for food in the presence of available food has been studied extensively. Responding for food appears to be a natural part of the behavior of animals whether or not other food sources are available. Again, these findings are not necessarily inconsistent with the three-term contingency. The light on the key, for example, is an S^D for responding to obtain food; the response is a key peck; the reinforcer is food. The free food is the reinforcer in a second three-term contingency involving the filled, freely available food cup (an S^D), the response of approaching it, and the reinforcer (food). What is surprising is the willingness of the pigeon to work for its dinner when free food is available.

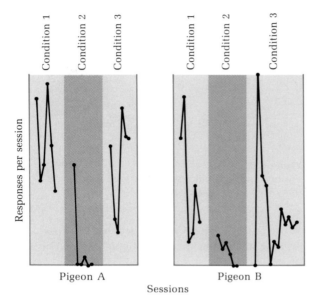

Figure 4.30
Responses per experimental session for each of two pigeons. In Conditions 1 and 3, responses produced stimulus change in addition to food. In Condition 2, responses produced food only, while pecks in the free-food cup produced stimulus change. The pattern of results shows that responding for food in the presence of freely available food depends upon the external stimulus changes that accompany such responding. [Adapted from R. F. Wallace, S. Osborne, J. Norborg, and E. Fantino, "Stimulus Change Contemporaneous with Food Presentation Maintains Responding in the Presence of Free Food." *Science*, 1973, *12*, 1038–1039. Copyright 1973 by the American Association for the Advancement of Science.]

The results of a recent experiment suggest that this phenomenon is due to the presence of conditioned reinforcers. The key-pecking response is reinforced not only by food (the unconditioned reinforcer) but also by the externally produced stimulus changes that accompany the presentation of food. When the pigeon pecks the key, the key-light turns off, the food tray rises into position with an audible click, and then is illuminated. Since all these stimuli are closely associated with the food, they tend to acquire the status of conditioned reinforcers. Figure 4.30 shows what happens when these stimulus changes are removed from the mechanical presentation of food and instead accompany pecks at the free food: the bird no longer pecks at the key (Condition 2 in the figure). When the experimental conditions are again reversed, so that the stimulus changes once more accompany only the response-produced food (Condition 3 in the figure), key-pecking is quickly resumed. It seems as if the "extra" stimuli that accompany the food have become conditioned reinforcers of such strength that, in this situation, they influence the choice response. In other words, the pigeon prefers food with external stimulus changes, rather than just food alone.

These findings suggest that the presence of conditioned reinforcers that accompany primary reinforcers have great importance in situations in which an organism must choose which response to make. The phenomenon of responding for food in the presence of free food seems analogous to many human responses.

Conclusion Psychology is an active field of scientific inquiry. Many of its crucial problems remain to be properly defined, much less solved. The study of operant conditioning has shed considerable light on the acquisition, maintenance, and extinction of behaviors and is continually uncovering new

phenomena as well. We have not offered definitive
explanations for all of the complex phenomena we
have discussed in the latter part of this chapter;
indeed, we chose many of them because they pose
challenges to reinforcement theory. But we have
shown that a thorough application of reinforcement
theory provides at least a plausible account of each
challenge.

Suggested Readings

Breland, K., & Breland, M. (1966) *Animal behavior.*
New York: MacMillan. [An engaging and
instructive account of the behavior and "misbehavior" of organisms.]

Nevin, J. A., & Reynolds, G. S., eds. (1973) *The study
of behavior: Learning, motivation, emotion and instinct.*
Glenview, Illinois: Scott, Foresman. [A more
advanced review of recent literature.]

Rachlin, H. (1970) *Introduction to modern behaviorism.*
San Francisco: W. H. Freeman and Company.

Reynolds, G. S. (1975) *A primer of operant conditioning.*
(2nd ed.) Glenview, Illinois: Scott, Foresman.
[The two foregoing books provide short, readable and authoritative treatments of operant
conditioning.]

Skinner, B. F. (1972) *Cumulative record.* (3rd ed.) New
York: Appleton-Century-Crofts. [Contains many
of B. F. Skinner's most important papers, most
of which are quite readable, even for the
beginner.]

Skinner, B. F. (1974) *About behaviorism.* New York:
Knopf. [Skinner's most recent, comprehensive
book on behaviorism.]

UNIT TWO

Motivation and Emotion

When we watch a runner strain every muscle to win a race, or a wrestler pin his opponent to the mat, or a gymnast (like world champion Olga Korbut, *opposite*) outdo all others on the balance beam, we are often tempted to explain the athlete's performance in terms of a "competitive drive" or a "need for recognition." But psychologists have to be cautious in their use of these everyday terms. All psychologists would agree that a runner exhibits basic *drives*—as when he gasps for breath after a race and later drinks a cup of water—because the physiological *needs* created by the depletion of oxygen and water are relatively easy to determine. But psychologists find it much more difficult to answer the larger question of *why* the athletes are spending every last ounce of their energy to excel.

"Motivation" is the general term used by us all to refer to the powers that lead us to act as we do, from satisfying basic physiological needs to engaging in complex social behaviors. But "motivation" means different things to different psychologists working in different areas; it cannot be defined to everyone's satisfaction. In this unit we shall only sample the range of behavioral phenomena that have traditionally been classified under the heading of motivation.

As suggested by the example of the runner, psychologists agree that behavior aimed at satisfying physiological needs is indeed motivated. All of us have suffered from strong thirst and hunger at one time or another, so we know that such states of deprivation are capable of preoccupying our thoughts and directing our behavior until they are relieved. Fortunately, few of us encounter truly extreme hunger or thirst. We should be thankful, because if we did, we would be spending much more time than we would like in satisfying basic needs. Suppose, for example, you were continually in a state of extreme thirst. You would be frequently uncomfortable and your behavior would appear rather odd. Consider the case of the "intemperate" drinker described in an intriguing letter written by a Dr. Thomas Atkinson in the nineteenth century:

Now, Messrs. Editors, whilst I regard the case which I am about to communicate, as a most extraordinary one, and altogether without a parallel, so far as I am informed; and whilst it may be rejected as exaggerated, or altogether apocryphal, by those to whom I am personally unknown, I, nevertheless, vouch for its accuracy, as it occurred under my own observation, and there are many persons yet living to whom an appeal might be had, were it necessary to sustain a statement made by one whose sole authority, he flatters himself, is sufficient to inspire confidence in any representation which he may make.

The case to which I allude, is that of Mr. J. H., who was my neighbor during my residence in the county of Halifax. He was a young man, below medium size, of sallow complexion, and more abdominous than is usual in persons of his age, presenting the appearance of one who, in his childhood, had been a *dirt-eater*. He was active and industrious, and enjoyed good health. He complained of nothing but *excessive thirst*. To such a degree did he suffer from this cause, that it was hard to resist the conviction that he been bitten by the "Dipsas," a serpent known among the ancient Greeks, whose sting produced a mortal thirst.

Although a sober man, he was the most intemperate drinker I ever knew, from *four to six gallons* of water being required to keep him comfortable during the night, while his daily ration of this, to him literal *"aqua vitae,"* amounted to not less than from *eight to twelve gallons*. He always placed a *large tubful* near his bed, on retiring for the night, which often proving insufficient, he was forced to hurry to the spring to obtain relief from the intense suffering occasioned by the scanty supply. He has frequently driven the hogs from mud-holes in the road, and slaked his thirst with the *semi-liquid* element in which they had been rolling, himself *luxuriating* in that which had afforded only a moderate degree of enjoyment to the swine.

He married quite a good-looking and respectable girl, and, in the year 1829, left Halifax for the Western District of Tennessee, whither several of his neighbors had emigrated a short time before; but arriving at a *first rate spring*, on the top of the Cumberland mountain, he "squatted" near it; where, at the last account which I had of him, (in 1854,) he was quaffing his nectar as in days of yore surrounded by his children, who had attained the age and arrived at the stature of full grown men.*

More than a century later we have a reasonably good idea of what was motivating Mr. J. H. He was suffering from a malady known as *diabetes insipidus,* which is characterized by *polydipsia* (excessive drinking), and *polyuria* (excessive urination). The malady was probably caused by a lesion or tumor in a critical area of the brain. Fortunately, Mr. J. H. was able to adjust successfully to his abnormality—by indulging his excessive thirst. We have chosen an example of motivation that is rather bizarre, but it is an example that illustrates motivation in action and is representative of the way in which motivation operates in more commonplace situations. A cat in heat, a human deprived of food for two days, the four-year-old boy who resists going to his room for a nap—all display the same kind of intense goal-directed behavior that characterized the intemperate drinker.

In Chapter 5 we will discuss the basic needs and drives that humans share with lower organisms. These include the *regulatory drives* (such as hunger and thirst), which are related to bodily needs that are essential for survival; and the *nonregulatory drives* (such as sex and curiosity), which, although not essential for the survival of the organism, are important either for the survival of the species or for the organism's optimal functioning. These drives have been the subject of much illuminating research over the past twenty-five years; consequently, we will have much to say about them.

In Chapter 6 we will investigate the problem of *complex motivation* in the light of different motivational theories. All human motives, and especially the most complex (such as artistic and political motives) develop through the individual's interaction, over a lifetime, with his environment. Thus we will emphasize the role of learning in complex motivation. The study of complex motivation is in a state of flux; thus, this chapter will ask more questions than it answers. We hope that some of these questions will stimulate the reader to pursue the elusive causes of complex behavior.

In Chapter 7 we discuss basic *emotions*—love, affection, fear, and others—which have been the subject of a fair amount of empirical work. We shall also discuss important theoretical treatments of emotional experience.

*A. V. Wolf, *Thirst: Physiology of the Urge to Drink and Problems of Water Lack.* Springfield, Illinois: Charles C Thomas, 1958, pp. 373–374.

CHAPTER FIVE

Needs and Drives

It was once assumed by experimental psychologists that all behavior could be explained as seeking to satisfy basic physiological needs, such as eating, drinking, and procreation. Animals seemed to learn only behaviors that produced opportunities for satisfying these needs. Hence *need reduction* was taken to be the mechanism of reinforcement in learning and performance. The strict theory of need reduction was put to rest in the early 1950s, however, by the studies of Fred Sheffield and his co-workers. Sheffield showed, for example, that rats would learn an instrumental response that would permit them to ingest saccharin, a nonnutritive sweetener from which the rats could not derive any nourishment. In another study, rats learned to run a maze in order to obtain access to a female rat with which they were prevented from copulating. Since no need was being reduced in either case, and since the behavior was learned and performed vigorously over a long period of time, need reduction was seen to be an incomplete theory of reinforcement. The theory of need reduction was also questioned because it was hard to imagine that an organism would remain completely inactive even if all of its physiological needs were satisfied. Finally, it was difficult to account for the complexity and variety of behaviors within a need-reduction framework.

Need reduction was superseded by a theory of *drive reduction* developed largely by Clark Hull and Neal Miller over a twenty-year period beginning in 1943. Unlike needs, which refer to basic states of deprivation, drives were depicted as strong stimuli that goad the organism into action. Thus, the infernal blare of your neighbor's TV set may impel you into action (for example, into closing your windows or complaining to your neighbor), even though no basic deprivation state may be affected by the noise. These strong "drive stimuli" may be related to needs—as when internal deprivation states related to the lack of food or water produce feelings of hunger or thirst—but, as the example of the loud TV suggests, they need not be. The important point is that the reduction of a drive stimulus ("drive-stimulus reduction") is reinforcing: behaviors that result in drive-stimulus reduction will recur with increasing frequency when the drive stimulus is again intense. The drive-reduction theorists thought that a limited number of drives—those corresponding to the basic needs plus a few others—would be sufficient to explain most behavior. If so, drive-reduction theory

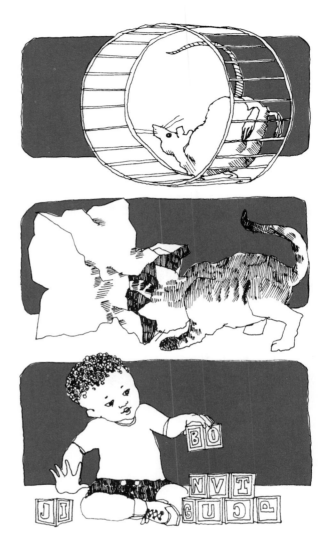

Figure 5.1
Some behaviors do not seem to be closely related to physiological needs like hunger and thirst. The opportunity to run (*top*), to explore (*center*), and to manipulate (*bottom*) all serve as reinforcers.

would represent an important improvement over need-reduction theory: it would avoid the incompleteness of need-reduction theory while retaining much of its simplicity. However, the number of drives seemed to proliferate as experimenters stopped restricting their attention to needs such as hunger, thirst, and sex, and started looking for other drives. It was found, for example, that rats would learn responses that led to the opportunity for activity, for exploration, or simply for visual stimulation. It therefore seemed necessary to postulate drives such as "the activity drive," "the exploratory drive," "the curiosity drive," and "the manipulatory drive" (Figure 5.1). It gradually became evident that almost any behavior that the organism normally engaged in could serve as a reinforcer for the learning of some new behavior. This finding, which should be familiar to the reader from our discussion of *Premack's theory* in Chapter 4, was largely ignored until the early 1960s because it was inconsistent with the notion that a limited set of drives motivated behavior.

Although drive reduction may not be a completely adequate theory of reinforcement, the drive terminology does provide a means of describing concisely much of the behavior in which humans and animals engage. The best argument for retaining the concept of drive in modern psychological theory is Neal Miller's, which stresses the usefulness of intervening variables in the description of behavior.

DRIVE AS AN INTERVENING VARIABLE

What do we mean when we refer to a concept such as "a thirst drive"? In empirical terms, thirst refers to a constellation of behavioral effects that may be produced by any one of a number of independent variables. If we did not invoke the concept of thirst, the relationships among all the independent variables manipulated and all the dependent variables affected (behavioral measures) would be overwhelmingly complex. Miller points out that by utilizing an *intervening variable* such as thirst we actually gain in conciseness, in the sense of reducing the number of descriptions of possible relationships involved. This reasoning is clearly illustrated in Figures 5.2–5.4.

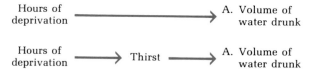

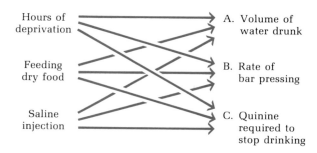

Figure 5.2
In this example, the intervening variable, "thirst," is
an unnecessary complication. [Figures 5.2, 5.3, and 5.4
are adapted from Neal E. Miller, "Liberalization of Basic
S–R Concepts: Extensions to Conflict Behavior, Motiva-
tion and Social Learning." In S. Koch, ed., *Psychology*:
A Study of a Science, Volume 2. New York: McGraw-
Hill, 1959, pp. 196–292.]

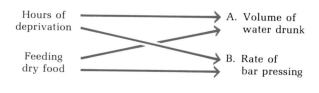

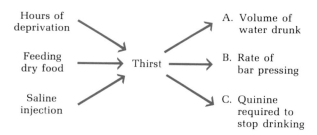

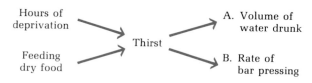

Figure 5.4

Figure 5.3
As Neal Miller's argument demonstrates (see text), the
use of intervening variables sometimes brings order
and conceptual simplicity to the study of motivation
(as shown in this figure and Figure 5.4).

Suppose first that thirst is defined as the volume of
water drunk following a period of water deprivation.
If this were all we intended to convey by the term
"thirst," then its use as an intervening variable would
add unnecessary complexity to our description.
When only two variables are present, as Figure 5.2
shows, it is simpler to represent the direct relation-

ship between them than to postulate an intervening
variable, such as thirst. But the volume of water
drunk may also be affected by feeding the organism
dry food. Similarly, there is a second dependent
variable, the rate of bar-pressing to obtain water, that
is affected by the operations of water deprivation
and dry-food feeding. Figure 5.3 shows that in
expressing all the relationships among two independent variables and two dependent variables, the use
of an intervening variable such as thirst no longer
increases the total number of relationships we must
talk about. There are four, whether or not we employ
an intervening variable. As soon as we have more
than two independent and two dependent variables,
however, the use of an intervening variable permits a
more efficient statement of the relationships between

them. This is shown in Figure 5.4, in which saline injections—which produce dehydration—are added as a third independent variable, and the amount of bitter quinine that an organism will tolerate in its water is added as a third dependent variable, or measure of thirst.

As Miller's argument and the figure demonstrate, the use of intervening variables, such as thirst and hunger, actually brings a measure of order and conceptual simplicity to the study of motivation. Intervening variables should be utilized with caution, however, since they often paint an oversimplified picture of the processes being studied. The effects of saline injections, for example, are not precisely analogous to those of water deprivation. Nor is the volume of water drunk directly related to the amount of quinine that will be tolerated by a thirsty animal. Since the independent variables that produce thirst are not interchangeable (nor are the dependent variables that are supposed to measure thirst), it is clear that use of the term "thirst" constitutes an oversimplification. In a rough sense, however, it is true that all the independent variables produce changes in the same general direction in all the observed behaviors. As long as we keep in mind the fact that the different independent and dependent variables are only approximately equivalent, we are on safe ground in using intervening variables such as thirst for the sake of convenience.

REGULATORY DRIVES

According to the drive theory of motivation, the basic physiological needs of the individual organism give rise to the first important class of drives—the *regulatory,* or *homeostatic, drives* such as hunger, thirst, respiration, and all the other drives related to the maintenance of body functions. The second important class of drives includes the *nonregulatory* drives,

which are important but not necessary for the survival of the individual organism. These include sex, curiosity, activity, and exploration, among others. In this section we will consider the regulatory drives, particularly hunger; in the next section we will consider the nonregulatory drives, with special emphasis on sex.

HOMEOSTASIS

Regulatory drives are those that must be satisfied if we are to survive. We must, for example, breathe, eat, and drink. In addition, we must avoid prolonged exposure to painful stimuli and to abnormally high or low temperatures. The amount of conscious time and effort we must devote to satisfying regulatory drives is far less than what was required of our primitive ancestors. Instead of hunting and gathering food to eat, we can walk into a restaurant or heat up a TV dinner. We can maintain adequate body temperatures by wearing manufactured clothing or by turning up the thermostat or turning on the air conditioner. If we put our minds to it, we can actually arrange to spend very little time consciously satisfying the regulatory drives. Many of us spend most of our time pursuing the satisfaction of nonregulatory drives and wondering what to do with our leisure time.

Homeostasis refers to the maintenance of a steady-state level of functioning by self-regulating mechanisms. When a physiological equilibrium is disrupted, biological and behavioral processes are automatically set into motion to restore the equilibrium. Some processes are normally under almost exclusive physiological control. For example, the level of oxygen in the blood stream is regulated by respiration, over which we normally exert no conscious control—except when swimming underwater or holding our breath to cure the hiccups or doing yoga exercises. If, however, a room is stuffy,

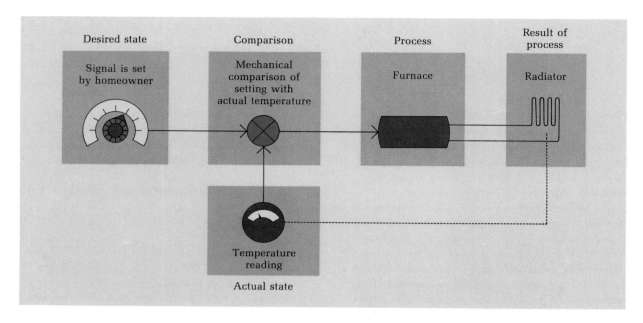

Desired state   Comparison   Process   Result of process

Signal is set   Mechanical   Furnace   Radiator
by homeowner   comparison of
                       setting with
                       actual temperature

                       Temperature
                       reading

                       Actual state

Figure 5.5
The household thermostat. Its operation resembles that of the *homeostats* that regulate the human body's metabolic functioning. [Adapted from H. Rachlin, *Introduction to Modern Behaviorism.* San Francisco: W. H. Freeman and Co. Copyright © 1970.]

we may open a window to facilitate respiration (by letting more oxygen into the room). When our body temperatures are too high, we perspire; evaporation of the perspiration lowers body temperature. On the other hand, when our body temperatures are too low, we shiver; this muscular activity has the effect of raising body temperature. Heart rate and blood pressure are other homeostatically regulated processes, which, for the most part, are internally controlled. External control becomes much more important when it comes to hunger and thirst. When the concentration of salt in the blood stream is too high, we make both physiological and behavioral adjustments to restore biological equilibrium. Physiological adjustment involves the release of an *antidiuretic hormone (ADH)*, which stimulates the kidneys to resorb water; the key behavioral adjustment is drinking. Our species has evolved in such a way that our bodies must regulate the important biological equilibriums both by automatically setting in motion the internal regulatory mechanisms and by inducing drives that cause us to behave in ways that restore equilibrium.

The homeostatic functioning of the body is so efficient that it has often been compared to a ther-

mostat (Figure 5.5). Of course, an organism must regulate not only body temperature but many other functions as well. Where are the *homeostats* in the body that are responsible for detecting physiological disequilibriums? As we shall see, the *hypothalamus*, located in the brain, is intimately involved in the regulation of hunger, thirst, sex, and certain other regulatory and nonregulatory drives. However, the exact mechanisms of control have yet to be determined.

Engaging in behavior that helps to restore physiological equilibrium is often reinforcing. Opportunities to eat and drink, for example, are effective reinforcers of other behaviors for deprived animals, and experiments have shown that animals will learn responses that restore physiological equilibrium with respect to temperature and respiration. In one study, when goldfish were placed in water lacking sufficient oxygen, they learned to interrupt a light beam when that response produced a brief exposure to oxygenated water. A more striking and unusual example, reported early in this century by C. P. Richter, involved a young boy who had a spectacular craving for salt. He would eat food only if it had mounds of salt on it. Moreover, he would go to great lengths to obtain salt. For him, the surreptitious scaling of heights to the cookie jar was replaced by similar behavior directed toward salt. The parents indulged this abnormality, but, realizing that it was strange, consulted their family physician. The physician was unable to explain it but advised that since the salt didn't seem to be harming the child, he saw no reason for alarm. Sometime later the boy was hospitalized for observation and was placed on a diet of normal salt intake. Within a week the child had died.

Thanks to several decades of research into the psychology of motivation, we now know that the child's salt-seeking behavior was an adaptive and indeed necessary effort at salt regulation. The boy apparently had an adrenal gland deficiency and, because of this, required massive ingestion of salt to remain healthy. The boy therefore had made a successful behavioral adjustment to an abnormal physiological situation. In the jargon of motivation, the boy had an "enhanced" drive for salt. This drive was manifested in his craving for and procurement of the needed substance. We shall see later in the chapter that much has been learned in the past decade about such *specific hungers*. First, we shall turn to a more general discussion of food regulation, an area of interest for several reasons: (1) most of us enjoy eating, (2) some excellent research has been done on hunger, and (3) the study of hunger well illustrates the study of motivation.

HUNGER

The two most important questions psychologists have asked about the regulation of food intake are "What

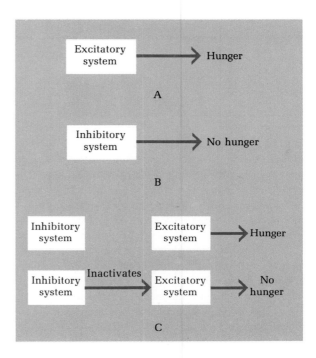

Figure 5.6
Three possible models of food regulation. The third appears to best describe food regulation in the normal human (see text).

causes hunger?" and "What determines the choice of food?" Although the question of hunger is complex, research over the past decade has shed a fair amount of light on the mechanism of hunger. The question of why we eat what we do is even more fascinating and has recently been the subject of much important experimental work.

The Mechanism of Hunger Do animals eat because the brain sends out an *excitatory* message, inducing hunger, when bodily stores are depleted? And do they stop eating when the excitatory signals stop? Such a simple excitatory model of hunger is shown in Figure 5.6 (Part A). A logically equivalent possibility is that animals eat *except* when the brain is sending out *inhibitory* signals that prevent them from eating. According to this model, depicted in Part B, when bodily stores are depleted, inhibitory signals from the brain cease and hunger is experienced. A third possibility, depicted in Part C, is that excitatory impulses initiate hunger and are later turned off by inhibitory impulses. This last model has been demonstrated by much recent research to be characteristic of normal humans, as well as many lower organisms; nevertheless, under some circumstances, food regulation appears to resemble one of the simpler models.

Some ingenious experiments by Vincent Dethier and his associates in the 1960s have shown that hunger in the blowfly, a close relative of the familiar housefly, appears to be regulated by a simple inhibitory model such as that illustrated in Part B of Figure 5.6. Their work indicates that hunger in the blowfly can be equated to an absence of stimulation from the recurrent nerve located in the fly's foregut. When the fly has a sufficient amount of food stored in the foregut, the recurrent nerve fires and prevents (inhibits) eating. When the recurrent nerve is severed, therefore, there is no possibility for inhibitory output and the fly eats continuously. Although Dethier has also discovered other factors that control hunger in the fly, the fundamental conclusion to be drawn from his work is that in some animals food regulation is primarily under inhibitory—as opposed to excitatory—control.

In contrast to this finding, food regulation in higher organisms is under the dual control of inhibitory and excitatory mechanisms. An important regulating structure is the *hypothalamus*—a vital subcortical brain structure intimately involved in the control of most motivational and emotional behaviors (see Chapter 7). Research on the physiology of motivation over the past three decades has placed increasing emphasis on the role of the hypothalamus in many motivational, as well as emotional, states. By means of such techniques as the electrical stimulation or surgical lesioning of discrete hypothalmic regions, behavior associated with each of

Figure 5.7
A rat with *hypothalamic hyperphagia*, caused by a lesion in the satiety connection system. With the satiety system—corresponding to the inhibitory system of Figure 5.6, Part C—inoperative, the rat does not stop eating as soon as normal rats do. Note that the rat's weight is not 80 grams but 1080 grams—this rat had outgrown the scale. [Courtesy Neal Miller]

the normally recognized drives can be drastically altered. Included among the behaviors affected by such procedures are those associated with hunger, thirst, sex, sleep, defense, and temperature regulation.

As early as the turn of the century it was suspected that some neural mechanisms were associated with hunger. Not until much later, however, were eating behaviors demonstrated to be specific to particular neural connection systems in the brain. In the 1940s, it was found that when lesions were made in a certain area of the brain, animals overate, became extremely obese, and often maintained weights three to four times their normal free-feeding weights (Figure 5.7). This phenomenon of chronic overeating is called *hyperphagia*.

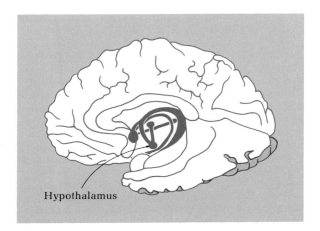

Figure 5.8
The hypothalamus is known to regulate basic physiological processes.

It was believed, until 1973, that the hypothalmus, which was known to influence so many motivational states, must play the central role in the satiety of hunger. We now suspect, however, that this function is controlled by nerve fibers in the *ventral noradrenergic bundle,* a system of connecting fibers that happens to pass through the hypothalamus (Figure 5.8). Because the destruction of this system results in a failure to stop eating, the ventral noradrenergic bundle can be thought of as an inhibitory, or satiety, connection system. The importance of the *satiety connection system* to food regulation in humans is shown by clinical cases in which overeating and obesity have been found to be correlated with tumors in the satiety system. That it took so long to identify this system is not really surprising: the brain is extremely complex, and the systems of nerve fibers are so interconnected that it is difficult to determine which system is associated with which behavioral effect.

Long-term study of hyperphagic (overeating) animals has revealed two distinct stages of overeating. The preliminary dynamic phase, an active phase of overeating with continual weight gain, may last as long as three months. This is followed by a static phase during which the hyperphagic animals eat no more than the amounts required to maintain the abnormally high but stable weight. If, during the static phase, the animals are starved to their normal preoperative levels, dynamic hyperphagia will resume when the animal has access to food and continue until the elevated plateaus are again reached. Thus, during the dynamic phase of hyperphagia, animals behave somewhat like the blowflies whose inhibitory control of eating was impaired.

Richard Nisbett (in 1972) and others have recently argued that there are several striking similarities in the behavior of hungry (nonobese) humans, obese humans, and hyperphagic rats. These similarities involve not only eating behavior but also emotionality, sexual behavior, and general activity. Hungry and obese humans and hyperphagic rats all tend to be more irritable, more apathetic, and more responsive to taste—but less active, less interested in sex, and less responsive to internal cues following ingestion than nonhungry humans and animals. We will return to a discussion of differences in the eating behavior of obese and nonobese humans shortly.

If the satiety connection system only inhibits hunger, what stimulates it? Is there another physiological mechanism involved in food regulation? Lesions in an area of the brain known as the *lateral hypothalamus* often produce total *aphagia* (failure to eat), as well as a marked *adipsia* (failure to drink), in rats and cats. Animals with such lesions will starve to death in the presence of food! On the other hand, electrical excitation of this area results in marked increases in food intake—even in satiated animals—within seconds of the onset of the electrical

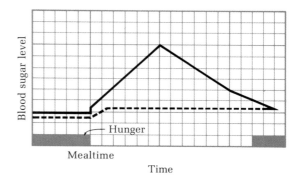

Figure 5.9
Jean Mayer's *glucostatic theory* of hunger stresses that the crucial variable is the amount of blood glucose being utilized by the organism. Glucose utilization is measured by the difference in the blood glucose levels in the arteries carrying blood away from the heart (solid line) and in the veins carrying blood back towards the heart (dashed line). When this *arteriovenous difference* is large, blood sugar is being utilized by the cells and the organism is not hungry. In the diagram, hunger occurs when the difference is small (before a meal and several hours following a meal). [Adapted from J. Mayer "Regulation of Energy Intake and the Body Weight: The Glucostatic Theory and the Lipostatic Hypothesis," *Annals of the New York Academy of Science*, 63 Art. 1, 15–43.]

stimulus. On the basis of these findings, it appears that the lateral hypothalamus is part of a *feeding system*. When animals are given lesions in both the feeding and satiety systems, the effects are the same as those produced by the lateral hypothalamic lesions alone: the animals become aphagic, adipsic, and eventually die. This suggests that normal food regulation requires first the stimulation of appetite by the lateral hypothalamus and later the inhibition of the lateral hypothalamic activity by the satiety connection system. When neither the feeding system nor the satiety system is functioning, therefore, the result is the same as when only the feeding system is destroyed.

Long-term investigation of the nature of the neural deficits produced by lateral hypothalamic lesions indicates that the effects may not be permanent. If kept alive by force-feeding and drinking, many lesioned animals will recover. Their recovery, which follows a fairly regular course, called the *lateral hypothalamic recovery syndrome*, progresses through a series of stages that reflect the regulatory as well as motivational deficits produced by the lesion. The recovered animals will drink water and regulate their caloric intake; but subtle differences between their eating habits and the eating habits of normal rats suggest that motivational deficits may remain even after metabolic function appears normal.

We have seen how the feeding and satiety systems affect eating behavior. But what activates these systems? Up to now we have been talking loosely about their sensitivity to the depletion of bodily "stores." But what, for example, is the specific mechanism that triggers the lateral hypothalamus—or the fibers leading into it—to send out hunger signals? The answer is not known with any certainty. The nutritionist Jean Mayer has formulated the *glucostatic theory*, which stresses that the crucial variable is the amount of blood glucose being utilized by the or-

ganism (as opposed to the simple blood-glucose level, which does *not* correlate well with hunger). The body's utilization of blood glucose is measured by comparing the glucose levels of the arteries and veins. Since blood is pumped out to the body through the arteries and returns to the heart through the veins, a significantly higher glucose level in the arteries indicates that glucose is being removed from the blood and utilized or stored as fat before reaching the veins. While glucose is being utilized, the organism is not hungry. When the arteriovenous difference becomes minimal, however, glucose is not being utilized and hunger results. The glucostatic theory is illustrated in Figure 5.9. This theory is attractive because it is consistent with the results of many (but not all) hunger experiments, and also because it makes sense intuitively. Hunger is more likely to be cued by glucose, which is utilized rapidly when available, than by protein or fat, which are utilized more slowly. Mayer postulated that the central nervous system has *glucoreceptors* that are sensitive to changes in the utilization of blood glucose. Apparently such receptors do exist; however, it now seems likely that they are located in the liver.

Other Factors in Hunger Now that we have discussed the role of the central nervous system—particularly the lateral hypothalamus and the ventral noradrenergic bundle—in the regulation of food intake, we should note a few of the many other factors that influence hunger and eating behavior. Peripheral impulses, such as stomach contractions ("hunger pangs"), are correlated with hunger to some extent; however, they play a much smaller role than was once imagined. Similarly, although gastric distention (the swelling or stretching of the stomach) plays a role in the cessation of eating, it is far less important than caloric intake. For example, if the stomach is loaded with bulky foods (such as celery) or noncaloric substances (such as cellulose), caloric intake is reduced but by no means stopped. Indeed, over the long term, most organisms regulate their food intake fairly well on the basis of caloric content. Another factor in food regulation is hormonal activity. Recent evidence suggests that hormones include a satiety factor, which presumably helps trigger the satiety connection system after the organism has eaten. The mouth also plays a small but significant role in hunger. For example, if food is loaded directly into the stomach, bypassing the mouth, it depresses subsequent oral intake less than if the same amount of food is actually eaten.

Although most of the factors we have been discussing have been studied primarily in lower animals (such as rats, cats, and monkeys), they are also known to influence hunger in humans. Human eating habits are further influenced by learning and cultural factors. Some of us acquire tastes for fattening foods such as candies, desserts, and beer, which we find appetizing even after our caloric needs

have been satisfied (and, presumably, even after the satiety connection system is active). Similarly, most of us in this culture eat three meals a day more out of habit than out of physiological hunger. The eating behavior of obese people seems to be especially influenced by environmental factors.

Research carried out in the past few years by Stanley Schachter, Richard Nisbett, and their associates, has pointed to a striking difference between the styles of food regulation of obese and normal (average weight) people. In one ingenious study, subjects were left alone with sandwiches. The number of sandwiches on the plate varied from subject to subject, but there was a large supply of sandwiches in the refrigerator, and each subject was encouraged to have as many sandwiches as he liked. The normal subjects tended to eat about the same number of sandwiches regardless of how many were on their plates. Thus, if the number was small, the normal subject went to the refrigerator and got more; if the number was large, he did not finish all the sandwiches on his plate. The obese subjects, on the other hand, tended to eat whatever was on their plates and avoided going to the refrigerator. In other words, if his plate was loaded with sandwiches the obese subject would finish them all, but if he received only a few sandwiches he would eat those and not go to the refrigerator for more.

In another experiment, obese and normal subjects were asked to rate the taste of two flavors of ice cream. They were told to eat as much from each bowl as they needed in order to make an accurate assessment of which ice cream tasted better. In fact, one kind of ice cream was of high quality and the other was adulterated with quinine and had a bitter taste. The normal subjects took a taste from each bowl. The obese subjects, on the other hand, took only a spoonful from the adulterated bowl, but then ate huge amounts of the high-quality ice cream,

Figure 5.10
Given an excuse—in this instance, that of an experiment—obese humans are more likely than thin ones to indulge their appetites (see text). This may not be surprising in view of recent work, suggesting that obese people are in a state of almost perpetual hunger because they are *underweight* relative to their biologically programmed set points.

apparently using the experiment as an excuse to indulge their appetites (Figure 5.10).

These and other studies suggest that normal human subjects, like the lower organisms, tend to regulate their food intake on the basis of internal cues. Obese subjects, on the other hand, are much more influenced by external factors—such as whether or not the food is visible, how easy it is to obtain it, and how it tastes.

Responsiveness to taste seems to be a particularly significant factor in hunger. In one experiment, reported by M. Cabanac in 1971, nonobese people given a concentrated solution of sugar water to drink reported that it tasted good, but their appreciation of it declined when they were tested fifteen minutes later. Obese people, on the other hand, were more

likely to continue to judge the sugar solution tasty, even after drinking it once. Again, the obese people seemed to respond more strongly to external factors, such as taste, than to internal factors.

We commented earlier on the striking behavioral similarities between obese humans, hungry organisms, and organisms with lesions in the satiety connection system. The possibility exists that obese people are in a state of almost perpetual hunger because they are in fact *underweight* relative to their biologically programmed level. According to this argument, social pressures prevent them from reaching their level, and, as a result, they are continually in a state equivalent to the "dynamic" phase in hyperphagic organisms. Not only are they not "gluttons"—as popular lore would have it—but they are continually exercising self-control.

Specific Hungers   Why do organisms select certain foods, and not others, to satisfy their hunger? (Figure 5.11.) All organisms, including rats, monkeys, and humans, exhibit specific hungers and aversions for particular foods. Human food preferences are culturally determined: thus fried grasshoppers and raw fish are delicacies in some cultures, but the mere thought of them produces shudders in members of other cultures. To a large extent, of course, we eat the foods that are accessible to us. But do our choices among those foods depend primarily on learning, or something else? The study of *specific hungers*, first carried out by C. P. Richter, P. T. Young, and others in the 1930s and 1940s, has shown that organisms are remarkably adaptive in choosing the foods their bodies need. For example, an organism deprived of a particular nutrient in an otherwise adequate diet appears to seek out the appropriate food necessary to relieve the deficiency. Hence the study of specific hungers, interesting and important in its own right, has implications not only for food regulation but also for our knowledge of learning.

Figure 5.11

It also illustrates the interplay of biological and environmental factors in the determination of behavior—a subject we shall explore in Chapters 15 and 16.

Human infants given the opportunity to select their own food in cafeteria-style experiments do remarkably well at choosing a nutritionally sound diet. Offered their choice of a wide variety of foods for a period of several months, the infants may choose a disproportionate amount of some foods on some days, but over the course of the experiment they will select an adequately balanced diet and experience normal growth and health. Such experiments have also shown that organisms exhibit specific hungers for foods containing specific nutrients in which the organisms are deficient. For example, selectively depriving the organism of vitamins B or C, protein, carbohydrates, or fats leads to a compensatory increase in the intake of specific food substances that will eliminate the deficiency. Cases have also been reported in which people with salt defi-

ciencies (brought about by dysfunction of the adrenal gland) have developed a spectacular hunger for salt. One such case was discussed earlier in this chapter.

What is the mechanism controlling specific hungers? For some time it was assumed that the physiological deficiency resulting from the lack of an essential nutrient produced a specific drive directed toward relieving that deficiency. One early hypothesis suggested that specific hungers developed because the organism's peripheral nerves became more sensitive to the required nutrient. This hypothesis was disproved, however, by demonstrating that a rat whose adrenal glands had been surgically removed had the same sensitivity to salt as a normal rat, even though it had a specific hunger for salt and consumed several times more than the normal rat.

Another theory suggested that specific hungers represent inborn taste preferences for foods capable of relieving vital deficiencies. If such evolved preferences existed in a species, they should be expressed only for foods present in the environment—not for pure nutrients, which rarely if ever occur naturally. However, in an experiment by Richter in which adult rats were provided with an assortment of pure nutrients (minerals, vitamins, carbohydrates, and proteins) not only did they select a well-balanced diet, but they actually selected a *better* diet—as revealed by their growth and health—than did a control group of rats that ate "lab chow" that had been selected by a dietician. These results suggest that the rats' performance was not due to inborn preferences, since animals were "self-selecting" on the basis of completely novel tastes.

It now appears that many specific hungers depend on experience. Until recently, most investigators believed that somehow the organism learns to associate the taste of a food containing the needed nutrient with the partial recovery from the deficiency that follows eating that food. Consequently, the organism eats more of that food until the deficiency is eliminated. When faced with a similar deficiency in the future, the organism will seek the food previously associated with recovery. One problem with this theory is that the deficiency is often not remedied for some time after the appropriate selection of food. How can the organism associate recovery from the deficiency with the much earlier ingestion of the responsible food? Moreover, many other behaviors, including ingestion of other substances, may have occurred in the interim. How can the organism correctly single out the one food responsible for recovery? Finally, there is the difficulty of explaining, in terms of the recovery theory, the "preference after recovery": if a deficiency is remedied either by injection or by allowing the organism to ingest the appropriate nutrient, and the same organism is *later* given a choice between the old deficient food and a new food, it will choose the new food. But this new food is not chosen for its association with recovery, since recovery was induced *before* the food was presented.

A series of experiments by Paul Rozin and his associates has made considerable progress in solving the riddle of specific hungers. They subjected rats to thiamin (vitamin B_1)–deficient diets for twenty-one days. The rats were then given a choice between the deficient diet and a thiamin-supplemented diet. As expected on the basis of earlier research, the deficient rats chose the thiamin-supplemented diet. In a second experiment, Rozin placed thiamin in the old deficient food and presented the thiamin-deprived rats with a choice between the familiar food (now enriched with thiamin) and some new food lacking thiamin. If the organism were seeking out thiamin—if it had a "thiamin sensor" of some kind—it obviously should choose the familiar but thiamin-enriched food. Instead, the rats chose the new food whether or not it contained thiamin.

One possible explanation of this finding is that the organism develops an aversion to the deficient food. An alternative explanation is that the organism will choose any new food, or, in other words, that an organism suffering a deficiency becomes generally *neophilic* ("loves new"). The neophilia hypothesis suggests that the organism tries out a variety of new foods and learns to choose the ones that help rectify the deficiency. Rozin tested the two hypotheses in an experiment in which thiamin-deficient rats were given a choice of three foods. Two of the choices were the standard pair: a new food and the familiar thiamin-deficient food. According to either hypothesis ("loves new" or "fears old") the organism should choose the new food. In addition, Rozin presented a third alternative consisting of an old familiar food that had never been associated with deficiency (that is, a food that the organism had ingested prior to the thiamin-deficient regimen).

Now, consider the possible outcomes of these three choices. If, as a result of its deficient diet, the organism has developed neophilia, it should choose the new food, as it does in the two-choice situation,

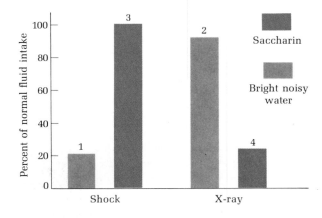

Figure 5.12
When rats are either shocked for drinking bright-noisy water or nauseated (with X-radiation) for drinking sweet-tasting water (Groups 1 and 4, respectively), their future intake of this water is suppressed. X-radiation is relatively ineffective when paired with bright-noisy water (Group 2), as is shock when paired with sweet-tasting water. The significance of this surprising interaction is discussed in the text. [Adapted from S. Revusky and J. Garcia, "Learned Associations over Long Delays." In G. H. Bower, ed., *The Psychology of Learning and Motivation*, Volume 4. New York: Academic Press. 1970, pp. 1–84.]

and display indifference between the two familiar foods. On the other hand, if the organism has developed an aversion to the deficient familiar food, it should spurn that food and try both the new food and the safe familiar food. Rozin's results are more consistent with the latter (learned aversion) hypothesis. He found that the rats preferred the familiar safe food and avoided the familiar deficient food, apparently having developed an aversion to the deficient foods. The fact that the familiar safe food was preferred over the new food indicates that the rats were somewhat *neophobic* ("fears new"), not neophilic. Given two foods that were nonaversive, the rats would prefer the familiar one.

Rozin's experiments show that at least some specific hungers result from the development of a learned aversion to deficient foods. In a sense, then, the phrase "specific hunger" is a misnomer; a more appropriate phrase would be "specific aversion." These results also explain the phenomenon of "preference after recovery" referred to earlier. "Preference after recovery" was puzzling only because the organism was assumed to be seeking a food to correct an already corrected deficiency. Now we can see that the organism is merely continuing to shun a diet for which it has developed an aversion.

Rozin's results do not by themselves solve all the questions regarding specific hungers. Why should the organism develop an aversion for food at all? Many events may have intervened between ingestion of a deficient or poisoned food and the resultant sickness. In order to obtain a partial answer to this question, we turn now to a series of ingenious experiments conducted very recently by John Garcia—experiments that have implications not only for the study of specific hungers but for the theory of reinforcement in general.

Garcia and his colleagues studied the development of learned aversions in rats by comparing the effec-

tiveness of two different punishments in inhibiting the drinking of two types of solutions. Half of the rats in their experiment drank water flavored with saccharine. The other half drank unflavored water that was accompanied by visual and auditory stimuli ("bright-noisy water"). (In this condition, each time the rat licked its water bottle, a light flashed and the bottle made gurgling sounds.) For half of the rats in each of these groups licking was followed by an immediate electric shock. For the other half licking was followed by exposure to X-rays, which produced symptoms of nausea. Thus there were four main groups of conditions: (1) bright-noisy water paired with nausea; (2) flavored water paired with nausea; (3) bright-noisy water paired with shock; and (4) flavored water paired with shock. Following a number of trials under these conditions, water intake was measured for all groups. The main results are shown in Figure 5.12. It is evident that punishment was indeed effective both for rats made nauseated after drinking the flavored water and for rats shocked while drinking the bright-noisy water. The important finding, however, is that these same aversive events (X-ray and electric shock) were not effective in suppressing drinking in either of the other two groups. That is, the aversive event was *not* effective either for the group that had shock paired with flavored water or for the group that had X-ray paired with bright-noisy water. In each case, the rats ingested close to their normal fluid intake in spite of the previous punishment.

These studies therefore indicate that the effects of reinforcers and punishers depend critically upon the particular stimuli that they follow, as well as the particular response of which they are consequences. It may be that the effects of pairing a stimulus and an aversive event (or reinforcer) are more pronounced if both are either internal (like nausea and taste) or external (like shock, and light and noise.) This interaction illustrates the principle of *belongingness*, originally advanced by the early American behaviorist Edward L. Thorndike.

One aspect of Garcia's results could have particularly broad consequences for our understanding of learning. He found that aversion would develop to taste stimuli even if nausea did not occur until several hours after ingestion. This result suggests that in certain situations learning can occur even though a long delay intervenes between the ingestion and its aversive consequences. The mechanism for this *long-delay learning* is not presently known. Revusky and Garcia have suggested that since taste stimuli occur infrequently and are thus well protected from interference by other stimuli, reinforcers acting upon them may have long temporal gradients—the reinforcers will be effective after unusually long delays. The only effective taste stimuli are chemical stimuli that occur while the animal is eating. The lack of interfering stimuli makes more probable the occurrence of long-delay learning—the

association of the taste stimuli with nausea occurring several hours later. Such learning does *not* take place when the organism is exposed to many other effective taste stimuli during this time. Nor does long-delay learning occur with visual or auditory stimuli, because interfering stimuli are continually impinging upon the visual and auditory senses.

THIRST

Like hunger, thirst is controlled by both internal and external factors. We may be stimulated to drink by an ad picturing a foaming glass of beer or a chilled soft drink. We are also more likely to drink when people around us are drinking; what we drink is in large measure determined by the culture we live in and by our past experience. (An American might be startled if he were served a glass of lemonade and beer—a common summertime drink in Paris.) Despite these influences, the most important factors controlling drinking, particularly of water (as opposed to drinks with nutritive value, alcohol, or sodas, which may satisfy drives other than thirst) are internal factors related to water deprivation. These include neural factors, the distribution of bodily fluids (for example, cellular dehydration and total fluid volume), oral factors, and hormonal factors.

Cellular dehydration seems to be one of two critical variables controlling thirst. It is believed that *osmoreceptors* located in the brain detect the occurrence of cellular dehydration—a condition in which bodily fluids are hypertonic, or contain a higher proportion of salt than is optimal—and somehow signal the lateral hypothalamus to trigger thirst. We have already noted that when the lateral hypothalamus is removed, animals become *adipsic* (will not drink).

In contrast to *osmotic thirst* (the kind we just discussed), it now appears there is a second kind of thirst called *hypovolemic thirst*, which depends on total fluid volume in the body. Several experiments have demonstrated that fluid volume loss (which need not affect osmotic pressure) produces thirst. For example, bleeding—which does not alter osmotic pressure— may induce thirst.

Oral factors appear to play approximately the same role in thirst as they do in hunger. For example, water loaded directly into an animal's stomach does less to suppress drinking than does the same amount of water taken orally. In addition, a dry mouth may serve as a thirst signal. It is also possible that some mechanism located in the mouth or throat signals the animal to stop drinking.

A hormone importantly involved in water regulation is the *antidiuretic hormone (ADH)*. When the amount of water in the blood is less than optimal, secretion of ADH causes the kidneys to resorb more water than they usually do, thereby producing a relatively more concentrated urine and at the same time recycling water into the blood. On the other hand, when the amount of water in the blood is more than optimal, secretion of ADH is inhibited, the kidneys resorb less water, and the resultant urine is less concentrated than usual. If the ADH secretion is impaired by a brain lesion, *polydipsia* (excessive drinking) results. Water regulation by ADH is thus a physiological counterpart of the behavioral regulation that occurs when we drink. In the introduction to this unit, we cited a case of "intemperate drinking" or polydipsia. It is fairly likely that Mr. J. H. had a brain lesion that impaired his ability to produce ADH; hence, he had *polyuria* (excessive urination) and polydipsia.

The foregoing detailed analysis of hunger and the briefer treatment of thirst suggest how the regulatory drives operate to maintain homeostasis and promote survival and health. It is now time to consider the nonregulatory drives, which take up so much of our behavioral time and energy.

NONREGULATORY DRIVES

In addition to the basic *regulatory drives* such as hunger and thirst, animals seem to have other drives whose satisfaction is not essential to maintaining the life of the individual. These have been called the *nonregulatory drives*. Unlike the regulatory drives, they do not result from any known depletion of bodily stores. Moreover, if nonregulatory drives are left unsatisfied, the animal will not die, as would be the case with regulatory drives.

The most familiar and extensively studied of the nonregulatory drives is the sex drive. Recent research has suggested a number of others, however, including drives for curiosity, activity, and exploration.

THE SEX DRIVE

Sexual activity serves a biological function that is vital not to the individual organism but rather to the species. Reproduction occurs in a wide variety of forms, ranging from mitosis in asexual unicellular organisms to complex mating rituals in vertebrates. Among the most thoroughly investigated influences on mating are hormonal factors, neural factors, and factors related to learning and early experience.

Hormonal Factors Hormones play an important part in energizing and organizing the sexual behavior of most animals. Sex hormones—the *androgens* in the male and the *estrogens* in the female—are secreted by the testes and the ovaries. As an animal approaches sexual maturity, hormones called gonadotrophins, secreted by the anterior pituitary gland, accelerate the secretion of these sex hormones; eventually ova and sperm are produced, and the *secondary sexual characteristics* begin to develop. Once sexual maturity is reached, the gonadotrophic hormones regularly stimulate the gonads, or sex glands, creating cyclic ovulation in the female and the regular production of sperm in the male. The extent to which the secretion of sex hormones actually determines sexual behavior varies markedly among different species. In some lower mammals and birds, hormones play a very large role in sexual behavior. In humans, however, as we will see, the role of hormones is considerably reduced.

Females of most species—excluding humans—are sexually receptive only at certain times. For most higher animals, these periods of sexual readiness, called *estrous periods*, coincide with the occurrence of ovulation (the production of ova). The appearance of estrus is highly dependent on the secretion of hormones. Female rats whose ovaries have been removed will no longer engage in sexual behavior; but sexual behavior will resume if the ovariectomized females are given regular injections of appropriate female hormones. Similarly, precocious sexual activity can be produced in sexually immature female rats and dogs by regular hormone administration.

Except for those animals that mate only during certain seasons, males are much more likely to be continually sexually active than are females. However, their sexual behavior, like that of females, is highly dependent on hormones. Castrated male rats will eventually cease mating, though the decline in sexual activity may occur over a period of many weeks, rather than immediately. Sexual behavior can be restored in castrated males (or initiated in sexually immature males) by the administration of male hormones.

Figure 5.13
Many factors may be at work here, but, as an old song puts it, "Oh, what a little moonlight can do!"

As we move up the phylogenetic scale, this dependency on hormones is seen less and less. Some female monkeys and chimpanzees have been observed to engage in sexual behavior during periods corresponding to the low point of ovarian activity in the menstrual cycle, though the frequency of copulation is much higher around the time of ovulation. Similarly, castrated male monkeys and cats have been known to engage in sexual activity for as long as years following castration, even in the absence of hormone administration. Finally, in sexually experienced adult humans, we see still more freedom from hormonal controls. Castrated males and ovariectomized females sometimes experience little or no decline in sexual activity or satisfaction. Females may also remain sexually active after the natural decline in ovarian function that occurs with age. (In this case, it is likely that adrenal hormones are partially responsible for sexual arousal.) It appears that in humans, experiential, social, and cultural factors can—to a large extent—override hormonal variables in their control of sexual behavior (Figure 5.13).

Neural Factors Neural factors seem to exercise profound control over sexual behavior in all species studied. In mammals, lesions in the *hypothalamus*, the subcortical structure that plays a vital role in many types of motivation and emotion, may extinguish all sexual activity in both males and females. Females become extremely indifferent and males are rendered essentially impotent. Moreover, all this occurs in spite of the maintenance of normal levels of circulating sex hormones. Stimulation of particular areas of the male rat's hypothalamus with a mild electric current will immediately produce coordinated sexual responses, including erection and mounting of a female. The vigor and frequency of copulation are greater than in normal copulation, but as soon as the stimulation is turned off, copulation ceases abruptly. In some species, stimulation of a given brain area will produce male sexual behavior in *either* males or females. Male *or* female opossums under the influence of such stimulation can be taught to run a maze for the reward of reaching a female sexual partner. (Indeed, these animals would continue to run the maze and vigorously attempt to copulate when the only reward at the end of the maze was a toy woolly dog.) These and other experiments indicate that the brain contains neural systems that serve as activators and coordinators of many components of sexual behavior.

Experiential Factors A third major determinant of sexual behavior—and for some species, including our own, the most decisive factor—is that of early experience. For humans, this includes social and cultural factors passed on from generation to generation via learning.

Studies of rats and monkeys, many of them conducted by Harry F. Harlow and his associates since the late 1950s, have shown that early experience is an important influence on the development of sexual behavior. For example, male rats raised in isolation are unable to copulate successfully the first time they try. Monkeys also require some degree of peer interaction for the development of normal sexual relationships. Harlow has found that if infant rhesus monkeys are raised in isolation and fed only by wire or cloth surrogate mothers for a period exceeding the first three months of life, they will later perform poorly as sexual partners and neglect their own offspring. Total isolation produces the most severe social deficits, but partial isolation is also harmful. Infant monkeys raised in neighboring wire cages, where they can see and hear—but not touch—each other later exhibit both disturbed sexual behavior and heightened aggression. We shall discuss Harlow's work in more detail in Chapter 7.

In humans, of course, the effects of learning and early experience are not only more varied, but also more profound. The extent to which biological factors can be offset by experience in humans is clearly illustrated by studies of *hermaphrodites* and *pseudohermaphrodites*—individuals with all or many of the biological and psychological characteristics of *both* sexes.

Of what sex are you? Although the answer may seem—and usually is—obvious, sex is a complex concept, and your sex depends upon many factors. Recent investigators have outlined several variables that play a part in sex or gender determination. Among these are the sex chromosome pattern (XX for female, XY for male), the morphology of the external genitals, the morphology of the gonads (the sexual glands), the balance of sexual hormones, and the morphology of the internal accessory reproductive structures such as the fallopian tube in the female. In addition to these five predominantly biological variables, two psychological factors must be added: the sex of assignment and rearing—that is, whether your parents and peers treat you as a female or as a male; and gender role—the personal sexual identification of the individual.

In most cases, these seven variables are largely congruent with one another and the task of determining whether someone is a female or a male is a simple one. Occasionally, as in the case of hermaphrodites and pseudohermaphrodites, the seven factors of sex are not clearly consistent with one sex or the other. Here gender determination becomes much more difficult.

A *true hermaphrodite* is an individual who possesses *both* male and female genitals (external sexual structures) and gonads (sexual glands). This condition is an extremely rare one. Much more common, however, is the condition of *pseudohermaphrodism*. A pseudohermaphrodite typically has a normal chromosomal pattern (either XX or XY), but with some of the remaining six factors suggesting the male sex, and others suggesting the female sex. (Unlike the true hermaphrodite, however, both sexual systems are not completely represented.) A female pseudohermaphrodite may, for example, in addition to female internal sexual organs and female chromosomes, have masculinized external genitals. Or a male may have normal male sexual glands and an XY chromosomal pattern, but in addition possess a partial vaginal tract and no well-developed penis. Often, such individuals possess hormone systems incongruent with their genetic sex. The presence of these hormones at critical embryological periods results in the development of an external genital morphology consistent with the unusual hormonal pattern. The realization that a child is a pseudohermaphrodite may not occur right at birth, when inspection of the external genitals is the predominant method of sex identification. The individual is likely to be assigned to the (genetically and gonadally) wrong sex; it may be only at puberty that the mistake is discovered. Most individuals, however, choose to remain the sex they were reared, even though genetic and gonadal evidence indicates that they are more appropriately considered members of the opposite sex. The strong persuasion sometimes offered by parents to change sexual roles is usually ineffective in negating this preference for the genetically wrong sex. In these cases, therefore, the interaction between hormonal effects prevailing during embryological development and early psychological experience is able to negate the effects of the genetic and gonadal determinants of sexual behavior. These findings on the importance of the organism's experience in embryo and early learning are supported by evidence of unsuccessful attempts to alter homosexuality, impotence, and frigidity by hormone administration. These conditions seem to result largely from learning, and are frequently not reversible by biological treatment in adulthood.

A final index of the extent to which human sexual behavior is dependent on experience is the large range of sexual practices observed in different cultures. Anthropologists tell us that behavior that is acceptable in one culture may be forbidden in the sexual mores of a second culture. The degree of complexity of the sexual practices that result is staggering and once again attests to the importance of experience in the determination of human behavior. We shall deal with love and sex in humans more extensively in Chapter 20 and in the units on human personality and psychotherapy.

EXPLORATORY, MANIPULATORY, AND CURIOSITY DRIVES

Partly because of its great success as a meaningful concept in biology, the notion of *homeostasis* (introduced at the beginning of this chapter) was eagerly,

Figure 5.14
This curious monkey learned to open the little door to see what was going on around its isolated cage. [Figures 5.14 and 5.15 originally illustrated R. A. Butler's "Curiosity in Monkeys" (*Scientific American*, February 1954, pp. 70–75). Photos by Myron Davis]

and in some cases uncritically, extended as a basic postulate in the explanation of behavior. It was assumed that a living organism's ideal behavioral state was a maximally quiescent one. All behavior was presumably an effort to produce this blissful steady-state condition by the avoidance or counteraction of stimulation. Gradually, however, data collected on nonregulatory drives such as exploration, curiosity, and manipulation produced serious doubts about the utility of homeostatic explanations of behavior.

Organisms seem to need a certain level of stimulation and will, in fact, actively seek it out (Figures 5.14 and 5.15). A monkey kept in a barren wire cage surrounded by an opaque box will learn a color discrimination for the reward of being allowed to peek through a window for thirty seconds, even though the window exposes nothing more than the normal laboratory setting. Similarly, access to auditory stimulation has been shown to be rewarding. Exploratory tendencies evident in many animals seem also to reflect a preference for novelty or for increments in stimulation. Animals tend to explore actively any novel environment, and may actually prefer an environment that permits more exploration over one that permits less. Moreover, animals will learn a response that is rewarded by the opportunity to explore. Rats choose the arm of a Y-maze that leads to a checkerboard maze over one that leads to a blind alley. Exploratory tendencies appear to be independent of general activity, and their occurrence does *not* require the accompanying state of deprivation that is characteristic of the regulatory drives such as hunger or thirst.

Curiosity and manipulation seem to provide their own rewards. Rats given a choice between two same-sized goal boxes generally choose the one containing various objects over the one that is empty, and once inside, investigate the objects actively. Extensive experiments with primates indicate that manipulation, too, may be engaged in for its own sake. Monkeys given mechanical puzzles to keep over a period of days will repeatedly disassemble them for no apparent reward other than the chance to manipulate. Similar data on chimpanzees indicate that an object with more stimulus heterogeneity (many colors or patterns) will elicit more manipulative behavior than a more homogeneous object.

These stimulus-seeking behaviors have been variously categorized as exploratory drives, manipulatory drives, curiosity drives, activity drives, and so forth. As more and more data are collected, distinctions between the various classes become progressively more difficult to draw. It may be best to categorize them all as stimulus drives, which differ

Figure 5.15
The interior of the curious monkey's cage. [Myron Davis]

along several dimensions from the regulatory drives created by internal bodily needs.

That genuine stimulus needs exist is best illustrated by a series of experiments designed to study *sensory deprivation* in humans. The subjects in these experiments were college students who were paid twenty dollars a day for the tedious task of lying on a cot in a small sound-deadened room for twenty-four hours a day (with time out for meals). Stimu-

lation in the room was kept at an absolute minimum. The subjects wore goggles that minimized patterned vision, in addition to gloves and cuffs that reduced tactile stimulation as much as possible (Figure 5.16). After an initial period of sleeping, subjects became bored, restless, and irritable. They began to invent ways to stimulate themselves—for example, touching their fingers together and twitching their muscles. They would eagerly anticipate periods during which they were allowed to listen to otherwise boring stock market reports provided on tape. The most dramatic result of the isolation was that after a day or two, many subjects began to have hallucinations, which became increasingly more complex as time went on. These subjects were apparently producing their own sensory stimulation in the absence of any in the external environment. Cognitive abilities began to deteriorate after three or four days in isolation: isolated subjects did quite poorly on simple arithmetic tests and on anagrams. Eventually, the subjects were unable to tolerate the isolation and all asked to be excused from the experiment. The results of this experiment provide further evidence that living organisms need external stimulation.

AGGRESSION

A final note is required in this section on the topic of aggression. Much discussion in psychology has centered on the question of whether there is an independent aggressive drive or whether animals become aggressive only in an effort to satisfy some other drive state. Is aggression a means to an end, or is it an end in itself? Instances of aggression as a means to an end frequently fall into one of two categories: (1) aggressive predation to obtain food, as when chimpanzees attack and eat other mammals and even other, smaller, primates, and (2) defense of one's territory from intruders, as when a male stickleback fish attacks another male when the latter

Figure 5.16
Experiments on *sensory deprivation* dramatize the importance of external stimulation.

intrudes on his breeding territory. Most examples of animal aggression (human aggression is a much more complex phenomenon and is dealt with in Chapter 20) represent either predation or territorial defense. However, examples that fit neither category, such as the aggressive displays of Siamese fighting fish and the mouse-killing response seen in some rats, suggest that aggression may also exist as an independent drive.

The male Siamese fighting fish engages in aggressive display whenever it is confronted with another male fighting fish. If allowed access to one another, the two males will fight to exhaustion or even to death. A fish will fight in any location—his own territory, the other's territory, or neutral ground—so the fighting behavior does not represent territorial aggression. The conclusion that this behavior is evidence of aggression as an end in itself is supported by J. Hogan's finding that the opportunity to aggressively display can serve as a positive reinforcer sufficient to maintain a learned response. Moreover, when Siamese fighting fish are maintained at moderate levels of deprivation, they will engage in a response that produces a stimulus (that elicits aggressive display) more often than they will engage in one that produces food (as we shall see in Chapter 15).

Mouse-killing—studied by James Myer and others—is also difficult to interpret as either predation

or defense. Some rats will attack and kill the first mouse they ever see. Other similar rats (even littermates) never do. No special training is required to produce the killing response, and the killers are not under any kind of externally imposed deprivation. Like the Siamese fighting fish, mouse-killers will learn new behaviors that are reinforced by the opportunity to attack. A killer rat can be taught to press a bar that will introduce a mouse into the cage. The rat then immediately kills the mouse and continues pressing to produce another. Obviously the rat would not work to introduce the mouse into an otherwise mouseless environment if territoriality were the motive behind its aggression. Brain lesions that produce a total cessation of eating behavior in rats have no effect on the killing response; therefore, though it may be related to predation, mouse-killing is not supported by hunger alone.

These two apparent examples of aggression as an end in itself leave open the possiblity that an aggressive drive does exist—at least for some organisms—as a nonregulatory drive independent of the maintenance of any regulatory-drive state.

ACQUIRED DRIVES

In addition to the regulatory and nonregulatory drives that we have been discussing, there are other drives that are acquired in the individual's lifetime. In Chapter 3, we related the tale of little Albert's acquired fear of furry objects—perhaps the first experimental demonstration of an acquired drive. Such conditioned fear has subsequently been studied more extensively and systematically. In one experiment, rats received shocks in one side of a two-compartment box. Subsequently, they learned to jump a hurdle, *without any further shock*, just to escape from the conditioning compartment into the adjacent "safe" compartment. The more dissimilar were the stimulus cues that differentiated the safe compartment from the conditioning compartment, the more rapidly the hurdle-jumping response was acquired. These results suggest that conditioned fear (of the conditioning compartment and its stimuli) brought about the acquisition of a new response (the hurdle-jump).

Other acquired drives include such human tendencies as patriotism, affiliation, and achievement (which we shall discuss in the next chapter), and some forms of human aggression (which will be treated in Chapter 20).

THE STRENGTH OF DRIVES

What determines the strength of drives, and which of our drives is strongest? The answers to both of these questions, though tentative, fit in well with our intuitions. Undoubtedly the most important determiner of the strength of a given drive is the amount of deprivation—at least where regulatory drives such as breathing, hunger, and thirst are concerned. The importance of deprivation has also been demonstrated for drives such as sex, activity, and exploration. It is much less clear, however, to what extent deprivation affects acquired drives. For some, the sweet smell of success seems to serve an appetitive rather than a satiating function. Many a shrewd businessman may eagerly seek a new venture after closing a big deal. Similarly, behaviors associated with nationalism and aggression do not always seem

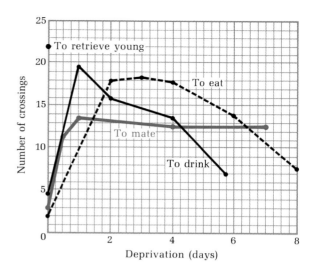

Figure 5.17
The strength of various drives as a function of deprivation in the rat. Drive strength was measured by the number of crossings of an electrified grid within a given period of time. [Adapted from C. J. Warden, *Animal Motivation: Experimental Studies in the Albino Rat.* New York: Columbia University Press, 1931.]

to depend upon any obvious deprivation state. With these possible exceptions, however, the strength of drives tends to increase with increasing deprivation. (Where the regulatory drives are concerned, of course, the drive eventually subsides in strength as the organism becomes weaker and ultimately dies.)

A Comparison of Drive Strength The classic comparison between the strengths of different drives was performed in the 1920s and 1930s by C. J. Warden and his associates at Columbia University. Warden utilized an obstruction box consisting primarily of an electrified grid which the rat had to cross in order to obtain reinforcement. As Figure 5.17 shows, rats deprived of food, water, or sex for varying lengths of time had to cross an electrified grid to obtain a nibble of food, a drop of water, or brief exposure to sex objects (in every case the reward was minute—a possible defect in Warden's work). The dependent variable was the number of times the rat would cross the electrified grid within a given period of time. Note that the figure reveals a sharp increase in drive strength with increasing deprivation. Note also that the hunger and thirst drives reach higher peaks than the sex drive. The decline at extreme levels of deprivation for hunger and thirst reflects the onset of weakness. (Sex shows no such decline, but is remarkably level after the first day.) Note that, at least in this experiment, the maternal drive is strongest of all. In a companion study that produced virtually the same results, the behavioral index was the highest level of shock that the rat ever tolerated in order to cross the grid. Here, too, the maternal drive was the strongest: a mother rat will tolerate an extremely intense shock in order to reach her pup.

Suggested Readings

Berlyne, D. E. (1960) *Conflict, arousal, and curiosity.* New York: McGraw-Hill. [A review of some important nonregulatory drives.]

Dethier, V. G. (1962) *To know a fly.* San Francisco: Holden-Day. [A short, fascinating account of Vincent Dethier's work with the blowfly, stressing food regulation. Very entertaining.]

Harlow, H. F. (1971) *Learning to love.* San Francisco: Albion. [A lively paperback on the five forms of love identified by Harlow in his work with primates.]

Kimble, D. P. (1973) *Psychology as a biological science.* Pacific Palisades, California: Goodyear. [Contains a good treatment of hormones and sexual behavior, including hermaphrodism.]

Mayer, J. (1968) *Overweight: Causes, cost and control.* Englewood Cliffs, New Jersey: Prentice-Hall. [An interesting book on obesity.]

Miller, N. E. (1952) Liberalization of basic S-R concepts: "Extensions to conflict behavior, motivation and social learning." In Koch, S., ed., *Psychology: a study of a science,* Volume 2, New York: McGraw-Hill, pp. 196–292.

Nisbett, R. E. (1972) "Hunger, obesity and the ventromedial hypothalamus." *Psychological Review, 79,* 433–453. [An interesting article on food regulation, stressing the behavior of humans and rats.]

Revusky, S., & Garcia, J. (1970) "Learned associations over long delays." In Bower, G. H., ed., *The psychology of learning and motivation,* Volume 4. New York: Academic Press. pp. 1–84. [An interesting and comprehensive account of work on long-delay learning and "belongingness".]

Rozin, P., & Kalat, J. W. (1972) "Specific hungers and poisoning as adaptive specializations of learning." *Psychological review, 78,* 459–486. [An excellent overview of the problem of specific hungers, including a summary of the authors' own important work.]

Schachter, S. (1971) "Some extraordinary facts about obese humans and rats." *American Psychologist, 26,* 129–144. [See the comment concerning the Nisbett article.]

CHAPTER SIX

Complex Motivation

What motivates human behavior? This is one of the most intriguing—and difficult—questions that psychologists face. For the behaviorist, whose experimental approach focuses on the effects of reinforcement on learning (see Chapter 4), *motivation* refers primarily to conditions within our bodies and in our external environment that make particular events reinforcing—for example, food deprivation makes food reinforcing. For the humanistic psychologist, whose approach emphasizes human needs and goals, motivation refers more to the hypothesized process by which needs arouse and learning directs complex behavior.

Behaviorists are by no means oblivious of the complex problems of human psychology. Experience has taught them, however, that scientific principles can best be established by limited, controlled studies. Much as anthropologists seek out less complex cultures in which social processes can more easily be identified, behaviorists often attempt to analyze in simpler organisms the behavioral processes that underlie human behavior. As we have already discussed, a number of important discoveries about human behavior have emerged from studies of other animals.

Although humanistic psychologists agree that humans exhibit many of the basic physiological drives and learning processes observed in lower animals, they emphasize that the human capacity for thinking, language, and complex social organization has created multifarious expressions of the basic drives, and in addition has given rise to motives that appear to be uniquely human (Figure 6.1). They argue that we can discover the origins of artistic, sporting, intellectual, criminal, and political activity, and so on, only by studying human behavior itself; granted that the study of human motivation is somewhat speculative, we can no more postpone the study of our own behavior than political and social scientists can postpone their studies until all the anthropologists' findings are in.

In this chapter, we will consider different views of human motivation and different methods of measuring motives, as well as investigate some of the processes that influence the development of learned motives. Finally, we will turn to some current issues in human motivation.

VIEWS OF HUMAN MOTIVATION

From one perspective, that of mechanistic psychologists stressing the importance of innate behavior and classical conditioning, humans have been viewed as mere bundles of instincts and reflexes—with no more intrinsic motivation than thermostats. From another perspective, that of psychoanalytic theory,

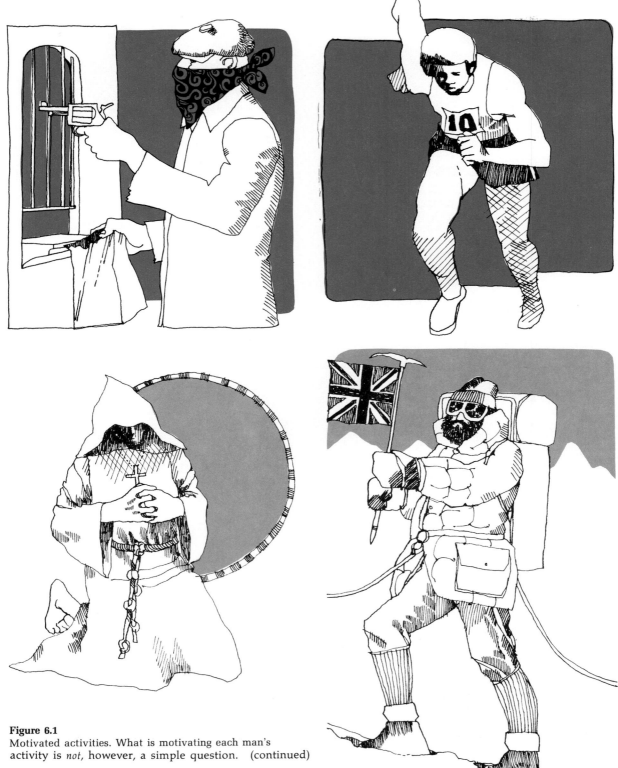

Figure 6.1
Motivated activities. What is motivating each man's activity is *not*, however, a simple question.   (continued)

Figure 6.1 (continued)
More motivated activities. Why does the politican praise his audience? Why does the soldier carry out orders with precision?

humans have appeared to be driven by motives arising from the depths of their unconscious minds (as we shall see in Chapter 24). Although these two views seem very different, they share the assumption that human behavior is determined and driven, rather than spontaneous.

A third important view of human motivation stresses its *cognitive, goal-oriented* character. Cognitive views of motivation go back at least as far as the philosopher-psychologist William James (1842–1910),

who pointed out that the concept of motivation was necessary to bridge the "psychomotor gap" between ideas and actions. This view was further elaborated in the 1960s by George Miller, Eugene Galanter, and Karl Pribram in their influential book *Plans and the Structure of Behavior*.* According to the theory set forth in this book, the psychomotor gap is bridged by the construction of *plans* for achieving certain ends

*New York: Holt, Rinehart and Winston, 1960.

and by continual testing to determine whether or not the operation of the plans has produced the desired end. The concept of the *TOTE*, an acronym standing for "test, operate, text, exit," was introduced to describe the unit of planning and performance. Only when the end is achieved—and the psychomotor gap has been successfully bridged—does the organism "exit," thereby completing the TOTE. Another important cognitive view of human motivation, *dissonance theory*, will be considered in detail later in this chapter.

MEASURING HUMAN MOTIVES

There are scores of methods of assessing human motives. The methods most widely used by psychologists are of three general types: direct, indirect, and experimental. Although these three types of measurements are not sharply defined, and even overlap somewhat, it is useful to consider them separately. *Direct measurement* of motivation refers to a variety of techniques that permit the subject to express his motives through verbal or other overt behavior. *Indirect measurement*, on the other hand, requires the examiner to infer the subject's motives from his responses to fairly ambiguous stimulus situations. Finally, *experimental measurement* involves the laboratory testing of empirical predictions based on particular motivational hypotheses. Since the direct and indirect methods for measuring human motives will be considered in more detail when we discuss the measurement of individual differences in Chapter 26, the present section will place greater emphasis on the other approaches.

Direct Measurement of Motives   For many purposes, the most accurate methods of assessing human motives are those employing direct measurement. These methods adhere to the dictum of the social psychologist and personality theorist Gordon

Allport, who recommended that if you want to find out what a subject is doing and why, "ask him." The validity of Allport's dictum has been underscored recently by the results of a variety of investigations into the relative efficacy of direct and indirect measurement of individual differences. (These will be discussed at length in Chapter 26).

What are some of the direct techniques? One powerful technique is simple observation. By observing what a person spends most of his time doing you can get an exceptionally good idea of what is motivating him. Indeed, this measure may be even more effective than asking the subject to account for his own behavior. Often these two measures—overt behavior and self-description—covary. Thus, if you ask a person to indicate which part of a newspaper he finds most interesting, you will probably find that it is the same section that he spends the most time reading. Occasionally, however, you may come upon a subject who stresses that he is most interested in national news, but who appears to spend most of his time reading the sports section. In this instance, you would probably conclude that his overt behavior (reading the sports section) gives a more accurate index of his interest than his self-description (preferring national news). Even behavioral observation can lead one astray, however. It could be, for example, that our subject really doesn't enjoy the sports section but is reading it in order to chat with his boss, an avid sports fan.

In addition to behavioral observations, direct measurements include interviews (often used in the assessment of job applicants), questionnaires, and checklists.

Indirect Measurement of Motives   Although direct measurement is suitable for many assessments of human motivation, there are certain situations in which subjects are unaware of their motives. In other

instances they may choose *not* to express their real
motives. An applicant to medical school, for
example, may prefer to tell the interviewer that his
interest in medicine is theoretical or altruistic,
rather than a reflection of an overriding urge to make
as much money as possible. A politician may tell his
electorate that he intends to serve the common good,
when in fact he expects to serve his financial
backers.

The basic idea behind indirect tests is that the
subject's true needs and drives are likely to affect his
responses to *unstructured* (ambiguous) *stimulus
situations*. On the basis of what the subject *projects*
into his interpretation of a stimulus situation, the
psychologist is able to assess the subject's true
motivation. Such tests (which will be discussed in
Chapter 26) are called *interpretive* or *projective* tests.
Here we shall simply mention some of the more
common ones. The most commonly used projective
tests require the subject to interpret—by relating a
story or description—a grossly unstructured stimulus
such as an inkblot, as in the *Rorschach test,* or an
ambiguous picture, as in the *Blacky Test* and the
Thematic Apperception Test (TAT). For example, the
Blacky pictures include twelve cartoon-like drawings
featuring a dog named Blacky, who appears with
other dogs in various poses; the subject, usually a
child, is to tell a story about each picture (Figure
6.2). The Thematic Apperception Test (TAT) consists
of a series of standard pictures about which the subject is asked to make up a story. The subject's story
is structured only to the extent that he is expected
to relate what is happening in the picture, who is
doing what to whom and why, what the characters'
motives, hopes, and fears are, what has happened in
the past, what will happen in the future, and so on.
How the reports are scored depends upon the reason
for administering the test. For example, if the experimenter is interested in measuring the subject's
need for achievement (*n Ach*) or his need for power

Figure 6.2
Items from *The Blacky Pictures.* Children are asked to
tell a story about each picture. The Blacky test is a
popular projective test. Each of the cartoons illustrates
a stage of psychosexual development or portrays a type
of relationship within that development. The test is used
primarily with children. [Reprinted, by permission, from
G. S. Blum, *The Blacky Pictures.* New York: Psychological Corporation, 1950.]

(*n Power*), the subject's story will be scored in terms of how much achievement orientation or power orientation it displays. (The procedure for scoring TAT tests is taken up in Chapter 26.)

Although the TAT was designed to assess the motives of individual subjects, David McClelland has used the TAT to assess the motives of whole nations. McClelland measured the strength of achievement motivation exhibited in the elementary textbooks used by school children in 1925 in each of several different nations. He then compared the strength of achievement motivation as measured in these 1925 textbooks with changes in various economic indices, such as the gross national product, from 1925 to 1950. His hypothesis, which was generally confirmed, was that the stronger the achievement motive in the 1925 culture, the greater the economic gains made by that country in the next twenty-five years. Later work has shown the achievement motive to be a double-edged sword. Along with economic growth comes a predisposition to develop serious psychogenic disorders such as ulcers and high blood pressure. Thus the need-achievement measure obtained from the 1925 textbooks also predicted the 1950 death rate from ulcers and high blood pressure! The expression of need for power in the 1925 textbooks also proved to be a good predictor of the death rate from aggression-related causes such as murder and suicide. While these correlations must be interpreted with caution, they are surprisingly elegant in the following sense: measures of the power motive in 1925 bore no relation to economic growth or psychogenic disorders, whereas need for achievement was similarly unrelated to the 1950 death rate due to murder and suicide. In summary, the effects of the need for achievement and the need for power were surprisingly selective.

As a group, the indirect measures of motivation have special value in situations in which direct measures appear to be inappropriate, as when the

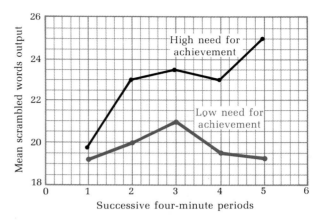

Figure 6.3
The average number of scrambled words made by a group of male college students above and below the mean in n achievement (n Ach) scores in each of five successive four-minute periods. [Figures 6.3 and 6.4 are adapted from E. L. Lowell, "A Methodological Study of Projectively Measured Achievement Motivations." M.A. thesis, Wesleyan University, 1950.]

subject is not willing or able to give accurate self-reports. At the same time, the interpretation of indirect tests is a complex business, as we shall see in Chapter 26.

Experimental Measurement of Motives David McClelland and his associates have reasoned that if n Ach (need for achievement) scores are a useful index of the strength of achievement motivation, then persons with high n Ach scores should differ in a number of predictable ways from persons with low n Ach scores. In 1951, McClelland provided experimental support for his hypothesis by showing that subjects who score high in need for achievement—in a test similar to the TAT—are also faster at unscrambling anagrams (scrambled words) and solving arithmetic problems. These results are illustrated in Figure 6.3. In the figure, which shows the anagram results, note that the subjects with a high need for achievement improve during the course of the experiment, whereas those with a low need for achievement do not. McClelland attributes this increase to the fact that subjects who are highly

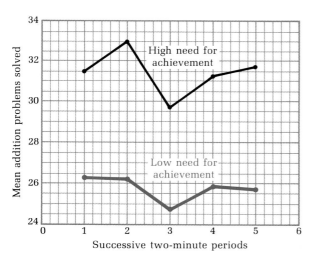

Figure 6.4
The average number of addition problems solved by a
group of male college students above and below the
mean in n Ach in each of four successive two-minute
periods. [Adapted from Lowell's study.]

motivated search for a better strategy of solving the
complex anagrams and thereby improve with
practice. Next, note that in Figure 6.4, which shows
the arithmetic results, no such improvement is
evident for either of the groups represented. This
may be explained by the supposition that all subjects
are already at about a maximum level of efficiency
when they begin (the ten minutes of practice with
addition is not likely to produce any significant
breakthroughs). In this case, subjects with a high
need for achievement do better because they try
harder and solve the problems more rapidly. Thus,
these experiments by McClelland and his associates
lend support to the notion that need for achievement,
as measured by indirect tests, can be used to predict
performance.

Other experiments on the measurement of human
motives stem from Leon Festinger's ingenious theory
of *cognitive dissonance.* In a dissonance experiment, a
person is induced to act overtly as if he had a certain
belief that he really does not have. For example, we
might induce him to advocate publicly a position
that he does not really hold. The overtly expressed
opinion conflicts with the real belief and produces
cognitive dissonance. The dissonance can be reduced
by changing the unexpressed belief. Moreover,
according to Festinger, the opinion change will be
in inverse proportion to the pressure put on the
subject to induce him to advocate the contrary
position. In other words, the less pressure there is,
the more the opinion changes. Assume, for example,
that you are in favor of anti-abortion laws and that
you are asked to read publicly a brief statement
against such laws. If you agree to do so with
minimum pressure to comply (say a request that you
fill in for a absent participant in a panel discussion),
you are more likely to weaken your stand in favor
of anti-abortion laws than if you are put under
stronger pressure to comply (say you are offered an
all-expense-paid week for two in Mexico City). In
either case, the dissonance you perceive between
your beliefs concerning abortion and your public
reading of the statement is presumed to be unpleasant. If the pressures bringing about a change in
behavior are substantial (a free trip to Mexico), then
the pressures themselves *justify* the overt expression,
and your internal opinion need not change. However,
where the pressures to comply are at a minimum
(a simple request), then the overt expression may be
justified only by an internal opinion change. In
effect, you change your opinion so that it is more
in accord with your overt behavior.

Consider the example of new-car owners, who,
according to recent data, continue to read automobile
reports and advertisements, but *only* about the brand

WARNING: THE SURGEON GENERAL HAS DETERMINED THAT CIGARETTE SMOKING IS HAZARDOUS TO YOUR HEALTH.

Figure 6.5
Cigarette smokers may reduce cognitive dissonance by avoiding reading the warning on the pack. Of course, one purpose of the warning is to encourage the smoker to kick the habit. That too would eliminate dissonance, leaving the ex-smoker fully to believe data linking smoking to cancer and heart disease. Indeed, many ex-smokers have stronger opinions against smoking than those who have never smoked. This result is consistent with dissonance theory, since strong opinions about the damages of smoking helps justify the decision not to smoke.

of car that they have already purchased. According to cognitive-dissonance theory, these people are trying to keep their opinion of their new car consonant with their behavior of having bought it. They therefore avail themselves only of information that adds to their positive opinion of the product purchased, and thus avoid dissonance. Similarly, inveterate cigarette smokers, who place a high value on their lives and for whom reports linking smoking with cancer and heart disease are highly dissonant, might decrease thier dissonance by discounting the validity of the reports or by avoiding reading the warnings on the pack (Figure 6.5). In either case, in Festinger's terms, a state of dissonance has motivated dissonance-avoiding or dissonance-reducing behavior.

ORIGINS OF MOTIVATION

How are motives established? Are there motives that are "derived" through learning? We saw in the previous chapter that several powerful drives, such as hunger, thirst, and sex appear to be closely tied to our innate physiological make-up. Although we know much less about other drives, such as curiosity and activity, it is likely that they too originate to a large extent in hereditary factors. At the same time we should caution that, owing to the complex interactions between organisms and their environments, it is usually fruitless to draw sharp distinctions between innate and learned behaviors (as we shall see in Unit V).

Consider sexual behavior, for example. It is clear that the glandular and hormonal changes that occur with physical maturation contribute greatly to sexual motivation; but so do experiential factors. If one's first sexual experiences are unpleasant, sexual motivation may well be less powerful than it would have been had the initial experiences been highly pleasant. Sexual motivation may also be influenced by what is taught about sex in the home, in church, in school, and in popular media.

The more complex human motives are, the more difficult it becomes to separate their learned and un-

Figure 6.6
How would you account for the artist's behavior? In
terms of reinforcement? *sublimation*? or—? (Accounts
in terms of reinforcement and sublimation are not
incompatible.)

learned components. How, for example, can we
explain artistic motivations (Figure 6.6)? Has this
motivation been gradually acquired because environmental influences—for example, parents, teachers,
or peers—have encouraged, or reinforced, artistic
behavior? (This would probably be closest to the
behaviorists' view of human motivation.) Or does
the artistic motivation reflect sublimation of a more
basic, unsatisfied sexual motivation (as is suggested
in Chapter 24)? (This would reflect the dynamic view

of motivation.) Finally, can artistic motivation be
explained by its goal directedness? (This is the aspect
that cognitive theory would stress.) Thus, several
explanations can plausibly be given for the origin of
the artistic motive. It is more difficult, however, to
trace the actual development of this motive and to
determine whether it is primarily learned or
unlearned.

One possible approach is through the results of
cross-cultural research. Motives that appear regularly
in widely disparate cultures are more likely to be
inherited than those that are peculiar to particular
cultures. Interpretation of cross-cultural findings is
difficult, however. Consider Henry Murray's theory
of universal human needs; Murray postulated
twenty-eight universal *psychogenic needs*, which he
contrasted with what he called the twelve *viscerogenic
needs* produced by physiological deficits. One of these
psychogenic needs is *affiliation*—the tendency to form
associations and friendships with other people.
Since affiliation is a fairly universal phenomenon,
one might conclude that the affiliation motive is unlearned. A moment's reflection, however, will reveal
that this conclusion is unwarranted. Beginning at
birth and continuing throughout infancy, a child is
dependent upon (and reinforced by) other people.
There is thus more than ample opportunity for
affiliation to become a learned motive. A child may
readily learn that many of his physiological needs
are satisfied only when others are present. And so
the presence of others becomes a derived reinforcer.
Similar arguments can be raised with regard to other
complex motives such as "autonomy," "aggression,"
and "orderliness."

Learned Motives   One class of motives that
clearly reflects learning is addiction. If a person
ingests alcohol, heroin, or LSD and finds the effect
pleasurable, he is likely to ingest it again (as we

might expect from our discussion of operant conditioning in Chapter 4). Repeated administrations may lead to psychological, as well as physiological, dependence. Dependence on caffein, generally ingested in coffee and tea, is commonplace the world over. Many people believe that they cannot wake up or think straight in the morning unless they have had a cup of coffee. They continue to ingest coffee throughout the day as a "pick-me-up," often continuing until the evening, when they may unwind with a "couple of good stiff drinks."

Addiction and psychological dependency are maintained not only by their physiological effects but by the reinforcement obtained from indulging the desire for them, and also to a large extent by social and cultural factors. The coffee break and the cigarette break and the cocktail hour provide the individual with a socially approved excuse to take a rest from work and to engage in social interaction. Advertisers, of course, try to perpetuate these social phenomena. (The problem of addiction is treated in more detail in Chapter 27.)

In general, motives develop with a person's experiences. This generalization is consistent with the behaviorist and dynamic views of motivation, which stress the influence of past experiences, as well as with the cognitive view, which stresses goal-orientation. Obviously a person's history and his current goals are related. Indeed, the extreme behaviorist view would explain "purpose" by stressing that the apparently goal-directed character of human behavior is really based on reinforcement for past behaviors. Thus, the associate professor spends seventy hours a week in scholarly pursuits not because he is striving for a promotion and for future recognition from his colleagues, but because he has been reinforced in the past for his scholarly pursuits (by receiving a doctorate, a teaching job, a promotion from assistant

to associate professor, and the praise of his colleagues for past work). The cognitive theorist, on the other hand, would probably turn the argument around. Acknowledging the role of reinforcement, he could minimize it and say that all of the individual's behavior had been goal-oriented towards future reinforcements. The two views are difficult to distinguish on empirical grounds, especially since both agree that the consequences of behavior (reinforcement) are intimately involved with the development of learned motives.

Examples of learned motives are cravings and tastes, art and sports appreciation, and, possibly, ambition. In addition, levels of aspiration—the goals we strive for and expect—certainly depend upon past successes and failures. Complex learned motives seem to be generally derived from more basic motives. Specifying their development, however, is often impossible. We can only speculate that social approval and companionship are often crucial in the development of such motives as art and sports appreciation. For example, many of the people who regularly attend concerts might not do so if no one else were in the audience. Similar arguments could be made about other psychogenic motives.

THE PROBLEM OF AGGRESSION

Aggression is a label that is applied to diverse human behaviors. For our present purposes, it is sufficient to restrict our attention to two broad classes of aggressive behavior. The first, which is largely unlearned, is *elicited aggression*. This is aggression that occurs instinctively and automatically as the result of particular stimulus situations. Early work in the 1940s singled out frustration as a main cause of aggression. The *frustration-aggression hypothesis* stated that frustration inevitably causes aggression, but did not rule out other causes as well. Thus, if a

Figure 6.7
Frustration may lead to aggression.

door fails to open on the first push, we push harder and finally aggressively shove; a frustrating failure at work may result in kicked wastebaskets or pounded desks. (Figure 6.7 shows an instance of aggression on the golf links.) More recently, it has been shown that *pain* elicits aggression. Animals that are electrically shocked or suddenly deprived of expected food bite other animals or even inanimate objects in their cages. Humans, too, tend to strike out aggressively when subjected to painful stimuli of all sorts. It may be that frustration owes its close link to aggression to its painfulness.

It has been shown that an organism in pain will learn an operant response in order to obtain another organism to aggress against! Thus, pain seems to set up an aggressive drive that is the basis of reinforcement when it is reduced by the chance to be aggressive.

The second class of aggressive behaviors, which is clearly learned, is referred to as *operant aggression*. When a child finds that he can obtain a piece of candy by taking it away from a smaller child, his

aggressive behavior is reinforced by the acquisition of the candy. A few such reinforcements and we may have a bully in the making.

Finally, many complex aggressive responses probably involve both elicited and operant components. For example, an aggressive response may initially be elicited but may provide the organism with reinforcement; in this case, it may become operant aggression.

FUNCTIONAL AUTONOMY

Some psychologists—notably, Robert S. Woodworth and Gordon Allport—have argued that motives often develop because behaviors that have led to reinforcement in the past become self-motivating or rewarding in themselves, after they have stopped being mechanisms for achieving other rewards. This concept has been called *functional autonomy*; the current motive functions autonomously, independent of previous motives.

Two animal studies are often cited in support of the theory of functional autonomy—one of sand-digging in mice, the other of ear-scratching in rats. The sand-digging study, reported by R. Earl in 1957, showed that mice that had learned to dig nine pounds of sand in order to reach a box containing food continued to dig nine pounds of sand even when food was no longer reinforcing—that is, even when the mice had eaten their fill. More recent studies—for example by J. A. King and Ron Weisman in 1964, and by E. J. Fantino and Michael Cole in 1968—however, have shown that digging is itself reinforcing for mice. Mice will dig nine pounds of sand even when they are not hungry and when no food is ever present in the "goal box" (Figure 6.8). This result illustrates a problem raised in Chapter 5: when psychologists assumed that reinforcement depended upon the satisfaction of one of a limited

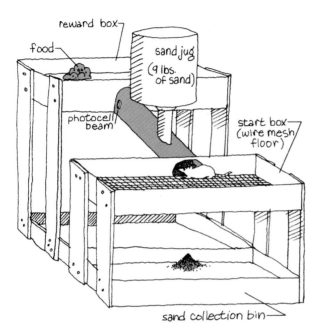

Figure 6.8
The mouse will dig nine pounds of sand from the tunnel even when it is not hungry and even when it has never found food at the other end of the tunnel.

Figure 6.9
Why do some people hoard money?

number of basic needs or drives they were often blind to some of the other possibilities—in this case, that digging itself was reinforcing. Now we know that an unhungry mouse will even *eat* in order to gain a chance to dig—an application of Premack's principle. In 1974, R. G. Isaac and G. L. Rowland reported that rats are also vigorous diggers. Thus, there is no need to invoke functional autonomy to explain the sand-digging results. The ear-scratching results are also open to question. In this study, it was found that when an irritant (collodion) was placed on rats' ears, the rats would scratch their ears for several weeks after the application of the irritant. Further experimentation, however, showed that when the experiment was carried out for a longer period of time (seventy days instead of twenty-five), ear-

scratching virtually disappeared in all rats. Apparently the ear-scratching behavior was independent only of the stimulus narrowly defined as application of the irritant—not of the stimulus defined more broadly and correctly as the application of the irritant and its subsequent irritation. Again, the concept of functional autonomy proves unnecessary.

How, then, can we explain seemingly antonomous human behaviors such as the miser's hoarding? Perhaps the miser's behavior persists because it continues to be reinforced from time to time. The miser (Figure 6.9) must eat, maintain a home, and otherwise provide for the necessities of life. All of this requires money, so the reinforcing power of money is maintained.

Despite our conclusion that the concept of functional autonomy—as originally conceived—has little utility for contemporary psychologists, there is an important grain of truth in the concept that must not be overlooked. Many behaviors that are initially maintained by primary reinforcement may ultimately become reinforcing themselves—although *not* because they have been associated with primary reinforcement. A child may take violin lessons only because his parents provide him with contrived reinforcers such as money, play privileges, or praise. After the child's violin-playing skills develop, however, the music he produces may be sufficient to reinforce his violin playing. Similarly, pupils whose classroom performance is enhanced by token-reinforcement systems and by teacher attention and praise for effective classroom behavior often come to appreciate the subject matter, which becomes reinforcing. (We shall discuss the use of tokens in human reinforcement in Chapter 32.) In each of these cases, reinforcers maintain the behavior until the behavior produces its own reinforcing consequences; at that point, the contrived reinforcers become unnecessary.

ISSUES IN HUMAN MOTIVATION

We will conclude this chapter by considering two important current issues in the field of human motivation: (1) the significance of sex differences in achievement motivation, and (2) the question of self-control of motivation.

Sex Differences in Achievement Motivation   The motives of men and women differ largely, if not entirely, because of the different roles they are expected to play in society. Men in our society are generally rewarded for competitiveness and individual achievement—traits considered useful in the job market. Women, on the other hand, are rewarded for sympathy and helpfulness to others—traits valued in family life. Hence certain behaviors are widely considered "masculine" and others "feminine." Recent research, conducted primarily by Matina Horner, has indicated that many women

are motivated to *avoid success* in competitive achievement. Women's TAT stories show much more "fear of success" imagery than men's, and women are more likely to become anxious in competitive situations. Whereas competitive situations facilitated performance in some circumstances for more than two-thirds of the men tested, fewer than one-third of the women performed better in competitive situations than they did in the noncompetitive situations. These results and others suggest that women who fear success can realize their potential best in noncompetitive situations, particularly those free from competition with men. Horner's results apply only to group differences between men and women. Thus, there are many women who show no fear of success. As more women pursue careers outside the home, society will undoubtedly be forced to modify its definitions of "masculine" and "feminine," and will change in the direction of egalitarianism, moving away from the male dominance that has so pervasively colored our image of the roles of men and women in Western society (Figures 6.10 and 6.11).

Self-Control   "Self-control" was once thought to be exclusively a province of humans, and perhaps some of the higher nonhuman primates. In the last decade, however, research has shown that self-control can be demonstrated for lower organisms as well. The data in Figure 6.12 show the results of an early study of self-control in pigeons. In this study, pigeons could obtain a reward either by pecking at a key immediately after it was illuminated with a red light or by delaying their pecks until the light turned green. If the pigeon pecked at the red key, reinforcement was followed by a period of extinction that is, a period in which no reinforcement was available. On the other hand, if the pigeon waited until the light turned green, it could obtain reinforcement without a subsequent penalty. Although the pigeons did not often exhibit self-control by delay-

Figure 6.10
A female lineworker. [Courtesy Pacific Telephone. Photo by Paula Condon]

Figure 6.11
A male telephone operator. [David Powers]

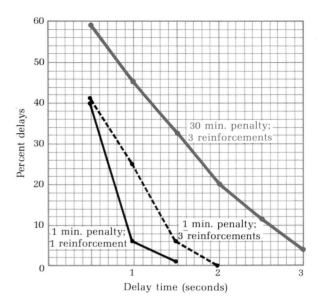

Figure 6.12
Data from an experiment in rudimentary self-control in the pigeon. Food—followed by a penalty—could be obtained immediately by pecking a red key. If the pigeon waited until the key turned from red to green, a peck would produce food *without* a subsequent penalty. The advantage to delay was greatest when the penalty for *not* delaying was thirty minutes of darkness (during which there was no opportunity to earn food) and the pigeon could earn three reinforcements if it waited for the green key light. The advantage to delay was least when there was only a one-minute penalty and one reinforcement. The figure shows that the percentage of trials on which pigeons delayed ("Percent delays") in each condition is a function of the length of time (from one-half to three seconds) it had to wait for the change from red to green. Comparison of the three curves shows that the pigeon delayed more, the greater the advantage to delay. [Data from E. Fantino, "Immediate Reward Followed by Extinction vs. Later Reward without Extinction," *Psychonomic Science*, 1966, *6*, 233–234.]

ing, their tendency to do so increased in proportion to the advantages of delaying. In other words, the frequency with which the pigeons exhibited *self-control* by not pecking at the red key depended upon the relative attractiveness of conditions following pecks at the red and green keys. The top curve in the figure represents the conditions most conducive to waiting for the green light: a thirty-minute penalty for pecking at red, as opposed to three food reinforcements consequent upon waiting for green. At the other extreme, the bottom curve shows the amount of self-control exhibited when the penalty for picking up an immediate reinforcement by pecking at the red key is only one minute and only one reinforcement is available if the organism waits for the green key. The middle curve portrays a condition in which the advantages of delaying are intermediate between those shown in the first and third curves.

The technique employed to demonstrate the kind of self-control shown in Figure 6.12 is a rudimentary one. Nevertheless, it did show that pigeons would delay their responses in order to maximize reward and that their delays increased as the number of reinforcements for delaying increased and also as the penalty for *not* delaying increased.

Much self-control demonstrated by humans, of course, is of a considerably more sophisticated and cognitive variety. Consider the classic example of Ulysses, who tied himself to the mast of a ship in order to avoid being tempted by the Sirens (Figure 6.13). Ulysses determined at a distance that the avoidance of crashing upon the rocks outweighed the pleasure of approaching the Sirens. Moreover, Ulysses was shrewd enough to realize that the closer he got to temptation, the less likely that he would resist it. Thus he tied himself to the mast so that, should his value structure change, he would have to stick by his original decision not to be tempted. Many of us follow the same logic when we put an alarm clock out of easy reach so that we will not be able to turn it off without getting out of bed the following morning. This is done when the consequences of one behavior—getting up on time—are valued more highly than the consequences of another—sleeping late. In the morning, this preference may be reversed; but we are forced to get out of bed to turn off the alarm.

Howard Rachlin and Leonard Green were able

Figure 6.13
Ulysses tied himself to the mast of a ship in order to avoid the temptation of the Sirens. He was clever enough to realize that he would not be able to resist the temptation when it was close at hand. This is a more sophisticated form of self-control than that demonstrated in Figure 6.12 (see text).

to demonstrate a similar effect with pigeons in 1972. They showed that preference for a small immediate reward over a delayed large reward could be reversed by simply adding a constant amount of delay to both rewards. When the delays were both short the pigeon always chose the immediate, smaller reward. When the delays were both long, however, the pigeon always chose the larger reward. Rachlin and Green's interpretation of these results is a good illustration of the behavioristic viewpoint. They note that self-control is a product of immediate environmental contingencies and that learning self-control consists of learning these contingencies, whether we are referring to Buddhist monks, six-year-old children, or pigeons. Although the pigeons in Rachlin and Green's experiments are less likely than humans to be thought of as having "ego strength" or other complex cognitive and motivational systems, they nonetheless exhibited "self-control."

The reader is certainly free to accept or reject Rachlin and Green's behavioristic explanation. Similarly, the more cognitively oriented theorist is free either to attribute or deny cognition to the pigeon. Actually, the cognitive and behavioristic views, though stated in different terms and stemming from different theoretical orientations, really do not differ much with respect to their empirical predictions: both predict that the organism's behavior will be goal-oriented, at least in the sense of being affected by reinforcement.

McClelland, D. C. (1961) *The achieving society.* Princeton: Van Nostrand, 1961. [An interesting study of McClelland's work on the need for achievement, utilizing projective measures of motivation.]

Rachlin, H., & Green, L. (1972) "Commitment, choice and self-control." *Journal of the experimental analysis of behavior,* 17, 15–22. [An interesting study and analysis of self-control from the behaviorist viewpoint.]

Suggested Readings

Birney, R., & Teevan, R. (1962) *Measuring human motivation.* Princeton: Van Nostrand. [A good paperback collection of some milestone papers.]

Fantino, E. J. (1968) "Of mice and misers." *Psychology today,* July. [A review of studies examining Allport's doctrine of functional autonomy and analyzing the problem of the miser.]

Haber, R. N. (1966) *Current research in motivation.* New York: Holt, Rinehart and Winston. [A comprehensive book of readings containing many important papers in all areas of motivation, including anxiety, guilt, and unconscious processes.]

Horner, M. (1970) "Femininity and successful achievement: A basic inconsistency." In Bardwick, J., Dorwan, E., Horner, M., and Guttman, D., *Feminine personality and conflict.* Belmont, Calif.: Wadsworth. pp. 45–74. [Horner's fascinating work on sex differences in achievement motivation.]

CHAPTER SEVEN

Emotion

We all know what an emotion is in an everyday sense: it's what we *feel* when we meet an old friend, or escape a falling rock, or find someone crowding in ahead of us—in short, *emotion* suggests an agitated or excited state. Because of a great variety of opinions as to the precise nature of emotion, contemporary psychology does not possess a standard definition of the term. However, there is agreement that there are indeed emotions or emotional responses and that they are an important component of any human personality.

In this chapter we shall first consider the problem of identifying emotions—focusing on the methods of self-description, observation of facial expressions, and measurement of physiological changes. Then we shall briefly discuss the major theories that have been advanced to explain the activation of emotional behavior. Although several elegant studies have examined pleasant emotions such as love and joy, most of the important work in the study of emotion has dealt with unpleasant emotions such as anger and fear, and the effects of prolonged stress on emotional and physical well-being. We shall consider the most significant and revealing studies of both the pleasant and unpleasant emotions.

THE IDENTIFICATION AND MEASUREMENT OF EMOTIONS

It is possible to identify and even quantify emotions according to a subject's own *introspective reports*; however, observations of a subject's expressive movements and physiological changes have proved to be more reliable indices of emotion. Often these *behavioral indices* yield a better picture of what the subject is experiencing than do his own verbal reports. For example, if someone is having a miserable time visiting relatives he doesn't like, he may say "I'm really enjoying this" in answer to the question "You seem quiet today—are you having a good time?" But his expressive behaviors may give him away: he may fidget, be unusually silent or talkative, or escape frequently on various contrived errands. Physiological indicators—such as brainwaves, blood pressure, and muscular tension—would reveal that he is tense or drowsy, depending upon his personal style of dealing with unpleasant social gatherings. In a somewhat similar way, a criminal may well deny his guilt, but it is unlikely that he will foil the lie-detector (which we shall discuss later in this chapter).

Another problem with verbal reports is that they are difficult to compare. Although a subject may respond consistently to certain internal changes that he has learned to label "joy," "terror," "fear," "anxiety," and "sorrow," his use of these terms may not correspond exactly to that of another subject. Behavioral expressions thus permit more accurate measurement and comparison of emotions than do self-reports. It is important to note, however, that expressions of emotion are influenced both by a person's culture and by their immediate situation.

Cultural Relativity   Emotions are expressed differently in different cultures, and this suggests that learning plays an important role in the expression of emotion. Otto Klineberg has pointed out that Chinese are taught to display emotional restraint— a fact that helps explain the relatively reserved behavior that is considered "inscrutable" by many Americans. Given the cultural differences in emotional expression, observers must take special care to construe emotions in their proper cultural contexts. Spontaneous interpretation of others' emotions may sometimes tell us more about our own perceptions than about the expressions we perceive. Nevertheless, certain expressions of emotion—for example, laughter—appear to be universal. Probably there are certain basic human emotions—such as joy and fear—that represent innate responses to certain stimuli. These basic responses, particularly fear, become readily conditioned to previously neutral stimuli, as we explained in Chapter 3.

The Schachter Experiments   The influence of the social situation on the experience and expression of emotion was studied in a series of experiments by Stanley Schachter and J. Singer in 1962. In one experiment subjects were given injections of adrenalin and either told, truthfully, to expect the symptoms of physiological arousal characteristic of adrenalin, or misinformed as to the nature of the drug and told to expect other symptoms—for example, aching or numbness in parts of their bodies. Control subjects were given placebo injections of saline but were told to expect physiological arousal. All of the subjects except the saline controls should have had the same degree of physiological arousal, but only the correctly informed subjects should have been able to correlate these physiological cues with their expectations. The misinformed subjects could be expected to interpret their internal reactions as emotional responses to the situation (not being able to ascribe them to the effects of the drug).

To test their hypothesis that the situation would help determine what emotions were experienced after administration of the drugs, the experimenters manipulated the social environment in various ways. Subjects were told to wait for about twenty minutes so that the drug could take effect and the vision test (the sham pretext for the study) could proceed. Individual subjects were then joined by the experimenter's confederate. In one condition, the confederate was high-spirited—his euphoric behavior included crumpling up paper into balls and shooting them into a waste basket—in the other condition the confederate behaved disagreeably. It was thought that the confederate's behavior would provide the subjects with information about how they should be feeling (whether high-spirited or depressed). The subjects' actual emotions were measured (1) by observing their behaviors through a one-way mirror and (2) by having them fill out a questionnaire later.

The results showed that the misinformed subjects experienced emotion more like that suggested by the confederate's behavior than did the correctly informed subjects, both in terms of their actions, as observed through the one-way mirror, and in terms

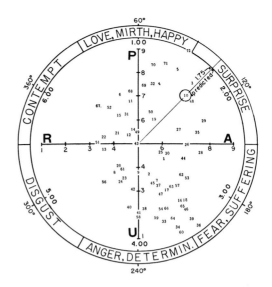

of their moods, as reflected in the questionnaire. The control subjects, who were given saline injections and misinformed about the effects were less likely than their adrenalin-injected (and equally misinformed) counterparts to exhibit and report emotions like those being expressed by the confederate. Therefore, it appears that physiological cues do play a role in emotion—otherwise, the saline-injected subjects would have exhibited the same effects as the other misinformed subjects—but environmental and social factors also have roles. These findings point to an important generalization about emotion: *internal (physiological) and external (especially, social) stimuli jointly determine the experience and expression of emotion.*

Facial Expressions Facial expressions are the most readily observable indicators of emotion. But do observers belonging to a common culture agree on the emotions indicated by various expressions? And if so, what variables determine their judgments? Robert S. Woodworth asked observers to identify, on a six-point scale, the emotions being expressed by a professional actor. His scale included (1) love, happiness, mirth, (2) surprise, (3) fear and suffering, (4) anger and determination, (5) disgust, and (6) contempt. A remarkably high correlation was found between the actor's intended emotions and the judged emotions. Although subjects sometimes misjudged the intended emotion, they were rarely off by more than one scale value. For example, if the intended emotion was disgust (5 on the scale), it was most likely to be correctly identified as disgust; if an error was made, however, the emotion likely to be chosen was either 4 or 6 on the scale (that is, either anger and determination, or contempt).

Later experimental work showed that Woodworth's scale was circular. According to subjects' judgments of facial expressions, Category 1 (love, happiness,

Figure 7.1
Harold Schlosberg located each of seventy-two pictures of actor Frois-Wittman's poses on a circular chart of facial expressions according to the judgments of subjects. This work showed that subjects reliably classify facial expressions on the basis of two dimensions: (1) pleasantness–unpleasantness, the P–U axis; (2) rejection–attention, the R–A axis. For example, Picture 10 (circled) is plotted at coordinate values (7,7), based on subjects' ratings of this picture on the P–U and R–A dimensions. The radius of a circle drawn around the center (0,0) through (7,7) hits the scale at 1.75—a scale value that closely agrees with the 1.65 value obtained using the older six-category scale in the earlier study. [Figures 7.1 and 7.2 are reprinted, by permission, from H. Schlosberg. "The Description of Facial Expressions in Terms of Two Dimensions." *Journal of Experimental Psychology*, 1952, 44, 229–237. Copyright 1952 by the American Psychological Association.]

mirth) was close to Category 6 (contempt). Thus, for some expressions whose modal (most frequently selected) category was 1, the next most frequently selected category was 6, and vice versa. Figure 7.1 shows how seventy-two pictures, used in an experiment conducted by Harold Schlosberg in 1952, were located on a circular scale similar to Woodworth's. The major axis of the circular scale is *pleasantness–unpleasantness,* extending from Category 1 (love, happiness, mirth) to Category 4 (anger and determination). The other axis is *attention–rejection,* extending from the border between categories 5 (disgust) and 6 (contempt) at the rejection end, to

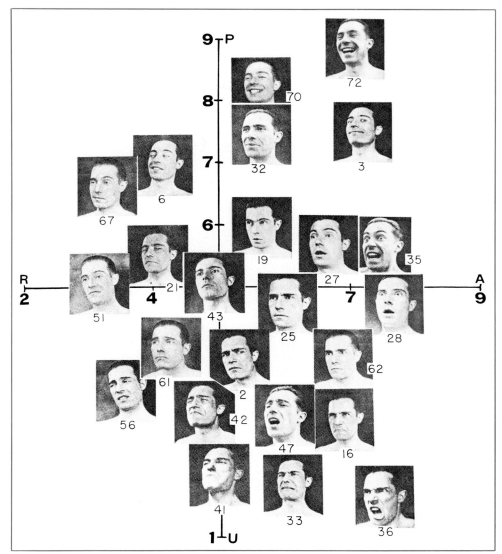

Figure 7.2
Some typical pictures of Frois-Wittman located on Schlosberg's circular surface of facial expressions.

the border between categories 2 (surprise) and 3 (fear and suffering) at the acceptance end of the axis. Judges were asked to rate pictures on a nine-point scale for pleasantness–unpleasantness and on a second nine-point scale for attention–rejection; their judgments were then used to locate each of the pictures on the circular scale. The results were in close agreement with those obtained when the

subjects classified the pictures in terms of emotional labels. The finding—that subjects can reliably classify facial expressions even when utilizing only two factors—suggests that all emotions can be described in terms of their values on these two axes (plus an intensity value). A more graphic description of Schlosberg's circular scale of facial expressions is given in Figure 7.2.

What determines the correlation between facial expressions and emotion? To some extent the correlation is culturally determined, and to some extent expressions may represent innate responses to particular situations, as when we grimace with pain or laugh with joy. Evidence for such innate determinants of facial expressions also comes from the work of Charles Darwin, who wrote *The Expression of the Emotions in Man and Animals* in 1872. Darwin stressed the *utility* of the responses that constitute emotional expression, as when an angry dog bares his teeth in preparation for biting (Figure 7.3). Darwin noted that when an angry man sneers, he is not preparing to bite an adversary, but his expression of hostility is probably a vestige of what, in an evolutionary sense, was once a biologically useful act. Other innate emotional reactions may still have utility. For example, when we are startled by a sudden noise and jump (the "startle reflex"), we may be avoiding danger.

Physiological Changes We have already seen that physiological changes accompany and are sometimes responsible for the experience and expression of emotion. Some of the more common physiological measures of emotion include changes in electrical skin resistance, blood pressure, blood volume, respiration, pulse rate, skin temperature, and brain waves, as well as the pilomotor reaction involving erection of body hairs often associated with rapid chilling of the skin (as in "goose pimples" and "hair-raising experiences").

Of these physiological measures, changes in electrical skin conductance, blood pressure, and respiration form the critical components of the popular *lie-detector test*. In this test, lies are detected when they are accompanied by changes in these physiological indicators that did not accompany truthful answers to innocuous questions, asked during an early part of the interview in order to obtain a baseline. For example, a subject may be asked for his name, his age, and his address in order

Figure 7.3
Charles Darwin pointed out the utility of many emotional expressions—as when an angry dog bares his teeth—and contended that many of man's expressions are vestiges of these biologically useful acts.

to set the baseline. Then queries about the crime, if truthfully answered, should produce the same changes. It should be noted, however, that considerable skill and experience are needed to interpret the results and that changes in these variables may occur for many reasons. For example, changes in skin conductance following a lie are far less reliable than those following strong and sudden stimulation. Moreover, a given change in electrical skin conductance—as measured by the *galvanic skin response* (GSR)—may be attributable to any one of several factors (for instance, temperature) that may be changing while the lie-detection procedure is in progress. Such variations make interpretation difficult. Finally, it should be pointed out that the lie detector may be "beaten" by a knowledgeable subject who has learned to control his emotions and who can either produce emotions such as anxiety during the phase of the lie detector test when innocuous questions are asked or suppress it when lying. The change in the GSR that occurs when anxiety-provoking questions are asked or when the subject lies, will therefore not appear to be substantially different from the subject's reactions during baseline testing. In addition, people with serious personality disorders, such as psychopaths, may beat the lie detector test simply because they do not experience stress when lying. They lie effortlessly. On the other hand, lie detectors may be fallible with highly anxious subjects who may display large changes in the GSR even when they are telling the truth. The question "You did attack those people, didn't you?" may disturb a perfectly innocent person who has been brought in for questioning and hooked up to the complicated apparatus. For all of these reasons, results from lie-detector tests are normally inadmissible as court evidence in this country unless agreed upon by both contesting parties.

The lie-detector test has its historical precursor in the "ordeal by rice" practiced in some cultures. If a suspect could not swallow a handful of rice, he was judged guilty. The rationale was that the guilty person would be anxious, and would therefore not be salivating—thus, he would have difficulty swallowing the rice.

In general, the more physiological measures that are taken, the more likely it is that they will permit an accurate assessment of emotion. Nonetheless, emotions are generally hard to distinguish on a purely physiological basis. For example, extensive investigations of fear and anger have shown that the two emotions have many physiological symptoms in common, including increases in heart rate and blood pressure. There is evidence, however, that whereas fear is characterized by a greater increase in the rate

of breathing, anger is characterized by a greater increase in muscular tension.

Self-Description of Emotions The *self-description* of emotion involves the *introspective approach*, developed by Wilhelm Wundt (1832–1920). Wundt founded the school of psychology known as *structuralism*, which searched for the mental elements (or "structure") composing complex experience. When applying the technique to emotion, the structuralist sought to analyze feelings into their conscious contents. From these analyses, Wundt concluded that there were three dimensions along which emotions vary: *pleasantness–unpleasantness, excitement–depression*, and *strain–relaxation*. According to this *tridimensional view* of emotion, any given feeling could be located, through *introspection*, somewhere within the space defined by these three dimensions.

One of the problems with Wundt's theory was that other psychologists did not agree on the dimensions defining feelings. A more serious problem, however, was the dependence on introspection itself. The basic problem with introspection—as we saw in Chapter 1—is that subjective reports are unreliable, and there is never any assurance that different people are experiencing the same emotions even when they describe them in the same terms.

Despite the difficulties of introspectionism, some psychologists, utilizing modern statistical techniques, have succeeded in developing useful classificatory systems for describing emotions. For example, the use of the technique of *factor analysis* to describe correlations among various emotions has revealed that most emotions can be described in terms of two dimensions that correspond closely to those of Schlosberg's circular scale (Figure 7.1) and Wundt's tridimensional theory. One is an *evaluative dimension*, which resembles Schlosberg's and Wundt's pleasantness–unpleasantness dimension. The other is

Table 7.1
The Mean Judged Intensity of Synonyms for Each of Eight Emotion Dimensions

DIMENSIONS							
DESTRUCTION	REPRODUCTION	INCORPORATION	ORIENTATION	PROTECTION	DEPRIVATION	REJECTION	EXPLORATION
Rage (9.90)	Ecstasy (10.00)	Admission (4.16)	Astonishment (9.30)	Terror (10.13)	Grief (8.83)	Loathing (9.10)	Anticipation (7.30)
Anger (8.40)	Joy (8.10)	Acceptance (4.00)	Amazement (8.30)	Panic (9.75)	Sorrow (7.53)	Disgust (7.60)	Expectancy (6.76)
Annoyance (5.00)	Happiness (7.10)	Incorporation (3.56)	Surprise (7.26)	Fear (7.96)	Dejection (6.26)	Dislike (5.50)	Attentiveness (5.86)
	Pleasure (5.70)			Apprehension (6.40)	Gloominess (5.50)	Boredom (4.70)	Set (3.56)
	Serenity (4.36)			Timidity (4.03)	Pensiveness (4.40)	Tiresomeness (4.50)	
	Calmness (3.30)						

Source: Robert Plutchik, *The Emotions: Fact, Theories and a New Model*, New York: Random House, 1962.

Note: The particular dimensions listed correspond to those developed by Robert Plutchik but need not concern us here. The judgments were made (by thirty college students) on a scale of from one ("very, very *low* intensity") to eleven ("very, very *high* level of intensity"). Note that *terror* and *ecstasy* are judged the most intense emotions. The interested student should consult Plutchik's book.

an *intensity dimension*, which was incorporated in Schlosberg's system and which bears some similarity to Wundt's dimensions of excitement–depression and strain–relaxation. The fact that terms describing emotions can be reliably measured and placed in classificatory schemes suggests that the terms are meaningful and useful. Moreover, such classifications show that each of the hundreds of words composing the vocabulary of emotions can be located on a scheme similar to that of Figure 7.1 and each can be characterized in terms of just two basic dimensions.

Judged Intensity of Emotional Terms In order to gain an appreciation of how people react to emotional terms, the terms used to describe emotion have been scaled according to intensity. In one study, college students rated the intensity of emotions described by each of the terms in Table 7.1 on an eleven-point scale (with 11 being "very, very intense," 6 "moderate," and 1 "very, very low"). Note that terror, ecstasy, and rage were rated the most intense emotional experiences. Some of the other judged emotions are listed in the table. They are grouped according to eight emotional dimen-

sions. Ecstasy, for example is judged as the most intense emotion along its dimension, followed by its weaker synonyms: joy, happiness, pleasure, serenity, and calmness, in that order.

THEORIES OF EMOTION

The fact that we can identify and measure emotions tells us very little about what causes them. There have been dozens, if not hundreds, of theories of emotion advanced throughout the history of psychology. Most of them have proven inadequate. Today, however, we may be on the verge of developing, at long last, a useful and comprehensive theory of emotion. Stanley Schachter and George Mandler have devised a model that appears to encompass many of the best features of the important earlier theories. In this section we shall review the three historically most important theories of emotion—the James-Lange theory, the Cannon-Bard theory and other activation theories—and show how the modern Schachter-Mandler theory grew out of the older theories and out of Schachter's experimental work.

The James-Lange Theory The *James-Lange theory* of emotion, formulated in 1884 by William James and elaborated in 1885 through the independent work of the Danish scientist, Karl Lange, stated that visceral and other somatic (bodily) reactions generate the conscious component of emotion. In other words, the emotional response *precedes* the emotional experience: emotion is the result rather than the cause of the behavior associated with an emotion. Fear, for example, is said to be our awareness of bodily changes that have been triggered by the fearful stimulus: we are afraid because we find ourselves running from danger; we do not run because we are afraid. One of the most important by-products of this early and influential theory of emotion was that it generated a large number of experiments designed to refute it. The theory was important, however, not only for generating significant research in the area of emotion but also for being one of the first to identify emotion as primarily a physiological event.

In 1927, the American physiologist Walter Cannon unleashed an attack against the James-Lange theory, raising three major criticisms. In the first place, Cannon noted that whereas emotions were held by James to depend upon preceding visceral arousal, organisms deprived of sensory input from the viscera continued to manifest emotional behavior. Cannon also pointed out that the visceral changes accompanying emotion are too diffuse to be responsible for the clearly differentiated emotions that humans appear to experience. More recently, some experiments have indicated that it is possible to differentiate certain emotions such as fear and anger according to their different patterns of physiological reaction; but these are, at most, extremely subtle differences in physiological patterns that must mediate dramatic differences in emotional experience if James is to be supported. A third difficulty with the James-Lange theory is that emotional reactions

appear with a shorter latency than would be possible given the known latencies of conduction from the viscera to the brain. In other words, the afferent nervous system (that portion of the nervous system carrying input to the central nervous system) probably cannot act fast enough to account for the rapid development of consciously experienced emotion.

Cannon's arguments, and experiments supporting them, appear to have rendered the James-Lange theory untenable. Recall, however, that the Schachter experiment (introduced at the beginning of the chapter) supported the notion that visceral arousal was implicated in emotions. We shall see that there is an important truth in the James-Lange theory that must be incorporated into modern theories of emotion. First, however, we must discuss the other historically important theory, that of Cannon and Bard, which has important modern descendants in the activation theories of emotion.

Activation Theories Activation theory refers to the general view that emotion represents a state of heightened arousal rather than a qualitatively unique type of psychological, physiological, or behavioral process. Arousal is considered to lie on a continuum that extends from states of quiescence, such as deep sleep, to such extremely agitated states as rage or extreme anger. The *Cannon-Bard theory* of emotion—developed in 1934—moved from criticism of the James-Lange theory to a real attempt at theoretical integration. It held that the conscious experience of emotion, rather than being the result of impulses from the viscera and blood vessels, as James and Lange had supposed, was the result of an upward discharge to the cerebral cortex from the thalamus, which was assumed to be the seat of emotions. The central problem in the debate between the advocates of the James-Lange theory and the Cannon-Bard theory was the difficulty of pinpointing the determinants of conscious experience. The important aspect of Cannon's theory for the present discussion is neither its emphasis on the thalamus—which turned out to be incorrect—nor its attack on the James-Lange theory. Instead it is Cannon's suggestion that emotions serve an *emergency function* by preparing the organism for appropriate action. Thus the Cannon-Bard theory was an important precursor of modern activation theories of emotion.

The term *activation theory of emotion* was actually coined in 1951 by Donald B. Lindsley, who pointed out that when subjects are in an emotional state there are clear effects on an electroencephalogram (EEG)—a record of electrical changes in the cortex obtained from electrodes attached to the scalp. Specifically, Lindsley pointed out that emotion produces an *activation pattern* in which the *synchronized (alpha) rhythms* of the relaxed organism are largely replaced by low-amplitude, fast-activity brainwaves (as we shall see in Chapter 10).

The physiological activation pattern, it should be noted, is similar whether it is caused by emotional events, sensory stimulation, or complex problem solving. In other words, although we may concede that emotional behavior always involves activation, it is not clear how we can distinguish between activation produced by emotional events and activation produced by other causes. The activation concept, therefore, cannot provide us with a definition or a complete theory of emotion, except insofar as we identify emotion with activation. If we do that, of course, then we need not retain the concept of emotion. Emotion is, after all, an intuitive concept, and it is not intuitively appealing to describe a person solving a calculus problem as being in a state of emotion, although his brainwaves display an activation pattern.

Lindsley's activation theory of emotion did point to a physiological correlate of most emotional

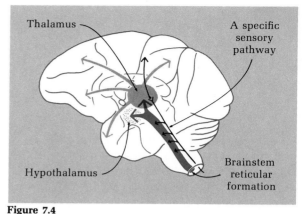

Figure 7.4
A schematic representation of the important neural structures and pathways involved in emotional behavior. According to Donald Lindsley's activation theory of emotion the *reticular formation* must be activated if significant emotional behavior is to occur. [Adapted from H. Magoun, "The Ascending Reticular System and Wakefulness." In J. F. Delafresnaye, ed., *Brain Mechanisms and Consciousness*. Oxford: Blackwell, 1954.]

behavior, and his experiments produced evidence that is interesting in and of itself. For example, they demonstrated that the activation pattern of the EEG can be reproduced by appropriate electrical stimulation of brain structures, especially in the *brainstem reticular formation* (Figure 7.4). When appropriate lesions are made in this structure, the activation pattern of the EEG is abolished and the alpha rhythms are restored. In this event the organism becomes relatively nonexpressive or apathetic.

Figure 7.4 presents a schematic representation of the primary structures and pathways of the central nervous system that are, according to activation theory, implicated in emotional behavior. The reticular formation itself contributes impulses both upward toward the cortex and downward toward the musculature. The descending fibers permit impulses from the activating mechanism to influence muscular movements and visceral activity. At the same time, the ascending fibers permit ascending impulses that form the basis of the activation patterns manifested in the EEG. Thus, electrical stimulation of the activating mechanism—or any other novel or significant stimulus occurring in the organism's field of attention—alters the EEG pattern in the direction of increased activation, whereas lesions in the same area or in its upward projection pathways can alter an activated EEG pattern into a sleep pattern. These inverse effects of electrical stimulation and lesions upon behavioral functions are an example of a generalization that holds for many brain structures and behavioral functions: removing an area has the opposite effect of stimulating the same area.

To summarize, the essence of Lindsley's activation theory of emotion is that the reticular system must be activated in order for significant emotional behavior to occur. The activating system appears to serve only a general energizing function, however. It is currently believed that structures in a different portion of the brain, the limbic system, organize the input and determine the particular form of the expressed emotion.

The Jukebox Theory of Emotion   In 1962, George Mandler noted that there seem to be two stages in the production of an emotion, which correspond to the two stages in selecting a tune on a jukebox. The first step in the jukebox process is to insert a coin to activate the machine. This corresponds to the physiological arousal that Schachter's experimental work implicates in the production of emotion. But an additional step is required to play the jukebox: the appropriate button must be pressed to select a tune. This is analogous to the fact that the stimulus situation determines which emotion occurs. Mandler points out that the same stimulus situation can produce both steps simultaneously.

The Current Theory of Emotion   Activation, then, whether produced by social situations, drugs, or other stimuli, is probably necessary but not sufficient for the occurrence of an emotion. Although

it is somewhat premature to speculate about the physiological correlates of this activation, they no doubt include the reticular activating mechanism, the viscera, and the hypothalamus. Internal emotional events are apparently modulated by environmental stimuli (including social stimuli) to produce the experience and expression of a particular emotion. In general, this provides a broad and vague, but probably adequate, theory of emotion.

THE DEVELOPMENT OF EMOTIONS

John B. Watson stated that an infant is born with three basic emotions: *love*, elicited by contact and stroking; *fear*, elicited by loud noises and by loss of support; and *anger*, elicited by constraint of movement. Watson believed that other emotions become differentiated later, through conditoning.

A more panoramic developmental view was advanced in 1932 by Mildred Bridges, who performed the classic study of the development and differentiation of emotions in infants and young children. Figure 7.5 presents data, based on observer ratings, indicating the approximate ages at which emotions evolve or are differentiated from their more general predecessors. Note that the first emotion is a generalized excitement reaction. As the infant grows older, its reactions become more specific. Thus, soon after birth the emotion of distress is observed. After about four months, the distress reaction differentiates into more specific emotional reactions: first anger, and later disgust and fear. These changes represent developmental processes that may occur without any particular experiences. Although Bridges placed a greater emphasis on development that did Watson, she did not deny that emotions could be conditioned. She agreed with Watson, for example, that fear can both (1) be elicited as an unconditioned response to particular stimuli and (2) be conditioned to previously neutral

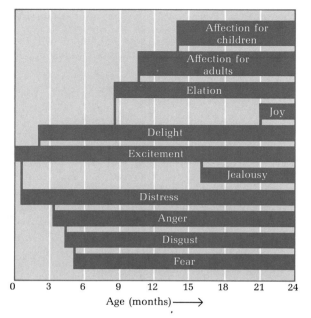

Figure 7.5
The development and differentiation of emotions based on the observations of infants and young children. [Adapted from M. Bridges, "Emotional Development in Early Infancy," *Child Development*, 1932, 3, 324–341.]

stimuli. Recall that Watson himself conditioned young Albert's fear of furry objects, by pairings with an unconditioned stimulus for fear (a loud noise).

Maturational processes and conditioning both play important roles in the acquisition of emotional expression; however, the precise contribution made by each cannot be specified. It might be said that whereas we feel emotions such as love and fear without learning, *whom* we love and *what* we fear depend on learning. Finally, although it is probably true that many basic emotions are unlearned, the full range of rich emotional experience and expression that characterizes humans develops through the course of experience.

STUDIES OF SPECIFIC EMOTIONS

In this section, we shall consider some of the more important findings that have emerged from the

experimental study of specific emotions. We shall first consider the positive, pleasurable emotions such as love and pleasure itself, and then the negative, generally unpleasant emotions such as fear, anxiety, anger, and terror.

POSITIVE EMOTIONS

Less experimental work has been carried out on the positive emotions than on the negative emotions; the negative emotions are more readily identified and produced in the laboratory. However, thanks to the work of Harry Harlow and his students, we have learned a good deal about the development of affection in primates. In addition, studies involving self-stimulation of pleasure centers in the brains of both humans and lower animals have shed considerable light on the neurological basis of pleasurable emotions.

Love. Love, of course, refers to affection that one organism shows for another. Working with monkeys in the late 1960s, Harlow delineated five affectional systems: *maternal love, infant love, peer love, heterosexual love,* and *paternal love.* These affectional systems develop in sequences, each to some extent building on preceding ones. Maternal love, characterized by care and *contact comfort*, appears to be a largely innate response of the normal mother to her infant's dependence. Maternal love passes through stages of care and comfort, during which the infant is totally dependent upon the mother for satisfaction of its physical and psychological needs, through a transitional stage, to the final stage of *relative separation*, during which the mother begins to leave the infant alone while the infant is simultaneously developing an increased curiosity about its environment.

Nearly coincident with maternal love is infant love, characterized by the infant's close attachment to its mother. Harlow has demonstrated that this love

Figure 7.6
Harlow with infant monkey. [Figures 7.6, 7.7, and 7.8 were provided by courtesy of Harry F. Harlow.]

Figure 7.7
Normal mother and infant.

is elicited by the contact comfort that the mother provides (Figure 7.7), rather than by her satisfaction of such basic needs as food and warmth, as was previously assumed. This has been shown by experiments in which infant monkeys have been raised with "surrogate mothers"—terry-cloth or wire mother substitutes (Figure 7.8). Harlow found that infant monkeys spend more time with *cloth* mother surrogates than with wire mother surrogates, regardless of which surrogate mother provides them with their milk. Figure 7.9 shows that the infants spent much more time in contact with "dry" cloth mothers than they did with "nursing" wire mothers. This striking finding is a major advance over older notions that infant love was a result of the mother's association with the reduction of hunger and thirst. Instead, there seems to be more to being a mother than supplying food.

The stages through which the infant-love system progresses include the stage of reflexive love (related to nursing), the stage of comfort and attachment (characterized by the infant's physical attachment to the mother), the stage of solace and security (in which the infant develops curiosity, but soon returns from brief exploration to re-establish contact with the mother), and the stage of relative independence (which is jointly determined by the infant's enhanced

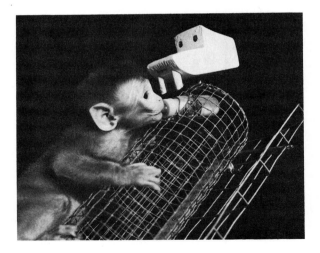

Figure 7.8
Infant on "nursing" surrogate mother. Some surrogates were wrapped with terry cloth.

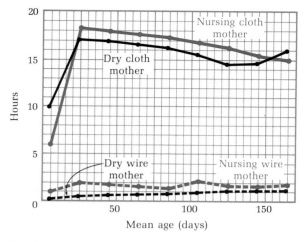

Figures 7.9
Number of hours per day spent on dry and nursing cloth and wire surrogates as a function of the baby monkey's average age. [Adapted from Harry F. Harlow, "Love in Infant Monkeys," *Scientific American*, 1959, *200*, 68–74. Copyright © 1959 by Scientific American, Inc. All rights reserved.]

curiosity and by the mother's behavior during her stage of relative separation).

After the mother-love and infant-love stages have run their course, the infant is ready to enter into peer relationships. The peer affectional system begins with very tentative, presocial play and moves progressively through rough-and-tumble *free play*, which includes the learning of sexual posturing, and *creative play*, in which the primate begins to see that objects may be used in many different ways. The peer affectional system is vital for the normal development of the heterosexual affectional system. This has been amply demonstrated in studies by Harlow in which primates of both sexes were raised in individual wire cages throughout the stages of the infant and peer affectional systems. Adults that have been deprived of early affection fail to display normal heterosexual behavior when they are tested in heterosexual dyads. One result of their deprivation is a failure to learn how to control aggression during the peer-love period. Thus the deprived male, in the company of a normal female, displays an unusual amount of aggressive behavior, which may even

culminate in severe physical attacks. The deprived female initially displays similarly heightened aggressive tendencies, but quickly learns to suppress them when they elicit counteraggression by a normal male. Nonetheless, socially deprived females tend not to develop normal heterosexual relations; they generally avoid prolonged social proximity with males.

The last of the five important affectional systems, the paternal affectional system, seems to depend primarily on experiential factors rather than on biological ones, which play a more important role in the first four stages. The paternal affectional system appears to function as a secondary source of protection for the infant.

Pleasure. Pleasure, according to most behavioral indicators, is an emotion similar to love. The study of this emotion has centered on experiments involving intracranial self-stimulation (ICS) of "pleasure centers" or "reward centers" in the limbic system of the brain. The milestone work in this area began in 1954 when James Olds showed that rats would learn a response, such as pressing a bar, in order to deliver electrical stimulation to certain areas of their brains (Figure 4.16). Differences in the rate of bar-pressing seem to be dependent on the location of the tip of the stimulating electrode. Olds found both rewarding and punishing electrode placements. They were defined with reference to the operant level of responding—that is, the rate of responding when no stimulation was provided. When the animal responds significantly more often than at its operant level, the electrode location is defined as rewarding; on the other hand, when the animal responds *less* often than at the operant level, the location is considered punishing. Olds has reported particularly high scores for self-stimulation in several limbic-system areas. Of course it could be argued that a rat responding to obtain stimulation of limbic areas is not necessarily doing so because of resultant pleasurable sensations. Studies of two human mental patients—reported by Dr. Robert Heath and his colleagues at Tulane University in 1963—are illuminating in this respect. (One patient suffered from narcolepsy, uncontrollable sleeping, and the other suffered from cataplexy, sudden attacks of extreme weakness.) Verbal reports of these patients indicated that stimulation at certain points of the brain is indeed "pleasant," a sort of emotional reinforcement. Self-stimulation with certain electrode placements is so reinforcing for rats that they will sometimes continue to press for many hours, at the expense of eating and drinking, until they drop from exhaustion.

NEGATIVE EMOTIONS

All of us have at one time or another experienced the potentially destructive emotions of anger and rage; protective emotions ranging from timidity through apprehension, fear, panic, and terror; emotions related to deprivation or loss, such as gloominess, dejection, sorrow, and grief; and emotions related to rejection, such as boredom, dislike, disgust, and loathing. As with the positive emotions, few successful efforts have been made to distinguish between closely related emotions, except by means of self-reports or the interpretation of facial expressions.

Physiological studies have succeeded to some extent in differentiating the complex patterns of physiological changes that characterize fear, anger, and certain other emotions. But more work has been done on the overt behavioral expressions of particular emotions. Probably the most studied is aggression, which is an outward manifestation of anger. Aggression will be considered in some detail here and again in Chapter 20 when we consider human interpersonal relations. Following our discussion of aggression, we shall briefly touch upon some of the other negative affective states, including anxiety, fear, terror, and emotional stress.

Aggression   If two animals are enclosed together in an experimental chamber and occasionally administered shocks through the floor of the chamber, they are likely to attack each other. This phenomenon, called pain-elicited aggression, was demonstrated for a variety of species in a number of experiments by Nathan Azrin and his associates in the early 1960s. Aggression is *elicited* in the sense that aggressive responses reliably follow the shock, provided that an appropriate object is present against which to aggress. Hence, strictly speaking, the eliciting stimulus is the shock *plus* an appropriate stimulus object. In order to eliminate the possible influence of social factors, subsequent studies of elicited aggression used single animals with inanimate objects to bite or attack; pain-elicited aggression was observed in these studies also. Further experimentation has shown that the appearance of an object against which to aggress can maintain operant behavior in squirrel monkeys subjected to shock. For example, shocked squirrel monkeys will pull a chain in order to produce a ball to attack. More recent studies have also demonstrated that aggression can result from types of stimuli other than physically painful ones—for example, stimuli associated with extinction schedules or with high fixed-ratio requirements.

Some animals show a greater tendency toward aggression than others. In Chapter 5 we noted that some rats "spontaneously" attack and kill the first mouse they ever encounter, whereas other rats of seemingly similar genetic and environmental backgrounds are never observed to kill. The percentage of killers found in the given population of rats has been shown to vary with species, sex, breeding, and developmental experience. For example, a higher

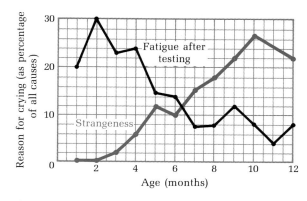

Figure 7.10
The amount of crying due to fatigue and to strangeness is plotted as a function of the infant's age in months. Note that the reasons for crying change with age. Indeed, as we continue to grow older, different events set the occasion for emotional expression. [Adapted from N. Bayley, "A Study of the Crying of Infants during Mental and Physical Tests." *Journal of Genetic Psychology,* 1932, *40,* 306–329.]

percentage of killers is found among wild rats than among domesticated ones. Killer rats will eat the mice after killing them; nevertheless, the killing itself is so rewarding for these rats—even in the absence of hunger—that the opportunity to kill can serve as an adequate reinforcer for the maintenance of a learned response.

Finally, aggression, once expressed, can be maintained by reinforcement (operant aggression). For example, organisms will emit aggressive responses if they produce food rewards. Children who are reinforced for aggressive behavior may carry the aggressive style into adulthood. Thus, aggressive behavior may represent either elicited aggression, provoked by aversive stimuli, or operant aggression, maintained by rewards.

Fear, Anxiety, and Terror Although certain emotions appear to be innate in response to certain stimuli, the situations that lead to particular emotions also depend in large measure upon what the organism has experienced in the past and upon his age. Evidence with humans and chimps suggests that as the young organism learns to recognize familiar features in its environment, it also begins to display fear of the unfamiliar. For example, as the child learns to discriminate between its parents and strangers, it usually begins to show a fear of strangers. Figure 7.10 shows that infants cry with increasing frequency throughout the first twelve months of their lives when they are confronted by strangers or when they are put in strange places. Since crying due to fatigue diminishes throughout this period, the results cannot be attributed to a greater general tendency to cry. Strangeness also produces fear in chimpanzees, as was demonstrated in 1946 by Donald Hebb. Chimps show fear when confronted with strangers and with strange objects that bear a close similarity to some familiar object—for example, the disembodied head of a chimpan-

zee(!), a biscuit with a worm in it, or a familiar person unusually dressed or masked.

Whereas a three-year-old child might be afraid of the dark, of lightning and thunder, and of being left alone, by the age of ten he might begin to fear bad report cards, tests, and bad dreams. As the child gets older, social and school-related situations are added to those that are sometimes fearful. Beginning in adolescence, fears of inadequacy in social situations increase and, in some cases, never abate. At the same time, fears related to competence and achievement usually become more important to the individual than fears of physical harm and the supernatural.

A quantitative measure of anxiety, known as *conditioned suppression,* has been used extensively in animal laboratories and has been used, in modified form, with humans as well. In this procedure, an animal that is emitting a standard operant response, such as the bar-press, and obtaining food reinforcement on an intermittent basis is presented at specific intervals with an originally neutral stimulus, and immediately afterward administered shock independent of its behavior. The effect of pairing a neutral stimulus with shock and superimposing the two on a schedule of food reinforcement is to lower the rate of responding in the presence of the stimulus as compared with the rate of responding in its absence. This suppression of responding can be measured in several ways. One measure is the suppression ratio, which divides the rate of responding in the presence of a stimulus by the rate of responding in its absence. Since the stimulus precedes shock, it is generally called a pre-aversive stimulus; the suppression of responding in the presence of a pre-aversive stimulus is often called *conditioned suppression*, or a *conditioned emotional response*, or *anxiety*. The conditioned suppression paradigm has been used with many species of animals, including pigeons, rats, monkeys, and humans to assess the conditions under which a stimulus paired with an aversive event will suppress ongoing behavior.

The conditioned-suppression procedure establishes conditions in which we would all feel anxious—in the presence of a stimulus that regularly precedes a painful event. For that reason, we think of the effects of conditioned suppression *as* anxiety, even though it is overt *behavior* that is *suppressed*, rather than a *feeling* that is *expressed* and felt. But it is still a safe guess that the procedure does produce a genuine feeling of anxiety. And we may, paradoxically, learn even more about the feeling by publicly studying its overt correlates than by privately observing our own experience of it.

We have encountered other instances of conditioned emotions in Chapter 3. Conditioning also plays an important part in learning how to *express* emotion. For example, fear may be expressed by aggressive behavior, submission, or flight—which of the three an individual will tend to display may well depend on how successful the behavior has been in his past. The importance of learned and cultural factors in the expression of emotion was considered at the beginning of the chapter.

Terror is extreme fear and is generally considered the most intense emotion we can experience. Striking examples of terror have been obtained with infant chimpanzees and rhesus monkeys. Harlow has shown that the distinction between a brave and a cowardly infant chimp is the presence or absence of a natural mother or her effective substitute. A chimpanzee raised with a cloth mother surrogate will not panic if placed in a strange test room with his cloth mother. After making contact with the mother, the chimp will explore the chamber and play with the toys it contains. On the other hand, when placed in the same room without the cloth mother, the chimp displays prolonged terror.

EMOTIONAL STRESS AND PSYCHOSOMATIC DISORDERS

The negative affective states are not without their positive value. At the very least, pain and fear help the organism avoid or escape from dangerous or harmful situations, and emotions such as anger may help to mobilize the organism for effective action—although this point has been disputed by P. T. Young and others, who have claimed that all emotional states are disruptive and disorganizing. It has long been held that emotions such as sorrow and grief enrich life by challenging human understanding. Furthermore, some have maintained that in order to experience and appreciate fully the joys of life, one must have first experienced its sorrows. Unfortunately, there is no empirical evidence with which we could resolve this point one way or another.

We can say with certainty that prolonged negative emotional states may create serious somatic problems. The body initially reacts to stressful situations with successful adaptation and adjustment. Prolonged emotional stress, however, can produce serious disorders such as ulcers or migraine headaches. We shall briefly turn to a discussion of emotional stress and psychosomatic disorders.

Emotional Stress   Not everything in the world is as we would like it to be, and our daily lives are filled with pressures and stresses resulting from responsibilities, frustrated desires, and unfulfilled ambitions. One approach to solving these problems is to change our environment so as to eliminate the factors causing the stress and discomfort. But this is not always possible. Another approach is to change our aspirations or our reactions to situations in order to become better adjusted to them. (This is in large measure the aim of the psychotherapeutic techniques that we shall be discussing in Chapters 30 through 32.) Since it is probably impossible and perhaps undesirable to eliminate all emotional stress, it is important to understand how we react to emotional stress.

Hans Selye, a Canadian endocrinologist and physiologist whose work on stress began in the 1930s, pointed out that the amount of time that we are exposed to emotional stress affects our reactions to it. He described the *general adaptation syndrome*, which consists of three successive stages in our physiological reactions to stress. The first stage, the *alarm reaction*, consists of heightened responsiveness of the autonomic nervous system, resulting in decreased blood pressure and body temperature, and the release of hormones that alter our emotions and motivations. Under severe or prolonged stress, the reaction enters the second stage, *resistance to stress*. In this stage many of the reactions of the first stage are reversed; for example, blood pressure and body temperature rise. Eventually, the third stage, *exhaustion*, is entered, in which physiological reactions are no longer sufficient for adjusting to the stress. Instead, death or serious injury (such as an ulcer) may occur.

Psychosomatic Disorders   Selye pointed out that the body's ultimate reaction to prolonged emotional stress tends to be a *psychosomatic* disorder. The nature of the disorder will vary from individual to individual. Each of us has his own characteristic pattern of psychosomatic reactions, which may produce a wide variety of more or less specific disorders such as ulcers (caused by a malfunctioning of stomach secretions), asthma, chest or back pains, migraine headaches, hives, shortness of breath, or hypertension (high blood pressure).

An important investigation of psychosomatic disorders, involving the experimental inducement of ulcers in monkeys, was conducted by Joseph Brady and his colleagues in 1958. In Brady's experiment, "executive" and control monkeys were subjected to electric shock every twenty seconds. The executive monkey could push a lever that would prevent both animals from receiving the shock; the control monkey, on the other hand, could not do anything about the shocks. Which monkey developed the ulcers? The one with responsibility, of course! The executive monkey developed a serious (perforated) ulcer within three weeks and died. Later research showed that the timing of the stressful situations was critical. Brady's original study alternated six-hour experimental periods with six hours of rest. The ulcer effect was harder to obtain with other on-off patterns, ranging from thirty minutes on and off to twenty-four hours on and off. These studies suggest that emotional stress produces ulcers when the stress is intermittent, rather than continuous, and when the occurrence of stress coincides with the natural periodicity of stomach secretions. In support of this hypothesis Brady noted that stomach secretions did not occur *during* the stressful situation, but occurred *after* the session was over, beginning following two hours of rest and reaching peak flow after six hours of rest. When the stressful situation was reinstated before the secretions reach maximal levels, further secretions were sharply decreased. These findings substantiate what is known about psychosomatic ulcers in humans, particularly business executives: much of the extra gastric secretion occurs not during the eight-hour workday but during the subsequent evening and night.

It is important to note that Brady's work made use of fairly predictable shocks, which occurred every twenty seconds in the absence of avoidance responding. It turns out that *unpredictable pain* is even more likely to cause ulcers than predictable pain. This was discovered in a study by M. E. P. Seligman, in 1968, which compared the effects of unavoidable but predictable shocks with unavoidable and unpredictable shocks in a group of male rats. Both group of rats received the same number of shocks, but one group received a warning signal for three minutes prior to each shock. The remaining forty-seven minutes of each fifty-minute session was a period of safety for these rats. Rats that did not receive a reliable warning signal spent the entire fifty-minute session in fear. Of the eight rats in this group, six developed stomach ulcers, whereas none of the rats in the predictable-shock group had ulcers.

Taken together, these studies suggest that several factors help determine whether or not an aversive experience will lead to psychosomatic disorder. For example, it appears that the more responsible the individual is for controlling the unpleasant events, the more he will be likely to experience stress and develop ulcers. Also, the less predictable the occurrence of the aversive event, the greater the anxiety and the higher the likelihood of developing ulcers. Finally, the duration of the stressful experience and the timing of rest periods are crucial in determining whether or not ulcers will develop. It may well be that an eight-hour workday, followed by a restful period of dinner, television, and sleep, in a life filled with responsibility and unpredictable stress, is most conducive to the development of serious psychosomatic disturbances.

Suggested Readings

Cofer, C. N. (1972) *Motivation and emotion*. Glenview, Illinois: Scott, Foresman. [This paperback provides a good basic treatment of motivation and emotion, although the emphasis is on motivation.]

Fantino, E. J. (1973) "Emotion." In Nevin, J. A., & Reynolds, G. S., eds., *The study of behavior*. Glenview, Illinois: Scott, Foresman. Pp. 280–320. [A comprehensive review of research and theory in emotion—with emphasis on historical roots—primarily from a behavioristic perspective.]

Darwin, C. (1965) *The expression of the emotions in man and animals*. Chicago: University of Chicago Press. [Darwin's classic work on emotion. Still important and interesting reading more than a century after its first appearance (in 1872).]

Harlow, H. F. (1971) *Learning to love*. San Francisco: Albion. [An engaging treatment of Harlow's work on love, ending with a chapter on man's social behavior.]

Mandler, G. (1962) "Emotion." In Brown, R. M., Galanter, E., Hess, E. H., & Mandler, G., eds., *New directions in psychology*. Vol. 1, New York: Holt, Rinehart and Winston. Pp. 267–343. [An enjoyable and informative statement of the Schachter-Mandler theory of emotion.]

Young, P. T. (1961) *Motivation and emotion: A survey of the determinants of human and animal activity*. New York: Wiley.

Young, P. T. (1973) *Emotion in man and animal*. (2nd ed.) Huntington, New York: Krieger. [Young's treatment of emotion.]

UNIT THREE

Thought and Language

Thought and language are believed by many psychologists to be manifestations of man's unique mental powers—powers that set man apart from dumb animals. This notion has been strongly challenged by some who have observed much similarity between the ways in which humans and animals solve problems. But advocates of human supremacy can still argue that man—and man alone—has developed both speech and a complex and highly structured language, and that these are evidence of man's uniqueness.

Contemporary psychology recognizes that there are many similarities between humans and other organisms—and that the behavior of all organisms, including humans, is governed by many of the same fundamental principles. Most psychologists are comfortable with the notion that organisms like chimpanzees can communicate by means of sounds and symbols and that such behavior may not be vastly different, *in principle*, from the ability of humans to use language. In recent years, psychologists in several laboratories across the country have even demonstrated the capacity of chimpanzees to learn rudimentary languages composed of symbols and gestures. But before we discuss these interesting and significant studies of animal language, let us return briefly to the topic of man's mental powers in order to discuss the ways in which psychologists have approached the subject of "thinking."

Many psychologists have attempted to study the process of thinking by means of experiments that permit them to analyze the behavior of human subjects who are confronted with particular well-specified problems. An independent variable in such an experiment (as in any experiment) is a variable that is manipulated by the experimenter. An example is the *difficulty* of the problem the subject is asked to solve by thinking: when a subject is asked to unravel an anagram (a word or phrase formed with the letters of another word or phrase), the experimenter may use an anagram that is relatively difficult or relatively easy; in a "concept-formation" experiment, where a subject is asked to classify various stimuli (for example, words) according to specified characteristics, the experimenter may set a relatively difficult task for the subject or a relatively easy one. As we know, a dependent variable is a factor that is affected by an independent variable—in this case, the independent variable is the degree of difficulty of the problem chosen by the experimenter. In studies of human thinking and problem solving, the dependent variables that are generally observed and recorded include one or more of the following: (1) the amount of time the subject takes to solve a problem, (2) the accuracy of the solution, (3) the subject's strategy for solving the problem.

Although, as we shall see, psychologists know a substantial amount about the overt behavior that occurs during the solution of problems, there is unfortunately little agreement about the nature of the thinking that is taking place while problems are being solved. As we shall see in Chapter 8, some psychologists favor the pragmatic assumption that thinking *is* behavior, and that the laws that describe the overt behavior describe the thinking as well. We shall also discuss the views of a group of psychologists who maintain that the essence of thinking is the utilization of symbols—that is, a person who is thinking is using symbols (words, for example) to represent objects and events that are not present. Although many other definitions exist as well, these two are perhaps the most important and will be the basis of our own working definition of thought. Whatever one's definition, thinking is an amorphous topic that has given rise to many points of view and to many different research approaches. In Chapter 8, which is devoted to the nature of thought, we have tried not to impose our own biases, but rather have adopted an eclectic approach, sampling several of the more important contemporary theories and types of research.

People who seem to be adept at thinking—flexible in confronting new problems, and insightful and efficient in solving them—are considered more "intelligent" than those who appear to be less mentally competent. However, any contemporary definition of intelligence is necessarily as incomplete and arbitrary as that of thinking.

The common measure of intelligence (and general aptitude), the IQ test, has proved to be a successful device for predicting academic achievement.

But, since it has been shown that performance on all aptitude tests is influenced by experience, the predictive validity of an IQ test may mean only that children who have learned easily or efficiently in the past are likely to continue doing so. In that case, IQ tests measure simply the general ability to transfer what has been successfully learned, in school or in the home, to novel reasoning tasks. As a gauge of such ability, these tests may be useful to the admissions staff of a professional or graduate program wishing to assess the potential performance of a particular applicant. Although the tests are employed as reliable screening devices, we must not adopt the erroneous and potentially harmful assumption that the relationship between an IQ score and subsequent performance will be unaffected by the applicant's future experience, for, in fact, his IQ may be drastically altered by environmental circumstances.

A person's problem-solving ability, then, is in great part determined by the tasks he has encountered previously and the ways in which he has coped with them; similarly, his performance on intelligence tests is conditioned by his prior experience in verbalizing, reasoning, and interacting with his world. In planning an educational experience for others, a teacher or psychologist should realize that the challenge presented is as much a test of his or her own experimental ingenuity as it is a test of the pupils or subjects. Our discussion of problem solving will show that even the most intelligent of subjects can be easily trained to appear embarrassingly inept when confronted by a trivial task. On the other hand, when a given program of instruction is properly organized, individuals who have previously manifested subnormal intelligence (as measured by IQ tests) can show dramatic improvement in learning ability (and in IQ).

The importance of experimental ingenuity is probably nowhere better demonstrated than by the example of teaching a rudimentary language to a chimpanzee. Before the first of these dramatic demonstrations in the mid-1960s, man had for centuries (and especially since the acceptance of Darwin's theory of evolution in the late nineteenth century) singled out his ability to communicate by means of language as the one attribute that distinguished him from other animals. Research on man's nearest phylogenetic neighbors, the great apes, had strengthened the belief that language was indeed unique to human beings: in fact, before 1966, the most successful attempt to teach an ape to speak produced a disappointingly low vocabulary of four words in a chimpanzee named Viki. We know now, however, that those early studies failed not because of the chimp's basic inability to communicate with symbols but because of our own insistence that a humanlike spoken word be the form of communication.

In 1966, Beatrice and Allen Gardner of the University of Nevada found that the chimp's failure to use more words was due to its inability to make a variety of sounds. Thus, they began to teach their female chimp, Washoe, to communicate by means of a nonverbal language—American Sign Language, originally developed for use by the deaf. In the years following 1966, Washoe's accomplishments became increasingly more impressive. By 1970, she had developed a vocabulary of 160 manual gestures. Moreover, not only could Washoe make a sign to refer to a specific object but she could also generalize. For example, once she had learned the sign for flower, she would apply it to all flowers, including flowers she had not seen before. Occasionally she would even make the flower sign to refer to any prominent scent present at the time. Within a year after her training began, Washoe began constructing her first sentences: that is to say, she began combining signs in patterns roughly resembling grammatical constructions; for example, she constructed an original sentence, "Gimme tickle," which she used when she desired to be tickled. Any number of gestures can, of course, be randomly combined to form strings, but all the combinations that Washoe constructed seemed to convey sensible meaning. Indeed, the Gardners observed that Washoe's sequential development of various sign combinations was similar to the development of initial word combinations that occurs in very young children.

Apparently, the talents demonstrated by Washoe are representative of chimpanzees in general. Several researchers in other laboratories have had equally successful results, using somewhat different procedures on their own chimps. Among them are David Premack at the University of California and Duane Rumbaugh at Georgia State University.

Premack gave his chimp, Sarah, a set of differently colored plastic forms, each one being the symbol for a different word. Sarah, too, learned more than a hundred words, which she could combine into sentences. Moreover, Sarah expressed conceptual terms, such as "same" and "different," and she seemed to have excellent command of the use of negatives, questions, and even the conditional "if—then" constructions. Both the Gardners and Premack now have younger chimps in training. Several chimps are learning language at the Institute for Primate Studies in Norman, Oklahoma (where initial evidence indicates that the chimps may be able to use sign language to communicate with one another). To date, then, findings suggest that the capacity for language learning is quite general within the species.

Duane Rumbaugh taught his chimp, Lana, to type on a specially made typewriter, which reproduced the symbols for her own language. The typed messages were then projected onto a screen from which Lana was able to check her own sentences as she worked. That is, once she had produced a message and it was displayed on the screen, Lana determined whether her message was correct or incorrect. If she found errors, Lana pushed her erase button and began again. Thus, Lana not only had to be able to "speak" her language, she had to *read* it as well!

Some scientists do not believe that these chimps are really functioning as humans do when they produce human language. Nevertheless, until we have a better understanding of exactly what this behavior of the chimpanzee is, the overwhelming amount of evidence to date suggests that, though these animals may not yet be able to express themselves as elegantly as humans have been known to do, they appear to share at least some of the linguistic aptitude once attributed to man alone.

CHAPTER EIGHT

Thought

A scientific description of *thinking* is elusive at best because it is impossible to observe another's thoughts directly. Like dreams, memories, and perceptions, the thoughts of another person are revealed to us only by that person's own verbal reconstructions of past events. And such verbal reports are notoriously unreliable from the scientific point of view. In this chapter we will sample several of the more important areas of theory and research on thinking: it is a field in flux, and one in which several illuminating but diverse theories have been proposed.

ASPECTS OF THOUGHT

Even though thinking is a difficult phenomenon to define—or perhaps *because* it is difficult to define—literally dozens of different definitions exist. Most of them belong to one of two major categories. In the first category are the definitions proposed by those who maintain that thinking is the construction of internal representations of external events, including the anticipation of external events. (As shown in Figure 8.1, if a child sees an object being hidden under a carton, for example, he can anticipate that the object will still be there when the carton is lifted. In order to make this kind of prediction, he must have in his mind an internal representation of the object's placement, and such a representation is an example of thinking.) In the second type of definition, thinking is described as problem solving in which the person transfers what he has learned from previous experience and applies it to his present situation. This definition is more concrete as well as more functional than the first one, because it does not rely on unobservable internal representations but rather defines thinking as problem-solving activity that can be readily studied and measured.

Actually the two classes of definitions—the functional and representational—are not contradictory: in fact, problem-solving behavior provides evidence for the existence of internal representations, which, in turn can be seen to aid in solving problems. In this chapter, we shall draw from both points of view. First, we will treat thinking as a form of behavior in which one integrates perceptions experienced in the course of time and also grasps patterns or relationships existing in what has been perceived. Since the integration of perceptions is internal, our own definition, then,

Figure 8.1
After the parent hides the child's toy under the carton, the child points at the carton, suggesting that he may have some sort of internal representation of the hidden toy.

necessarily incorporates the approach of the first class of definitions. Yet, since the grasping of relations can be most accurately tested by posing problems, we must also make use of the second class of definitions. Our working definition of thinking will be: *behavior that solves problems through the use of symbols—or internal representations—of things and events that are not currently present.*

Aside from our subjective convictions, how do we know that thinking occurs? Several specific types of events suggest that thinking, as defined in the preceding paragraph, does indeed take place. First, a "sudden idea"—an idea that is not obviously related to one's prior experience or perception—suggests that some kind of purely mental (internal) reorganization occurs from time to time. For example, we sometimes suddenly remember something that we have failed to remember on an earlier occasion, despite strenuous efforts to do so. Similarly, the solution to a vexing problem may unexpectedly come to mind after a period of *incubation* during which we have made no conscious effort to find the solution.

A second type of event, which manifests more directly the integration of perception and the grasping of relations, is observed in experimental studies of problem solving. In the course of solving a problem, both humans and animals often make a significant advance at a particular point, demonstrating a sudden and penetrating comprehension of a situation. This type of experience is usually referred to as _insight,_ or an *"aha!" experience.* It is as if certain aspects of the problem suddenly become clear, or some relation between the component parts of the problem were suddenly grasped, thereby permitting rapid and sudden solution. Examples of insight are illustrated in Figures 8.2 and 8.3.

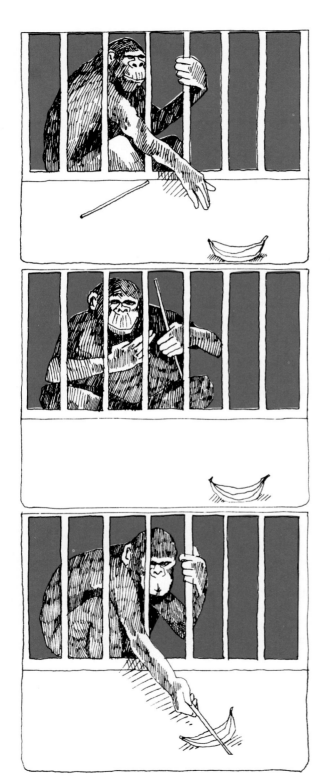

Figure 8.2
The chimp can't reach the banana, but it suddenly gains the *insight* that the stick may be used to gather in the banana.

Another source of evidence suggesting that representational thinking does indeed occur is the existence of mental imagery. For example, many chess masters are able to play the game skillfully even when blindfolded. This ability lends strong objective support to their claims that they have a mental image of the chessboard upon which they can register an opponent's moves and plan their own. (Individuals differ greatly in the extent to which they experience, utilize, and report mental imagery, a fact we have discussed in Chapter 2 and shall return to in this chapter.)

ORIGINS AND DEVELOPMENT OF THINKING

Two of the principal authorities on the development of thinking are Jean Piaget and Lev Vygotsky. The Swiss psychologist Piaget has developed an important theory in which he proposes that the development of thinking occurs in several stages. According to Piaget's theory, in the first major stage—the *sensorimotor period*—language is absent, and thinking is primitive. This stage endures for about the first two years of life, during which a child develops the idea of *object constancy*, which permits him to recognize an object despite variations in its placement or appearance from moment to moment. The child also develops anticipation of events during this initial period, which suggests that he is beginning to think. For example, if a ball rolls under a couch, the child will anticipate that it will be there if he crawls in after it. This recognition, that he himself can retrieve the ball, shows the child's ability to anticipate events, organize separate items in the perceptual field into patterns, and solve a problem. Although it is clear that such is the stuff that thinking is made of, the child in the sensorimotor stage still cannot perceive most relationships, not to mention symbolic and logical operations. (In Chapter

Figure 8.3
The pigeon in this detour problem (developed by the German psychologist Wolfgang Köhler) can get to the food cup behind the wire screen only by moving *away* from the cup and around the screen. The solution to the detour problem is often executed suddenly, suggesting sudden insight.

17, we shall discuss Piaget's theory of the development of thought.)

The Russian psychologist Vygotsky studied the relationship that existed between thinking and language during the early stages of child development. He proposed that thinking is produced by language, that language is learned first and then becomes internalized as thinking. (According to this view, of course, the sensorimotor child is not producing true thought.) However, Vygotsky also correctly pointed out that language and thinking should not be *equated*. We cannot, for example, express everything we are thinking, as exemplified by the tip-of-the-tongue phenomenon (see Chapter 2). When we grope for words and find ourselves unable to express a thought adequately, we are demonstrating that thinking is more than language.

THE RELATION OF LANGUAGE AND THINKING

Is language the expression of thought or does language in fact determine thought? Aside from Vygotsky's proposal on the origin of thinking (which we shall examine in more detail in Chapter 17), one of the strongest hypotheses relating language and thought is that of the anthropologist Benjamin Lee Whorf, who has contended that language determines thinking. He has argued that people in different parts of the world, speaking different lauguages, view the world in different ways. They have different modes of thinking, because thinking is determined by language and their languages differ in certain important ways. (See Figure 8.4.) Whorf's view is discussed in more detail in the following chapter. Although, in our view, Whorf's theory is probably not correct, it is fair to say that he has accurately recognized the close correspondence between language and thinking. Indeed, the two are so closely related that arguments about which one causes the other, or which is primary, have not proven very fruitful.

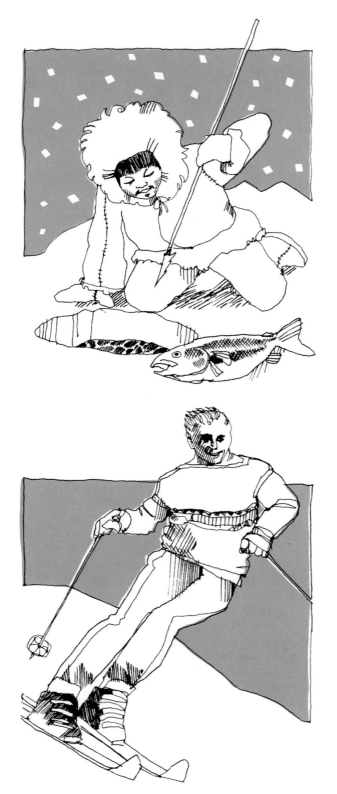

Figure 8.4
Eskimos have a very large number of terms for different kinds of snow, skiers have several, and many people have just one. But do Eskimos *think* differently about snow than skiers—or from people for whom "snow is snow"? The answer would be "yes" if thinking were determined by language—as the Whorf hypothesis suggests.

THOUGHT AND DREAMS

Do we think while we dream? Are dreams distinguishable from thinking? These are difficult questions to answer because the nature and content of an individual's dreams must be reconstructed from his memory. Nonetheless, there is no reason to believe that there is any fundamental distinction between thinking in the waking state and mental activity in dreams. Some theorists have insisted that thinking is more coordinated and generally clearer in the waking state. Although this hypothesis may be true, it is difficult to test. First of all, the mental activity that takes place in dreams may seem less clear because reports of dreams are only recollections in the waking state of what has transpired during the dream state, whereas descriptions of one's thinking during the waking state may be much more immediate and do not require resurrecting mental activity from one conscious state to another, that is, from dreaming to waking (as we shall see in Chapter 10). Second, a significant insight into a problem or the achievement of the solution itself during dreaming has occasionally been reported. Although it is difficult to evaluate such reports, they suggest that dynamic and even creative thinking may indeed occur during dreaming. In any event, whether or not one accepts the idea that dreaming is a form of thinking, it is safe to say that reports of dreams, like reports of thinking, necessarily constitute verbal reconstructions of internal events. Therefore, as such, they are influenced by the perceptions, experiences, memories, and motivations of the person making the report and are subject to the same kinds of inaccuracies that may occur in any report or recollection.

One type of dreaming—daydreaming—occurs in the waking state, but has a mind-wandering quality that seems distinct from normal thinking, and indeed from most dreams. Little is known scientifically about daydreaming, but the subjective reports of many people indicate that it too is strongly affected by factors such as perception and motivation.

THE FUNCTIONALIST VIEW: WHAT THINKING DOES

The functionalist point of view maintains that mental activity, such as thinking, enables us to adapt to fluctuations in the environment. From this point of view, then, the importance of thinking lies in its effects on us and on our world. Much of our thinking is directed toward achieving long-term goals or helping to regulate our behavior as we satisfy short-term goals.

But if we maintain that thinking is vital for regulating adaptive behavior, we should be able to specify how we get from thought to action—how do we bridge what has been call the *ideomotor* gap? What enables us to bridge this ideomotor gap is *psychomotor action,* which unfortunately is as poorly understood today as it was at the turn of the twentieth century when the American psychologist William James coined both terms. We can view language and other overt behavior as the public embodiment or expression of thinking, but exactly how psychomotor action makes this possible is not known. Also, we cannot say with any certainty why some of our thoughts are expressed in action and others are not: surely we all think about things we are not doing now nor ever will do. Which of our thoughts we select for public expression depends on many variables, such as the nature of the situation, our momentary motivation, our values, and our ability or willingness to put thought into action.

THEORETICAL APPROACHES TO THINKING

In this section we shall briefly consider the six most influential theoretical approaches to the subject of thinking. The ideas put forward by Freud, Piaget,

and B. F. Skinner have probably had the most significant impact on contemporary psychology. The views of the early behaviorists, the Gestalt psychologists, and, more recently, the information-processing theorists have also had an important impact. We shall see, however, that none of these theories has proven to be completely adequate. Most psychologists find that the various views complement one another, each making a valuable contribution to an understanding of the subject. It seems certain that all of them will be taken into account in any complete and adequate treatment of thinking that may ultimately be devised.

THE EARLY BEHAVIORISTS: THINKING AS SPEECH

John B. Watson (1878–1958), the founder of American behaviorism, equated speech and thought. This equation was directly based on the behaviorist position: behaviorists chose to study only observables, and therefore to circumvent the elusive problem of thought by defining it as *subvocal speech,* which obeyed the same rules as vocal speech. The behaviorist could then presumably study thought by observing the variables controlling speech.

If thought were merely subvocal speech, then some muscular correlate of thinking should be detectable in the vocal apparatus; it is for this reason that most of the experiments inspired by Watson's theory were attempts to find such correlates. Some experimenters tried to determine which tongue movements might be correlated with thought. Others looked for any similarities between thought and speech that might be apparent in tiny movements of the vocal cords. In retrospect we can see that this approach was unlikely to produce conclusive findings that would either prove or refute this *motor theory of thought,* for it was founded on the assumption that the muscular movements would be faint replicas of those required for real speech. It did not take into account the possibility that thought could possess all the functional properties of speech and still not possess its muscular properties. Moreover, most of the experimental work was inconclusive, since any positive results that supported the motor theory were subject to alternative interpretations, and negative results could always be dismissed on the grounds that the measuring instruments were not sensitive enough.

Some of the more interesting work on the behaviorist motor theory was done with deaf-mutes. Since deaf-mutes communicate with their fingers, they might be expected, when they think, to move their fingers more than would a control group of normal adults, whose thinking would be linked to muscular movement in their vocal apparatus. In one series of experiments, the subjects were given a variety of abstract problems to solve mentally. The correlation between motor activity in the fingers and thinking was considerably higher for deaf-mutes as a group than for their non-disabled counterparts. These results suggest that the motor theory cannot be entirely discounted. But it was also found that the higher the intelligence of a deaf-mute subject (as measured by a standard test), the lower was the correlation between thinking and motor activity. This finding has raised the interesting possibility that mediation of thought by motor activity is more common, or even more essential, in subjects with less intelligence. This hypothesis is in accord with the observation that children engage in more overt mediation than do adults; in other words, certain overt behaviors appear to have the function of facilitating thought—for example, counting on the fingers or pointing to words when reading.

Studies with animal subjects have shown that, as we move up the phylogenetic scale, the dependence on overt mediating activities in problem solving

decreases. In addition, observations of humans under stress have demonstrated that many regress to a greater dependence on overt mediation. All of these findings suggest that some kinds of motor activity in thinking may be important, or even essential, for the development of advanced symbolic abilities, but that they become increasingly less important once symbolic development is accomplished.

Although it is certainly not productive to view thinking simply as subvocal speech, it should be acknowledged that the motor theory of thinking, though incomplete, is partly correct. However, interest in the theory has faded as it has become increasingly evident that it is virtually untestable and is at best incomplete.

SKINNER AND VERBAL BEHAVIOR

A more modern behaviorist view of thinking was expounded by B. F. Skinner during his William James Lectures at Harvard University in 1947. Skinner viewed thinking as private behavior, which he maintained was determined by stimulus control and reinforcement in the same way as overt behavior. Skinner has written an important book, *Verbal Behavior,* in which he attempts to show that overt behavior and thinking are both determined by operant conditioning (see Chapter 4). In the following chapter on language (Chapter 9), Skinner's treatment of verbal behavior is discussed in some detail. In general, he maintains that a speaker-listener interaction is overt behavior, whereas, in thinking, the speaker is his own listener. The important point he makes is that thinking is behavior—be it covert or overt:

> When we study human thought, we study behavior. In the broadest possible sense, the thought of Julius Caesar was simply the sum total of his responses to the complex world in which he lived. We can study only those of which

we have records. For obvious reasons, it is primarily his verbal behavior which has survived in recorded form, but from this and other records we know something about his nonverbal behavior. When we say that he "thought Brutus could be trusted," we do not necessarily mean that he ever said as much. He behaved, verbally and otherwise, as if Brutus could be trusted. The rest of his behavior, his plans and achievements, are also part of his thought in this sense.*

Skinner also confronts the related and equally difficult problem of knowledge, which he designates as *potential behavior.* When we say, for example, that we "know the alphabet," what we mean is that we have the potential for reciting it.

FREUD AND UNCONSCIOUS THOUGHT

The Viennese psychiatrist Sigmund Freud (1856–1939) showed that some thinking is unconscious, in other words, that a person is unaware of some of his thoughts (there are examples in Chapter 24, where Freud's ideas are discussed in more detail). In essence, his theory centered on the unconscious memories and desires that affect attitudes and influence behavior, rather than on the mechanism of thought. Concentrating on the fact that thinking and "lapses" of thinking do occur, Freud attempted to infer their motivational sources.

PIAGET'S DEVELOPMENTAL APPROACH

As we mentioned previously, Piaget maintains that man's thinking evolves in a series of successive stages of development. His theory is discussed in detail in Chapter 17, and therefore, like Freud's, need be considered only briefly here. For Piaget, the

*Skinner, B. F. *Verbal Behavior.* New York: Appleton-Century-Crofts, 1957, pp. 451–452.

mind of the adult that has emerged from the developmental process is qualitatively different from the mind of the child. In the early stages of development, the child sees world and self as one: for example, he believes the sun moves because it is following him. In a subsequent stage he thinks that the sun *wants* to move, and then that it moves because of primitively conceived mechanical forces—because it is being "pushed." Still later, the child develops the adult's abstract view of the sun's movements. As the child's thinking progresses through each stage, it becomes less self-oriented and more complex, permitting the child to perceive and understand increasingly more of the world around him, until abstract thought and reasoning ultimately develop.

THE GESTALT PSYCHOLOGISTS: THE HOLISTIC APPROACH

The *gestalt psychologists*—whose school was founded in Germany in the early part of this century—emphasized the importance of organization in thinking and perception. The gestalt movement had its greatest impact on the study of the comprehension of perceptual phenomena, as we shall see in Chapter 14. With respect to thinking, the gestalt psychologists stressed the usefulness of looking at the whole field, or the context, in which thinking is occurring, and demonstrated this usefulness in a series of experiments on problem solving, in which thinking was studied in various goal-oriented situations. From these studies, the gestalt psychologists derived the concept of *restructuring* the problem to achieve an optimal solution. They maintain that such reformulation is necessary for many problems to permit one to grasp the relations that are crucial for gaining the insight that will lead to the solution. Examples of restructuring will be given in the discussion of empirical studies of thinking later in this chapter.

THE INFORMATION-PROCESSING APPROACH

The *information-processing approach* to thinking bears some similarity to the gestalt approach. Both have focused on problem-solving behavior, and both stress the importance of reformulating problems to make them more readily solvable. In addition, psychologists subscribing to the information-processing approach have contributed many innovations to the study of thinking and have tightened experimental methodology in that area. For example, information processors have developed elaborate models that are proposed descriptions of human information processing and problem solving. In their work, they have relied on computers as devices for simulating human thinking and problem-solving.

The basic reason for employing computers in the study of problem solving is that computers can be programmed to simulate human behaviors, even though no computer yet devised has the elegance or complexity of the human brain. By programming a computer to solve certain kinds of problems the way a human being does, we may gain an understanding of human problem-solving—by analogy—because we know how the computer has been programmed.

The use of computer-simulation models of thinking raises several basic questions. First, can the computer think? (Figure 8.5.) Although we may be inclined to reject such a proposal out of hand, it nevertheless deserves thoughtful consideration. If the computer can play a brilliant chess game and flawless checkers, and if it seems to employ the same game-playing strategies that some humans do, on what basis can we refute the proposition that the computer is thinking? Obviously we can do so only if we know that there are certain additional dimensions of human thinking that are not present in the machine's problem-solving operations.

Figure 8.5
Can the computer think?

One obvious basis for rejecting the suggestion that computers think is our subjective impression of what our own thinking actually is; nevertheless, although the computer may not "experience" thinking in the way we do, its overt behavior in regard to a given problem may be shown to manifest the same strategies and actions as our own. Moreover, the computer program provides the computer with internal representations that are indisputably as effective as our own. Although the skeptic may insist that the computer's behavior is limited to what it has been programmed to do, the fact remains that our own behavior is determined—or programmed—jointly by our genetic endowment and our previous experience (see Chapters 15 and 16). Theoretically, then, there may not be that much difference between the computer's problem solving and our own. But it must be noted that, even though a computer may behave in exactly the same way we do in regard to a given problem, there is no guarantee whatsoever that it is following the same principles.

In developing computer-simulation models, one begins with an analysis of the actual problem-solving behavior of humans: for example, to construct a chess-playing program, one first determines the strategies of chess masters and the actual moves of competent human players. On the basis of such analyses, computer programs are designed with the purpose of simulating human problem solving. If a program's output successfully simulates human problem solving, the premises that have been incorporated into the program are accepted as valid. However, if the computer fails to behave in the way that the human does, the experimenter realizes that his model is either incomplete or in error, the program is modified, and the simulation is attempted again. Gradually, a program emerges that directs the computer to simulate human behavior.

The pioneer investigation of computer simulation was made by H. A. Simon, A. Newell, and J. C. Shaw in the late 1950s. Their information-processing model, the "Logic Theorist," was able to prove thirty-eight of fifty-two symbolic-logic theorems taken from *Principia Mathematica,* a major work published by the English mathematicians and philosophers Alfred N. Whitehead and Bertrand Russell over a half-century ago. The significant feature of the Logic Theorist was that its computer program did not test every possible sequence of logical operations in performing the proofs. Such an exhaustive task, like surveying every possible consequence of every available move on a chess board, would not reflect human problem solving at all accurately. Instead, the Logic Theorist used *heuristic strategies* for problem solving. There are several types of heuristic strategies, each of which is a kind of "restructuring of the field" reminiscent of gestalt theory. One type of strategy is *working backwards,* so that the human (or computer) begins at the desired result and tries to work backwards until the initial state is attained. The *means-end strategy* is an analysis of the difference be-

tween the initial state and the desired goal, followed by attempts to minimize the differences between them. Operations that are successful in reducing the difference are repeated until the desired state is achieved. A third strategy is the *make-a-plan* strategy, in which the human (or computer) formulates a problem—with a known solution—that is similar to the problem to be solved; the known solution is then used to devise a solution for the new problem.

Scores of computer-simulation models have been developed since the introduction of the Logic Theorist. They include models for game playing, attitude change, verbal learning, pattern recognition, decision making, and even forms of neurotic behavior. Although many of these information-processing models have proved valuable in helping us to understand complex behavioral processes, one limitation is that each addresses itself only to one specific type of problem solving. In contrast, Newell, Shaw, and Simon's "General Problem Solver" (GPS) has proved particularly exciting and promising. The GPS incorporates some of the heuristic strategies, concepts, and analyses common to the specific information-processing models and applies them to a wider variety of problems. Although it has successfully solved a large number of problems that differ sharply in content, it has been inadequate for others. Nonetheless, it is an excellent beginning for the development of a truly comprehensive problem solver.

STUDIES OF THINKING AND PROBLEM SOLVING

In this section, we shall attempt to convey the general spirit that has prevailed in the research recently conducted in the area of thinking, particularly in problem solving. Most of the work has been rooted in one or more of the theoretical perspectives discussed in the preceding section, but some approaches to particular problems have not been drawn from any particular theory of thinking.

INTROSPECTION AND SELF-REPORT

Around 1900, an introspective approach to thinking grew out of the *structuralist school of psychology,* whose followers searched for the "structural elements" of experience. Emulating the chemists of the period, who were analyzing chemical compounds into their component elements, the structuralists tried to analyze human subjective experience into its elements. This analytic technique, called experimental *introspection,* was applied to thinking primarily by German psychologists at the University of Würzburg. A common procedure would be to present the subject with a "stimulus" (the word "night," for example) and ask him to respond with words describing his conscious reaction to the stimulus. However, the technique yielded little information about the mental operations of thinking, because—although the subjects reported images, and the images could be influenced to some extent by the experimenter—both the subjects' conscious reports and the experimenters' analyses clearly indicated that the chain of images was not a sufficient description of thought. Thus, although the word "night" might be reliably expected to produce one or a number of images, the subject could rarely describe any intervening mental activity between his initial perception of the stimulus word and the utterance of his response. Thus he would say that a particular response ("day," for example) had simply "sprung to mind." The introspectionist work by this Würzburg school revealed that although images often accompany thought, *imageless thought* can also occur and is in fact common.

Why did work by the introspectionists fail to reveal much about the thought processes? One reason was the marked difference among individuals in their imagery (that is, the ability to produce images). For example, the French geometrician Poincaré said that he lacked the ability to visualize space. Obviously this deficiency did not hinder his brilliant geometric feats. This does not mean, of course, that imagery may not sometimes be helpful to thinking: Beethoven's auditory imagery enabled him to compose masterworks after he went deaf; Emile Zola's acute olfactory imagery permeates his prose; and the psychologist Francis Galton was capable of such vivid visual imagery that he was shocked to find that other scientists could get along without it. The introspective method is also inadequate because it depends on people's descriptions of their thoughts, and there is never any guarantee that these reports from two different subjects are indeed reports of similar conscious experience. In addition, the only descriptions available are those of images, and thinking is made of deeper stuff than conscious images: there is more to thinking than meets the mind's eye.

STUDIES OF THINKING WITH ANIMALS

Gestalt psychologists, such as Wolfgang Köhler (1887–1967), as well as behaviorists, such as Edward C. Tolman (1886-1959), have demonstrated that animals think. This finding should not be surprising, of course, since many of the complex learned behaviors of which animals are capable (see Chapter 4) would be very difficult indeed without some form of internal representation. This is not to say that thought processes in lower organisms are even remotely equivalent to those in man; man is presumably more symbol-oriented, more analytical, and capable of processing and remembering more information than any other organism. Nonetheless, animals exhibit many forms of behavior that have traditionally been assumed to be solely products of human thinking.

Tolman and his followers adequately demonstrated that animals develop expectancies and exhibit insight. (1) Expectancy has been demonstrated in experiments in which a less preferred food is substituted for a preferred food as a reward for a learned response: the result is an immediate decrement in responding, accompanied by obvious distress, suggesting that the subject had learned to expect the preferred food. (2) Tolman and his followers demonstrated insight in rats confronted with detour problems, such as those shown in Figure 8.6. After a rat had become acquainted with the runway, blocks were placed in one of two places. When the animal found that the short path to the goal was blocked it naturally took the next shortest path. When the block was placed in the portion of the maze common to both the shortest and next shortest path, however, the rat demonstrated that it had developed a *cognitive map* of the runway: after finding the short path closed, it shunned the next shortest path (which would also have led to the block) and chose the longest, but unblocked, route to the goal.

In 1917, Köhler published an account of his observation of insight in the chimpanzee. Köhler devised a double-stick problem, in which the chimp Sultan had to reach a banana lying outside his cage. Not only was the banana outside Sultan's grasp but also neither of the two sticks in his cage was long enough to reach it. The key to the solution was that the two sticks were hollow, and the end of one could be fitted inside the other, to form a single long stick. After a few minutes had elapsed, Sultan pushed one stick as far out of the cage as it would go and then pushed it with the second stick. Al-

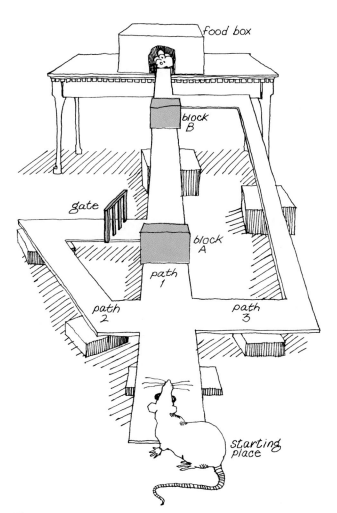

Figure 8.6
This drawing is based on a diagram of a maze used to test insight in rats: Path 1 is preferred to Path 2, and Path 2 is preferred to Path 3. If Path 1 is closed by Block A, the rats run by Path 2 after finding Path 1 closed. The placement of Block B, however, closes both Paths 1 and 2. The rat demonstrates insight by shunning Path 2 (after finding Path 1 closed) and runs by Path 3 instead. [Adapted from E. C. Tolman and C. H. Honzik, "Insight" in Rats," *University of California Publications in Psychology, 4*, 1930, 215–232.]

though this action enabled him to move the banana, he could not bring it within reach. The experimenter returned the second stick and, after about an hour, Sultan picked up the two sticks, played carelessly with them, and, suddenly, inserted the end of the thinner one into the thicker. Having done so, he went immediately to the side of the cage nearest the banana and attempted to bring home the banana. On his first try, the sticks came apart, but Sultan promptly reconnected them and obtained the banana. (See Figure 8.7.)

Figure 8.7
Köhler's chimp Sultan learned to assemble a long stick from two shorter ones.

PROBLEM SOLVING

We have all been confronted by many types of problems, and we can usually evaluate the efficiency and success of our solutions. Indeed, we devote much of our lives to solving problems. Almost

LIST A	LIST B	LIST C
mawon	idtio	isad
nclue	oofl	rwtoe
hcild	ldot	ldot

Figure 8.8
Some anagrams. Try them.

everything we do is directed toward some goal or other, most of which are attainable only after we have managed to cope with certain problems. Often the means for realizing some of life's more important goals—such as a successful career, a happy marriage, a peaceful life—are not at all discernible; that is to say, the problems that must be solved are not clearly specified. Moreover, even when they are, the possible solutions may not be well defined, nor is it clear what strategies should be undertaken for obtaining them. Finally, we may fail to recognize a successful solution, or may make the mistake of thinking we have attained one when we have not. However, studies of problem solving in the laboratory circumvent these difficulties by establishing a fairly precise specification of the problem to be solved, a reasonably well-defined set of possible solutions, and a reasonably clear method for evaluating success. Although generalizations formulated from the extensive experimental work on problem solving are not likely to help an individual choose a career, select a spouse, or obtain a sense of self-fulfillment, they do provide information that is applicable to solving the more mundane problems that we must cope with from day to day.

In a problem-solving experiment, the delineation of the problem and the evaluation of the solution are done by the experimenter, but the identification of the possible solutions generally rests with the subject. One effective procedure for achieving the correct solution is to determine whether or not an *algorithm* exists for the problem. Algorithms are sets of rules, which, when followed, must lead to a solution because they are systematically applied, in a specified order, to all possibilities and their outcomes. But algorithms, though exhaustive, are tedious and often completely impractical, except for very simple problems. More useful are simpler strategies for finding a solution. Basically, heuristic strategies are rules of thumb for restructuring a

problem in a certain way, thus permitting the problem solver to conserve his time by limiting his efforts to the more productive of the alternative strategies. Some examples of heuristic strategies were given in the preceding section, when we discussed the Logic Theorist.

Trial-and-error Solution   Often we solve simple problems, such as anagrams, by simple trial and error. Rather than applying an elegant strategy, we try out each alternative solution in turn until we happen on one that appears to be correct. Since it is the solution, and not the number of errors, that is important, a more appropriate name for this approach woud be *trials-until-success.*

The facility and speed with which an individual arrives at a solution to an anagram can be affected by his *set*—his predisposition to approach the problem in a certain, restrictive manner. For example, the third anagram in Figure 8.8 will be more readily solved by a subject who has just worked the first two anagrams, because he will then have a "set" for references to people ("woman," "uncle," and "child"). Similarly, the anagram "ldot" will probably be approached differently by subjects who have already experienced "idtio" and "oofl" than by those who have been presented with "isad" and "rwtoe."

Concept Learning   Another group of studies of problem solving involves concept learning. *Concepts* refer to learned symbolic responses that occur in reaction to each of the members of a given class of stimuli. The classes are based on the form, function, or other common properties of the stimuli making up the class. In one of the pioneer studies of concept formation, experimenters used figures similar to those shown in Figure 8.9. After looking at a few of the positive and negative examples of the nonsense words, "tibs" and "doxs," a person should be able to

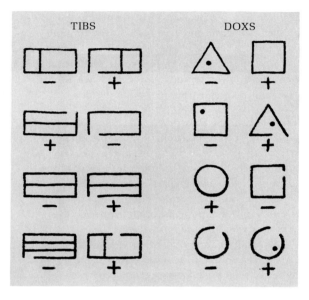

TIBS   DOXS

Figure 8.9
Positive (+) and negative (−) examples of nonsense
words ("tibs" and "doxs") of the type used in concept-
learning tasks.

generate the concepts. Moreover, he should be able
to identify whether or not a new example belongs to
either class. Research has shown that subjects can
sometimes label new figures correctly even though
they cannot consciously state the defining characteristics of the concept.

Jerome Bruner's work on conceptual development
in children has been extremely revealing. For
example, in one study, Bruner showed that young
children tend to group objects according to their
perceptual characteristics, whereas older children
tend to group them according to functional characteristics: thus, a five-year-old will probably group the
set of objects shown in Figure 8.10 by color, whereas

most older children will group them according to
their potential use. We will discuss the child's
development of concepts in Chapter 17.

Insight   For many problems, the solution depends
on our ability to restructure the field, and such
restructuring often requires insightful behavior.
An important characteristic of insight is that apprehension of the solution generally *precedes* the
problem-solving behavior. For example, when Sultan
solved the double-stick problem, he appeared to
have gained insight into the solution immediately
prior to inserting the thinner stick into the thicker
one (see Figure 8.7). This conclusion can, of course,
only be inferred from the fact that Sultan looked
at the two sticks, surveyed the visual field including
the banana, and then suddenly and smoothly
executed the novel solution.

What determines how insightful we are? Are there
factors that facilitate insightful behavior? Certainly
there is no doubt that *experience* can be very helpful.
If animals solve successive series of problems, they
tend to solve them progressively more quickly—in
effect, they are *learning to learn*. In part, learning to
learn depends on *transfer of training* (see Chapter
2), including the transfer of appropriate strategies.
But there are important exceptions to the generalization that experience teaches us how to solve
problems and increases the likelihood that we will
demonstrate insight when faced with future
problems. In some cases, prior problem-solving
experiences can actually *hinder* subsequent problem
solving, as illustrated in the following discussion.

Figure 8.10
These objects tend to be grouped according to perceptual
characteristics (e. g., color) by young children, but
according to functional characteristics (e. g., potential
use) by most older children.

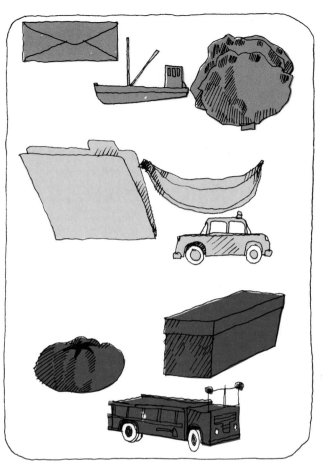

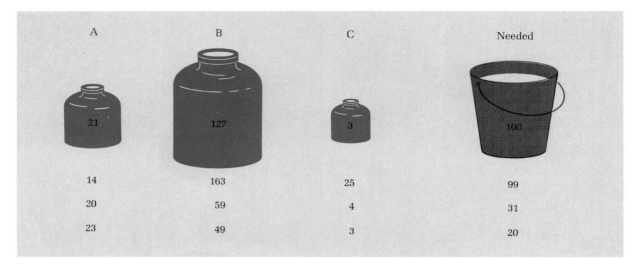

A	B	C	Needed
21	127	3	100
14	163	25	99
20	59	4	31
23	49	3	20

Figure 8.11
Subjects in Luchins' experiment were required to use three measuring jars, whose capacities are indicated by numbers, to obtain a given amount of water. [Adapted from A. S. Luchins, "Mechanization in Problem Solving," *Psychological Monographs*, 42, (Whole No. 248), 1942. Copyright 1942 by the American Psychological Association.]

Rigidity, Set, and Creativity In 1942, A. S. Luchins reported an exhaustive study of the problem solving of children, college students—and even college instructors. The basic task was a computational one, performed on the blackboard, in which subjects were required to state how they would obtain a given amount of water, using three measuring jars. They were required to work out a series of these problems; the amount of water required and the sizes of the empty measuring jars varied for each one (see Figure 8.11). For example, in the first problem, the three empty jars (A, B, and C) could hold 21, 127, and 3 units of water, respectively, and the required amount of water was 100 units. In the next problem Jars A, B, and C held 14, 163, and 25 units, respectively, and 99 units of water were required. In the third problem, the measures were 20, 59, and 4 units, and 31 units of water were required. Note that in each of the problems, the requisite amount of water can be obtained by filling Jar B and then reducing that amount by pouring enough from it to fill Jar A once and Jar C twice. In other words, the equation, $B - (A + 2C)$, provided the solution to all of the problems in this first series. Then, in the next problem, Jars A, B, and C held 23, 49, and 3 units, and subjects were required to figure out how to obtain 20 units. Those who had worked on the first series continued to

employ the strategy that had been successful in all of the previous problems [that described by the equation, $B - (A + 2C)$]. Observe, however, that a much simpler solution is $A - C$. When this was pointed out to subjects, they were embarrassed. Control subjects, who had not had the prior experience with the first series of problems, readily solved this problem by means of the simpler approach.

Luchins' study demonstrated that problem-solving experience often provides the subject with a "set" for solving a problem in a particular way, and this set may interfere with subsequent problem solving. In his final problem, the set that had been gained from solving the preceding problems led to a correct, though unduly complex, solution. In addition, Luchins showed that subjects would persist in trying an old solution, even when it failed to solve a new problem. This reliance on a habitual solution interfered with the thoughtful consideration of potential solutions that is required for effective problem solving. In a sense, the subjects became

Figure 8.12
Charlie Chaplin, as an assembly-line worker in "Modern Times," often overcame functional fixedness. Here, he finds a novel use for his wrenches. [The Museum of Modern Art/Film Stills Archive. © The Roy Export Company Establishment.]

fixated on the older solution, so that *rigidity* hindered their problem-solving ability.

Other dramatic examples of fixations in problem solving, based on the interference of prior experience, are found in the work of N. R. F. Maier, Karl Duncker, and others, on *functional fixedness.* Whereas the fixation in Luchins' studies was a fixation of *method*, functional fixedness refers to fixation of *function*, that is, a tendency to assign only one function to a particular tool or object: thus, experience in using a tool or object in a certain way decreases the likelihood that the same item may be used in a novel way in the future. (See Figure 8.12.) For example, experimental subjects may be given a number of tools and required to perform a task, such as building a stand. In one study, those who

were first given a problem that required them to use a tool, such as a pair of pliers, in one of the usual ways (for example, to unfasten nuts) had difficulty later in using the pliers for a novel application (for example, as a simple weight on a pendulum). On the other hand, subjects who were not first required to use the pliers in the standard way were adept at employing them successfully for the novel task.

To overcome functional fixedness and the kind of rigidity illustrated by Luchins' experiments, subjects must undergo training in a variety of problems, so that they will learn to try a variety of responses in a problem situation: in other words, so that they will acquire *creativity*. One means of increasing the likelihood of obtaining creative solutions is the technique of *brainstorming*, developed by industrial psychologists. In brainstorming, a group of employees is brought together and asked to generate ideas as rapidly as possible, often stating the first thing that comes to their minds. The aim is to come up with some suggestion that, though wild and impractical, may contain the germ of an original idea, which, in turn, may be extracted and subsequently refined by others in the brainstorming group. In essence, brainstorming is a method for generating scores of ideas rapidly in the hope of coming up with creative suggestions that are ultimately workable. It is thus a kind of mental trial and error, in which novel verbal behavior is reinforced and developed by other members of the group.

INTELLIGENCE

What do we mean by intelligence? If you were to say that a certain student is "intelligent," you would probably mean that he is verbally facile, does well in school, and appears to have a knack for solving

problems and devising ingenious solutions. In
general, then, we tend to equate intelligence with
creativity and verbal fluency, and we usually infer
its presence in an individual from his achievements,
or at least his success in avoiding failure. Unfortunately, our everyday definitions of intelligence are
not very precise or entirely adequate. There is an
old story about a motorist who was stranded near
a mental hospital when a wheel on his Cadillac
started wobbling because three of six lug nuts had
worked loose and dropped off. As the motorist stood
scratching his head, a shabbily dressed patient came
over to the fence and suggested that the motorist
stagger the remaining three lug nuts so the wheel
would stay on until he could drive the car to a
garage. When the man looked surprised to get such
good advice, the patient smiled and said, "I may be
crazy, but I'm not stupid."

When we actually attempt to measure intelligence,
its definition becomes very difficult. Indeed, the most
precise statement we can make is that intelligence is
what an intelligence test measures: the degree of intelligence is designated by the score obtained on
the test. Although this definition may seem superficial, it is impossible to substitute one that is better,
unless perhaps we rely on some everyday explanation—for instance, that intelligence is a combination
of creativity, verbal fluency, and intellectual accomplishment. In spite of the difficulty in defining
intelligence, tests have long been used as devices
for measuring the intelligence of school children
and often for assigning them to different programs.

BINET'S CONTRIBUTION
TO INTELLIGENCE

The French psychologist, Alfred Binet, constructed
the first formal *intelligence test* in 1905. He did so at
the request of the French government, which wanted
to identify those children who were unlikely to profit
from a standard educational program.

Figure 8.13
Alfred Binet. [Historical Pictures Service, Chicago]

Binet's basic strategy, and the strengths and
weaknesses of the test that he constructed, are
representative of the contemporary intelligence tests
that will be discussed in the next sections. The
general structure of the test was founded on Binet's
assumption that "dull" or "subnormally intelligent"
children should perform in the same manner as
younger children of normal intelligence. The test
consisted of a series of questions on a graded scale,
each level of difficulty supposedly corresponding
to a year of chronological age. Thus, if a child could
answer as many questions as an average six-year-old,
he was said to have a *mental age (MA)* of six. If his
real or *chronological age (CA)* were in fact eight, he
would be retarded; if it were four, he would be
gifted. This basic notion was incorporated by Stern
and Terman into their formula for determining the
intelligence quotient (IQ):

$$IQ = \frac{MA}{CA} \times 100$$

WHAT DOES IQ MEAN?

The formula above shows that a child with a mental age of precisely 6.0 but with a chronological age of 8.0 would have an IQ of 75. The gifted child with the same mental age but with a chronological age of 4.0 would have an IQ of 150. Binet employed a work-sample approach to assess the validity of the questions for each year of his scale: he selected skills—including simple perceptual tasks, such as recognizing the difference between two lines of un-equal length, and verbal tasks, such as identifying the definition of abstract words—many of which were obviously related to school achievement. He used them to predict overall achievement in suc-cessive grades (and at the corresponding age levels). Thus a child of seven who has the demonstrated verbal and arithmetic ability of an average eight-year-old is judged to have a higher *aptitude* for accelerated achievement than an average seven-year-old. In other words, a student who has learned at a pace that is more rapid than normal will probably continue to do so. However, this predictability is complicated by the possibility that a particular student might have had a better-than-average op-portunity to acquire the requisite intellectual skills, just as another seven-year-old might manifest a mental age of six years as a result of an impov-erished educational environment.

Is there a way to assess aptitude without confusing it with previous achievement? The typical approach has been to try to ensure that all subjects will have about the same degree of acquaintance with the items on the test. Thus, all items might be com-pletely novel: for example, those in a so-called "culture-fair" test might consist of abstract geometric forms that no child has seen before. Thus the nature of the test items does not place children raised or residing in one particular culture at an advantage or disadvantage over those from another culture. Or, conversely, an effort might be made to include only

items that will be familiar to all subjects: for example, reasoning tasks using only words that every child is expected to know (such as "mother," "food," and "steps"). However, neither type of test is definitive. For one thing, even if we judge the items of a test to be thoroughly familiar, we can never be certain that a child has been taught the meaning of what we assume to be the simplest of words. Another more important element of uncertainty—applicable whether test items are familiar or novel—is due to the fact that reasoning or inference is required on the part of the child. Critics correctly point out that this faculty itself may have been taught. In other words, IQ tests may simply measure the general *transfer of training* from reasoning tasks successfully learned in school or in the home to novel reasoning tasks. It is evident, then, that it is impossible to talk of tests that measure pure aptitude. *All aptitude tests necessarily measure achievement.*

The real difference between *aptitude* and *achievement* tests lies in their different objectives. Achievement tests (such as final examinations in courses) are simply attempts to measure what a subject has al-ready learned, whereas aptitude tests (such as IQ tests) measure what a subject has learned so that some aspect of future performance may be predicted. The IQ tests have proved to predict academic achievement successfully; that is, it has been shown that most children who have achieved well in the past continue to do so.

CURRENT IQ TESTS

The modern descendent of Binet's original scale is the *Stanford-Binet test*. In one form of the test, six widely varying items are presented for each year of mental age. Each question is worth two points (or two months). Thus, if a child correctly answers all of the thirty-six items through Year Six, he earns seventy-two points (two for each answer). Assume further that he correctly answers four of the six items for Year Seven, five of the six items for Year Eight, two of the items for Year Nine, and none of the items for the more advanced levels. He has, then, answered an additional eleven items, worth an additional twenty-two months, so that his total score (72 + 22) is 94 months. What is his IQ? Obviously this depends on his chronological age. If he is ninety-four months old, his IQ is 100. If he is, for example, exactly seven-years-old (eighty-four months), his IQ is 112 (94 divided by 84, multiplied by 100). The Stanford-Binet test has undergone frequent revisions, but the basic significance of the IQ score remains the same: it is a relative score, assessing the performance of the individual child in relation to that of the general population of children to age sixteen; thus, scores above or below 100 are *relative* to the *average* score of 100 obtained by an average child within a given age group. On the basis of their scores, children are placed into one of several arbitrary categories ranging from *mentally retarded* to *mentally gifted*. Thus, the bottom 25 children in a typical sample of 1,000 (scores below 70) are arbitrarily described as *mentally retarded*, whereas the top 25 children (scores above 130) are arbitrarily described as *mentally gifted*. The distribution of IQ scores within a typical segment of the population is shown in Figure 8.14.

The other popular IQ test is the *Wechsler Intelligence Scale*. The Wechsler test, like the Binet test, includes several types of items. Unlike the Stanford-Binet test, however, the Wechsler test scores each type of item separately, producing Wechsler Intelligence Scales of verbal comprehension, arithmetic comprehension, vocabulary, picture completion, picture arrangement, block designs, and several others. These can all be classified into two basic types of scales: verbal and performance. Items on the verbal scales, which include the vocabulary, arithmetic, and verbal-comprehension scales, can be answered with pencil and

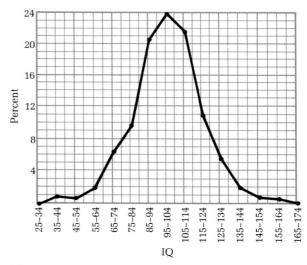

Figure 8.14
A typical distribution of IQ scores for children and youths aged two to eighteen. [Adapted from L. M. Terman and M. A. Merrill, *Measuring Intelligence*. Boston: Houghton Mifflin, 1937.]

paper. Items on the performance scales, such as the block design, picture completion, and picture-arrangement scales, require manipulation of objects. There are separate Wechsler scales for adults and children, although both are similarly constructed. The scores on the Wechsler test, particularly those for the verbal scale, are quite well correlated with scores on the Stanford-Binet test, suggesting that both tests measure the same sorts of abilities.

FACTORS AFFECTING IQ

It appears that IQ is affected by a *combination* of inherited and environmental factors, as we will see in Chapter 16. Although we cannot determine with any certainty the extent of the influence of either heredity or environment, most studies have suggested that genetic influence is often substantial, accounting for a significant amount of the variation in IQ. This finding does not indicate, of course, that environmental influence is not significant. It is possible that the less stimulating the environment, the less its effect on IQ, leaving a correspondingly greater proportion of the variation to be contributed by hereditary

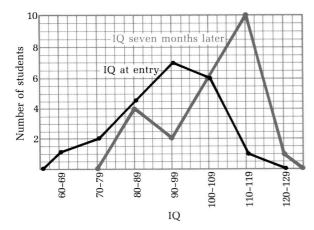

Figure 8.15
The distributions of IQ scores for twenty-four students in a Washington, D.C., reform school, both before and after introduction of a remedial education program using monetary incentives in order to improve performance in academic subjects. [Adapted from H. L. Cohen and J. Filipczak, *A New Learning Environment*. San Francisco: Jossey-Bass, Inc., 1971.]

factors. Thus, by providing children with a rich variety of intellectual and perceptual stimulation, we may be able to increase the environment's contribution to IQ. Recent studies have shown that intensive remedial education of poor children can sometimes produce IQ increases of fifteen points or more within a period of a few months. Figure 8.15 gives the results from one such study, utilizing a monetary incentive system—to maximize motivation for learning academic course material—with reform-school teenagers. In this study, the average IQ of the students rose twelve-and-one-half points after seven months of such motivated academic study—a remarkable increase. This emphasizes the strong relationship between IQ and academic achievement. Just as problem-solving ability derives in large part from the nature of a person's past experience, performance on intelligence tests is greatly influenced by the person's prior experience in verbalizing, reasoning, and interacting with the world.

Suggested Readings

Bartlett, F. (1958) *Thinking.* New York: Basic Books. [A classic overview of thinking.]

Cohen, H. L., & Filipczak, J. (1971) *A new learning environment.* San Francisco: Jossey-Bass. [The techniques of operant conditioning successfully applied to problem learners.]

Lindsay, P. H., & Norman, D. A. (1972) *Human information processing.* New York: Academic Press, Inc. [A modern overview of human information processing.]

Neisser, U. (1967) *Cognitive psychology.* New York: Appleton-Century-Crofts. [A good treatment of psychological research on thinking.]

Newell, A., Shaw, J. C., & Simon, H. A. (1958) "Elements of a theory of human problem solving." *Psychological review,* 65, 151–166. [One of the pioneer articles on the new human information processing.]

Piaget, J. (1953) *The origins of intelligence in children.* London: Routledge and Kegan Paul. [Piaget on intelligence.]

Skinner, B. F. (1957) *Verbal behavior.* New York: Appleton-Century-Crofts. [Skinner's challenging treatise on the behavioral approach to language.]

Vygotsky, L. S. (1962) *Thought and language.* Cambridge: M.I.T. Press. [Vygotsky's classic work on thought, language, and their interrelation.]

Wertheimer, M. (1945) *Productive thinking.* New York: Harper. [An excellent book on the gestalt approach to thinking and problem solving.]

Whorf, B. L. (1956) *Language, thought and reality.* New York: Wiley. [An engaging exposition of Whorf's hypothesis.]

CHAPTER NINE

Language

What is _language_? We shall approach this question in three very different ways and shall consider language as a form of behavior, as a mental activity, and as a vehicle of communication. When focusing on language as behavior, we attempt to explain its intricacies and complexities by applying the rules that govern other forms of behavior. When treating it as a mental activity, we are interested in the competence an individual must possess in order to speak and understand any language, even at an elementary level. When concentrating on language as a vehicle of communication, we ask _what_ is communicated as well as _how_ communications are received and interpreted. This broad range of questions explains why the different branches of psychology have proposed varying descriptions of language.

In this chapter, we shall first examine language as a vehicle, or medium, man makes use of for communicating meaning to others; then we shall examine language as a set of rules necessary for competent communication; finally, we shall build a case for defining language as behavior that exists not merely to communicate nor as an expression of knowledge, but rather because of its effects on the world of the speaker and his listeners. The reader should realize from the start that an understanding of language rests on a recognition that language is _highly regular and structured human behavior that is employed as a means of communication between individuals because of its effects on listeners._

Be careful not to equate language with speech: there is much more to language than vocal sounds. People communicate with each other and affect each other with many kinds of behavior besides speech— by written words, silent movies, pictures, gestures (see Figure 9.1), facial expressions, and even by the transmission of odors and tactile sensations.

THE MEANING OF MEANING

When someone speaks to you, what is communicated is the meaning of what is said. Only part of that meaning is conveyed by the words actually used. At least an equally large part is communicated by how the words are said and by how you interpret them. For example, the meaning of "There is a bug in the living room" depends not only on the meaning of the words in the sentence, but also on how the speaker says it, who the speaker is, and the

Figure 9.1
Joyce Lynch appears on "Newsign Four," a daily television news program for the deaf, broadcast in San
Francisco. Here, she announces the name of the program.
In American Sign Language, the word "news" is conveyed by the flowing motion that starts in the upper
left-hand photograph and ends in the upper right-hand
photograph. The word "sign" is shown in the lower
left-hand photograph. The word "four" is shown in
the lower right-hand photograph.
[Photographs courtesy of KRON-TV, Channel 4, Chron-
icle Broadcasting Company]

context in which the sentence is spoken—that is, what the speaker has just been talking about and doing, what he does when he utters that particular sentence, and what you, as a listener, expect him to be talking about. For example, if a small child runs out of the living room, agitated, white-faced, and screaming, the meaning you extract from the sentence will be quite different from what you will discern if the speaker is an FBI agent calmly describing his plan to obtain evidence on a gang of narcotics smugglers by planting eavesdropping equipment in the home of the suspected ring leader (Figure 9.2).

Such dissimilar interpretations of the same string of words have promoted linguists, philosophers, and a few psychologists to dissect the concept of "meaning" into various kinds of meaning. Hence, there is a difference between the *denotative meaning* and the *connotative meaning* of a word or symbol. Denotation is the reference to a real and describable item (it is the kind of specific meaning contained in a dictionary definition, for example) whereas connotation suggests the emotional tone of a word or sentence—such as that conveyed by the agitated scream in the first example. A similar distinction is often made between *intentional meaning* and *extensional meaning*, the one referring to what the speaker intends to convey and the other to all of the other bits of information that he conveys without necessarily intending to do so.

To reiterate, a listener's interpretation of a particular sentence depends not only on what is said but also on the context. There are two fundamental types of context: (1) the situation in which it is spoken (the environmental situation), and (2) the set of associations that the listener has already acquired. In the reference to the bug in the living room, then, your interpretation of the speaker's meaning is partly determined by the situation you see him in as well as which association ("insect" or "radio")

Figure 9.2
The meaning of an ambiguous sentence is often clarified by the context in which it is uttered. Each of the above situations suggests different meaning for the sentence: "There is a bug in the living room."

occurs to you when you hear him speak. Each type of context has traditionally been identified with a different psychological view of language. The *environmental situation of the speaker* has been emphasized by behaviorists, who maintain that it acts as a stimulus that controls the listener's behavior just as the actual words do. In contrast, the mentalists have stressed the *associations of the listener,* or his <u>*apperceptive mass*</u>—the listener's accumulated knowledge, based on his prior experience. Obviously, both types of context are important to an understanding of meaning: even a behaviorist thinks about what he reads or hears; even a mentalist is influenced by the environmental stimuli he encounters. Both types of context contribute to meaning.

Is there any accord between the behavioristic and mentalistic approaches to meaning? For both, meaning is more than that which is conveyed by the situation and words of the speaker. For the behaviorist, it is really the *effect of the words* of the speaker *on the listener.* For the mentalist, the meaning of an utterance lies in the associations and the understanding of the listener. Insofar as one of the effects on the listener is a change in his apperceptive mass (his associations), the behaviorist and the mentalist begin to agree.

THE SEMANTIC DIFFERENTIAL

A listener can examine his own associations to a word and can rate them in terms of various dimensions. Charles Osgood and his collaborators have tried to formulate a quantitative statement of a word's meaning by asking people to rate the meaning of the word on a variety of common dimensions, expressed as adjective pairs, such as "strong-weak," "good-bad," "fresh-stale," "tense-relaxed," and so on. In practice, each member of a pair is printed at the end of a line that is divided into seven sections.

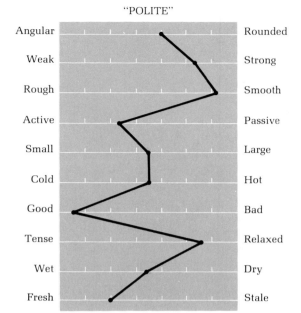

Figure 9.3
Osgood's *semantic differential* shows where people, on the average, rank words on scales described by pairs of adjectives, such as "angular-rounded" or "fresh-stale." The figure shows that "polite" is judged to connote "smooth," "strong," "relaxed," "active," "good," and "fresh"; "polite" is judged not to connote "rough," "weak," "tense," "passive," "bad," or "stale." [Adapted from C. E. Osgood, "The Nature and Measurement of Meaning," *Psychological Bulletin,* 1952, 49, 197–237.]

The subjects rate the meaning of a word by marking the section of the line that corresponds to their rating of the word in terms of that pair of adjectives. When this is done for various common words, there is considerable agreement among people. The diagram in Figure 9.3 shows the average rating of the meaning of the word "polite" on a variety of dimensions.

It is clear that there must be a maximum number of dimensions for any set of associations—and that beyond that number we will obtain little additional information by adding more. Sooner or later, the adjective pairs that we add will produce ratings identical to those produced by adjective pairs already used. Surprising as it is, *three* dimensions are sufficient to exhaust people's ability to read meaning into words: *evaluation* (for example, "good-bad"), *potency* ("weak–strong"), and *activity* ("active–slothful"). Ratings on other dimensions correspond so closely to ratings on one or another of these three that they add no new information about the meaning of the word.

Osgood's work is compatible with both mentalistic and behavioristic ideas about meaning. But, statistically correct, carefully controlled, and ingeniously insightful though it is, the *semantic differential* has yet to convince psychologists that it is the ultimate way to determine the meaning of meaning—it seems too simple. Its simplicity is the reason for its appeal as well as for its lack of acceptance, for scientists look for the simplest possible explanations of phenomena but are distrustful of oversimplification.

THE LINGUISTIC STRUCTURE OF LANGUAGE

A speaker of a language has the ability to generate and to understand an enormous number of expressions or sentences in that language. The number of possible sentences is so large—indeed, it seems almost infinite—that obviously a person cannot learn them all individually. Rather, as he acquires *competence* in a language, what he apparently learns is a system of rules—called a *grammar* by linguists—that he employs in conjunction with a vocabulary, a wish or a need to communicate, and an idea of what he wants to say in order to generate appropriate sentences. By careful analysis of grammatical sentences, linguists have constructed grammars for a variety of languages.

A grammar is a set of *rules* with which one can generate any grammatical sentence in a language. By a grammatical sentence, we mean any appropriate or meaningful sequence of words that is judged grammatical by a competent, educated speaker of the language. For example, if we hear the sentence, "The young man went home," we recognize it immediately as a grammatical sentence. However, if we hear the same words rearranged into "Man went young the home," we automatically reject it as ungrammatical. Since a speaker of a language can discriminate grammatical from ungrammatical sentences in that language, he obviously can be said to know the rules—he has learned them and knows them *intuitively*—although he is unlikely to be able actually to write down and describe them. A person shows that he knows the rules by speaking the language competently, if not always entirely according to the rules of "standard grammar" prescribed by schoolbooks. Thus, a speaker who utters the sentence "I ain't coming" manifests his *competence in the language*, even though his usage is substandard. Linguists speak of the rules that are required for such competence as the *knowledge* the speaker has of the language.

The grammar of a language consists of several different sets of rules: *syntactic rules*, governing the permissible ordering and placement of words in a sentence; *semantic rules*, determining which words can be used meaningfully in a particular syntactical position in a sentence; *phonological rules*, governing the actual sound system of the spoken language. These sets of rules are quite independent. For example, a sentence can be meaningful, but syntactically incorrect ("They not came yesterday.") or syntactically appropriate but semantically nonsensical ("Square, green notions bark quietly.").

In *phonology*, the study of the sounds of a language, sounds are categorized into *phonemes*, the elementary sound groups that can in some way be distinguished from each other: thus the consonant phonemes *p* (in the word "pit") and *b* (in the word "bit") provide the distinction between two otherwise identical words. In English, there are some forty-five phonemes, each corresponding to acceptable pronuncia-

Table 9.1
Differences among the Sounds b, p, **and** t

DISTINCTIVE FEATURE	b	p	t
Voiced (sounded)?	Yes	No	No
Anterior (front of mouth)?	Yes	Yes	Yes
Labial (lips used)?	Yes	Yes	No

tions of English sounds. Within a phoneme, there is great variation in the actual acoustical properties of the sounds; for example, a child, a woman, and a man each produce the b in "bit" and the p in "pit" with different sound frequencies and intensities, but all three of the sounds will be identified as that phoneme by a listener who is competent in that language.

Phonemes, or speech sounds, are distinguishable from one another by one or more *distinctive features.* For example, one distinctive feature is voicing: thus a sound may be voiced (like the b in "bit") or unvoiced (like the p in "pit"). Table 9.1 shows how the sounds of b, p, and t are differentiated by three distinctive features. Differences such as these allow us to discriminate the sounds of our language.

Phonological rules also determine the ways in which phonemes can be ordered or joined. For example, in English, they govern the ways in which plurals are pronounced: thus, they specify that "girls" is pronounced *girl* $+$ z (or that the voiced l is followed by the voiced z), but that "tacks" is pronounced *tack* $+$ s (because the unvoiced k must be followed by the unvoiced s). The native speaker of English demonstrates his knowledge of these rules whenever he forms and pronounces these plurals correctly.

Phonemes are combined into larger units that have meaning, and another set of rules is applied to these units of meaning. For example, let us consider the rules for forming adverbs from adjectives. In English, they are formed by adding the suffix -*ly* to the adjective. In French and Spanish, the adverb is also formed by the addition of an adverbial suffix (-*ment* or -*mente*), but the rules in those languages further specify that the addition must be accom-

panied by another change, that of the adjective to its feminine form. Thus, in English, "complete" becomes "completely"; in French, "complet" becomes "complètement"; in Spanish, "completo" becomes "completamente." These meaningful units in a language (such as the root adjective *complete* and the suffix -*ly*) are called *morphemes.*

A competent speaker must also possess other semantic information: that is, he must know the *meanings* of the morphemes (words, prefixes, and suffixes) of his language. In the preceding section, we discussed the different views of meaning held by the behaviorists and the mentalists. The linguists' view is founded on a concept like the semantic differential. Linguists maintain that the competent speaker acts as though he had ready access to a mental dictionary (or lexicon) that defines the morphemes of his language by listing their properties. Thus, in uttering or listening to the sentence "The dog ate the bone," the speaker consults his lexicon for the properties of "dog," "ate," and "bone" and infers the meaning of the words from the properties. Just how this process works is unclear. Certainly, what we have just described is an analogy rather than an actual mechanism. The image of a listener laboriously looking up each word of a sentence in a dictionary is in conflict with the high speed with which we can understand the sentence. We shall return to this question later in this chapter.

In many ways, the most fascinating of the sets of rules are the *syntactic rules* governing the syntax, or the structural relations between the words of a sentence or utterance. These relationships are diagrammed in Figure 9.4, in which each element or word in the sentence is identified as a part of speech (noun, adjective, and so on) as well as by its function (subject, direct object, and so on).

Knowledge of the syntactic rules is demonstrated by a speaker when he generates acceptable and

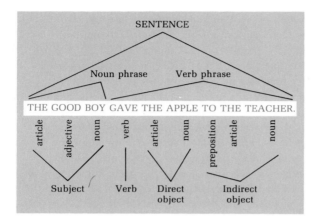

Figure 9.4
The grammatical structure of a simple sentence.

competent sentences, and by a listener when he
recognizes them as grammatical and is able to
decode their meaning. In generating a sentence, a
speaker starts with the idea of a sentence and then,
according to some linguists (notably Noam Chomsky
and his followers), successively applies rules from a
transformational generative grammar in order to transform the sentence into its various parts. A few of
the basic rules are as follows:

1. Sentence → noun phrase + verb phrase
2. Noun Phrase → article ± adjective + noun
3. Verb Phrase → auxiliary verb + verb + tense
   marker (for example, a marker indicating past
   tense) + noun
4. Noun → article ± adjective + noun

The ways in which these rules are applied to define
the *structure* of the sentence are shown in Figure 9.5.

Thus, after all transformations have been applied,
the structural order of the sentence is as follows:

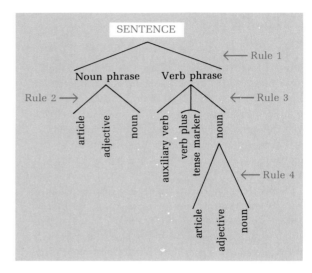

Figure 9.5
According to linguists, transformational grammar re-
fines a sentence by applying the various rules described
in the text at the appropriate level in the transformation
from idea to sentence.

[article + adjective + noun] + [auxiliary verb +
verb + tense marker] + [article + adjective +
noun]. At this point, the rules governing the appropriate sequences of phonemes and combinations of
morphemes are applied in order to transform this
structure into properly pronounced and hence intelligible words that express the speaker's meaning.

The importance of syntactic rules is illustrated by
the following ambiguous sentence: "They are
playing cards." Since it is completely out of context,
this sentence could be interpreted in one of two
ways: (1) some people are engaged in the activity
of playing cards (2) an object is being identified as
a pack of playing cards. Each alternative has a
different underlying, or *deep structure*. Thus the
sentence could be diagrammed in either of the two

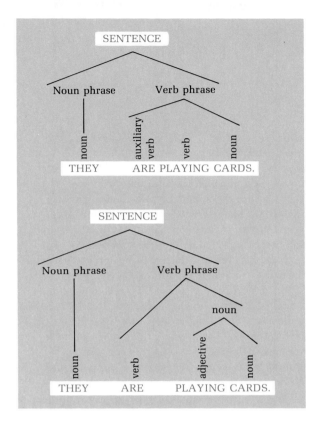

Figure 9.6
The meaning of a given surface structure (for example, "They are playing cards.") differs depending on the deep structure. The *context* of a sentence is usually helpful in reacting properly to the meaning.

ways shown in Figure 9.6, depending on which transformational steps the speaker, in generating the sentence, has applied to the verb phrase "are playing cards"; that is, whether he has transformed it into (understood it as) auxiliary verb + verb + noun, or into verb + adjective + noun. Either is possible. There is nothing in the written sentence itself—the *surface structure*—that enables us to discriminate between these two deeper structures, which carry totally different meanings.

PSYCHOLINGUISTICS

We have just discussed the elegant sets of rules that linguists have devised to explain, at least in theory, the production of grammatical sentences. But is this sequential application of rules actually what a person does when he creates sentences? The answer to this question is not yet known.

As we have already suggested, the linguistic analogy of looking up words in a mental dictionary in order to understand their meaning seems to be in conflict with the extraordinary speed with which we can comprehend sentences. Similarly, the linguist's rules for generating sentences would not appear to have psychological reality: in ordinary discourse we simply do not have the time to process utterances, at least consciously, from a basic sentence core into the final complex and detailed product that constitutes a complete, grammatical sentence. In fact, if you were to transcribe a series of conversations exactly as they were spoken, you would discover that people rarely, if ever, speak in complete sentences of much complexity. Most ordinary speech is an assemblage of fragments: we deliver information to each other in small, incomplete, but grammatical chunks, which are easily processed. For the most part, it is only when we engage in the formality of writing down our ideas that the grammatical details of an utterance or a body of utterances appear.

On the other hand, there is some evidence that the linguist's structure may influence a person's linguistic behavior. For example, it can be demonstrated that sentences of increasingly complex grammatical structures require correspondingly more time to comprehend or to memorize. And more complex sentences seem to require more "space" in our memory: if we ask a subject to recall both a list of words as well as a sentence that has preceded that list, the number of words recalled drops as increasingly complex sentences are used. In this kind of experiment, the psychologist (1) varies the grammatical complexity and (2) measures differences in his subjects' performance on each item. However, it is extremely important to eliminate other nongrammatical influences by controlling the lengths of words and sentences and also—the most difficult of all—by trying to assure that all subjects' previous experience and familiarity with all of the material will be as uniform as possible. Thus far, results suggest that grammatical complexity has some effect on psychological functioning, but we are not yet certain of this.

The psychological reality of grammatical rules has also been suggested by certain experiments showing the way in which grammatical structure can affect our perception. For example, if a subject listens to sentences consisting of clearly distinct grammatical elements, and other stimuli, such as clicks, are introduced, he will tend to hear those stimuli as occurring at the grammatical junctures, or pausing points, between the elements in the sentence, even though they are really occurring slightly before or slightly after a juncture. It is as if the grammatical junctures are places of perceptual relaxation that allow some attention to be diverted to the clicks.

In addition to the psychological relevance and reality of grammars, psychologists are interested in the way language is learned, but that is a topic for Chapter 18.

THE BEHAVIORAL FUNCTIONS OF LANGUAGE

We have said that a behaviorist defines meaning as the *effect* of an utterance on a listener. He views *verbal behavior* in general as a form of behavior that (1) occurs in response to the presence of particular stimuli, (2) has effects on the environment, including other people, and (3) is, in turn, modified by these effects, which are either reinforcing or punishing

(see Chapter 4). Behaviorists, then, have a different perspective on language than most linguists; that is to say, they are concerned not only with speech itself (or with the system of rules underlying its production) but also with speech as a form of communication—behavior that affects another person (and in that sense communicates "meaning").

In studying verbal behavior, behaviorists analyze a verbal episode into its various *functions* (rather than into its grammatical elements). Such functions are illustrated in the following exchange: a child asks its mother for butter; the mother passes the butter; the child says "Thank you"; the mother, "You're welcome." The child initiates this episode by emitting vocal, verbal behavior in a deprived state (no butter) and in the presence of certain *discriminative stimuli* (see Chapter 4), such as bread, mother, and distant butter. The child has learned previously that such a request will be reinforced by his receiving the requested object. Many behaviorists call an expression such as "Pass butter," which specifies its own reinforcer (the butter), a *mand* (a neologism coined from the word *demand*). The naming of the object "butter" is called a *tact* (meant to suggest the idea of making *contact* with a certain object or event), as is all verbal behavior in which something is named. The tact "butter" has been learned as the response that is reinforced in the presence of butter. "Pass" is also a tact of the movement of the butter. The word "please" is included because past experience has shown that a reward is received more frequently if it is used than if it is not; that is, the uttering of this particular word increases the likelihood that the mother will behave in a reinforcing way (by passing the butter). A verbal expression like "please" is called an *autoclitic*: it affects, in a positive way, the mother's response to the mand "Pass butter," but is not really needed for any other reason.

For the mother, the expression "Pass butter, please" is a discriminative stimulus in whose presence her behaving in the specified manner has been reinforced. It is also a mildly aversive stimulus, since her child indicated a lack of something (and awareness of such a lack can be of concern to her) and also since the child has in the past become unpleasant when the butter was not passed. In this situation, the mother passes the butter, thereby reinforcing the child's mand.

The arrival of the butter is more than a reinforcer; it is also a discriminative stimulus to which the child responds "Thank you," which reinforces the mother's response of passing the butter. Finally, the "thank you" is, for the mother, a discriminative stimulus that—because of her previous training in etiquette—determines her response, "You're welcome."

The mand, tact, and autoclitic, then, are important concepts in the behaviorist's approach to verbal behavior. Other categories of verbal behavior are also important, notably *echoics*, *textuals*, and *intraverbals*. All are operant behaviors that are controlled by discriminative stimuli and that owe their existence to experience—and their continuance to reinforcement.

An *echoic* is a response that is an echo or duplicate of its discriminative stimulus. A parent says, "Say 'dinner,'" and this prompts the echoic "Dinner" by the child. Echoing behavior takes place from the very beginning of a child's vocalizing. It makes the child sound like a person, and is therefore strongly reinforced by the parents, because they find it highly reinforcing to them. Thus echoing is intrinsically taught by the parent, and the young child soon learns that there is no more certain guarantee of parental reinforcement than production of the right words, properly pronounced—that is, approximately the way in which the parents pro-

nounce them. A child's initial verbal echoics probably constitute the first learning experiences related to what later becomes a generalized tendency to emit *imitative* behavior.

A *textual*, like an echoic, is a duplicate response, but this type of response is in a medium different from the discriminative stimulus that is being reproduced. For example, reading aloud is a vocal reproduction of written stimuli. By means of echoics and reinforcement, the child learns that certain sounds are reinforced in the presence of letters and groups of letters. As the child develops his reading skills, the size of a controlling stimulus usually becomes larger, expanding from groups of letters and short words to longer words, phrases, and—for practiced, rapid readers—whole sentences.

An *intraverbal* is one step further removed from the strictly imitative behavior of echoics: it is a verbal response to a verbal stimulus, but the stimulus and response bear no formal (one-to-one) relationship to each other. For example, the large number of historical facts—such as key events and dates—that most of us automatically know without having to reflect is composed of intraverbals that are readily emitted. Thus, if presented with the stimulus question "Date of Columbus's trip?", the answer "1492" has already been reinforced so many times that we automatically produce that response. Similarly, the stimulus "1492" will prompt the response, "Columbus's trip." A substantial amount of this kind of intraverbal material is mastered in schools by today's students under various degrees of duress.

Behaviorists have not yet devised a detailed description of grammar, as linguists employ the term. Although there is not necessarily a contradiction between a transformational generative grammar and a behavioral view of language as verbal behavior, the behaviorists have been slow to accept such a grammatical model as a behavioral reality. This is an area of psychology in which significant progress can be expected to occur in the near future.

Animal Languages? If language is learned behavior, and if animals can learn, then animals might be able to learn a language. The evidence is that they can, but that their linguistic competence is greatly inferior to that of man.

David Premack has trained chimpanzees to talk with small plastic chips, which refer to objects and to various linguistic concepts of relationship, such as "and," "or," "part of," and so on, in the same arbitrary way that a human's words do. The chimp can become quite good at certain linguistic operations: recognizing and answering questions, tacting and manding objects, and completing sentences. For example, if shown a slice of an apple and a whole apple, the chimp can indicate the relation between them by choosing, from a variety of plastic chips, that chip representing "part of."

The training is long and arduous, consisting of many thousands of trials in the course of a period of years. The competence attained by the chimp is not great, but it exists; the chimp does master a language of sorts.

It is doubtful if any animals that are less highly developed than chimps could attain even a chimp's limited competence. The type of communication observed among bees and talking birds does not qualify as real language because these organisms cannot rearrange the parts of their "sentences" to convey a variation in meaning: their language capacity, then, is limited by the number or range of distinguishable signals they can produce but cannot recombine to form new utterances. In fact, some linguists will not admit that the chimp's behavior is truly language; to them, man's position as the one talking beast still seems secure.

LANGUAGE AND THOUGHT

Although much of our thinking occurs through the medium of words, much is also nonlinguistic; for example, we do not rely on words when we recall scenes we have seen, or when we review in our minds a musical performance or the movements of the participants in a sports event. And there may be thought so far removed from words that words cannot even be used to describe it.

Nevertheless, our ability or inability to put things into words—to code them—seems to affect our perception of them and also our ability to think about them. Indeed, the anthropologist Benjamin Lee Whorf concluded from his studies of American Indian languages that different linguistic communities perceive their worlds differently. He further hypothesized that these differences in perception were directly caused by differences in language. The first part of this proposal was the result of direct observation. For example, he found that certain tribes of Indians distinguish colors differently than we do, in accordance with the different words for colors in their languages; similarly, he noted that Eskimos have many more words for snow than we do, each word identifying a different type (as we noted in Figure 8.4). But the second part of his hypothesis—his assumption about the nature of the cause—is not as easily verifiable. Is the lack of a linguistic symbol for a given uncodable object the reason why that object is not perceived? Is it true that if there is no name for an item (or even a concept, such as *past time*), one does not see it or think about it?

An alternative proposal is that perception is not determined by naming, but that the two are correlated—that both have the same origin in the individual's experiences in his culture. According to this theory, then, an individual learns to name the things at the same time that he learns to see (or discriminate) them.

Psychologists in general reject as inadequate *Whorf's theory* that perception is determined by language, although they admit that it may have some applicability. Thus a well-developed linguistic code or system of notation certainly facilitates our perception of things and our ability to think about them. Indeed, learning the names of the parts of a flower or of an airplane sharpens our perceptions of those objects and offers us new perspectives for thinking about them. On the other hand, it is a fact that we are able to discern things for which we have no names. For example, we can discriminate colors for which we have no names; if we look closely at a tree, we notice many features of the tree that we cannot describe in very accurate terms. The real value, then, of such a hypothesis, and of the controversy it provokes, lies in the extensive development of conflicting points of view that ensues and in the research on psychological phenomena it stimulates.

Suggested Readings

Menyuk, P. (1971) *The acquisition and development of language.* Englewood Cliffs, N.J.: Prentice-Hall. [Discusses the linguist's approach to meaning, grammar, and the generation of sentences.]

Osgood, C. E., Suci, G. J., & Tannenbaum, P. H. (1957) *The measurement of meaning.* Urbana: University of Illinois Press. [Meaning and its measurement as well as the semantic differential.]

Skinner, B. F. (1957) *Verbal behavior.* New York: Appleton-Century-Crofts. [The behaviorist's approach to language.]

UNIT FOUR

Sensation and Perception

How is a firewalker able to walk on hot coals without feeling pain? Presumably, his nervous system is intact: the pain receptors in the skin of his feet are sending signals via nerves to the appropriate part of his brain. Yet he *feels* no pain. At least, this is what he tells us, and his behavior seems to confirm it. On the other hand, perhaps he is feeling pain but is somehow able to ignore it. What do you think?

The information in this unit may help you form an answer to this intriguing question. It should certainly help you understand the answers to some of the broader and more fundamental questions concerning how we gain information about our world.

When you think about it, we are all like the firewalker in the sense that what we don't feel is often just as important as what we do. As many commentators have remarked, we would be overwhelmed and bewildered if we were always aware of all of the fantastically complex activity that composes our environment—what would our perceptual world be like if we could hear high-frequency sonar signals and see in both ultraviolet and infrared light? In reality, as rich and complex as our sensory world is, the ranges of stimuli to which our sensory receptors respond are relatively quite limited samples of what is going on around us. Visible light, for example, is only a tiny segment of the available spectrum of electromagnetic waves.

Let us consider how the human eye detects visible light and enables us to form a picture of the world around us. When we look out on our world, we perceive a distinct image with straight lines, contours, colors, objects at varying distances from us, and various shadings of light and dark. What we see looks somewhat like a photograph, and, as we all know, the eye is somewhat like a camera: it contains a lens that focuses rays of light into an upside-down image on the retina.

At the retina, light stimulates visual receptors. Oddly enough, before it reaches these visual receptors, the light must pass through a layer of blood vessels and nerve fibers. Furthermore, the eye is continually quivering. At this point, our camera analogy has broken down: if we either laid a layer of tissue over the film in our camera or caused the camera to vibrate constantly, the resulting photograph would be decidedly blurred and distorted. Yet neither of these features have an adverse effect on our visual system; we see the world clearly. How this comes about is discussed in Chapter 12.

Even though it is a relatively small sampling of the world around us, our own perceptual world consists of an enormous number and variety of stimuli. Thus the brightest light that we see is some 700 times brighter than the dimmest light we can see. We are also sensitive to an enormous range of colors and gradations in color; it is estimated that a human being can distinguish among some 150 different colors, though we have separate names for only a few—those of the rainbow. And, although the images on our retinas are essentially two-dimensional, our vision is three-dimensional, and we are thus able to judge the distance of objects. It is obvious that the phenomena of vision—and of the other senses—are varied and complex; all of them pose special problems for the sensory psychologist who must describe and explain them.

One remarkable feature of perception is the constancy of the objects we perceive. For example, a man appears to be man-sized both when he is close to us and when he is far away, even though the man's image on our retina is drastically reduced in size when he is far away. Some perceptions are nothing more than illusions: some drawings, as we shall see, can be seen in either of two contradictory ways. Indeed, they may seem to shift magically from one image to another. These phenomena, too, must be explained by any model that is to be proposed as an accurate representation of the visual system.

Although vision is the sense that has been most studied by sensory psychologists, the perceptual phenomena in the other senses—such as hearing, taste, smell, the skin senses, balance, and others—are also under study. Perhaps we can appreciate the many challenges facing the study of sensation and perception if we ask what sort of a machine could be constructed to keep track of as many stimuli as we do, as competently as we do, and as consistently as we do, not only from day to day but from moment to moment? At present, any such man-made reproduction is impossible. It is true that those pursuing the study of sensation and perception have succeeded in describing certain sensory phenomena in detail and have proposed credible explanations of the ways in which they work. But if we consider the process of perception itself, in all of its manifestations, the fact remains that no one can say exactly how it works. In this unit we shall discuss the data and the theories that are available to contemporary psychology.

CHAPTER TEN

Some Factors Influencing Perception

Our normal, wide-awake perception of reality may be influenced by numerous factors—ranging from our needs, motivation, and values to our various states and levels of awareness. In this chapter, we shall discuss a variety of these influences, beginning with a particular state of consciousness that occupies about one-third of our lives: sleep.

SLEEP

As a physiological state, sleep allows the body to rest and restore itself after the exertion that has taken place during the waking state. To a psychologist, sleep is also an altered state of awareness, in which perception is not so much turned off as dramatically altered and in which the motor functions are ordinarily reduced to those reflexes necessary for life (plus a few twitches). Moreover, sleep is a regularly occurring state that comes to infants for about an hour every few hours and to adults for between six and nine hours once a day. To date, we know comparatively little about perception during sleep. The tools employed to investigate the changes in perception that occur during sleep have only very recently been developed, and our knowledge of perception in this altered state of consciousness is

limited. There is considerable folklore about sleep and dreams; numerous claims about perception and learning in the sleep-state have been made. Some of these claims—for example, stories of learning during sleep as a tape recorder plays softly under the pillow—are of doubtful validity. However, there is apparently less forgetting during sleep than during wakefulness. Tales of solving problems while asleep are probably based on ideas that occur during drowsy periods late at night and early in the morning, although the chemist August Kekulé, who discovered the ring-structure of the benzene molecule, claimed that his idea originated in a dream. Organized activity does not commonly occur in sleep as we experience it, although sleepwalking is one rare instance of such activity. And, of course, dreams are consistently recurring evidence that our minds can be vividly active even when we sleep.

The Psychophysiology of Sleep Until the discovery of the *electroencephalogram (EEG)* made the scientific study of sleep possible, only speculation and verbal reports had been available. The EEG is a record of the gross electrical activity of the brain: electrodes fastened to the scalp detect rather minute fluctuations of electrical activity in the brain that are recorded as waves by pens on a moving strip of paper. Distinguishable *wave patterns* come from the different locations of the electrodes.

If a person is awake but inactive, mentally and physically, most of his brainwaves occur at a frequency of about 10 cycles per second. Waves of this frequency are called *alpha waves*. If the person fixes his attention on something, or becomes mentally or physically active, the waves become more irregular and shift to a higher frequency. The waves are then called *beta waves*. Beta waves (20 to 25 cycles per second) are of lower amplitude than alpha waves (that is, the high and low points of the waves are not as great). Since a person can control his own attention voluntarily, to some extent, he can somewhat determine which type of brainwaves he will emit. If an electrical *biofeedback* device is set up so that a person can see what proportion of his EEG is alpha, he will probably be able to increase the alpha activity by "letting go" and relaxing more. When properly used, such a device is a useful tool for the treatment of tension, because the presence of a large amount of alpha may well be a better indicator of true relaxation than the therapist's or patient's judgment.

As one goes to sleep, a regular series of changes can be seen in the EEG. These changes allow us to divide sleep into four fairly clear-cut stages or levels (see Figure 10.1) Although significant differences can occur among individuals, the average subject progresses from the waking state to a stage of light sleep and then quite soon to the two deeper levels (Stages 3 and 4), in which he remains during the first part of the night. Later, sleep is primarily at the lighter two levels, and mostly at the lightest level (Stage 1).

Stage 1 sleep can be divided into two phases: periods of rapid eye movements (abbreviated "REM") and periods in which rapid eye movements do not occur (non-REM sleep). The REM periods

are of particular interest in the study of sleep for several reasons. First of all, certain physiological processes are more active: brain activity is greater; breathing and heartbeat rates increase; in males, enlargement or erection of the penis often occurs. Also, people who are awakened during or just after a period of REM sleep report that they have been dreaming. Frequent interruption of REM periods (and hence presumably of dreams) leads to an increase in the number of REM periods later that night and often on succeeding nights. These findings allow us to pinpoint the periods during which dreams occur. They suggest that we need to dream— at least, they show that we do compensate for lost dreaming time. Finally, the concurrence of dreaming and physiological activity lends some support to Freud's emphasis on the sexual significance of dreams. (Freud's theory of dreams will be discussed in Chapter 24.)

Recent work on dreams, stimulated by the discovery of REM periods, has revealed that much dream content has its roots in the reality of the dreamer's everyday world rather than solely in the unconscious mind, with which Freud was concerned. The reason for this focus may be in the rapidity with which the REM-awakening method allows us to get a report of the dream. Obviously, all that we can know about a person's dream is what he tells us about it. Even if we can assume that (1) the subject is completely honest, (2) the image of the dream remains vivid in his mind, (3) he has an adequate vocabulary with which he can describe the image, and (4) there is nothing in the dream that he wants to hide or consciously distort in his reporting, he is still describing a phenomenon that has occurred in one state of consciousness (sleep) from the viewpoint of another state (the waking state), and he is describing it in the language of the waking state. This disparity between the state in which the experience occurs and that in which it is reported leads

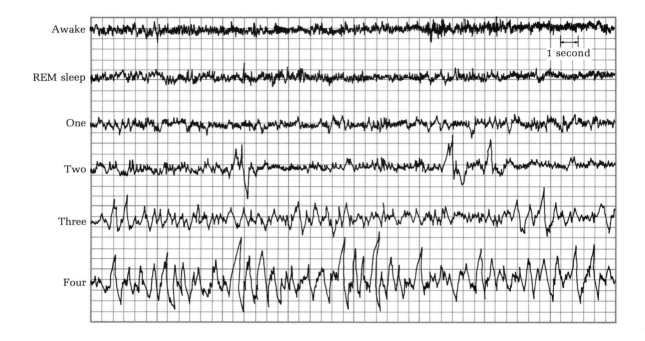

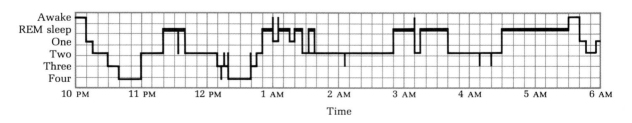

Figure 10.1

The diagram (bottom) shows the various levels of sleep during a typical night for a representative individual. These levels are inferred from the sleeping individual's electroencephalogram (EEG), samples of which at the various levels of sleep are shown in the upper part of the figure for one electrode location. (An EEG is recorded by a machine that amplifies the electrical waves that the brain produces and records them on the moving strip of paper.)

us to question the reliability of even the most seemingly straightforward dream report. Given our present incomplete knowledge about the various states of awareness, probably all we can predict with certainty is that such a description will be more accurate if it is given just after the dream rather than later in the day.

THE WAKING STATES

Just as there are several stages of sleep, there are several states of waking perceptual activity, many of which we have all experienced. Our normal waking state of consciousness fluctuates in a variety of ways: the degree of our attentiveness influences our perceptions of the world around us, as do our short-term moods and our long-term values and motivations. Some "altered" states of awareness are induced by external influences, such as drugs and hypnosis. Still other altered states are self-induced by meditation. These different influences on our waking perceptual activity will be discussed in subsequent sections of this chapter.

Attention   Our ability to shift attention, as well as the capacity of the world around us to attract our attention—often against our will—suggests that there is considerable selectivity in our perception of the world. We focus on only one of many available objects or sounds; or our attention shifts from one type of sensation to another, for example, from listening to seeing.

To illustrate the way in which our attention can shift from one sense to another, let us draw on a typical example that all of us have experienced. If you read a book while listening to familiar music, you find that you either pay attention to the book or the music—only occasionally to both, and then inefficiently. You may find that you have turned a

couple of pages while listening to the music, but you do not know what you have "read." Similarly, a theme in the music that you especially like can suddenly remind you that the music has been on but that you had not been listening while you were engrossed in your reading.

Experimental research on animals has suggested that the phenomenon of *selective attention* has a psychophysiological basis. Russian investigators have found that an *orienting reflex* accompanies the arousal of attention. This reflex can be observed in a dog when he "pricks up his ears," and it can be precisely measured as changes in selected blood vessels. Changes in the brain also take place when attention is directed from one item to another. These changes can be demonstrated in a cat whose brain has been implanted with electrodes to give us a reading of the electrical activity in the brain's auditory areas (see Figure 10.2). First, the cat's ear is exposed to some auditory clicks. If the cat is then presented with the sight of a cage of mice, a large decrease in the auditory activity evoked by each click results. Close attention to visual stimuli can result in an inhibition, or a decrease, in the brain's response to auditory stimulation.

Shifts in attention can be even more dramatic when they occur within the same type of sensation. For example, we have all had the experience of being engaged in conversation with a friend and simultaneously overhearing a nearby discussion that, for one reason or another, is of some interest. Although you may switch your attention between the two conversations at will, it is difficult to follow them both at the same time (and impossible to follow one's own conversation plus *two* others). Your attention may be drawn automatically from one conversation to the other for various reasons: something of vital significance or interest might be mentioned, someone might momentarily speak more loudly or

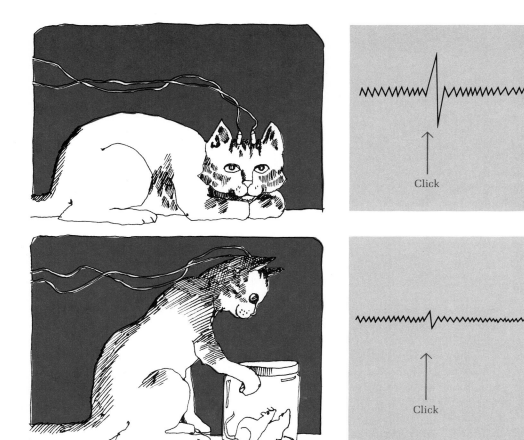

Figure 10.2
The cat's attention is reflected in its brain's response to external stimuli. The brain responds much less to auditory clicks when the cat's attention is diverted by the mice than when the cat is free to attend to the clicks.

forcefully than anyone else, or someone may mention a key word or phrase such as your name. At other times we seem to monitor other conversations even though we do not directly attend to them: for example, even if we have not been listening carefully to what our friend has been saying, we will give him our attention if he pauses for an unusual length of time or mentions something of particular interest.

We can also process at a low level several sources of information at once. Although such *parallel pro-*cessing of different sources of information is possible, it is also apparent that not very much information is extracted from a message to which we do not pay attention. These conclusions have been verified in the laboratory, where we can make a more formal and controlled study of parallel processing by playing a separate message over each of two earphones, rigidly controlling the content of the messages, instructing the subject to process the information in various ways, and finally asking him what he has heard.

Vigilance Sustained attention is called vigilance. Its characteristics and determinants are important and have been studied in some detail. For example, the question of how long one can keep one's mind on a dull and repetitive task is a practical problem of increasing importance in an industrial society that consigns many of its people to incredibly routine jobs. The graph shows that tired people can perform accurately for a time, but that the more tired they are, the shorter will be the period during which they are able to keep up their accuracy (see Figure 10.3). A tired person's attention wanders faster than a rested person's.

Although the act of attention is an internal one, there have been attempts to make it externally observable. In one experiment, subjects were asked to observe the movements of a small mechanical pointer that was inside a dark box, and to note all deflections of the pointer away from the vertical. Subjects could observe the pointer only by pushing a button to turn on a light in the box for a quarter of a second. The subjects were told to push the button, observe pointer deflections, and report all deflections as soon as they occurred. The act of pushing the button, then, was the external manifestation of the subject's attention to the pointer. The results showed that observing (button-pushing) was partly determined by whether the pointer deflections occurred at regularly spaced or random intervals. When deflections were randomly programmed, observing occurred quite consistently. But when they occurred regularly at one-minute intervals, the subjects made little effort to observe just after a deflection, probably because they had never been successful in finding a deflection at that time; as the minute elapsed, observing became more frequent. These effects closely resemble the effects of schedules of reinforcement on performance. They indicate

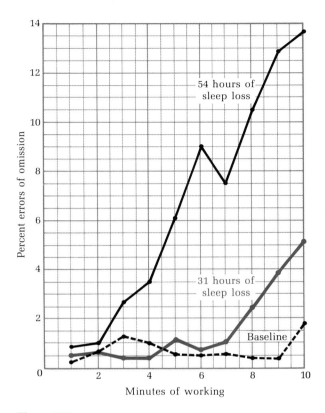

Figure 10.3
The effect on performance of fatigue caused by sleep loss. Rested subjects ("baseline") and tired subjects (thirty-one or fifty-four hours of lost sleep) are nearly identical in accuracy at the start of the task, but the number of errors increases earlier and more rapidly, the more tired the subject. [Adapted from H. L. Williams, A. Lubin, and J. J. Goodnow, "Impaired Performance with Acute Sleep Loss," *Psychological Monographs*, 73 (Whole No. 484) 1959. Copyright 1959 by the American Psychological Association.]

that the frequency and pattern of finding things influence our persistence in looking for them.

Effects of motives and values There is also evidence that the various motives of an individual and the values he holds affect what and how he perceives. For example, in one experiment, groups of children from rich and poor families were asked to indicate how large various coins appeared to be by adjusting the size of a circle of light projected on a screen until it seemed to be the same size as the coin. The low-income children, who presumably had learned to place more emphasis on the value of money, significantly overestimated the apparent size of some coins. In another study, children were asked to estimate the size of poker chips and did so correctly at first. But then they were allowed to use them as "currency" to exchange for valuable objects, and, when asked again to indicate the perceived size, overestimated it. These experiments demonstrate a tendency to perceive highly valued objects as larger than they are—a tendency that is not limited to children. For example, most of us tend to think of people we admire as being tall; we overestimate their size. If our admiration for a person diminishes, we are also likely to perceive him as shorter.

Apparently, our motives and values also cause us to erect perceptual defenses against certain stimuli, and to maintain perceptual vigilance for certain other stimuli—although whether these mechanisms of defense and vigilance are strictly perceptual is open to question. One way of observing them experimentally is to measure the threshold of recognition for words that are presented to a subject by means of a tachistoscope, a device that illuminates a word for a very short period of time—a few milliseconds—and allows the duration of illumination to be precisely regulated. A word's recognition threshold is the duration of the illumination period required for recognition; the longer the period, the higher the threshold is said to be. Thus, if the thresholds of socially unacceptable words, such as the traditional four-letter words, are higher, it is inferred that a person's perceptual defenses are operating. Similarly, a person's vigilance may cause

the thresholds to be lower for words related to his values, motives, or interests: for example, an investor might see the word STOCK after a shorter period of illumination than he will STEAK; but a butcher who puts his money in a savings bank instead of investing it might require less time to see STEAK.

But, are defense and vigilance really perceptual? For example, when defense seems to occur, it is possible that the observer really identifies the word perceptually at the same threshold as he does other words, but merely waits for longer periods to elapse before reporting his recognition, owing to embarrassment or surprise at finding a word like SHIT in a psychologist's tachistoscope. And what we call "vigilance" may be simply an indication of an individual's familiarity with a word, based on the frequency with which he has encountered it in the past. It is known that frequently occurring words have lower recognition thresholds than infrequently occurring words. When every effort is made to present words having equal frequencies of occurrence, the differences in threshold on which the concept of vigilance is based become smaller but apparently do not always disappear altogether.

Psychopharmacology   Our perceptions of ourselves and of the world can be altered by *psychologically active drugs*—those drugs that affect one's behavior or state of mind in some way. For any person, at any given time and in any given environmental or behavioral situation, there exists a drug that, in some dosage, can alter his experience in some way. This broad statement is meant to suggest the breadth of drug effects that modern psychopharmacology has made possible. It also illustrates the dangers inherent in taking drugs: their effects depend on variable and uncertain factors that are often poorly understood—the drug itself, the dose, the form in which it is taken, the individual taking the drug, his personality, his mood, and his expectations at the time. We shall examine these factors and discuss the use of various psychologically active drugs in Chapters 27 and 29.

Self-control of perception   Some states of "altered awareness" can be reached entirely by one's own efforts and without the aid of external experiences or drugs: such are the states of heightened inner perception attained by techniques of _meditation_—for example, those practiced in Zen and Yoga. An extreme example of such self-control is the Hindu or Moslem fakir's ability to exclude various stimuli of the external physical environment and to walk barefoot on hot coals or to lie down on a bed of nails. As inconceivable as such feats seem to be to members of most Western cultures, they evidently occur (as shown in our unit-opening photograph). Studies have revealed genuine changes in the functions of the bodies of Yoga practitioners and Zen monks in meditation. The amount of oxygen utilized is lower; the resistance of the skin to electricity is greater; alpha waves predominate in the brain. Although this much control of one's body is impossible for most of us, presumably we all have the potential for developing or learning it. Indeed, in the last few years, some clinical psychologists have begun to use biofeedback instruments for the purpose of enabling patients to observe—and thereby learn to modify—various physiological processes, including brainwaves.

Another way such physiological control might be achieved has been demonstrated by a Russian psychologist, K. M. Bykov. He reports experiments in which nearly every bodily function was conditioned by means of Pavlov's conditioning procedure. In his experiments on body control, Bykov showed that Pavlovian conditioning could influence an astoundingly large number and variety of the body's reflexes and bring them under conscious control. Bykov studied the production of white blood cells and various reflexes connected with kidney, heart, and skin functions.

Hypnosis   The _hypnotic trance_ seems to cause alterations in many functions, especially in perception, motivation, and memory. The hypnotized subject can be instructed to ignore pain (as does the fakir), to do whatever the hypnotist suggests, to fail to remember what happened under hypnosis, and even to perform certain tasks after the trance ends without knowing why (this is called _post-hypnotic suggestion_). The subject devotes his attention to the hypnotist, ignoring those intrusions that might normally distract him. He is passive, and waits to be told what to do, rather than initiating action. He follows the hypnotist's orders, even when they require him to distort what he knows (or strongly suspects) to be true of himself and the world. And, like a child, the hypnotized subject willingly plays games, particularly games in which he pretends to be someone or something else.

It is not known why people act in the particular way they do when under hypnosis. Nor is it certain whether the ritual of hypnotic induction—the process of being hypnotized—is necessary. The function of the ritual is particularly difficult to assess, because whatever the hypnotist does can be conceived as "hypnotizing." For example, a person who is normally terrified of mice can be confronted with a mouse in a cage and gently but firmly told again and again that she is no longer afraid of mice and that she can prove it to herself by opening the cage and picking up the mouse. This common type of hypnotic demonstration will work with some individuals without the preface of a formal hypnotic "induction." But it can always be claimed that the continual gentle reassurance was enough to induce a valid form of trance.

Individuals differ greatly in their suggestibility, that is, their susceptibility to suggestion and other external influences and thus to hypnosis. Some are highly suggestible, whereas others are so resistant to suggestion that they cannot be hypnotized. This variation can be observed in one's everyday inter-action with other people. For example, try saying, "It's cold in here," to friends in the course of a period of several days, and keep track of the answers. Many will simply agree or ignore your remark; some will deny it; but the most suggestible will agree that they do feel a little cooler, and per-haps even close a window or turn up the heat.

In general, experts have concluded that one does nothing under hypnosis that one would not do under normal conditions, given the right circumstances. Hypnosis imposes strong persuasive demands, both social and individual, on the subject, helps him to focus his attention in a given direction, and pro-poses suggestions to which he may be receptive already, at least unconsciously. Whether or not any-thing else is involved in hypnosis has yet to be scientifically and unambiguously established.

EXTRASENSORY PERCEPTION

It seems to be an enduring characteristic of man to try to escape from his normal bounds and to expand his capabilities. In technology, this urge has led to space travel. In the field of perception, it is expressed in speculation about, and attempts to demonstrate, extrasensory perception (ESP). The basic notion is that some people can perceive without the use of the known physiological senses: such perception is called "extrasensory" (outside the senses). Let us examine some of the different types of ESP that are alleged to occur.

Mental Telepathy   In *mental telepathy*, one person is believed to perceive what another is thinking. For

Figure 10.4
Cards like these are often used in ESP experiments.

example, if Person A selects successive letters of the alphabet and concentrates on them, the telepathic person (Person B) should be able to report the cor-rect letters more frequently than chance guessing would lead us to expect. Experiments on telepathy have been conducted with the use of simple ma-terials, such as a set of three cards, each with a distinctive geometric design (see Figure 10.4). One person selects a card on which to concentrate, and the other tries to determine which card it is. The chances that the receiver will guess correctly on any given trial is one out of three, or $33\frac{1}{3}$ percent. Some receivers, some of the time, can average better than $33\frac{1}{3}$ percent correct choices in the course of a hun-dred or so trials. Such performances are often taken as evidence supporting the occurrence of ESP. Indeed, suppose a person chooses the correct card every time in the course of one hundred trials; the *probability* of this happening is so low that it would convince many people that ESP was at work. But even this dramatic evidence would fail to convince the skeptics: statistically, *any* percentage of correct guesses can be expected to occur by chance alone—every now and then, someone will win five straight bets at a roulette table, someone will win the Irish Sweepstakes, and someone will even make a hundred correct choices on an ESP test.

Clairvoyance and Precognition   Other types of ESP that are alleged to occur are *clairvoyance* and *precognition*. Clairvoyance is the visual perception, in the mind, of a distant object or event (in the past, present, or future) without any direct knowledge of it, and without the aid of the senses. *Precognition* is the foreknowledge of an event. For example, many people, upon hearing bad news, say thay they "had a feeling" that such an incident was going to happen. It is difficult to make a statistical evaluation of this type of phenomenon, based on probability of occurrence, because we do not know how many times the person has "had a feeling" about a distant or future event when in fact nothing at all has actually taken place, and he has since forgotten the feeling.

Psychokinesis   In *psychokinesis*, a person is said to produce or control the movements of objects by mental activity alone. In evaluating psychokinesis, statistics again are significant. Commonly, a psycho-kinetic person attempts to affect the roll of a die (one of a pair of dice). Since there are six sides, each number has one out of six chances of coming up on any given throw (provided the die is not loaded, a possibility that must be checked carefully before the experiment). The psychokinetic concentrates on each throw, trying to influence the die to roll to a stop with, say, the number four on top. In 1,200 throws, for example, according to the *laws of probability*, we could expect one-sixth of them (200) to be fours. How many fours in excess of 200 would

be required before we believe that psychokinetic influence had been involved?

As in a mental-telepathy experiment, if all 1,200 throws should come up as fours, the results might seem quite convincing. However, since even that incredible outcome has a probability of occurrence, although an extremely small one (1 divided by 6^{1200}), it would not be *conclusive* proof of psychokinesis. Indeed, if the experiment were performed enough times—say, 6^{1200} (a number larger than the estimated number of atoms in the universe)—we could expect that on one occasion, based on probability alone, a string of 1,200 fours might occur. This outcome would be so newsworthy that it would no doubt be widely publicized without mention of the $(6^{1200}-1)$ failures, thus lending credence to the occurence of psychokinesis.

Skeptics might be convinced of a person's psycho-kinetic ability if he demonstrates that he can exceed chance with more than one die, and with more than one number, or in several successive runs of 1,200 throws each. But we must still decide what propor-tion of successful throws, on how many successive occasions, are necessary before we will truly *believe* in a subject's psychokinetic powers. As the required number of successful throws increases, the proba-bility of that number's occurring decreases. The lower the probability at which we will believe, the higher is our threshold of belief. Among most scien-tists, including psychologists, this threshold is high for all of the alleged "extrasensory" phenomena, and has not yet been attained. For this group, the observable data have not been convincing, and the concept of extrasensory perception remains an im-plausible one. The general consensus is that an individual can readily influence himself by his un-expressed thoughts alone but probably cannot influence other people or objects. Contemporary psychology places ESP in the realm of the un-proved—and perhaps the unprovable.

Suggested Readings

SLEEP AND RAPID EYE MOVEMENT

Aserinsky, E., & Kleitman, N. (1953) "Regularly occurring periods of eye motility and concomitant phenomena during sleep," *Science*, *118*, 273–274. [The start of the study of REM.]

Kleitman, N. (1963) *Sleep and wakefulness*. (2nd ed.) Chicago: University of Chicago Press. [Good introduction to field.]

Luce, G. G., & Segal, J. (1966) *Sleep*. New York: Coward-McCann. [A good overview of the various lines of work in the field.]

ALTERED STATES OF CONSCIOUSNESS

Bykov, K. M. (1957) *The cerebral cortex and the internal organs*. (Edited and translated by W. H. Gantt.) New York: Chemical Publishing.

Tart, C. T., ed. (1969) *Altered states of consciousness*. New York: Wiley.

Wallace, R. K., & Benson, H. (1972) "The physiology of meditation," *Scientific American*, *226*, 84–90. Reprinted as Scientific American Offprint 1242.

HYPNOSIS

Barber, T. X. (1969) *Hypnosis: A scientific approach*. New York: Van Nostrand.

Hilgard, J. R. (1970) *Personality and hypnosis: A study in imaginative involvement*. Chicago: University of Chicago Press.

Shor, R. E., & Orne, M. T., eds. (1965) *The nature of hypnosis*. New York: Holt, Rinehart and Winston.

EXTRASENSORY PERCEPTION

Rhine, J. B., & Brier, R. (1969) *Parapsychology today*. New York: Citadel.

CHAPTER ELEVEN

Psychophysics

We gather information about what goes on around us through the *receptors* in our sensory organs, which are activated by the various *stimuli* in the outside world. The range of stimuli that unimpaired human sensory systems are capable of receiving is remarkable—consider the range of our auditory sensitivity: the most intense sound we can tolerate without severe discomfort is millions of times more intense than the faintest sound we can detect; if we were much more sensitive, we would detect the random motion of air molecules around us. Obviously, our sensory world would be chaotic if we responded to all available stimuli. But we process only a proportion of them, because our receptivity to stimuli is influenced by numerous other factors: by the degree of our attention to a given stimulus object; by our tendency to be more responsive to changing stimuli than to those that are constant; and by our motivations, needs, and values.

THE STUDY OF PSYCHOPHYSICS

That branch of psychology which is concerned with the relationship between stimulation and sensation is called *psychophysics*. In this chapter, we shall study

this relationship primarily as it is observed under controlled laboratory conditions. Let us begin by defining three important laboratory procedures that are employed by the psychophysicist: *detection* involves deciding whether or not an object is present, or an event has taken place; *discrimination* is the application of careful analysis to determine whether one object or event is different from another; *scaling* is the systematic comparison of the measurable aspects of objects or events. These three procedures are applicable to the investigation of all of our sensory systems—including vision, hearing, taste, and smell.

Stimuli and Sensations It is important to distinguish between (1) a stimulus, (2) a stimulus object, (3) the process of stimulation, and (4) the sensation that is produced. A *stimulus* is an amount of physical energy that produces an effect in one of the sensory systems of an organism. A *stimulus object* is the source of the physical energy that ultimately produces the effect; it is an entity that can be described in physical terms. This book, for example, has a particular size and weight, pages of a particular texture and thickness, and a cover that reflects a particular pattern of physical energy. When stimuli coming from the stimulus object affect our sensory organs in some way, we say that the stimulus object has provided us with information, or a stimulus, by the process of *stimulation*. Thus, if we touch the pages of this book with our fingers, the sensory receptors in the fingers are tactually stimulated; as we read a page, our eyes are visually stimulated by the pattern of light reflected from the paper; and, if the book is dropped, our ears are aurally stimulated.

The quality of the stimulus itself that finally reaches the appropriate sensory receptor depends on a number of situational factors: the auditory stimulus produced by the book hitting the floor will be influenced by such conditions as the composition of the floor, the height from which the book is dropped, the angle at which it hits the floor, the acoustic properties of the room, the location of the listener, and so on. Similarly, if a pocketful of change falls on a sandy beach, the sounds of the coins hitting the sand may be unnoticed, although the same coins dropped on the floor in a quiet library will produce an embarassingly effective auditory stimulus. The relationship between the properties of a stimulus object and the stimulus or stimuli affecting the organism is never invariable. Rather, the stimulus object, the conditions in which it exists, and its surroundings—all jointly determine the quality of the stimulus reaching an organism. Moreover, each of the many variables that influence the relation between a stimulus object and the stimulus may assume an almost infinite number of values. For example, a book that has been dropped will never fall in precisely the same way on two different occasions, and, except in the most controlled environments, no two patterns of echos will be the same. Similarly, if we close this book and look at it, the pattern of physical energy activating the receptors in our eyes will depend not only upon the pattern

Figure 11.1
Identical sensory stimuli may be produced by different stimulus objects. The right-hand figure could be either a trapezoid or a rectangle tilted away from the viewer.

of light reflected from the cover but also upon the general illumination of the room and the characteristics of the lens that focuses the light rays upon the retina, among other variables. Thus, the same stimulus object may produce a vast number of patterns of stimuli. Also, identical patterns of stimuli may be produced by different stimulus objects: for example, the form shown in Figure 11.1 could easily be seen as either a rectangle tilted backward or a trapezoid.

The stimulus or pattern of stimuli is ready for processing when it reaches the receptors. First, the physical energy must be converted (transduced) into nervous energy, a process known as *sensory transduction*. Next, neural transmission conveys the neural message to the brain (we shall discuss sensory transduction and neural transmission in Chapter 12). The resulting electrical stimulation of the brain produces the *sensation*—that is, the consciousness or awareness of that stimulus. For all of our senses, the same processes of sensory reception, transduction, neural transmission, and the ultimate electrical stimulation of the brain produce sensation.

Unfortunately, it is extremely difficult for the psychologist to observe sensation directly. The early *structuralists*—followers of Wilhelm Wundt—attempted

Figure 11.2
Wilhelm Wundt. [Historical Pictures Service, Chicago]

to study sensory experience by means of an *introspective approach*. The structuralist asked his subjects to look into their own minds, to describe their conscious experiences. He wanted to identify the various sensations of which complex experience is composed: in effect, he tried to determine the "structure" of mental experience, much as chemists tried to find the component elements of substances. However, the inherent defect in this approach is that subjective reports of conscious experience are extremely unreliable. For example, it is impossible to ascertain that two subjects, who both report that they see the color red, are in fact experiencing the same or even similar sensations. Sensations caused by more complex patterns of stimuli are even more difficult to analyze.

A more fruitful approach to the observation of sensation is psychophysics, the study of the relation between stimulus and sensation. Although psychophysicists, too, solicit verbal reports from their subjects, they differ from the structuralists in that they require only very simple statements. The experimenter's questions are so designed that the responses will be as unambiguous as possible and interpretation by the subject will be minimal. For example, the subject might be asked to answer whether or not he senses the presence of a stimulus (the detection procedure), to specify whether two stimuli are different from one another (the discrimination procedure), or to assign numbers to the various sensations corresponding to the magnitude of each (the scaling procedure). Using these three procedures, the psychophysicist reduces ambiguity and subjectivity to a minimum. The ways in which these three methods can be applied are treated more fully in the following discussion.

The Attributes of Sensation Just as a stimulus has physical dimensions—such as the intensity and frequency of a sound stimulus, for example— sensation has psychological dimensions (called *attributes*), such as loudness and pitch. It was once thought that a simple one-to-one correspondence existed between the physical dimensions of a stimulus and the subjective attributes of sensation; for example, that the loudness of a sound corresponded only to its intensity and that its pitch was determined only by the frequency of the sound wave. Today we know that the relationship is more complex: loudness depends, to some extent, upon frequency, and pitch also depends partly upon intensity. Moreover, we know that there are two other attributes of sound: one is volume, or the "bigness" of a sound (for example, the voice of a tenor is heard as "bigger" than that of a soprano, though

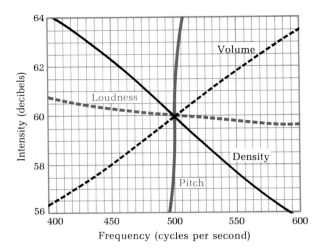

Figure 11.3
The four attributes of an auditory sensation—its loudness, pitch, volume, and density—depend on both the intensity and frequency of the auditory stimulus. The graph shows isophonic contours for the four attributes. Each combination of frequency and intensity from along any of the four curves sounds the same in terms of the attribute. Example: A tone of 400 Hz and 64 dB has the same density as tones of 500 Hz and 60 dB or 600 Hz and 56 dB.

both may be equally loud); the other is density, which refers to the "solidity" of a sound (for example, a bugle tone is denser than that of an organ).

Nineteenth-century observers defined an attribute of sensation as a quality that satisfied the criterion of *independent variability*: in other words, it could be varied by altering the physical dimension of the corresponding stimulus while the other attributes of the sensation remained constant. For example, if the attribute of loudness could be varied by manipulating the intensity of the sound waves while the other auditory attributes of pitch, volume, and density remained unchanged, then loudness would satisfy the criterion of independent variability.

It was subsequently found, however, that changes in the intensity of a tone affected all four attributes of the tonal sensations (Figure 11.3 illustrates the interrelationship of the four and their dependence on intensity and frequency.) In one series of experiments, for example, S. S. Stevens asked subjects to listen to a standard tone with a frequency of 500 cycles per second (Hertz or Hz) and an intensity of 60 decibels (dB, referring to the units used for measuring the relative loudness of sounds). The task was to compare another (comparison) tone to the standard tone by distinguishing between the attributes of each. When a particular attribute, such as loudness, was being examined, subjects were given a number of comparison tones that varied in frequency and intensity from the standard. They were then asked to adjust either the intensity *or* the frequency of each comparison tone until its loudness was equal to that of the standard tone. If we examine Figure 11.3, we can see that if a comparison tone had a frequency of 600 Hz and an intensity of 60 dB, the subject would have to lower the intensity of the stimulus tone somewhat in order to match its loudness to that of the standard. As the subject lowered the intensity,

he did indeed succeed in adjusting the loudness, but the other three attributes changed also. In general, then, as can be seen in the figure, each of the tonal attributes is a joint function of intensity and frequency; in fact, none of the four can be varied independently of the others. As Stevens' experiments showed, if one of the four is to be changed, either intensity or frequency must be varied, and this variation will, in turn, affect each of the other tonal attributes as well.

Stevens asserted that, instead of independent variability, the proper criterion for identifying an attribute should be *independent constancy*: that is, any one attribute can be held constant while the other three change, but this constancy can be held only by adjusting both physical dimensions; thus, if the subject wishes to maintain constant loudness while increasing the frequency of the tone, he must decrease the intensity at the same time. In Figure 11.3, each line is the *isophonic contour* (a line showing the constancy of the particular acoustic quality) of an attribute: in other words, a given attribute sounds the same along that particular line.

Investigators have observed similar relations between the physical dimensions of light (intensity and wavelength) and the attributes of visual sensation (brightness, hue, and saturation). Much less is known about the attributes of other sensations. But since corresponding relationships of stimulus to sensation have been found for both hearing and vision, it is highly possible that similar relationships will be discovered for the other senses. Indeed, some psychologists have proposed the concept of a "unity of the senses," suggesting that the attributes of the different sensations may correspond to one another. For example, the attribute of brightness seems significantly similar to that of loudness, in that the two are closely related to the physical dimension of intensity. Furthermore, every other sense has a quantitative attribute, and it has been suggested that this corresponds, at least in part, to the intensity of the stimulus, no matter what the sense. Similarly, each sense has a qualitative attribute, and each of these may be analogous to hue (color) in vision and pitch in hearing.

THE DETERMINATION OF THRESHOLD AND THE CLASSICAL PSYCHOPHYSICAL METHODS

Absolute Thresholds Simply stated, the *absolute threshold* is the minimum value of a physical stimulus that reliably produces sensation. The absolute threshold, therefore, separates the sounds we can hear from those we cannot, the odors we can smell from those we cannot, and so on. The measurement of this threshold requires considerable experimental expertise. The major problem is largely technical: the stimuli must be presented under experimental conditions that permit assessment of maximal sensi-

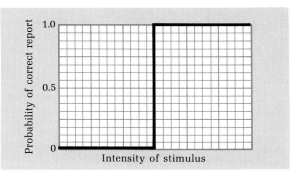

Figure 11.4
If our senses were perfect, the threshold would appear as shown here. As the intensity of the stimulus increases (to the right), no intensities would be perceived until, suddenly, an intensity was perceived 100 percent of the time.

tivity. For example, if a subject's maximal sensitivity to brightness is measured in a room that is anything less than completely dark, or if the subject has not adapted to the dark, the eye will be unable to detect stimuli that may actually be several times stronger than the true absolute threshold, stimuli that are readily detected by a dark-adapted eye.

Let us assume, however, that we have made all the technical refinements necessary to insure maximal sensitivity of, for example, the ear. In order to determine one's absolute threshold of sensitivity to sound, we present the subject with several sounds of different intensities in a series of trials. The sounds are presented by means of earphones, so that extraneous sounds will not be heard and the subject will be able to devote all his attention to those presented. On each trial the subject is asked to report whether or not he has heard a sound. "Catch trials," in which no sound is presented, are interspersed to determine whether a subject might report hearing a sound when none has been perceived.

If determination of the absolute threshold were simple and straightforward, we might expect to find a stairstep relationship between the intensity of the stimulus and the probability of the subject's reporting that he has heard the sound (see Figure 11.4); that is, the intensity at which that probability changed from 0 to 100 percent would be the subject's absolute threshold of sensitivity to that stimulus.

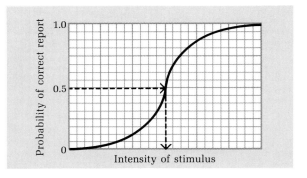

Figure 11.5
The actual findings are that the probability of perceiving the stimulus increases gradually as the stimulus increases. (By convention, psychologists agree to call the stimulus intensity that is perceived on half of the trials the "absolute threshold.")

Instead, however, the data on detection by any given subject are likely to generate a curve like that in Figure 11.5. This curve describes the relation between the physical intensity of the stimulus and the probability of the subject's positive response on a given trial. The range of values to which the subject is likely to respond positively is quite broad.

Where, then, is the absolute threshold? By convention, psychologists have defined it as the intensity of the stimulus that will produce a "yes" response on 50 percent of the trials. Thus, the point on the horizontal axis (showing the range of stimulus intensities), at which the curve in Figure 11.5 passes through 0.5 on the vertical axis is the value that we designate as that particular subject's absolute threshold of sensitivity to the stimulus. Precise measurements of absolute thresholds have revealed the remarkable sensitivity of all of our sensory systems. (Long ago, it was noted that a single candle flame can be seen from a distance of thirty miles on a dark clear night; this places the human light-detection threshold at about 10 quanta.)

In a particular situation, a number of factors can affect the determination of a given subject's absolute threshold of sensitivity to a sensory stimulus. Besides the degree to which the sensory organ has been adapted, the external conditions under which the measurement is taken are important. Thus, in audition (the capacity for hearing), the use of earphones

facilitates the subject's concentration on the stimulus by minimizing distracting noises. Also, other types of distractions should be removed; for example, if an experiment is conducted in a darkened room, visual distractions are eliminated. It is important that the subject's attention to the stimuli be undivided, because lapses in attention have been known to cause decreases in measured sensitivity. In addition, thresholds may vary subtly with the particular technique employed to measure them. Let us now examine the three most important psychophysical techniques for measuring thresholds.

The Classical Psychophysical Methods

Three classical psychophysical methods were devised by the German physiologist and physicist, Gustav Fechner (1801–1887), who is considered the father of psychophysics. These methods are widely used today for measuring absolute thresholds. They are (1) the method of limits, (2) the method of constant stimuli, and (3) the method of forced choice.

In the *method of limits*, the experimenter presents the subject with a series of stimuli that are changed in successive steps along a given dimension, such as auditory intensity. In an *ascending* series of trials, the experimenter begins with a clearly subthreshold value that is progressively raised until the subject reports that he hears the sound. The experimenter then raises the value of the sound well above the threshold and conducts a series of descending trials until the subject reports that he hears no sound. After several ascending and descending series are completed, the experimenter computes the average of those values at which the subject's judgment changed in each series. This average is designated as the absolute threshold.

By conducting both ascending and descending series of trials, the experimenter tends to minimize any of the effects produced by response perseveration, that is, the tendency to continue or persevere

Figure 11.6
Gustav Fechner. [Historical Pictures Service, Chicago]

in a given pattern of responses. In the ascending series, for example, the subject might become accustomed to reporting that no sound was heard, and his expectation to hear no sound in the subsequent trial might thus influence his perception. If perseverative errors do occur, their effects will be largely eliminated by averaging the results from the ascending and descending series.

In the *method of constant stimuli*, also known as the method of right and wrong cases, the experimenter begins with a number of stimuli selected from a wide range of values along a given dimension. The stimuli include at least one sample that is well above the probable threshold value and another sample that is well below it. The stimuli are presented to the subject in random order, and the subject is asked to indicate whether or not he detects each. In this method, the experimenter relates the probability of a "yes" response to stimulus intensity (as in Figure 11.5), and once again, the point at which the curve crosses 50 percent on the vertical axis indicates

the value that is designated the subject's absolute threshold of sensitivity. The advantage of the method of constant stimuli is that it minimizes the likelihood the subject will commit errors of perseveration.

In either of the foregoing methods, there is always the possibility that the subject's report on whether or not he has perceived a stimulus will not be accurate. One way of offsetting this problem somewhat is to make it highly worthwhile for the subject to be correct: thus we might produce maximal sensitivity by offering a monetary reward for correct identification of stimuli or report of their absence. (We shall treat this approach in more detail at the end of this chapter, in the discussion of "Signal-Detection Theory.") However, even for highly motivated subjects, stimulus values near an absolute threshold are extremely hard to detect, and a subject may, for example, be convinced that he has not perceived when in fact he has. An experimenter can often show that a subject has indeed perceived a stimulus if he employs the *method of forced choice*.

In this method, a subject is presented with a choice of stimulus items and required to select that which he perceives. Thus if the absolute threshold of sensitivity to brightness is being measured, a series of dim stimuli are presented in any one of four quarter sections on the screen. Each time, the subject must choose the quarter in which he thinks the stimulus is being presented. Given another viewing situation, when one of the other methods is employed, a subject might honestly believe he has not perceived a stimulus; but the forced-choice data of this method may prove that he actually has perceived a stimulus, at least in some of the trials. Given four choices, there is a 25 percent chance that a subject will choose correctly, and one whose performance is better than chance is apparently detecting stimuli at low intensities.

The three psychophysical methods for determining absolute thresholds yield somewhat different results.

This fact emphasizes the underlying complexity of psychological events that at first appear quite simple. We shall now examine the discrimination problem, the difference threshold, and what is perhaps psychology's oldest sensory law, Weber's law.

Difference Thresholds and Weber's Law   The *difference threshold* is the minimum difference in value between two stimuli that can be perceived by the subject. Sometimes called the *just noticeable difference (jnd)*, it is the smallest difference that is noticed in 50 percent of the trials. Both the absolute threshold and the difference threshold are statistical concepts, and both are measured in much the same way. An experimenter can employ the method of limits to determine the difference threshold: he begins by presenting two stimuli, a standard stimulus and an easily discriminable comparison stimulus. He then gradually changes the comparison stimulus in successive steps so that it more and more closely resembles the standard, until, finally, the subject reports that he perceives no difference between the two. Then, in another series of trials, the experimenter begins with two stimuli that are judged "not noticeably different" and progressively changes the comparison stimulus until the subject reports a difference. The difference threshold is the average of these two determinations.

One interesting aspect of difference thresholds is that they vary with the value of the stimulus. This relationship is known as *Weber's law* and may be stated mathematically as follows: $\Delta I/I = k$ (or $\Delta I = kI$), in which the constant k depends upon the kind of sensation. Weber's law states that the difference threshold (ΔI) is proportional to the value of the stimulus (I). The proportion is constant for a given sensation. Thus, the greater the value of the stimulus, the greater the value that must be added or taken away to create a "just noticeable difference." For example, if we have two twenty-

five-pound weights and a half pound must be added to one of them in order for the two to be judged as different, then twice that amount, or one pound, must be added to a fifty-pound weight in order for it to be discriminable from another fifty-pound weight.

The values of the constant k for the various attributes of sensation are called *Weber fractions*. For example, the Weber fraction for judged weight is 1/50. Weber fractions may be calculated for each attribute of sensation and range from as little as 1/333 for the pitch of a tone to 1/5 for the taste of salt. Thus, a very small change in the frequency of a sound will produce a discriminably different pitch: under optimal conditions, a subject can discriminate between a pitch of 1000 Hz and one of 1003 Hz. At the other extreme, a 20 percent change in the salinity of water is necessary, under optimal conditions, before the subject notices a difference. The Weber fraction for brightness, about 1/60, falls between those two extremes. The smaller the fraction, the greater our sensitivity to changes in a given attribute of sensation. Weber fractions provide us with a good index of our sensitivity to different attributes, and their range shows us how much our responsiveness to sensory change varies. It should be noted that Weber's law holds quite reliably for the middle ranges of stimulus intensity but not as well for the extreme values. Nonetheless, it remains a useful and generally valid approximation.

SENSORY MAGNITUDE AND THE NEW PSYCHOPHYSICS

Fechner's Law   Taking Weber's Law as a starting point, Fechner developed the first general psychophysical law describing how the magnitude of a sensation varies with the value of the stimulus. The *Weber-Fechner law*, as it is now called, states that,

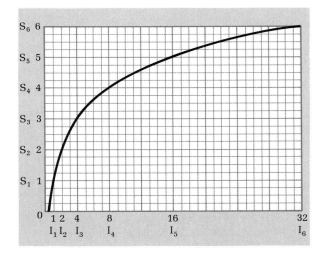

Figure 11.7
In this graph of the Weber-Fechner law, both coordinates are linear (arithmetic).

as the physical stimulus is increased logarithmically (that is, by multiplication such as 10, 100, 1,000, and so on), the resultant sensation increases only arithmetically (1, 2, 3, or 10, 20, 30, and so on.). In other words, sensation increases in equal steps as the stimulus increases in proportional, or ratio, steps. The Weber–Fechner law can be simply stated: $s = k \log I$, in which s refers to the magnitude of the sensation, k refers to a constant, whose value depends upon the particular sensory attribute in question, and I represents the magnitude of the physical stimulus. The Weber–Fechner law was remarkable in that it sought to describe the growth of sensation as a function of the growth of stimulation for any sense. The formula is illustrated in Figures 11.7 and 11.8. Note that in Figure 11.7 the units along the vertical axis (corresponding to the magnitude of sensation) are equal, whereas the units on the horizontal axis (corresponding to the value of the stimulus) are unequal but proportional. When the same relation is plotted on semilogarithmic graph paper, which has a linear vertical axis and a logarithmic horizontal axis (as in Figure 11.8), the Weber-Fechner relation appears as a straight line.

Although the Weber–Fechner Law was subsequently shown to be inaccurate, at the time that it was proposed it seemed to be a reasonable description of the remarkable sensitivity of our various sensory systems. As we already know, many of our sensory organs are responsive to an enormous range of stimuli. For example, the ear can detect sound stimuli ranging in intensity from a pressure of 0.0002 units of force (dynes) per unit area of one square centimeter (cm^2) to a pressure of 2,000 dynes per cm^2 (or from 0 dB to 140 dB): that is, the ear responds to sounds ranging from one as low as the tick of a watch twenty feet away to noises louder than those produced by jet aircraft flying immediately overhead (indeed, noises that are so intense that they can actually cause pain). Thus, if the Weber–

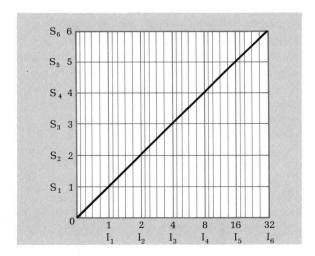

Figure 11.8
In this graph of the Weber-Fechner law, the horizontal axis is logarithmic, so that (1) equal multiplicative steps in stimulus intensity are equal steps on the axis and (2) the logarithmic function becomes a straight line.

Fechner law were applicable—and our sensations did increase only *arithmetically* in response to *logarithmic* changes in stimulation—this relationship would explain the remarkable capacities of the ear and other sensory organs to respond efficiently to such wide ranges of stimuli.

One reason for the inadequacy of the Weber–Fechner law was Fechner's misinterpretation of the Weber fraction. He had assumed that the "just noticeable differences" described by the Weber fraction were psychologically equivalent—in other words, that for each single just-noticeable increase in stimulus value that occurred, the degree of difference that was perceived in the sensation would be the same. For example, if the addition of a half pound to 25 pounds, and of one pound to 50 pounds was required for a subject to detect a difference in weight, the increase in heaviness caused by the addition of the half pound to the first weight was assumed to be psychologically equivalent to the increase in heaviness caused by the addition of the one pound to the second weight. Fechner's assumption was certainly plausible, but subsequent experimentation has proved that it was a false one. Although Fechner was justified in drawing upon Weber's law, which has been shown to be essentially correct, the use of modern techniques for the direct measurement of sensation—to be discussed in the next section—has established that just noticeable differences are not psychologically equal.

Although the Weber–Fechner Law has been refuted, it remains a monumental step in the history of psychology. Fechner's enduring contribution to psychology was the assertion that virtually every sensation bears the same mathematical relationship to its stimulus, despite the fact that he incorrectly formulated the details of that relationship.

Since the early 1950s, however, new methods for measuring sensory perception have been devised; these methods constitute the "new psychophysics."

They were conceived largely by S. S. Stevens (1906–1973), and the Stevens power law, which he developed from those methods, is today considered an accurate description of many psychophysical relations. The new methods and the Stevens power law clarify further the relationship between stimulus magnitude and the magnitude of sensation.

The New Psychophysics   In the new psychophysics, four principal methods are employed. Recall that Fechner's classical techniques are used to determine absolute thresholds and difference thresholds, and that from the thresholds a curve relating sensitivity to the intensity of the stimulus can be constructed. In comparison, the new psychophysical methods allow one to measure perceived magnitude *directly*.

The first two methods, *ratio estimation* and *magnitude estimation*, are similar in that both require the subject to make an estimate. In each, the subject is first given a standard stimulus: for example, if the stimuli consist of lines of varying length (so that the subject will be asked to report perception of apparent length), the standard might be a line that is one foot long. In ratio estimation, the experimenter presents two or more stimuli (such as lines of varying length) and asks the subject to estimate the ratio of one to the other. In magnitude estimation, the standard stimulus is assigned an arbitrary numerical value. The subject is then presented with one or more comparison stimuli and asked to give each stimulus a number that will describe its value in relation to the standard: thus if a line is twice as long as the standard, the subject will give it a number twice as big; if it is only half as long, he will give it a number half as big, and so on.

In the other two methods, *ratio production* and *magnitude production*, the subject is given the standard stimulus and then asked to produce comparison stimuli that conform to specified ratios or degrees

Table 11.1
Four Important Methods Employed in the New Psychophysics

	RATIO	MAGNITUDE
ESTIMATION	The subject is presented with a standard stimulus. He is then given a comparison stimulus, and asked to estimate the ratio of one stimulus to the other.	The subject is presented with a standard stimulus, which has been assigned an arbitrary numerical value, often 10. He is then given one or more comparison stimuli, and asked to estimate the numerical value of each, in terms of a ratio to the standard, 10. Thus, if the comparison stimulus seems twice the value of the standard, the subject calls it 20.
PRODUCTION	The subject is presented with a standard stimulus. He is then given a prescribed ratio, and asked to produce or adjust a comparison stimulus, so that the ratio of one stimulus to the other corresponds to the ratio he has been given.	The subject is presented with a standard stimulus, which has been assigned a numerical value, often 10. He is presented with comparison numerical values and asked to produce or adjust comparison stimuli so that they correspond to the comparison values.

of magnitude. In ratio production, a person might be required to draw a line that he thinks is three times as long (or one-third as long) as the standard. In magnitude production, the subject is given the standard stimulus, such as a one-foot line, and told to assign the number 10 to that line. Then he is presented with a series of numbers, one at a time— 5, 2.5, 12, 15, for example—and asked to draw a line, that, in his opinion, conforms to each number. The four methods are summarized in Table 11.1.

All of these methods can be applied to other sensations as well. For example, if the experimenter is using the fourth method, magnitude production, to measure someone's perception of loudness, the subject is first presented with a standard sound stimulus, say, a 20 dB tone that is assigned the number 10; he is then presented with a series of numbers, for example, 5, 40, 2.5, 80, and is required to adjust the tone's intensity until he thinks it corresponds to each number.

Using the preceding four methods, Stevens and his associates demonstrated that the Weber–Fechner

Law was incorrect. A stimulus that is 25 jnd's above threshold is not perceived to be half as big as one that is 50 jnd's above threshold. Instead, the perceived size of the jnd increases with the value of the difference itself. Thus, Fechner, who mathematically integrated jnd units in the belief they were equal, was actually equating unequal units.*

After demonstrating the inadequacy of the Weber–Fechner law, Stevens developed what is known as Stevens' power law, which more accurately describes the relationship between stimulation and sensation. This law states that equal stimulus ratios correspond to equal sensation ratios and is expressed

---

*Actually, Fechner was almost right. Had he made a somewhat different assumption about the subjective size of the jnd, his law would still be valid today. In particular, he should have assumed that equal *ratios* of jnd's result in equal ratios of sensation rather than assuming that equal differences in jnd's yield equal differences in sensation. The ratio assumption would have led Fechner to postulate the power relation between stimulation and sensation that Stevens was to propose almost a century later.

as follows: $s = k(I)^n$, where s refers to the magnitude of the sensation. k is a constant determined by the choice of units, and I is the stimulus that is raised to a particular power, n. The exponent n varies with the particular attribute of sensation. (An exponent indicates the number of times a particular value is to be multiplied by itself: thus the exponent "2" in I^2 indicates that the stimulus is to be squared to obtain the magnitude of sensation; I^3 would mean that the stimulus is to be multiplied by itself twice: $I \times I \times I$; and so on.) In Figures 11.9 and 11.10, the increases in magnitude of three psychological sensations—perceived electric shock, apparent visual length, and brightness (each having different exponents)—are plotted on two kinds of graph paper, one with both coordinates logarithmic, the other with both coordinates linear. Note that when the psychophysical relations are plotted in logarithmic coordinates (Figure 11.9), the lines are straight; when the same relations are plotted in linear coordinates (Figure 11.10), the line is curved and increasingly more upward if the exponent of the attribute is greater than 1 (as is that of electric shock, which is 3.5) and curved and increasingly more level if the exponent is less than 1 (as is that of brightness, which is 0.33). Since apparent length has an exponent of 1.0, the psychophysical relationship between the sensation and the stimulus is a straight line, even on linear coordinates.

If an attribute has an exponent of 1.0 (such as the visual perception of length, or the sensation of cold), psychological magnitude bears a one-to-one relationship to physical magnitude. If an exponent is greater than 1.0, psychological magnitude increases more rapidly than physical magnitude, and if it is less than 1.0, psychological magnitude increases less rapidly than physical magnitude. For example, let us assume that a stimulus increases in value from 5 to 10 to 20. If the exponent is 2, the psychological

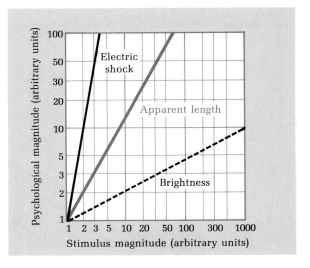

Figure 11.9
Graph of the Stevens power law in which both axes are logarithmic, and the power functions consequently appear as straight lines.

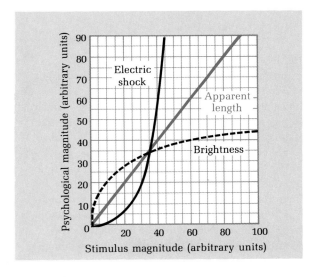

Figure 11.10
Graph of the Stevens power law in which both axes are linear, illustrating the different rates of growth of psychological magnitude with different exponents in the power functions.

magnitude will increase more rapidly than the physical magnitude: from 25 to 100 to 400. But if the exponent is 0.5, the psychological magnitude changes more slowly than the physical magnitude: from 2.2 to 3.2 to 4.5. Finally, if the exponent is 1, the psychological magnitude will increase at the same rate as the physical magnitude: from 5 to 10 to 20. Stevens' data appear to demonstrate conclusively that the power relations accurately describe the relationship between stimulation and sensation—equal stimulus ratios correspond to equal sensation ratios.

SIGNAL DETECTION THEORY

We have defined the absolute threshold as the minimum value of a stimulus that produces a sensation in a subject on 50 percent of the trials. But why is it that a person will detect a stimulus 50 percent of the time, and not the other 50 percent? *Signal detection theory*, developed by D. M. Green, J. A. Swets, and W. P. Tanner, is an attempt to distinguish between the subject's *ability* to detect signals and the *probability* that he will correctly report them.

First of all, the theory introduces the concept of spontaneous neural activity, or "background noise." This noise occurs constantly in sensory nervous systems and is not caused by any external stimulus. Thus if an external signal is very weak (as one near the absolute threshold always is), the subject may not detect it—that is, his response will be a "miss"—because he does not distinguish it from his own spontaneous neural activity (see the distribution at the bottom of Figure 11.11). Or a subject may report detection of an external stimulus signal even though none has been presented (in a catch trial): the sensation has in fact come from his own spontaneous neural activity, or noise. If he does make this par-

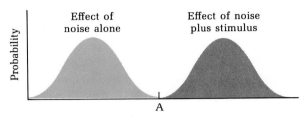

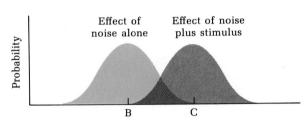

Figure 11.11
Frequency (or probability) distributions for the occurrence of different intensities of stimulation for background noise alone and noise plus stimulus. *Top*, the stimulus is so intense that its effect is always greater than that of noise alone. *Bottom*, the overlap of the two distributions shows that many events that are really stimulus plus noise are indistinguishable from noise alone and vice versa. How such ambiguous events are judged by the subject depends on his criterion. If it is low, at B, he will call them all stimulus-plus-noise, making a larger number of false alarms. If the criterion is high, at C, he will interpret all of the ambiguous events as background noise only, missing a large number of stimuli. Criteria usually are placed between B and C, and can be changed by the subjects' expectations and his motivation.

ticular type of error, he emits what experimenters call a "false alarm." When the signal *is* presented, the subject experiences a sensory effect that is produced by both the signal *and* the noise (see the distribution at the bottom of Figure 11.11, describing variability of the combined effects of signal-plus-noise). If he correctly reports having detected a signal, he scores a "hit." If the signal is strong enough, there will be no overlap between the distribution for noise alone and that for signal-plus-noise (Figure 11.11, *top*), and the subject will probably always be correct in his evaluation of whether or not a signal has been presented. Thus the strength of the signal, which in part determines the degree of overlap between the distributions for signal-plus-noise and noise alone, is one important factor influencing a subject's decision on whether or not he has perceived the stimulus.

Another factor influencing the subject's number of correct responses, misses, and false alarms is the *criterion* he sets for determining whether or not he has perceived a signal. When the signal is moderately intense, so that there is no overlap between the two distributions (Figure 11.11, *top*), the criterion naturally falls between the two distributions, allowing for optimal performance. However, the criterion becomes more significant when stimulus signals are weak, so that the two distributions overlap (Figure 11.11, *bottom*). Then the subject might establish his criterion anywhere in the overlapping area (that is, anywhere along the horizontal axis between B and C in the figure). If a person's criterion is very relaxed, for example if he establishes it at B so that his reaction to spontaneous neural activity is maximal, he will never miss a signal when it is presented, but he will make a larger number of false alarms. If one's criterion is very rigid, that is, if placed at C, so that his reaction to spontaneous neural activity is minimum, he incurs no risk of making false alarms,

but he will miss a large number of the signals. If the criterion is placed anywhere between B and C, an intermediate proportion of misses and false alarms will occur. Thus, in any individual, the proportions of correct responses, misses, and false alarms will depend on two factors: the amount of overlap between the two distributions, and the subject's individual criterion for deciding whether a stimulus has been perceived.

As might be expected, individual subjects vary widely in the criteria they establish. A person's expectations and motivation influence his placement of this criterion, even if either the stimulus signal or the background noise is constant. In some signal-detection experiments, the primary aim has been to explore these influences of expectation and motivation. For example, if one is to assess the effect of the subject's expectation in an experiment, the expectation must be influenced in some way. One way is to vary the probability of signal presentation. Thus if the subject has heard a signal in 90 percent of the preceding trials, in subsequent trials he will be more likely to report a signal, whether or not one has been presented, than if the signal occurred only half the time. Similarly, if a signal is rarely presented, then the subject will come to expect no signal and the probability of his reporting none will be higher.

The subject's criterion can also be dramatically altered by his motivations. In an experimental situation for example, the experimenter might inform the subject that false alarms are more serious than misses. Thus the subject will set a more rigid criterion (closer to C in Figure 11.11), diminishing his chances of making false alarms but increasing the probability that he will make misses. The experimenter might influence the subject's motivations even more directly by introducing a *payoff matrix*, such as those shown in Figure 11.12, in which four

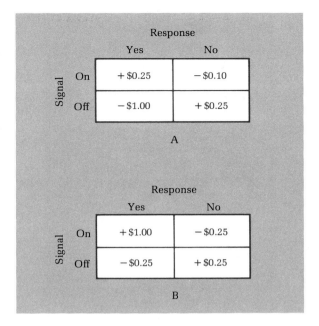

Figure 11.12
Two payoff matrices. They show the financial outcome, gain or loss, for each possible response of the subject on each detection trial. The stimulus may occur or not and the subject can say that it did or not, making four possible outcomes. The entries in the cells of the matrix give the gain or loss. For example, in A, a "yes" response without a signal loses $1.00, while in B, the same response loses only $.25. In detection theory, the payoff matrix alters the subject's placement of his criterion.

different monetary values, either rewards or penalties, are assigned to the four possible outcomes of the subject's report on a trial. Note that in the upper matrix, the penalty for false alarms is quite severe (one dollar); therefore subjects that have been presented with this matrix will probably establish their criterion so that they make considerably fewer false alarms than misses. In the lower matrix hits are amply rewarded (one dollar apiece) and, although the penalties for false alarms and misses are the same, the subject will probably make more false alarms than misses in order to maximize the number of hits.

Even outside of an experimental setting, a subject's criterion can be dramatically altered by his motivations. For example, if a doctor is attempting to detect

a certain disease, and it is one that is serious and contagious, he is likely to establish a loose criterion (one that is nearer to B than to C in Figure 11.11); thus he may diagnose a person's symptoms as that disease, when in fact it is not. However, if the illness he is attempting to detect is not contagious or particularly grave, the doctor's criterion will be more rigid (and closer to C than to B). These kinds of motivations affect anyone in an important decision-making situation—not only doctors, but safety inspectors, radar operators, clinicians, scientific investigators, and others.

Both the subject's expectations (which are based on his past experience with signal frequencies) and his motivations (which are influenced by the consequences of the responses he makes) combine to form his *response bias*. In an experiment, this response bias, together with the subject's own sensory capabilities and the strength of the signal, determine the point at which that subject will establish his criterion. These important variables and the ways in which they influence a subject's responses are diagrammed in Figure 11.13. Although the variables themselves have already been discussed, it is important to add that, in most signal detection experiments, the background noise is provided by the experimenter, so that he can determine its strength and control its fluctuations.

Signal detection theory has provided us with an approach for investigating the relationship between the two recognizable types of errors—false alarms and misses. Also, it has enabled us to recognize that we cannot eliminate both at the same time, but that we can minimize one type of error by committing more of the other. It has demonstrated that the concept of a flexible criterion is more viable and productive than the classic concept of the absolute threshold; that detection is a complex psychological process; and that seemingly straightforward psycho-

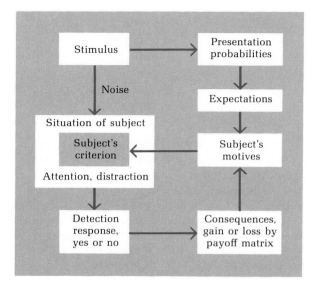

Figure 11.13
A diagram showing some of the factors involved in detection experiments.

physical judgments depend not only on the strength of the signal and on an individual's sensory capabilities, but also on his expectations and motives. The theory has enabled us to conduct studies of the detection process that have been both elegant and extremely fruitful in furthering our understanding of detection and the psychological factors that influence it. Signal detection theory and the new psychophysics are to date the two most significant psychophysical advancements of this century.

Suggested Readings

Boring, E. G. (1942) *Sensation and perception in the history of experimental psychology.* New York: Appleton-Century-Crofts. [This work includes an excellent historical treatment of psychophysics.]

Marks, L. E. (1974) *Sensory processes: The new psychophysics.* New York: Academic Press. [A comprehensive and elegant treatment of the new psychophysics.]

Stevens, S. S. (1971) "Issues in psychophysical measurement." *Psychological review, 78,* 426–450. [One of Stevens' last papers on his new psychophysics.]

Swets, J. A. (1973) "The relative operating characteristic in psychology." *Science, 182,* 990–1000. [A recent and readable introduction to signal detection theory. The mathematically sophisticated reader may want to follow this up with portions of: Green, D. M. and Swets, J. A. (1966) *Signal detection theory and psychophysics.* New York: Wiley.]

CHAPTER TWELVE

Sensory Processes

As we mentioned in the introduction to this unit, the stimulus information that is available to us is relatively limited. For example, the only objects that we can see are those that emit or reflect electromagnetic waves of energy within a certain range of wavelengths. Thus our eyes are sensitive only to wavelengths of between 400 and 700 *nanometers* (*nm*). If we were able to see objects or surfaces that emitted or reflected wavelengths outside of that range, our visual world would be very different. If, for example, our eyes perceived radio waves, which bounce off clouds at night, then we could see the images of distant cities reflected in the sky as easily as we see the images projected on a television screen.

The information available to our auditory system is also limited. Our ears are sensitive only to a specific range of vibratory frequencies—from approximately 20 to 20,000 *Hertz* (*Hz*). Thus, we are unable to perceive higher or lower frequencies directly. Indeed, if we could, our auditory world would be greatly altered: we would even be able to hear a dog's tail wag at two shakes per second!

To illustrate the selective nature of our perceptual world, consider the bat (Figure 12.1), who flies in pitch-darkness, judging the position and distance of objects by bouncing ultrasonic waves off them.

Our sensations and perception are, then, restricted by our sensory capacities. In Chapter 11, in our discussion of absolute thresholds, we noted that our sense organs could not perceive physical stimuli below certain intensities. In this chapter, we will consider other perceptual limitations: (1) those imposed by the physical properties of the stimuli we can perceive, (2) those imposed by the structure and function of the sense organs that collect and transform (*transduce*) stimulus energy into nervous energy, and (3) those imposed by the nervous system, which transmits the transduced energy to the brain.

THE STIMULI

In this section, we will be concerned primarily with visual and auditory stimuli, both of which are *periodic waves*. A wave is a disturbance or variation that travels through the air or another medium. A wave is periodic if its form repeats itself regularly. Three important properties of periodic waves are: *frequency* (the number of high points, or peaks, per second); *wavelength* (the length of one cycle in the wave, or the

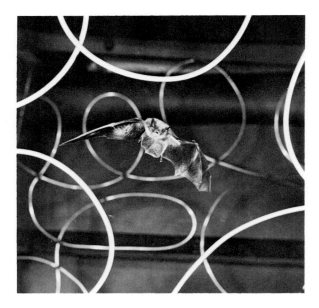

Figure 12.1
This bat can fly through tangled tubing in total darkness because it detects objects by means of echolocation—a kind of animal-radar. The bat emits a series of "sounds" that are too high in frequency for us to hear. (If we reduce their frequency—by playing back a record of them at a much slower speed, they sound to the human ear like a series of squeals.) The sounds hit objects and bounce back to the bat's ears, which are sensitive to them. The bat senses how far away the object is from the time it takes a "squeal" to get there and back; it senses the direction of an object from the angle and the timing of the returning echo striking its ears. [Bernard Hoffman, Time-Life Picture Agency]

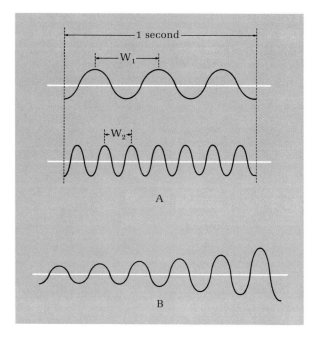

Figure 12.2
Waves are graphed by plotting their intensity (vertical axis) against time (horizontal axis). In A, an increase in frequency from 3 to 7 cycles per second (a unit now called a "Hertz" after a German physicist and abbreviated "Hz") results in a decrease in wavelength from W_1 to W_2. The distance between the peaks (the wavelength) must be less if there are more peaks (frequency) in the same amount of time. In B, we see that the intensity of a wave may change without any change in either frequency or wavelength.

physical distance between peaks); and *intensity* (the height of the peaks or the depth of the low points). Figure 12.2 shows several representations of periodic waves that differ in these three properties. Frequency and wavelength are obviously interrelated, because if the frequency is increased the peaks will occur closer together. But neither frequency nor wavelength are affected by intensity. We can specify almost completely the physical character of any wave stimulus arriving at one of our body's receptors if we know the intensity and either the wavelength or the frequency. As we shall see later in this chapter, these physical characteristics are important in determining our perceptions.

In general, stimuli are actually combinations of waves. Figure 12.3 gives three simple examples of the ways in which two waves combine. In each example, the intensities of each wave at each point along the time axis have been added together, but the resulting combination is different for each pair of waves. The differences are due to the different *phase* relations between each pair. In the first example, the peaks of each wave occur at exactly the same point on the time axis; they are in perfect correspondence, that is, exactly *in phase*. Consequently, the two reinforce each other—the peaks and valleys of the combination wave are exactly twice those of either of the single waves. In the second example, the peak of one wave and the low point of the other wave occur at exactly the same point along the time axis: the two are exactly *out of phase*. As a result they exactly cancel each other—the combination wave

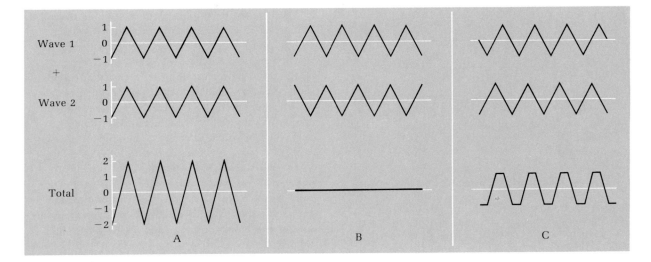

Figure 12.3
Two or more waves can be added together. The resulting
combination wave depends on the phase relation
between the waves. This figure shows the combination
waves that result from the addition of two simple waves
of the same frequency when the waves are exactly in-
phase, perfectly out-of-phase, and half-way between
these two extremes.

always has an intensity of zero. In the third example,
the two waves are one-half cycle out of phase, and
the combination wave is the result of that particular
phase relation. In reality, most stimuli are much
more complex. Indeed, an infinite number of waves,
of all intensities, can be added together to produce
literally any variety of combination wave. The significance of wave combinations will be illustrated
in greater detail in Chapter 13, where we shall
examine the qualities of sensation, such as pitch
and loudness.

Light Waves Vision is produced by those wavelengths of electromagnetic radiation that stimulate

the visual receptors in the eyes (Color Plate I,
facing page 258). The human visual system does
not react to wavelengths outside of the range
of 400 to 700 nanometers, and we therefore do not
perceive that radiation. Radiation of wavelengths
within the specified range is perceived as light, and
different wavelengths of light produce in us sensations of different colors.

The intensity of the visual stimulus is an important characteristic, for it determines our perception
of brightness. It is measured by determining the
amount of light falling on a given area during a
given period of time.

Sound Waves The auditory stimuli are also
periodic waves, but unlike the electromagnetic light
waves, they require a material medium, such as air
or water, to travel through. Only those waves within
a given frequency range—approximately 20 to 20,000
Hertz—activate the human auditory receptors, and are

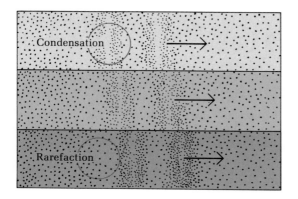

Figure 12.4
When a vibrating body waves back and forth, it alternately compresses (or condenses) and releases (or rarefies) the air or water or other medium around it. The condensations (and the rarefactions) are conducted through the medium. If we drop a stone into a still body of water, we can watch the condensations caused by the stone spread out from the point of impact in a matter of seconds. When the condensations in a medium —usually air—reach our ears, we hear them, provided that they occur more than about 20 times a second and fewer than about 20,000 times a second. [Adapted from *Psychology Today: An Introduction*, 2nd ed. Del Mar, California: CRM, Inc., 1972.]

hence called sound waves. Sound waves are emitted from a physical object that has been set into vibration. For example, if the string of a guitar is plucked, it gives off sound waves that travel through the air as a series of regularly spaced condensed areas (increased pressure on the air) and rarefied areas (decreased pressure on the air). Those waves that are within the specified frequency range produce the sensation of hearing when they reach the sensory receptors in the ear. These physical characteristics of sound waves are illustrated in Figure 12.4.

The *intensity*, or amplitude, of a sound is usually expressed in units of physical pressure (dynes) per square centimeter (cm^2). Also, for convenience, we usually measure the intensity of a sound in terms of the ratio between it and the intensity of a standard sound of 0.0002 dynes per cm^2, which is the lowest intensity that a person can ever hear under the best circumstances (the human threshold of sensitivity to sound intensity). The unit for measuring this relative loudness is the *decibel (dB)*.

The decibel value of a given sound pressure is equal to 20 × the logarithm (to the base 10) of the ratio between the sound pressure in question and the standard value. All this means is that a decibel scale on a graph is logarithmic, or multiplicative, rather than linear, or additive: each increase of 6 dB means that the sound pressure has doubled. A value of 12 dB thus means the pressure has quadrupled. And 18 dB means the sound pressure has increased eightfold. Every addition of 6 dB doubles the pressure.

Other Stimuli   Although visual and auditory stimuli are probably of most interest to the psychologist, we should also examine chemical, mechanical, thermal, and electrical stimuli, which produce sensations in other sensory systems. Chemical stimulation of the receptors in the tongue and in the nose evokes sensations of taste and smell. Mechanical stimuli give rise to a variety of sensations: those detected by receptors in the abdomen produce internal sensations (such as hunger); those reaching the nonauditory (vestibular) organ in the inner ear help to produce the sense of balance and enable us to regulate it; those stimulating the receptors in our joints, muscles, and tendons enable us to feel stress on our limbs and to be aware of the position and movement of our body or the different parts of the body. For the various sensations felt on the skin, thermal, mechancial, and chemical stimuli are received by a highly complex system of skin receptors. Finally, electric stimuli can evoke a response in any or all of our sensory receptors because of of the electrical characteristics of our nervous system.

The Doctrine of Specific Energies It is essential to recognize that the sensation produced by stimulation is caused by the nature of the receptor, not by the stimulus. This principle is called *the doctrine of specific nerve energies*. It specifies that although each receptor may have its natural stimulus—for example, the receptors in the eye respond to light waves; those in the ear, to sound waves—the stimuli themselves do not cause the sensation (such as that of vision or hearing). Instead, they cause an effect specific to a particular sensory organ, and that effect is transmitted to the brain and is perceived as the sensation. In fact, any stimulus that stimulates a particular sense organ will produce the specific effect of that organ: if we use electricity instead of sound waves to stimulate the receptors in the ear or the eye, we will still evoke the sensation of hearing or sight. Our sensory knowledge of the world is determined not only by the capacities of our sensory receptors, but also by *which* receptors are stimulated.

THE SENSORY RECEPTORS

We have seen that the receptors in our sense organs are stimulated by only a limited amount of the available stimulus information. In this section, we will discuss the way in which these organs collect the physical energy of the stimuli and deliver it to its receptors, which transform it into the nervous energy that is carried to the brain. We will examine in detail the way in which these organs, especially the eye and the ear, work.

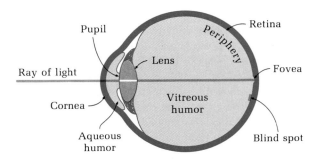

Figure 12.5
A cross-section of an eyeball. The structures mentioned in the text have been labeled in the diagram.

The Eye Although we should realize that physicists describe the electromagnetic energy we call light both (1) as wavelike and (2) as composed of discrete units of energy (*quanta*), let us simplify our discussion of the process of visual perception by thinking of visual stimuli as rays of light that travel in straight lines.

The human eye is one of the most amazing devices ever designed or evolved. Let us appreciate it first by reviewing how it is constructed physically—by following some rays of light that happen to enter the eye. The surface of the eye consists of the transparent cornea, which resembles a mirror bulging out like a bubble (see Figure 12.5). When light rays reach the cornea, about 3 percent of them are reflected off its surface. The remaining rays proceed through the corneal shield, the liquid *aqueous humor*, the *pupil* of the eye, and into the lens. The lens causes the rays to bend, and the degree of the bend depends on both the angle at which the rays enter and their wavelength. Coming out of the lens, the rays pass through the *vitreous humor*, which fills the eyeball and helps to keep it rigid. They continue toward the back of the eyeball, where the rays are focused on the back of the eye, which is about three-fourths of an inch away from the cornea.

When the rays focus on the back of the eyeball, they form an image of the object from which they were emitted or reflected. The size of the image is determined by both the size of the object and the distance of the object from the eye (see Figure 12.6). Note also that, as the arrows in the figure indicate, the image on the back wall of the eyeball is inverted, but it—like all images—will be perceived right side up by the brain.

If the rays of light from a given object were to stop at the back wall of the eye, we would see nothing. The *retina*, site of the *photoreceptors* for vision, is buried inside the wall of the eyeball, sandwiched between blood vessels and nerve fibers on one side and the opaque outside coating of the eye, the *choroid*, on the other (see Figure 12.7). Thus the light must travel through layers of blood vessels and nerve fibers to reach the retina, where it finally makes contact with photoreceptors. Near the middle of the retina, we find a *blind spot*, where nerve fibers stream like telephone wires out of the eyeball. There are no photoreceptors in the blind spot; thus, any waves that reach it strike nerves, not receptors, and are not seen.

Now we must complicate matters further. The eye is constantly quivering. Consequently, no ray of light entering the eye or any point on a given retinal image ever falls on the same photoreceptor for more than the barest fraction of a second. Instead, the quiver causes each point on the image to fall successively on a variety of neighboring receptors. Far from blurring our vision or hindering our visual ability, as you might expect, this quiver and resultant variation in the location of the image on the retina are actually necessary for vision. If we nullify the effect of the quiver by arranging artificially (see Figure 12.8) to have an image always fall on exactly the

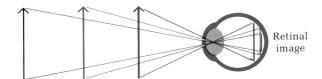

Increased distance of constant-size object with decreased size of retinal image

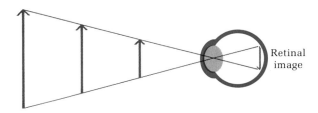

Increased size of distant object with constant size of retinal image

Figure 12.6
An object in the real world is focused by the lens as an upside-down image on the retina of the eye. The size of the image depends on both the size of the object and its distance from the eye. The closer an object, the larger its image on the retina. Thus, a small close object can produce a retinal image as large as that produced by a large distant object.

same part of the retina all of the time, we find that the image disappears: in a short time we see nothing but a gray blur! The explanation of this surprising fact is that the visual system is stimulated by *changes* in light; it is a *detector of differences*. When the effect of the quiver is nullified, no single receptor is exposed to any changes in light falling on it—each receptor is constantly exposed to the same ray of light. But the receptor *does not report* the presence of light without changes, and hence we *do not see anything*.

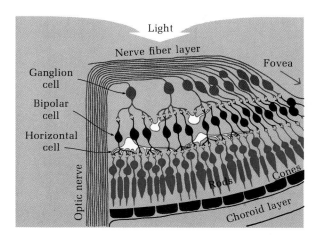

Figure 12.7
A cross-section of the rear wall of the eyeball shows the nerves and blood vessels through which light travels before stimulating the visual receptors.

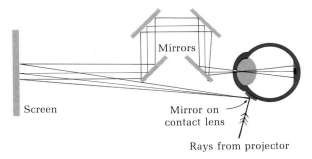

Figure 12.8
The eye's normal quiver assures that the image on the retina moves. If an image on the retina does not move, we do not see it. This diagram shows how we can stabilize an image on the retina by means of a trick: the image is reflected off a mirror attached to the eyeball itself. [Adapted from L. A. Riggs, F. Ratliff, J. C. Cornsweet, and T. N. Cornsweet, "The Disappearance of Steadily Fixated Visual Test Objects," *Journal of the Optical Society of America*, 1953, *43*, 495–501.]

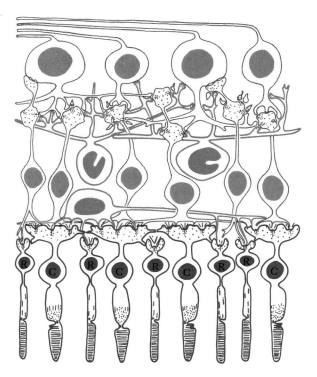

Figure 12.9
A highly schematic cross-section of the retina, showing rods (R) and cones (C) and the nerve fibers that lead from them to the optic nerve. [Adapted from Dowling and Boycott, *Proceedings of the Royal Society* (*London*), 1966, 166B, 80–111.]

The retina's photoreceptors, which are buried deep in the eye's back wall, are classified into two groups—long thin *rods* and short squat *cones* (see Figure 12.7 and 12.9). The retina is composed of millions of these two types of receptors. The *fovea* (see Figure 12.10), which is in the center of the retina and is the area on which the normal eye, observing an object in a normal manner, focuses its image, is composed exclusively of cones. However, the number of cones decreases, and the number of rods increases, as we progress from the fovea toward the *periphery* of the retina. Rods are much more sensitive to light of low intensity than are cones, but the cones enable us to see color. (We will discuss the significance of these differing functions in Chapter 13.)

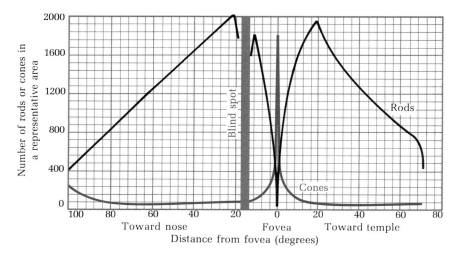

Figure 12.10
The number of cones is greatest in the fovea and negligible elsewhere, whether we move across the nasal retina (toward the nose) or the temporal retina (toward the temple). Rods are negligible in the fovea but predominant elsewhere. Note that there are neither rods nor cones in the blind spot, which is why light that falls there is not seen. [Adapted from G. Østerberg, "Topography of the Layer of Rods and Cones in the Human Retina," *Acta ophthalmolgica*, Copenhagen, 1935, *61*, Supplement, 1–102.]

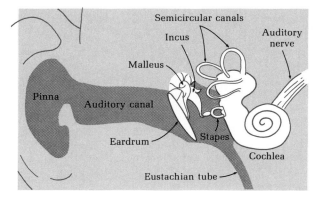

Figure 12.11
An overall view of the anatomy of the human ear in cross-section.

The Ear Our auditory apparatus transports sound waves from the air into the inner ear, where transduction of the stimulus energy into neural impulses occurs. The path of the sound wave through the ear is shown in Figure 12.11. First, the *pinna* (the outer ear) collects the wave and channels it into the auditory *canal*. As the wave travels down the canal, it bounces off the walls until it reaches the eardrum (*tympanic membrane*). The wave causes the eardrum to vibrate in synchrony with it, because the wave's condensed areas push the drum in, and its rarefied areas allow the drum to spring back.

The wave proceeds to the other side of the eardrum and into the middle ear, now having traveled perhaps an inch or so in all. Below the middle ear is the Eustachian tube, which leads to the throat and which opens when we swallow, thus relieving pressure in our ears. Within the middle ear is a structure composed of three tiny bones: *the hammer* (malleus),

which is connected to the eardrum; the *anvil* (incus); and the *stirrup* (stapes), which is joined to the *oval window* of the *cochlea* in the inner ear. The three bones are delicately but firmly linked together, and they are so balanced and levered that they vibrate in unison and thus transmit the sound wave from eardrum to oval window (Figures 12.11 and 12.12).

Once transmitted across the oval window and into the inner ear, the sound wave sets up a disturbance in the liquid-filled cochlea (Figure 12.12). As Georg von Békésy observed, this disturbance takes the form of a *traveling wave*, and it stimulates the auditory receptors within the *organ of Corti*, which is within

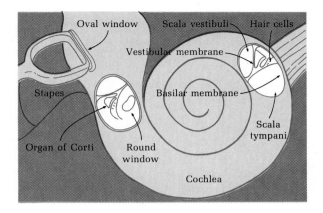

Figure 12.12
A close-up of the inner ear, where sound is transported from the eardrum into the cochlea, where the hearing receptors are stimulated.

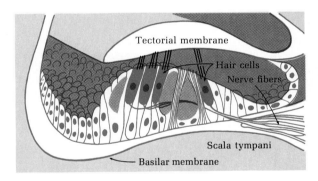

Figure 12.13
An enlarged cross-section of the organ of Corti, which is located within the cochlea and contains the hearing receptors.

the cochlea. The cochlea (as its Latin name suggests) is coiled, as is the *basilar membrane* within the cochlea, which supports the organ of Corti. If we imagine these structures as uncoiled (as in Figure 12.14), we can more easily visualize a traveling wave and its effect. Imagine further that this uncoiled cochlea is a rope extending along the ground: if you pick up one end of the rope and start moving it up and down, the amount of displacement of the rope will gradually increase along its length until it attains a maximum and then it will subside to almost none.

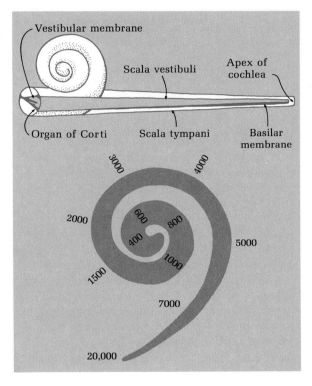

Figure 12.14
When we imagine what the cochlea would look like uncoiled, we see that the basilar membrane and organ of Corti stretch down the whole length of the cochlea canal.

If you move it slowly (at low frequency), the point of maximum displacement is quite far from your hand; if the movement is faster (at high frequency), the point of maximum displacement is closer to your hand rather than farther away. Similarly, when sound waves of high frequency move the basilar membrane, the maximum displacement of the membrane is near the oval window, where the stirrup is attached;

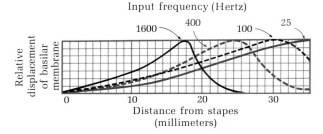

Figure 12.15
As the frequency of the stimulus to the oval window increases, the point of maximum displacement of the basilar membrane moves closer to the oval window. [Adapted from G. von Békésy, "Variation of Phase along the Basilar Membrane with Sinusoidal Vibrations," *Journal of the Acoustical Society of America*, 1947, *19*, 452–460.]

when the waves are lower in frequency, the maximum displacement is further away from the oval window and closer to the apex, or top, of the cochlea (see Figure 12.15). The organ of Corti lies on the basilar membrane and moves with it.

A cross-section of the organ of Corti itself is pictured in Figure 12.13. In the organ are *hair cells*. Tiny hairs extend from these cells across a gap and into another structure, the tectorial membrane. As waves travel through the cochlea, the hairs are moved, and the hair cells are pulled by their movement. As we shall see in the discussion of auditory transduction, these hair cells are the actual sensory cells of audition.

The Receptors for Taste and Smell   The sensations of taste and smell result from chemical sensitivity. Some chemical receptors are located in the tongue (Figure 12.16), and some (the olfactory receptors) are located at the very top of the nasal cavities (Figure 12.17). Only four basic tastes are discriminated by the taste buds: sweet, salty, sour, and bitter. The olfactory sensations are more com-

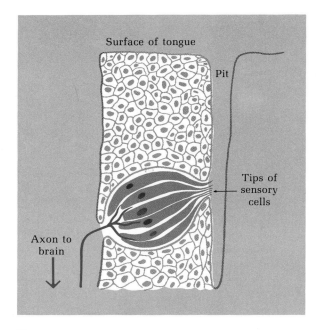

Figure 12.16
A schematic cross-section of a taste bud; the taste buds are located beneath the surface of the tongue. The tips of sensory cells in the taste bud protrude into an adjacent pit in the tongue. When solutions in the mouth fill the pit, the sensory cells are stimulated. [Adapted from R. S. Woodworth, *Psychology*, 4th ed. New York: Holt, Rinehart and Winston, 1940.]

Figure 12.17
The receptors for smell are located at the top of the nasal cavity, where they are stimulated by molecules of substances that come in through the nose or rise up from the base of the mouth. [Adapted from C. Pfaffman, "Studying the Senses of Taste and Smell," in T. G. Andrews, ed., *Methods of Psychology*. New York: Wiley, 1948.]

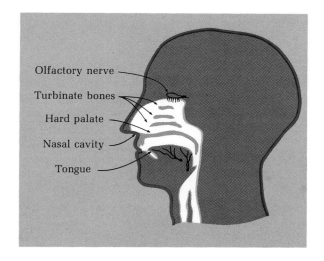

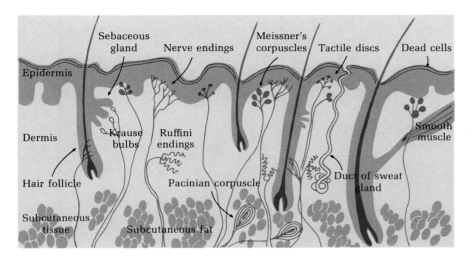

Figure 12.18
The skin is one of the most elaborate and interesting of the body's sense organs. It contains a multitude of different receptors that respond to a variety of stimuli. [Adapted from *Psychology Today: An Introduction*, 2nd ed. Del Mar, California: CRM, Inc., 1972.]

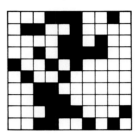

Figure 12.19
An example of the locations within a square centimeter of skin in the forearm where cold was felt when a chilled pin head touched the skin.

plex, and as yet, no one has produced a classification that seems wholly satisfactory. We should note that much of what we ordinarily think of as taste is produced by the olfactory receptors, as we notice if we hold our nostrils shut and try to distinguish between a bite of an apple and a bite of a raw turnip or potato.

Interesting research is being conducted on chemical sensitivity, but the technical nature of the data and theories places the topic outside the scope of this volume. We must refer the reader to more specialized texts for further information on chemical sensitivity.

The Skin Receptors The skin harbors an elaborate and varied array of receptors (see Figure 12.18). These receptors respond to mechanical pressure, heat and cold, and electrical stimulation. However, there is no absolutely clear evidence that one type of receptor consistently responds to a particular type of stimulus, although one group, the so-called free nerve endings, seem to be consistently correlated with pain. We can demonstrate this lack of specificity by pressing a chilled metal pinhead lightly to different spots on someone's forearm. If

we were to map out all those spots at which the person feels the cold, we would find that only some of the spots we press actually sense the cold (see Figure 12.19). If we then examined the receptors underneath each cold spot, we would not usually find one particular type of receptor for each. Most of the receptors in the skin do not seem to be specific for a certain sensation. Together, they somehow enable us to perceive a wide variety of sensations: warmth and cold, touch and pressure, pain, as well as more complex sensations, such as itch, tickle, wetness, and so on.

Helen Keller (1880–1968), the famous writer and lecturer who was both deaf and blind, learned to read words that were traced on her skin. In recent years, researchers working on the problem of blindness have begun to develop a new use for the skin receptors. With the aid of television cameras and other modern electronic equipment, these researchers have translated patterns of light into dot patterns (of pressure or electric stimulation) on areas of the skin of blind subjects. If this research proves successful, the skin may eventually become a substitute retina for the blind. To date, blind subjects using such systems in the laboratory have been able

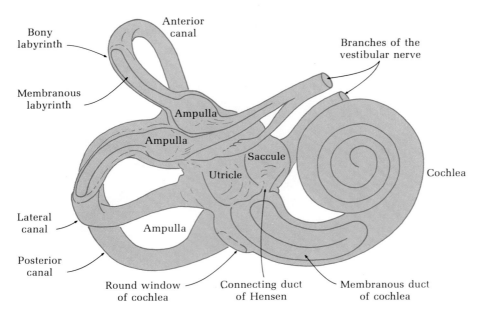

Bony
labyrinth

Anterior
canal

Branches of the
vestibular nerve

Membranous
labyrinth

Ampulla

Ampulla

Saccule

Cochlea

Utricle

Lateral
canal

Ampulla

Posterior
canal

Round window
of cochlea

Connecting duct
of Hensen

Membranous duct
of cochlea

Figure 12.20
Located next to the cochlea is a labyrinth of three semi-circular canals that provides the largely unfelt sensory input that allows us to maintain our balance. When these receptors are stimulated harshly or abruptly, we become dizzy—and aware of our sense of balance. [Adapted from F. A. Geldard, *The Human Senses.* New York: Wiley, 1953.

to read large printed words and to discriminate among a few simple objects.

The Receptors for Position, Movement and Balance Receptors in our muscles, tendons, and joints enable us to sense the position of our limbs (the kinesthetic sense) and to perceive our body movements. These receptors are stimulated by the pressure and stress that is applied to them when our muscles move our limbs and hold them in various positions.

An elaborate system in the inner ear (the *vestibular system*) is responsible for the sensations of balance, and (when we lose our balance) for the sensation of dizziness. This system consists of three *semicircular canals*, arranged at right angles to one another, and two sac-like chambers, the *utricle* and the *saccule* (Figure 12.20). The semicircular canals have enlarged ends containing receptor cells that respond to any

movement or rotation of the head. The receptors in the utricle and saccule respond to the forces of gravity. Extreme or repetitive disturbance of the vestibular senses—such as those that can occur when we are in a boat on rough seas—can cause dizziness and nausea. Fortunately, however, we can adapt to nearly any disturbance: thus sailors overcome sea sickness, and astronauts eventually find weightlessness an almost normal condition.

TRANSDUCTION

In the preceding sections we have briefly examined the physical characteristics of the stimuli to which we are sensitive, the way in which these stimuli come into contact with our sense organs, and the nature of some of the major sensory organs and their receptors. We shall now consider *transduction*, the process by which the physical energy of stimuli is converted into neural energy. But first we need a basic understanding of the neural energy itself, and the system in which it is conducted.

The nervous system is composed of tissues that are *electrically excitable: nerve fibers* and clusters or layers of nerve *cells* (see Figure 12.21), and the supportive tissue that fleshes out and separates the

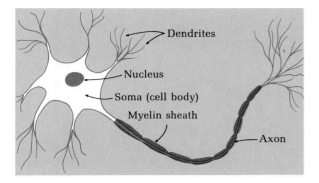

Figure 12.21
A representative nerve cell. The dendrites collect electrical impulses from other cells and the axon sends the impulses on to the next cell.

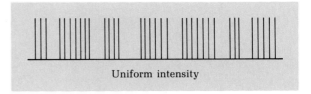

Uniform intensity

Figure 12.22
If we record the electrical activity in a single nerve, we find that the nerve either fires or does not—there are no intermediate effects. Each firing produces on our record a spike that marks a brief period of electrical activity. The individual spikes may be frequent or infrequent, but they are always uniform in intensity.

groups of fibers and cells. Electrical events in the nervous system can be recorded by means of very tiny *electrodes* inserted into either fibers or cells. Studies show that cells communicate with each other by means of *electrical impulses* sent along nerve fibers. Other studies of these events have produced two concepts that are particularly important for our purposes: the *all-or-none-law* of the nervous system and the *refractory period*.

The all-or-none-law describes the way in which nerve fibers perform their basic task of communicating between groups of nerve cells by electrical impulses. According to the law, a nerve fiber at any given instant is either active or inactive, either it is transmitting an impulse, or it is not (see Figure 12.22). No nerve fiber is partially active. The *refractory period* determines the rapidity with which a nerve fiber can send impulses: that is, the activity of sending the impulse temporarily depletes the fiber's resources, and the fiber requires a short period (the refractory period) of a millisecond or less to recover before it can transmit an impulse again. Consequently, the frequency with which any nerve fiber can send impulses is limited to a few thousand or so per second.

What initiates any given nerve impulse is the generation of electrical activity in a quantity sufficient to initiate a "send" signal to the nerve fiber in question. The means by which that electrical activity is generated is the process of transduction. Just as

the sensory organs vary in structure and function, the transduction that takes place in each sensory system operates in very different ways. In the following paragraphs we will briefly examine two different processes of transduction—visual and auditory.

Visual Transduction   The visual receptors (rods and cones) each contain *photopigment*, which absorbs light energy. Light causes the pigment to decompose temporarily. As a result of this decomposition, a visual nerve fiber is triggered into electrical activity. (The pigment subsequently recomposes in the absence of light.) The rods' pigment, *rhodopsin*, which has been isolated from the retinas of animals, has properties that explain several important visual phenomena.

Astonishingly little energy is needed to initiate enough activity in the nerve for a person to be aware of a visual sensation. Indeed, if only seven rods simultaneously absorb just one quantum of light energy each, vision will occur. A flashlight bulb produces some 2,000,000,000,000,000 quanta in one millisecond; the total of 7 quanta required for vision is minute indeed. The eye is obviously a highly sensitive device.

Auditory Transduction   Transduction of waves in the cochlea to nerve impulses in the acoustic nerve is accomplished by the hair cells of the organ of Corti (see Figure 12.13). Movement of the hairs triggers neural impulses. There is much about auditory transduction that we still do not know, but we do know where it takes place. We also know that the ear, like the eye, is extremely sensitive. Movements of the eardrum over distances smaller than the diameter of the hydrogen atom result in our hearing a sound.

TRANSMISSION OF NEURAL IMPULSES

If we are to experience sensation, it is necessary that activity in the brain, mainly in the cerebral cortex, take place. The cerebral cortex is an intricate layer of nerve cells and fibers that covers the top, sides, and crevices of the brain. Once the receptor has transduced physical energy into electrical or neural energy, bundles of nerve fibers called *tracts* carry the neural impulses from the receptor to the cortex. There are different nerve tracts for each of our sensory organs. In this discussion, we shall examine only the visual tracts, which should give us a sufficient appreciation of the basic principles—and the complexities—of the transmission of neural impulses.

Figure 12.23 shows the visual tracts, which run from the receptors in the retina to the occipital lobes of the cerebral cortex. Figures 12.7 and 12.9 illustrate the neural connections between receptors and the nerve fibers attached to them. In the fovea, one cone connects to one bipolar cell, and a number of bipolar cells go to a *ganglion cell* (a ganglion is a small aggregate of nerve cells). Cones, then, have more individual direct contact than do rods, which are generally connected in groups of several to one or more bipolar cells. (It is as if the rods need to pool their resources). The nerves that emanate from the rods are interconnected by an extensive system of *amacrine* cells. Thus there is more communication

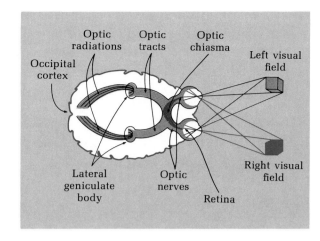

Figure 12.23
This schematic diagram shows how information is transported from the retina to the occipital cortex in the brain.

between individual rods and groups of rods than there is between the individual cones.

The nerve fibers from the retina converge at the blind spot on the rear wall of each eyeball and run out the back of the eye as the optic nerve. The optic tracts from each eye meet at the base of the brain, at the *optic chiasma* (from the Greek letter χ). Here, both tracts divide and about half of the fibers of each tract go to each half of the brain. As Figure 12.23 shows, visual stimuli originating from an object to the right of the person (and hence falling on the left side of each eye) are routed to the left side of the brain, and stimuli originating from an object to the left of the person (and falling on the right side of each eye) are routed to the right side of the brain. Damage to one side of the brain cannot, therefore, eliminate all of our vision.

Beyond the chiasma, the optic tracts on each side ascend via relay stations to two complex masses of nerve cells, the lateral *geniculate bodies*. From there, the nerve fibers coming from the retina fan out and continue to the occipital lobe of the cortex, where the final processes that transform the neural impulses into visual sensation actually take place.

All of our sensory systems are characterized by a similar transmission of nerve impulses from the receptors through relay stations to the cerebral cortex.

NEURAL PROCESSING

What sort of information is carried by the nerve tracts of our sensory systems, and what forms does it take? How are sensory stimuli coded for neural transmission? How are they converted into information for the brain? To date, complete answers to these questions are not known, but certain experimental findings on *stimulus coding* suggest that at some time in the future someone will be able to propose descriptions and theories that are more specific.

Stimulus Coding Since we are aware of both the intensity and the frequency of sounds, information about at least these two properties must be carried by the nerves to our brains. How could this be done? At first glance, it appears that nerves have very little capacity for carrying information. They are, after all, limited by the refractory period to a highest frequency at which they can send impulses, so that there is only a limited number of frequencies that a nerve can encode directly for the brain. The intensity of the nerve impulse is essentially useless for carrying information because it is limited to only one intensity by the all-or-none law. But there is more to the story than this.

Nerves are, we have seen, specialized to the sense that they serve. The optic nerve always carries information that leads us to see; the nerves from the skin carry information that is interpreted as pertaining to the skin, no matter how the nerves are stimulated. Electrical stimulation of the optic nerve produces a sensation of light even though light is not the actual stimulus. So, *which nerves* are active carries

a great deal of information to the brain. This idea can be carried further, since, in the eye, *which part* of the retina is sending out nerve impulses tells the brain where in the visual field the stimulus is located, just as *which part* of the skin tells the brain where the stimulus is located on our body.

Additional ways of encoding information arise from the fact that there is communication between nerve fibers and cells. Thus, a given nerve can be affected not only by what is directly impinging on it but also by what is happening to its neighbors. There is both horizontal and vertical communication. At the retinal level, for example, there are horizontal connections between nerves coming from individual receptors. As we move vertically up the optic tract toward the brain, we find nerve cells that respond to what is happening to many nerve fibers at a lower level. This sort of structure allows a quite complex encoding and a rich and patterned array of information to be carried to the brain.

A closer examination of vertical communication between nerves reveals more of the complexities of neural encoding and processing. In ways that are not completely understood, several nerves from receptors converge at nerve cells closer to the brain and make it possible for these cells to have very complicated functions.

The following information comes from studies with cats and monkeys. In these studies, an animal's eye is immobilized and pointed at a screen on which lights can be projected in various locations corresponding exactly to points on the animal's retina. The experimenter records the electrical activity of various cells in the animal's brain by means of electrodes inserted through the skull and down into the cells.

These studies have furnished knowledge about several kinds of responses to light by individual cells. One type of brain cell has quite a lot of electrical activity in the dark and responds with a decrease in activity when light is directed to the part of the retina that sends nerves to the cell. Other cells can be found that respond with increased activity only to darkness, that is, when a light is turned off. And still others increase their activity when a light comes on, just as we would expect from a light-detecting system. But the first two kinds of responses indicate that the visual system is more than just a light detector. This suspicion is enhanced when we learn that many responses to the onset or offset of light are transient: the cell's activity changes but only for a short time, quickly returning to its level before the light changes. This, like the fixed-image experiment, suggests that the visual system is a difference detector designed to respond to changes in light.

Even more complex response systems have been found. Some brain cells respond only to spots or bars of light or dark that move in particular directions. One such cell increases its electrical activity whenever a bar of light moves horizontally across the screen but not when it moves vertically. Others respond only to other highly specific stimuli in a seemingly endless variety of ways. It is thought that these specialized responses by single brain cells to complex stimuli are due to the structure of the visual nervous system. Various bits of information from a number of different receptors converge at a single brain cell in a way that allows that cell to respond only to specific stimuli, such as horizontally moving bars of light.

INTERPRETATION

We have briefly surveyed (1) some of the stimuli we perceive, (2) the way in which they come into contact with our receptors, (3) the transduction of stimulus energy into neural impulses, (4) the way in which these impulses are conveyed to the brain, and (5) a few of the ways in which the nervous system apparently converts and processes stimulus information.

Although we have some understanding of the elementary structures and functions of our sensory apparatus, no one has yet been able to provide a wholly satisfactory answer to the basic question: how do we perceive? All that we can really ascertain is that somehow the complex and intricate activity of the nervous system produces perception. But our inability to offer a more concrete explanation at this time need not deter us from studying perception. Just as we can inquire into the facts of the earth's rotation on its axis, even though we do not know how, why, or when it began to spin in the first place, so we can ask about the properties of our sensory systems without knowing why we experience sensation. We shall examine some of the properties of our perceptual world in the next chapter.

Suggested Readings

Grossman, S. P. (1967) *A textbook of physiological psychology*. New York: Wiley. [The accounts and bibliographies in Parts 1 and 2 are a good starting place for further reading.]

Von Fieandt, K. (1966) *The world of perception*. Homewood, Illinois: Dorsey. [Another good source for further readings.]

CHAPTER THIRTEEN

Sensory Phenomena

The big question, "How do we perceive?" is still essentially unanswered. If we fully understood the workings of our sensory systems, we would be able to explain in orderly and logical fashion the various sensory phenomena that we experience. Since we do not have such knowledge, we are obliged to study the sensory phenomena themselves because they may furnish clues and indications that may eventually enable us to describe the entire process of perception. Futhermore, they are intrinsically interesting. Whatever answer is ultimately devised—if indeed one is ever possible—it will have to explain all of the sensory phenomena we are about to discuss.

Sensory systems—vision, hearing, taste, smell, the skin senses, and others—have many characteristics in common. For each of them, we can (1) distinguish between intensity and quality, (2) identify the minimum stimulus energy needed to activate them, and (3) observe the changes in degree of sensation produced by varying the values of the corresponding stimuli. This chapter is organized around these characteristics that the senses have in common. Our discussion will center on vision and hearing, about which the most is known, but we shall also refer to the other senses when it is useful or specially interesting.

THE THRESHOLD

Every sensory system has a lower limit of sensitivity and cannot detect less than a minimum amount of energy. In Chapter 11 we discussed these *absolute thresholds* and described various ways of measuring them. In this chapter, we shall continue our discussion.

In vision, the amount of energy necessary to attain the threshold of sensation depends on the wavelength of the stimulus (Figure 13.1); and in hearing and vibratory sensation on the skin, the minimum amount of energy (or the intensity of the stimulus necessary to reach the threshold) depends on the frequency of the sound or vibration (Figures 13.2 and 13.3). A similar dependence probably exists for the other senses as well, but not enough is known about the physical dimensions of the stimuli for us to be sure.

Figure 13.1 shows the relationship between energy and wavelength at threshold in vision, and Figures 13.2 and 13.3 illustrate that between threshold energy and frequency in hearing and in the sensation of vibration. Since the *amount* of energy required to produce a first noticeable sensation increases along the vertical axis, the points of maximum sensitivity

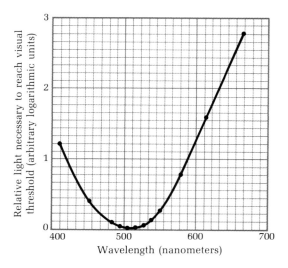

Figure 13.1
The smallest amount of light energy that can just barely be seen varies with the wavelength of the light. This graph shows the relative amounts of energy required to reach absolute threshold as a function of the wavelength of the light. Notice that the eye is most sensitive to light of around 510 nanometers and is less sensitive to shorter and longer wavelengths. [Adapted from F. A. Geldard, *The Human Senses*. New York: Wiley, 1953. Data from Hecht and Williams.]

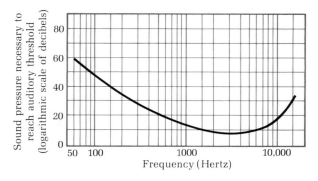

Figure 13.2
The smallest amount of acoustic energy that can just barely be heard varies with the frequency of the sound. The ear is most sensitive to frequencies around 3,000 Hertz. [Adapted from L. J. Sivian and S. D. White, "On Minimum Audible Sound Fields," *Journal of the Acoustical Society of America*, 1933, 4, 288–321.]

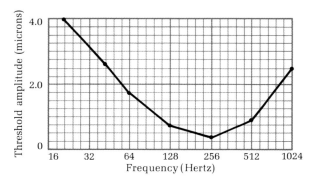

Figure 13.3
The intensity of a vibration that can just be felt by the fingertip depends on the frequency of the vibration. Our fingers are most sensitive to frequencies around 250 Hertz. [Adapted from F. A. Geldard, "The Perception of Mechanical Vibration: The Frequency Function." *Journal of General Psychology*, 1940, 22, 281–289; data of four researchers have been averaged.]

are where the curves are lowest: about 510 *nanometers* (*nm*) in vision; about 3000 *Hertz* (*Hz*) in hearing; about 250 Hertz in the vibratory sense.

THE MAGNITUDE OF SENSATION

The sensory magnitudes for a large variety of sensations have been measured by such methods as *ratio estimation, ratio production, magnitude estimation,* and *magnitude production* (see the discussion on "The New Psychophysics" in Chapter 11). No matter which method is used, the question to be answered is always how much more or less intense is the sensation produced by one intensity than the sensation produced by a higher or lower intensity? The result is a psychophysical function: a statement or curve describing the relationship between growth in sensation magnitude and growth in stimulus magnitude.

As we also discussed in Chapter 11, these psychophysical relations have been plotted according to the Stevens power law, which is today accepted by many as the universal psychophysical law. Recall that equal stimulus ratios correspond to equal sensation ratios. In other words, if we must *multiply* the stimulus by four to double the sensation magnitude, we must

Table 13.1
Representative Exponents

Continuum	Exponent	Stimulus Condition
Loudness	0.60	Binaural
Loudness	0.54	Monaural
Brightness	0.33	5° target (dark-adapted eye)
Brightness	0.50	Point source (dark-adapted eye)
Lightness	1.20	Reflectance of gray papers
Smell	0.55	Coffee odor
Smell	0.60	Heptane
Taste	0.80	Saccharine
Taste	1.30	Sucrose
Taste	1.30	Salt
Temperature	1.00	Cold (on arm)
Temperature	1.50	Warmth (on arm)
Vibration	0.95	60 Hertz (on finger)
Vibration	0.60	250 Hertz (on finger)
Duration	1.10	White-noise stimulus
Repetition rate	1.00	Light, sound, touch, and shocks
Finger span	1.30	Thickness of wood blocks
Pressure on palm	1.10	Static force on skin
Heaviness	1.45	Lifted weights
Force of handgrip	1.70	Precision hand dynamometer
Vocal effort	1.10	Sound pressure of vocalization
Electric shock	3.50	60 Hertz (through fingers)
Tactual roughness	1.50	Felt diameter of emery grits
Tactual hardness	0.80	Rubber squeezed between fingers
Visual velocity	1.20	Moving spot of light
Visual length	1.00	Projected line of light
Visual area	0.70	Projected square of light

Source: S. S. Stevens, *In Pursuit of Sensory Law*; second public Klopsteg lecture (Evanston, Ill.: Technological Institute, Northwestern University, November 7, 1962, p. 7.)

multiply the stimulus by sixteen (4 × 4) to quadruple (2 × 2) the sensation magnitude and so on—every time we multiply the stimulus by 4, we multiply the sensation by 2. Mathematically, this relationship is expressed as $s = k(I)^n$, where s refers to the sensation, k is a constant determined by the choice of units, and I is the stimulus that is raised to a particular power, or exponent, n. One of the important advantages of this law is the description of psychophysical relations in terms of their exponents. For example, if you consult Table 13.1, you will notice the large range of exponents, from the lowest, 0.33 for brightness, to the highest, 3.5 for electric shock. Note also that warmth and cold have different exponents, indicating that the two are separate sense modalities thoughout the skin; and that, although many substances, including saccharine and sugars, taste sweet, each has its own exponent. (The significance of this variation is not yet understood.)

Referring back to Figure 11.10, where a few psychophysical relations have been plotted within arithmetic coordinates, note that a sensation with an exponent greater than 1.0 (such as electric shock) increases more and more rapidly as stimulus magnitude increases (it is positively accelerated), and that a sensation with an exponent of less than 1.0 (such as brightness) increases more and more slowly (it is negatively accelerated). One interesting aspect of this variation is that some sensations with exponents greater than 1.0 seem to be signs of danger (for example, electric shock rapidly becomes painful), whereas those with exponents of less than 1.0 are all phenomena from which we extract information (such as the perception of light). Sensations that signify danger seem to increase rapidly, functioning as early warning systems, but those that provide us with information invariably increase slowly, thus permitting us to respond to a large range of stimulus magnitudes without overloading our sensory systems.

Defects in Magnitude Perception Certain kinds of deafness and blindness are reflected in psychophysical relations. _Nerve deafness_ is a condition in which hearing is normal if the stimulus is above a certain intensity but severely hindered below that intensity. In an experiment measuring sensory magnitude, a person with this disability generates the relation shown in Figure 13.4: below the critical intensity, his sensations decline in magnitude much more rapidly than those of normal people. _Night blindness_ is a condition in which vision is normal in daylight but seriously impaired in faint light or in the dark. A person with this disability generates the relation shown in Figure 13.5: below a given level of illumination, there is no sensory magnitude whatsoever. The person's visual system cannot _adapt_ to the dark.

ADAPTATION

The most intense sound pressure that we can hear is more than one million times greater than the pressure at the threshold of sensitivity to loudness. The amount of light energy on a bright, clear day is at least that much larger than the amount at the threshold of sensitivity to brightness. Yet we can perceive

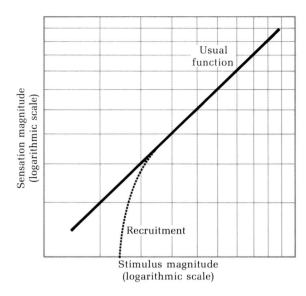

Figure 13.4
In some forms of deafness, the reported loudness of sounds (the sensation magnitude) is normal when the intensity of the sound (the stimulus magnitude) is above a certain level. Below that level, though, the reported loudness declines more rapidly than is normal as the intensity is decreased. Conversely, as the intensity increases the sensation grows more rapidly than is normal. (This is called "recruitment.")

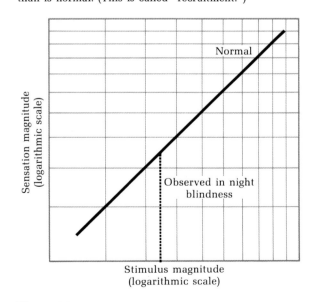

Figure 13.5
In night blindness, the sensation magnitude drops abruptly to zero. Thus, nothing is seen below a certain stimulus level.

stimuli for hearing and seeing not only at these extremes, but also at every intensity in between. This capacity of our sensory systems to operate effectively across such a wide range is called *adaptation*. All of the sensory systems have this capacity, but the mechanisms and the degree of adaptation differ.

Visual Adaptation   The visual system is really two systems in one. One system consists of the rods, the receptors in the eye that respond to low intensities. At these intensities, the other system of receptors, the *cones* do not function at all; rather, cones require considerably more light, and also it is the cones that enable us to perceive color. Consequently, at night our vision is dependent almost solely on the *rods*, which are sensitive to the lower intensities of light; but because the rods do not allow us to perceive color, we see only gradations of brightness in a world that is achromatic (lacking in color) unless we are exposed to lights intense enough to excite the cones. (The eye and its receptors were described in Chapter 12.)

The way in which this dual system works can be demonstrated by two experiments, the first of which you can perform yourself at home. Go into a very dimly lighted room and just sit and wait for about ten to twenty minutes without looking directly at any sources of light. Notice that you become gradually able to see more of the room and its objects in dim illumination. The process your visual system has undergone is called, not surprisingly, *dark adaptation*. What has occurred is a switch from color (cone) vision to rod vision, and, if the room is dark enough the cones will be totally inactive and your vision will be totally achromatic. This transition has been formally and exactly studied in the laboratory, by means of such experiments as the following.

This experiment is similar to the first one, but conditions are more tightly controlled and exact

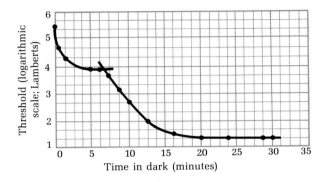

Figure 13.6
Normal eyes that have been exposed to daylight will adapt to the dark. At first, the threshold intensity declines rapidly. Soon, it levels off: the cones have become a little more sensitive in the dark. After about seven minutes in the dark, the cone portion of the curve ceases because the more sensitive rods allow us to see at intensities well below those that excite the cones. [Adapted from S. Hecht and S. Schlaer, "An Adaptometer for Human Dark Adaptation," *Journal of the Optical Society of America*, 1938, *28*, 269–275.]

measurements are taken. The procedure is nothing more than the measurement of threshold, which we have already discussed (in Chapter 11). The subject is removed from sunlight abruptly into a room that is totally dark. In the room, there is a source of light that can be illuminated at any time and at any given intensity. Periodically—about once a minute—the subject is asked to pay close attention to the source of stimulation and to report the instant at which he sees the light, which is turned on and gradually increased in intensity. As soon as the subject reports perception, we record the intensity of the light.

The results can be represented by a curve such as that in Figure 13.6, which shows that the intensity necessary to stimulate vision is determined by the amount of time the observer has been in the dark. Note the two parts of the curve: the first part shows that the intensity required for a stimulus to be just barely perceived (the threshold of sensitivity to brightness) is highest at first and gradually declines until it levels off at an intensity that is still quite high, during the first five minutes or so in the dark; the second part describes a sharper decline in required intensity in the course of the next ten to twenty minutes. The first part of the curve describes the increase in sensitivity of the cones in the dark, and every light that is perceived during those first minutes of the experiment can be identified by its color. The second part describes the increasing sensitivity of the rods, which take longer than the cones to become active in the dark after exposure to light, but which become more sensitive than the cones at about seven minutes and continue to increase in sensitivity thereafter. This shift, in dark surroundings, from the moderately insensitive cones to the extremely sensitive rods is the primary adaptive mechanism of our visual system.

We can investigate this mechanism in greater detail by making a few simple modifications in the foregoing laboratory experiment. One modification is to locate the stimulus and focus the subject's eye in such a way that light falls only on the fovea, that part of the retina consisting solely of cones (see Chapter 12). Obviously we will obtain only the first part of the preceding results: since the rods are not stimulated, there are no receptors to pick up lower amounts of light energy, and the threshold will remain constant after about five minutes because the cones have attained their maximal sensitivity in dark surroundings.

An interesting variation is to conduct the experiment with different wavelengths of light. For each wavelength, the threshold that each part of the curve attains as the receptors develop sensitivity in the dark differs. These results can be summarized by

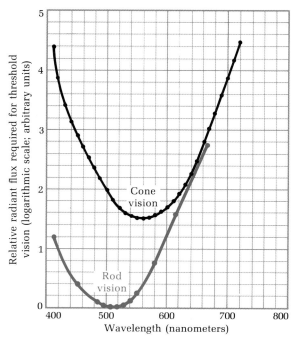

Figure 13.7
Threshold curves—of intensity plotted against wavelength—for the rods (*lower curve*) and the cones (*upper curve*). [Adapted from F. A. Geldard, *The Human Senses.* New York: Wiley, 1953.]

threshold curves for both rods and cones, describing the different thresholds attained for each wavelength of the light (see Figure 13.7). Notice that the threshold curve for the cones is at its lowest threshold (and maximum sensitivity) at about 555 nanometers, a wavelength that is perceived as greenish-yellow; and that the threshold for the rods is lowest at about 510 nanometers, which is green. Notice also that the thresholds of sensitivity to wavelengths of around 700 nanometers (the red hues) are very high for the cones, although these wavelengths are not perceived at all by the rods. This explains why in dim lighting—for example, in twilight—the reds and yellows (the longer wavelengths) lose their brightness and the blues and greens appear brighter by comparison. As night continues to fall, those colors that are the brightest by daylight will disappear and be replaced by gray, whereas green objects will continue to appear green for a longer time. This shift in visibility—from the longer wavelengths to the shorter—is called the *Purkinje effect*, after the Czech observer who first described it.

Auditory Adaptation   Moderate and strong acoustic sensations fade slightly in the course of a long period of time. Thus, loud music seems a little less loud as we become accustomed to it, but only a little. This kind of reduction, then, is a form of adaptation, but not a pronounced one. Apparently, the auditory system does not need as elaborate an adaptive mechanism as the visual system: indeed, extremely intense acoustic stimuli are not common in nature whereas highly intense visual stimuli, such as the rays coming directly from the sun, are. In short, the auditory system is well suited for detecting faint sounds, but has no natural need for a separate system of "auditory cones" to perceive intense stimuli.

Chemical Adaptation   Unlike the auditory system, the systems of smell and taste adapt quite markedly to the chemical stimuli that activate them (Figure 13.8 illustrates the rate of olfactory adaptation to certain stimuli). Continued exposure to any taste or smell results in a greatly diminished sensitivity to that stimulus. A flower garden, for example, is extremely fragrant when we are first exposed to it, but if we remain in it for even a short length of time, we are soon totally unaware of the aromas around us.

Thermal Adaptation   A final example of sensory adaptation is that of our skin senses to a wide range of thermal stimuli. This can be illustrated by the following classic demonstration, which you can try yourself. Get three glasses or other containers and fill one with tap water, one with hot water, and the

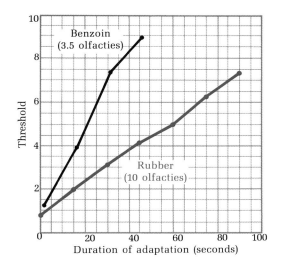

Figure 13.8
Adaptation to two different odors—that of benzoin and that of rubber. As a person is exposed to the odors for longer and longer periods of time, a larger and larger amount of the substance is needed in order to detect its odor. [Adapted from H. Zwaardemaker, *L'odorat*. Paris: Doin, 1925.]

third with ice water. Then put your left hand into the hot water and your right hand into the cold water. At first, the left hand will feel warm, the other cool. But soon they will both feel normal, for thermal adaptation has taken place. At this point, put both hands into the tap water. The hand from the cold water will feel the tap water as warm, and the hand from the hot water will feel the same water as cold.

THE QUALITY OF SENSATION

The variety of sensory qualities—such as colors, pitches, odors, and flavors—are, to borrow a phrase,

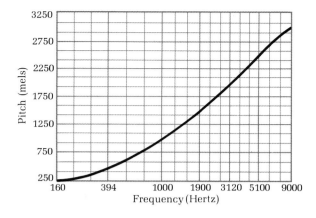

Figure 13.9
How the pitch of a sound (measured in mels) increases with increases in the frequency (in Hertz) of the sound. [Adapted from S. S. Stevens and J. Volkmann, "The Relation of Pitch to Frequency," *American Journal of Psychology*, 1940, *53*, 329–353.]

the spice of life. But the perception of such qualities poses difficult problems for the psychologists and physiologists who try to understand it. The fundamental phenomena are not difficult to comprehend: for example, the colors we see are correlated with the wavelengths of light emitted or reflected by objects; the pitches we hear are correlated with the frequencies of sound; and the ways in which visual or auditory stimuli combine to produce combination colors or sounds have been understood for a long time. That there are defects in our perception of the qualities in each modality is also known and these have been studied extensively. As a result, reasonably plausible theories of the mechanics of both color perception and the detection of different pitches of sound have been formulated, but there remain unresolved areas for which the prevailing descriptions do not furnish satisfactory explanations. In this section, we will be concerned with the perception of sensory qualities in vision and hearing, beginning with hearing since it is less complex and more clearly understood.

HEARING

Pitch Perception The physical frequency of a sound is measured in Hertz and the sensation of pitch is measured in *mels*. Figure 13.9 shows the psychophysical relation between pitch and frequency, that is, the way in which the sensation of pitch (in mels) increases with increasing frequency of the stimulus (in Hz). Thus if we have several pairs of stimuli, each differing by the same number of mels, the number of Hz by which each pair differs will not be constant. For a further explanation of these psychophysical relations, review the section on the new psychophysics in Chapter 11.

Tones can be combined in an infinite variety of ways. If two of the same frequency occur together and are in phase—that is, both are compressing and

rarefying the air simultaneously—they reinforce each other; if they are of the same frequency and intensity but are totally out of phase—so that one compresses as the other rarefies—they completely cancel each other and there is no sound at all; in general, however, two waves will be neither exactly in phase nor exactly out of phase, but somewhere in between. If two or more tones of different frequencies are combined, we hear combination tones. When sound waves of all frequencies, each with the same intensity, occur in random phase, they combine to produce a random fluctuation called *white noise*—sounding much like the whisper "shhh."

A remarkable feature of the ear is that it perceives a complex tone not as a single sound but as a combination of the component elementary tones: thus, when we perceive such a complex tone, we can discern at least some of the component tones. For example, if we listen to a recording of a symphony, we can distinguish certain orchestral sections—for example, the flutes and the bass viols—and with additional muscial training or ability, one can distinguish all of the sections. The formal description of our ability to perceive individual tones that compose a combination tone is called *Ohm's acoustic law*. This law implies that a great deal of information about the individual components of the wave is

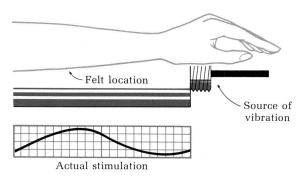

Figure 13.10
This model of the cochlea (which is simply a person's forearm with a tube of fluid attached) provides added evidence for the place theory of frequency coding. Different frequencies of vibration imparted at the indicated source are felt on the forearm at different locations. Although each frequency makes a large area of the arm vibrate, the vibration is felt at a specific location for each frequency. How can one feel in only one place when the stimulus covers a large area? Békésy proposed that the effects of energy at more intensely stimulated locations inhibits the effects of energy at less intensely stimulated locations. The result is that the total effect of the energy over the large area is *funneled* into the location of maximum stimulation.

somehow encoded in the auditory neural apparatus. This law is therefore significant enough that it must be incorporated into any theory of pitch perception.

Theories of Hearing   Theories of hearing attempt to explain the way in which the nervous system codes information about sound. Theorists have worried mainly about frequency, apparently the most difficult to encode.

The *volley theory* states that the auditory system somehow duplicates the frequencies in a sound wave. The cochlea responds to a sound wave by reproducing the wave's frequencies. However, recall that the *refractory period* limits the rate at which any single nerve can discharge impulses (see the section on transduction in Chapter 12). Consequently, one nerve alone cannot fire rapidly enough to follow a high frequency; instead several nerves would have to alternate in transmitting volleys of impulses; and that is what is proposed by the volley theory. This sort of direct representation of physical frequency in neural frequency may indeed occur, but it is almost certainly not a complete explanation of the auditory coding underlying our perception of pitches.

The *place theory of pitch* is supported by compelling evidence from several lines of research. Although any theory can be discredited by the discovery of a new fact that it cannot accommodate, the place theory remains the most acceptable theory of auditory coding. It proposes that the coding of physical frequency is determined by the place of stimulation on the organ of Corti, which extends along the length of the cochlea. Recall that incoming sound waves vibrate the basilar membrane and that those of different frequencies displace different parts of the membrane and stimulate different portions of the organ of Corti. The place theory says that we hear different pitches because different places on the organ of Corti have been stimulated.

The validity of the place theory has been supported by a variety of demonstrations. (1) Recall that stimulating the cochlea with different frequencies of sounds produces traveling waves that maximally stimulate different locations on the basilar membrane and organ of Corti. (2) A physical model of a stretched out cochlea has been used to determine the location of the sensation produced by stimuli of different frequencies. The model is a plastic tube, large enough to support someone's forearm. The tube is filled with fluid, a subject's forearm is placed on the tube, and the fluid is set in motion by a vibrating piston that produces traveling waves like those in the cochlea. It has been demonstrated that waves of different frequencies will produce localized stimulation of the skin at different places on the arm (see Figure 13.10). (3) It has been observed that damage to the organ of Corti by prolonged, very-high-intensity sounds occurs at different locations in the organ, depending on the frequency of the damaging stimulus. (4) Experimental surgical removal of localized places on the organ in animals produces loss of hearing for quite specific frequencies. In short, the place theory is quite well supported by the available evidence.

VISION

Color Perception   Most of us can see between 125 and 130 separate colors. Figure 13.11 shows how this is possible in terms of the minimum change in any wavelength that is required for an observer to distinguish a different color or shade of a color. Notice that a stimulus of 500 nanometers need only be changed by one, to 501, in order for the normal observer to detect a change in color. Since such changes are extremely small, many different colors can be seen. There is no contradiction between this fact and the fact that we have only a limited number of names for colors. Rather, most of us—those who are not painters or printers or artists—simply choose to ignore many differences that we can distinguish clearly and consistently under ordinary circumstances, as well as numerous other variations that can be reliably perceived only in the tightly controlled conditions of the psychologist's laboratory.

In addition to brightness and hue (the psychologists' term for color), a chromatic sensation has saturation, meaning the degree to which it differs from gray. Color Plate II shows the Munsell system of colors, arranged according to hue, brightness, and saturation.

Just as we can combine tones for the ear or create a mélange of tastes for the palate, so can we mix colors for the eye. Let us begin by distinguishing between the two types of *color mixing*, *subtractive* and *additive*. Subtractive mixing occurs when we mix paints; additive when we mix lights.

In subtractive mixture, each paint absorbs (and thus subtracts) some wavelengths from the light falling on it; when two or more pigments are combined, still more wavelengths are absorbed. The

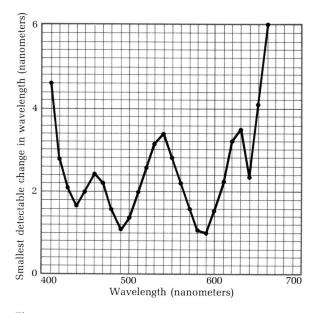

Figure 13.11
This graph shows how much *change in wavelength* is needed in a given stimulus in order for an observer to notice a *change in the hue* (color) of that stimulus. Note that the changes are extremely tiny. [Data from L. A. Jones, "The Fundamental Scale of Pure Hue and Retinal Sensibility to Hue Differences," *Journal of the Optical Society of America*, 1917, *1*, 63–77.]

wavelengths that have not been absorbed are reflected back to our eye and cause us to perceive the color we see. Thus, when blue and yellow paints are mixed, green results because the green wavelengths have not been absorbed by either the blue or the yellow, and therefore it is these that are reflected back to the eye. In other words, the color that we see is determined by which wavelengths are *not* absorbed.

In additive mixture, we combine lights of different colors (wavelengths). We do not have pigments that absorb certain wavelengths, but rather light waves themselves. Consequently if two colors of light are mixed, none of the component wavelengths are subtracted; rather, all of them go on to the eye. From the eye, these combined stimuli are then transmitted to the brain, and by some process that we have no way of directly observing, the various wavelengths are mixed in the brain to produce the color that we ultimately perceive. Additive mixing can be demonstrated by projecting lights of different colors onto a screen and then combining them by overlapping them: for example, if red and green are combined in this way, the perceived result will be yellow.

Studies of additive color mixing have shown that red light, blue light, and green light can be mixed to produce any color in the spectrum: for this reason they are called the three *primary colors*. (The primary colors of pigments are red, blue, and yellow, which can be combined with the same effects—subtractively). Thus, with the wavelengths, red and green produce yellow; red and yellow, orange; red and blue, purple; and green and blue, blue-green. A combination of all three primary colors produces gray, and—if they are bright enough—pure white light.

Every primary color has a single *complementary color*: mixing any two complements results in gray. The complement of blue is yellow; of red, blue-green; of green, magenta. If we combine appropriate amounts of any two complementary colors—for example, a blue light and a yellow light—the result is gray, or, if the two lights are bright enough, white. Figure 13.12 enables us to determine the complement of any given wavelength: if we select a wavelength region along the horizontal axis of the graph, the vertical axis will show the complement of that wavelength.

Color Blindness   Before discussing theories of color vision, we will examine some defects in color

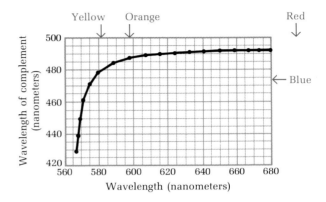

Figure 13.12
Complementary colors. To find two wavelengths that will produce gray if properly mixed together, find one on the horizontal axis, note its location on the curve, and read the other off the vertical axis. [Adapted from J. G. Priest, "Note on the Relation between the Frequency of Complementary Hues," *Journal of the Optical Society of America*, 1920, 4, 402–404; data from seven researchers have been averaged.]

vision, because an understanding of these defects will help to explain color perception. The most extreme form of color blindness is due to a genetically determined absence of cones in the retina. Such eyes see no color at all and have a second blind spot, or *scotoma*, in place of the normally cone-laden fovea. A person with this color defect normally perceives a world that is colorless. Studies of this type of color blindness have helped to confirm the cones as the organs of color perception.

Less extreme are the other forms of color blindness, which are more appropriately termed color anomalies because they permit some perception of color. In observing color-anomalous persons, experimenters have determined which colors are perceived—by such means as questioning subjects directly, analyzing the ways in which these subjects add lights together in order to match colored stimuli, and by soliciting reports from those very rare and valuable subjects who have the anomaly in only one eye.

The more common of these partial defects is the red-green anomaly, permitting a viewer to see only variously saturated yellows and blues as well as gray. Those having this anomaly see all wavelengths above about 500 nm (blue-green) as either yellow or gray, and all wavelengths below 500 nm as either blue or grayish. They can be further divided into two groups, who differ in that the first group, the *protanopes*, perceive reds as gray rather than yellow, and the second group, the *deuteranopes*, perceive a small band of wavelengths just below 500 nm as grayish rather than blue. Thus the colors that a person with normal vision perceives as

RED   ORANGE YELLOW GREEN   BLUE   VIOLET

are perceived by the protanope as

<u>GRAY</u>   YELLOW   YELLOW   YELLOW   BLUE   BLUE

and by the deuteranope as

YELLOW   YELLOW   YELLOW   YELLOW   <u>GRAY-BLUE</u>   BLUE

Aside from the red-green anomaly, a rarer defect is the yellow-blue anomaly (tritanopia). *Tritanopes* see all of the reds and greens, but perceive blues and yellows as white or—if these colors are dim—as gray.

People with color anomalies compensate for their defect somewhat by learning that certain objects are always called the same color, even if they themselves cannot perceive the color. Thus protanopes and deuteranopes, for example, learn that grass is "green," and that stoplights are "red." The main difficulty faced by people with color-defective vision, then, is that they confuse certain colors in unfamiliar objects or in multicolored items: for example, they will always have trouble selecting clothes that match or complement each other, without the help of someone with normal color vision.

Theories of Color Vision   There are two major sets of theories of color vision. Both originated in the nineteenth century, and both have been elaborated by current efforts to explain color vision. The *Young-Helmholtz theory* postulates that there are three types of retinal receptors for color—one for each of the three primary colors, red, green, and blue; and that various combinations of excitation of these receptors result in the perception of the colors that mixtures of the corresponding primary colors produce. In short, it is assumed that the process of color mixing that occurs in the person's nervous system is analogous to that which is known to occur when different wavelengths combine. Recently, this theory has gained additional support from data demonstrating that different wavelengths of light are absorbed by different pigments extracted from the retinas of chickens; thus, the retina has the capability of recognizing the three primaries.

The second theory—proposed by Ewald Hering—is based on the fact that mixing two colors—such as red and green—leads us to see neither color but rather gray. This suggests that the mechanisms responsible for red and green sensations may somehow oppose each other. This theory is most applicable as an explanation of the color anomalies and of our perception of complementary colors. It proposes that there are three different mechanisms in the retina, each producing two opposing qualities of sensation. The first is a "black-white" mechanism: when stimulated by visible light, it induces the perception of white; in the absence of light, this mechanism produces the sensation of black. The black-white mechanism accounts for our perception of brightness. The other two mechanisms account for color. One, a "red-green" mechanism opposes the sensation of red against the sensation of green. The other, a "yellow-blue" mechanism, opposes the sensation of yellow against the sensation of blue. Color

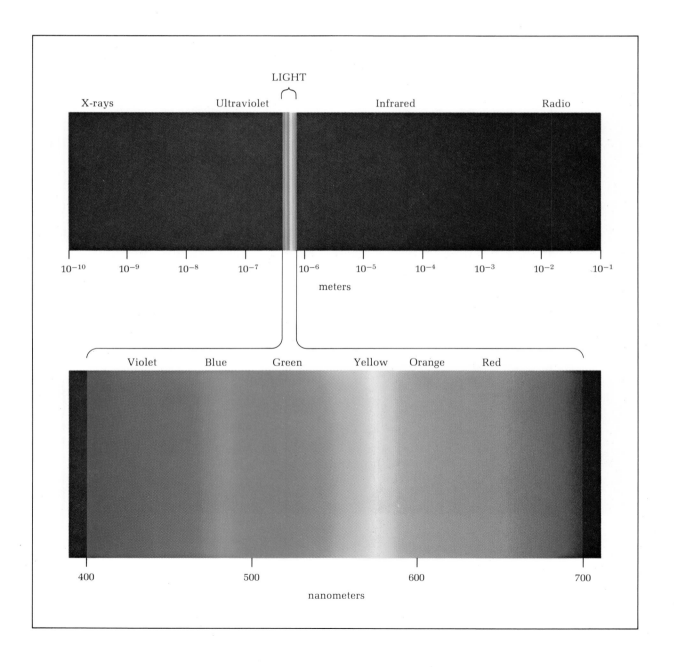

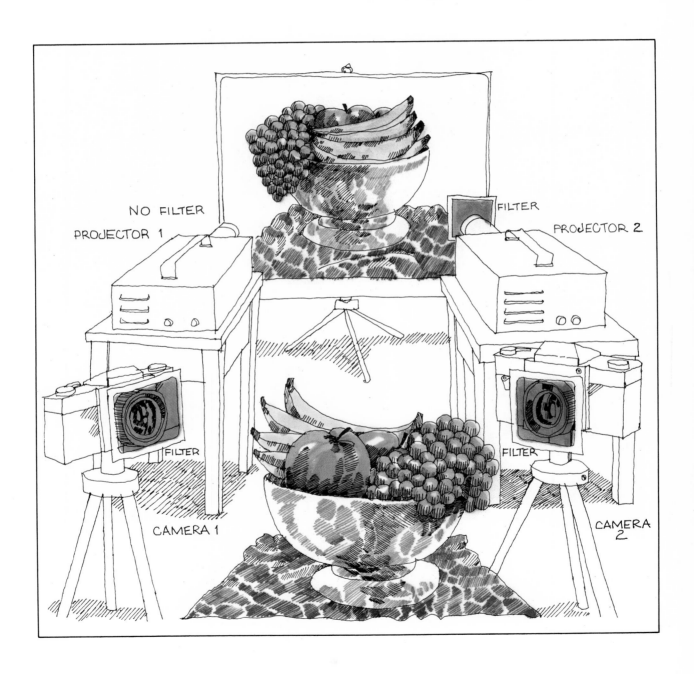

PLATE IV
The four central gray patches are all identical. A white surround makes the gray look darker; a black surround makes the gray look lighter. Colored surrounds tend to induce the complementary hue in the central gray. To see this, stare at the pictures in a moderate level of illumination.

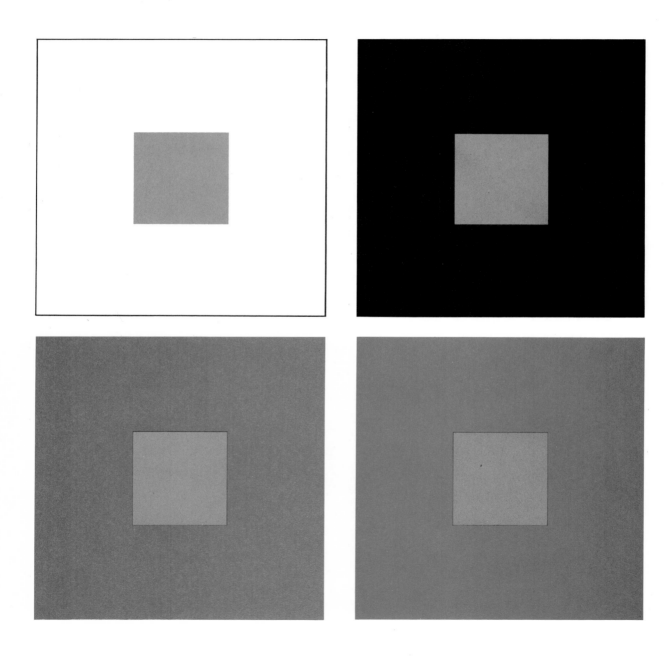

PLATE V
You will see a complementary afterimage of this scene if you first stare at the central dot for a minute and then look at the white space below. (Hold the book in a position that prevents glare but provides good illumination.)

PLATE VI
In good illumination without glare, stare at the center of the red and black figure for fifteen seconds, then at the center of the green and black figure for fifteen seconds, and then continue alternately staring at the two for fifteen seconds each until you have stared at each eight times. Then look at the black and white figure on the facing page. Note which white bars appear what color. Finally, rotate the book 90° and look for changes in color. You should observe the McCulloch effect. Its causes are not currently known.

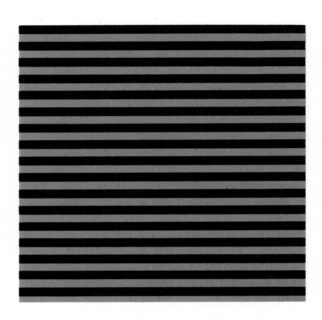

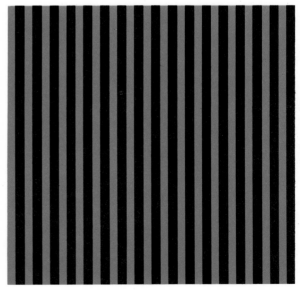

PLATE VII
Focus on the black dot at the center of the green
square for one minute. Then gaze at the white square
below it and observe the red afterimage. After a few
seconds, transfer your gaze to a more distant light-
colored surface (such as a white wall). Note that the
size of the afterimage seems larger when you look
at the more distant surface. The direct proportionality
between size and distance of the afterimage is
known as *Emmert's Law.*

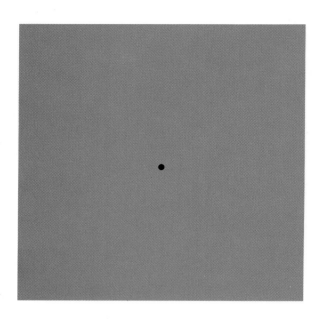

anomalies occur if either the red-green or the yellow-blue mechanism does not function properly.

If two complementary colors—blue and yellow for example—simultaneously stimulate the blue-yellow mechanism, their effects oppose and counteract each other, and only the effects of the white mechanism, which is activated by all visible wavelengths, remain. Hence we see gray. The Hering theory is called the *opponent-process theory* because the two processes in each mechanism oppose each other.

Certain studies of nervous systems lend support to the opponent-process theory: for example, it has been observed in the ganglia of fish that the response of these nerve cells to wavelengths of reds and yellows is a definite "off" discharge, while the response to the shorter wavelengths of blues and greens is an opposing "on". There remains, however, much in the theory that is not wholly satisfactory: for example, the ways in which the opponent processes of the three substances would have to react to various wavelengths in order to account for the results of color mixing do not seem wholly plausible to some researchers. Nevertheless, the theory is not impossible, and, since there is much that is not yet known about vision, the concept of opponent processes may continue to contribute significantly to our knowledge.

Land: Beyond Color Theory? In the traditional studies of normal color vision, the number of basic colors has always been considered to be at least three and the information about color mixing and color anomalies has been used as the fundamental data to be worked with and explained. Different wavelengths do cause different colors, and mixtures of only three wavelengths can produce all colors; but is that how the eye really works? Edwin Land, founder of the Polaroid Corporation, jogged conventional thinking by his demonstration that mixtures of *only two colors* (or of white and one color) could produce sensations of all colors under certain circumstances.

For example, Land took two black-and-white photographs of a natural scene from different positions. One photo was taken through a red filter and the other through a green filter. He made them into black-and-white slides and projected both on the same screen from separate projectors positioned at exactly the same distance and angle from the screen as the cameras had been from the photographed scene (see Color Plate III). The slide taken through the red filter was to be projected with red light and the slide taken through the green filter with white light. If he turned on only either the red or the white projector, the scene appeared in various shades of red or gray. When he turned on both together—all the colors were reproduced, as naturally as in the original scene. The question remains, how does one obtain yellow, green and blue from a mixture of red and white. Nobody is certain of the answer.

SENSORY CONTRAST

We speak of *sensory contrast* when the effect of one stimulus is altered by another stimulus that occurs before, afterward, or at the same time. If the two stimuli occur together, there is *simultaneous contrast*; if in succession, *successive contrast*.

Visual Contrast Although sensory contrast occurs in the other senses, the effects that are studied most are those occurring in vision. Visual contrast may involve either changes in apparent intensity or changes in apparent hue.

Color Plate IV illustrates the effect of simultaneous contrast on apparent intensity, that is, on the apparent darkness of the four gray squares. The gray of each square is in fact identical, but the brightest surroundings of one make it appear the darkest. The effect of simultaneous contrast on apparent hue is also illustrated in Color Plate IV. If this figure is viewed in a moderately bright light, the gray squares tend to take on the hue complementary to the hue of the surrounding area. This effect was noted by Hering, and it influenced his opponent-process theory of color. He discovered what are called *Hering shadows*: that is, the shadow cast by an object in colored light appears to be of a hue that is complementary to the light. It has been suggested that simultaneous contrast explains the appearance of the additional colors in the Land demonstration: thus, that red and green combine into yellow, and that the yellow generates its complementary color blue, much as a Hering shadow would be produced. However, it is not at all clear how this might work in practice.

Successive color contrast also occurs: for example, if one is exposed to colored light for a long time, the hues of scenes he views subsequently appear different than they otherwise would.

Auditory Contrast and Masking   In hearing, when two acoustical stimuli are presented simultaneously, the usual result is that one of them becomes harder to hear, rather than subjectively altered: this effect is called *masking*. For example, speech can be masked by presenting other sounds along with the speaker's voice. The degree of masking depends on the relationship between the signal (the voice) and the masking "noise." For any signal, masking increases (1) with the intensity of the masking stimulus, also called the *masker*, and (2) with a greater resemblance of the masker to the signal. The most effective masker for human speech is that produced by three or four other people of the same sex speaking the same language: for example, think

of how difficult it is to hear one person in a group of three or four if everyone speaks at once. Similarly, the effectiveness of a given masking noise will depend on the characteristics of the signal. For example, one's voice (the signal) can be heard more clearly on a moving subway train if it is high-pitched, because it differs more from the predominantly low-frequency subway noise (the masker) than does a voice of normal pitch.

Contrast in Other Senses   Sensory contrast affects our other senses as well. *Successive* contrast can alter a variety of sensory perceptions. Orange juice tastes surprisingly sour after the taste of something sweet, like sugar; ammonia smells unbelievably sweet after a waft of chlorine gas; a person has difficulty keeping his balance on land after several days at sea; and to a baseball player, one bat seems much lighter than usual after he has swung two. *Simultaneous* contrast can alter sensation in yet another way, because the person perceives the separate stimuli differently in blends. This type of contrast helps to determine why certain blends of odors make up a more pleasing perfume than others, and which combinations of aromas and tastes distinguish a really fine wine or sauce.

AFTERIMAGES

The final type of sensory phenomenon that we will discuss in this chapter is the *afterimage*. An afterimage occurs when the effects of sensory stimulation persist after the stimulus has gone. One that you can readily observe for yourself is "Bidwell's ghost." In a dark room, move a lighted cigarette (or penlight) slowly back and forth at arm's length in front of your eyes. Let your eyes go out of focus and look straight ahead, but do not move your eyes to follow the cigarette. The ghost is the spot of light that trails

behind the moving embers on the end of the cigarette. If you stop moving the cigarette, the ghost
rapidly catches up to it. The ghost is a *positive afterimage* of the ember—"positive" because it looks the
same as the ember. This image persists wherever
the moving cigarette has been, but for only a half
second or so; the sensory impression is of a second
ember trailing the first. (Compare "immediate
memory" in Chapter 2).

A *negative afterimage* is an image that is complementary in hue to the original sensation. To observe
one yourself, first look at Color Plate V, in moderately good light, and stare at it for about a minute.
Then look at the white space below the picture. The
afterimage that you see will be negative.

In this chapter, we have progressed from phenomena that appear to be quite simple and fairly
well understood to those that are harder to
understand. We conclude with a phenomenon that
has caused nearly everyone who is concerned with
sensory processes to marvel—something that has
doubtless driven a few people into more relaxed
pursuits than trying to understand how the senses
work.

We refer to the *McCulloch effect* (see Color Plate
VI). In good light, stare alternately at the left and
the right figures for thirty seconds each until you
have looked at each ten times. Now look at the third
figure. Note the hues of the lines oriented in the
different directions. Now, continue to look at the
third figure and rotate the book ninety degrees.

The direction of the bars changes when the book
is rotated, indicating that information about direction
is somehow preserved in the afterimages. Nobody
really understands this process; apparently the direct-
tions of the lines have some definite visual significance. What does seem certain is that when we are
able to explain in detail the McCulloch effect and

Land's demonstration, we will know quite a bit more
than we currently do about vision—and about
sensory processes generally.

Suggested Readings

Corso, J. F. (1967) *The experimental psychology of sensory
behavior*. New York: Holt, Rinehart and Winston,
Inc.

Geldard, F. A. (1972) *The human senses*. (2nd ed.)
New York: Wiley.

Kling, J. W., & Riggs, L. A. (1971) *Woodworth and
Schlosberg's experimental psychology* (3rd ed.),
New York: Holt, Rinehart and Winston.

Teevan, R. E., & Birney, R. D., eds. (1961) *Color
vision*. Princeton, N. J. : Van Nostrand.

CHAPTER FOURTEEN

Our Perceptual World

Perception is the organizing process by which we interpret our sensory input. Perception is in part determined by several principles of organization, which our nervous system imposes on the stimuli. In addition, perception is affected by our past experiences, by our present expectations, and, sometimes, by our hopes and fears. Of course, perception also depends on the quality and intensity of the stimuli and upon our attentional state.

Our sensory receptors are bombarded continuously by stimuli. Our nervous system processes stimulation from all of our receptors in a manner that brings order and continuity to our perceptual world. If perception were not an organizing process, our view of the world would correspond more directly to the jumble of sensory stimulation. The result would be chaotic: we would have difficulty identifying many objects; we would be hard pressed to perceive size and depth or to judge distance. For example, if you look at a friend standing across the street, your retinal image is just a fraction of the size of your image of the same person when he is standing next to you. Yet, your friend appears to maintain a constant size. We shall discover why this is so when we discuss the perceptual constancies that account

for much of the stability and order in our perceptual experience. We shall also learn how we are able to see in three dimensions despite the limitation imposed by more or less two-dimensional retinal images. We shall also deal with "failures" in perception: cases in which perception is not veridical (truthful) and we experience illusions. For an example of the latter, see Figure 14.1.

Perception begins with the excitation of the sensory receptors. The variety of stimuli perceived by our sensory organs is more apparent if we concentrate on the perceptions of a single organ. (1) Close one eye and spend about a minute examining the perceptual world revealed by your open eye. Note that you see a portion of your nose, your cheeks, upper lip, and, if you are wearing glasses, the rims and temple pieces of the frames. Your perceptual field probably includes the ceiling, floor, and walls, if you are indoors, or the ground and the horizon, if you are outside. (2) You can become more aware of the various sound stimuli reaching your ears if you close your eyes and listen carefully to the sounds around you. Depending on where you are, you may find that you are experiencing dozens of auditory experiences, perhaps including people

Figure 14.1
The viewer perceives a most unusual waterfall in this lithograph by Maurits Escher. [*Waterfall.* Escher Foundation, Haags Gemeentemuseum, The Hague]

chattering in the distance, the hum of traffic (itself composed of distinguishable sounds), and the sound of music drifting from a radio in the distance. If you are in a library, you may hear the sounds of pages turning, footsteps, whispers, and the usual assortment of creaking chairs, coughs, and so forth. If the library is quiet enough, the hum of fluorescent lights, the ticking of your wrist watch, and the sound of your own heart beat may also be part of your auditory world.

In concentrating on the other sense modalities, particularly smell and taste, you will not experience as much. But you can feel the pressure on your skin produced by your clothes and by contact with the chair beneath you. If you try, you can also perceive visceral cues from the functioning of your internal organs and kinesthestic cues from your muscles.

Normally, however, one is not aware of the nose on one's face, or the hum of fluorescent lights, or the feel of clothing. Instead, one generally attends only to stimulation that is relevant to the task at hand, shutting off most of the rest.

Since vision is considered by many to be man's most important sense, and since most research on perception has been done in the visual modality, we will concentrate primarily on visual perception. However, the principles of organization operating in visual perception are generally applicable to our other senses, and we shall treat perception in other modalities, especially hearing, where comparison seems interesting or valuable.

THE ORGANIZATION OF PERCEPTION

In the preceding chapters on psychophysics and the visual sense (Chapters 11, 12, and 13), we discussed the conditions under which seeing occurs, the ways in which the attributes of sensation are measured, and some of the physiological processes occurring in reception, transduction, and neural transmission in vision. But what enables us to see objects as such? What causes the accumulated stimuli on the retina to be perceived as integrated patterns? Why do certain portions of our two-dimensional retinal image stand out from the rest?

Let us begin by examining the process of *object perception*, whereby we perceive various shapes (objects) as standing out from the rest of the perceptual field (the background). *Contours* (outlines) are extremely important in this process. Imagine that you had been blind from birth but could suddenly see. Your visual world would be a strange jumble. One person who underwent this experience said that the first object he recognized was an orange—because of its tactually familiar round contour.

Object perception is of course determined partly by the _retinal stimulus_, the pattern of light energy reaching the eye. Recall that in Chapter 11 we made a distinction between the stimulus and the stimulus object. In perception, a stimulus (also called the _proximal stimulus_) is used to make inferences about a stimulus object (the _distal stimulus_): that is, sensory information is employed to construct a representation of reality. However, other factors also contribute to that representation; the visual representation that we construct is not determined by the proximal stimulus alone. For example, look at Figure 14.2: do you see a vase or two faces? To demonstrate further the way in which perception of the same distal stimulus can vary, conduct the following experiment on a few friends. First, ask some of them to look at the figure and estimate how tall the vase is; they will undoubtedly perceive the vase. Then ask a few others to look at it and describe what the two people are doing; these people will probably perceive the faces rather than the vase. Though the reality does not change, our perception changes with out expectations, or _set_.

Another factor influencing our perception is illumination. For example, look at the staircase pictured in Figure 14.3, Part A. Are the stairs portrayed from above or below? Again, by selecting a set, you can perceive them from either perspective. Now, look at Part B and Part C, to which light cues have been added: the staircase in Part B appears to be viewed from above, and that in Part C, from below. Thus, the illumination cues influence the observer's perspective and remove much of the ambiguity of Part A.

The patterns that we have just discussed, Rubin's vase and Schröeder's staircase, illustrate the phenomenon of _figure–ground reversal_. Each can be perceived in two plausible ways. In Figure 14.2 in particular, two very different items can be seen, depending on which of the two shapes is perceived as the object

Figure 14.2
An ambiguous figure that can be seen either as a vase or as two faces.

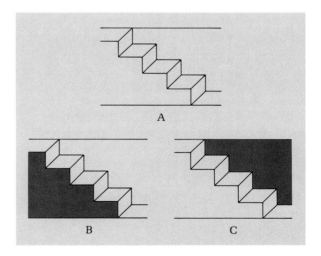

Figure 14.3
Schröder's staircase is a reversible figure. Which figure is seen can be affected by adding illumination cues, as in Parts B and C.

and which as background. However, both illustrations are deliberate presentations of ambiguous situations. In normal perceptual situations, one configuration is more meaningful than the other, and there is no ambiguity about which is object and which is background. Although it is possible for one to concentrate his attention on characteristics of the background, it is difficult to avoid noticing the objects or figures first. This perception of objects or figures as the salient items is believed to be due to structural features of our nervous systems. Thus newborn infants are observed to look more at objects or figures than at the background; so are adults who are seeing for the first time. And the same is true of rats that are exposed to light after having been reared in darkness.

What are the characteristics of an object? We know that it tends to stand out from its background even if it is the same distance from us as its background, like a word printed on a page. Also, objects tend to be unbroken, whereas the background is interrupted (by objects).

The school of gestalt psychology has contributed concepts that enable us to specify more explicitly the determinants of shape (or pattern) perception. The word *gestalt*, coming from the German, means "form" or "whole," and gestalt principles of perception are concerned with why we perceive shapes and patterns as whole objects. The *gestalt psychologists* (especially Max Wertheimer, Kurt Koffka and Wolfgang Köhler) described several principles of organization that apply to the perception of objects and patterns of objects.

Gestalt Laws of Pattern Organization The *principle of proximity* is illustrated by the dot pattern in Figure 14.4, Part A. Note that the pattern appears as three groups of two horizontal rows, but that it is not necessary to perceive it that way rather than as a group of vertical rows or as a rectangle com-

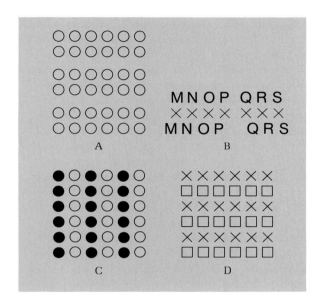

Figure 14.4
The principle of proximity. Items that are close together tend to be seen as groups. (See text.)

posed of thirty-six circles. If, instead, the spacings were larger between pairs of vertical dots, then vertical rows would be seen. The principle of proximity states that, all other factors being equal, objects that appear close to one another will be seen as belonging to the same group. This principle is reliable (it can be depended on to produce the same results again and again), verifiable (it can be tested) and quantifiable (it can be objectively measured—that is, the degree of proximity necessary to produce such perceptual grouping can be specified). To test the principle yourself, you could make up a number of patterns like that shown in the figure, varying the space between rows or columns, and then ask a few people how they perceive each of the patterns.

The principle of proximity applies to hearing as well as vision. If five notes are played on the piano at random, and a pause is inserted between the third and fourth notes, a listener will hear the first three as making up one group and the last pair as making up the second. But if the notes occur in some recognizable pattern, the grouping may be less obvious: for example, if the first five notes of the scale are played, the pause between the third and fourth will have to be longer before two groups are perceived.

Our perception of groups of visual stimuli can also be influenced by the imposition of a recognizable pattern or structure. For example, if a subject is presented with the top row of letters in Figure 14.4, Part B, he will probably ignore the space between the P and the Q and report seeing seven consecutive letters of the alphabet. Yet the same spacing in the next row of X's gives the impression of two groups. Thus, the meaningful structure imposed by the subject's own familiarity with a given pattern or sequence overrides the proximity principle in the perception of the top row of letters, and a much wider space, such as that shown in the third row, will be required for the subject to perceive two distinct groups of letters. Thus the similarity of certain items—such as alphabet letters from P through S and the consecutive notes of the scale—influences perceptual groupings; this effect is called the *principle of similarity*.

The principle of similarity states that, all other factors being equal, objects that appear similar to one another will be seen as belonging to the same perceptual group. The principle is illustrated in Figure 14.4, Part C, in which vertical rows of dots are seen, and in Part D, where the squares and crosses are perceived as forming six horizontal rows. Like the proximity principle, the similarity principle is reliable and readily testable. In many situations, it is also easily quantifiable.

What happens when similarity and proximity operate against each other? Figure 14.5, Part B,

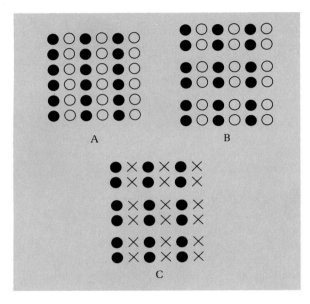

Figure 14.5
The principle of similarity. In Part B, the principles of proximity and similarity oppose each other.

presents a dot pattern that has the same spacing as Figure 14.4, Part A but the same similarity cues as Figure 14.4, Part C. Note that this pattern is readily perceived as either six horizontal or six vertical rows. By manipulating the degree of proximity (by adjusting the spacing between rows, as in Figure 14.5, Part A) or that of similarity (by changing the unfilled circles to X's, as in Figure 14.5, Part C), the tendency for either orientation to predominate may be varied.

Another important principle of organization is *closedness*: closed contours define figures more readily than do open contours. For example, in Figure 14.6 the same curved lines are repeated from left to right; they differ only in the way they are joined together.

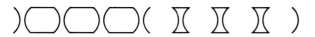

Figure 14.6
The principle of closedness. [Adapted from J. E. Hochberg, *Perception*. Englewood Cliffs, N.J.: Prentice-Hall, 1964.]

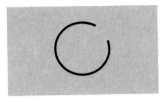

Figure 14.7
The principle of closure.

Figure 14.8
Another illustration of the principle of closure. We tend to see lines as forming meaningful whole objects.

Thus the areas within the closed contours on the left of Figure 14.6 are seen as outlines of TV screens; those on the right are seen as outlines of apple cores.

A related principle of organization is that of *closure*: when viewing an incomplete pattern we tend to "close" the pattern and perceive it as a meaningful whole. For example, the curved line shown in Figure 14.7 is likely to be perceived as a circle, particularly if the subject sees it for only a brief period of time. Even if the subject has ample opportunity to perceive the gap, he is still likely to describe the figure as a circle with a gap in it rather than as a curved line.

The principle of closure is also illustrated in Figure 14.8. The lines in Part A will probably be perceived as the letter M. The lines in Part B, however, are more likely to be seen as the letter N, perhaps followed by "a period" or "a smudge of ink." The line in Part C is intermediate: different people will report perceiving different patterns. The best illustration of closure is Part A, which subjects almost

Figure 14.9
The principle of good continuation, which here overpowers the principle of proximity. (See text.)

Figure 14.10
Here the principle of good continuation operates to achieve closure, the achievement of a good perceptual whole.

invariably perceive as "M." Perception of all three examples, however, obeys the following generalization: *the organism interprets the stimulus object in a manner that is as simple as possible, and as consistent as possible with his sensory information and his past experience.*

All of the foregoing principles of organization are reliable, verifiable, and often quantifiable. Other principles are less so, but their influence on perception can nevertheless be readily demonstrated. One such principle, *good continuation*, is illustrated in Figure 14.9. When asked to fill in one of the four dots, people will probably select c although it is no closer to the last filled dot than is b or a. The arrangement of the preceding filled dots, however, predisposes one to continue the line by filling in c, instead of breaking the pattern by filling in b or a. Even d, which continues the pattern of prior dots, will probably be selected over b or a, despite its greater distance from the rest of the figure. In this situation, the principle of good continuation outweighs the principle of proximity.

What does the pattern shown in Figure 14.10 look like? Note that this is the same pattern as was seen in Figure 14.8, Part A, except that the final half line is continuous with the rest of the figure. You probably perceive this figure as an M, but you are

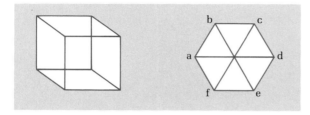

Figure 14.11
Two drawings of the same wire cube. In one, the effect
of depth is virtually unavoidable; in the other, the
principle of good continuation tends to prevent us from
seeing the figure with depth. [Adapted from J. E.
Hochberg, *Perception*. Englewood Cliffs, N.J.: Prentice-
Hall, 1964.]

obeying the principle of good continuation rather
than the principle of closure: you are not filling in
a perceptual "gap" but extending or "continuing"
the figure to compose a meaningful figural whole.

Now look at the patterns drawn in Figure 14.11.
They are each drawings of a wire cube. The left-
hand drawing looks like a three-dimensional cube;
the right-hand drawing appears to be a flat pattern.
Note that it is possible (though difficult) to see the
left-hand drawing as two-dimensional. It is reasonably easy to see the right-hand drawing as a three-
dimensional cube, but in order to do so, we must
break the good continuation of the lines. For
example, if lines a–d, b–e and c–f are seen as continuous unbroken lines, they suggest a flat pattern.
In order to see a cube, we must perceive each line
as terminating at the center (which becomes a corner
of the cube) and joining other lines at what appear
to be right angles.

Note that all of the organizing principles suggest
that perception will be as simple, as meaningful,
and as good (in the sense of a "good configuration")
as possible. This is the gestalt *law of Prägnanz*, which
has also been called the principle of simplicity: we

tend to interpret our sensory stimulation so that we
perceive the simplest possible pattern. This principle
is so pervasive and important that it is desirable that
we be able to define "simplicity" objectively rather
than relying on our intuitions about what is and
is not simple.

Perceptual psychologists Julian Hochberg (b. 1923)
and Fred Attneave (b. 1919) have been at the fore-
front of the effort to determine what conditions permit us to perceive a simple figure. Their research
has suggested ways in which the gestalt concept
of "configurational goodness" can be measured.
Attneave found that simple figures are those that
obey the following rule: information about the parts
provides knowledge of the whole. What are the characteristics that such a figure might be expected to
have? First, if it has symmetry, it is "good," because
information about one side of the figure is all that
is needed for accurate prediction of what the other
side looks like. In addition to symmetry, unbroken
lines and curves and compact areas contribute to
figural simplicity because they enable the perceiver
to construct the whole from some of its parts. In
addition, the observer's familiarity with the figure is
an important factor: thus if we have already seen
a figure several times or more, we can more readily
construct the whole figure after only a brief view of
its parts. Similarly, we recognize old friends by the
sounds of their voices or a glimpse of their backs,
but we need more perceptual cues before we recognize new acquaintances.

Hochberg utilized the reversible figures shown in
Figure 14.12. Each figure may be seen as either two-
or three-dimensional. Each figure within a set has the
same three-dimensional shape, though the orientation
varies from figure to figure. Within each set, the
two-dimensional complexity varies. Two-dimensional
complexity is measured by the number of continuous
lines, the number of different angles, and the total

melody. The important determinant of a melody is the relation of the notes to one another, or their *pattern*. Unfortunately, the specification of melodic goodness is not yet as advanced as that of configurational goodness.

DEPTH PERCEPTION

Several effective visual cues to depth perception allow us to make effective use of our two-dimensional retinal patterns to interpret the location and distance of the stimulus object or, in other words, to perceive a three-dimensional world. Although these cues collectively furnish us with a reasonably accurate representation of space, they can sometimes fail us, as is demonstrated by illusions. An illusion can occur when the cues provided by two-dimensional patterns are ambiguous, as demonstrated by Figure 14.3 for example. The cues to depth perception are divided into two classes: *monocular cues* (those that are effective even if one eye is closed) and *binocular cues* (those which require perception by both eyes).

Monocular Cues Most of the monocular cues to depth perception have been known for centuries. Several were discovered and elaborated by Leonardo da Vinci, who, like other artists, was naturally interested in understanding how man perceived depth in order to create the impression of depth in his work. Philosophers were also concerned with the problem of depth, and particularly with the knotty question of how a two-dimensional retinal pattern could result in three-dimensional perception. Bishop Berkeley, for example, pointed out that depth perception is influenced by kinesthetic cues (that is, cues related to bodily position and movement).

Certain kinesthetic cues occur during the *accommodation* of the lens to object distance—that is, when

Figure 14.12
Figures used by Hochberg to investigate the relationship between the increasing complexity of a figure and a subject's increasing tendency to see depth in the figure. [From J. E. Hochberg, *Perception.* Englewood Cliffs, N.J.: Prentice-Hall, 1964.]

number of angles in the figure. Note that the more complex the two-dimensional figure, the greater the possibility that subjects will view it as three-dimensional. Thus the apparent three-dimensionality of the figure is a direct function of its two-dimensional complexity.

The general gestalt principle of goodness, too, appears to apply to the other senses. To draw again on the example of musical notes, a given selection of notes played in a given order might be perceived as melodically pleasing, whereas the same notes in a different order would not be. If the first selection is then played an octave higher, or even in a different musical key, it will still be perceived as the same

the lens changes shape in order to focus upon an object that is near or far away. As the lens changes shape, the pull of the eye muscles causes kinesthetic stimuli that we use to judge distances. The nearer the object on which the eye is focused, the rounder the lens; the farther away, the flatter the lens. However, kinesthetic cues are effective only for the perception of objects that are relatively near, since only a minute degree of additional flattening occurs when the eye focuses on objects more than a few feet away.

The other cues we use in depth perception are visual. They include the *interposition* of objects (Figure 14.13). Interposition is the partial obscuring of one object by another, enabling us to tell which object is in front and which in back.

Illumination cues are the effects of light and shade on depth perception. These provide a strong and reliable impression of depth, as illustrated in Figure 14.14. First, cover the right-hand side of the figure and look at the left-hand side. Is Corner 1 or Corner 2 the closer? After deciding, cover the left-hand side of the figure and look at the right side. Is Corner 3 or Corner 4 closer? Most subjects see 1 and 4 as being closer. Note that the figure is a reversible one and that in order to have judged both 1 and 4 as being closer, we had to reverse the figure. Why did we do so? When we look at the left-hand side of the figure, the illumination appears to come from the right and we take the gray portions to be shadows. When we look at the right side of the figure, however, the illumination appears to come from the left, and the "shadows" make 4 seem nearer than 3.

Straight lines appear to merge in the distance, and the more the lines converge the greater is our impression of the distance. Such *linear perspective* can be a powerful cue to distance (see Figure 14.15). Another cue, size perspective, arises from the relation between the perceived size of the retinal image and

Figure 14.13
Interposition enables us to judge which of two objects is farther away from us. But sometimes we can be fooled into judging distance (and size) by apparent, unreal interposition, as the bottom picture shows. [David Scherman. Photographs appeared in W. H. Ittelson and F. P. Kilpatrick, "Experiments in Perception," *Scientific American*, August 1951, 50–55.]

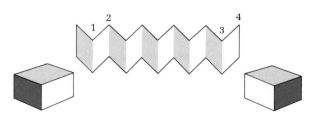

Figure 14.14
Illumination cues can create an illusion of depth. [From J. E. Hochberg, *Perception*. Englewood Cliffs, N.J.: Prentice-Hall, 1964.]

Figure 14.15
Linear perspective is an important cue to depth.

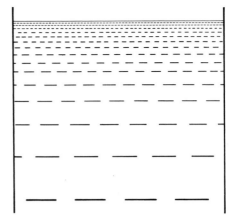

Figure 14.16
Gibson's artificial textural density gradient produces the appearance of depth. [Adapted J. J. Gibson, *The Perception of the Visual World*, 1950. Houghton Mifflin Co.]

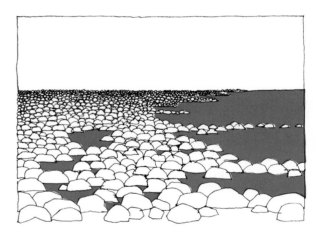

Figure 14.17
A natural textural density gradient.

the perceived distance. Since objects are smaller (they subtend a smaller retinal angle) in the distance, a decrease in apparent size causes an increase in apparent distance (Figure 14.16). (The complex relation between size, distance, and the size of the retinal angle will be explored in more detail when we discuss size constancy.)

Of the monocular cues to depth perception, the most comprehensive is the concept of *textural density gradients* developed by J. J. Gibson (b. 1904). What this concept demonstrates is that surfaces extending outward from us have textures, which are projected on the retina in such a way that a texture appears to increase in density as the surface extends away from us. The greater the distance, the more dense the texture of a surface seems. Figure 14.16 illustrates one of Gibson's artificially constructed textural

gradients. Note the perception of depth. The lines at the bottom of the figure are quite widely spaced (so that they appear as foreground), and those at the top more densely packed, producing the impression of distance. The textural density gradient is an important cue to depth perception in the natural world. An example of a natural textural gradient is shown in Figure 14.17. As Gibson has pointed out, the concept of textural gradients may be considered to encompass most of the other traditional cues for depth perception. For example, in linear perspective, lines seem to come closer together and, in so doing, become denser; in size perspective, as objects become smaller in the distance they also appear to be closer together and thus denser.

Other cues are those of *relative movement* (or *motion parallax*). These occur when we move our heads in relation to the environment, or when objects in the environment move in relation to us. For example, when the perceiver is stationary but objects are moving, the faster objects tend to be perceived as closer.

Binocular Cues One of the best cues to depth perception, and the only important one requiring both eyes, is *binocular parallax*, or *binocular disparity*. When you look at an object first with one eye and then with the other, you do not see an identical image, because the two eyes do not view the same object from exactly the same perspective. This disparity in images is illustrated for a single solid object in Figure 14.18. Yet when we perceive an object with both eyes, we perceive a single fused image. How fusion occurs is unknown, but we do know that it takes place in the brain and that the result is an impression of depth, or of the object's solidity. Two eyes are indeed better than one, because the disparity between the two images provides important information about the object's three-dimensionality.

Binocular disparity has been used as a determinant of depth perception since the early nineteenth century, when Wheatstone contructed a stereoscope to show that a striking impression of depth could be obtained by presenting disparate two-dimensional images to each eye. Nor is it necessary to present only familiar objects in order to convey an impression of depth; powerful stereoscopic effects can be obtained with the use of meaningless, randomly generated patterns. In addition, it has been shown that binocular disparity is a powerful cue for depth perception even when it is the only cue available.

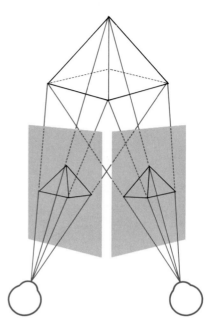

Figure 14.18
Each of our two eyes sees a single object from a slightly different perspective. This binocular disparity is an important cue to depth. [Adapted from J. J. Gibson, *The Perception of the Visual World*, 1950. Houghton Mifflin Co.]

A less important binocular cue to depth perception is *convergence*. Like the monocular cue of accommodation, convergence is a kinesthetic rather than a visual cue, and one can feel its effect quite strongly by rapidly shifting focus from a near to a far object. Both eyes "converge" upon an object in order to focus it. If the object is distant, the degree of convergence is slight. On the other hand, if the object is near (as the nose on your face) both eyes are directed markedly inward. Convergence is a useful cue to distance because the degree of eye-muscle movement varies with the degree of convergence. Like accommodation, however, convergence is a useful cue only for objects that are relatively close (within 40 or 50 feet), because there is little convergence for more distant objects, the lines of regard from the two eyes to a distant object being essentially parallel.

Thus a variety of different distance cues facilitate our perception of depth. Usually, several are present at once. When they seem to contradict each other, we rely on the single most compelling cue, which is probably interposition. But gradient cues and binocular disparity can also predominate. Under normal circumstances, the cues that have previously served us most adequately in a particular context will be the most influential determinants of depth perception under similar conditions.

ACOUSTIC LOCALIZATION

How do we respond accurately to the direction and distance of a sound? As in visual depth perception, we make use of various cues in the auditory stimulus that reaches the ear (the proximal stimulus) to determine the location of the sound source (the distal stimulus). As in vision, some of the cues require perception by one receptor alone (the *monaural cues*), and others require perception by both (the *binaural cues*).

Monaural Cues   Important monaural cues are the cues to *distance*. We judge the distance of an object by the loudness of the sound. Loud sounds are cues for near objects, soft sounds for relatively distant ones. Obviously, these cues can often mislead us: a clap of thunder, the sound of a truck backfiring, and a sonic boom may all give the frightening impression of coming from sources that are much nearer than they really are. Fortunately, although distance cues are often ambiguous, we generally obtain a fairly good estimate of distance from them, especially when we interpret them along with other information about the potential source of the cues. For example, in an electric storm, we judge the distance of lightning not by either visual or auditory cues alone, but rather by the amount of time, if any, elapsing between them. Also, we know what degree of loudness to expect from familiar sound sources, such as jet planes and ringing telephones; if we are in our front yard, we can usually tell, for example, whether the phone that is ringing is ours or our nextdoor neighbor's. Sometimes, of course, we are wrong. Most of us, at one time or another, have started to answer our phone when in fact the ringing came from elsewhere, or we have opened a front door because we mistakenly thought we heard a knock. In Edgar Allan Poe's short story "The Telltale Heart," a frantic villain confesses his crime after he mistakes the sound of his own pounding heart for that of the heart of his victim under the floorboard—a fatal error in acoustic localization.

Echolocation   A different sort of auditory cue to distance is *echolocation*, in which an organism judges the distance of an object by emitting sounds and judging the time until their echoes return. Echolocation is of vital importance for bats and dolphins, for example. Thus bats rely on echolocation for normal (nocturnal) flying; a highly developed "sonar" system has evolved within this species. (See Figure 12.1.) Bats emit high-frequency cries (far above our range of hearing) at a rate of almost fifty per second. The echoes produced by such frequently emitted sounds enable the bats to perceive the distance and location of even small objects, including the moths on which they prey. Similar elaborate and highly successful mechanisms have been identified in the dolphin, which emits sounds underwater; the echoes allow the dolphin to determine the location of food and other objects.

Echolocation can be important for man also. Although we could readily learn to employ echolocation, most of us never become proficient at it, since visual depth cues are so effective. However, it is largely because of echolocation that the blind can get around as well as they do. The sounds blind people make as they walk are echoed from nearby objects and enable the blind to avoid them. It should be noted that many blind people are not aware they are making use of auditory cues. Nonetheless, experimentation has shown that they do: for example, if a blind subject's ears are plugged, his ability to avoid obstacles is seriously impaired.

Estimating the distance of sounds is a fairly simple process requiring the use of only one ear. When sounds grow louder, we judge that the distal object is moving closer; when they become softer, we judge that the object is moving away. These cues are fallible, but serve us reasonably well most of the time. However, judging the *direction* of sounds becomes a bit more complicated, and for this, the use of both ears is necessary.

Binaural Cues   In Chapter 12 we learned that sound waves, regardless of the direction of origin, must progress through the outer ear flap (the pinna) and through the ear canal before they strike the ear drum (tympanic membrane), cross the three bones of the middle ear, and enter the inner ear where they set the basilar membrane in motion. Given this long and intricate route of sound waves, it seems remarkable that we are able to identify the location of a sound source (or to *localize* the sound) quite accurately.

Most studies of auditory localization have been conducted in controlled laboratory settings, but even an informal experiment will yield essentially the same results. One such experiment was conducted on top of a building, where tones of different frequencies were presented from various directions to a blindfolded observer, sitting on top of a high chair. Each of two subjects' task was to point in the direction of the sound. The results are shown in

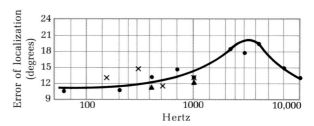

Figure 14.19
Errors of localization of a tone depend on the frequency of the tone. [Adapted from S. S. Stevens and E. B. Newman, "The Localization of Actual Sources of Sound," *American Journal of Psychology*, 1936, *48*, 297–306.]

Figure 14.19, in which the average error of auditory localization is plotted against the frequency of the tone. Note that despite our expectations that localization should be extremely difficult, low and high tones are localized quite accurately—within 12° to 15°—out of a maximum possible error of 180° (see Figure 14.19). In the paragraphs that follow, we shall discuss the different binaural cues that permit such accurate localization of high and low frequencies, and finally we shall see why localization is so poor for intermediate frequencies (around 3,000 Hz).

First of all, evidently both ears are necessary for localization. Individuals who are deaf in one ear have difficulty localizing sounds, as do subjects who have one ear plugged. Just as retinal disparity (produced by the perception of an image by two separate receptors in different places) is an important determinant in visual space localization, so the spatial separation of the two ears affects our perception of arriving sound waves and hence our perception of sound direction. Careful experimentation has isolated two important binaural cues: time-difference cues and intensity-difference cues.

A sound does not arrive at both ears simultaneously, because one ear is usually farther from the sound source, so that the sound reaches it slightly later. What appear to be trivial *binaural time differences* are important cues that permit accurate localization. For most people, tested under optimal conditions, a difference of only .1 millisecond—that is, one ten-thousandth of a second—is sufficient for accurate localization of tones of certain frequencies!

We are best able to distinguish sounds that come from far to the left or to the right of the median plane (the vertical plane passing though the middle of the head from front to back). The farther a sound is from the median plane, the more easily we localize it. But sounds in the median plane (those directly in front of, behind, above, or below the listener) are difficult to localize because they are equidistant from our two ears, and hence there can be no binaural time differences.

When binaural time differences are lacking, we tend to create them automatically by moving the head slightly (often imperceptibly) and thus permitting accurate localization. When the subject moves his head slightly to the left, for example, a sound originating from a source directly in front of him now arrives at his right ear before his left. This fact permits the subject to perceive that the sound's source is in front of him: if the source is behind him, a turn of the head to the left causes the left ear to receive the sound first. If the sound source is located either above or below the listener, a lateral rotation of the head will not create binaural differences; instead, one must tilt the head. Thus, in a normal perceptual situation if sounds are in the median plane—so that time-difference cues are absent—localization is difficult but nevertheless can be accomplished by head movements.

Although binaural time cues are not reliable for high-frequency tones, the other principal cues to auditory localization—*binaural intensity-difference* cues—are effective only for high-frequency tones. Intensity-difference cues account for the improvement in local-

ization for high-frequency sounds shown on the right in Figure 14.19. The portion of the curve describing poor localization corresponds to the range at which neither set of cues is very effective for tone localization.

What causes binaural intensity differences? Sound waves coming from the right or left side of the subject must bend around the head to reach the farther ear. Some are blocked and do not reach the far ear at all. Thus, the far ear receives a slightly less intense sound. Such binaural intensity differences are effective only for the high-frequency tones because the long wavelengths of the low-frequency tones can bend around the head with little loss of intensity. Like the time differences, intensity differences will not occur if the sound source is in the median plane. Thus, an absence of intensity differences is a cue that the sound may be somewhere in the median plane, and head movements enable us to determine the location.

To summarize the binaural cues, there are two important types—time-difference cues and intensity-difference cues. Together they provide us with a remarkable ability to localize sounds in space.

PERCEPTUAL CONSTANCIES

When we look at the same object on different occasions the stimulus object itself does not change, but the stimulus pattern—the pattern of light energy falling on the retina—is almost never identical on separate occasions. Nevertheless, we perceive familiar objects as having the same or constant size, shape, and color, even though the retinal images vary widely. Similarly, the loudness of a sound will be heard as fairly constant, even though the distance between sound source and hearer varies. The various perceptual constancies enable us to perceive our world as stable, regular, and consistent.

Figure 14.20
Increasing familiarity affects shape constancy.

Object and Shape Constancy This book
(at least when closed) looks like the same book
regardless of its position on a table, its distance from
us, or varying light conditions. This tendency of an
item to appear as the same object in spite of shifting
conditions is called *object constancy*. *Shape constancy*
refers to the fact that an object appears to retain the
same shape despite the fact that the retinal images
may vary greatly, depending on the object's position.
The shape that we perceive is determined by the
retinal image, in conjunction with (1) cues to the
location and tilt of the distal object, and (2) whatever
knowledge we have about its true shape. For example, try to imagine you are a child viewing for the
first time the unfamiliar object of unknown shape
shown in Figure 14.20.

Size Constancy When we see someone we know
in the distance, the retinal image produced by that
person is a mere fraction of the size of the image
produced by the same person when he is standing
directly in front of us. Why then, in spite of the
variation in distance between him and us, do we
perceive the person as being of constant size? Our
immediate response might be "because we know he
is the same size," and although there is some truth
to this answer, it is not an adequate explanation of
size constancy, the tendency of an object to be perceived as the same size, in spite of the different sizes
of our retinal stimuli. Indeed, we usually perceive

Figure 14.21
Size constancy may obtain even for unfamiliar objects
(horizontal lines) if there are cues provided by familiar
objects (trees).

even unfamiliar objects of which we have no prior
knowledge, as size constant. To verify this phenomenon yourself look at the row of horizontal lines
in Figure 14.21. Why are the lines not seen as a
set of lines varying systematically in size on a two-
dimensional piece of paper? The answer lies in the
cues to apparent distance that are present in the
figure. When cues are ambiguous, what we see is
often influenced by our expectations, which can be
based on past experience or on a prior acquaintance
with the object or objects. If we have no expectations
about the size we may simply guess that one of
several possible hypotheses is correct; or we may
shift our perception from one possibility to another,

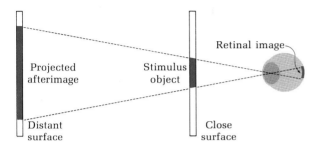

Figure 14.22
Emmert's law. The size of the afterimage increases with increases in the distance of the surface against which it is seen.

as we can when viewing reversible figures. Normally, however, cues are not ambiguous, and our judgment of size is reasonably straightforward.

Our perception of size is jointly determined by the size of the object's retinal image and by its apparent distance. If two stimuli have retinal images of the same size, the one that is farther away will appear larger. To demonstrate this joint influence of retinal size and apparent distance on perceived size, focus the eye on the black dot at the center of the green square in Color Plate VII for at least thirty seconds. Then, immediately gaze at the white square below it, and observe the red afterimage. After a few seconds, transfer your gaze to a more distant light-colored surface, such as a white wall. Note that the size of the larger afterimage varies directly with the distance between the eye and the surface on which the image is projected. This direct proportionality between the size and the distance of the afterimage is known as _Emmert's Law_, which is illustrated in Figure 14.22.

In the perception of an object, the smaller the retinal image becomes, the more the apparent distance increases. Since the two factors of retinal image and apparent distance work together, the perceived size remains constant: the increase in distance compensates for the decrease in size of the retinal image.

The relationship is summarized in the equation: $S = sD$, where S is the perceived size of the object, s is the size of the retinal image, and D is the apparent distance of the object. If the cues for distance are reliable, the actual size of an object can be instantly (and unconsciously) inferred.

Ordinarily, we have little difficulty judging true size and distance. Occasionally, however, cues may be conflicting or misleading and can cause some interesting perceptual distortions.

Figure 14.23 illustrates the perceptual distortion known as the _Ames room_ after its architect, Adelbert Ames, Jr. Is the child on the right a giant? And is the child on the left a midget? We perceive an extreme difference in sizes because the two figures appear to be an equal distance away. According to our equation, if the figures are equally distant the one casting the largest retinal image must also be correspondingly larger. However, our assumption of equal distance is in error, because the room is not rectangular. It is in fact constructed quite asymmetrically (see Figure 14.24). The rear wall slants sharply back to the left, and becomes progressively larger. Thus, in the Ames room, misleading distance cues produce a grossly distorted impression of size—and that is at variance with our normal expectations and experience. It is interesting to note that if subjects are allowed to explore actively a room of this type, say, with a long pointer, the distortion will be greatly diminished.

What the Ames room illustrates is the way in which size constancy can be manipulated by manipulating distance cues. When distance cues are largely eliminated, size constancy breaks down and the observer relies on the size of the retinal image and past perceptual experience for judging the size of familiar objects and on the retinal image alone for judging the size of unfamilar objects. (A jungle-dweller, on his first visit to flat open country, insisted that distant cattle were "insects.") As shown in

Figure 14.23
An Ames room produces distortions of perception by means of confusions in size and distance. [Peeter Vilms]

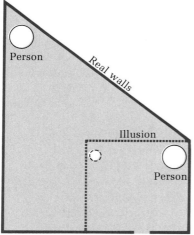

Figure 14.24
This diagram shows how the Ames room was constructed in order to appear rectangular to a viewer in a particular location.

Figure 14.23, the size of familiar objects will be badly misjudged if misleading distance cues are present.

Brightness Constancy Constancies of brightness (as well as of color) are determined in great part by the contrast relations within the visual field, for example, the relation between the light coming from an object and the light coming from its surroundings. The disk-surround arrangements shown in Figure 14.25 have been used to study these relations. The luminance of a single disk and of its surrounding ring of light may be varied independently of one another in order to assess the contribution of each to perceived brightness. It has been learned

Figure 14.25
The surround of a disk influences its perceived brightness.

that the luminance of the disk may be varied over a wide range and yet appear to be constant—provided that the luminance of the surround is varied correspondingly. In other words, subjects will report no change in the brightness of the disk if a constant ratio is maintained between the luminance of the disk and that of the surround. The importance of such contrast cues is also illustrated in experiments utilizing two disk-surround arrangements (Figure 14.25). Each disk-surround setup is projected, a sizeable distance apart from one another, onto a screen in a darkened room. The disk-surround on the left is called the standard, since the luminance of both the disk and the surround remain constant (although different from one another). The subject is instructed to adjust the intensity of the disk on the right until it appears equal in brightness to that of the disk on the left. The numbers on the two outer rings in Figure 14.25 indicate that the experimenter has set the standard surround at a luminance of 300 millilamberts (mL) which is twice the luminance of the comparison surround (150 mL). The figure also shows that the luminance of the standard ring on the left (300 mL) is twice that of the disk it surrounds (150 mL). What luminance value will the subject set for the comparison disk on the right? If he is to make the two equal in units of intensity,

he should set the comparison disk at 150 mL. Instead, he tends to set it at around 75 mL because the disks appear equally bright when the ratio of surround-luminance to disk-luminance is about equal for each disk.

The conclusion that brightness constancy results if a constant ratio is maintained between an object and a surround—though not precisely true for all luminance values—is a useful generalization that is applicable under most light conditions. For example, you probably judge the lightness of the white background of the pages of this book to be fairly constant, although you have probably been reading this book under a wide variety of lighting conditions, perhaps ranging from dim lighting in the evenings to the full light of the noonday sun. A good deal of constancy is achieved because the luminance of the book's "surround"—adjacent and nearby objects, such as your desk and various items on top of it—is varying at the same time.

Although perceived brightness is greatly influenced by contrast cues, and brightness constancy is generally achieved by maintaining a constant ratio of background-luminance to object-luminance, certain perceived cues to illumination are also important if constancy is to be maintained. The importance of illumination cues can be nicely illustrated by the following demonstration. Take a piece of gray cardboard and fold it down in the middle as shown in Figure 14.26. Place it so that it is illuminated from the left side. Since the illumination is coming from the left, the right side of the cardboard will be in shadow. An observer will see the surface of the cardboard for what it really is: a uniform shade of gray with one side in the path of illumination and the other side in shadow. In other words, an observer's perceptual system will attribute the diminished brightness of the right side to the direction of light—that is, to the observed fact that the shaded side is not in the direct path of the illumination. However,

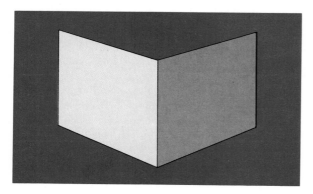

Figure 14.26
The perception of an object as one thing or another can
influence the perceived brightness of the parts of the
object (as is explained in the text).

a piece of cardboard folded in this way is reversible:
that is, it is possible to view this three-dimensional
object as a flat surface. If a subject succeeds in
reversing the figure, his perception "somersaults,"
and he reports seeing a flat surface of two distinct
shades of gray (the left side is seen as medium
gray, the right side as dark gray). This reversibility
demonstrates that illumination relationships alone do
not determine perceived brightness. (When a subject
reverses the figure, the illumination of the physical
stimulus remains unchanged, and yet perception
changes radically.) When the subject perceives the
surface as flat, he cannot attribute the difference
in shading to the direction of illumination. Consequently, the subject concludes that the flat surface
consists of two distinct areas of different shades
of gray (since one half—the half in shadow—is reflecting less light and therefore appears less bright),
a conclusion that is contrary to his intellectual
knowledge that the cardboard is indeed a homogeneous gray. It must be emphasized once again that

such *perceptual inferences* (also called *unconscious
inferences*) that a person makes in judging illumination
cues for perception of size, distance, shape, and so
on, are quite unconscious and automatic. The various
illumination cues—those for contrast as well as for
direction of illumination and spatial position—largely
determine perceived brightness.

Loudness Constancy   Perceptual constancies
are not restricted to vision alone. They occur in hearing and other senses as well, although they have
been studied much less extensively than in vision.
Loudness constancy, for example, refers to the fact
that the actual loudness of a given sound stimulus
will be perceived as fairly consistent, even if the
distance between the perceiver and the sound source
varies. One reason is that, in judging the true intensity of a sound source, we automatically account for
the distance between ear and source. Also, one's past
experiences influence loudness constancy. Familiar
sounds (such as noise from an aircraft or the ringing of a telephone) may exhibit loudness constancy
even when the cues to distance are poor.

As we have seen, perceptual constancies are governed by various cues. However, the very cues that
enable us to perceive a stable and ordered world
are often misleading or misjudged. When cues are
misinterpreted, instead of perceptual constancies,
we experience perceptual illusions.

PERCEPTUAL ILLUSIONS

We have already pointed out that perception *never*
precisely reflects the physical characteristics of distal
stimuli. In a way, then, all perception is illusory!
Nonetheless, we usually speak of "illusions" only
when there is a *gross misjudgment* of some characteristics of the distal stimulus. Thus, perceptual illu-

sions are phenomena that differ only in *degree* from normal perception. We shall discuss one or two examples of each of the most important categories of these illusions.

Illusions of Size   Why does the moon appear much larger when it is on the horizon than when it is directly overhead? The moon is virtually the same size in both locations, and its retinal image cannot vary enough to account for the difference in apparent size. What causes such a striking perceptual difference? When the moon is on the horizon there are often scores of buildings, landmarks, and other distance cues between the observer and the moon (see Figure 14.27). These cues allow the perceptual system to infer that the moon is very distant, but there are no perceptual cues when the moon is overhead. It then appears smaller, because, as we have already seen, given a constant retinal image, the greater the perceived distance of an object, the larger it will look. Similarly, if the moon is on an ocean horizon, it does not look quite as big as it does against a metropolitan backdrop, because there are fewer distance cues on the water between the observer and the horizon.

Other examples of the same type of size illusion were presented earlier. For example, the distortion illusion of the Ames room was also produced by misleading distance cues (owing to the illusory rectangular appearance of the room).

Another type of size illusion is illustrated by the two squares in the center of Figure 14.28. Although both center squares are the same size, the one on the left looks larger. The perceptual context of *frame of reference* imposed by the small outer squares makes the center square on the left appear bigger than its identical counterpart on the right, contained in the larger squares.

Figure 14.27
The moon tends to appear larger when it is near the horizon than when it is high in the sky. A horizon has been simulated in the bottom photograph. [Stephen Greenberg]

Figure 14.29
The Müller-Lyer illusion is an illusion of length.

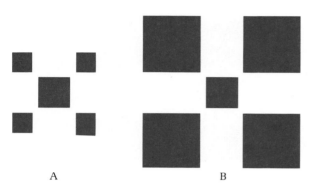

A   B

Figure 14.28
An illusion of size can be created by surrounding same-sized squares with larger or smaller squares.

Frame-of-reference illusions are best understood if we examine Harry Helson's theory of *adaptation level*. Briefly, Helson (b. 1898) maintains that whenever we estimate the magnitude of any sensation, such as perceived size or weight, we interpret the magnitude of a given stimulus by reference to the other stimuli that have been presented in the series. If the subject has been presented with a series of weights, for example, he constructs (as usual, unconsciously) some personal scale of subjective heaviness. This scale is based largely on weights that have been presented in the series, but it is also based partly on the subject's past experience with weights. One point along the scale is neutral and therefore is the subject's "adaptation level." Stimulus values above the adaptation level are judged "heavy," and those below it are judged "light." The adaptation level varies constantly, since the stimuli that act on a person at any given moment vary. Subjective judgments of sensation magnitude, then, vary according to the other stimuli that make up one's standard of comparison at a particular time. Similarly, a person's subjective judgments of the center

squares in Figure 14.28 depend on the other stimuli (the peripheral squares) that are presented at the same time, and are therefore standards against which the judgments can be made.

Illusions of Length   Look at the two abutting lines in Figure 14.29. Although the line on the left looks longer, both are of identical length. Whether a line appears longer or shorter depends on whether it is between the closed arrowhead figures or the open ones. This is the famous *Müller-Lyer illusion*: according to one theory, the illusion is caused by the varying angles at which the line of the shaft meets the line of the arrowhead.

Illusions of Perspective   Look next at the two dogs standing on the railroad tracks in Figure 14.30. The dog at the bottom of the figure appears smaller. Yet the same two dogs away from the railroad tracks (a misleading perspective cue) appear to be the same size (and indeed occupy the same portion of the page).

Illusions of Shape, Curvature, and Direction Many factors may influence our perception of shape, direction, and curvature. Look at the illustration of the man blowing a smoke ring (Figure 14.31). Most people view the ring as circular. Without the supporting cues provided by the context, however, the same ring is seen as elliptical.

Figure 14.32 illustrates two established distortion figures created by two of the earliest experimental psychologists, Ewald Hering and Wilhelm Wundt. In each figure, the two horizontal lines are parallel. However, in the Hering figure (A), the parallel lines appear to be bowed and thus farther apart at the center than at the end. In the Wundt figure (B), the motif of background lines has been reversed so that

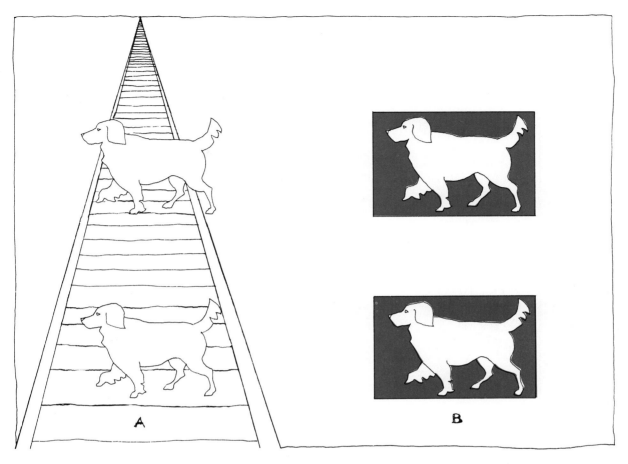

Figure 14.30
An illusion of perspective. In A, the top picture of the dog appears larger because it seems to be farther away.

Figure 14.31
An illusion of shape. Smoke rings appear rounder than do identical but meaningless ovals.

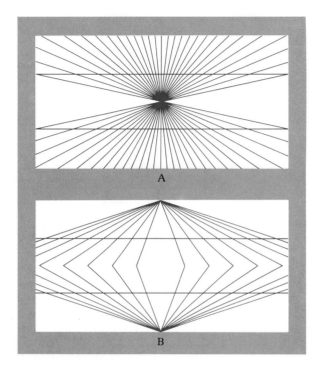

Figure 14.32
Two illusions of curvature. The horizontal lines are
actually straight and parallel.

the lines now appear bowed in the opposite direction. These illusions are poorly understood but are
believed to result from eye movements and a tendency to overestimate acute angles.

   The known types of illusions are numerous
indeed, and it would take many pages to list them
all. What they demonstrate is that the accuracy of
our perceptual judgment of a stimulus object
depends in great part on various cues in the visual
field. Although we can readily explain some of the
illusions by using the established principles of size
constancy, distance cues, and familiarity to analyze

them, others remain enigmatic. We know that much
of what is illusory largely results from what is
brought to the situation by the perceiver—his needs,
his expectations, and past experiences. When interpreting ambiguous figures, not only do we tend to
form them into "good" figures but we also interpret
them in terms of our expectations and hopes (this
is called "wishful perception"). The influence of
such wishful perception, or motivation, on one's
interpretation of ambiguous stimulus situations forms
the basis of a number of the projective tests of personality, which we shall discuss in Chapter 26.

PERCEPTUAL LEARNING

Perceptual psychologists have traditionally been
divided into two schools—the *nativists*, who believe
that perceptual mechanisms are largely inherited,
and the *empiricists*, who emphasize the contribution
of experience to one's perceptions. Neither group
has had any trouble finding phenomena to study or
arguments to support their positions—probably
because they are both partly right. As we now realize, both inherited and learned factors are important
in perception.

   As a consequence of this debate, considerable
research has been done on the role of early experience in perceptual development. For example,
animals were once experimentally raised in total
darkness for as long as sixteen months; since that
time, it has been learned that some light is necessary
for the development of the retina and brain. Hence,
in subsequent experiments, animals have been raised
in unpatterned light (provided by halves of ping-
pong balls firmly fixed over each eye). After one to
three months, such animals are exposed to the patterned stimuli of the real world. The purpose of
these experiments is to determine which visual
stimuli the animals perceive merely as a result of

innate perceptual ability. It is evident that the visually deprived animals can see and can make use of certain visual stimuli to guide their behavior: they do not run into objects, as a blind animal will; they can scamper under a couch or behind a stove when silently pursued, indicating that they see their pursuer. But their discriminative abilities are often very poorly developed. For example, they may have great difficulty distinguishing between certain spatial patterns.

Sensory deprivation has also been studied in people who were born with cataracts that were later removed. Although people might seem to be better subjects than animals, one problem is that a human has other contact with sensory stimuli, since he can touch and feel objects, and therefore the deprivation is not as complete as it is for animals, which can be denied these additional contacts in an experimental situation. In addition, a human being describes his world in words rather than actions, and words can be as misleading as they are informative. However, these drawbacks aside, the reports of people who acquired vision some years after birth have been useful, as an early example in this chapter suggested.

The reports indicate that the newly sighted are able to see gradations in brightness, the various colors, and figure-ground relationships. If we assume that their visual systems are normal, then these perceptual abilities would seem to be innate. What they cannot see indicates that some learning is necessary for normal perception. They report that straws of different lengths look "different," but they must touch the straws before identifying the longer ones. Faces, statues, or everyday utensils such as knives and forks are not identified just by looking at them, even though they are familiar to the touch. And they initially cannot distinguish squares from triangles without counting the edges or corners, but they do note that they look different. It is not certain whether the deficiency is in perceptual ability or in the ability to *use words to describe* visual perceptions (or in both), but it is clear that visual experience has an important function in the development of our normal perception of the world.

Another approach to the influence of learning on the perceptual system is the study of the effects of drastic alteration of the normal perceptual field. Can a person adjust to a radically altered visual world? Suppose, for example, that we were to wear special glasses that turned retinal images, and thus our visual world, upside down. This kind of rearrangement would be most inconvenient at first, but experiments have shown that people can adjust to even this radical change in their visual world. Indeed, we would find that we gradually adapted to our distorted world, even to the point of being able to ride a bicycle safely in heavy traffic. But the inverted world would never seem normal; it would be too much in conflict with our sense of balance, which tells us that we were still upright, and with our movements, which we would still *perceive* as up and down even though they appeared to be reversed when observed through the prisms. Evidently a person in this predicament continues to feel that his body is normally upright but that his head is upside-down.

PERCEPTION OF MOVEMENT

The ability to detect and to judge movement is vitally important. Many lower organisms depend upon movement detection for their survival; some, like frogs, have specialized movement detectors that reliably respond to moving prey. Human beings, too, make use of movement perception, not only when they estimate the location, speed, and path of moving objects—an ability that is often necessary for survival—but also when they indulge in such distinctly human pursuits as watching the shifting

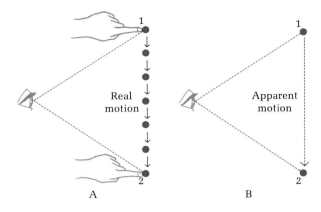

Figure 14.33
Part A shows the perception of a moving object. Apparent movement occurs between two lights lighted in sequence, as in Part B.

shadows on television and motion-picture screens. As is true of all perception, perceived motion does not bear a one-to-one relation to physical motion. Rarely is there a simple correspondence between actual physical movement (of the distal stimulus object), the patterned movement on the retina (the proximal stimulus), and our subjective impression of movement (perception). As we shall see, we sometimes perceive movement that is not represented in either the distal or proximal stimulus; on the other hand, we sometimes fail to perceive movement even when the retinal image accurately reflects the movement of distal objects.

Although the mechanisms of movement perception are complex and poorly understood, three basic operations can be illustrated with the following demonstrations: (1) hold a finger in front of your face at arm's length and move it from left to right across your visual field; (2) next, keep your finger stationary in front of you and move your eyes from left to right (3) finally, close one eye and press on the outer corner of your open eye a few times. For each demonstration, you will experience a different perceptual experience. The first demonstration illustrates the perception of normal movement: as the finger crosses the visual field, it stimulates successive groups of receptors on the retina and causes movement perception. In the second demonstration, when the eyes move while the finger remains stationary, different receptors on the retina are again successively stimulated by the finger but the finger is correctly perceived as stationary. The perceptual apparatus discounts the movement registered on the retina, because it has received kinesthetic cues from the eye muscles indicating that eye movements are responsible for the change in the finger's position on the retina. Thus, our perception of movement is jointly determined by the movement of the retinal image and by cues from the muscles that are

employed in eye movements. This interaction of movement on the retina and muscular cues also explains the apparent "jumping" of the visual image in the third demonstration: when we press the corner of one eye, the resultant change in the retinal image is not offset by normal eye-movement cues; hence, the image is perceived as moving, although the distal objects are not moving.

Apparent Movement If two lights in close proximity to each other are successively flashed on and off, within a given period of time, the observer will perceive movement of the light from one position to the other, even though no real movement has occurred. Figure 14.33 illustrates the difference between real movement and this particular type of apparent movement: note that the apparent movement only seems to occur between Points 1 and 2 in Part B of the figure. A common example of apparent movement is the motion picture.

The apparent movement itself can vary, depending on the amount of time elapsing between presentation of the stimuli, the distance between the stimuli, and the intensity of each. In order to obtain *optimal movement* (that is, the strongest illusion of continuous movement), an interval of about 6 milliseconds between presentations is desirable. If the intervals are longer, the phenomenon that gestalt psychologists called *phi movement* occurs: the light does not actually appear to move continuously from one place to the other, but the observer nevertheless has the impression that a stimulus has moved. Another variation of apparent movement is the _delta movement_: for example, if there are two lights, such as those in Figure 14.33, Part B, and the second stimulus is sufficiently brighter than the first, the direction of movement will be reversed so that the light appears to move from Point 2 to Point 1. Other variations result from the influence of additional stimuli: for example, if a vertical line is placed in the path between two flashing lights, the movement (called a _bow movement_) appears to bend around the line.

A second type of apparent movement occurs when a small spot of stationary light is viewed in an unstructured perceptual field, such as a dark room—after a short time, the spot of light appears to move around. This _autokinetic effect_ is an example of "self-generated" movement. The distance of the apparent movement can be affected by our expectations. For example, if an experimenter's accomplice reports that the spot of light is moving across long distances, the subject too will perceive greater movement. Similarly, the autokinetic effect can be reduced by having an observer present who insists that no movement occurs. You can demonstrate the autokinetic effect to your own satisfaction if you set up a point source of light in a darkened room: even though you know that the light is not moving, you will probably still obtain the effect. If you do not have a point source of light, try staring at a single star in the sky for a while; you may experience movement and may even be briefly convinced that the star is really a moving satellite! However, the effect will be reduced if the star is surrounded by other stars, since they provide a frame of reference that reduces the illusion.

Other illusions of movement, called perceptual _aftereffects_, seem to result from satiation of visual receptors. For example, if one stares at a waterfall

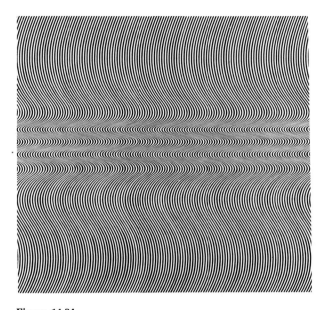

Figure 14.34
A stationary stimulus can create an illusion of movement. [Bridget Riley, _Current_, 1964. Synthetic polymer paint on composition board (58¾ inches by 58⅞ inches). Collection, The Museum of Modern Art, New York. Philip C. Johnson Fund.]

for some time and then turns the eyes away to focus on other objects, the objects will appear to be moving upwards. A similar phenomenon is experienced by children when they spin themselves around in one direction for a length of time and then stop: for a moment, the world seems to spin around them in the opposite direction.

Another type of apparent movement is more of a riddle and is illustrated in Figure 14.34. Although this is a two-dimensional figure of a stationary pattern, a strong perception of movement is obtained. The dynamics of this kind of apparent movement are poorly understood.

Induced Movement The kinds of apparent movement illustrated in the foregoing examples are largely indistinguishable from real movement although neither the stimulus object nor the retinal image moves. Just as we can perceive movement when no physical movement has taken place, we can also fail to perceive movement when movement has in fact occurred. Thus, in *induced movement*, the observer · incorrectly perceives a moving object to be stationary and a stationary object to be in motion. For example, on a cloudy night the moon may appear to be moving swiftly in the sky behind a sea of clouds. Although the clouds are moving, they appear to be stationary and their movement induces the apparent movement of the moon. Although the representation of the moon and clouds on the retinal image faithfully represents the state of each, we perceive the opposite. The reason is that if one object in the field is more readily seen as a figure (the moon), and the other more readily seen as background (the clouds), the movement will usually be attributed to the figure. Another common example of induced movement is that perceived from a train, when we have difficulty in judging whether our train or the one across the tracks is moving: we receive no cues about the nature of the movement from our own limbs because we ourselves are stationary; therefore, we must rely totally on visual cues, which are ambiguous. Subjects' perceptions of induced movement can also be manipulated in the laboratory, either by manipulating figure-ground cues or by providing cues about the nature of the physical movement.

Perceived Causality in Movement   When one billiard ball strikes a second ball, and the second one then moves, we say that the impact of the first ball has imparted motion to the second. Such perception of *causality* can also be induced by moving light stimuli, such as those used to demonstrate the phi phenomenon. For example, if movement of a light from Point A to Point B is followed closely in time by movement of a second light from Point B to Point C, subjects will perceive the first movement as causing the second. It is important to note that subjects are not consciously inferring that the first movement gave rise to the second, but rather they are reporting their perception that it did so.

PERCEPTION OF TIME

Although the stimulus for the perceived passage of time is not known, some aspects of time perception are understood, and several theories have been proposed. First, it has been observed that subjects perceive the duration of a short period of time (say, less than one minute) as increasingly longer, the greater the number of events (or "filler activities") that occur during that period. Thus, filled intervals (those containing explicit, discrete events, such as a series of clicks or the reading of meaningful passages) appear to last longer than unfilled intervals, marked simply by two signals, one at the beginning and the other at the end of the period. For periods that are longer than one minute, these generalizations do not necessarily hold and may even reverse. Indeed, time appears to "slow down," if there is nothing to do.

Also, psychopharmacological research has shown that as a general rule, drugs that speed up bodily processes cause one to perceive time as passing more quickly. Similarly, depressants—such as tranquilizers—slow down the perceived passage of time. Such research lends support to the theory that *apparent duration* is somehow correlated with "biological clocks" (time-correlated internal processes). It has been suggested that the body has two such biological clocks: a short-term mechanism for estimating short durations (one that is correlated for example, with heartbeat or brain rhythms, both of which vary with the nature of filler activities) and a long-term mechanism correlated with the rhythms of certain natural bodily sensations, such as sleepiness, hunger, or the need to eliminate. The importance of natural body rhythms in the perception of time has been demonstrated in certain isolation studies in which subjects have spent several days without explicit cues to time (such as clocks or outside illumination). Often, subjects in these experiments become surprisingly accurate in estimating what the real time is. Also, anyone who travels across several time zones on an overseas or transcontinental flight learns that a period of several days, or even weeks, can elapse before the body adjusts to a significant time change.

PERCEPTION OF SPEECH

One of our most marvelous and complex perceptual systems is the one that enables us to perceive speech accurately. Although auditory patterns vary dramatically from person to person, we are nonetheless able to recognize and respond to meaningful utterances. Moreover, the experimental analysis of speech perception has shown that even if the speech waveform is rendered unrecognizable by systematic distortion, intelligibility often remains high. For example, the amplitude can be distorted by an electronic process called "peak clipping." Thus if the peaks (or high-amplitude portions) of the wave form are removed, speech remains intelligible. Even if the speech wave is so distorted that only the one-sixteenth of the wave nearest the center axis remains, more than 95 percent of monosyllabic words are perceived correctly! These findings indicate that the central portion of the speech waveform is more critical for intelligible perceptions. Apparently, it is this center portion that contains the consonant sounds that affect intelligibility much more strongly than the vowel sounds do. Speech can also be distorted by removing the upper or lower frequencies of the sound spectrum. Yet conversations are quite intelligible even when the information contained in either the lower or upper half of the sound spectrum is deleted.

It is obvious, then, that the intelligibility of speech does not depend upon either amplitude or frequency alone. Apparently, normal speech contains so much *redundancy* (redundant, or repeated, information) that

comprehension occurs even when listening conditions are far from optimal and even when the speech is being systematically distorted. Thus perception of speech (or comprehension) is similar to the perception of other sensory phenomena in that it is not too closely dependent on the precise characteristics of the distal stimulus. For this reason, the word "barefoot" is understood even though its acoustic wave form is never identical from enunciation to enunciation even by the same speaker. Speech perception, like all other perception, is a process of organizing and interpreting sensory input.

Suggested Readings

Beardslee, D., & Wertheimer, M. (1958) *Readings in perception*. Princeton: Van Nostrand. [An excellent selection of classic readings in perception, including the *gestalt* perspective.]

Gibson, J. J. (1966) *The senses considered as perceptual systems*. Boston: Houghton-Mifflin. [An authoritative and challenging treatment.]

Gibson, E. J. (1969) *Principles of perceptual learning and development*. New York: Appleton-Century-Crofts. [A comprehensive treatment from the developmental viewpoint.]

Hochberg, J. E. (1964) *Perception*. Englewood Cliffs, New Jersey: Prentice-Hall. [A short, excellent introduction to perception.]

Koffka, K. (1953) *Principles of gestalt psychology*. New York: Harcourt Brace Jovanovich. [Old but definitive statement by one of the original members of the gestalt school.]

UNIT FIVE

Instinct and Heredity

Like newborn birds and mammals of many species, young rhesus monkeys instinctively form a strong and specific attachment to a parent. Separated from its own mother, the young monkey shown on the facing page has formed a filial attachment to a large woolly dog. The monkey and dog were part of an experiment by William A. Mason and M. D. Kennedy that we shall describe in Chapter 15.

In this unit, we shall take a look at how an organism's genetic inheritance influences its behavior. There is general agreement that among the lower organisms, heredity governs a large proportion of behavior. Even in animals as complex as dogs, birds, and monkeys, instinct clearly plays a substantial role in behavior. When it comes to humans, though, there is often considerable disagreement over the role of instinctive behavior.

For example, consider the highly controversial problem of human aggression: is hostile action toward others instinctive or learned? Too often in the past, psychologists have approached the controversial question of human aggression with an oversimplified answer. The data are the same regardless of the psychologist's point of view: man may strike out when threatened or when injured or when frustrated; he may kill for gain, or revenge, or in obedience to a superior, and so on. Explanations of the data differ considerably: (1) some psychologists see aggression as innate, (2) others as learned, and (3) still others as imposed on man by social and economic conditions. While defending their own particular approaches to the issue, psychologists often fail to integrate their valid but limited points of view with those equally valid and likewise limited points of view of other psychologists.

Konrad Lorenz, the ethologist, sees aggression between members of the same species as an instinctive reaction to specific environmental stimuli. He draws this conclusion from his lengthy and detailed studies of animal behavior.

Behaviorists hold that aggressive behavior is largely the result of pain and frustration; and that, as these are reduced, there is less reason for aggression to occur. Furthermore, situations leading to aggression can be avoided if peaceful behavior is rewarded. Thus, for behaviorists, there is no innate need for aggression: when the environment can be correctly arranged, aggression will not occur.

Erich Fromm, a socially oriented humanistic psychologist, sees aggression as the product of civilization. Fromm admits that an individual who is threatened may act in a hostile manner in order to protect himself. He calls such behavior *benign* aggression. He describes other aggressive urges as *malignant* aggression resulting from the exploitation, oppression, and helplessness forced on people by contemporary civilization. He feels that aggression will always be a problem as long as some segments of society are exploited and oppressed, and most people feel that their ability to control and influence the world around them is small or nonexistent.

When it comes to eliminating aggression, psychologists range from strongly to mildly pessimistic. The behaviorist is perhaps least pessimistic. Believing that it is possible to modify behavior through training, the behaviorist holds that aggression can be eliminated when the proper adjustments in the environment can be made. Fromm feels that only a complete overhaul of society would be effective in eliminating aggression. Lorenz' opinion, that human aggressiveness is innate, seems to offer little hope for its elimination.

But are these points of view truly incompatible? (1) One of the fundamental tenets of behaviorism is the assumption that certain events serve as rewards for all members of a given species. This implies that heredity does indeed affect the way animals respond to their world. It would do no harm to the behaviorist's position to admit that the connection between certain kinds of stimuli and responses (frustration or pain and aggression, for instance) is innate, just as reflexes are innate. (2) The oppression, exploitation, and frustration that predominate in Fromm's view of civilization could be described as complicated instances of aggression-provoking stimuli from the behavioristic viewpoint. (3) Lorenz, in turn, concedes that aggression is triggered by particular environmental circumstances, even though the relationship between stimulus and response is innate. Although each psychologist looks at the same data from a distinctive point of view and comes up with a different interpretation, there seems to be no reason to believe that these interpretations are necessarily incompatible.

Naturally, differing viewpoints about the nature of human aggression lead to different opinions on the elimination of aggression. If there were a world in which pain and frustration—in either the behaviorist's or Fromm's sense—did not exist, then perhaps aggression would not occur. But is it realistic to suppose that such a world might exist? Isn't suffering a part of life? And will there not always be relative differences among individuals that can serve as occasions for frustration and hence for aggression? Moreover, is aggression entirely devoid of social value? Many ethologists, including Lorenz in his book *On Aggression*, suggest that if aggression is innate in man, it may serve some kind of adaptive function. For instance, by fostering competition, it may be the force behind many social improvements and much progress in various fields of human endeavor.

In the chapters that follow, we have emphasized the hereditary aspects of behavior and have traced those genetic mechanisms that are believed responsible for their transmission from generation to generation. We approach these with the attitude of that branch of psychology that believes them to be paramount. But the reader has been forewarned that there are other, not necessarily incompatible, points of view.

CHAPTER FIFTEEN

Ethology

Why study animal behavior? Can the study of nonhuman organisms tell us anything about human behavior? There are many possible answers, but two are most important. First, general principles of behavior that apply to all organisms, including man, may be discovered and developed more conveniently and efficiently with lower organisms. Second, there are continuities between the behavior of different species, owing to evolutionary processes. The more we learn about other organisms and about the behavioral similarities and differences between organisms at different places on the evolutionary scale, the more we will appreciate both man's unique abilities and those that he shares with other organisms.

The first point—that certain fundamental laws of behavior may apply to all organisms (at least those equipped with a central nervous system)—has been well documented in studies of operant and classical conditioning (see Chapters 3 and 4). To say that humans, pigeons, and chimpanzees are governed by the same laws is not, of course, to say that the organisms are the same. That would be as incorrect as maintaining that the fact that feathers and bowling balls both obey the law of gravity makes them the same. The second point—regarding the continuity

of organisms on the evolutionary scale—emphasizes the comparative study of different species rather than a search for general principles governing the behavior of all organisms.

Finally, we should stress that the study of animal behavior is fascinating—and often is fun. For this reason alone, the behavior of "lower" organisms has attracted the attention of psychologists, biologists, zoologists, and others with a natural curiosity about behavior.

Ethology is the study of behavior as practiced, primarily, by zoologists. The ethological approach stresses the study of _species-specific behavior_, or behavior that is fairly uniform across all members of a given species. In other words, any two normal, same-sexed members of the species will react to certain stimulus situations in virtually the same way. For example, spiders spin webs that are characteristic of their particular species, birds build nests and sing songs that typify their species, and all normal male stickleback fish launch the same type of attack on other male sticklebacks that intrude into their territory during mating season.

Such behaviors, which are controlled by environmental stimuli (as we shall see in the next section), result from hereditary predispositions that have been shaped by natural selection. In general, behavior that is more adaptive—more favorable to the survival of the species—becomes more likely to recur over generations. For example, we can imagine that sticklebacks that emitted the attack behavior and held their territory were more likely to mate and have offspring than those that did not. Over many generations, only sticklebacks with this hereditary predisposition bred and hence, eventually, only those were born. Much can be learned about the _ontogeny of behavior_ (the development of behavior within an individual organism's lifetime) by appreciating the principles of _phylogeny_ (the evolutionary development of the behavior that is characteristic of a species).

INNATE VERSUS LEARNED COMPONENTS OF BEHAVIOR

With regard to behavior, the question "What is inherited?" is a deceptively simple one. _Behavior_ itself is not inherited, although the capacity and predisposition to behave in certain ways is.

Organisms enter the world with a particular biological structure that helps determine much of their behavior. For example, humans can develop the necessary neuromuscular coordination for walking or swimming but not for flying. In other words, what a normal organism inherits is the physical capacity for engaging in the behaviors characteristic of its species.

Our pupils contract when stimulated by light. This pupillary contraction is an example of a _reflex_—a simple, specific, unlearned response to a specific type of stimulus. Another well-known reflex is the knee-jerk (or _patellar reflex_) that occurs when the patellar tendon is struck. Every organism is born with reflexes that are intimately linked to basic biological functions and are often vital to its survival.

The fact that these reflexes do not have to be learned means that they are ready to function as soon as the organism is born (sometimes even before it is born).

Many behavior patterns more complicated than reflexes also appear to require no learning; such complex unlearned behaviors are called _instincts_. Instincts, like reflexes, occur in response to particular stimuli (_sign stimuli_). We say that sign stimuli "release" instinctive responses. For example, the red spot on the belly of the male stickleback fish is said to release attack behavior in other males of the species who enter his territory, as illustrated and described in Figure 15.1. Instinctive behavior, like a reflex action, does not have to be learned and thus does not depend on prior experience. As we shall see in this chapter, instinctive behavior patterns are elicited by unconditioned stimuli, without the expectation of a reward. Furthermore, it is a very mechanical and stereotyped form of behavior—for instance, the males of some species of insects will perform complete mating rituals in the presence of a mere chemical stimulus.

A given species is also inherently responsive to a given set of reinforcers. For example, the presentation of a slice of prime rib may influence the behavior of most hungry humans and dogs, but not that of horses or guinea pigs. The distinction lies not in the organisms' different experiences with prime rib but more fundamentally in the value of roast beef for organisms with different types of digestive tracts. By the same token, a helping of hay will reinforce the behavior of horses, but not that of humans.

Learned behavior, on the other hand, is dependent on consequences, or on reinforcement. It alters as the reinforcement alters, and is thus much more flexible than instinctive behavior. An organism that is capable of learning from experience can make individual alterations in its behavior during its own

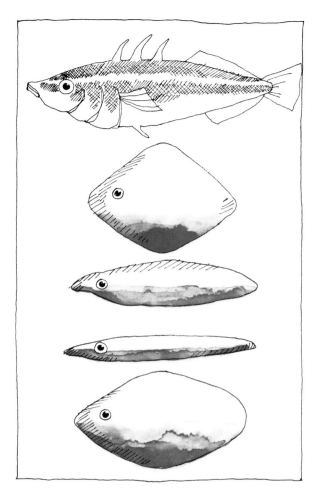

Figure 15.1
Models used to determine the stimulus that releases attack in the male stickleback fish. Lacking a red belly, the realistic model at the top does not release attack, but the unfishlike lower models with red undersides do. Hence the red belly is the releasing stimulus. [Adapted from N. Tinbergen, *The Study of Instinct.* Oxford: The Clarendon Press, 1951.]

lifetime; it may even develop actions that are different from those of any other member of its species. More than any other organisms, humans show this potential for a rich variety of behaviors.

Examples of Innate Behavior Whereas reflexes refer to behaviors that involve only a portion of the organism, *tropisms* are behaviors that consist of move-

Figure 15.2
Eleanor J. Gibson and Richard D. Walk found that birds, human infants, and other mammals, like this kitten, seem able to perceive and avoid a sharp drop as soon as they can move about. In the experiment, a strong sheet of transparent glass covered the cliff so the subjects could not fall. [William Vandivert. This photograph appeared in E. J. Gibson and R. D. Walk's "The Visual Cliff," *Scientific American*, April 1960, 64–71.]

ments of the entire organism: the moth is attracted to light, and the roach flees it. Tropisms have been studied most extensively with invertebrates, but they are also found in vertebrates and higher organisms. For example, infant mice and rats will climb up an inclined plane, thereby exhibiting a *negative geotaxis* (a tendency to move away from the earth, or against the force of gravity). Figure 15.2 shows another interesting example of a tropism.

Two classes of tropism have received most attention: *kineses* and *taxes*. Kineses are the more primitive *undirected* locomotory reactions to changes in stimulus intensity. Among these reactions are speed of movement and frequency of turning. For example, the wood louse will move more quickly as the air becomes less humid. Taxes are directional responses in which the organism moves either directly toward or away from the stimulating source. One familiar example is the way moths fly towards light. Another one exhibited by many insects, including locusts and other grasshoppers, is flying directly into the wind. The mechanism for this taxis is a kind of "aerodynamic sense organ" in the form of hair tufts on the front of the locust's head. Air currents cause the hair tufts to bend; bending of the tufts stimulates flying. When the wind direction shifts, the tufts on one side of the head are bent more than those on the other, resulting in a change in orientation that again puts the locust on a direct course into the wind. When the hair tufts are removed, or covered with paint, none of these reactions, including flying, occurs.

Examples of Learned Behaviors Learned behavior involves the modification of an individual's behavior by experience, as discussed in the first unit of this book. Examples of learned behaviors in humans are commonplace: among other things, you have learned to read these words.

The ability to learn from experience, which many higher organisms share, but in which humans excel, means that an organism can alter many of his actions according to their consequences; he need not react blindly to whatever stimulus the environment may present. Figure 15.3 illustrates an experiment in which a kitten, though able to observe its environment, was prevented from interacting with it. Unable to move about and thus observe the consequences of its own actions, the kitten failed to learn normal responses.

Even learning itself is affected by hereditary factors. Although there are great individual differences, the members of each species seem able to learn just so much, and no more. The responses making up the learned behavior sequence must be

Figure 15.3
In this apparatus, used by Richard Held and his colleagues, one kitten could walk around, turn to the right or left, and make up and down movements. The other kitten was confined in a gondola that duplicated the movements of the first kitten but prohibited the confined kitten from interacting with its environment. [Ted Polumbaum. This experiment is described in R. Held's "Plasticity in Sensory-Motor Systems," *Scientific American*, November 1965, 84–94.]

ones that the organism is physically capable of performing: pigeons cannot learn to talk, and humans cannot learn to fly. Similarly, the primary reinforcer for performing the behavior must be one that has value for the organisms: pigeons will not respond for an ultimate reward of sirloin steak, nor men for pigeon feed. This value is also determined by the organism's inherited biological structure.

STUDIES OF INSTINCTIVE BEHAVIOR

Although there are many definitions of instinct, one that has survived since the time of the Stoics in

300 B.C. defines instinctive behavior as *unlearned, uniform within a species*, and *adaptive*. The way in which instincts are adaptive is readily apparent: they are behaviors that enable the organism to feed, procreate, escape from predators, and perform other functions essential for the survival of the species. In this section we shall discuss several examples of instinctive behaviors and the principles governing them.

In order to understand the use, and misuse, of the term "instinct" for such unlearned species-specific behavior patterns, it is helpful to know something of the history of psychology.

Around the turn of this century, at a time when little was known about the determinants of animal behavior, the term "instinct" came into wide use as an *explanation* of behavior. The great American social psychologist William McDougall claimed that all behavior, including human behavior, had instinctive origins. Unfortunately, all McDougall could do was to name instincts—accordingly, a person is pugnacious, or motherly, or gregarious because he or she has a fighting instinct, a parental instinct, or an instinct to congregate. Such labels, of course, tell nothing about the factors that actually control the behavior in question. The lists of instincts drawn up by different theorists were long, extensively varied, and often contradictory. Indeed, when the different lists were combined, the total number of instincts came to several thousand. Even the great philosopher and psychologist William James took to list-making, noting that man was particularly rich in his instinctive repertoire.

Merely to label behaviors such as "suspicion" and "sociability" as "instinctive impulses," however, is not a very fruitful approach to understanding the behaviors. Moreover, there is obviously more than one kind of "suspicious" or "sociable" behavior. With the rise of American behaviorism in the 1920s,

there came an emphasis upon learning and the environment as determinants of behavior. The disparity between this view and that of the instinct theorists led to an "anti-instinct" revolt among the behaviorists.

An important consequence of the anti-instinct revolt, spearheaded by the Chinese psychologist Zing-Yang Kuo and other behaviorally oriented experimental psychologists, was the realization that the notion of instinct should not be used as an explanatory principle replacing deeper understanding of the factors giving rise to the behavior in question. To respond to questions such as "Why do cats kill rats?" with answers like "It's an instinct" is often an admission of ignorance. In any case, it constitutes a "nominal fallacy," a mistaken belief that one has explained a phenomenon simply by naming it. Today, we realize that behavior patterns develop as a result of the constant interaction between organism and environment.

For the purposes of discussion, we will continue to use "instinct" in this chapter to describe complex behaviors that are significantly dependent upon hereditary factors and that are elicited by specific environmental stimuli. It should be understood, however, that this description does not constitute explanation.

A *sign stimulus*, or *releaser*, is a particular object, or part of an object, that elicits a particular response or set of responses in a particular species of organism. The red spot on the belly of a male stickleback has already been cited as one example of a sign stimulus (see Figure 15.1). The sight of it deep within his territory induces another male stickleback to prepare for battle, but the sign operates only for males of this one species of fish. The word "sign" emphasizes the fact that the releasing stimulus may not be a whole object; it is likely to be only one aspect or part of an object—a colored area, an odor, a call, an attitude, or a gesture. A red spot on the belly of the crudest of artificial models will still provoke the fighting behavior of a male stickleback in his own territory.

Sign stimuli play important roles in communication between members of the same species (in courtship, for example), between members of different species (in the discouragement of predators), in reproductive behavior, feeding, and many other situations. They are crucial to the survival of the individual organism and the species. Their adaptive function can be seen rather dramatically in the case of certain species of moths (see Figure 15.4) that have evolved large spots resembling owl eyes on their wings. Because owls are among the natural predators of insectivorous birds, such insect-eaters fly away from any rapidly moving stimuli resembling owl's eyes. The moth's wings, therefore, release an instinctive flight response in their bird predators, thus contributing to the survival of the moths.

But isn't this instinctive flight response maladaptive for the birds? Not very. Certain behaviors, such as fleeing from predators, are so vital to the organism's survival that it is adaptive for it to respond to the sign stimuli that release them, wherever they occur, even if they lose a few meals by doing so. When sign stimuli appear in inappropriate locations, they often trigger instinctive behaviors that have no practical function at that time—we could call such incidents "false alarms."

The ethologists Konrad Lorenz and Niko Tinbergen, both Nobel Prize winners, have coined the term *social releaser* to describe that class of releasers that triggers interaction with other organisms, including members of one's own species. An example of a social releaser is provided by the behavior of the male Siamese fighting fish *(Betta splendens)*. When confronted by either another male Betta, its own mirror image, or an appropriate

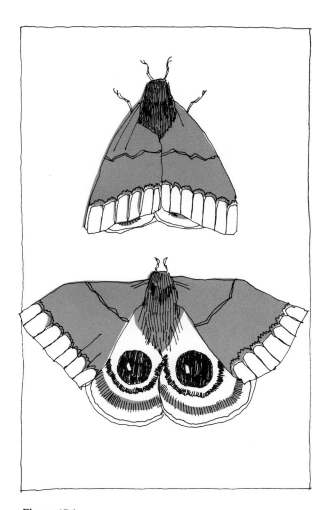

Figure 15.4
In the natural food chain, insectivorous birds eat moths but are themselves eaten by owls. The design on the wings of this moth resembles an owl's eyes, which frighten away the insectivorous birds that might otherwise eat the moth. Apparently the birds recognize dangerous owls by their eyes and so treat the moth as an owl!

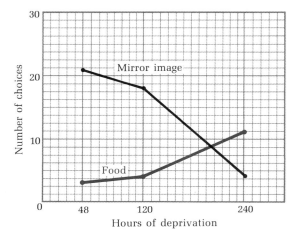

Figure 15.5
A male Siamese fighting fish could choose to swim
through a loop leading to food or through a loop leading
to a mirror at which he displayed a fighting response to
his own image. The graph shows the number of times
the fish chose each alternative as he was more and
more deprived of food. Only when the fish had not
eaten for 240 hours did he clearly prefer food to the
fight-eliciting mirror image. [Adapted from E. Fantino,
S. Weigele, and D. Lancy, "Aggressive Display in the
Siamese Fighting Fish (*Betta Splendens*)," *Learning and
Motivation*, *3*, 1972.]

model, the fish engages in a highly stereotyped
aggressive behavior pattern consisting of a deepening
of body and fin color, gill-membrane extension, and
frontal approach toward the other Betta, accompanied
by undulating movements. The fighting response is
a powerful one; two confined male *Bettas* may
combat until death or, at least, until exhaustion.
Moreover, the Siamese fighting fish will learn a new
response in order to obtain this social releaser for
aggressive display as a reinforcer. A Siamese fighting
fish that has been deprived of both food and the
opportunity to display for a moderate length of time
(either 120 or 48 hours) will choose the response
that produces its mirror image more frequently than
he will choose the response producing food. If
deprivation is sufficiently increased, however, (240
hours) food is preferred. The results, shown in Figure
15.5, suggest that the effectiveness of social releasers
may depend critically upon the organism's internal
physiological state.

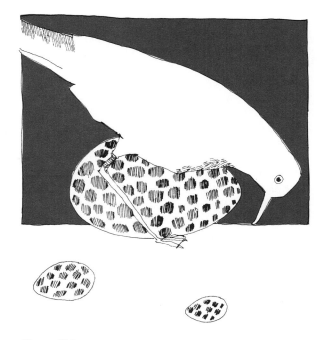

Figure 15.6
A supernormal stimulus. The oyster-catcher prefers the
larger to the normal egg, even though it cannot sit on it
properly. Notice that the bird ignores normal-sized eggs
that it could brood properly.

Supernormal Stimuli What happens when an
organism encounters a stimulus that resembles the
sign stimulus except that it is more salient and conspicuous? Using models, ethologists have found that
supernormal stimuli may be *more* effective in releasing
behavior. For example, oyster-catchers and other
birds prefer to sit on a huge *supernormal* egg rather
than on an egg of normal size, as shown in Figure
15.6. In the case of the stickleback models (shown in
Figure 15.1) the larger the red spot on the male's

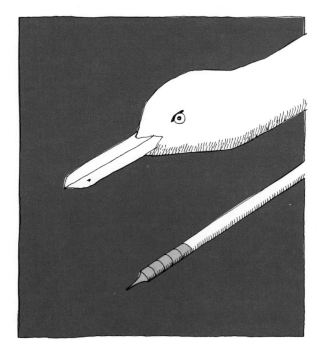

Figure 15.7
Young chicks peck more at the lower model, which contains the sign-stimulus, red, than at the realistic model of a parent's head without the red. The color, not the shape, of the object is the sign stimulus.

belly, the stronger the aggression. A final example, reported by Tinbergen, is that of the herring gull chick which obtains food by pecking a red spot on the parent's bill. When the chick pecks at the red spot, the parent opens its mouth, which contains regurgitated food, such as fish. When the chick is presented with models of bills, such as those shown in Figure 15.7, it gives the strongest pecking response not to the most realistic looking bill, but to models that are longer and show the most red. On the other hand, something that looks very beaklike

(at least to humans), but which is short and lacks redness, will release very little pecking on the part of the chick.

Experiments like these confirm the idea that what operates as a releaser is not the object itself, the egg, the intruding stickleback, or the parent gull's bill, but certain signs or characteristics of that object, such as size, shape, or color.

Vacuum and Displacement Activities   Specific sign stimuli tend to release specific behavior patterns, but there is rarely a perfect one-to-one relationship between them. For example, instinctive behaviors sometimes occur in the absence of the *appropriate* sign stimulus *(displacement activity)* or in the apparent absence of *any* sign stimulus *(vacuum activity)*.

We noted (Figure 15.1) that the male stickleback will attack another male stickleback that enters its territory. If the same stickleback intrudes on another's territory, he will flee before the enraged male proprietor. The red spot is, therefore, a sign stimulus for either attack or flight, depending on the environmental context in which it is presented. The stickleback's behavior is controlled by an interaction between the sign stimulus and its location in relation to his own territory. What happens when two male sticklebacks meet at the border of their respective territories? Under these circumstances, each fish will display conflicting tendencies to flee and to attack. After alternating between aggression and flight for a few moments, each fish may simultaneously engage in displacement activity, so named because the organism apparently *displaces* its conflicting tendencies to a seemingly irrelevant behavior, in this case, digging as if in preparation for nest-building as shown in Figure 15.8. (Among humans, whistling nonchalantly might be an equivalent activity.)

Displacement digging can also be artificially produced by the experimenter who punishes the stickleback for attacking an appropriately colored model in its own territory. When the model is presented to the stickleback and actually used to hit him, the fish first fights, then flees, then returns to the scene of the battle but begins to dig instead of fight. After a time, however, the fish will fight again. This suggests that the displacement digging occurs under stressful conditions when the tendency to flee (caused in this situation by being counterattacked within the borders of his territory) is equal to the tendency to fight (released by the presence of an intruder bearing the appropriate sign stimulus).

Vacuum activity is instinctive behavior occurring in a psychological or environmental "vacuum," that is, in the apparent absence of stimulation. For example, Lorenz notes that a starling, deprived of food, may perform an entire sequence of fly-catching behavior—including searching for, catching, and killing the nonexistent fly!

Chained Responses Many instinctive behaviors consist of a *chain* of responses; that is, each response produces a new stimulus situation, which, in turn is the sign stimulus for the next response in the chain. This is not the same as the conditioned response chain studied in Chapter 4. In instinctive behavior chains, the separate responses are linked to an invariable sequence of preceding stimuli. As we shall see in our discussion of the reproductive cycle of the ring dove later in this chapter, it is difficult, and sometimes impossible, for an experimenter to manipulate these chains so that they can begin in the middle.

Courtship behavior in the stickleback involves such a response chain (Figures 15.9–15.12). The swollen abdomen of the female stickleback releases the male's zigzag courtship dance. The zigzag dance in turn induces the female to swim toward the male who then turns and leads her to the nest, where he

Figure 15.8
Displacement activity (here, digging in the sand) may occur when there is a conflict between two behaviors, such as fight and flight. [Figures 15.8, 15.9, 15.10, 15.11, and 15.12 are adapted from N. Tinbergen, "The Curious Behavior of the Stickleback," *Scientific American*, December 1952, 22–26. Copyright © 1952 by Scientific American, Inc. All rights reserved.]

Figure 15.9
The courtship ritual of the stickleback fish is a complex chain of stimuli and responses, as is shown in this and the next three figures. Stage 1: The egg-filled abdomen of the female releases the male's zig-zag dance. [Copyright © 1952 by Scientific American, Inc. All rights reserved.]

Figure 15.10
Stage 2: The zig-zag dance induces following in the female as the male goes to the nest and points to it. [Copyright © 1952 by Scientific American, Inc. All rights reserved.]

Figure 15.11
Stage 3: Then the female enters the nest and lays her eggs in response to the male's prodding at the base of her tail. [Copyright © 1952 by Scientific American, Inc. All rights reserved.]

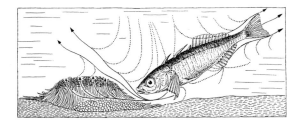

Figure 15.12
Stage 4: The male enters the nest after the female leaves, fertilizes the eggs, and then fans them to insure that they are all fertilized and adequately oxygenated. [Copyright © 1952 by Scientific American, Inc. All rights reserved.]

points his head to the entrance. This behavior stimulates the female to enter the nest, which induces the male to tremble, prodding the base of her tail with his nose. The trembling causes the female to spawn. She then leaves the nest, which is a signal for the male to enter and fertilize the eggs. Chained responses are obviously crucial for the performance of complex behavior patterns, and are particularly important in social interaction between two or more individuals of the same species.

Imprinting The classic example of imprinting comes from Lorenz' work with ducks. He has reported that the chicks of precocial birds—those that can walk within hours of hatching and therefore do not remain in the nest—will follow virtually any moving object to which they are initially exposed after hatching. The response of following, which usually constitutes the chick's first social interaction with its own species, remains specific to the initially followed object. Lorenz termed this phenomenon *imprinting*. It substantiates the idea (commonly found in human psychology as well as in ethology) that an organism's earliest social experiences have a profound effect on the course of its life.

Imprinting serves an effective social-identification purpose, since the first moving object seen by a young organism is normally its mother. Laboratory and field studies have shown, however, that almost any moving object presented soon after hatching will elicit the following response. Slightly older chicks, however, do not imprint on moving objects. Thus, some researchers have maintained that there is a hereditarily determined "critical" time in the life of the young chick during which imprinting is most likely to develop, and after which it may not occur at all. Despite Lorenz' contention that imprinting is a special learning process that fixes irreversibly on one object and occurs only within a narrowly delimited

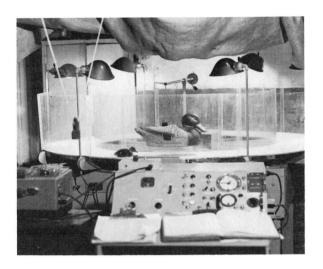

Figure 15.13
Eckhard H. Hess's early apparatus for studying imprinting. The baby bird follows the model (here of a female duck) as it moves around the circular track. The model that the bird follows during the critical period is the one that the bird will imprint on and tend to follow later. The apparatus in the foreground controls the movement of the model and records observations of the bird's behavior. [Photograph courtesy of Eckhard H. Hess.]

critical period, we now know that imprinting is sometimes reversible, and the critical period is by no means sharply defined.

In Mallard ducks, the critical period peaks around fourteen hours following hatching. At that time, the largest proportion of ducks is most easily imprinted (Figure 15.13). The onset of the critical period apparently coincides with the onset of the chicks' ability to walk. The offset of the period is more of a puzzle. There seem to be two main reasons why the chicks' susceptibility to imprinting apparently vanishes. In the first place, as time goes on, the chick may already have imprinted on a stimulus in its sur-

roundings. Evidence for this hypothesis comes from an experiment in which chicks were isolated for three days (well past the end of the critical period for normally raised chicks) and then tested with various models to see which they preferred to follow. The chicks tended to follow models with visual patterns that resembled the walls of the cage in which they had been housed. These results suggest that during their confinement the chicks had already imprinted on the cage walls: what appeared to be the absence of imprinting was actually imprinting on an unsuspected object. Another important factor in the apparent termination of the critical period, stressed by Eckhard H. Hess and others, is a growing aversion to unfamiliar objects. Once the chicks have become familiar with a particular environment, they go through a phase in which they appear to avoid novel stimuli and are therefore unlikely to imprint on them.

Recent investigations by Hess have provided new insights into the imprinting process. This work is also important for the soundness of its method, an ingenious synthesis of laboratory and field research techniques. Hess and his co-workers tried to make their laboratory setting as "natural" as possible in order to employ the benefits of the naturalistic environment that characterizes the field study while still retaining the controlled environment of the typical laboratory study. Hess placed infertile Mallard eggs in a nest located in the wild. This nest was equipped with a microphone and speakers which were connected to the nests of fertile eggs being incubated in the laboratory. This arrangement is illustrated in Figure 15.14.

The female Mallard sitting on the infertile eggs in the wild received any sounds produced by the unhatched ducklings in the lab nest. At the same time, any sounds made by the maternal duck were transmitted to the laboratory incubator. Thus both the

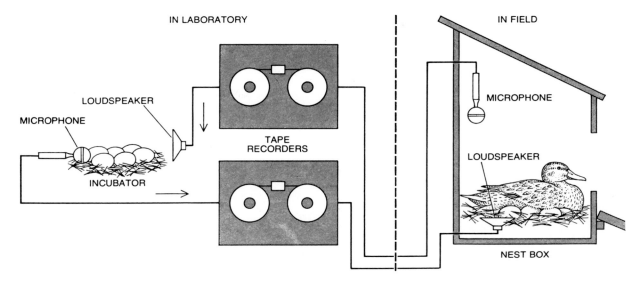

IN LABORATORY

MICROPHONE

LOUDSPEAKER

INCUBATOR

TAPE RECORDERS

IN FIELD

MICROPHONE

LOUDSPEAKER

NEST BOX

Figure 15.14
Hess's apparatus for combining laboratory and field research. Unhatched ducklings in an incubator in the laboratory heard the sounds of a mother duck in the field. The mother sat on infertile eggs and heard the sounds from the hatching ducklings over a loudspeaker. [From Eckhard H. Hess, " 'Imprinting' in a Natural Laboratory," *Scientific American*, August 1972, 24–31. Copyright © 1972 by Scientific American, Inc. All rights reserved.]

duck and the eggs were in a relatively natural situation that was largely undisturbed by the experimental manipulations, but permitted precise recording and control. Hess found that the mother Mallard sitting on infertile eggs responded to the duckling sounds coming from the laboratory in much the same way as did Mallards sitting on fertile eggs. His findings suggest that female Mallards become prone to respond to sounds of hatching ducklings after sitting on eggs for two or three weeks.

Of greater interest is the extent to which the unhatched ducklings responded to the clucks of the mother Mallard. Hess found that, as the time of scheduled hatching approached, ducklings emitted the largest proportion of their cries in response to their mother's clucks, while the female Mallard clucked at her highest rate during the hatching period. Hess concluded that "the sounds made by the female Mallard and by her offspring are complemen-

tary. The female Mallard vocalizes most when a duckling has just hatched. A hatching duckling emits its cries primarily when the female is vocalizing."

Another intriguing aspect of Hess' results is that the ducklings apparently learn to recognize the mother Mallard's sounds prior to hatching. Moreover, the prehatching vocal stimulation later influences the ducklings' ability to recognize the mother's call, and may in fact facilitate the ducklings' imprinting on the appropriate object. Ducklings that had been deprived of experience with maternal vocalizations imprinted just as easily on a decoy duck crying "Come, come, come" as they did on a decoy emitting normal Mallard sounds. In contrast, ducklings that had been exposed to a maternal call prior to hatching were more likely to imprint on decoys emitting natural sounds than on decoys crying, "Come, come, come."

Hess' results suggest that the normal imprinting process begins with a vocal interaction between the prehatched duckling and the mother Mallard and that some degree of learning occurs prior to hatching.

An experiment by W. A. Mason and M. D. Kennedy in 1974 showed that infant rhesus monkeys raised with their mothers or with age-mates or with cloth surrogate mothers for a period of from one to ten months developed strong filial bonds to dogs if they were removed and placed with the dogs (as shown in the photo at the opening of this unit). These results demonstrate that the filial bonds developed in early rearing need not be irreversible—that is, the infant monkeys transferred their attachment to the canine mother substitutes.

The study of imprinting suggests that subjects imprinted on unnatural objects may be unable to engage in effective courtship with members of their own species when they mature. Instead, they may attempt to court the unnatural object. In one case, cockerels that had been imprinted to cardboard boxes attempted to court and mount the boxes. Similarly, male subjects imprinted on other species may try to court females of that species rather than females of their own species. Fortunately, animals in nature are rarely imprinted on unusual objects because they rarely encounter them during the critical period. It is important to note how hereditary and environmental factors contribute to imprinting: the tendency to follow something and the span of the critical period may be determined by heredity, but the object that the organism happens to follow is determined by the environment.

Early experience has also been shown to affect many human responses, such as the development of language and perception. For example, feral children, who have not had contact with humans during childhood, appear to be permanently incapable of normal language acquisition. In the discussion of the development of bird songs in the next section, we will encounter another striking example of the effects of early experience.

THE INTERACTION OF ORGANISM AND ENVIRONMENT

With imprinting, we have already demonstrated how behavior may result from the interaction of hereditary and environmental factors. In this section, we

will discuss three further examples of organism-environment interaction: (1) the development of bird songs and alarm calls; (2) parental behavior in the ring dove; and (3) rat-killing by cats.

Bird Songs and Alarm Calls The white-crowned sparrow is a small finch that makes its home on the Pacific Coast, among other places. The song of the male finches occurs exclusively during breeding seasons, supporting the contention that the main function of the male song is to establish its territory by warding off other males, and to attract females. Perhaps because of its crucial function, the male song is extremely elaborate and distinctive. Moreover, these complex song patterns vary widely from region to region. Peter Marler has investigated the effects of different early experiences on the adult sparrow's song. His basic findings are summarized in Figure 15.15. The left side of the figure shows the results of isolating young male white-crowned sparrows at various times following hatching. When mature, the birds produce a simple, but phrased, song (clearly less complex than the mature song of the normal male). The same is true even if, while in isolation, the young birds are exposed to the songs of other species of birds. Again, in contrast to the song of normal adult males, the simple song of the isolated male is the same regardless of the region from which the finch was obtained. Thus, all male finches appear to have the innate potential for developing this simple song regardless of their locale and of their auditory experience while in isolation. White-crowned sparrow chicks who never have an opportunity to hear an adult's song, never develop a normal elaborate adult song. However, young, isolated sparrows that are exposed to the song of an adult white-crowned sparrow from any region, will, upon reaching maturity, produce that song. This is a rather striking piece of data, because several

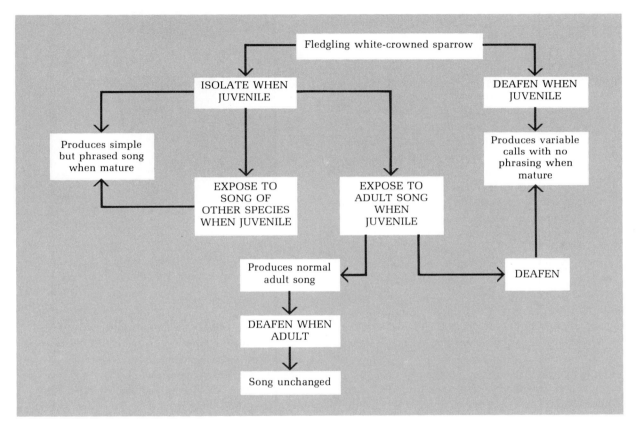

Figure 15.15
A diagram of the experimental procedures used by
Marler, Tamura, and Konishi. The effects of the proce-
dures are also shown. [Adapted from A. Manning,
An Introduction to Animal Behavior (2nd ed.). Reading,
Mass.: Addison-Wesley.]

months intervene between the isolated chick's
exposure to the adult song and his own singing.
of the same song.

It would appear that the sparrow retains a memory
of the song. When the bird becomes mature enough
to produce the appropriate sounds, he learns to

match his sounds to those he remembers. If this is
the case, deafening the young sparrow just before
maturity would interfere with the development of the
adult song, since the bird would not then receive
the auditory feedback required to compare its own
vocalizations with the memory of the adult song
it had heard months before. The right side of the
diagram shows that, in fact, the adult sparrow that
has been deafened before maturity can produce variable calls but lacks the ability to phrase. The same
type of abnormal song is obtained from white-

crowned sparrows that have been deafened as juveniles and never exposed to the adult song. (That the abnormal song is not merely the result of the deafening procedure is shown by the fact that adult birds deafened *after* they have already learned to produce the normal adult song continue to sing normally.)

It seems, then, that exposure to the adult song as a juvenile is in itself not sufficient to produce normal singing. In addition, after reaching maturity, the bird must be able to hear in order to produce a song matching the one he heard months earlier. These experiments further support the contention that the sparrow compares the song it is producing with its memory of the adult song.

These observations of the white-crowned sparrow's song provide an excellent example of *species-specific behavior*. Within the species of finch studied, the young birds will copy the dialect of any white-crowned sparrow they hear; the song of other species will, however, have no effect. In addition, these results provide further evidence for the existence of a critical or sensitive period that determines the development of a given behavior. Moreover, the complex interaction between hereditary predispositions, infant experience, and later learning is also evident here. Apparently the sparrow is genetically equipped to memorize the adult song in its first three months. Learning occurs much later on, when the finch modifies its own sounds according to the remembered sounds.

Many instinctive behaviors must be perfectly executed right from the start, as in the case of those that enable the organism to eat or to escape from a predator. For example, alarm calls and the escape responses they elicit occur normally even in birds raised in total auditory isolation; the first time a bird hears an alarm call, it flees. Yet, in the same organism, prolonged experience may be required for the development of songs and other less immediately essential vocalizations.

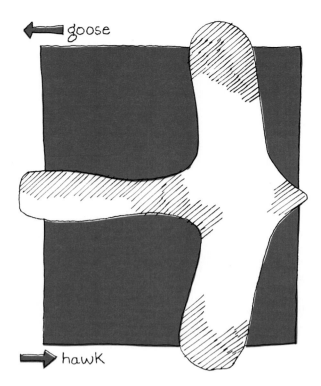

Figure 15.16
A bird's ambiguous figure. If this figure moves to the left, it simulates a goose, if to the right, a hawk.

Experience often plays a part in *modifying* even such relatively simple instinctive behaviors as alarm calls, however. Researchers have asked the question: how does a bird recognize its predator and give the alarm? Alarm calls have been studied extensively with geese and other game birds, in experiments utilizing the ambiguous goose–hawk figure shown in Figure 15.16. Note that when the figure is seen as moving to the left, it resembles the shadow of a goose flying overhead; when moving to the right, it resembles the shadow of a hawk. It has been known for some time that the hawklike figure constitutes a sign stimulus for the release of an alarm call in geese and other fowl. As Tinbergen has shown, a model of the same figure facing the opposite direction (the gooselike direction) is not a stimulus for an alarm call.

The experiments demonstrate that the relationship between a hawklike stimulus flying overhead and the resultant alarm call is not nearly so specific as was originally thought. Making the correct call to the correct flying stimulus seems to involve habituation (see Chapter 3). Studies in which models are presented to geese raised in isolation show that the goose emits an alarm call to almost any form moving overhead at an appropriate speed. This nondiscriminative response, like that of the birds to owl-like eyes, is adaptive in that it is essential for an organism to have a reliable mechanism that enables it to flee from a predator.

However, it is still more adaptive to learn to flee only in response to true predators. In time, the goose apparently becomes habituated to familiar forms flying overhead and stops emitting alarm calls to them. The goose has essentially learned to *withhold* the alarm call to stimuli that have in the past flown overhead without adverse consequences. Thus, the initial tendency to sound an alarm call to any object flying overhead at the appropriate speed is modified through experience so that alarm calls eventually occur only when danger is imminent.

Once again we see how animal behavior develops through a complex interaction between an organism's inherited tendencies and its environment. The organism's genetic endowment predisposes it to respond to particular stimuli. This response may then be modified and/or elaborated by the organism's further interactions with its environment.

Parental Behavior of the Ring Dove   Perhaps the most interesting example of the interaction between the organism's biological structure and its environment (including members of its own species as part of the environment) can be found in Daniel Lehrman's comprehensive study of parental behavior in the ring dove.

The ring dove's reproductive cycle consists of several successive events: courtship, nest-building, egg-laying, incubation of the eggs, and feeding of the young. These are executed with such invariable precision that they appear to be a classic example of a complex cycle of instinctive behavior. Lehrman's work shows that each stage in the cycle of reproductive behavior is determined by the interaction of stimuli in both the internal and external environments. In this way, the cycle is an instinctive behavior chain similar to that of the sticklebacks.

When two experienced breeding doves who have never mated with each other are paired, courtship behavior occurs on the first day and is characterized by the "bowing coo" of the male, depicted in Figure 15.17 (Part 2). The doves then participate in nest-building for the next week or so (Parts 3 and 4), during which time they also copulate. As the week of nest-building progresses, the female dove becomes increasingly attached to the nest. If a human hand examines the nest, for example, the female will doggedly remain on the nest, perhaps slapping the hand with her wing. When this occurs, it is a sign that egg-laying is imminent. Somewhere between the seventh and eleventh day, the female produces her first egg, usually between four and five o'clock in the afternoon. Forty hours later, she lays her second egg (Part 5). Incubation of the eggs is accomplished during the next two weeks with both parents participating alternately: the female always sits for eighteen hours of the day, while the male sits for the remaining six (Part 6). Once the eggs hatch (Part 7), the final two weeks of the five-week cycle are spent in feeding the young (Part 8).

During incubation of the eggs, the walls of the parents' crops become thick, and the inside layers begin to slough off, falling into, and eventually filling, the crop. In feeding, the parent regurgitates this "crop milk," which the young then ingest. As the two-week period comes to an end, however, the parents become increasingly unconcerned with the feeding requests of the young. During the same period, the young doves develop the ability to peck

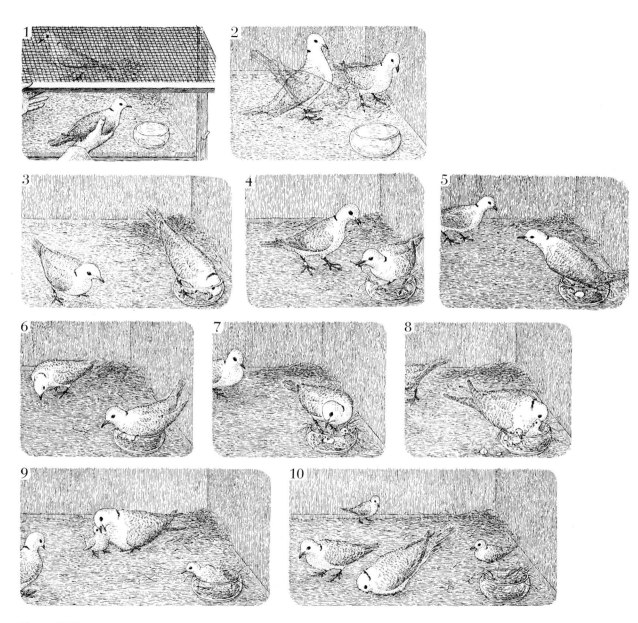

Figure 15.17
See text for explanation. [From Daniel S. Lehrman, "The
Reproductive Behavior of Ring Doves," *Scientific
American*, November 1964, 48–54. Copyright © 1964 by
Scientific American, Inc. All rights reserved.]

for grain on the cage floor. Within a week or two, the adult male once again begins to strut about, his bowing and cooing signaling renewed courtship and the advent of a new reproductive cycle.

Lehrman investigated the determinants, both internal and external, of each kind of behavior in the reproductive cycle. He determined that the entire process of nest-building and egg-laying must be completed before incubation of the eggs can occur. A pair of doves presented with a nest they have not built and eggs they have not laid will only incubate if they have been together for a period of at least seven days and during that time have constructed a nest of their own. A single dove, given a nest and eggs, will never incubate. If two doves that have been together are given a ready-made nest and eggs, but no nest-building material, they will tear the nest apart and rebuild it. Only after this does incubation begin, suggesting that the initiation of incubation is critically dependent upon the prior experiences of both courtship and nest-building.

Lehrman has further demonstrated the critical part played by hormonal stimuli in sustaining the cylce of reproductive behavior. Hormonal secretion induced by environmental events (including the behavior of either partner) must precede certain stages of the cycle. In the male, the hormone *progesterone*, necessary for incubation of the eggs, is stimulated by nest-building behavior. Nest-building is in turn dependent upon the hormone *estrogen*, which is stimulated by the courship ritual. The behavioral effects of hormonal secretion stimulated by preceding environmental events may be artificially induced by the direct injection of hormones. Thus, doves that have not experienced courtship and nest-building will nonetheless incubate eggs if first injected with *progesterone*.

To summarize, Lehrman has shown that each of the successive components of the cycle of reproductive behavior is determined by a different set of interacting external stimulus conditions and internal hormonal states. The hormones that modulate behavior are themselves stimulated by events in the external environment, including the behavior of the other organism of the pair.

Rat-killing Behavior in Cats In the 1930s, Zing-Yang Kuo did a number of important experiments intended to discredit the old concept of "instinct" as an explanation of behavior and to gather evidence for the theory that all behavior develops through learning. He asked, "Do cats have an instinctive tendency to kill rats?" To answer this question, he raised some kittens individually with one rat pup; others he raised in isolation, that is, these kittens were exposed neither to rats nor to other cats; and a third group of kittens was raised with cats and exposed to the sight of their mother and other cats killing rats. Zing-Yang Kuo reasoned that if rat-killing were an instinct, all of the kittens should kill rats irrespective of their environmental rearing conditions.

Most of the kittens raised in the normal rat-killing environment killed rats by the age of four months when given the opportunity to do so. However, when given the same opportunity, less than half of the kittens raised in isolation killed rats. Most of the nonkillers learned to kill, however, after being allowed to watch other cats kill. Finally, the kittens that were raised with a single rat pup did not kill rats at all when given the opportunity. Only one of eighteen was finally trained to kill, although three others would kill rats of a different strain than their old cagemate. In other words, they were not instinctive rat-killers, nor was it easy to instruct them in the art of rat-killing.

Similar results have been obtained with bird-killing in cats, with rabbit-killing in dogs, and with

Figure 15.18
The early experiences of a cat have a profound effect on how the cat treats rats. A cat raised with a rat will not kill its cagemate.

mouse-killing in rats. Typically, a cat raised with a single rat (and a dog raised with a single rabbit) display signs of affection for their cagemate. If the rabbit or rat is removed from the cage, the dog or cat shows signs of missing its companion. This observation led Zing-Yang Kuo to ask whether the results showed that cats have a rat-*loving* instinct. (Figure 15.18).

In a subsequent study, Zing-Yang Kuo raised *groups* of kittens and rat pups together. Under these conditions, signs of affection between the kittens and rats were largely absent, yet the cats did not kill the rats. From all appearances, it seemed that the animals displayed a mutual indifference. Once the rats had offspring of their own, however, the situation changed. Twelve of seventeen cats were seen eating the young rat pups when the mother rat (with whom they had been raised) was absent. What was the difference between the new rat pups and the older rats? Kuo found that the decisive characteristic was the *hairiness* of the adult rat. The same cats that ate rat pups would also eat shaved adult rats. Kuo separated the cats and rats and found that, even after four months, the cats would not kill the normal adult rats. The cats were then given imitation training; they were allowed to observe other cats killing and eating rats. The training had little effect. Of the sixteen cats tested, six tried to kill rats and only three of these succeeded. Yet these same cats routinely killed and ate shaved adult rats. Their behavior was clearly under stimulus control, with the relevant stimulus being the rat's fur (see Chapter 4). These experiments demonstrated nicely both the conditions under which rat-killing behavior reliably developed and occurred, and those under which it reliably failed to occur. The studies also demonstrated the profound influence of early experience upon later behavior. The fact that the cats killed and devoured shaved rats, and ignored hairy ones, suggests that the eating of shaved rats is a continuation of their earlier behavior of eating naturally hairless newborn rats.

Zing-Yang Kuo concluded:

> The cat is a small-sized tiger. Its bodily makeup is especially fitted for capturing small animals; its body and legs are fitted for swift movements, its sharp paws and teeth are fitted for capturing and devouring; and its eyes and ears too, are very helpful in guiding its capturing responses. Here we have a machine so manufactured that under ordinary circumstances it will kill or even eat animals smaller than itself, such as rats, birds, etc. But its swift bodily make-up may also make it playful in response to small animals or small objects especially moving objects. Is it necessary to add that this machine has been endowed by heredity, through its nervous system, with the instinct to kill rats and other small animals, and also another instinct to play with them? Should this machine become as large as a tiger it may even ignore smaller animals such as rats, etc., but will seek to kill much larger ones including men. Shall we say then, that this larger machine possesses an instinct to kill man, and another instinct to pity and forgive rats and other smaller animals? To me, the organismic pattern (please note that I do not mean neural pattern!) or bodily make-up and the size should be sufficient to tell why the cat behaves like cat, the tiger like tiger, or the monkey like monkey. The cat has a cat-body and hence the rat-killing behavior; the tiger has a tiger-body and hence man-killing behavior. The chimpanzee has a chimpanzee body, and so uses sticks and does many things almost human. Have the cat and the tiger any instincts? Does the chimpanzee possess any insight? Is the cat's behavior toward the rat hereditary or learned through trial and error, or by imitation? To me all such questions are useless as well as meaningless.*

*From Z.-Y. Kuo, "The Genesis of the Cat's Behavior toward the Rat." *Journal of Comparative Psychology*, 1930, *11*, 1–35.

LONG-TERM INTEGRATED BEHAVIOR PATTERNS

The homing and migratory behaviors of many birds, fish, turtles, mammals, and insects have long been a source of puzzlement and interest. In a sense, however, they are no more puzzling than other behavior patterns we have considered in this chapter. In the first place, like the behaviors we discussed in the previous section, homing and migratory behavior involve subtle interactions between the organism's innate drives, its physical ability to respond to certain environmental stimuli, and the environment itself. Moreover, most examples of homing and migration differ in complexity but not in kind from the orienting reactions (kineses and taxes) that we discussed near the beginning of the chapter. In most cases, however, the stimuli controlling the orientation have not been identified. The problem seems not to be that the behaviors are so extraordinarily complex but that our knowledge of the animals' senses is so poor.

Homing is defined as the individual organism's ability to return to a familiar breeding or roosting area. For example, a pigeon or starling released at any point within a mile of its roost or nest will invariably find its way back, and they will often return home over far greater distances. G. Matthews, who has studied homing extensively, believes that the successful homing pigeon "homes" by using an innate ability to orient itself to familiar landmarks, at least when it is released within eighteen miles of the roost. He showed that the homers learned landmarks after just two releases in which they flew over both the landmark and the roost. It is also fairly certain that pigeons and other birds use celestial cues, particularly the position of the sun. If the apparent position of the sun is changed by mirrors, or if the sun is obscured by a heavy cloud layer, accurate homing is impaired, especially long-distance homing where landmarks are relatively ineffective. Just *how* birds utilize the sun's position to home successfully, however, is not yet known.

Migration is defined as a periodic journey undertaken by all the members of a species, either at fixed seasons of the year or at a particular point in the individual organism's development. The annual movements of many birds, of mammals such as the caribou, and of the Atlantic salmon represent the first type. The journeys that mark the life cycles of many fish, such as mackerel, eels, and all species of Pacific salmon, are examples of the second type. The two-year-old salmon migrates from the stream or river where it had been spawned to the sea. Two years later, many of the fully mature salmon manage to return to the very same stream or river, where they spawn and die. Some migrations, such as that of the sea cod, are even more striking: although the fertilized cod eggs drift many miles before hatching, the adult cod still returns, four years later, not to its hatching place, but to the spawning area.

The precise internal and external stimuli controlling these migrations—the time of year or the age at which they begin, the urge to leave and then to return to the starting point, and the cues used on the journey itself—have yet to be identified. Regarding the salmon, we do know that cues from the position of the sun are important, whereas the nature of the currents, surprisingly enough, does not appear to be critical. Yet even when the sky is overcast, the salmon can orient to a certain degree, suggesting the operation of additional cues, as yet unknown. As for the ability to locate the exact spawning place, experiments indicate that salmon choose the streams that lead home on the basis of chemical cues present in the water. Thus, the salmon appears to have an "olfactory memory" that rivals the white-crowned sparrow's "auditory memory"!

Migration is a prime example of an exceedingly complex system of behaviors—strongly influenced by hereditary factors—that requires the individual organism to respond to specific biological and environmental cues so that it can retrun to a specific place—the place where it was born, or spawned.

HUMAN INSTINCTS

Do humans display instinctive behavior patterns? The answer is a qualified "yes." Human behavior, like that of other species, results from a complex interplay between the individual's inherited biological structure and its environment. The "yes" is qualified because human behavior is extremely flexible and is far more susceptible to learning and experience than is the behavior of lower organisms. It is even more difficult, therefore, to distinguish between learned behavior patterns and instinctive ones in humans. At birth, many organisms are already able to walk, feed themselves, and perform other basic functions relatively independently of their parents. They grow up quite rapidly, because so much of their behavior is built in, in the form of reflexes, tropisms, and instinctive behavior patterns. The human infant, however, is almost entirely dependent upon adults. Because of this initial dependency, the human being has a long childhood in which it develops an increasingly greater ability to deal flexibly and intelligently with the environment. Much of this development is accomplished through learning, yet, as we shall see in Chapters 17 through 19, the individual's ability to learn certain skills often seems to depend on his level of development, and the schedule of maturation for each individual seems largely to be fixed by heredity.

Suggested Readings

Bermant, G. (1973) *Perspectives on animal behavior.* Glenview, Illinois: Scott, Foresman. [An interesting collection of ten original essays by experts in the field.]

Birney, R. C. & Teevan, R. L. (1961) *Instinct.* New York: Van Nostrand. [A collection of classic articles and experiments including important contributions by William James, Zing-Yang Kuo, Konrad Lorenz, Eckhard Hess, Karl Lashley, Niko Tinbergen, Daniel Lehrman, and Frank Beach.]

Denny, M. R., & Ratner, S. L. (1970) *Comparative psychology: Research in animal behavior.* (Rev. ed.) Homewood, Illinois: Dorsey. [A thorough treatment.]

Lorenz, K. Z. (1952) *King Solomon's ring.* London: Methuen. (Reprinted 1959 by Pan, London.) [A delightful reading experience.]

Lorenz, K. Z. (1966) *On aggression.* London: Methuen. [A controversial and interesting treatment.]

Manning, A. (1972) *An introduction to animal behavior.* (2nd ed.) Reading, Massachusetts: Addison-Wesley. [An excellent, highly readable, and balanced overview.]

Tinbergen, N. (1951) *The study of instinct.* London: Oxford. [The master's classic.]

CHAPTER SIXTEEN

Behavior Genetics

The science of *genetics* is concerned with the way biological characteristics are transmitted through the species and through a family to an individual organism. Its primary tasks are identifying which characteristics are capable of being transmitted and discovering how they are transmitted. By contrast, *ethology*, discussed in Chapter 15, is the study of the kinds of behavior (particularly animal behavior) that occur throughout an entire species, and the degree to which these behaviors may be inherited. Of particular interest to psychologists is behavior genetics, which is concerned with the way in which heredity may influence such behavioral and psychological characteristics as intelligence, aggressiveness, and various types of mental illness and retardation.

Every species is distinguished by certain characteristics that are transmitted as the species reproduces itself. Although individual organisms within a species may differ widely, they still resemble each other more than they resemble other species. Human beings, no matter how different in appearance and behavior, have more in common with each other than they do with apes, cats, birds, or fish.

In addition to species-specific characteristics, individuals also display a family resemblance. Organisms tend to resemble their parent organisms in certain ways. They also resemble the other organisms those parents have produced. For this reason, it is sometimes possible to follow a certain trait—a particular kind of stem on a plant, the shape of an ear on a dog, or the shape of a jaw on a person, through many generations. Yet, at the same time, the offspring of one set of parents may differ widely from those parents and from each other. Each organism is unique—although it may be very similar to others, it is never exactly like any other member of its species.

The variation that gives each organism its individuality is attributed both to its heredity and to its environment.

Each organism that reproduces sexually has a biological inheritance determined by the genetic information encoded in the two germ cells from which it developed. Very complex structures called _genes_ determine many vital characteristics of an organism (the general shape of the body and the way its systems function), as well as less important characteristics. In humans, blood type, fingerprints, eye color, and the color and texture of the skin and hair are examples of characteristics associated with particular genes.

The environment—meaning the organism's surroundings and the kind of stimuli that they provide, the kind of food it eats, and also the social context

Figure 16.1
Genetically identical forms develop differently in different environments.

in which it lives—is another source of variation. Differences in environment produce differences in both physical characteristics and behavior.

A third source of variation is the interaction between an organism's genetically determined characteristics and its environment. Size and weight, for example, are influenced both by heredity and by the kind and amount of food the organism gets.

The respective roles of heredity and environment become clearer if we consider relatively simple organisms: a group of trees scattered over a hillside in a way that gives different trees slightly different climatic environments with respect to temperature, rainfall, sunlight, and soil. The kind of leaves that the tree has—oak leaves or maple leaves or pine needles—is strictly determined by the genetic inheritance of the tree. On the other hand, such characteristics as the slant of the trunk are mainly determined by the environment—those exposed to steady wind

at the top of the hill will develop a permanent slant; those sheltered at the bottom of the hill will grow straighter. Other characteristics of the tree, such as its eventual height, are determined by a combination of these two influences. The maximum and minimum potential height of a healthy tree is determined by its genes, but exactly how tall it grows within this range is determined by the environment— sunlight, rainfall, wind, and soil—in its location. It is important to note that either genetic or environmental factors can influence the survival of any given tree. Poor soil at the top of the hill can kill a tree that has a full genetic potential for growing perfectly in richer soil at the bottom of the hill. Likewise, a defect in a tree's genetic endowment that prevents the tree from using food for growth would kill the tree in even the best of all possible environments. (See Figure 16.1.)

Speaking generally, a similar kind of analysis can be applied to the variations exhibited by humans.

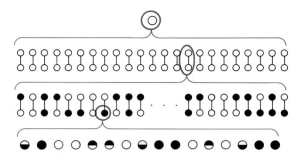

Figure 16.2
A schematic diagram of the arrangement of genetic material within a cell. A closer look at the twenty-three pairs of chromosomes (*top row*) shows that they carry many genes also arranged in pairs (*middle row*). Examination of one gene reveals its construction from nucleic acids (*bottom row*).

One's genes are completely responsible for the color of one's eyes and the various natural characteristics of one's hair. One's environment, past and present, is totally responsible for the specific language one speaks. Other characteristics are jointly determined: one's height, like that of a tree, depends both on one's genes and on adequate nourishment; one's occupation (as a football player or a jockey, for example) may depend in part on inherited bodily characteristics and in part on environmental factors.

The observed characteristics, or *phenotypes*, of the members of a group exhibit variation—similarities and differences. Likewise, the genes also exhibit variation. The totality of genes possessed by an organism is referred to as its *genotype*, and we thus speak of the variation in genotypes among organisms. Behavior genetics seeks to determine to what extent similarities and differences in phenotypes can be traced to (1) similarities and differences in genotypes of the individuals, (2) to environmental factors, or (3) to interactions between the genes and the environment.

Genetic experiments are often indirectly verified by examining the resulting phenotypes in successive generations, since it is not yet possible to watch the operations of individual genes within a cell. In the last hundred years, our knowledge of genetic mechanisms has, however, been greatly increased by careful experimentation and observation. Geneticists can predict the results of mating two organisms with markedly different phenotypes, as far as known hereditary characteristics go. It is also becoming possible to define more precisely which characteristics are hereditary, and how different genes interact with each other and with the environment. Thanks to technological advances in electron microscopes and microphotography, scientists can observe and record many of the basic events of heredity within the cell itself.

ELEMENTARY GENETIC PRINCIPLES

Each cell in your body (and there are trillions of them) contains exactly the same genetic material that was produced by the union of two germ cells, one from each of your parents. Taking a closer—but a very brief and schematic look—at this genetic material within a cell, we find that it is composed of structures called *chromosomes*. Except in the germ cells, the chromosomes are in pairs, with the two members of a pair being called *homologues*. In human beings, each cell normally contains twenty-three different *pairs* of chromosomes, making forty-six chromosomes in all (Figure 16.2). Each chromosome contains two tightly linked *DNA macromolecules*, which are long stringlike structures composed of smaller molecules. Segments of the two-stranded DNA have been identified as the functional units—genes—that determine the particular biological features of an organism. A chromosome may comprise more than a thousand individual genes. The two chromosomes in a pair are like nonidentical twins, in that the corresponding genes in each are not always identical. Each member of a pair of genes is called an *allele* (an alternate). The pairs of alleles influence a specific characteristic of the person—hair color, eye color, type of hair, and so forth.

Take a minute to reflect on the marvelous economy of this very complex organization of a cell's genetic material, which is itself only one very tiny

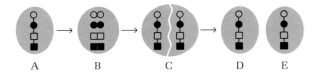

Figure 16.3
A schematic diagram of the major events that take place
during mitosis as a cell (A) first duplicates its genetic
material (B) and then divides (C) into two cells (D
and E).

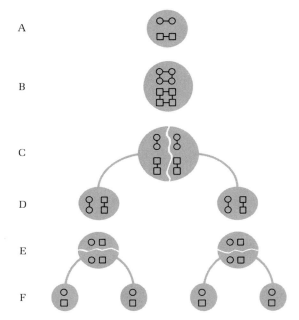

Figure 16.4
A schematic diagram of the major events that take place
during meiosis as a cell divides twice, resulting in the
formation of gametes (germ cells).

part of the cell. Each chromosome pair carries
hundreds of pairs of genes. And there are twenty-
three pairs of chromosomes in each and every
human cell.

When a cell divides in two during growth, it
first duplicates its genetic material exactly and then
sends a copy into each new cell. This process, diagrammed in Figure 16.3, is called _mitosis_.

Every individual grows and develops from a single
cell by this process of successive cell divisions. Since
each cell receives an exact duplicate of the chromosomes in the original cell, we need only understand
the origin of the chromosomes and genes in the
original cell in order to understand the basis of
genetic inheritance.

At the moment of human conception in the
ovarian duct of the mother, a single germ cell from
the father (a sperm or _spermatozoan_) merges with
a single germ cell donated by the mother (an egg
or _ovum_). The result is a _zygote_, the single cell from
which the entire individual organism will develop.
The sperm and the egg are exceptional among all
human cells in each having, not twenty-three _pairs_ of
chromosomes, but rather only twenty-three _single_,
unpaired chromosomes. These germ cells, or _gametes_,
are formed in the male and female reproductive
glands by a combination of two processes: a form
of mitosis and _meiosis_. Since this double process is

a basis for the laws of genetic inheritance, we shall
look at it rather closely.

In meiosis (see Figure 16.4), the chromosome pairs
first duplicate, as in mitosis, and the cells then divide
twice, producing four cells, each containing only
twenty-three chromosomes. During fertilization, each
parent contributes one gamete, bringing the total
number of chromosomes in the zygote back up to
forty-six, in twenty-three pairs. The zygote then
divides by the process of mitosis, and in due course,
all the specialized cells of the human body develop,
including the reproductive cells that can start the
process all over again.

It is the combination of meiosis and the sexual union of gametes from each parent that determines the hereditary variations between individuals. In order to understand this, it is necessary to examine what happens before the cells divide into gametes, and what happens when the gametes combine into a zygote.

A gene may have two alleles that determine different phenotypes. For example, of a pair of alleles for eye color, one may be for blue eyes, the other brown eyes. A person who has one allele of each type will have brown eyes, and the allele for brown eyes is thus said to be _dominant_. The allele for blue eyes is said to be _recessive_—it is there, and may find expression in blue-eyed offspring if it goes into a gamete which merges with a gamete that also carries the recessive allele for blue eyes rather than the dominant allele.

In genetic notation, dominant alleles are designated by capital letters and recessive ones by small letters; and the same letter is used for alleles that are a pair: our simplified alleles for eye color can be expressed as A and a.

As we have seen, during fertilization, each parent contributes one gamete to the zygote. If either gamete contains a dominant allele, that determines the phenotypic trait of the adult that grows from the zygote. It is only a matter of chance which gamete combines with which, but that chance dictates many of the physical characteristics of the child. To an unknown extent, it also affects psychological traits and behavior.

Before meiosis occurs, however, segments of homologous chromosomes may exchange places, or _cross over_, thus shuffling the combination of alleles on the two chromosomes. Which alleles a gamete receives thus depends on whether there were crossovers before meiosis, as well as on which chromosome of a pair it receives.

The number of different gametes that are possible depends upon the number of gene pairs in the original cell, on the crossovers, and on the process of meiosis. In humans, this number is very large.

Genetic mechanisms are still not completely understood, partly because of their complexity. Geneticists have been able to identify a lack or a surplus of genetic material as the cause of certain kinds of mental retardation and metabolic disturbances, as we shall see, but they do not as yet know exactly how genes affect cells in such a way that some become specialized as kidney cells, others as skin cells, others as brain cells, and so on. Until we understand which genes control which parts of development. and how, no genetic theory of human behavior can be positively verified. Moreover, some of our present estimates about correspondences or correlations between the genotypes of different individuals may turn out to be incorrect.

THE MEASUREMENT OF INHERITANCE

If there is still much to learn about genetic mechanisms, if we do not know exactly how genotypes affect phenotypes, then how do we know that a human characteristic has been inherited? We know this simply because members of a family often exhibit the same characteristics. All the phenotypic traits that have been mentioned as being largely hereditary—general body type, blood type, hair color, and so forth—have been identified by careful examination of family trees.

Trying to determine the laws of genetics from a study of human families, however, would take a long time, because one human generation lasts so long. Moreover, humans do not usually keep records of the kind of data that geneticists need, and human matings cannot be arranged for experimental purposes. Therefore, in order to discover how heredity works, geneticists have done what so many other scientists (including psychologists) have done: they have worked with lower organisms, both animals and plants. In fact, the basic principles of genetics were first worked out in the 1860s by a Moravian monk, Gregor Johann Mendel (1822–1884), who experimented by crossing different types of peas, a fast-growing, sexually reproducing plant. By *selective breeding*, geneticists can create experimental family trees in a relatively short time, and keep accurate records of the characteristics they wish to trace.

Of course, the practice of selective breeding predates the science of genetics by thousands of years: all varieties of domestic plants and animals have been developed in this way. In genetic experiments, selective breeding is accomplished by mating particular members of the species that excel in the desired trait, such as size. The differences between the average sizes of males and females in the parental generation and the average sizes of the male and female offspring (the *selection gain*) are noted, and then the largest offspring are bred, and so on. Since such experiments are conducted in a laboratory, the environmental conditions can be kept nearly the same for each generation, so that any differences in phenotype should be almost entirely due to heredity. Experimenters also breed particular organisms that differ markedly in the trait of interest— guinea pigs with black coats may be bred with guinea pigs with white coats, for example—in order to follow the distribution of alleles through a number of generations.

The results of selective breedings are often measured by a *heritability index*, which is a fraction expressing how much of the phenotypic variation between individuals is due to variations in their genotypes if the environmental factor is kept constant. The figure can be used to predict, for a

Figure 16.5
Identical twins are believed to develop from a single zygote and are of interest to geneticists because of their presumably identical genotypes. [Courtesy of Frances Riley]

large group of individuals, the degree to which a certain characteristic—birth weight, adult weight, facial markings—will, on the average, reappear in successive generations. The establishment of a heritability index for certain species of organisms is obviously very useful for commercial breeders of livestock, but it is of little practical use in estimating the heritability of human traits.

Geneticists have also studied records of human families, of course, as far as they are available. The hereditary aspects of many human traits, diseases, and functional disorders has been established by comparing naturally occurring inbred populations (such as isolated villages), or large numbers of

Table 16.1
Sample Percentages of Concordance

DISEASE	MONOZYGOTES	DIZYGOTES
Schizophrenia	69	10
Tuberculosis	54	16
Cancer	10	6

individual family groups, or the different generations of one family. In particular, twins are of great interest to geneticists, especially identical twins, whose genotypes, it is assumed, are also identical. Geneticists theorize that identical twins, called _monozygotes_, occur when, for unknown reasons, the first division of the zygote produces two identical cells that then develop into separate individuals (Figure 16.5). Any phenotypic differences that emerge between such twins as they grow up should then be due only to environmental influences, or to different types of interactions between the genotypes and the environment. Although at present we cannot be absolutely certain that identical twins share exactly the same genetic makeup, studies of identical twins show that, both in appearance and in behavior, they do tend to resemble each other more than fraternal twins, and far more than brothers and sisters (siblings) that are not twins. (See Tables 16.1 and 16.2).

Fraternal twins, called _dizygotes_, result when two ova are for some reason available for fertilization at the same time, and both are penetrated by separate spermatozoa. Such twins may be quite different phenotypically, and their genotypes may be as different as those of siblings born at different times. (Incidentally, twinning itself seems to be hereditary for certain humans.) Fraternal twins are also interesting to geneticists because they provide a kind of experimental control for identical twins. That is, they share the environmental qualities of being twins, being born at the same time and being regarded in a special way. Their test scores also are closer than those of nontwin siblings.

Survey studies of twins and other types of family relationships often use _concordance_ as a measurement of whether a certain characteristic has been inherited or not. A pair of individuals are said to be concordant for a characteristic if they both exhibit that characteristic and discordant if they do not. Concor-

dance is usually expressed in terms of the percentage of the pairs of individuals in a group of pairs, such as twins, that resemble each other in some aspect of appearance or body functioning or behavior.

Table 16.1 shows an example of the percentage of concordance between monozygotic and dizygotic twins with respect to three characteristics: schizophrenia, tuberculosis, and cancer. For example, in 69 percent of the cases in which one twin had contracted schizophrenia, the other twin had also. The pronounced difference in the percentage of concordance between monozygotic and dizygotic twins seems to suggest a closer genetic similarity between the monozygotic twins. However, the study does not take into account environmental influences, which may have a substantial effect on all three characteristics, as we shall see.

PSYCHOGENETICS

So far, we have been concerned primarily with the mechanisms of genetics and the influence of genotypes on phenotypes. There is also considerable evidence that genotypes may affect the individual organism's behavior in various ways.

It is obvious from Chapter 15 that a given species of organism inherits the potentiality for certain kinds of behavior, as well as a certain type of body structure. Yet the higher a species stands on the evolutionary scale, the less its behavior seems to depend on heredity, and the more on learning from experiences with the environment. It is quite difficult to separate environmental from hereditary factors in the behavior of higher organisms; this has been one of the greatest obstacles in determining how much of an organism's behavioral tendencies might be derived from its parents. Even an animal's size, for example, is a partially heritable factor that greatly affects its relationship to everything in the environment, including members of its own species. It may quite literally determine its position in a social group, and thus it affects its behavior as well, although indirectly.

Despite these difficulties, selective breeding has shown that certain behavioral tendencies can be passed from one generation to the next, in all species of organisms that have been studied. It is well known that dogs can be bred for different behavioral traits, such as wildness, obedience, and the tendency to bark. Cocks and bulls have been bred for aggressiveness. In experiments with fruit flies (*Drosophila*), a favorite organism in many genetic studies because the generation time is short, flies can be bred for such traits as duration of copulation and the tendency to fly either up or down, toward or away from a light. If birds of related types, each of which exhibit a different mating dance, are bred together, it is sometimes possible to obtain offspring whose mating dance has bits and pieces of the dance of each of its parents—striking evidence of the genetic basis of some instinctive behavior.

It is sometimes difficult to draw clear-cut conclusions from selective breeding experiments, however. It is always possible that the characteristic itself is not inherited, but rather that some other predisposition controlling that characteristic is the genetically determined trait. For example, in one type of experiment on maze-running in rats, one breeding group consisted of rats that ran a certain type of maze rapidly; another, of rats that ran the same maze slowly. These abilities appeared to function as a rough measure of intelligence: the "fast" rats seemed to learn what to do more quickly. After several generations, the scores of the respective offspring consistently diverged, the fast becoming faster, and the

slow, slower. This would seem to be a case in which selective breeding promoted a particular characteristic of behavior, speed or slowness in getting through a maze. Yet the psychogenetic implications of the study would have been invalidated if it had been discovered that the respective families also diverged in health and vitality, or in the length of their legs, purely physical qualities that would differently affect running. It is also important to note that the behavior that was transmitted was quite specific: the running behavior cannot really be equated with any general abstract quality such as intelligence. Moreover, when the same rats were tested on other tasks, the fast ones were no longer always fast, nor the slow ones slow.

The same difficulties of obtaining clear evidence of the role of heredity in behavior in lower organisms also applies to humans. In most cases, it is extremely difficult to tell whether a person's behavior resembles that of his parents and siblings because he shares certain hereditary traits or because he has shared a certain environment and experiences. It is also possible that, although certain personality traits may not be hereditary, they are affected by physical traits that are: a very short human being may compensate for his shortness by being extremely aggressive, a tendency produced by a combination of an inherited body type and social attitudes toward smallness rather than by inherited aggressiveness.

Psychogenetic studies tend to concentrate on those forms of behavior that can be measured on standardized tests (such as IQ tests) and distinct abnormalities (such as mental retardation and mental illness). In some such studies, especially those involving mental retardation, it has been possible to identify a specific genetic basis. In others, such as those concerned with intelligence, it seems impossible to separate genetic from environmental influences.

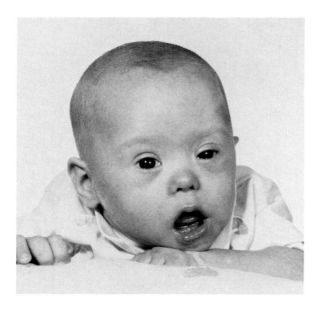

Figure 16.6
A victim of Down's syndrome, a genetic defect whose genetic causes have been determined. [Courtesy of the March of Dimes]

Mental Retardation   Certain forms of mental retardation have been traced directly to genetic anomalies. *Down's syndrome*, for example, can be traced to the presence of additional chromosomal material. As a result, the child develops in a very abnormal way, becoming characterized by low IQ and reduced behavioral capability, short stature, and a peculiar fold of the eyelid (Figure 16.6), a shortened life span, and a kind of dull and child-like demeanor. Other genetic anomalies resulting in mental deficiency are *phenylketonuria* (PKU) and galactosemia. The problem in such cases is a malfunction in a gene responsible for producing an

enzyme that promotes an essential sequence in the body's metabolism of certain foods. Without the enzyme, metabolism of these foods is incomplete, and the residue of these substances becomes toxic, causing physical and mental deterioration. Since the discoveries that these diseases were linked to a genetic cause, early detection of possession of the defective gene has become possible, and in many cases the actual disease can be prevented by limiting the child's diet to foods his system can handle.

These and other studies provide firm evidence that genes are intimately involved in normal psychological development.

Psychological Characteristics of Twins   Cases in which a psychological characteristic has been traced to a specific genetic source are still rare. Studies using identical twins are widely cited, not because twins constitute the ideal research population, but because such studies are the only ones in which one of the factors, heredity, can be assumed to be constant. Since identical twins are presumed to have developed from a single zygote and to possess the same genes, phenotypic psychological differences between them can theoretically be ascribed to differences in their environments. Conversely, if identical twins are separated, so that they grow up in different environments, similarities between them ought to be due to similarities in their genotypes. Table 16.2, which gives correlation coefficients obtained between measurements of several physical and psychological characteristics, tends to confirm this idea.

Notice first the higher coefficients of correlation for such measures as height, weight, and even IQ for monozygotic twins, indicating a genetic influence on these measures. This influence is supported by the fact that the correlation for height and weight fails to diminish significantly when the monozygotic twins are reared apart. The correlation does diminish

Table 16.2
Sample Correlations Between Pairs of Twins

CHARACTERISTIC	MONOZYGOTES		DIZYGOTES
	REARED TOGETHER	REARED APART	
Height	.93	.97	.65
Weight	.92	.87	.63
IQ	.87	.75	.53
Introversion–Extroversion	.42	.62	
Neurotic tendency	.38	.53	

slightly for IQ, indicating that genetic influences may not be as strong for this characteristic as they are for less complex traits such as height.

When we turn to measures of personality, such as introversion-extroversion, and the "neurotic tendency" (which we shall discuss in later units), we find that the correlations are larger for monozygotic twins reared apart. This anomaly, it has been argued, may arise because of competition between twins who are reared together, making for an environmentally induced decrease in their correlation.

Some very extensive studies by Irving Gottesman have shown the plausibility of assuming a genetic basis for certain personality traits. In one study that we choose as an example, he worked with thirty-four pairs of monozygotic and dizygotic twins, who answered questions from an inventory of personality characteristics developed at the University of Minnesota (the Minnesota Multiphasic Personality Inventory). He found that the measures of social introversion, psychopathic deviation, and depression produced significantly higher correlations (ranging

from .47 to .57) between the monozygotes than between the dizygotes (.07 to .08). He argued that the fact that monozygotes presumably share the same genotype had something to do with the difference.

There are, of course, problems in interpreting these figures. All of these characteristics are somewhat affected by the environments in which the persons live. A shared environment tends to produce similarities, so that higher correlations for twins reared together may be due to environmental influences as well as genetic ones. Even for twins reared apart, the environments may not have been completely different. Also, all twins, especially those who live together, share the experience of being twins—whether they are identical or fraternal, they share the same uterine environment, are exactly the same age, and are close to the same stage of physical and mental development. Also, all twins living together (and particularly identical twins) share the unusual situation of being regarded as twins by the people around them, who may expect them to act more or less as a unit.

Table 16.3
Sample Intra-Pair IQ Correlations

CATEGORY	THEORETICAL GENETIC CORRELATION	EMPIRICAL CORRELATION
Unrelated persons		
Reared apart	0	0
Reared together	0	.23
Foster parent + child	0	.22
Parent + child	.50	.50
Siblings	.50	.48
Twins		
Dizygotic	.50	.52
Monozygotic		
Reared apart	1.00	.75
Reared together	1.00	.87

Intelligence   There is evidence of genetic influence on intelligence. Table 16.3 lists various categories of people who are assumed to share a common genetic background or a common environment or both. Along with this information, the table gives a sample of correlations that have been obtained between the IQ's of these people. The correspondence between the theoretical genetic correlation and the empirically determined IQ score suggests that genotype does have something to do with how well an individual can answer questions on an IQ test. It is important to note, however, that, as yet, no one knows the precise biological basis of intelligence.

The table also indicates considerable environmental influence on IQ. The correlation between the IQ's of unrelated persons raised together is .23, although their genetic correlation is zero. The IQ correlation between such persons raised apart is essentially zero, as geneticists would argue. More particularly, the IQ correlation between foster parents and foster children is .22; if their genetic correlation is really zero, then such results can only be explained by environmental influence. The fact that the already high correlation between the IQ's of monozygotic twins increases when they are raised together is additional evidence for an environmental effect on intelligence.

Intelligence is only one example of how genetic and environmental influences exert a combined influence on human characteristics. There is really no question that this combined influence exists; the question is how it works to produce the specific traits of each individual, and to what extent the traits can be altered by altering either environment or genotype. There is also the awesome question of the morality of altering genotypes, if this ever becomes possible. The advantages of early diagnosis of genetic problems that could lead to severe mental retardation (as in PKU) and mental illness seem obvious. Potential dangers of genetic engineering will be obvious to anyone acquainted with the eugenics programs of Nazi Germany.

Great advances are being made in our knowledge of genetics. Geneticists can observe and measure phenotypes, personality traits, and intelligence, and they can argue, often convincingly, that some of these traits are more or less determined by heredity. With the help of ingenious and sophisticated technology they can also observe some of the principal events of genetics on a microscopic scale: cells, chromosomes, and even genes, mitosis, and meiosis. But as yet they cannot perceive the finer details of reproduction: the chemical reactions in mitosis and meiosis, and the ways in which cells become specialized. But even though the results of the genetic process cannot be fully explained, they are clear: the single zygote develops into a complete organism, capable of living independently and ultimately reproducing itself, bearing a resemblance both to its species and to its parents, and yet being a unique individual.

Suggested Readings

Gottesman, I. I. (1963) "Heritability of personality: A demonstration." *Psychological monographs, 77* (9, Whole No. 572). [Good example of studies of the inheritance of complex characteristics.]

McClearn, G. E., & DeFries, J. C., (1973) *Introduction to behavioral genetics*. San Francisco: W. H. Freeman and Co. [Excellent and simple introduction to this difficult field, with a summary of the work on the inheritance of intelligence.]

Stern, C. (1973) *Principles of human genetics*. (3rd ed.) San Francisco: W. H. Freeman and Co. [A more difficult but complete account.]

MAJOR AREAS OF CONTEMPORARY PSYCHOLOGY

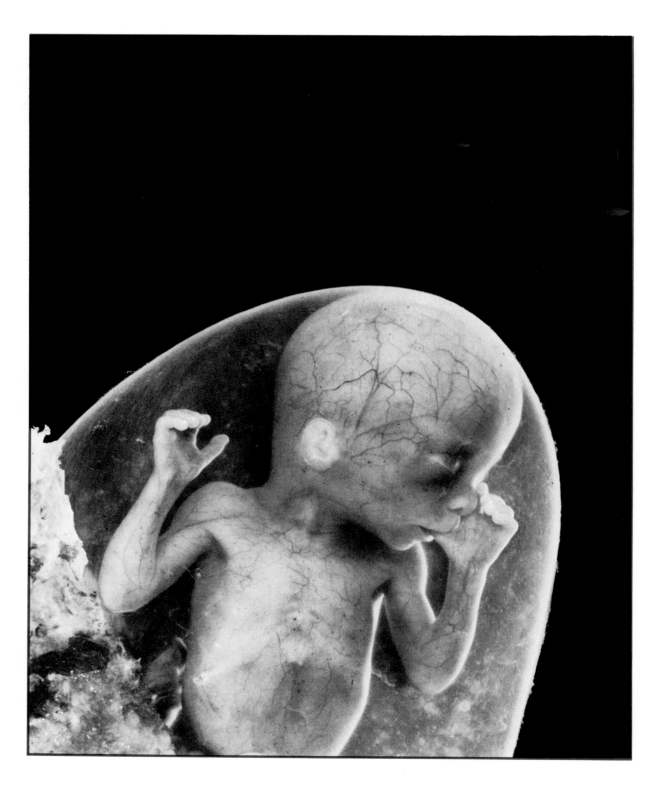

UNIT SIX

Developmental Psychology

At the age of eighteen weeks, when a fetus is only six inches long, thumb-sucking has already evolved from earlier and simpler behaviors. At birth, a human infant is at once a very dependent and a very skilled organism. It cannot take care of itself, and it will die if it is not conscientiously attended. But if its basic needs are met, it is equipped for survival as a separate organism. It can respond appropriately to a wide variety of relevant environmental stimuli. A newborn infant will suck on a nipple that is presented to its lips. An infant will grasp, quite strongly, an object that is pressed on its palm. An infant can follow moving objects with its eyes. It has a complete system of internal reflexes that allows it to digest its food, to regulate its temperature, to breathe, to eliminate wastes, and to grow. And there is evidence that newborn infants can learn—that their behavior can be modified by the consequences that it has on the environment.

Early growth and development is varied and rapid. By the time the third year of life is well under way, the wholly dependent infant has grown into an organism that stands on its own two feet, walks around, explores its world, manipulates objects, and communicates in short sentences. Already a recognizable and real personality has emerged. And there are usually distinctive styles of social interactions: the personalities of three-year-old children can be described with many of the same terms that we apply to adult personalities—they can be characterized as outgoing or introverted, friendly or antagonistic, and so on.

The emotions develop also. The young infant seems to have but three emotional states: unhappy crying, contented cooing, and a nondescript and level state associated with sleep and the minutes before and after sleep. But by the age of three the child may display happiness, fear, anger—nearly the whole spectrum of adult emotional responses. But he still differs from adults in the way he expresses emotions. These differences gradually disappear as development continues and the child comes to control its emotions and to refine them. The young child may burst into tears at each disappointment, but the older child accepts mild frustrations without pronounced emotional display. Young children typically fear strangers; older children may actively seek interaction with children they do not know well.

While all of these changes are occurring in the social and emotional life of the child, it is learning to speak his language in the way adults do, and it is coming to think about its world in increasingly advanced and complicated ways. Because intellectual development is not only one of the most studied but also one of the most interesting and informative developmental areas, we shall begin this unit with a discussion of how a child's intelligence evolves.

The study of how infants become adults is at the heart of developmental psychology. The course of human development brings into play all the basic processes we have been studying: learning, memory, motivation, thought, language, sensation, perception, and heredity. In the study of development, the differences of opinion held by different schools of psychology become acute, because the different processes—talking, walking, seeing, feeling—are all taking place simultaneously in one child. The study of development thus raises many of the issues previously encountered—for example, the old dichotomy of heredity versus environment. Although it is now generally agreed that a human being is shaped by both (as we saw in Chapter 16), the relative effects of heredity and environment on a child's ability to talk, think, or learn from experience are still to be determined. While ethologists and geneticists are making new discoveries about the mechanisms of genes and inherited patterns of behavior, psychologists are endeavoring to find out just how it is that inheritance combines with experience to create an adult human being.

CHAPTER SEVENTEEN

Intellectual Development

In the course of becoming an adult, an infant will develop in many ways: physically, emotionally, socially, intellectually, and so on. Some kinds of development are segmented—children grow by *stages* that are relatively distinct psychologically. Other kinds of development are continuous—physical growth begins at conception and continues after birth at varying rates of speed until about the age of twenty-five. The rate of growth is greatest during the first year; it continues less rapidly until about the age of four. Between four and about twelve, the growth rate slows down considerably. It takes a final spurt during adolescence; the body reaches adult proportions at about eighteen, and then slows down again.

Motor development, the increasing capacity for controlled movement, also seems to proceed gradually in a regular sequence that follows the pattern of neuromuscular development. Stages in motor development are readily observable in infants and young children (Figure 17.1). Actions of the head and neck appear first: raising the head, attending to sounds or visual stimuli, smiling. Muscular control spreads downwards and outwards from the head; as children acquire control over the more distant areas of their bodies, they are able to perform specific actions involving those muscles: from

a vague reaching for objects, to grasping them, to picking up and dropping them. This is called the *principle of motor primacy*; it states that children cannot acquire a more complex skill until their bodies have achieved enough size, strength, and coordination to allow them to do so. Thus, raising the head, raising the chest, sitting up, rolling, wriggling forward by pulling with the elbows, standing with support, creeping, walking with support, standing alone, are all preparations for independent walking.

Some of these activities overlap: children may continue to creep for some time after they walk alone. Sometimes an activity is skipped: children may begin walking even though they have done relatively little creeping. Some children walk long before others; the *rate of maturation* is different for each child, but the general pattern of development is the same for all children. The idea of definite stages of development is also useful in understanding other types of development, as we shall see.

STAGES OF DEVELOPMENT

Nowhere is the concept of *developmental stages* better illustrated than in intellectual development, the ways in which modes of thinking change as a person grows and encounters more and more of the world.

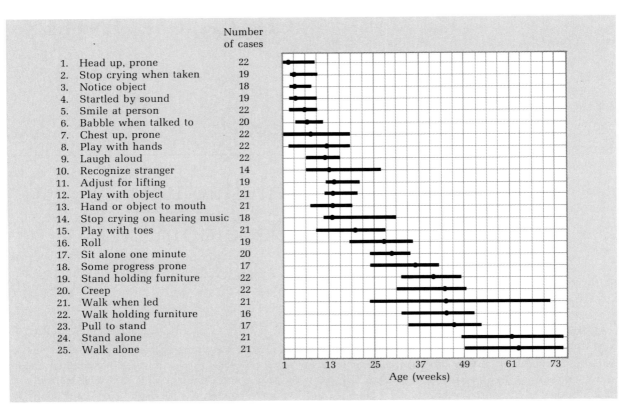

		Number of cases
1.	Head up, prone	22
2.	Stop crying when taken	19
3.	Notice object	18
4.	Startled by sound	19
5.	Smile at person	22
6.	Babble when talked to	20
7.	Chest up, prone	22
8.	Play with hands	22
9.	Laugh aloud	22
10.	Recognize stranger	14
11.	Adjust for lifting	19
12.	Play with object	21
13.	Hand or object to mouth	21
14.	Stop crying on hearing music	18
15.	Play with toes	21
16.	Roll	19
17.	Sit alone one minute	20
18.	Some progress prone	17
19.	Stand holding furniture	22
20.	Creep	22
21.	Walk when led	21
22.	Walk holding furniture	16
23.	Pull to stand	17
24.	Stand alone	21
25.	Walk alone	21

Age (weeks)

Figure 17.1
An infant gradually and progressively develops behaviors that permit it mobility and independent action. [Adapted from M. M. Shirley, *The First Two years, Vol. 1: Postural and Locomotor Developments.* University of Minnesota Press, 1959.]

Consider two experimental studies that illustrate the idea of stages:

1. An eighteen-month-old girl lies on a couch with two blankets in front of her. An adult—perhaps a researcher or the mother—attracts the child's attention with a toy that makes music when it is squeezed. The researcher puts the toy under one of the blankets as the child watches. The child pulls the blanket aside and grabs the toy. The researcher hides the toy again and again under the same blanket, and the child finds it. Then the person openly hides the toy under the second blanket. But the child looks for it under the *first* blanket.

A short time before, the child would not have looked for the toy under any blanket: if she could not see it, she assumed it didn't exist. Now she does look for hidden objects: she knows they have *permanence*—even though she doesn't see them. But more development will have to take place before the child will begin to realize that *where* the person causes the object to be hidden has a lot to do with *where* it will be found. These three stages of a child's behavior (not looking, active looking, looking where it may be found) reveal substantial changes in the structure of its mental world (Figure 17.2).

2. Set up a three-mountain scene, like that in Figure 17.3, for several children ranging in age from three to seven and ask them which of the profiles of the three mountains will be seen from each of the four sides of the table.

At around the age of three, children will think that all views are the same, and that each view looks like the one they see from their own perspective.

Figure 17.2
Once a child appreciates the permanence of objects, it
will search for them when they are hidden. But the child
will not necessarily search in the place where the object
was last seen.

(This is called *egocentrism.*) A year or so later, children
will realize that scenes appear different depending
on the perspective of the viewer; they will be able
to identify what some views will look like. By the
age of seven children will easily identify exactly
what is seen from each perspective. These are stages
in the development of *perspectivism.*

These two as well as many other studies and
observations have shown that the stages of intellectual development always occur in the same order
and that none are omitted. This is strong evidence
for the validity of the stage concept. It is also clear
that more advanced stages *include* preceding stages:
in our second example, children do not lose their
own views of the three mountains, rather they add
the ability to imagine the world as viewed from the
perspectives of others. Furthermore, all stages seem
to be necessary. This has been demonstrated by
attempts to speed up intellectual development.
Where this has proved at all possible, it has only
been possible to go to the next stage and never to
skip over a stage. Corresponding to this is the existence of some overlap of *adjacent* stages. As children

move from one stage to another, they may have
occasional relapses to modes of thinking proper
to the previous stage as well as occasional insight
into the modes they will eventually use in the next.
The mechanisms for going from stage to stage are
still in doubt, but the existence and order of stages
in intellectual development is well established.

The custom of attaching age-ranges to different
stages and the use of the phrases, "as the child
grows up" and "later in life" should not confuse the
reader into equating chronological age with developmental stages. Although the stages unfold in unvary-
ing order, children progress through the stages at
different rates. This is similar to the varying rates of
maturation found in motor development. It is not
uncommon to find a four-year-old whose thinking is
at the same level as that of a six-year-old. They both
passed through the same stages, the four-year-old
just went faster. It is likely, however, that the six-
year-old will advance to the next stage sooner than
the four-year-old.

There has always been speculation about the
relative contributions of *maturation* and *learning* to
the progress of development. The question is

Figure 17.3
The three mountains look different depending on the
perspective of the viewer. A young child does not
appreciate this fact—egocentrically believing that everyone sees the mountains from his perspective.

especially important for educators and social psychologists. If a child's rate of maturation is hereditarily determined, can it be altered? There is evidence that environmental changes do alter school performances and intelligence test scores, at least temporarily. How can such improvements be made permanent? At what age should they be made? Is it possible to influence a child's genetic makeup before birth? We shall discuss some experiments on these questions later in this chapter. As we have seen, both maturation and experience are essential to development—as usual with theoretical dichotomies, we must be wary of oversimplification.

PIAGET'S THEORY OF INTELLECTUAL DEVELOPMENT

In 1923, a Swiss zoologist-turned-psychologist published a book entitled *The Language and Thought of the Child.* Jean Piaget followed this with *Judgment and Reasoning in the Child* in 1924, *The Child's Conception of the World* in 1925, *The Child's Conception of Physical Causality* in 1927 and, after a wartime hiatus and a couple of other books, *The Psychology of Intelligence* in 1947. These books and others that followed, as well as the supporting work of Piaget himself, his students, collaborators, and followers, have caused a revolution in our views of children, the meaning of intelligence, and the meaning of development. For example, it was Piaget who advanced the idea of developmental stages. Piaget built an edifice of theory and fact that ranks with the works of Sigmund Freud and B. F. Skinner in its influence on twentieth-century psychology.

Building an Understanding Children, says Piaget, are always intellectually active. They are striving to take in, or *assimilate,* information and make it fit their concepts of the world, changing their con-

Figure 17.4
The Swiss psychologist Jean Piaget, whose work has transformed our understanding of the psychology of development. [New York Times/John Soto.]

cepts in order to *accommodate* information that disagrees with them, and trying out various activities in order to test their concepts further. Out of all this activity there eventually arises an adult's abstract, conceptual view of the world where there was once only an infant's reflexive, motor responses. There is nothing passive about Piaget's version of development. All humans work all the time to assimilate information gained from experience (their interaction with the environment) into a concept or *schema* of how things work. *Schemata* are conscious or unconscious ideas of what the world is, how it operates, and how to respond to it. In the example cited earlier, the stage at which the infant will not even look for an object that it sees a person hide under a blanket clearly involves a different schema about objects than the stage at which a child looks for the hidden object.

When the information received by the child conflicts with the child's *schema*, the schema and the behavior associated with it must be adapted to *accommodate* the discrepant information. In the blanket experiment, the schema might be interpreted as follows: "If an object disappears, it must still exist. Look for it where you have found it before, under the blanket." But when the toy is hidden under the *second* blanket, the schema is upset. "Looking where you looked before" does not produce the toy. It may take some time for the logical conflict to be resolved into a new schema that fits the new information: "Object and location are not the same. An object may be in different places at different times. Look for it where you *last* saw it."

For Piaget, changes in *schemata* forced by conflict *are* development. Once the logical conflict is resolved and the child has reached a new understanding, a new logical conflict comes along and upsets his schema again. The idea that intellectual development occurs only in the presence of such conflicts is one of Piaget's most controversial theories.

The idea of developmental stages also implies Piaget's conviction that a child seems to reach the next stage all at once. For example, in one type of developmental study, infants may be given the task of *tracking*, or following with their eyes, a train that moves, stops, moves on, stops again. In other words, they are being asked to deal with an object that is sometimes stationary and sometimes moving. Studies have shown that, instead of a gradual decline in errors, the infants will make about the same number of tracking errors in each training session until one day they suddenly make no errors at all. And they continue to make no errors during subsequent sessions, indicating that they have indeed stepped up to a higher level of development. (This contrasts sharply with the progress of motor development described at the beginning of this chapter, in which complicated motor activities such as walking are achieved gradually by successive approximations.)

Piaget's Concepts   According to Piaget, there are two aspects to the human mind, just as there are to any vital system. One is *structure*, the other is *function*. With regard to the body, structure refers to anatomy (how it is built) and function to physiology (how it works). With regard to the mind, structure refers to the schemata, and function to the *organization* and *adaptation* of the schemata. Piaget developed the idea of the basic organizing function relatively little. He infers its existence from close observation of the behavior of very young children; the observations seem to indicate that from the moment they are born, human beings are continually trying to make some kind of order out of their surroundings. Piaget studied adaptation—the function essential to development—thoroughly.

Adaptation is accomplished by the processes of *assimilation* and *accommodation*. As we have seen, the schemata are formed from information gathered from the environment. A baby reaches under the first blanket and touches the object it expected to find. The sensations of touching and grasping the object provide the child with information that the object is indeed there. This confirms the child's schema of where to look for things. But if the object is not there, the information "not there" conflicts with the schema. The schema and the looking behavior must change in order to accommodate the new information about objects. When the schema seems to "work," that is, when an action achieves the expected results, the child is in an *equilibrium*. The child's concepts of the world and the results of its actions are in balance. It will continue to practice the action of looking under the first blanket as long as it finds the object there. But if the object is not there, the tactile information "not there" again conflicts with the schema. At this point, the schema and the looking behavior must change again in order to accommodate the latest information about objects, and so on. The accommodation provides a new equilibrium at a higher conceptual level.

Obviously, schemata can get quite complicated, since they ultimately account for all the adult's capacity for complex behavior and abstract thought. They provide the basic strategy for all problem-solving behavior, whether the problem is to find the missing toy, or the missing pair of mittens, or the missing number in an equation. A schema always includes an element of anticipation that calls for a specific strategy and predicts a result: the infant's schema for objects might be stated, "If you look for an object where you last saw it, you will find it." Long-term schema are equivalent to plans: career-building activities are based on the assumption that if you perform a number of actions or tasks in a certain order, such as going to a succession of schools and holding a number of progressively more challenging jobs, you will one day find yourself successful in your field.

PIAGET'S STAGES OF INTELLECTUAL DEVELOPMENT

We can do little here beyond sketching Piaget's stages of intellectual development, but we shall at least describe Piaget's views on the most important changes in the mental structure of a person in the first fifteen years of life (see Table 17.1).

Sensorimotor Stage   Piaget calls the first stage of intellectual development the *sensorimotor stage* because the infant's schemata are limited to direct sensory and motor interactions with the world. Only later, when symbols become available, does abstract

thought begin in earnest. The four most important developmental trends in this period, which covers roughly the first two years of life, are (1) the expansion of *reflexes* into *circular reactions*, (2) the *differentiation* of objects and the appearance of *intentions*, (3) the development of the concept of *object permanence*, and (4) the evolution of the idea that objects can be disassociated from the actions they evoke (meaning is more than movement). It is safe to say that the reader who can understand these developmental changes in the context of Piaget's concepts will have a good grasp of what Piaget is saying. Before delving into this, though, we need to examine a methodological fact and one more concept, *contents.*

The fact is, as investigators of a child's thought, we can never know its mind and its schemata directly. We can only infer how its mind is structured and what it thinks from its overt behavior—what it does, what it says, how it looks, what part of the environment it manipulates, and how it responds to deliberate changes in the environment during experimental or teaching sessions. These visible aspects of the child and its world are called *contents* by Piaget. We deduce how the mind works from these contents. Piaget often speaks of *contents that exemplify a schema* without bothering to refer directly to the schema itself, because he holds that contents are simply manifestations of schema.

1. Although intellectual development probably begins before birth, when reflexes first begin to operate, it is customary to consider that the sensorimotor stage starts at birth. The infant initially has *contents* that are limited to reflexes. It first exhibits *simple circular reactions*—*simple* because they involve only the infant and its manipulation of its own body and *circular* because the infant repeats the manipulation over and over again as if it were going around in a circle. An infant's thumbsucking is an example of such a circular reaction.

Table 17.1
An Outline of Piaget's Stages of Intellectual Development

SUBSTAGE	APPROXIMATE AGES*	SOME CHARACTERISTIC DEVELOPMENTS
SENSORIMOTOR STAGE		
	0–2 years	Reflexes become circular reactions Object differentiation and permanence Intentions appear Meaning becomes more than movement
Simple circular reactions	0–5 months	Repeated actions on body (e.g., thumb sucking)
Secondary circular reactions	5–6 months	Repeated actions on objects (e.g., rattle shaking)
Tertiary circular reactions	18–24 months	Experimental manipulation of environment (e.g., dropping objects)
CONCRETE-OPERATIONS STAGE		
	2–11 years	Symbols and language Reversible operations
Preoperational period	2–7 years	
Preoperational phase	2–4 years	Broadens schemata, egocentric
Intuitive phase	4–7 years	Absolute number, perspectivism, conservation
Concrete operations	7–11 years	Cardinal and ordinal number
FORMAL-OPERATIONS STAGE		
	11–15 years	Abstract conceptualizations Form as well as content Operations on operations

*These age ranges are approximate, since they may vary by as much as a year or two or more in particular cases. The order in which the stages appear is very reliable, however.

Secondary circular reactions appear at some four or five months of age when circular reactions formerly applied to the body are applied to objects in the environment outside the body. Shaking a rattle is an example. What is involved in shaking a rattle (a *synthesis* of a reach-and-shake schema and a hear-the-funny-sound schema) illustrates how mental structures can combine during intellectual development. The infant realizes that the ability to manipulate an external object (reaching and shaking something) can be used to reproduce interesting sensory effects (hearing the rattle). This is an important extension of its ability to deal with the world.

As development continues, *tertiary* circular reactions appear. The child begins to alter its environment experimentally in order to see, hear, or feel the effects. An example of this "experimental stage" is the interest in falling objects that appears during the second year. The child repeatedly drops, puts down, rolls, and tilts all kinds of objects. Careful observation seems to confirm the fact that babies are fascinated not by the particular object or their own activity alone, but by the phenomenon itself and the different ways they can make different objects fall. This indicates an advance in their understanding of objects and their relationship to them.

2. The bit of development we have just discussed shows that the child rapidly sets up schemata that clearly differentiate between itself and objects. Its direct manipulation of such objects as rattles seems to imply that intentional behavior has developed. But simple repetition of a behavior is not convincing evidence of intention, which appears unequivocally only toward the end of the sensorimotor period, when the infant forcefully pushes aside obstacles in order to get at the object it wishes to manipulate.

3. The development of concepts about *object permanence* and of permanent *object locations* are most important for future development. During the first two years of life, the infant comes to realize that (*a*) objects are separate from itself, (*b*) that they continue to exist even if hidden, and (*c*) that they are likely to remain in the place they were last seen. This is quite an intellectual accomplishment—one that represents a substantial developmental advance.

4. For the infant during the sensorimotor stage, the meaning of the world is action—its own action. The infant is limited in its ability to act on its environment. Without language, the child can only communicate with movements. Action and perception are nearly identical. In terms of contents, babies who usually throw balls or caress dolls will begin throwing or caressing motions when they merely see balls or dolls from a distance. The meaning of the objects is the movements that go with them. Just a bit later, their reaction will be to name or ask for the objects—to use *language*—but at this stage of development, the meaning of objects is just exactly what can be or has been done with the objects.

From Action to Symbol and Operations

Around the age of two years, the child begins to replace direct action with symbols. An obvious example is the use of language to ask for something rather than just reaching to get it. (At two years, children can speak in three- or four-word sentences.) But the creation of symbols and their integration into the mind's schemata lead to still more revolutionary developmental advances. Around this time, too, *operations* become important. Piaget has defined an operation as an *internalized action that is reversible and which can be integrated with other actions*. An internalized action is a mental act that cannot be directly observed by others, and the child itself may not be aware of it. Once again, the mind's operations must be inferred from observable contents. "Reversibility" refers to the fact that operations have an opposite that undoes them. For example, an operation becomes reversible when a little boy realizes not only that he has a brother but that his brother also has a brother—him. In arithmetic, subtracting 17 from 25 undoes the operation of adding 8 to 17. In movement, going from A to B undoes having gone from B to A.

Stage of Concrete Operations   The period between the appearance of symbols (around two years) and the appearance of truly abstract conceptualizations (around eleven) is called the *stage of concrete operations*. That operations are available to the child in its thinking distinguishes this stage from the sensorimotor stage, in which thinking was largely limited to direct motor interactions with the environment. The term "concrete" indicates that, during this stage, operations deal mainly with actual objects and the relationships between them. It is a preparation for the final stage of formal operations, which are mainly concerned with abstractions.

The stage of concrete operations is subdivided into stages and phases as follows:

1. Preoperational stage (approximately two to seven).
   (a) Preoperational phase (approximately two to four).
   (b) Intuitive phase (approximately four to seven).
2. Concrete-operations stage (approximately ages seven to eleven).

In the *preoperational phase*, operations begin to appear, but more important is the laying of the groundwork for their fuller appearance later. Categories expand; for example, a child may assimilate eating cocktail snacks with a toothpick by accommodating its schema of eating methods, and this schema may be further elaborated by experience with other ways of eating—with spoons, forks, fingers, chopsticks, and so on. Such broad categories with "interchangable parts" are essential to the development and effective use of operations.

As we indicated before, preoperational children are *egocentric*. They think that everyone sees things the way they do. It is a surprise to even a four-year-old boy that his tall parent can look down into things—a golf bag, say—that he cannot. Moreover, the child attributes his knowledge and modes of thought to others. He knows that he is a separate person, but he still assumes that he is the center of a world of people who all see and think about things the way he does.

In the *intuitive phase*, real operations are revealed in the child's contents or actions, but the child cannot describe its operations nor discuss them—hence, they are used intuitively. In this stage, children begin to classify objects into categories with less and less dependence on perceptual cues, such as the shape, smell, or feel of an object. For example, kindergarten children will agree that apples, oranges, and bananas are all fruit, despite the differences in their appearance. Children are also able to form the concept of absolute number. For example, they can count eight oranges and eight clothespins and agree that there are the *same number* of each, although the objects are different. This fails to arouse their interest, however; they do not yet realize its importance.

The greatest stride in intellectual development during these years is in the first recognition of the basic principle of *conservation*, the fact that the qualities that determine an object's physical characteristics, such as number, length, quantity, area, and weight, remain the same despite changes in the object's appearance (Figure 17.5). We will discuss the conservation of quantity as a general example. Suppose we show a five–year–old girl two identical

Figure 17.5
Before the development of conservation, the child thinks that there is more liquid in the taller container even when the child sees the liquid poured into it from the shorter container. [New York Times]

Figure 17.6
Which row has more beads? The preconservation child thinks that the longer row has more.

glasses, each containing exactly one pint of milk, and ask her which glass contains more milk. She will agree that both have the same amount. Now, we pour the milk from one of the glasses into a taller but narrower glass. The preconservation child will think that there is now more milk, because the column of milk looks taller and therefore bigger. (It often looks bigger even to adults, a fact exploited by bottlers of all kinds of liquids from milk to beer.) Only after developing the concept of conservation of quantity (usually sometime between the ages of five and seven) will the child realize that the amount of something does not alter even though its shape or the appearance of its container changes. Similarly, the conservation of number involves the realization that the number of beads in a row remains the same, whether they are spaced close together or far apart (Figure 17.6). In each case, the characteristic of quantity or number is detached from the physical appearances of the objects. These are very dramatic changes in a child's idea of the world.

When concrete operations finally become the *dominant* theme of a child's thinking—sometime between the ages of seven to eleven—some fairly complicated mental operations are finally possible. The child realizes the importance of _cardinal numbers_. The fact that there are eight oranges and eight clothespins may now become interesting. The child is also interested in ordinal numbers—being second rather than third becomes important, whereas earlier it was only winning or losing that was of interest. A combination of these two ideas allows the child to organize important parts of the world into useful numerical hierarchies.

Stage of Formal Operations   Complex abstract thinking—the *formal operations* that dominate adult thinking—begins at this stage of intellectual development. Children become interested in forms; they begin to construct relationships between concrete operations and between symbols. For example, the concrete operation of resemblance can be doubled and extended as an analogy. Operating concretely, children know that $4 = 4 \times 1$ and that $16 = 4 \times 4$. Operating formally, they think in terms of 4 is to 1 as 16 is to 4—that is to say, they operate formally on concrete operations. Children are also capable of abstract conceptualization. They actively push their mental world around in order to test and retest their schemata. In Piaget's terms, the person's mind is dominated by form as much as by content.

In intellectual development, a person moves from reflexes to sensory and motor contact with the world, to symbolic manipulations, to concrete mental operations, and finally to abstract formal operations. Each new stage incorporates the last stage into a more complex structure.

CONTRIBUTIONS BY PIAGET'S FOLLOWERS AND COLLEAGUES

We have sketched Piaget's ideas of intellectual development. His followers and colleagues have not significantly altered his theory, but their research has substantially increased the data that support it. We now turn briefly to a few extensions, applications, and modifications of Piaget's theory, in order to highlight their usefulness in explaining intellectual development.

Piaget constructed his theory on the basis of detailed observations of European children as they grew up during the 1920s, 1930s, and 1940s. His work has inspired a great deal of subsequent work, most of which supports his description of the stages of intellectual development and their order of appearance. The main departures from Piaget's reports have been in the chronological ages at which different stages appear. Thus, there have been demonstrations that children less than four years old can master conservation and that appropriate training can produce formal-operational thinking well before the age of eleven. If our society's dedication to rapid development continues to find expression in its educational practices, further modifications of Piaget's timetable may be necessary in order to conform to the observed facts of development.

Outside of Piaget's system, the most extensive developmental system has been constructed by Lawrence Kohlberg in an effort to explain moral development. Kohlberg has shown that the development of morality also has stages. Moreover, according to Kohlberg, people advance through the stages at different rates and do not necessarily ever attain the highest level of moral development (Figure 17.7). There is also cross-cultural evidence that the stages are the same and occur in the same order in the United States, in Europe, and in China.

The stages of moral development are revealed in research studies that note people's responses to hypothetical moral dilemmas, posed in such a way that they must choose one or another alternative action. In a typical dilemma, subjects must decide whether to (1) steal a drug that they cannot afford to buy or (2) let their mother die for lack of the drug. The subject is asked, "What would you do *and* why?" The choice, though interesting, is not as important as the reasons, because it is the *reasons* that define the level of moral development. If the decision to steal or not to steal is made in order simply to

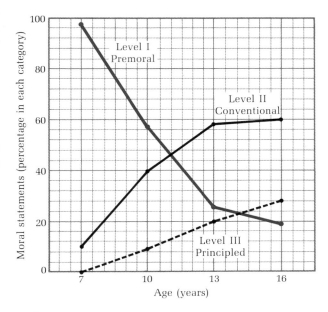

Figure 17.7
An empirical description of moral development. At age seven, nearly all (100 percent) of the reasons for choosing an alternative action are premoral (based on reward or punishment). Over the years, the premoral reasons decline as statements based on higher levels of morality increase. [Adapted from L. Kohlberg, "Moral Development and Indentification," in H. Stevenson, ed., *Child Psychology: 62nd Yearbook of the National Society for the Study of Education.* Chicago: University of Chicago Press, 1963, pp. 277–332.]

avoid punishment or *obtain a reward*, the person is in the *premoral stage.* If the choice is made on the basis of avoiding guilt from disapproval, censure, or dislike by other people, the person is in the stage of conventional morality, in which authority and the approval of others determine moral behavior. If the person's decision is based on the overall welfare of the community, he or she is in one of the most advanced stages of moral development. Even more advanced, according to Kohlberg, are those who base their decision on their own personal system of values.

Other theorists of development have differed with Piaget in point of view and emphasis. An example is Jerome Bruner, whose theory of the development of mental representation elaborates on a critical theme in Piaget's work—the development of symbolism. Bruner found three stages: (1) *enactive*

representation, basically sensorimotor and active, (2) *ikonic* representation, a primitive, presymbolic mode with literal "pictures" of objects and events instead of genuine symbols of them, (3) and the ordinary *symbolic* representation we have mentioned earlier in this chapter.

The Russian psychologist Lev Vygotsky differed with the school of Piaget over the issue of the relationship between language and thought during development. Piaget felt that language and intellect developed along parallel but separate paths. Vygotsky felt that *thought had its origins in speech,* which was driven inside the mind by two forces: one, the insistence of the world that a child not talk all of the time, and two, the clear advantage of talking inaudibly to oneself in order not to telegraph one's next move. Out of talking to oneself, Vygotsky proposed, emerged thought. (What actually happens may be a combination of both processes: speech does become subvocal, and modes of thought certainly do develop on their own).

The application of Piaget's ideas to education suggests that an ideal curriculum would present students with material that they are developmentally just ready to understand. Accordingly, developmental psychologist Jerome Kagan has proposed a "crest of the wave" theory of education. The child is seen as riding a wave in precarious balance. At any given age, he or she is just exactly ready for a few educational experiences. But the child is also in constant danger of either sliding back down the wave if it encounters too easy a lesson, appropriate to an earlier developmental stage, or of falling forward on its face if the lesson it encounters is too far beyond its capacity. The best curriculum should provide the appropriate experience at the right time. This intriguing idea has, unfortunately, not yet been developed to the point that teachers can identify with certainty what stages a particular child has reached and what lessons are best for him or her.

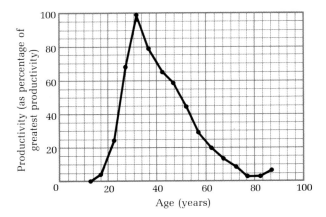

Figure 17.8
The ages at which inventors, scientists, and mathematicians made their outstanding contributions. Although the peak period is in the thirties and forties, there are substantial contributions in the fifties and sixties. [Adapted from H. C. Lehman, *Age and Achievement.* Princeton, New Jersey: Princeton University Press, 1953.]

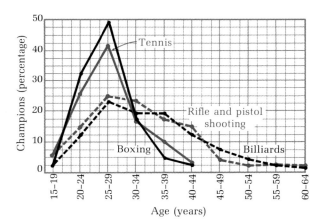

Figure 17.9
The ages of champions in a variety of skilled sports. Notice that the peak period in sports is only two or three years less than the peak period in intellectual contributions. [Adapted from H. C. Lehman, "The Most Proficient Years at Sports and Games," *Research Quarterly of the American Association for Health and Physical Education,* 9, 1938, 3–19.]

Intellectual Productivity   A person has matured intellectually by at least the age of fifteen. Some recent studies have even placed the stage of formal operational thinking at an earlier age for some people. If the tools of thought are mature at fifteen, why then is it that intellectual productivity in most areas peaks at about thirty, as shown in Figure 17.8? Part of the answer seems to be the contribution of experience. Interestingly, athletic success peaks in the mid-twenties (Figure 17.9). Besides experience, another factor seems to influence intellectual productivity: any given person has only a limited number of things to say, points to make, things he or she can do very well, or accomplishments that will satisfy him or her. This factor helps to put an upper limit on the age of productivity. Many people make intellectual contributions well beyond the age of forty, but truly original works produced after that age are relatively rare.

The Mechanisms of Development   Let's return now to the longstanding question of nature versus nurture and examine some experimental evidence.

Very young infants certainly show the ability to learn from experience. As we can see in Figure 17.10, if an infant's crib is modified so that by turning its head it can make a moving visual display appear over the crib, the infant will show an increased tendency to turn its head—this is an example of operant conditioning (as we recall from Chapter 4). There is also evidence that Pavlovian conditioning can be carried out with young infants. So learning does take place. But there are a lot of behavioral changes that do not seem to be clear instances of learning. For example, as an infant grows older, it tends increasingly to look at the corners and edges of geometric figures, rather than other parts of the figures. This increased concentration of looking behavior is relatively hard to understand in terms of

Figure 17.10
When the infant turns its head (*left*) it presses a switch
in its pillow that turns on a moving visual display above
the crib. Head-turning becomes more frequent, and the
infant learns to press the switch with a smaller movement (*right*) that allows it to watch the display continually. [Sol Mednick. These photographs appeared in
T. G. R. Bower's "The Visual World of Infants,"
Scientific American, December 1966, 80–97.]

simple learning. It probably represents both an
increased ability to control the eyes (motor maturation) as well as developments in the infant's perceptual system that make corners and edges more
attractive or important.

Studies of nature and nurture in intellectual
development have come from the *deprivation paradigm*—in which an infant is deprived by circumstances
of an opportunity to practice a skill until beyond the
age at which it normally appears, and then given a
chance at it. For example, there have been studies
of language deprivation (through correctable deafness), deprivation of experience with walking
(through the custom of swaddling infants in blankets,
which occurs in some cultures), and general intellectual deprivation (through a dull and unstimulating
early environment). The usual result is that the
deprived child is initially not as able as the
normally reared child, but then rapidly catches up by
mastering the skill more quickly than normal,

undeprived children mastered it. The compensatory
spurt and catching up occur only if the deprivation
has not been too radical or too prolonged. Just
exactly how much deprivation is too much is not yet
known with certainty.

The compensatory spurt has been demonstrated in
such national programs as Head Start, but in only a
limited way. Such programs fail to have more
significant effects because it is difficult to remedy a
deprived environment in only a short period each
day. More permanent compensatory spurts have been
found in studies of children from orphanages who
are moved to more adequate home environments on
a permanent twenty-four-hour-a-day basis. (See
Chapter 8.) Studies of the effects of deprivation in
humans are often conducted with victims of accidents, wars, disease, or poverty, because, for moral
reasons, we will not experimentally deprive human
beings of the conditions necessary for normal
growth.

With lower animals, however, psychologists
believe that it is occasionally justifiable to restrict
environmental conditions artificially during early life
in order to find out about development. Such studies
of animals have unequivocally shown the effects of
deprivation in early life. Dogs raised in closely
confined quarters and with very limited experience

show nearly incredible failures to learn from experience. In one set of studies, Scotty dogs raised in this way would repeatedly stick their nose into flames, even though they were singed every time. (See Chapter 15.)

Artifically enriched environments also have effects. It has been shown that rats from enriched environments (with many gadgets to operate and shapes to look at and areas to explore) tend to have bigger brains that contain more of some chemicals associated with rapid mastery of problems. In addition, the rats are relatively rapid learners. Whether artificial enrichment would also improve learning in humans is not certain, but the results support the notion that an organism's early exposure to the world can have far-reaching consequences.

Can Special Learning Accelerate Development?

Several attempts to move children into a higher stage of development by teaching have appeared to be successful. For example, children can successfully adopt an adult's attitudes when the adults are presented as models, and they can be taught to describe their moral behavior in terms borrowed from a higher stage of moral development. But perhaps the most interesting case to date concerns teaching the concept of conservation of amount. Suppose that we take a boy who insists that the taller glass has more milk than the shorter glass, even after he sees us pour the milk from the shorter to the taller glass. Now we tell him to drink milk out of the tall glass until he brings the amount down to the amount that used to be in the short glass. Some children will say that this is silly—clearly indicating that they know *intuitively* that you cannot drink *some* milk and still have the same amount. The confusion soon leads to an accommodation, which incorporates the concept of conservation.

But it is not necessarily that simple. Children who attain insight into conservation this way will not necessarily exhibit conservation in other situations. This insight is particular, rather than the general operational understanding that is characteristic of a true developmental advance. Similarly, teaching adult attitudes through modeling or adult morality through coaching often fails to attain true developmental advances. Children learn only particular answers without achieving the mental structure that characterizes an advanced stage and permits ready generalization to instances that have not been explicitly taught.

Of course, none of this means that development is not a product of learning. It may be that a particular, critical learning experience produces development, or that there are a large number of learning experiences that result in advance from stage to stage. Experience is certainly necessary for intellectual development, and someday psychologists may identify particular sets of experiences that are needed to advance an individual through the various stages.

Suggested Readings

Bayley, N. (1969) *Bayley scales of infant development.* New York: The Psychological Corporation. [A discussion of physical growth in infancy.]

Bruner, J. S. (1966) *Toward a theory of instruction.* Cambridge: Harvard University Press. [The developmental view applied to education.]

Flavell, J. H. (1963) *The developmental psychology of Jean Piaget.* Princeton: Van Nostrand. [A somewhat lengthier discussion.]

Kohlberg, L., & Turiel, E. (1971) *Research in moral development: The cognitive-developmental approach.* New York: Holt, Rinehart and Winston. [A discussion of moral development.]

Phillips, J. L., Jr. (1969) *The origins of intellect: Piaget's theory.* San Francisco: W. H. Freeman and Co. [Piaget's theory is neatly summarized.]

Piaget, J. (1950) *The psychology of intelligence.* (Translated by M. Piercy and D. E. Berlyne.) London: Routledge and Kegan Paul. [Although this is a very difficult book, it is one of the half-dozen true classics of twentieth-century psychology.]

Piaget, J. (1952) *The origins of intelligence in children.* (Translated by M. Cook.) New York: International Universities Press. [The student who gets through this and the preceding volume may wish to consult other works by Piaget and B. Inhelder, his chief later collaborator.]

Smedslund, J. (1962) "The acquisition of conservation of substance and weight in children: VII. Conservation of . . . etc.," *Scandinavian journal of psychology, 3,* 69–77. [The conclusion of a series of experimental studies on the acquisition (development) of conservation. The references in this paper will send the reader to earlier papers, which should be read first.]

Stevenson, H. W., Hess, E. H., & Rheingold, H. L., eds. (1967) *Early behavior: Comparative and developmental approaches.* New York: Wiley. [A good starting place for the reader interested in early experience in development.]

Vygotsky, L. S. (1962) *Thought and language.* Cambridge, Mass.: MIT Press. [Another perspective on intellectual development.]

CHAPTER EIGHTEEN

Development of Language

It takes a long time to master a new language. If you were suddenly dropped into a village in Saudi Arabia, it would probably be several weeks before you could ask for even a few of the things you would need, and at least several years before you could carry on a grammatical conversation on an abstract topic. Even then, you might find it difficult to follow an adult native speaker who spoke rapidly. So it should not be surprising that it takes the average human infant dropped into our midst three to four years to master the rudiments of English *grammar*. We can appreciate just how much is involved in this feat if we follow it a few months at a time, drawing parallels between the development of language and the development of other skills.

During the first few months of life, an infant does little linguistically but cry and coo. By around six months of age, the baby's neuromuscular system has matured enough for it to be able to sit up, grasp and play with objects, distinguish strangers from parents, smile and laugh, respond to adult speech by *babbling*, and babble spontaneously. During the babbling stage, the baby produces a continuous stream of apparently meaningless sounds that approximate the rhythms and intonations of adult speech. By one year of age, an infant is able to stand

alone for a short time, to try walking on its own, to respond pretty well to verbal directions like "No!", and to say its first word. One of our tasks in this chapter will be to find out how babbling develops into that first word.

Between one-and-a-half and two years, when the child can stand alone and walk, it has some understanding of speech and can point to objects as they are named. It can also put a vocabulary of twenty to two hundred words together in simple two word "sentences." These sentences are pointed and graphic—"Dad gone," "I full", "more milk"—and are referred to as *telegraphic speech*.

Right about the age of two, we find that the child spends most of its time running around, breathlessly using its vocabulary of about three hundred words to construct sentences that are frequently three words, and occasionally four words, long. Between two and three years of age, the child's vocabulary is growing faster than it ever will again. The sentences are becoming more elaborate. At the same time, the child is developing hand–eye coordination and learning to use its hands in finely graded movements.

By its third birthday, the child can balance on one foot but probably will not hop reliably on one foot for another twelve to eighteen months. It can ride a tricycle and use about a thousand words with almost unerring correctness, if not with unerring grammar. And by the age of four years, a child will speak with an almost perfect replica of an adult's grammar.

In this brief sketch of language development, we have paralleled changes in linguistic competence with changes in the child's motor capabilities. This correlation is a rather loose one—children who are not well coordinated may nevertheless speak very well—but the comparison still serves to emphasize the combined roles of both maturation and experience in determining development.

PSYCHOLINGUISTIC DESCRIPTIONS OF LANGUAGE DEVELOPMENT

Psycholinguists study the language of children partly because it plays such an important role in child development; children's ability to relate to other people and to use abstract ideas is closely related to their ability to handle language. Also, it is believed that the way in which language develops may give some insight into language itself as a unique human accomplishment, and thus into the question of what it means to be human.

There are two tasks in studying any type of development. One is to describe in proper order the changes that take place. This provides the data for the second task, which is to explain why and how the changes come about—the dynamics of development. We shall take up the description of language development in this section, leaving the dynamics for the next.

The process of learning to understand and use language can be broken down into changes in *phonology*, how to say and pronounce language; *syntax*, how to put words and phrases together according to clear grammatical rules; and *semantics*, what the groups of sounds that make up words mean to those who hear them. Taken all together, these three sorts

of changes make up the field of *developmental psycholinguistics*.

Phonological Development Phonology is the study of how we produce and discriminate the sounds of our language. A competent speaker of English, for example, has command of some forty-five *phonemes*, which are the accepted sounds that make up understandable English words. An infant's ability to make these sounds develops rapidly during the early months of life, but along fairly complex lines.

At birth and for several months afterwards, there are no sounds that qualify as phonemes: infants are limited to cries and coos. But at around six months of age, babbling begins. Babbling is composed of apparently random sounds produced by the same parts of the body—the larynx, the tongue, and lips—that will eventually produce the sounds of adult speech. It is thought that all children, regardless of what language they will eventually speak, are capable of forming all the sounds of any of the world's languages during the babbling stage.

Exactly what happens during the period between six months and one year, when the typical child comes up with his first word, is not thoroughly known, and probably differs from child to child. Studies show that phonemes that are going to be used later come and go in the child's daily babbling in just the same way as phonemes that are never used in the child's native language. It is clear that there is no simple learning process that selects the phonemes that will be needed and discards those that will not be needed. No parent could possibly reward a baby for every individual sound that belongs to a language. However, words and combinations of sounds do attract the interest and approval of parents.

Phonological development occurs at two different levels: what the linguists call *segmental* changes (in the

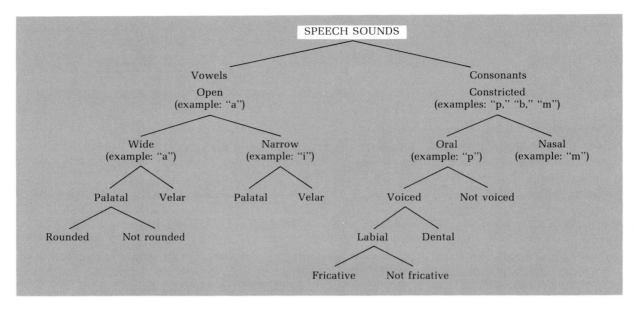

Figure 18.1
An example of the method by which English phonemes
(recognized speech sounds) can be defined in terms of
a series of serially applied two-valued distinctions.
Speech sounds are first divided into two classes: vowels
(open sounds) and consonants (constricted sounds). Each
class is further divided into two groups, for example,
oral consonants and nasal consonants. Each of these
groups is divided into two subgroups. This process is
continued until all forty-five English phonemes have
been defined. (Only a few of the divisions are shown
here.)

sounds themselves) and *suprasegmental* changes (in
combinations of sounds, intonation, and stress). We
will describe the latter first, from two points of
view—what the child says and what he shows that he
can understand.

Close observation has revealed that during the six
months preceding the momentous first word, the
individual utterances in a child's babbling increase
in number and length. They also become more word-
like in form and character. The mixture of consonants and vowels also becomes more similar in
composition to the words that the child will soon be
speaking. There are discernible patterns of intonation and stress that influence both the child's
production of speech sounds, and the child's
comprehension of them. For example, if we measure
the heart rate and general movement (level of

motility) of children as we read real speech to them,
we find at around eight months of age that their
heart rates and movements alter as we change from
declarative sentences to questions. Presumably
children of this age are sensitive to the differences
in intonation.

Segmental changes in individual phonemes are much
more difficult to measure and discuss. The reason is
that phonemes are hard to categorize and their
recognition is a matter of individual opinion.
Whether a certain phoneme is the "same" or
"different" from another, or whether it was said
correctly, depends on a judgment by a listener, and
listeners tend to disagree. But it nevertheless seems
that phonological development is a process in which
the child first recognizes that the available phonemes
fall into two large categories, those that are open
(vowels), such as "ah," and those that are relatively
closed (consonants), such as "p," "b," or "m." These
two categories are then subdivided and refined still
further until the infant arrives at the forty-five
phonemes necessary for speaking and understanding
English. The process resembles the system of
successive binary distinctions that occur in the
operation of certain types of computers (see Figure
18.1). There is evidence that a child's phonemes
actually develop in this way.

The exact linguistic circumstances just preceding the utterance of the first word are the subject of some disagreement among the most knowledgeable authorities. This probably reflects individual differences among the children who have been observed and different approaches to language instruction by parents. Some children seem to approach the first word gradually; others say it right out of the blue; others actually go through a period of silence just before the first word. Whatever precedes it, the first word has a distinctive characteristic: it is *always*, in any language, composed of consonants formed in the front of the mouth, a "p," "b," "m," or "t," and vowels formed in the back of the mouth, an "e," or "a." The first word often contains two identical syllables. It is not surprising that the first word frequently refers to a member of the child's immediate family—"papa," "mama," "bebe," "baba," etc. That the syllables in these words are identical reflects the fact that they were formed by very young children whose language development was at a low level.

We have talked about the "momentous first word." Momentous is an apt designation from the point of view of both the parent and the child. As we shall see when we discuss the mechanism and function of language as distinct from sound production and structure, parents are pleased when their child produces its first intelligible word. And the child, in turn, enjoys pleasing his parents with his speech. From now on the child relies principally on speech to manipulate the people who are the most important elements in the environment: parents, relatives, peers, and even family pets.

The "first word" might better be called the *first linguistic communication*. By the time it occurs, the child has gained enough control over emphasis and intonation to utter the word either as an abbreviated declarative sentence ("Mama." = There is mama.), a question ("Mama?" = Where is mama?), or an imperative ("Mama!" = Mama come immediately.) The reader can appreciate these differences if he tries to imitate them. Even a child's first word carries meaning.

Development of Syntax The sentence, initially one word long, expands rapidly both in terms of the number of word units that are combined in it and the complexity of the combinations. The discovery that there are rules underlying early combinations of words indicates that even the child's simplest of languages has a definite grammatical structure. These grammars are not adult types, and there is evidence that they may differ in complexity and type from child to child. These differences probably represent differences in both the actual language the child hears spoken and the strategy employed by the parents when actively teaching a child about language, but we do not yet have enough information to be certain.

Linguistic development progresses from this level toward the extraordinary intricacy of an adult's grammar. Development is spurred on by a combination of growth and social experiences. As children mature, their motor and mental capabilities increase. At the same time, listeners are demanding greater linguistic accuracy and specificity and rewarding them when they appear. Soon children are forming three-word sentences, and it becomes apparent that they have grasped the idea of subject–verb–object. (Strangely enough, this word order seems to be a natural one that appears first even in children whose parents speak a language, such as German, that uses a different order, subject–object–verb.)

From the stage of three-word groups, both the number of words and the complexity of their arrangement increase. The transformations of sentences, which we discussed in Chapter 9, become possible—for example, turning statements into questions, embedding subordinate clauses in the

Table 18.1
Development of Sentences

MODE	STAGES		
	1	2	3
Declarative	Bob go.	Bob going.	Bob is going.
Interrogatory	Bob here?	Bob's here?	Is Bob here?
Imperative	No go!		Don't go!
Negative	No do.	I no do.	I will not do (it).

middle of sentences, and forming one compound sentence by joining two simple ones. New forms are mastered, such as the progressive mode—"He is going out," instead of "He goes out." The child also develops the ability to use whole sentences in each of the adult modes: declarative, negative, interrogatory, and imperative. Table 18.1 shows how sentences in each of these modes typically fill out during development.

Children often *overgeneralize* new rules when they master them, and this tendency usually leads to grammatical errors. Forming the past tense of verbs is an example. Before children learn the rule of adding "d" or "ed" to form the past tense, they usually use "came" and "given" correctly. But once the general rule is mastered, it is temporarily overgeneralized: children say "comed" and "gived". These forms gradually disappear as the idea of exceptions to rules develops more fully. Overgeneralization is excellent evidence that children do learn rules of speech, not just separate vocal responses, and that they actively try to organize their linguistic world. In this task, the use of the regulatory function of grammar represents a great step forward.

Several studies of children's grammar have tried to determine whether children can understand expressions that they do not yet say themselves. Generally, the developmental sequence seems to be: imitation of the phrase first, followed by understanding, and finally by spontaneous production. Certainly children can imitate what they do not

understand. There is also evidence that children can understand expressions which they do not yet produce; an example is "yes." But, except possibly in word-play, it is rare for children to produce frequently an expression that they do not at least *think* they understand.

Semantic Development   Since we have discussed the meaning of meaning in Chapter 9, only a few comments on the development of meaning are needed here.

Children's first meanings are connotative and relatively simple—the "help-needed" meaning of the cry and the "happy-state" meaning of the coo. Denotative meanings develop and expand rapidly in number when children begin to speak words. One gross measure of the growth of meaning is illustrated in the graph in Figure 18.2, which shows the approximate number of separate words that a typical child uses correctly at various ages. Children also rapidly combine the two aspects of meaning: they recognize very early that *how* you say it can make as much difference as *what* you say.

The Language of the Deaf   Deprived of the ability to adjust their speech by listening to themselves, totally deaf children never develop any oral language at all without specific training. But they can master and use other kinds of communication, notably written language, lip reading, and sign language. Studies are unanimous in showing that the deaf, on the average, develop each of their linguistic

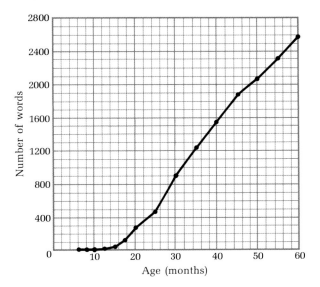

Figure 18.2
This graph depicts the growth of a typical child's vocabulary over the first six years of life.

skills much more slowly than do those who can hear. In one study of comprehension of passive sentences, normal eight-year-old subjects performed better than deaf seventeen-year olds.

Despite these differences in the level of linguistic functioning, there are similarities in the structure of the languages used by deaf and by normal subjects. The development of _sign languages_ has been studied by Ursula Bellugi-Klima in order to see if the principles found in ordinary spoken languages are generally found in sign languages as well. Substantial similarity has been found between the grammars that describe spoken languages and the grammars that describe the sign language of the deaf.

MECHANISMS OF LANGUAGE DEVELOPMENT

It may be that no single set of concepts as currently understood can explain how and why children acquire the ability to speak their own language. The learning approach favored by behaviorists offers an explanation of how children can learn to speak from their experiences with other people. However, the basic stimulus–response–reinforcement contingency (which we discussed in Chapter 4) must be modified, or at least carefully elaborated, in order to account for the child's overgeneralizations and his first verbalizations that contain material apparently not learned. Nor can learning alone yet account for the fact that only man among all the animals is able to master a complex oral language.

Imitation theory, the idea that children acquire language by imitating other people, obviously has a certain validity. Children do indeed imitate others, both in what they say and in how they say it. However, this explanation encounters many of the same objections as the learning approach. All children's speech cannot be traced to imitation, because children say things that they could not possibly have heard—even on television.

Recent biological theories mention the anatomical differences that limit the sounds that other animals, such as apes, can produce. They emphasize the structural differences between human and animal brains, and attribute human linguistic abilities to those differences. But these structural theories lack functional mechanisms—they do not explain how a child masters his own language or why he says what he does.

Cognitive theories, such as Piaget's (which we discussed in Chapter 17), assume that people have a basic, innate organizing function that sorts out and codifies information received from sensory perceptions such as sight and touch, and then forms general rules that dictate behavior. The structural biological details of this organization and rule formation are vague, however, and since the process is invisible, its mechanism can only be inferred from the child's behavior.

Although these theories of language are quite different, they are not necessarily incompatible. Each one regards the development of language from a different viewpoint, and each one can provide an adequate explanation of a certain aspect of the subject.

Imitation and Language Imitation theory holds that children either have an innate tendency to imitate others or that they acquire it very early in life. Choosing between these two alternatives is not important, since they probably cannot be definitely separated. Either way, we have to be clear about what imitation means, since there are many things it is not. We may infer imitation when one person behaves in a way that appears to be closely similar to the way another person behaves. *But we must be sure there is no other cause for the similarity.* Three other common causes for similar behavior are: inherited similarities in physical structure, similar environments, and similar experiences. For example, if a little boy walks with the gait of the parent because he has inherited a certain physical structure necessitating such a gait, the similarity is not due to imitation. In the same way, the exposure of a child to an environment or to experiences similar to those of the parent can account for quite a lot of the similarities in their behavior. What is left may legitimately qualify as imitation.

In the course of linguistic development, as we have seen, a child imitates not only the words and phrases that it hears but also the way in which they are said. But imitation cannot account for every word the child speaks, since he says many things that he could not have heard.

Biology and Language Man's apparently unique status as the talking animal owes much to the relatively advanced state of his nervous system. Only

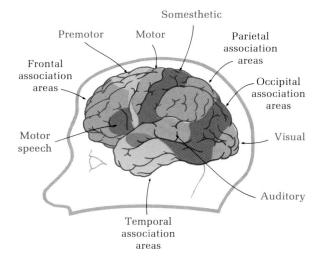

Figure 18.3
In this side view of the human cortex, six sensory and motor areas are identified: visual, somesthetic, motor, premotor, motor speech, and auditory. Activity in the visual area, for example, is correlated with the activity of visual receptors and with reported visual sensations. Cortical areas that have not been linked to a specific sensory or motor system are called "association areas" because they are thought to allow associations or connections between the other areas.

humans have a nervous system—and a bodily structure—capable of rapidly and accurately producing the complex patterns of sounds that make up spoken language and the intricate and structured system of marks that compose written language. In addition to these unique physical abilities, there seem to be deeper biological sources that encourage language. Claims that the structure of human grammar is inherent in the *nervous system*, and hence not derived from experience, are undoubtedly too strong. The "natural" order of subject before verb and object probably owes as much to human experience—the way people manipulate objects in their environment—as it does to heredity. But there is ample evidence for the importance of biological factors in normal language development.

Norman Geschwind has suggested that the key difference between animals and humans that allows humans to develop a spoken language lies not in the size of the brain but in its structure. He points out that a human's brain (Figure 18.3) vastly exceeds an animal's in the amount of cerebral cortex that cannot be connected with any specific type of sensory perception or modality. The unassignable cortex has developed in between *cortical areas* that *are* assignable to specific senses, such as hearing or vision. It is possible that these unassigned or *"association" areas of cortex* facilitate language by making connections between two senses, such as sight and touch. These associations, in turn, may help the naming of objects, an ability fundamental to the development of language.

This structural theory may have a certain validity, but studies of the connections between the nervous system and the brain indicate that it may be oversimplified. In the first place, the distinction between the motor, sensory, and association areas is blurred; for example, motor activity is much less restricted to the primary motor area than had been thought in the first half of this century. Moreover, although the modern concept of *localization of function* in the brain holds that specific psychological functions tend to be located in specific areas of the brain, each sense modality may also have alternate pathways that relay the same sensory information to other parts of the brain. These alternate routes enable higher organisms to continue to function almost normally even when a substantial portion of the brain is damaged. For example, if a stroke or wound damages a certain area of the brain of an adult (the lower outside frontal cortex, the third frontal convolution), his speech suffers drastic, but often only temporary, impairment. The fact that impairment occurs shows that this brain region is somehow linked to speech, but the *recovery of function* over a period of time indicates that the critical nerve pathways responsible for speech must be able to reestablish themselves elsewhere in the brain. Sometimes, humans recover a surprising amount of their former abilities after bodily paralysis from a severe stroke; this is another example of the plasticity which characterizes the nervous systems of humans and lower animals.

The *plasticity* of the brain is further illustrated by children who have lost an entire half of their brain from damage or radical surgery. In each person, one half of the brain dominates the other—the concept of *cerebral dominance*; severe damage or removal of that half can permanently impair many basic functions. For example, the separate abilities of understanding, speaking, reading, and writing language are controlled or dominated by the left half of the brain in right-handed people, and vice versa in left-handed people. In a very young child, the loss of either half apparently slows language development to a degree, but it does not prevent it. In an older child or an adult, however, the loss of the language-dominant half is accompanied by the loss of the ability to use language, and the loss is usually permanent. If the nondominant hemisphere is lost, however, only minimal speech impairment may result.

Such phenomena as recovery of function and cerebral dominance have led many theorists to reject a strictly structural and spatial account of how the brain handles language in favor of a functional theory—that something about how the brain works, or about how its parts work together, is responsible for the unique neurological events that allow humans to understand and reproduce spoken language. So far, what this specific something is, is not known.

Behavior and Language The approach of behaviorists to the phenomena of language development has of course emphasized how much of language development may be or must be dependent on learning by experience. Their views are unfortunately based more on intuition and the extension of principles derived from research on animals than on actual empirical studies of young children, but they still seem to make good sense.

The behaviorist starts from the observation that it is natural for infants to make sounds—babbling is innate. How is it, then, that babbling becomes more like human speech; how is the ability to imitate words acquired; how are vocabularies expanded and grammatical complexities and rules introduced? The behaviorist's answer is that the infant's speech is shaped when he is reinforced for emitting sounds that resemble real words in the presence of certain stimuli—for example, his teddy bear or his mother. Since the sounds have been reinforced, he tends to repeat them whenever he encounters those stimuli.

Parents want their children to become, eventually, normal adults. This obvious fact has far-reaching consequences; it means that parents will reinforce as frequently as they can any behavior, including speech, that indicates that their children are growing up normally. This, the behaviorist believes, is the primary developmental mechanism: children gradually become more like their parents because the parents generally reinforce behavior that resembles their own.

Behaviorists have traditionally found the acquisition of grammar more difficult to explain than any other phenomenon in language development. Their problem came from a reluctance to talk about the learning of *rules*, which grammar seems to require, instead of the usual learning of separate responses. Modern behaviorists, however, explain grammar as simply a set of responses by the speaker which set up the *relationships* between words that are necessary for bringing about the desired responses from the listener.

Suggested Readings

Bellugi, U., & Brown, R., eds. (1970) *The acquisition of language*. Chicago: University of Chicago Press. [Representative empirical studies.]

Geschwind, N. (1965) "Disconnection syndromes in animal and man," *Brain, 88*, (Part II), 237–294.

Lenneberg, E. H., ed. (1964) *New directions in the study of language*. Cambridge, Mass.: MIT Press. [Several of the many, mainly cognitive, points of view on the phenomena of language are presented.]

Lenneberg, E. H. (1967) *The biological foundations of language*. New York: Wiley. [The biological point of view is presented powerfully here and in the article by Geschwind.]

Menyuk, P. (1971) *The acquisition and development of language*. Englewood Cliffs, N.J.: Prentice-Hall. [A concise and highly readable summary of language development.]

Skinner, B. F. (1957) *Verbal behavior*. New York: Appleton-Century-Crofts. [The behaviorist's point of view.]

CHAPTER NINETEEN

Individual Development Within Society

In this chapter we shall trace the process by which the newborn infant becomes a member of the society in which he or she lives. The progress of individual social development has been elegantly outlined by Erik H. Erikson, a psychoanalyst who has done extensive research in the fields of child analysis and child development. In his well-known book, *Childhood and Society,* published in 1950, he described the growing child's changing relationship to society as a series of eight *psychosocial* stages, roughly paralleling Sigmund Freud's *psychosexual* stages (which we shall discuss in Chapter 24). Erikson differs from Freud in presenting social development as a continuing process that extends beyond infancy; according to Erikson, a person goes on developing and changing all his life. At each new stage, the person faces a new social conflict or crisis. The way in which a person meets it exerts a positive or a negative influence over his or her personality and affects behavior in the next stage.

The aim of this chapter is to present Erikson's general views with additions and digressions from several other theorists of special periods of development.

For the purposes of discussion, we shall add one stage (post-adolescence and youth) to Erikson's structure of the life span and divide the life of the individual into nine unequal periods:

1. Birth to one year
2. Years one and two
3. Years three and five
4. From six to puberty
5. Adolescence
6. Post–adolescence and youth
7. Adulthood
8. Mid–life crisis
9. Aging

The age ranges for these periods are approximate; each person passes through the nine stages at his or her own pace. In one person, adolescence may be prolonged; in another, it may be very short. The "mid-life crisis" in some may be so brief that it could hardly be said to have occurred at all. Sooner or later, however, every person encounters the specific problems belonging to each period, problems created both by the physical changes of his or her

Figure 19.1
Erik H. Erikson. [Courtesy W. W. Norton & Co.]

own body and by the necessity of relating to other people and clarifying his or her own role in society.

In the discussion that follows, based largely on Erikson's views, we shall consider the five most important characteristics of each period: (1) the important social developments, (2) the outstanding personal crisis, (3) the resolution of the crisis, (4) the social effects on the individual, (5) any special aspects of growth during the period.

THE FIRST YEAR OF LIFE

A person's orientation toward many of life's basic problems is decided during his or her first twelve months. That crucial first year determines whether a child will be primarily successful or unsuccessful in

seeking and giving both affection and material benefits. The child develops a basic trust or mistrust of the world and begins to express and control drives and hopes for success. Obviously, these issues are fought out on very primitive ground. But the things children learn in the first year become the basis for the way they will behave toward the world in the future. Symbolically, and with variable success, children will continue to try to solve each of the problems encountered in the future with the general types of intellectual, behavioral, and emotional reactions that were *initially* successful for them. The reactions are modified, of course, but the basic orientation tends to remain the same.

The most important social figure in the child's first year of life is the nurse, or _caretaker_, who is often but not always, the mother. Thus, almost all of us owe an important part of our basic outlook on life to heredity and to our mothers. How does this come about?

Babies bring to the world inherited temperaments and preferences for certain types of activities. Since they cannot care for themselves, they are wholly dependent on others to provide for immediate and intense needs: food, warmth, comfort, physical contact with other humans, especially with a mother's breast. The way in which the mother or caretaker satisfies these needs determines such basic personality characteristics as trust or mistrust, boldness or passivity, optimism or pessimism. Caretakers who meet a child's needs promptly, appropriately, and, perhaps most important of all, willingly and acceptingly, tend to instill trusting, hopeful traits. An accepting atmosphere allows infants to feel that they are important and effective participants in their worlds: not just *takers* of satisfaction but also *givers* of opportunities for the care the mother or nurse wants to offer. The child's feeling of effective, successful interaction with those who make up its world lays

Figure 19.2
The warm and accepting atmosphere created by a successful and mutually satisfying period of breast-nursing can instill in the infant a basic trust in its world and confidence in its ability to deal with it. [Graves/Jeroboam, Inc.]

the foundation for future social development. It means that the child will tend to be optimistic and trusting in meeting the problems, demands, and opportunities of the ensuing periods of its life.

Because of the importance of the relationship between the child and the caretaker, there has been a great deal of research done on one of the most outstanding parts of this relationship: nursing. It is not at all certain that this is the most important event during this period. It is difficult to compare the urgency of the infant's various needs and impossible to ask it which it considers most important. But nursing has attracted the most interest, perhaps because it is a source of genuine physical pleasure for both baby and mother.

A great deal has been made of the supposed increase in intimacy afforded by breast-nursing as opposed to bottle-feeding. It is likely this emphasis has been misdirected. What is important for the child is willing and accepting care in an atmosphere that communicates to the child that it lives in a reliable world that can be trusted. Most theorists agree that a successful breast-nursing relationship represents such an atmosphere (Figure 19.2). But it can be created in other ways too: mothers or other caretakers who do not breast-nurse can create such

a loving atmosphere. Moreover, breast-nursing alone, without acceptance and love, does not create an atmosphere conducive to basic trust. Without such an atmosphere, the child is likely to emerge from the first year with relatively more fear and self-doubt than confidence and basic trust in the world and other people.

THE SECOND YEAR OF LIFE

Both the mother and the father are the central social figures for the child during this year. The biggest developments center around toilet training, during which the child learns to control the parts of its own body that are involved in elimination. (Figure 19.3). This is a crucial period for two reasons. First, if the child does not learn bowel control easily, it feels inadequate. This can, in turn, produce feelings of shame and self-doubt that can last for many years. These feelings may become a permanent part of the child's personality, affecting its view of itself and the world. In an extreme case, the child feels that it is worthless, and the parents' behavior may seem to indicate that they fully agree. On the other hand, prompt mastery of control over toilet habits results in proud parents and children who feel confident and competent.

During the period of toilet training, there are at least three aspects of *control*. The parents control the child, the child controls itself, and also finds out that it can control its parents—that its toilet behavior has a noticeable effect on them. The important events of social development in the second year can thus be seen in terms of who controls whom. Normally, the outcome is balanced; neither the parents nor the child devise dictatorial controlling measures.

The modes of social control that the child discovers at this stage can become relatively permanent strategies for dealing with other people. The two

Figure 19.3
Early and easy mastery of its own body in toilet training can give a child confidence; failures can lead to
feelings of shame and self-doubt. [Graves/Jeroboam, Inc.]

essential actions in bowel control are *retaining* and
expelling. Some psychologists believe that these may
be translated into general personality traits. It is
thought that the child who successfully uses either of
these modes during toilet training is likely to continue to try them out in solving his future problems.
The extreme use of one mode results in a totally
effusive personality. Extreme use of the other mode
produces a compulsively incorporative personality
who makes a life–style out of restraint. Neither is

developmentally normal; the better outcome of this
period is a balance between the two extremes.

The appearance of a decided fear of strangers
during this period may be related to the problem of
control. It is as if the child were having enough
trouble coping with two parents without dealing with
another adult.

The first two years are spent in establishing what
can be called the *inactive integrity* of the child: trust,
confidence, autonomy, and cooperation are mainly
passive traits at these ages. In the next period, which
runs up to the age of entry into formal school, the
development of *active integrity* becomes a central
theme.

FROM THREE TO FIVE

The key social element in this period has been
described as the generalized family, in order to indicate that the child's horizon of socially influential
figures extends beyond mother and father to include
sisters and brothers (siblings), relatives, and others
that are close to the family. These people teach,
guide, criticize, and sometimes harass the child as it
struggles to find its place in this larger social group.

The critical personal conflict in these years is
between confident self-initiative (Figure 19.4) and
guilt. _Conscience_, the ability to distinguish between
what society considers right and wrong (equivalent
to Freud's superego), develops rapidly as children
learn what is expected of them, what behavior will
be rewarded, and what will be punished. Some of
society's expectations become part of a child's own
expectations of itself; when it violates them, it feels
guilty.

Between three and five years is thus a time of conflict between natural personal desires and the prohibitions and rules of society. The child must steer
itself by three standards: what it wants, what its
generalized family expects, and what it has come to

Figure 19.4
The three- to five-year-old is able to explore the world.
[UPI Photo]

expect of itself. If the child is successful in doing
this, it will be able to reach its goals satisfactorily
within the rules set by society and itself. If unsuccessful, the child's relationship to society will be
unbalanced. The rules it follows will either be so
prohibitive and rigid that its natural desires often
break them, causing crippling feelings of guilt, or
they will be so weak that they exert almost no control at all, resulting in frequent antisocial behavior.
Once again, the outcome of this period dictates the
growing child's continuing approach to its world.

The fear of strangers largely disappears during this
period but is replaced by an intense fear of being
abandoned by one or both parents. Some psychologists theorize that, in developing a conscience, the
child is actively trying to make the parents' view of
the world part of its own—to make a part of the
parents a part of itself—and so a threat of losing a
parent is a threat of losing a part of the child itself.
Hence the intensity of the fear.

The differing *sex roles* of boys and girls become
very important as the child establishes wider contacts

within the family and with other children of the
same age (peers). The child's sex has determined
how other people treat him or her right from the
moment of birth: girls and boys are differentiated by
names, colors (pink versus blue), clothes, etc. They are
also affected by the way each parent reacts toward
their sex. During the preschool years, the child
develops an awareness of the kind of behavior that
is considered appropriate to his or her sex. Little
girls usually become interested in their appearance
and in dolls; little boys generally concentrate on
constructive and destructive toys—blocks, trains, cap
pistols, and so forth (Figure 19.5).

These are strictly *cultural* differences. Children
raised in cultures with different expectations for
the two sexes just as rapidly conform to those
behavioral standards. What is the same in various
cultures, though, is the child's concern with sexually
appropriate behavior in these early years.

FROM SIX TO PUBERTY

The social scene continues to expand in the last
years of childhood. This is most dramatic on the
first day of primary school, when the child is
suddenly exposed for long periods of time to a social
group much larger than the family and close friends.
Children come to realize that their effective social
groups extend not only to a school class but to a
school itself, the general group of people of their
age, and, eventually the very general group called
young people.

What this all means for social development is an
expansion in *social competence*. Children learn to
express their aggressiveness in socially approved
ways (in competitive sports, for example). They also
learn to cooperate with others, in order to accomplish
jointly what no single child could accomplish by
itself.

Figure 19.5
A rowdy little boy and a quiet little girl may be conforming to cultural expectations. [David Powers]

These are also years of intensive *social comparison.* Children become aware of their standing in their groups. They find out that people differ physically, intellectually, racially, economically, and socially, and that they themselves can be classified and ranked in each of these ways. They learn, moreover, that their status affects how they are treated by the people around them. They experience both the advantages and disadvantages of holding a high rank in comparison with others in their group and a low rank in comparison with others. How well or how poorly a child develops socially during this period is often largely determined by previous experiences. A child who has acquired in its early years a basic trustful-

ness, optimism, and self-initiative is likely to make more progress socially than one who has acquired a pessimistic outlook and who experiences shame, self-doubt, and guilt because of its feelings and desires. Social development thus builds on itself.

The older the child becomes, the more difficult it is to separate the child's personal problems from their social context. The overriding personal challenge of the social struggles of these years seems to have become avoiding the urge to *escape,* either socially, by withdrawing into oneself, or both socially and physically, by means of artificial methods such as drugs. Such alternatives to building productive relationships with other people seem to be increasingly attractive to preadolescents as the complexities and hence the stresses of modern society increase. This trend is reflected in increases in drug abuse as well as in an increase in preadolescent suicide.

Balancing aggressive and hostile urges against the demands of an increasingly strict conscience becomes a major task around the middle of this period. Difficulties in controlling hostility are often expressed, especially around the age of nine, by the appearance of tics and superstitions. Tics—short, rapid, repetitive movements, such as twitches—appear during periods of stress or lack of adequate rest and may occur over periods of several months. Superstitions such as not stepping on cracks to avoid disaster or injury or frequent washing to avoid bad odors or germs usually express the developing child's struggles within himself. Once thought to be abnormal, these phenomena are now known to be so common among children at this period that their complete absence is considered unusual.

ADOLESCENCE

At just about the time that many children seem to have solved the social problems we have just discussed, the period called "adolescence" occurs,

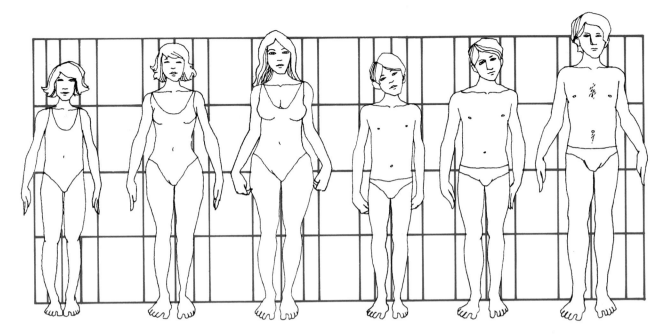

Figure 19.6
Among adolescents of the same age, there are dramatic differences in physical development and appearance, which no doubt affect the individual's search for identity. Each of these groups contains individuals of the same chronological age—12.75 years for the girls, 15.75 years for the boys—but they represent widely different degrees of physical maturity. [Adapted from J. M. Tanner, "Growing Up," *Scientific American,* September 1973, pp. 34–43. Copyright © 1973 by Scientific American, Inc. All rights reserved.]

adding a whole new set of challenges and opportunities. These tend to center around the establishment of personal identity, the development of sexual awareness, and the development of new relationships to the opposite sex.

The bodily changes that occur at puberty are well known: the enlargement and maturation of the sexual organs and glands, the appearance of *secondary sex characteristics* such as the growth of body hair, the male voice-change, and the final spurt in growth (Figure 19.6). The emotional changes are equally complex and even more important in terms of social adjustment. Differences in the rate of development of boys and girls can create difficulties at this age, since girls tend to develop sexually at an earlier age than boys. In our culture, the initial female emotional need seems to be for warmth and intimacy

with others—not necessarily with boys, but with close friends or family members. A boy's sexual maturity comes later, on the average, and although they experience greater intimacy in their personal friendships with other boys, their increased strength finds an outlet in competitive, even aggressive, behavior. Moreover, their capacity for overt and intense sexual arousal, expressed physically in erection, creates a compelling need for immediate and explicit sexual gratification that girls often do not experience until later in life. Variations of these sexual differences in development at puberty appear in all cultures. Given these differences, the central problem of a heterosexual society is the integration of the sexes.

The most urgent problem of personal development in this period has been referred to as a search for *identity*. One has begun to realize and face one's own destructibility, the fact that one will die sooner or later. Having been a child clearly different from one's parents, one has become an adult similar to one's parents; and one faces the necessity of caring for oneself, not only sexually and socially but, in the future, economically as well. The approach of complete independence also creates a need to explore one's own personality and one's new abilities.

Adolescents are subject to pressure from all directions: from the standards they set for themselves, from their peers, from their parents, and from other adults. It is impossible for them to act in a way that will appease all these pressures, and difficult for them to choose which one to yield to. They often feel that they must make important decisions without guidance because there seems to be no experienced person who understands the situation. Older people who have encountered the same problems may appear unsympathetic because these problems are no longer urgent for them; in addition, they may not remember their own feelings or solutions clearly.

The preoccupations of adolescence, like those of adulthood, reflect the current social and economic situation. As the world changes more rapidly, young people face dilemmas that older people may never have known. For example, a generation that grew up in a time of economic depression faced different problems from one that reached adulthood during a period of prosperity. It is naturally difficult for the first generation to comprehend the concerns of the second and vice versa. Inevitable misunderstandings result in the so-called *generation gap*, a product of imperfect memories, the accidents of experience, and perhaps a little envy as well.

POST-ADOLESCENCE AND YOUTH

There is no clear psychological or chronological ending to adolescence. Traditionally, it is said to be over around the time of graduation from high school, at about eighteen. However, by no means all people have solved the social and sexual problems of their essentially new adult life by the age of eighteen, although some have.

Leaving high school, either by graduating or dropping out, has certain social, economic, and personal effects. One may follow several courses: one may stay in the same town or move away; stay with one's family or move out; go to college, or get a job, or just "hang out"; get married or stay single. In any case, the bulk of one's time and energy is no longer taken up by enforced schooling and must be devoted to something else. One must assume responsibility for oneself (and sometimes for a spouse) to a greater degree than ever before.

The need to achieve a balanced and satisfying sex life and identity, which has been stressed as a primary concern during this period, is usually dwarfed by the need to find a direction for one's life, to determine its values and its goals, and to discover the means for attaining those goals. Those problems of adolescence that have not been solved become more urgent because the person is now more or less "on his own." Post-adolescent development begins when the person takes the initiative in solving these problems.

In the prosperous sectors of modern society, adolescence is sometimes followed by a period that Kenneth Keniston has called *youth*. It constitutes an extension of what Erikson has called "adolescence" and functions as a transtition between adolescence and adulthood. The duration of youth varies from individual to individual—it may be as long as ten years for a person who enters college and graduate school, or moderately short or nonexistent for the person who is committed immediately and wholeheartedly to training for a career or job. For those who immediately and *seriously* assume financial and marital responsibilities, the attitudes and responsibilities of adulthood follow directly upon adolescence.

ADULTHOOD

Adulthood may be said to begin with full commitment to a career or to marriage and a family or both. The birth of a child means that the individual has become a parent (the reverse of being a child), graduation from school or college changes his status from that of student to graduate and prospective employee, and promotions in a career may eventually change a person from employee to employer.

Descriptions of the ideal, well-adjusted, *mature personality* differ in point of view and emphasis, but they nearly all agree on the following characteristics advanced by Gordon W. Allport. The truly mature man or woman is capable of both loving and being loved, of working to benefit others as well as self, of being truly a participant in human affairs rather than withdrawn and isolated, of both commitment to living and its goals as well as renunciation of unrealistic goals and earlier dreams. Such a person, in short, gains satisfaction from his or her position in the world, while still realistically working for self-improvement as well as for improvement of the world. Few people fully meet this ideal, but many do approach it.

Personal crises continue to arise as adult lives unfold. One important source of such crises in the contemporary world is the institution of marriage. As husbands and wives grow older, they may change in different ways and at different speeds. It is not really strange that differences develop between people over the course of ten or twenty years or more—what is amazing is the numbers of couples for whom shared experiences make life together interesting and satisfying enough to more than compensate for their inevitable differences.

Sometime between the ages of thirty-five and fifty-five nearly everyone's life changes, abruptly or gradually, for better or worse. One of the forces responsible for negative change appears to be dissatisfaction with whatever particular life-style has been achieved. If people are successful in their work, they feel they should have become more successful. It they have not been successful, they may feel it is too late to become so. They may wish to enter a different profession, obtain greater power and

responsibility, switch from a private career to public service, or vice versa. Women who have been successful as mothers and/or housekeepers often find that their children's growing up has left them with nothing to do. Menopause usually occurs during or shortly after this age-range and may add a sense of inadequacy to the feelings of futility. Often, they redirect their energy toward a useful career, community work, or some other definite activity outside the home. The motive for such changes in both sexes is not necessarily money nor is it usually escape from any particular circumstance. It is rather a general conviction that there should be *more* to life than is being experienced.

During this period, people may let go of cherished dreams that they have carefully nurtured and cultivated for years. A scientist may admit that his personal contribution to his field will never be as remarkable as he had hoped. A family man may discover that, no matter how much he saves or how hard and long he works, he will never have enough money for the kind of life he had hoped to provide for his family. In such circumstances, people must base new goals on a realistic appraisal of what is possible. The period of crisis and reappraisal may take only a short time or it may be spread out over a number of years.

Not everyone, however, is able to make such an adjustment. Goals may be reluctantly, even angrily, abandoned, and nothing may take their place but unproductive and bitter resignation. We might say that such people stop developing.

AGING

For many people, two major concerns of old age are a threatened loss of sexual activity and an end to productive work. The former is physiologically based and the latter socially and economically based, but both have psychological effects. Women at the age of

Figure 19.7
Born in Russia well over a century ago, Shirin Gasanov (*left*) still takes an interest in the vineyards near his home. [TASS from Sovfoto.]

Figure 19.8
This German woman, who is picking hops on a farm near Gosselthausen, has taken part in nearly fifty harvests. [UPI Photo]

menopause no longer have the ability to bear children; men at that age may encounter difficulty in maintaining their previous sexual performance. Both sexes are subject to the physical and hormonal changes of aging. Those who are working may no longer be allowed to work for wages; thus, many lose an activity that has structured their days for forty or fifty years. Women who have made a career out of motherhood face the equivalent of early retirement when their children leave home. Many older people are thus threatened by idleness, illness, depression, self-doubt, and often, economic hardship. (But see Figures 19.7 and 19.8.)

As their friends age and die and their own physical condition deteriorates, the elderly are forced to recognize that their own lives are nearing an end. There are, of course, great differences in the ways elderly people react to these changes in their lives, depending on a host of psychological, social, and economic variables. According to Erikson, very well-adjusted people will develop a sense of "being ready not to be" during this period.

Finding a commitment and a role is not easy for the aged in our culture (Figure 19.9). In less "advanced" cultures, where several generations live together on the same ground and in the same house, there is work for the aged to do. They quietly slide into the responsibilities of being grandparents, which absorbs their time and energies. But that is not very common now, at least not in America. Life styles have changed so radically and rapidly over the last half-century or so that each generation tends to live in its own separate world. Like everyone else, the aged dislike being a burden and being useless, and they seek reassurance that they are neither. In our culture today, that reassurance often is not forthcoming.

Figure 19.9
The sounds of the city,
Sifting through the trees,
Settle like dust
On the shoulders
Of the old friends.

Can you imagine us
Years from today,
Sharing a park bench quietly?"

[Lyrics from "Old Friends" by Simon and Garfunkel. ©
1968 Paul Simon. Reprinted by permission of the
publisher.]

Suggested Readings

Allport, G. W. (1961) *Pattern and growth in personality.*
New York: Holt, Rinehart and Winston. [The
ideal mature personality as well as the normal
adult is discussed; for a discussion of maturity,
see pages 275ff.]

Bandura, A., & Walters, R. H. (1963) *Social learning
and personality development.* New York: Holt,
Rinehart and Winston. [The learning view of
social development.]

English, O. S., & Pearson, G. H. J. (1945) *Emotional
problems of living: Avoiding the neurotic pattern.*
New York: Norton. [A slightly different perspective.]

Erikson, E. H., ed. (1963) *The challenge of youth.* New
York: Anchor. [Describes several aspects of this
period, and contains Keniston's approach.]

Erikson, E. H. ed. (1964) *Childhood and society.* (2nd
ed.) New York: Norton. [Erikson's ideas provide
the framework for this chapter.]

Erikson, E. H. (1968) *Identity, youth, and crises.* New
York: Norton. [Erikson's views on identity and
youth.]

White, R. W. (1952) *Lives in progress.* New York:
Dryden. [Especially good on normal adulthood.]

White, R. W. (1964) *The abnormal personality.* (3rd ed.)
New York: Ronald. [See Chapters 3 and 4 in
particular.]

UNIT SEVEN

Social Psychology

As social beings, we humans depend on each other. As children, we need parental care and guidance. As adults, we are largely dependent on other people for the fulfillment of both our basic needs and our more complex motives. Especially in modern society, our peace and prosperity depend in some measure on other people throughout the country, and even the world—who may seem terribly remote from us. In fact, however, the world may be a somewhat smaller place than we generally imagine.

Consider the following problem: of the total American population, two people are selected at random, and one (the starting person) is to communicate a message to the other (the "target" person) via a chain of person-to-person communications. How many additional people will be required to relay the message if each person in the chain can contact only one other person, who is known to him on a first-name basis? For example, how many intermediaries would be required if a Kansas wheat farmer was to contact the wife of a divinity student in Cambridge, Massachusetts? Many people would estimate that as many as a hundred intermediaries would be required. However, when Dr. Stanley Milgram performed this "small world experiment" in 1968, he found that many fewer intermediaries were needed. Indeed, an average of only five intermediaries is typically required in experiments such as this, and the range is two to ten. For example, the link between the Kansas wheat farmer and the divinity student's wife was accomplished by only two intermediaries: the farmer sent the message to a local minister who in turn sent it to a minister who taught in Cambridge. The Cambridge minister happened to know the target person.

But simply because we are accessible to communication from even seemingly distant sources, it does not follow that we generally treat our fellow man in a neighborly fashion. The inhumane attitudes that often prevail are apparent in our daily experience as well as in newspaper and television reports. Some of the material we will be discussing in this unit forcibly illustrates such attitudes. In particular, experimental research on obedience has shown that the typical subject will comply with an experimenter's demands even to the point of administering what he thinks are extremely painful, and perhaps even lethal, electric shocks to a helpless experimental subject. And what is the likelihood that the typical person will phone for help if a stranger is, for example, undergoing an epileptic seizure? It has been shown that under many circumstances a large majority of people will *not* call for help. Although the observations and findings on obedience and on concern for others are disturbing, we must acknowledge their existence before we can decide on how to build a more humane and friendly world.

If interpersonal relations between strangers having no particular antagonisms toward each other are often callous and inhumane, consider how much worse the situation becomes when members of "lower-caste" groups are involved. Fortunately, studies in the psychology of prejudice have shown that large gains have been and are being made in the reduction of such prejudice. In the study of prejudice too, the first step is to acknowledge the magnitude and scope of the problem. For example, in the 1940s Kenneth and Mamie Clark showed that by the ages of three and four many black children were already convinced that being white was better than being black. This distressing finding was revealed in the way the children played with dolls: black children felt that white dolls were superior to black ones. The effect on self-esteem that this study points to is at least as important a consequence of prejudice as are more obvious forms of discrimination and violence that have been directed at blacks. More recent studies have found a similar lack of self-esteem among women. Phillip Goldberg gave college women several articles and asked them to evaluate the scholarly merit of the articles. Identical articles were attributed to male authors for some experimental subjects and to female authors for other experimental subjects. Regardless of the topics of the articles (which included some on which women commonly might be presumed to have expertise), the articles were judged to be more competently written and to have more scholarly merit when they were attributed to male authors. In other words, college women, like the young black children in the Clarks' study, had learned to believe that they were inferior. Thus does prejudice and discrimination breed further prejudice and discrimination.

But what are the original causes of prejudice? There are several, and we shall discuss the important ones in Chapter 22. In this introduction, it is sufficient to point out that competition and conflict often lead to prejudice. Muzafer Sherif and his colleagues were able to produce prejudice experimentally by taking a random selection of people, dividing them into two distinguishable groups, and placing the two groups in competition: each of a number of normally adjusted twelve-year old boys was assigned to one of two groups, "The Eagles" and "The Rattlers." Cooperation was stressed *within* each group by assigning each to various group activities such as constructing recreational facilities and preparing camp parties; conflict was created between groups by pitting them against one another in various competitive activities in which prizes were awarded to the winning group. Though the competitions began in a spirit of camaraderie and sportsmanship, these feelings soon disintegrated. Instead, the members of each group began to call their rivals names (such as "stinkers" and "cheaters"), developed low opinions of them, and maintained very few intergroup friendships. How could this situation be reversed? Sherif found that the elimination of competitive games and the institution of large amounts of intergroup social contact were *not* sufficient to eliminate the intergroup hostility. The hostility was successfully eliminated only when the two groups were forced by circumstance to cooperate for a common goal. For example, in one incident, the boys were required to pull a truck to get it started. They all pulled together (with the same rope they had used earlier in a fiercely competitive tug of war), and the truck was started. After a few such incidents (arranged by the experimenters), hostilities had ended and intergroup ratings and friendships had increased. Experiments such as these, which induce and eliminate prejudice, help us to understand the nature of prejudice and the ways in which it can be reduced.

In this unit, we are concerned with people as social beings, and we shall investigate their relations with other people in groups. In Chapter 20, we shall discuss the human dyad (two-person relationship), and examine the major dyads in life, how impressions of others are formed, and the bases for interpersonal attraction, including romantic love and sexual behavior. In Chapter 21, we shall discuss the important influences that groups of individuals have on our behavior, and we shall present some important studies of conformity and obedience. Intergroup relations are discussed in Chapter 22. Finally, we shall investigate the ways in which our attitudes and opinions are formed and modified in Chapter 23.

CHAPTER TWENTY

Interpersonal Relations: Impression Formation, Love, and Sex

Perhaps our most important social interactions are those between just two people. The term *human dyad* is used to describe two individuals engaged in such a one-to-one relationship. Some of the most significant dyads are those formed with a parent, a sibling, a lover, a child, a friend, or a spouse. Other important human dyads are those formed with a teacher—particularly in early adolescence and again in graduate school—a peer, a neighbor, a close relative, a doctor, a lawyer, a pastor, and even an enemy.

The human dyad as well as the relationships among more than two people are profoundly affected by the roles and the status of the members. First, the role someone is expected to play in a particular human relationship will dictate his or her performance to a large extent: indeed, different people engaged in similar roles will adopt similar modes of behavior. Conversely, one person acting in two separate roles may behave very differently in each role. Also, the status of a person may affect that person's performance of the roles. For example, if two physicians are interacting and one is far more eminent than the other, the behavior of the less eminent physician is likely to be somewhat deferential, perhaps more like that of a medical student than a doctor.

Different relationships are created to fulfill various functions or tasks. When the task becomes obsolete, the relationship is likely to end unless it has come to fulfill other functions as well. Thus the dyad formed by two neighbors is likely to terminate when one neighbor moves—unless, of course, it has served important subordinate functions, such as those of strong friendship or continuing business ventures. Since each of us is a member of many dyads and other relationships, and since many relationships (particularly certain dyads) require much of our time, effort, and attention, a particular one will survive only if its function is sufficiently important.

In this chapter, we shall discuss (1) various types of interpersonal relationships, (2) some of the factors that cause a relationship to exist, and (3) various factors that influence the type, quality, intensity, and durability of a particular relationship.

IMPRESSION FORMATION

The way we respond to incoming information about other people is one basis on which we form impressions of them. We shall now discuss some of the factors that are known to influence impression formation, such as the initial communication, both voluntary and involuntary, emitted by the other person, our perceptual set, our own values and *self-impressions*, and the order of incoming information. We shall also discuss the important contributions that *attribution theory* and *social-comparison theory* have made to our knowledge of how impressions are formed.

Forms of Communication   When interacting with another person, one picks up information from his or her verbal behavior and from other voluntary expressions (smiles and gestures), as well as from apparently involuntary nonverbal sources of communication—perspiration, posture, eye movements, some facial expressions, and some nonverbal aspects of speech (such as its smoothness, pitch, and speed). For example, rapid speech is often attributed to excitement and anxiety, and slow speech to depression. Since others often try to make the best impression possible on us, their voluntary behavioral communications sometimes may be less trustworthy than their involuntary ones. Therefore, in forming our initial impressions of others, we tend to take note of nonverbal, involuntary communication as much as verbal and other voluntary behavior.

Set   Our preconceptions and predispositions have a major effect on both our learning and our perception. Thus it is not surprising that our prior beliefs or sets crucially influence the impressions we form. If we are predisposed to have positive impressions about an individual before meeting him, we are more likely to react favorably than we would if we had no personal preconception of that individual. Also, our own favorable response may in turn cause the individual to respond more favorably to us than he otherwise would have.

In one study, after teachers were given false IQ scores for some of their students, the students whose scores had been raised actually did better on sub-

sequent IQ tests than students whose scores had been lowered (but who in reality had the same initial IQ as the others). This study not only shows that *set* can influence impression formation and that impressions in turn can influence the behavior of the person being judged but also underscores the importance of nonverbal communication. The teachers' initial impressions of the students were formed not from the student's own behavior but from information provided about each student by other sources. Presumably, from that time on, the teachers' own differential behavior toward the "high IQ" and "low IQ" students affected the students' subsequent performance. This interaction between impressions and behavior may have more profound, far-reaching effects because of the so-called "halo effect": that is, our rating of a person on a particular characteristic is likely to be influenced by our assessment of another characteristic or by our general impression of that person. In fact, once we form a *personal stereotype* of a particular individual, we are likely to interpret his future behavior in ways that are consistent with the stereotype, just as we often categorize people belonging to certain social or ethnic groups in accordance with social stereotypes that we hold for all members of that group.

Effects of Values and Emotions   To some extent, the impressions that we form of other people are in keeping with our self-image. For example, if one tends to place his own interests ahead of everyone else's to the point at which he lies and cheats, he is more inclined to impute similar conniving motives and behavior to others. Similarly, the happy-go-lucky, self-satisfied person may attribute similar traits to those he likes, since he will assume that they too are among the salt of the earth. If, for example, you value masculinity highly, you are more likely to attribute this quality to men you like or admire than to those you do not.

A person's emotional state can also influence the impressions he forms of others, as was demonstrated in the following experiment. Subjects were made to feel apprehensive by the administration of several electric shocks to them. When subsequently asked to judge a series of photographs of other people, the subjects were more inclined to attribute frightening and aggressive tendencies to the photographed individuals than they were before the shocks.

Attribution Theory   *Attribution theory* is concerned with the relation between impression formation and the source—either internal or external— to which we attribute an individual's behavior. The theory applies both to self-attribution (the ways in which we interpret our own actions and internal states) and to attributions about others (our judgments about a person, based upon our inferences of what is causing his behavior). If, for example, we attribute a person's advancement in a corporation to the fact that his father is president, the opinion we form of that person's intelligence and industry may be lower than it would be if he were a product of the slums (Figure 20.1).

An important series of studies by Stanley Schachter and J. E. Singer (discussed in Chapter 7) has demonstrated that our own emotional reactions may crucially depend upon the availability of external determinants to which we can attribute our reactions. In one study, several groups of healthy student subjects were administered a set dose of adrenalin (epinephrine) and were then joined by another "subject" who was actually the experimenter's confederate or stooge. In some groups, the stooge would act in a jovial high-spirited way in an effort to convey a mood of general euphoria to the group. Other groups would be joined by another type of stooge, who would be surly and disagreeable. Some of the subjects were informed that they had received adrenalin

FOLLOWS FATHER'S FOOTSTEPS

23-YEAR-OLD ELECTED TO BOARD OF DIRECTORS

AP (III) YORK

Figure 20.1
If we attribute this person's success more to favoritism than to ability, we are likely to downgrade his ability.

and that they would experience side effects of physiological arousal (as evidenced, for example, by tremors and palpitations). Other were deliberately misinformed about what they had been given, and were told to expect aching and numbness in parts of their bodies. Still others were told nothing about the expected effects of the drug. All of subjects were exposed, therefore, to identical doses of the same drug and to the same kinds of external experience (although some subjects of each group were exposed to one type of stooge, and the rest to the other type of stooge). Schachter and Singer found that the responses of the misinformed subjects—both their actions, observed through a one-way mirror, and their moods, reflected in the questionnaires they answered—corresponded more to the stooge's behavior than did those of the correctly informed subjects. The correctly informed subjects could attribute their internal feelings to administration of the drug and were less affected by the stooge's behavior. However, the misinformed subjects could attribute their internal feelings only to the stooge's behavior and were therefore strongly influenced by it. (The uninformed group fell somewhere in between.) These studies, then, illustrate the fact that our emotional responses can be modulated by their inferred external determinants.

In general, the more easily we can attribute a person's actions to external causes, the less inclined we are to base our inferences about his typical behavior or personality on those actions. Thus the more unconstrained a person's behavior seems to be—that is, the less it seems to be generated by external motives or a role he is obliged to play—the more his choice of actions will determine an observer's inferences about his true nature. For example, we make few character judgments about the salesman whose conduct toward a potential customer is warm, good-natured, and solicitous: he is constrained by his occupation to behave that way. But we will be much more inclined to attribute genuine qualities of warmth and concern for others to him if we see him behave in a like manner to his assistant.

Although the foregoing description of attribution theory is quite simple, in practice it can be much more subtle. In an important study by Edward Jones, subjects observed students taking an IQ test. The students' performance was manipulated so that one group of subjects did extremely well at the onset,

but then their performance deteriorated, whereas just the opposite pattern was displayed by a second group. A third group performed at an intermediate level throughout. Subjects were most impressed by the students from the group that started out well. They attributed high performance in the early stage to the students' basic intelligence, and the subsequent decline in performance to the unchallenging nature of the task. The students who started slowly were viewed as people of less intelligence, for whom practice and hard work were required to improve their scores. This study has at least two important implications (1) mental ability is commonly seen as an enduring, internal trait, whereas motivation is commonly seen as transitory and external (the competent students "grew bored" while the less competent "began to feel challenged"); (2) the early performance of the students had a profound influence upon the ultimate impression formed, suggesting that primacy is more important than recency in impression formation. As we shall see, however, recency is sometimes more important than primacy.

Primacy and Recency Effects　Primacy effects in impression formation were first reported by Solomon Asch in 1946. He read subjects a list of adjectives—such as "intelligent," "industrious," "envious," and "stubborn"—that were supposedly traits of an unknown person. He presented the list in one order to half of the subjects, and reversed the order for the other half. Although all subjects received the same list, subjects who heard the positive attributes first developed the more favorable impression of the person being judged. In a later experiment, A. S. Luchins read subjects two paragraphs describing the activities of a person called "Jim." The activities reported in one paragraph were those of an extrovert whereas the activities in the second paragraph were those of an introvert. Half of the subjects read the paragraphs in one order; the other half read them in the reverse order. Again, in assessing Jim's personality, subjects were most influenced by the paragraph they read first. Luchins attributed this effect to the set produced by the initial information.

More recent work by Norman Anderson and his associates is compatible with Luchins' interpretation. Anderson has shown that the primacy effect occurs because subjects assign progressively less weight to each successive piece of information in serial presentations, apparently because they discount material that is not consistent with prior information. Anderson has demonstrated that the final impression may be described by averaging the favorableness of each of the cues in the serial list. In his averaging (or "information integration") hypothesis, Anderson accounts for the primacy effect by making the assumption that early information is weighted more heavily before being averaged with later information. The model predicts that a subsequently presented favorable piece of information will enhance a favorable impression only when the bit of information is *more* favorable than the average of the preceding information. Anderson's model is consistent with most (but not all) data in the vast area of impression formation.

Recency effects can also be significant in the forming of an impression. There are two ways to produce a recency effect readily. One way is to tax recall by requiring the subjects to engage in an intervening activity before they make their judgments. Since recently presented items are more easily recalled than previously presented items (see Chapter 2), interference with recall will tend to cause the earlier items to fade more completely from memory, thereby enhancing the recency effect. A second way of producing a recency effect is to structure the task so that the later items appear to have more validity

than the earlier ones. This may be done, for example, by giving the impression that the information being judged is more intimate or is coming from a more relaxed, unguarded informant as the task progresses.

Social Comparison   In the *social-comparison theory*, originally developed by Leon Festinger, it is noted that in order to evaluate information one must be able to assess it against appropriate comparison information. Although social-comparison theory applies to all of our beliefs about the world, including impression formation, it is most relevant to an assessment of ourselves, our own beliefs and emotions, and our own abilities and achievements. A man assesses his ability to play tennis, for example, not so much by an absolute standard, but by comparing his performance to that of his peers. For example, a good recreational tennis player may be one of the best in, say, his college class, but if he watches any of the nationally ranked tennis players on television, he may realize that he is a poor player indeed in comparison with them. In other areas of endeavor, however, the situation is much more unstructured, and one may be able to assess one's abilities only with reference to one's own particular comparison group. Thus many an outstanding student in high school goes on to a prestigious college only to find that he or she is at best an average student there.

In forming an impression of someone, we often do not evaluate the person in an absolute sense. Instead, we compare him or her to others we have known. Here too the ratings can be dramatically influenced by the comparison group we are using. For example, we may use a different standard for judging the intelligence of members of an academic community than we do for assessing that of assembly-line workers. A college dropout who takes a routine job in an assembly line, for example, may appear outstandingly intellectual when compared with the other workers.

Social-comparison theory is also important in the evaluation and expression of emotion. Its significance has been demonstrated by Schachter in an ingenious experiment on the relation between fear and the need for affiliation, which we shall discuss in the following section.

INTERPERSONAL ATTRACTION

What attracts us to others? We shall first look at some of the reasons why we are attracted to other people in general. Next we shall review some of the more important determinants of attraction to a particular individual. Finally, we shall conclude with a discussion of love and sex.

THE NEED FOR AFFILIATION

From birth, human beings require contact with other humans. Infants depend on adults for the satisfaction of hunger and thirst, and for warmth and protection. In addition, a child learns that others are in a position to provide it with information and rewards. In the course of these early experiences, people develop a sense of their dependency upon other people.

If contact, or affiliation, satisfies emotional needs—as we are suggesting—then it is possible that interpersonal contact becomes even more important to us if we experience strong emotions such as fear and anxiety, since these emotions may be presumed to increase our emotional dependency. Schachter tested this hypothesis on two groups of college coeds—a high-anxiety group and a control group. The high-anxiety subjects had been led to believe they would receive severe electric shocks while taking part in an experiment. All subjects were then asked whether they preferred to wait for the onset of the experiment in a room with other subjects, or alone. A clear difference emerged between members of the two groups: more of the high-anxiety subjects preferred to wait with others. This result not only supports the view that affiliative behavior, or the need for interpersonal contact, is enhanced by anxiety-arousing situations, but it is also consistent with Festinger's social-comparison theory (discussed above) in the following sense: in states of extreme anxiety, people look toward others to help interpret their emotional feelings; they are confused and would like to compare their tentative anxious feelings with the behaviors shown by others in the same situation. Anxious and uncertain, they look for guidelines in the behavior of their associates.

The Schachter-Festinger view implies, however, that not just *any* human contact will suffice. In order to provide adequate social comparison, the human companions must be sharing similar experiences; if they are not, their behavior does not provide the subject with relevant guidelines. Schachter confirmed this general stipulation in a subsequent experiment: whereas subjects preferred to affiliate with other subjects in the same situation (who could therefore provide them with a basis for social comparison), they were less willing to affiliate with subjects who were waiting in the same room but for an unrelated reason—that of consulting their faculty advisors.

Harold Gerard further illuminated the tendency to seek social comparison in stressful situations. He subjected two groups to an anxiety-arousing procedure and gave subjects in one group a clear idea of what they would supposedly feel. This group showed a much lower tendency to seek affiliation, suggesting that uncertainty creates a greater need for social comparison and, hence, for appropriate affiliation.

All of these studies suggest that individuals seek to affiliate with people with whom they can identify—particularly in ambiguous situations—partly because the behavior of others can be used as a standard against which one can assess his own abilities, achievements, and emotional reactions.

INGRATIATION

We have seen that people have a basic need, perhaps originating in infancy, to affiliate with others, especially in times of uncertainty and stress. But there are additional rewards for associating with others. In fact, most of our everyday rewards are administered by others, not only the material items such as food and clothing but also more intangible benefits like affection and companionship. Indeed, many of us attempt to maximize the benefits that can accrue from interpersonal interactions by manipulating others. One of the most common ways of doing so is *ingratiation* or the attempt to flatter and please those in a position to reward us. Edward Jones has studied the circumstances under which ingratiation succeeds and those under which it fails. His work—and that of others, most notably Elliot Aronson—has demonstrated the following general principles: (1) we tend to like people who praise us, but most of this effect is negated when we sense that we are being manipulated, that is, when we realize that the praiser has an ulterior motive; (2) individuals tend to like people who do them favors; and (3) our appreciation for those who perform favors for us extends even to those who do so unintentionally.

Aronson has maintained that, although certain rewards are basic to life itself and, in a given situation, are totally gratifying to the receiver—such as food to the man who is starving or a rescue launch to one who is drowning—many others, such as those sought by means of ingratiation, vary in effectiveness with numerous subtle situational variables. When someone's life does not depend on receipt of particular "favors," he is more selective in his assessment of them and in the way in which he responds (favorably or negatively) to their source.

THE DETERMINANTS OF LIKING

Interpersonal attraction depends upon more than affiliative needs and ingratiation. We shall now review some of the reasons people have for liking a particular individual.

Similarity People tend to like people who have interests, values, and opinions that are similar to their own. In part, this response may be due to *social validation* of one's own characteristics; people who agree with us tend to reassure us that our beliefs and values are sensible. In Ira Levin's novel *A Kiss Before Dying*, the villain's courtship of the cautious copper heiress is facilitated by his previously acquired knowledge of her likes and dislikes. When he casually mentions that his favorite artist is Charles Demuth she is visibly impressed. Since Demuth is *her* favorite artist, and since few others have even heard of Demuth, she feels he must be an unusually sensitive and intelligent young man, worthy of her attention.

Similarity is also important for the potentially rewarding function of friendship. People who share *our views* are more inclined to respect and like *us*, and such attitudes on the part of someone else toward us have been shown to be the most important single determinant of our own responses to that person. If, then, we tend to like people who are similar to us, is there any truth to the old adage that "opposites attract"? The answer is "yes, sometimes." Two individuals with opposite characteristics tend to attract each other if they have complementary needs that can be mutually satisfied by friendship. For example, a domineering person may get along very well with one who is submissive.

Mutual Admiration As a rule, we like people who seem to like us. Elaine Walster demonstrated this maxim nicely in a study on college women in 1965. While each subject was in a waiting room, she was confronted by a good-looking, charming young man who was in reality a confederate of the experimenter. He talked to her, told her that he liked her, and then asked her for a date. In the experiment itself, the subject was asked to read a personality assessment of herself. Some subjects received a positive assessment, others a negative one. At the end of the experiment the subject was asked to rate a number of people she knew. On the pretext that there was one space remaining at the bottom of the rating sheet, the experimenter asked her to rate the fellow in the waiting room. The important finding is that when a subject's self-esteem had been bruised by reading the negative personality evaluation, her positive feelings for the young man were greatly enhanced. Walster's work shows that admiration from others, generally a powerful determinant of our liking, is particularly important when we are feeling insecure.

However, the generalization that we like people who like us is modified by several complexities. In the first place, individuals are more impressed by someone who likes them but who also hold opinions that are different from theirs. Apparently most of us rationalize that, since the other person obviously doesn't like us for our opinions, he must like us "for ourselves alone." Another variation, demonstrated by Aronson, is that we generally value a person's favorable opinion more if that person has previously held us in low esteem than we do if he has held us in high esteem all along. It may be that we have really "earned" the respect of someone who has disliked us at first but learned to admire us, whereas we "take for granted" those who like us from the start. Despite these complexities, however, the rule that we like people who seem to like us is

generally applicable. It follows, therefore, that if you would like someone else to like you, you should make it clear that you like that person.

Proximity In a classic experiment reported in 1963, Festinger, Schachter, and Back showed that friendship patterns in a college dormitory varied with the proximity of the students' rooms to each other. Proximity facilitates liking for several reasons.

1. *Frequency.* Proximity increases the likelihood and frequency of interpersonal contact; it is known that familiarity breeds liking and *not* contempt. For example, subjects who met other people without interacting with them liked them better the more often they met. The mere sight of a stranger's photograph a number of times is sufficient to enhance liking.

2. *Availability.* People who live in close proximity are more readily available for interpersonal contact. To the extent that such contact is rewarding (as suggested by the affiliation studies), mutual attraction should develop beyond the mere effects of frequency.

3. *Similarity.* In more extensive living areas than a dormitory—say, in the neighborhoods of a town or city—those living in proximity to one another are likely to be of similar socioeconomic status. Since people from similar status groups tend to have more in common than those from dissimilar groups, interpersonal attraction may be facilitated.

Cooperation People who engage in cooperative behavior tend to develop mutual liking, even if the cooperation is dictated by an external situation such as military combat, a natural disaster requiring a rescue operation, or a class assignment requiring two students to work together. Even anticipated joint effort facilitates liking.

Physical Attractiveness   Other things being equal, we like people we find physically attractive more than those we find physically unattractive. For example, subjects who examine people in photographs and then rate their personalities tend to give higher ratings to people whom they see as physically attractive.

Competence   The more competent a person is, the more we tend to like him. However, we also prefer the competent people we like and admire to be fallible as well. Thus Aronson showed that the person with superior ability who commits a blunder (for example, spilling a cup of coffee) may be liked more than a person with the same superior ability who does not commit a blunder. This fact may help explain why some respected public figures see their popularity rise after they have committed a miscalculation. For example, President Kennedy's popularity ratings soared after the Bay of Pigs episode in 1961. On the other hand, people of average competence are downgraded if they commit similar blunders. When a person of average ability commits a blunder, we tend to treat it as further indication that he is not especially competent.

LOVE AND SEX

What is love? Too complex and varied an emotion to be defined precisely, it has many variations, most of which we experience at some stage of our lives. Futhermore, in order to answer such a question even partially, it is necessary to deal with such aspects of love as the emotional sensations it evokes, its causes, its physiological and behavioral manifestations, and the functions it serves.

Harry Harlow, in his work with primates, has shown that monkeys experience at least five "affectional systems," including mother love, infant love, peer love, heterosexual love, and paternal love (see Chapter 7). The types of love experienced by these primates appear to resemble closely those that humans experience. Most of us remember the love we felt as children for our mothers (infant love). Those of us who are parents can attest to the reality of maternal or paternal love. Most of us have also experienced strong affection for close friends and relatives (peer love). Finally, many of us have experienced romantic love (roughly corresponding to what Harlow has identified in monkeys as heterosexual love). We also speak of various kinds of love for ideas or objects, for example, love of God, country, nature, and so on.

The extent to which the emotions and physical manifestations of the different forms of love resemble each other or vary is subject to question. However, it is known that the various forms are often determined by very diverse histories of conditioning. Maternal love, for example, clearly depends much less upon a woman's history of rewarding experiences and much more on hormonal changes and stereotyped behavior patterns than do friendship or brotherly love.

Which form of love is strongest? This question, too, is impossible to answer fully. It has been shown that maternal love is a powerful motivating force—apparently stronger than hunger, thirst, or sex, at least in rats (see Chapter 5). But if we were to assess the different forms of love, we would need an objective behavioral criterion with which each could be measured. One criterion that has been suggested is time spent with a loved one. But this criterion would be misleading in many situations. For example, a girl may want to spend much more time with a friend, who shares many common interests, than with her mother, but this does not necessarily mean she feels more love for the friend than for her mother.

Psychologists have traditionally exhibited little interest in the study of love. Indeed until very recently the empirical generalizations that could be made about this area of emotion were few. Yet, in contemporary Western culture, the link between love and the important dyad of marriage is extremely significant. We know that a person is more likely to fall in love with and to marry a partner who has a similar background and interests, who is attractive, and, most importantly, who rewards the lover by providing affection, companionship, and a feeling of being accepted. In other words, the determinants of love are quite similar to the determinants of interpersonal attraction, discussed in the preceding section. In this section, we shall describe some interesting experimental work that has been done recently on the psychology of romantic love; then we shall consider certain recent findings on the related topic of sexual behavior, many of which disprove many longstanding popular misconceptions.

Romantic Love Probably the most thorough psychological study of romantic love is that by Zick Rubin. Rubin's work originated with the assumption that love can be treated as one person's attitude toward another person. Rubin restricted his study to the mutual love and liking that existed between 158 pairs at the University of Michigan. The strategy was to develop an attitude scale for love that would be distinct in content from a similar scale for liking. A large number of questionnaire items were devised to determine the respondent's attitude toward another person (whom we shall henceforth call the "target person"). Half of the items selected were based on speculations about love that had been proposed by numerous writers, including Sigmund Freud and Erich Fromm. As Rubin noted:

> These items referred to physical attraction, idealization, a predisposition to help, the desire to share emotions and experiences, feelings of exclusiveness and absorption, felt affiliative and dependent needs, the holding of ambivalent feelings, and the relative unimportance of universal-

istic norms in the relationship. The other half of the items were suggested by the existing theoretical and empirical literature on interpersonal attraction. . . . they included references to the desire to affiliate with the target in various settings, evaluation of the target on several dimensions, the salience of norms of responsibility and equity, feelings of respect and trust, and the perception that the target is similar to oneself.*

The items were then sorted into categories of love and liking by panels of student and faculty judges. Those items on which there was reasonable agreement about their appropriate category were next assembled into a questionnaire and administered to introductory psychology students who were asked to complete the items, first with reference to a boyfriend or girlfriend, and then with reference to a platonic friend who was a member of the opposite sex. After statistical analyses had been made of these responses, two distinct scales, one for romantic love and the other for platonic liking, were generated. The following three items are illustrative of the kinds of components contained in the love scale:

> **1.** *Affiliative and dependent need*—for example, "If I could never be with _____, I would feel miserable"; "It would be hard for me to get along without _____."
>
> **2.** *Predisposition to help*—for example, "If _____ were feeling badly, my first duty would be to cheer him (her) up"; "I would do almost anything for _____."
>
> **3.** *Exclusiveness and absorption*—for example, "I feel very possessive toward _____." "I feel that I can confide in _____ about virtually everything." *

*Zick Rubin, "Measurement of Romantic Love," *Journal of Personality and Social Psychology,* **16** (1970) 265–273.

The items on the love scale and on the liking scale are shown in Table 20.1.

Having contructed the scales, Rubin conducted two experiments. In the first, he administered a questionnaire containing both categories of items ("love" and "liking") to the 158 dating couples. He found that the love scores that each partner gave the other were virtually identical. Interestingly, there was more variation in the liking scores, the females generally giving their partners slightly higher scores than the males gave them. This sex difference was largely attributed to the higher ratings males received from females on "task-oriented" characteristics such as leadership potential and intelligence. The corresponding ratings females received from males were substantially lower. This discrepancy may reflect cultural attitudes on the desirability of task-oriented prowess in males as compared to females, at least within dating relationships. (If so, it should gradually disappear if a more egalitarian society continues to evolve). Another finding that was in accord with cultural stereotypes was the differences between males and females in the love scores they gave for same-sex friends. Females tended to love (but not like) their same-sex friends more than males did. In American society, manifestations of affection among females have always been generally regarded with more favor than equivalent displays of affection between males.

This questionnaire study revealed an additional finding of interest: whereas both males and females *loved* their dating partners much more than they loved their friends, the *liking* scores that they gave for their same-sex friends and for their dating partners were almost equivalent.

In his second experiment, Rubin tested the relationship between love and gazing (Figure 20.2). He reasoned that, since the love scale contained a major item on "exclusiveness and absorption," the more dating partners loved each other the more likely

Table 20.1
Love-Scale and Liking-Scale Items

Love-Scale Items
1. If _____ were feeling badly, my first duty would be to cheer him (her) up.
2. I feel that I can confide in _____ about virtually everything.
3. I find it easy to ignore _____'s faults.
4. I would do almost anything for _____.
5. I feel very possessive toward _____.
6. If I could never be with _____, I would feel miserable.
7. If I were lonely, my first thought would be to seek _____ out.
8. One of my primary concerns is _____'s welfare.
9. I would forgive _____ for practically anything.
10. I feel responsible for _____'s well-being.
11. When I am with _____, I spend a good deal of time just looking at him (her).
12. I would greatly enjoy being confided in by _____.
13. It would be hard for me to get along without _____.

Liking-Scale Items
1. When I am with _____, we are almost always in the same mood.
2. I think that _____ is unusually well-adjusted.
3. I would highly recommend _____ for a responsible job.
4. In my opinion, _____ is an exceptionally mature person.
5. I have great confidence in _____'s good judgment.
6. Most people would react very favorably to _____ after a brief acquaintance.
7. I think that _____ and I are quite similar to each other.
8. I would vote for _____ in a class or group election.
9. I think that _____ is one of those people who quickly wins respect.
10. I feel that _____ is an extremely intelligent person.
11. _____ is one of the most likable people I know.
12. _____ is the sort of person whom I myself would like to be.
13. It seems to me that it is very easy for _____ to gain admiration.

Source: Zick Rubin, "Measurement of romantic love."

Figure 20.2
The item "exclusiveness and absorption" on Rubin's scale correlated with the amount of observed mutual gazing in which young couples engaged.

they would be to gaze into each other's eyes in a reasonably unstructured laboratory situation. In order to test his assumption, he asked dating pairs to come to the laboratory for an experiment. Before the experiment each participating couple was observed for a brief period without their knowledge and their gazing behavior was measured. Rubin found, in those preliminary observations, that couples whose scores on the love scale had been above the median engaged in much more mutual gazing than couples who had scored below the median. The validity of the love scale—or at least of the item "exclusiveness and absorption"—appears to have been supported by the results of the questionnaires.

Moreover, these results were in turn successfully used to predict subjects' behavior in a laboratory setting.

Rubin's work shows that romantic love can, in some ways, be measured and quantified, and in a way that distinguishes it from liking or normal interpersonal attraction. Although this work has yielded some interesting generalizations, it is still merely a beginning, and many more investigations will be necessary before we begin to understand the huge psychological domain of romantic love. Another contribution has been made by Elaine Walster and her associates, who have undertaken an ambitious program investigating love. Whereas Rubin's work explored attitudes and behaviors associated with already existing love, Walster's has been concentrated more on factors influencing the growth of heterosexual attraction. One of her research projects has been an attempt to ascertain why men prefer the "hard-to-get" woman to more accessible women.

Walster and her associates began with the premise that there was some truth to the general assumption that a man prefers a woman who is "hard to get." In a variety of studies however, they found that there was little basis for this cliché. In one study, high school students were shown biographies and pictures of a teen-aged couple. Part of the information conveyed to the subjects about the couple was the extent of one member's interest in the other. Thus, depending on the particular set of materials about the dyad, one member might be described as having feelings of either indifference, dislike, or extreme liking for the other member. The subjects in the experiment were then asked to rate how likeable and how physically attractive they thought each member of the pair was. The hypothesis under test was: the less romantic interest the person expressed in his or her partner, the more socially desirable she or he would appear to the subjects. Instead, the opposite effect occurred: the more romantic interest expressed by the person, the more desirable she or he was judged to be. These—and other—findings support the adage, "All the world loves a lover."

The idea that men prefer a hard-to-get woman is probably founded on the assumption that such a woman, once "gotten," will boost the male's ego. But a fact that evidently has not been taken sufficiently into account is that, in the course of the chase, the male ego is likely to be in for quite a bruising. Indeed, it has been proposed that the supportive behavior of an affectionate, if more easily obtainable, partner is likely to compensate for (and perhaps outweigh) the potential ego benefits gained by successful pursuit of the elusive woman. If this is true, then, a most desirable woman would be one who was uninterested in other men but openly affectionate toward one, thus providing that one with a maximum "ego-boost." Thus, a woman who is highly selective is likely to be very appealing to the man that she does show affection for. Walster and her colleagues were in fact able to provide data demonstrating the attraction of such a "selectively elusive woman" in an experiment on computer dating. Male college students, not aware of the true purpose of the experiment, were given descriptions that prospective dates had provided about themselves. Each was also informed of the ratings that some of these women had given his own background information as well as the information on other prospective male dates. Some of the women's evaluations were uniformly unenthusiastic. Others were uniformly enthusiastic. Finally, each subject received the appraisals of a "selectively elusive women," who had rated him—but not the others—highly. Almost all of the subjects were most attracted to the selective woman and were most anxious to date her.

Although sexual attraction and sex itself are important in romantic love, they are not the only considerations. Similarly, love is not the only factor, not even a necessary one, in a satisfying sexual relationship. Nevertheless, love and sex are closely interrelated in many situations and consideration of the one therefore leads naturally to a consideration of the other.

Sex Kinsey's studies a quarter of a century ago were the beginnings of increased insight into the sexual mores of Americans. At the same time the vast publicity awarded Kinsey's works, *Sexual Behavior in the Human Male*, in 1948, and *Sexual Behavior in the Human Female*, in 1953, caused sex to become less unmentionable in the mass media. Progress toward a widespread enlightened understanding of human sexual behavior was greatly expedited by the publication of Masters and Johnson's research, entitled *Human Sexual Response*, in 1966. Whereas Kinsey's projects had been largely attempts to gather quantitative data on the nature and variety of sexual behavior, Masters and Johnson attempted to provide a precise description of the physiological changes that precede and accompany sexual orgasm. Their subjects performed a variety of sexual acts, which were measured, observed, and filmed by the experimenters. From an extensive collection of data, Masters and Johnson then exploded several of the myths that many people still hold as truths today. For example, they have shown conclusively that the size of the penis, which varies among normal males, is irrelevant to sexual effectiveness. It is also clear that the so-called "forty-year deadline"—the idea that one's sexual behavior is limited to the period between the teens and the fifties is inaccurate; indeed, it is possible for people to enjoy sex into their eighties and nineties.

The findings of Kinsey and Masters and Johnson, however, are not the only causes of the striking changes that have taken place in American attitudes toward sex. Other strong influences have been advanced techniques of contraception, the increased availability of contraceptive agents and devices, as well as changing economic and social conditions, exemplified by the drive for equal rights for women. The Victorian notion that "women do not enjoy sex" is declining, and women are freer to approach sexual relations with the same expectations of fulfillment as do men.

This new attitude has of course created some problems. If a "liberated" female has unrealistic expectations of her male sexual partner, he may be inhibited in much the same way as a female can be inhibited when a male has unrealistic expectations of her. Indeed, Masters and Johnson recently found that some 80 percent of the failures to reach orgasm during heterosexual relations in their laboratory were by males. The relative success of the females is a marked departure from what probably would have been observed a number of years ago, when the female orgasm was generally considered an "unexpected bonus" by those who did not appreciate the nature of female sexual arousal. Although it is probable that these results may be attributed at least in part to the clinical and unnatural atmosphere of a laboratory, they may also be indicative of an increasingly widespread emphasis on male sexual performance, which, in turn, has the unfortunate side-effect of generating anxiety in some males, leading to an apparent decline of interest in sex, and even to impotence. Such problems may be aggravated if the goal of intercourse is a stringent requirement to achieve "mutual," or simultaneous, orgasms. In other words, though mutual satisfaction is obviously a desirable goal, unreasonable demands from a woman can cause her partner to feel that he is engaged in a test of sexual skill every time he makes love to her, thus impairing his pleasure and eventually his initiative and ability (much as a man's haste

and lack of tenderness can prevent a woman from deriving pleasure, and can eventually cause frigidity).

It has been estimated that problems of sexual inadequacy exist in more than half of the marriages in the United States. Such problems are probably important factors in the majority of divorces. Recently, Masters and Johnson have been remarkably successful in treating many of these problems such as impotence, premature ejaculation, and frigidity. Although the success of treatment varies with different problems, the total percentage of cures is 80 percent.

The most important aspect of the Masters and Johnson treatment consists simply of putting the couple under treatment at ease. For example, they may be instructed not to try to have intercourse until they are given permission by the therapist—instead, they are requested first to caress each other, being careful to take turns so that each partner has a chance to receive as well as to give pleasure. Since the partners are explicitly forbidden to engage in sexual intercourse at this time, there cannot possibly be any anxieties about failing to perform on the part of either partner. In the course of several successive sessions, the caressing becomes increasingly more intimate until the desire for intercourse is intensified and anxieties about successful performance are greatly diminished. Only at that time is the couple given permission to engage in intercourse. The great success of the treatment not only speaks well for the method but also provides support for the assumption underlying the treatment: anxieties about performance are a major cause of sexual inadequacies.

The procedure employed in the Masters and Johnson treatment is similar to that of *systematic desensitization* in that one's emotional sensitivity to an imagined defect is gradually lessened (see also Chapters 3 and 32). Systematic desensitization has been used with remarkable success in the relief of many anxiety-related behavioral debilities including impotence. For impotence, the treatment is basically one of inducing the subject to relax at sex play and, consequently, to become more sexually responsive. By avoiding intercourse until he has a very strong desire to have it, he easily overcomes any fears concerning his performance.

Whether the treatment is that of Masters and Johnson or the closely related one of systematic desensitization, such therapy has proven its effectiveness in many situations. It may become increasingly important in guiding those with sexual problems to happier sexual relationships.

Let us now examine certain other important human relationships that do not center on love or sex. We shall consider next aggression and cooperation.

INTERPERSONAL AGGRESSION

From sibling rivalry to organized warfare, aggression is prevalent in human society. Perhaps no other issue in psychology has as many pressing social implications as aggression. What causes aggressive behavior, and why does it pervade almost every human activity?

There are those who maintain that aggressive behavior is the manifestation of a physiological drive, much like hunger or thirst; that a need to aggress must be satisfied periodically just as the needs for food or water must be satisfied. According to this view, the event that satisfies the aggressive drive is the suffering of injury or pain by the victim of the aggression. Perhaps the most familiar example of a drive or instinct theory of aggression is that proposed by Sigmund Freud. Freud considered the aggressive instinct, which he termed *Thanatos*, one of the two major motivating forces of human behavior. The other major force was, of course, the sexual

instinct, *Eros*. According to Freud, the most extreme manifestation of the aggressive instinct was the death wish, which he held to be present in everyone.

Apparently, at least some aggressive behavior can be due to physiological causes. The human brain (as well as that in many lower organisms) seems to contain neurophysiological mechanisms that, when stimulated, cause the person to attack. For example, one well-known brain surgery case is that of the young woman who was subject to fits of rage that had provoked her to commit attempted stabbings on several occasions. When she underwent brain surgery, one area of her brain was found to produce these aggressive behaviors, and after it was removed, her fits of rage disappeared. This evidence alone, however, does not warrant the classification of aggression as a basic physiological drive. In fact, to insist that the numerous and varied forms of human aggression all result from one drive alone would seem to be a gross oversimplification of the problem.

For a long time, the most frequently cited explanation of social aggression was the classical *frustration-aggression hypothesis* (see Chapter 7). Though recently criticized as an explanation of aggression, this approach has proved a useful conceptualization of aggression, in addition to stimulating a great deal of experimental work on the topic. Containing remnants of the Freudian theory of aggression, the hypothesis states that the major cause of aggression is frustration. In fact, in some analyses, frustration is even seen as a necessary condition for aggression. Frustration is usually defined as the blocking of some goal-directed activity. The more intense the original activity, the greater the frustration, and therefore, the greater the resulting aggression. For example, in one series of studies, children were placed in a room adjacent to a playroom filled with attractive toys. However, they were not allowed to go in and play

Figure 20.3
To what extent is aggression and violence perpetuated through imitation?

with the toys, but were instead forced by a barrier to stay in the adjacent room and merely look at the toys. When they were eventually allowed into the playroom, their play was much more destructive than that of a second group that had been given immediate access to the playroom. The frustrated group even smashed many of the toys, once they had gained access to them.

Examples of aggression in everyday life also support the frustration-aggression hypothesis. Aggression is more prevalent during periods of economic trouble, and the groups engaging in the most aggression are usually those undergoing the greatest hardships, as we shall see again in our discussion of prejudice (Chapter 22).

When the frustration–aggression hypothesis was initially suggested, the proposal that learning could have a very significant role in the maintenance of aggression was a novel one indeed. Today, however, modern studies of aggression actually center on the importance of learning. The results of these studies indicate that *reinforcement* and *modeling* can be critical influences in one's acquisition of aggressive tendencies. As we recall from the discussion in Chapter 4, reinforcement is the administration of some kind of reward. Both humans and lower organisms can be trained to fight or aggress if aggressive action is required for the attainment of reward. Other studies on human subjects have indicated that verbal praise for administering punishment increases the amount and intensity of the punishment administered.

However, the aggression that we observe in our society is so significant and frequent that *modeling* may be a factor even more critical than reinforcement in the learning and maintenance of aggression. Modeling occurs when a behavior of one individual is acquired simply by watching and copying that of a second individual. That is, by observing the rewards and punishments given out to someone else,

the observer may actually change his or her own behavior to conform with the other person's in order to obtain the same rewards. Modeling is also referred to as observational learning, and it seems to be effective in eliminating unwanted behaviors as well as in developing new ones. The results of experiments performed on children suggest that aggression is quickly learned from models. Exposure to the aggressive behavior of a model has been shown to increase aggression, whether the model is a person who is observed directly, an actor on a television screen, or a character in a cartoon film. Even more aggression results if the child is simultaneously provided with a verbal narration describing the model's aggressive behavior. The identity of the model is also an important factor. Observation of aggression in peers causes more modeled aggression than does the observation of aggression in animated cartoon characters (Figure 20.3). It has also been found that modeling may not be manifest immediately, but can be retained and expressed at a later time. These experiments, and the phenomenon of modeling in general, suggest the extent to which aggression and violence may perpetuate themselves by providing models for further incidents of aggression.

Figure 20.4
Monkeys cooperate in an attack on a crocodile. This instance of cooperative aggression is described by Harry F. Harlow in *Learning to Love* (San Francisco: Albion, 1971).

COOPERATION

Cooperative behavior occurs when two or more people engage in a joint effort to work for their mutual benefit. This form of behavior is of course widespread in human society, but it occurs among a wide variety of other species as well. Social insects, such as bees, ants, and termites maintain highly cooperative efforts in which each member of the society may perform one function, unique to its particular group, but without which the society could not function. Thus, within a bee colony, some workers do nothing but gather pollen and feed others, whereas those who are fed may be the builders who construct and maintain the hive. A very different form of social cooperation in animals is suggested by a report on cooperative aggression in a monkey colony of the Madison, Wisconsin zoo. The monkeys, who lived on an island surrounded by a moat, cooperated to attack a crocodile that had been placed in the moat. As the crocodile swam

by, one group of monkeys would grab a front leg. Together, they would hold it against a concrete wall while a second group of monkeys grabbed and bit the crocodile's soft underbelly (Figure 20.4).

In the laboratory, animals are observed to cooperate to obtain rewards and avoid punishments. The essential feature of such studies is that the rewards or punishments presented to *one* animal are at least to some extent dependent on the responses of *another* one. If rewards are used, one animal's responses might produce a reward for the other instead of for itself. For example, monkeys have been trained to respond cooperatively in order to feed one another. If one monkey presses a lever thirty-two times, food is presented to a second monkey who is visible to the first. Then the second monkey reciprocates, emitting thirty-two responses to produce food for the

Table 20.2
Payoff Matrix for the Prisoners' Dilemma

| | | PRISONER B | |
		Not Confess	Confess
Prisoner A	Not confess	1 year for A; 1 year for B	20 years for A; 6 months for B
	Confess	6 months for A; 20 years for B	8 years for A; 8 years for B

Source: Roger Brown, *Social Psychology.* New York: Free Press of Glencoe, 1965.

first. As long as the animals alternate response sequences, that is, as long as one animal completes only one sequence of thirty-two responses at a time, cooperation is maintained by the two animals.

Similar experimental procedures have been used to observe cooperation in humans. In one study, children were organized into cooperative teams of two children each. Each team was then given a game to play if it wished. The game was one in which cooperative responses—the insertion of sticks into *opposite* holes on a partitioned board—were rewarded with a single jellybean. One cooperative response, therefore, required a single response on the part of each child, and one jellybean was awarded to the team for each cooperative response. Children were not expressly instructed to cooperate with one another; they were merely asked if they wanted to play the game and then told that they might be receiving jellybeans. Whenever jellybeans were used to reward cooperation, however, high rates of cooperative behavior were maintained. The children often reached verbal agreements on how the candy was to be divided within the team. When the jellybeans were no longer presented for cooperating, cooperative behavior gradually declined. These experiments demonstrate that rewards can be used to induce individuals to cooperate, even though the subjects have received no explicit instructions to do so. Similar results have been obtained with larger cooperative groups and in more competitive game situations.

The Prisoners' Dilemma The presence of risk, usually in the form of a possible loss of reward or possible penalty, has been found to disrupt coopera-

tion. The *Prisoners' Dilemma game* demonstrates clearly the disruptive effect that individual risk can have on cooperative behavior. In this well-known example of a two-person game, two captured prisoners are faced with the decision of whether to confess or not to confess. The prisoners are known to be guilty of their crime, and their interrogator wishes to elicit confessions from them. Since they are interrogated individually, neither has knowledge of what the other has said. The interrogator tells each prisoner that if both of them confess he will recommend leniency, and they will each get only eight years in prison. If one confesses and the other does not, however, the confessor might get as little as six months, whereas the nonconfessor will get at least twenty years. If, however, neither of them confesses, the interrogator insists that he can convict them on a lesser charge and send both of them to prison for at least one year. All of the possible consequences of the four combinations of events that might occur are described in the *payoff matrix*, presented in Table 20.2. The prisoners' best interests are to some extent conflicting. The best outcome for one produces the worst for the other. By cooperating, however they can arrive at the second best outcome for each: that is, if neither of them confesses, they both get off with only a year in prison. The risk for each is not knowing what his fellow prisoner is going to do. If you were one of the prisoners, should you refuse to confess? Let's see what happens when the game is adapted for an experimental study of cooperation in the laboratory.

When subjects are placed in an analogous situation in the laboratory, they tend not to cooperate. This tendency is not too surprising, because, in not knowing what Prisoner B will do, the best individual strategy for Prisoner A (though of course, not the best cooperative strategy) is to confess. If he does, at worst he will protect himself from losing to Prisoner B, and there is a chance that he may even come out ahead of him. What is surprising is that *even when given a chance to confer on the best cooperative strategy beforehand*, the two individuals do not carry out their agreement to cooperate when they are alone.

Among humans and other higher mammals, cooperation appears to occur most frequently in those situations in which it has been specifically reinforced in the past. In the following chapter, we will discuss a related type of cooperative behavior, "helping behavior," which most of us seem to exhibit toward our fellow man primarily when there is strong social pressure to do so. We will also re-examine aggression in our treatment of warfare and revolution. As this and the following chapters point out, studies on aggression and cooperation suggest that, fundamentally, man is neither aggressive and competitive nor loving and cooperative; rather, he is mostly what he has been taught to be and, within limits, his behavior conforms to prevailing social requirements.

Suggested Readings

Aronson, E. (1972) *The social animal*. San Francisco: W. H. Freeman and Co. [A lively, entertaining and instructive overview of social psychology.]

Bandura, A. (1973) *Aggression: A social learning analysis*. Englewood Cliffs, New Jersey: Prentice-Hall. [Bandura's important treatment of aggression.]

Brown, R. (1965) *Social psychology*. New York: The Free Press. [A comprehensive, well-written introduction to social psychology.]

Masters, W. H., & Johnson, V. E. (1966) *Human sexual response*. Boston: Little, Brown.

Masters, W. H., & Johnson, V. E. (1970) *Human sexual inadequacy*. Boston: Little, Brown. [This and the preceding are two important books describing the authors' work on human sexuality.]

Rubin, Z. (1973) *Liking and loving: An invitation to social psychology*. New York: Holt, Rinehart and Winston. [An engrossing and informative look at love and liking.]

CHAPTER TWENTY-ONE

Groups

Each of us, as an individual person, belongs to a number of different groups. It is sometimes surprising to stop and consider just how many groups we do belong to and why we belong to them. What determines the groups with which we are affiliated? What effects do our group memberships have on us? In how many ways and in how many situations are these effects felt? A major part of social psychology consists of cataloging, describing, and explaining not only groups themselves but also their effects on members and nonmembers.

KINDS OF GROUP MEMBERSHIP

A group is simply two or more people who share, or are thought to share, one or more characteristics in common. We belong to a particular group either because we exhibit the characteristics specific to that group or because others think that we do. Groups exert their effects on people by influencing both the behavior of their members and the behavior of nonmembers who interact with the group in some way or for whom it has some significance.

The general determinants of group membership are three, each differing in the degree to which it can be modified. The first set of determinants con-

Figure 21.1
A meeting of the Society of Friends in New York City.
[New York Times/Sam Falk]

sists of various unmodifiable characteristics, usually biological, that we exhibit. (For example, skin color often determines the racial group to which one belongs, and a person's sex determines whether he or she is assigned to masculine or feminine roles by parents, peers, and others.) The second set of determinants are those we voluntarily assume when we elect to belong to a particular group. (A person adopts a particular political position as he decides to become a Democrat or Republican; or he adopts a certain religious philosophy if he is converted to a religion.) The third set of factors determining our group memberships are modifiable in *theory*, but difficult to change in practice. These determinants are mainly social or cultural. If we are born and raised in the American culture, we can become a member of another culture—say, the French culture—only by adopting the many forms of behavior, including the language, that make a person recognizably French. Although such a shift in cultural affiliation is possible, it is unusual and difficult, requiring many years of living in the second culture. A more common example is a shift in socioeconomic class. Thus it is possible to move from a low or middle-class group to a higher socioeconomic group, but such a change requires not only the acquisition of money and goods but also the development of behaviors that constitute the distinctive characteristics of the higher class, such as its speech and manners. Such social mobility is more difficult in some cultures than in others and in some is impossible after a certain age, since some of the requirements for membership in the upper class are experiences shared in youth, such as attendance at particular schools.

Our affiliations are thus numerous indeed, and many of them are involuntary. Together, these various groups strongly influence a wide variety of our activities. The image that others have of us, as well as our own view of the world and of other people,

are in large part determined by what groups we belong to. When the influences of groups are studied by a social psychologist, the traditional method employed is to assess the *norms* established by the group and their effects on a person's social *status*.

STATUS, ROLES, NORMS, AND CONFLICTS

A person's membership in groups helps to establish his *status* (the position he holds in society relative to other members in that society), his *role* (the way in which he is supposed to function in given situations), and the *norms* he observes (the standards determining the types of behavior, thoughts, and emotions that are appropriate for given situations).

Status Membership in a group can confer status on an individual, or remove it. Election to a national honor society tends to enhance a person's status; being indicted by a grand jury as part of a criminal conspiracy tends to decrease it. However, most symbols of status, or of the lack of status, are more subtle. For example, to be identified as a father, an Asian, a physician, a member of Congress, a used-car salesman, or an unemployed person automatically implies familial, professional, racial, or socioeconomic affiliations that partially determine one's perceived status in society.

Role Group membership also confers a role on a person. A role is a set of expected behaviors. These expectations are maintained by the person as well as by others, both inside and outside of the group. For example, a father exhibits certain behaviors that he, other fathers, and people in general expect of him, such as earning a living to support his family. These expectations induce the father to behave in the expected manner, and cause others to be surprised and condemnatory if he does not. Similarly, a vocational role—be it that of minister, banker, astronaut, athlete, or college professor—is identified with expected behaviors that, in general, the person must display to be successful in that role.

Norms Groups expect their members to behave in certain ways and according to certain standards; people outside of the group also expect certain behaviors of those in the group. These two sets of expectations constitute a group's norms, or the standards of behavior and appearance considered appropriate for a group member at a given time in a given circumstance. Norms vary from group to group, and they often change within a single group in the course of time. For example, in recent years the norms of behavior among college students have changed significantly. Although proms and big games are still important on some campuses, they no longer dominate student life as they did until the early 1960s. And, in turn, the student activism of the 1960s, which was a direct response to major political and social crises, seems to have given way to a quest for more knowledge and understanding about the root causes of such complex problems as war, overpopulation, the waste of resources, pollution, and inflation.

Reference groups are groups whose norms we look to for guidance in deciding what our own behavior should be, whether or not we are actually members of that group. Children show the effects of a reference group (the family) when they make up their minds to behave in a particular way because they think it is what their parents would do. A reference group is a particularly powerful influence on our behavior when we aspire to belong to it and attempt to become a member by imitating the behavior of its members.

Conflict The status, roles, and norms dictated by our various group memberships are often in conflict. The status of two persons may come into conflict as a result of a sudden shift in external circumstances: for example, a banker who lends a judge money finds their relative positions reversed if he is called before the judge for breaking the law. Or two or more roles maintained by one person can come into sharp conflict: for example, a working parent may find that the role of hard-working employee conflicts with that of companion to spouse and children. And norms, too, may conflict: those imposed by the corporation world upon the young, single, junior executive may be decidedly different from those maintained by the young, single population of the city in which he lives. These sorts of conflicts exist for everyone, and to conform to one role at the expense of another in a given situation may be the only way some people can reconcile conflicting demands.

LEADERSHIP

Although almost all groups have leaders, and leaders must by definition be capable and efficient, it is impossible to sketch the ideal leader. The reason is that what type of person assumes a leader's role in a particular group depends on the type of group and its function. Studies of leadership have revealed that leaders vary on three main dimensions: (1) source of power—whether the leader derives his power from the friendship of the group members or by the exercise of some sort of authority; (2) style—whether the leader ever performs tasks himself; (3) source of advantage—whether the leader helps the group or is helped by it in the accomplishment of goals. But personality characteristics—that is, whether the leader is friendly, personally helpful, or authoritarian —depend primarily on the group and its task. Authoritarian leaders emerge in highly emotional and stressful situations. The friendly, helpful leader emerges under less trying circumstances. A great tank commander might be a poor business executive or school administrator.

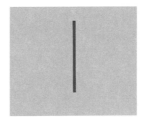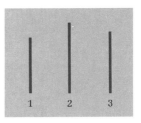

Figure 21.2
Subjects in an experiment by Solomon E. Asch were shown the two cards above. They were asked to choose the line on the right-hand card that was the same length as the single line on the left-hand card. [After S. E. Asch, "Opinions and Social Pressure," *Scientific American*, November 1955, 31–35. Copyright © 1955 by Scientific American, Inc. All rights reserved.]

In the 1950s, the social psychologist Richard Christie described a particular type of highly manipulative leader, whom he named a Machiavellian (or "Mach") after the Italian nobleman who wrote extensively on the techniques of power politics. Christie constructed a scale for determining how Machiavellian a given individual was. Though scores differed, showing some people to be considerably more Machiavellian than others, "High Machs" typically manifested a relativistic, or flexible, view of morality—a belief that the end accomplished by an action was more important than any characteristic of the action itself. They felt, for example, that other people often did not really know what was good for them and that deception was not wrong if it worked to everyone's advantage. "Low Machs" had a more absolute view of morality, believing that right and wrong were dictated by moral principles that transcended situational boundaries. They felt, for example, that not only should leaders act in a way that would benefit everyone but that the members of the group should choose a morally correct course of action.

By examining the outcomes of a series of three-person interactions, Christie was able to describe the situations in which High Machs emerged as leaders. In each interaction, a majority of two of the three persons compelled the group's decision. High Machs were found to be more effective than Low Machs in persuading one other member to support them in those situations (1) in which the issue was highly emotional, (2) in which either the task or the appropriate action of the group was ambiguous, and (3) in which face-to-face confrontations with the third member were required. It is possible that Low Machs would be more effective in less emotional and less ambiguous situations. In short, the type of person who becomes a leader of a particular group depends on the interaction of the members, the tasks and goals of the group, and the circumstances prevailing at the time.

CONFORMITY

Consider the set of three lines on the right of Figure 21.2. Suppose it is your task to indicate which of the lines was most similar in height to the "standard line" on the left. Suppose also that you are one of four subjects in an experiment in perceptual judgment and that each of the first three subjects says that Line 1 is closest in height to the standard. Would you be inclined to go along with their judgments and agree, even though it seems perfectly obvious that Line 2 most closely approximates the standard? You might indeed be a nonconformist in this situation and express your own perceptual judgment. Surprisingly, however, when the experiment was actually performed by Solomon Asch, he found that three-quarters of his subjects showed some tendency to conform to the judgments of the other subjects—who were, in fact, Asch's confederates—even though the judgments were extremely easy to make (so easy that mistakes occurred on less than 1 percent of the trials when individuals made the judgments in isolation). Subsequent testing indicated that subjects who had conformed did not actually believe the reports they had heard from the others and had given themselves. Although it may appear surprising that so many subjects would publicly

Figure 21.3
Two "stooges" and a subject in the Asch experiment on conformity. Subjects 5 and 7 are actually Asch's confederates who claim that Line 1 (in Figure 21.2) is closest in length to the standard line. Subject 6 is a subject who refused to conform. [William Vandivert]

conform to an opinion they privately knew was incorrect, we shall see that much more surprising, even distressing, instances of conformity occur in human behavior. The research we shall review in this section and in the subsequent discussion on (1) *obedience* and (2) *helping* suggests that social compliance is the single most powerful influence on our behavior in social situations. Indeed, most people can be made to behave in shocking and disconcerting ways—even without the threat of physical pain—in order to comply with social demands. We may even look back at Asch's pioneer study and wonder why only 37 percent of the subjects' judgments reflected acceptance of the incorrect judgments of others.

It is likely that if constraints had been placed on the nonconforming subjects, much more conformity would have occurred. In Asch's study, there were no explicit penalties or expressions of disapproval for making honest, nonconforming judgments. Most probably, incidents of conformity would have been sharply increased if frowns or other explicit signs of disapproval from the others had been directed toward subjects expressing nonconforming judgments (Figure 21.3). However, when one of the stooges also dissented and gave the correct judgment consistently, most—though not all—of the conformity effect was eliminated.

How many confederates need be present in order to influence conformity? If the number is great enough, will everyone conform? Studies have shown that one confederate is not enough to produce conformity. Instead, the subject apparently dismisses the other's judgment and assumes that his own is superior. In a one-to-one situation of this kind, the subject does not mock the confederates' mistaken judgment, but when a large group of uninformed subjects is presented with a single confederate, the confederate is often subjected to ridicule. When a single uninformed subject is presented with two confederates, the conformity effect appears, although the percentage of mistaken judgments is only between 10 and 15 percent. If there are three confederates, a more pronounced effect (about one inaccurate judgment in every three) is obtained. Interestingly, to increase the number of confederates even more (to as many as fifteen), causes no appreciable additional conformity.

Why do we conform? The reasons vary with the specific situation: probably the two most important ones are to gain social approval and to obtain information on how to behave correctly. Social approval is not the sole motive, as is demonstrated by incidents of conformity that occur when the subject makes his judgments privately. In these situations, the subject seems to be using the behavior of others to provide guidelines for appropriate behavior in difficult, ambiguous situations—for example, when making judgments of movement in the autokinetic phenomenon, which we discussed in Chapter 14. Hence, if the judgments in Asch's study had been very difficult—instead of patently easy—much more conformity would have resulted, and the additional conformity could have been attributed to the subject's genuine reliance on the perceptual judgments of others.

If you were asked whom you admired more—those subjects who sometimes conformed or those who consistently expressed their personal judgment—you would probably select the nonconformist. But, in your daily interactions with people, do you indeed like nonconformists better than conformists? In particular, do you prefer people who agree with you and with the goals of the groups to which you belong, or do you prefer the dissenter? The following research by Stanley Schachter in 1951 was addressed to this question.

A group of subjects—including three confederates—were read a case history about a juvenile delinquent named Rocco. They were then asked to decide on an appropriate disciplinary strategy ranging from "very lenient" to "very hard" treatment. Each of the three confederates played a different role. One, the "conformist," carefully took a position that represented the average of the real subjects' opinions—a group-consensus position. The second confederate took a nonconformist position, as far opposed as possible to the group consensus. Finally, the third confederate began by dissenting but gradually allowed his opinions to slide in the direction of total conformity. Who did the subjects like best? The conformist. Even the "slider," who did not appear to have the courage of his convictions, was preferred to the nonconformist. The results of Schachter, Asch, and others suggest that conformity is commonplace and that the conforming person is more likely to gain social approval than the nonconformist.

Given our preference for conformists, how do we react to "deviants," people who do not conform to prevailing patterns or standards of behavior? In 1968, Jon Freedman and Tony Doob administered a series of personality tests to groups of five or six subjects. In the tests, subjects were asked to indicate certain attitudes and opinions that would supposedly reveal information about various dimensions of their personalities. After the tests, "conformist" subjects received false feedback indicating that they and all but one of the other subjects, a "deviant," whose scores had been extremely variant, had scored near the mean in the various personality dimensions. The "deviant" subjects were each told that they were one of two members whose scores had been extreme whereas the scores of the rest of the subjects had clustered about the mean of each personality dimension. Next came the critical portion of the study. Subjects were told that one of their group would continue with a second test, this one on free association. The group was to decide which one of them would take the test. Some groups were led to believe that the test was pleasant, in that the person taking it would earn $2.50. The other groups were told that in the course of the test the person would receive painful electric shocks. Each member of the group ranked the others in the order in which he selected them for the additional task. The subjects who had been led to believe they were conformists selected other conformists for the pleasant task but selected deviant subjects for the unpleasant task. Subjects who believed their scores had been deviant tended to choose the other deviant for the pleasant task, and a conformist for the unpleasant task.

THE IMPORTANCE OF SOCIAL COMPARISON

A second important reason for the occurrence of conformity is our tendency to interpret *social reality* in terms of *social comparisons*. In other words, we rely strongly upon social cues from others when we ourselves are uncertain of what the appropriate conduct should be. For example, if after your first meal in a foreign country, your hosts shatter their brandy snifters in the fireplace, you may do the same. Yet you would hardly send your glass shattering to the floor after two four-year-olds had smashed theirs. In the first situation, you are using the behav-

ior of others as a cue for emitting appropriate behavior in an unfamiliar situation. In the second, you do not conform because the children's behavior does not function as an adequate social model on which to base your own behavior. However, as long as you have no reason to doubt your hosts' adequacy as models for your own behavior, you are likely to accept their actions, at least tentatively, as appropriate. Even if you have good reasons to believe they are drunk or for some other reason not in full control of their actions, you may "go along" with their behavior in order to gain acceptance or to avoid embarrassment (either yours or theirs), although in this situation you will be far less likely to do anything seriously at odds with your own sense of propriety or to emit the same behavior the next day in the presence of others.

We are, then, particularly inclined to rely on the judgments of others when the situation in which we are behaving is poorly structured. If the situation is completely unstructured, we will almost certainly conform. This phenomenon was shown by M. Sherif in his *autokinetic experiment*, which we described in Chapter 14 and mentioned in Chapter 20. Recall that in his observations of the *autokinetic illusion* of movement, Sherif used a stationary pinpoint of light in an otherwise dark room; subjects, when asked to judge the extent of the light's movement, invariably reported movement. It was also found that the perceived and reported movements were greatly influenced by the judgments of others. When subjects judged the movement in groups, their estimates gradually "funneled" or converged toward a consensus average as shown in Figure 21.4. Moreover, when the same subjects were subsequently tested alone, they continued to make judgments consistent with the group-established norms. When a situation is totally unstructured, and when we have no strong convictions of our own, we are likely to

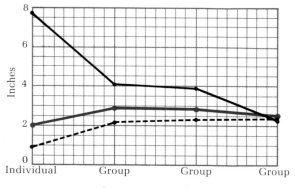

Figure 21.4
The degree of conformity to group norms shown by three subjects in Sherif's autokinetic experiment (discussed in the text). Note that the amount of movement of the stationary light reported by each subject tends to converge until all three are giving the same reports. [Adapted from M. Sherif, *The Psychology of Social Norms*. New York: Harper and Row, 1966.]

be receptive to suggestions about reality from others.

An important factor that determines the effectiveness of a social-comparison stimulus in producing conformity is the *perceived status* of the person exhibiting the behavior. This point was neatly illustrated in 1953 by Monroe Lefkowitz and his associates in a series of studies on jaywalking, in which several of the experimenter's confederates crossed a busy intersection against a pedestrian "wait" signal. Some dressed in suit and tie, suggesting a high-status position; others were slovenly. An observer recorded the number of pedestrians (the unknowing subjects of the experiment) who followed the jaywalking model and the number who did not on each of a large number of trials. Much more conformity—and thus disregard of the pedestrian signal—occurred when the high-status model jaywalked. The studies indicate that we are more inclined to violate a prohibition if we have a high-status social-comparison stimulus setting the example for us.

Additional studies have shown that the perceived status of jury members influences their effectiveness on the panel. In one study, a series of mock trials was conducted. Groups of twelve subjects actually heard a tape of a trial, received instructions from a "judge," elected a foreman, and then deliberated the case until arriving at a verdict. The subjects were classified into four status groups ranging from "proprietor" to "laborer," depending on their occupation. Results indicated that the higher the juror's status, the greater his or her influence on the group decision that was ultimately reached.

MASS HYSTERIA AND RIOTS

Social comparisons have a significant effect on the behavior that prevails in mass hysteria and riots. In the first significant study of mob behavior, in 1896, Gustav LeBon suggested that the mob had a collective "group mind" that usurped the individuality of its participants. He and others cited numerous examples of mass hysteria, lynching, and mob violence to support their proposal that a crowd's behavior was qualitatively different from the behavior of individuals acting alone—more uncivilized and more irrational.

Today we know that there is no reason to invoke a concept as nebulous as the "collective mind." Studies of conformity and obedience have shown that individuals may be made to comply with many social demands that might appear irrational if the controlling variables were not known. Floyd Allport noted this compliance long before the striking reality of social compliance was demonstrated in the laboratory. Indeed, he suggested that the person in a riot might be *more* "himself" rather than less so, and might rationalize his own behavior by noting that others were behaving as he would like to. For example, looting by others during a power blackout or a riot might provide adequate social-comparison stimuli for more looting; thus, the poor person who wants a color television set will be more inclined to steal one if he sees scores of his peers carting sets off for themselves. The anti-black bigot might normally refrain from violent action, but, if he sees others preparing to attack black demonstrators or a school bus, he may grow more willing to vent

Figure 21.5
Adults attacking a school bus carrying children—why?

his hatred. The harassed policeman may express his anger with his club when he sees others doing so.

However, social-comparison cues—though important—are not the only factors that foster mob behavior. A person at a riot also knows that he is less likely to be *caught* than if he attempts the same action in another setting, without the protection of the mob. Moreover, the *responsibility* for unlawful action is likely to be diffused among the members of the entire mob.

SOCIAL MOVEMENTS

The same factors that influence behavior in crowds—social-comparison cues, personal desires and emo-

tions, external rewards, and diffusion of responsibility—can significantly affect social movements. Such movements—whether directed toward economic, political, religious, or other aims—occur when individuals are dissatisfied with some aspect of their world. In 1941, Hadley Cantril, analyzing the rise of Nazism, noted that Hitler had become a spokesman for the frustrated desires and interests of many individual Germans belonging to the special-interest groups that he courted in his speeches. Once the movement had a following, it offered social-comparison cues for other would-be Nazis. Eventually, the pressure for conformity became almost overwhelming. Throughout the movement, of course, individuals rationalized various atrocious actions and absolved themselves from blame by diffusing the responsibility.

The same behavioral influences can be observed in contemporary movements, even nonviolent movements for social and economic reform. The women's liberation movement, for example, continues to gain momentum as many women who previously "kept their place" in the face of deeply felt inequities now find they have adequate social support for taking action to eliminate discrimination based on sex.

VARIABLES AFFECTING CONFORMITY AND DEVIANCE

Group Characteristics We have already noted that conformity is influenced by the size of the majority and that conformity to the behavior of a high-status model is likely to be greater than to that of a low-status model. Similarly, conformity is facilitated when the model is an expert (or when the majority consists of experts). Conformity is also enhanced when the model or models are important and/or similar to the subject. We are most likely to conform to a group of three or more people who are acknowledged authorities and who also happen to be our friends, employers, or colleagues, and who come from similar backgrounds.

Subject Characteristics   The more confident one is about his expertise in making a judgment, the less likely he is to conform. Such confidence can be developed experimentally in a person; for example, subjects who have made several successful perceptual judgments in Asch's experimental set-up are less likely to conform when the confederates begin making "mistakes." In general, subjects with high self-esteem are less likely to conform than subjects with low self-esteem. Finally, the more secure a subject feels in a given situation, the less likely he is to conform. Thus, individuals who are uncertain about their status in a peer group are more likely to conform to a group consensus than are those members who are more secure.

To complete our perspective on conformity and social compliance, let us now take a close look at some illuminating and disturbing experiments in two areas of topical interest: *obedience* and *helping*.

OBEDIENCE

Obedience became a topic of extreme interest during and shortly after the Korean War, when it became evident that the Chinese were using "brainwashing" techniques on American prisoners of war. Questions arose about the extent to which people could refuse to obey under extremely adverse circumstances. Moreover, given that they do obey, how are their values, beliefs, and attitudes altered by such forced compliance? Finally, if any such changes occur, are the effects permanent or are they temporary— persisting only as long as the threat of adverse consequences prevails?

Effective brainwashing techniques *do not* begin with the threat of physical harm if the subject fails to comply. Such treatment might confirm and even strengthen the individual's prevailing beliefs and attitudes, producing a result opposite to the desired one. Instead, the initial efforts are attempts to weaken the influence of whatever ideology governs the prisoner(s). This weakening is accomplished by disrupting an individual's faith in his own memory of how things were, by depersonalizing the prisoners (assigning numbers instead of names, taking away personal clothes, and so on), by developing in the person a mistrust for friends and relatives back home, and by planting suggestions that the prevailing ideology may encourage both individuals and society to forget the individual. Mistrust is engendered among the captives: leaders are removed and isolated; hints are left that informers have been planted in the group. Group cohesiveness declines, and communication among captives all but ceases. This rupture eliminates talk among the captives, not only of escape but, more importantly, of how things were back home—talk that might maintain and even strengthen the prevailing ideological structure. Eventually, personal isolation ensues.

The strain of isolation leaves the individual open to many new kinds of communication. Now desperate for companionship, the captive becomes less particular about the topic of conversation. This emotional need is coupled with the strain induced by such physical needs as hunger, ill health, muscular deterioration, and so on. At this point, the prisoner may be receptive to new ideological concepts simply because they come wrapped in a package labeled "the chance to talk to someone and dispel my loneliness." Once the individual begins to listen to new ideas, rewards that help to fulfill the induced needs can be used to encourage interest and enhance any glimmer of agreement. Other rewards might be subtle ones—a sympathetic smile or a cigarette— nothing overtly resembling a payoff, but rather the small gifts suggestive of friendship. Also, attempts are made by the interrogators to shift the blame for the prisoner's captivity away from the captor. The prisoner himself is made to feel responsible, guilty, and even ashamed. Meanwhile, however, the technique of rewarding any sign of receptivity is continually being used to instill in the prisoner a new set of beliefs and attitudes.

The use of these powerful techniques evokes the compliance of many individuals—as long as they remain directly under the stringent controls. Under these particular circumstances, captives do display obedience to their superiors. In large measure, they appear unable to disobey. However, this obedience is quite short-lived. When reexposed to familiar environments and conventional social restraints, the prisoners' behavior returns to normal. What is perhaps more surprising is that people seem to assume their original attitudes, beliefs, and values very soon after they have been reexposed to the conditions that originally produced and maintained them. It appears, then, that cognitive, or mental, as well as behavioral obedience can be modified and brought under the control of prevailing stimulus conditions. These new allegiances are, however, no more permanent than are any learned responses, once the stimuli that maintain them are removed.

In a more standard setting, when no complex and involved schemes are devised to insure compliance, how strong is the tendency to obey? Some experiments done at Yale University by Stanley Milgram in 1963 and 1965 have revealed the tendency to obey under pressures that are no more compelling than mere request. Obedience, it seems, may be a very deeply ingrained behavioral tendency.

In Milgram's studies, volunteer subjects were asked to take part in a set of experiments ostensibly investigating the effects of punishment on memory. The subjects were grouped in pairs. One, designated the "learner," was sent to an adjacent room, where he was to receive a list of word associations to memorize. After he had been seated in the room, he was connected to a set of impressive looking equipment apparently used to deliver the punishment. The other subject, designated the "teacher," observed all this. The teacher was then taken into the next room and seated before a control panel of labeled buttons, which appeared to be part of another maze of equipment. The teacher was instructed to test the learner's memory by quizzing him on a list of word associations. If the learner did not choose the correct association, he was punished. The punishment, electric shock, was to be delivered by the teacher. For each incorrect response, the teacher was instructed to press one of the buttons on the panel, giving an electric shock to the learner. The label on the button indicated the strength of the shock being delivered; with each incorrect response the voltage was to be increased by 15 volts. The range of punishment voltages was from 15 to 450 volts. The range of voltages from 375 to 420 was marked with a sign "Danger: Severe Shock." Voltages beyond 420 were ominously marked "XXX."

The "learner" was, in fact, a trained confederate acting a part and responding with a standard set of correct and incorrect answers. Although the teacher believed he was actually delivering shocks, and the confederate responded at times with protesting outbursts, no shocks were actually given. The object of the experiment was to determine how much shock the teacher was willing to inflict on the often protesting learner merely in response to the request of the experimenter.

At the outset of the experiment, the teacher was told that he could excuse himself from the experiment whenever he wished to do so. If at some point during the experiment the teacher expressed a wish to stop, however, the experimenter responded with a standard series of moderate requests to continue. It was the teacher's obedience to these requests that was being observed. How far would the teacher go in inflicting what appeared to be extreme pain upon another individual, in response to the moderate requests of a third person?

A group of Yale psychology majors was given a description of this situation and asked to predict what they thought the outcome of this experiment might be. The most pessimistic prediction was that as many as three out of a hundred subjects would continue along the entire range and inflict 450-volt shocks on their victims. Predictions were also made by forty psychiatrists from medical schools. They felt that less than 1 percent of the subjects would administer the most severe shocks and that only 4 percent would continue to administer shocks after the subject ceased to respond (at 300 volts).

The results were stunning. No subject stopped at less than 300 volts. Of the total of forty subjects, twenty-six administered the strongest shock (450 volts) to their learners! Rather than the 1 to 3 percent that had been predicted, about 65 percent displayed maximum obedience in the situation. (See Figure 21.6.)

It must be stressed that the subjects in the experiment represented a cross-section of professional people, laborers, clerks, and businessmen—a fairly random sample of Americans. Also, these results cannot be refuted by arguments that the subjects did not know what they were doing or that they did not believe the act being put on by the learner. That the teachers were convinced of the validity of the results of their actions is suggested by the signs of extreme stress many of them displayed as they progressed along the voltage scale. Many teachers were observed to groan, tremble, sweat, and even dig fingernails into their flesh. A few of them were actually overcome by uncontrollable seizures. More-

over, after the experiment had ended, and the true situation had been revealed, all subjects reported that they had been convinced by the learner's apparent reactions. These admissions are particularly remarkable when one considers the behavior of the learners. Before the shocks reached the strength of 100 volts, the learner moaned in pain; by 150 volts, the learner asked that the experiment be terminated; by 200 volts, he screamed that he could not endure the pain; later he stopped responding and instead pounded on the walls of the room; finally he was ominously silent. Throughout, the teacher—with some prodding from the experimenter—continued to shock the learner when he failed to make the required correct response—even though he had stopped responding altogether sometime before! Milgram concluded that the tendency to obey, having been practiced from childhood, is indeed strong, and can outweigh other moral dictates that have also been ingrained in the individual by extensive moral and ethical training since childhood.

Milgram's findings that most people can be made to administer massive and dangerous punishment to others, created an understandable pessimism. Some observers have found a similarity between those results and historically shocking examples of obedience, such as that exhibited by those Nazis who, obeying orders, slaughtered enormous numbers of civilians. And we know that the American officer who was convicted of the murder of elderly people, women, children, and infants in a Vietnamese village stated that he thought he was carrying out the orders of his superior officers.

Of course, Milgram's subjects were obeying a Yale scientist, and might have inferred that no irreversible harm would come to the victims in such a highly respectable setting. If they had so rationalized their actions, then it should follow that less compliance would occur if the scientist was not from a reputable

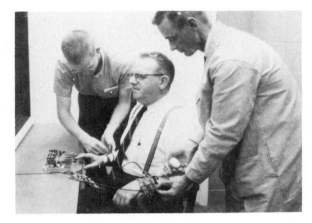

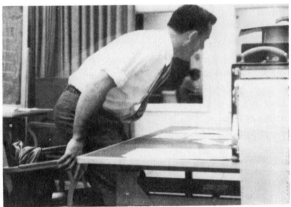

Figure 21.6
In Stanley Milgram's experiments on obedience, a shock
generator (*upper left*) played a crucial role. Subjects
saw their "victim" (*upper right*) having electrodes
attached to his arms. They also received a sample shock
(*lower left*). A few subjects, like the man at the lower
right, refused to carry out their assigned task. [Copyright
1965 by Stanley Milgram. From the film *Obedience*,
distributed by the New York University Film Library.]

institution. To test this possibility, Milgram repeated
the study in Bridgeport, Connecticut, where the
experimenter was, in the eyes of the subjects, an
unknown scientist operating out of a downtown
shopping area. At the same time, Milgram replicated
the study at Yale also. Although the proportion of
completely obedient subjects continued to be about
two-thirds in the Yale setting, it dropped to just
below one-half (48 percent) in Bridgeport. The
figure—still astonishingly high—would doubtless drop

further still if the experimenter posed not as a
"scientist" but, say, as an "electrician exploring
human memory as a hobby."

In both settings, Milgram did find that the visible
presence of the experimenter was important in maintaining compliance. When the experimenter was not
present, but instead conveyed his instructions over
earphones, two changes occurred in the results:
(1) several subjects cheated by administering low-
intensity shocks while assuring the experimenter
that they were complying, (2) the proportion of
completely obedient subjects dropped to about one
in five. Even so, Milgram's results are sobering in
demonstrating how compliant, how terribly obedient,
we can be.

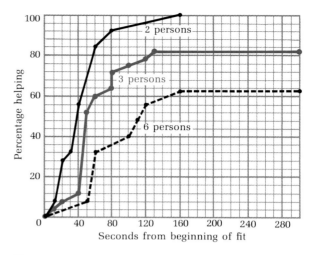

Figure 21.7
The cumulative number of helping responses made plotted against the number of seconds from the onset of the feigned epileptic fit. The curve marked "2 persons" describes results for the condition in which the group consisted only of the victim and the subject; in the "3 persons" group, a nonhelping stooge is also present; finally, in the "6 persons" group, four nonhelping stooges are present. Note that the smaller the group, the more likely people are to offer help. [Adapted from John Darley and Bibb Latané, "Bystander Intervention in Emergencies: Diffusion of Responsibility," *Journal of Personality and Social Psychology*, 1968, 8, 377–383. © 1968 Amer. Psych. Assn.]

HELPING

How about the other side of the coin? Is it probable that people will extend themselves to help someone else in serious trouble?

The answer is a distressing "no," although the course of action chosen does depend on the type of situation. Social psychologists became interested in this question in the early 1960s when a woman named Kitty Genovese was murdered in the Kew Gardens section of Queens, New York. At least thirty-eight ordinary middle-class citizens saw the killer make three separate attacks upon the woman in the course of a three-hour period. Three attacks were necessary because on each of the first two occasions the killer was frightened off by the voices of the onlookers, and by the sudden glow of their bedroom lights. On the third attempt he was successful. It was only then, after the woman was dead, that one of the thirty-eight witnesses called the police.

In a series of studies, John Darley and Bibb Latané investigated bystander intervention in an emergency. In one study—in 1968—a group of subjects, participants in a psychology experiment, communicated with other subjects in the group via an intercom system. After a period of time, one of the subjects (a confederate of the experimenter) simulated an epileptic attack. After making a few "relatively calm comments" the victim's voice grew increasingly loud and incoherent and culminated in the following outburst:

> I-er-um-I think-I-I need-er-if-if could-er-er-somebody er-er-er-er-er-er-er give me a little-er-give me a little help here because-er-I-er I'm-er-er-h-h-having a-a-a real problem-er-right now and I-er if somebody could help me out it would-it would-er-er-s-s-sure be-sure be good . . . because-er-there-er-er-a cause I-er-I-uh-I've got a-a one of the-er-sei——er-er-things

coming on and-and-and I could really-er use some help so if somebody would-er give me a little h-help-uh-er-er-er-er-er c-could somebody-er-er-help-er-uh-uh-uh (choking sounds) . . . . I-m . . . gonna die-er-help-er-er-seizure-er-[chokes, then quiet].*

Darley and Latané found that if the subject had been led to believe that he was the only one tuned in to the victim, he was much more likely to help by calling the experimenter than if he believed others were listening in also. Indeed, the greater the number of subjects believed to be tuned in to the intercom, the smaller the likelihood that the experimenter would be summoned. This result is shown in Figure 21.7.

*J. M. Darley and B. Latané, Bystander Intervention in Emergencies: Diffusion of Responsibility. *Journal of Personality and Social Psychology*, 1968, 8, 377–383.

These results suggest that "a diffusion of responsibility" seems to underly the failure to help. This conclusion was tested in an additional experiment, in 1969, by Latané and Rodin, in which a "lady in distress" was employed. In this study, a female experimenter left one or two subjects alone in a room after instructing them to complete a questionnaire. Moments later, a scream and a loud crash (intended to simulate the sound of someone falling) were heard. Subsequently, the woman's voice was heard moaning and crying for help. Although 70 percent of the subjects sitting alone offered to help, only 20 percent offered if they were paired with someone. Again, the mere presence of others decreased the likelihood of someone's acting to help another, thus further demonstrating the adverse effect of the diffusion of responsibility.

In other circumstances, however, helping does occur more frequently. In the first place, it increases if modeling occurs: in particular, it has been observed that subjects who see an experimenter's confederate help someone are more inclined to do so themselves when a similar situation arises subsequently. Moreover, if the victim remains in full view, and the bystander cannot readily escape from him, he is more likely to offer help. In such situations, it is possible that the embarrassment of not helping overcomes a basic reluctance to expend the effort to expose oneself to potential danger, to participate in an unpleasant scene, or to risk any of the other possibilities that constitute reasons for "not getting involved."

What are the chances, then, of help being offered if the situation is so arranged that escape is impossible? Irving Piliavin and his associates explored this very possibility in 1969 with the aid of a "laboratory on wheels," New York's Eighth Avenue subway. The experiment was conducted during the long nonstop run between 59th and 125th Streets in Manhattan,

so that passengers could not hope to leave the scene within a minute or so by getting off at the next stop. A confederate of the experimenter would feign illness or drunkenness (in the drunk condition, he would be reeking of liquor and would hold a liquor bottle). Approximately one minute after the train departed, the victim would stagger, collapse, and then remain lying on the floor and staring at the ceiling. On 95 percent of the trials, one or more people came to the aid of the stricken individual when he appeared to be sick, Even when he seemed to be obviously drunk, the victim received aid in 50 percent of the trials (in those trials in which assistance was not extended, another confederate aided the victim after the train stopped). Thus, these findings indicate that a greater degree of helping behavior occurs in those situations in which bystanders are somehow unable to escape. It is possible that, no matter what the situation is, what helping behavior does occur is merely (like obedience) another instance of social compliance; that with a few exceptions, we are most inclined to help only when some kind of social pressure to do so is applied. Ironically, however, social pressure does not derive from the mere presence of others; rather, their presence may strengthen the inclination not to help, since the responsibility becomes diffused, and social pressure is minimized. In fact, by not helping, the inactive bystanders are conferring a kind of social acceptability upon not helping.

GROUPS AND DECISION-MAKING

In the preceding sections, we have analyzed the ways in which an individual's behavior may be profoundly determined by social influences, including group expectations. Indeed, the mere presence of other people may affect the behavior of each individual. Unfortunately, the result is often a lowered quality of performance, especially in problem-solving. One of the reasons appears to be a subject's apprehension about having to perform in the presence of others—and anxiety about possible evaluation of the performance. Despite the fact that individual performance is sometimes impaired by social influence, groups of people working together can, in many situations, arrive at solutions or develop programs much more efficiently than would the same number of people working alone.

Critical factors that determine such group effectiveness are the nature and size of the undertaking and the talents of the group members: whereas a good poem is usually an individual effort, the galley proofs for a book are more efficiently proofread for typographical errors if two people work together; similarly, it is probably better to memorize alone, whereas the designing of a mass-transportation system or a space vehicle requires a group approach, in which the special skills and talents of the members are drawn upon. Generally, two or more heads are better than one when the group consists of people with complementary skills, well-suited to an efficient division of labor. Within the general area of group psychology, a number of interesting studies have been conducted on group decision-making. In this section, we shall examine briefly two important phenomena that have recently been shown to occur when groups make decisions.

The "Risky-Shift"   Consider the following situation. Mr. G. is an accomplished chess player who is entered in a major tournament. The odds that he will win are slight, since he has not done especially well in major tournaments before. After winning the first round, he finds himself playing the top-seeded player in the tournament. Early in the game, Mr. G. conceives of a plan which, though fraught with risk, might result in victory. But should the plan fail,

Mr. G. would likely be checkmated soon thereafter. Should Mr. G. take the gamble? Assume that you are advising Mr. G. Would you consider the risky play acceptable if the chances were only one in ten that it would succeed? Three in ten? Five in ten? Seven in ten? Or nine in ten? What is the lowest probability you would deem acceptable before advising Mr. G. to take the risk.

Hypothetical *choice dilemmas* such as these were actually presented to groups of subjects in an ingenious series of experiments initiated by Michael Wallach and Nathan Kogan. Individual subjects first checked the possibilities and then engaged in a group discussion with other participants. After the group discussion, subjects had a chance to reevaluate their answers. A striking result was the occurrence of a so-called *risky-shift*: after group discussion on most choice dilemmas, subjects tend to be willing to take more risk.

Originally, Wallach and Kogan concluded that group discussion diffused the responsibility for a decision in risk-taking, and that this lessening of personal responsibility produced increasingly risky decisions. Subsequently, other workers presented evidence indicating that mere familiarity with the issues tended to result in increased confidence and thus greater willingness to take larger risks. Although each of these factors may be partially responsible for many occurrences of risky-shift, more recent evidence suggests that the most important factor is what Roger Brown has called the "value hypothesis." Brown observed that the shifts tended to occur when one's cultural values favored riskiness. The effect of the discussion is then to support the individual's tentative assumptions that risk is indeed desirable in the situation, and to encourage him to assume a riskier position. Although such subjects might want to be "moderately risky" before the discussion, most have difficulty in judging which

odds constitute moderate risk. In other words, they lack an adequate frame of reference for assessing risk subjectively. It is probable, then, that group discussion helps people to see that risk is more valued by others than the subject had anticipated, and it also provides a frame of reference (or a social comparison) for estimating what is risky. Opinions are then free to shift toward the more admired and valued, riskier, point on the risk continuum.

Groupthink   Irving Janis has analyzed a feature of group decision-making that he has labeled _groupthink_. Janis notes that in group decision-making, considerable group pressure for consensus often occurs, effectively suppressing dissent and permitting poor and even disasterous decisions. Janis notes that groups that are particularly susceptible to becoming victims of _groupthink_ are cohesive groups with high morale. He has suggested that the inner circle of the Kennedy administration, as they launched the New Frontier early in 1961, was such a group. Janis analyzed the decision-making that led to the Bay of Pigs fiasco (an aborted invasion of Cuba by CIA-sponsored forces) early in that year and noted several symptoms of groupthink.

Probably the most salient feature of groupthink is the _esprit de corps_—the spirit of enthusiasm and dedication shared by group members for the group

and its goals—and the _illusion of invulnerability_ that arises. Although such optimism can be a positive trait in certain kinds of groups, such as athletic teams or encounter groups, it is a particularly dangerous trait for a group engaged in high-level policy planning. For one thing, it can lead to highly risky behavior, often a questionable and potentially deadly exercise, particularly in such an area as foreign policy. Recall too, that such risk-taking may be intensified by the risky-shift phenomenon, which generally occurs in group decision-making even when the members of the group are strangers.

Janis offers several examples to support his proposal that an illusion of invulnerability pervaded the Kennedy administration during the planning of the Bay of Pigs (Figure 21.8). For one thing, he states that Kennedy was convinced that the responsibility of the United States for the invasion could be kept secret. However, in spite of a widespread news blackout, a few news reporters warned of the invasion before it occurred, and no one was deceived by the time the United Nations Assembly met to discuss the invasion immediately after it began. The continued insistence of the American ambassador to the United Nations, Adlai Stevenson, that the United States was not a participant probably added to the worldwide revulsion that the invasion provoked, as Stevenson had been widely regarded as an honest and eloquent spokesman for democratic ideals.

The other examples of the illusion of invulnerability cited by Janis include the belief held by members of the Johnson administration that North Vietnam would retreat from a confrontation with the United States in the face of the continued "escalation" of bombing raids and other military operations.

The second symptom of groupthink noted by Janis is *rationalization*: that is, a group tends to respond to valid warnings, or other suggestions that it may not be on the best course, by ignoring them—and rationalizes its behavior by inventing new reasons to justify it. For example, Janis notes that when contact with Japanese aircraft carriers was lost prior to Pearl Harbor, not only was this danger signal ignored, but the American commander, when informed, joked about it, saying that the carriers might be rounding Honolulu's Diamond Head at that very moment! American military leaders, relying on long-term strategic superiority to the Japanese forces, rationalized that the Japanese simply wouldn't *dare* try a lightning-like knock-out blow.

A third symptom is a group's belief in its own *morality*. Victims of groupthink feel no need to question the moral consequences of their decision. Janis maintains that most evidence for this comes from what is left *unsaid* at meetings. One of the examples he offers is the reaction to Senator William Fulbright's remarks at one of the planning sessions for the Bay of Pigs invasion. Although Fulbright was not a member of the Kennedy inner circle, he had been asked to address the group. In his remarks,

Fulbright questioned the morality of the planned invasion. When the Senator finished speaking, President Kennedy did not ask for the group's reaction but swiftly passed on to the next item on the agenda.

Groupthinkers tend to *stereotype* their opposition, that is, to hold negative but oversimplified views of them. Stereotyping can be particularly destructive because it can mislead the group to underestimate the abilities of the enemy. For example, the Kennedy group believed Castro's army was so weak that a small brigade of armed exiles could launch a successful uprising. The Japanese in World War II were similarly underestimated as were the NLF and North Vietnamese in the Vietnam War. Presumably, the same kind of unrealistic evaluation of Israel's strength occurs in the Arab world.

Other symptoms include the *pressure* that is applied against even momentary dissension and a consequent *self-censorship*. For example, Arthur Schlesinger, Jr. has acknowledged that, during group discussions, he suppressed his personal objections to the Bay of Pigs invasion, though he had previously noted his objections in a memo to the President. A final symptom of groupthink is the illusion of *unanimity* shared by group members.

Groupthink, then, tends to produce poorly informed, poorly deliberated decisions that can have disastrous and unforeseen consequences. Obviously, these adverse effects can be counteracted only by an open discussion of any drawbacks or reservations, by thorough and impartial exploration of assumptions and alternatives for action, and by provisions for input by outside evaluators. In addition, at least one member of the group should play the "devil's advocate"—challenging the group's assumptions, and questioning the merits of its tentative decisions. If these measures are taken, the group approach to decision-making has far more to offer than decisions made either by individuals or by groups who are prey to groupthink. Moreover, if sufficient precautions are taken, a cohesive group instilled with genuine devotion to group tasks and goals may be much more effective than a loosely structured one whose members feel only somewhat committed to the efforts of the group and to the ultimate achievement of its goals.

LOSS OF GROUP AFFILIATION

Group affiliations tend to coincide with our social and economic status. As we noted earlier, all of us have roles, norms, and values appropriate to each of the groups to which we belong. When our position changes in some way, for example, when we move from a neighborhood, change jobs or interests, or improve our financial status—to name just a few possible changes—our group affiliations change as well. The most influential changes in group affiliation probably occur as we pass through adolescence, go on through college, embark on a career, and perhaps marry and raise a family. The changes in group affiliations that result are regarded as quite natural. Sometimes, however, forced or even abnormal changes occur, for example, if one is sentenced to prison, or if he is avoided by friends for some real or imagined wrongdoing, or if his social or economic position somehow changes dramatically, causing him to let many of his former group ties and friendships lapse.

In modern societies, there is great social differentiation, influenced in part by the industrial demands for a division of labor. The greater the social differentiation, the stronger the likelihood that changes in group affiliation will occur. These changes may be detrimental to the people undergoing them when modern society does not provide adequate new group affiliations. The sociologist Émile

Durkheim noted (in 1897) that a condition of *anomie* —or the absence of supportive group affiliations— may arise. In such a state of alienation, the individual is maladjusted and feels directionless. Durkheim reasoned that anomie would be most prevalent in periods of economic prosperity, during which upward mobility and concomitant changes in group affiliation are common. To support this hypothesis, he cited statistics showing that suicides occurred most frequently during periods of great prosperity. On the other hand, millions of contemporary people have endured many changes in group affiliation, some of them requiring very challenging and difficult adjustments.

Suggested Readings

Asch, S. E. (1955) "Opinions and social pressure." *Scientific american*, November, pp. 31–35. Reprinted as Scientific American Offprint 450. [A classic article on the social psychology of groups.]

Insko, C. A., & Schopler, J. (1972) *Experimental social psychology: Text with illustrative readings.* New York: Academic Press. [A very sound and comprehensive overview of social psychology, including some well-selected readings.]

Janis, I. L. (1971) "Groupthink among policy makers." In Sanford, N., & Comstock, C., eds. *Sanctions for evil.* San Francisco: Jossey-Bass. [Janis' engrossing theory of groupthink.]

Sherif, M. (1956), "Experiments in group conflict." *Scientific american*, November, pp. 54–58. Reprinted as Scientific American offprint 454. [Another classic.]

See also readings suggested for Chapter 20, especially those by Aronson and Brown.

CHAPTER TWENTY-TWO

Intergroup Relations

We have examined the important determinants of social behavior between two or more people, and the influences that a group can have on the behavior of its members. In this chapter we shall explore some important intergroup relations. The types of intergroup relationships that can evolve are varied, and many are mutually beneficial, as when groups share common goals. For instance, parents' and teachers' groups might collaborate to achieve certain educational improvements.

In this chapter we will emphasize interactions that are often mutually harmful: prejudice and warfare. Why? First, because a significant amount is known about them; second, because they are of central importance in modern society. In addition, much of what we learn from the study of prejudice and warfare is applicable to other intergroup relations. Although the phenomena themselves are generally negative, each has a positive counterpart: the absence of prejudice is openmindedness; the absence of warfare is peace. The more we learn about the causes and remedies of prejudice, for example, the better will be our ability to reduce its occurrence.

In the introduction to this unit, we saw that prejudice could be experimentally created and then eliminated. Specifically, group conflict engendered group hostility and prejudice; hostility and prejudice were then eliminated by requiring the groups to cooperate to achieve a common goal. We shall begin our study of intergroup relations with a closer look at the nature of prejudice, its causes, and its remedies.

PREJUDICE

Prejudice refers to a *prejudgment* made on the basis of faulty generalizations or incomplete information. Such a prejudgment may occur, for example, when an opinion or attitude is formed without consideration of the facts that would enable one to make an independent, objective judgment. Prejudices may be favorable as well as unfavorable. Thus, if we are politically liberal, we may be predisposed to accept the voting recommendation of a liberal organization if we lack independent information about a particular ballot measure. Similarly, a landlord may welcome a married couple as new tenants because he has had good luck with married tenants in the past. Note that these examples are the types of prejudgments that we all make most of the time: that is, we rely on past experience to predict future events.

If our prejudices are indeed the results of our own past experience, and if they are accurate, they provide us with a convenient way of dealing with new events. Even when our generalizations are somewhat reliable, however, we may fail to realize that they are no more than generalizations that can in fact mislead us if they do not accurately correspond to the specific situation before us. Surely not every married couple is a responsible renter, nor is every single person—even one of unconventional appearance—an irresponsible one.

Prejudice is therefore risky in that a generalization about a group of people or events is used to assess an individual person or event. The risk is particularly evident, of course, when the generalization is false to begin with, that is, when the generalization does *not* apply to the majority of persons in the group. It is difficult to know how accurate our generalizations really are, because although some of our beliefs that are based on experience may be valid, others may be based on experience that is *invalid* or unrepresentative. Finally, many of our beliefs are not based on personal experience at all, but on the word of others: parents, politicians, group spokesmen, or the mass media. Many of our prejudices, therefore, have been passed on to us from other sources.

Prejudices tend to be self-perpetuating. When we entertain a prejudice, we tend to interpret events in ways that are consistent with it. Moreover, we are likely to be emotionally resistant to change, and, in order to maintain our prejudice, we may seize upon any piece of information (or misinformation)—however insignificant—that supports our belief, while ignoring or rationalizing much more substantial evidence that appears to contradict it. Furthermore, we tend to regard events that we misinterpret from a biased point of view as confirmation of the bias. The irony, then, is that misconstrued events actually strengthen the prejudice that gives rise to the misconstruction.

The Functions of Prejudice Prejudices may help us to justify our behavior. For example, if the old settlers believe that the new immigrants are lazy and amoral (or militant and after their jobs), they can better rationalize unfair treatment of them or a vote against egalitarian legislation.

Prejudice can provide a means of venting our anger and frustration. If someone is unable to confront his boss for not giving him a raise, or a professor for not giving him an "A," or society for not recognizing his talents, he may vent his frustration elsewhere: perhaps by playing handball or running on a track—or less constructively, by slamming doors or kicking the cat. Or, still less constructively, he may direct his anger toward a *scapegoat*—someone for whom retaliation is difficult. In recent years, "people on welfare" have often been assigned this role. Historically, many groups, including poor immigrants, Indians, and blacks have all been treated as scapegoats. The origin of the term "scapegoat" is explained in Figure 22.1.

The Selection of a Scapegoat If an inability to retaliate is an important characteristic that one looks for in selecting a scapegoat, then there should be less interracial aggression if retaliation from the target can be expected. In 1972, Edward and Marci Donnerstein and colleagues conducted a laboratory study to test the specific prediction that the amount of aggression directed against black targets by white subjects would decline when the situation was constructed to maximize fear of black retaliation. Results showed that although white subjects displayed more aggression against black targets than against white targets when retaliation was unlikely, they delivered less direct (but more indirect) aggressive behavior toward black than white targets when the target had the opportunity to retaliate. The white subjects in this study generally expected more direct retaliation from black than from white targets. These results are consistent with the idea that whites have learned to fear black retaliation and that such fear

Figure 22.1
The term "scapegoat" is derived from a practice of the ancient Hebrews, who symbolically placed all of their sins on the back of a goat on an annual Day of Atonement. The goat, which had been chosen by lot, was then driven into the wilderness. It escaped (hence, "scape") the fate of a second goat, also chosen by lot, which was sacrificed as an offering to Jehovah.

may minimize direct forms of aggression. Although this conclusion concurs with black author James Baldwin's prediction that fear of the blacks' power to retaliate will be a crucial factor in the achievement of racial equality, it also suggests that indirect forms of aggression may be increased by such fears.

Inability to retaliate is one of the characteristics of the ideal scapegoat enumerated by the late Gordon Allport in his classic work, *The Nature of Prejudice*. Another characteristic Allport lists is membership in a group that is clearly identifiable, so that the chosen targets may be easily recognized. Thus black Americans are a convenient scapegoat for white Americans. In Hitler's Germany, the Jews were not as readily identifiable, and it may be that this was the reason they were required to wear a special insignia.

The third characteristic of a scapegoat is his accessibility. Obviously, one cannot use someone as a scapegoat if he is inaccessible. For example, at about the turn of the century, many whites in certain parts of the South were frustrated with sharply declining cotton prices. The northern industrialists who were in part responsible for the lower prices were inaccessible. However, throughout that period of economic distress, from 1882 to 1930, numerous lynchings of blacks occurred. Moreover, Carl Hovland and Robert Sears showed that the number of lynchings in a given year during this period could be predicted from cotton prices that year. Perhaps, to some extent, aggression against the northern industrialists was *displaced* to the blacks.

The fourth characteristic of scapegoats is being historically identified as such—Allport points out that if a particular group has been successfully used as a scapegoat in the past, then the same group is more likely to be used in the future. Moreover, the very fact that a group has been blamed for wrong-doing in the past can be employed to justify repeated aggressions. Indeed, people who have been punished

Figure 22.2
In Germany in the 1930s, these Nazi stormtroopers displayed signs warning Germans against Jews and calling for a boycott of Jewish merchants. [Brown Brothers]

or penalized simply as the result of chance or bad luck are subsequently viewed as deserving of their shabby treatment. For example, in one study, observers watched two people working with equal diligence on a task, but then as the result of a coin toss one of the two individuals received the entire reward. Upon learning this, observers actually rated the luckless person as having worked less hard!

Examples of Displaced Aggression In the preceding chapter we described a laboratory study demonstrating that people, when led to believe they conformed in attitudes and opinions to the pattern prevailing in a group, selected someone who supposedly did not conform to undertake an unpleasant task and to be exposed to the risk of receiving electric shocks. If deviants can be chosen as targets of aggression even in situations created in the laboratory, imagine how much stronger the tendency must be to displace aggression toward deviants in the real world. For example, we noted that Hitler used Jewish people as scapegoats against whom he could channel the frustration and anger stemming from defeat in World War I and Germany's subsequent social, political, and economic turmoil (Figure 22.2).

Displaced aggression is not a peculiarly human phenomenon. For example, a pigeon switched from a schedule of frequent reinforcement to one of *extinction* (in which rewards are terminated altogether) will emit emotional behaviors such as wing flapping, and, if given the opportunity, will aggress against a defenseless "target pigeon." Such aggression, which occurs as a result of the removal of positive reinforcement, has been labeled *extinction-elicited aggression.* Another type of displaced aggression, *pain-elicited aggression,* has been shown to occur in some animals after the administration of electric shock.

The Effects of Prejudice on Perception   Some psychologists—including Allport—have restricted the working definition of prejudice to cases in which the holder of an opinion is resistant to accepting contradicting evidence. Thomas Pettigrew has related several examples of *immunity to information,* which suggest that the prejudiced person may be "blind" to information that is inconsistent with his prejudice. For example, in one interview—conducted in the late 1950s—a friendly white North Carolina farmer confided that the family "always" turned their television set off when Negroes were performing. As Pettigrew was completing his interview he noticed that in the adjoining room the rest of the family was watching some black entertainers perform on television. Pettigrew reports additional examples revealing the large discrepancy that can exist between what people apparently sincerely believe to be true and what is actually happening before their very eyes.

Two or more individuals who view an indentical sequence of events may indeed receive very different impressions from them. Such *selective-perception* effects are well known and can be demonstrated by showing films of a sports event to the fans of both teams: most people exhibit a strong tendency to see the favored team as committing fewer infractions. Such an experiment on selective perception was performed

in 1951 by Albert Hastorf and Hadley Cantril after a major football game between Princeton and Dartmouth. The game had been rough, particularly on the part of the Dartmouth players, and Princeton's All-American tailback—Dick Kazmaier—had suffered a broken nose. Students at each university who had seen the game were later shown the game on film and asked to record rule infractions as they occurred. The Princeton undergraduates reported that the Dartmouth players were responsible for the rough play and that Dartmouth had committed twice as many infractions as had Princeton. The Dartmouth undergraduates, however, believed both teams were equally to blame for the roughness and that each team had committed the same number of infractions.

Another, more striking example of prejudice, so strong that no amount of corrective information would be likely to alter it, is illustrated in the following dialogue between "Mr. X" and "Mr. Y" from Allport's *The Nature of Prejudice:*

X The trouble with the Jews is that they only take care of their own group.
Y But the record of the Community Chest campaign shows that they gave more generously, in proportion to their numbers, to the general charities of the community, than do non-Jews.
X That shows they are always trying to buy favor and intrude into Christian affairs. They think of nothing but money; that is why there are so many Jewish bankers.
Y But a recent study shows that the percentage of Jews in the banking business is negligible, far smaller than the percentage of non-Jews.
X That's just it; they don't go in for respectable business; they are only in the movie business or run night clubs.*

*Gordon Allport, *The Nature of Prejudice,* (Cambridge, Mass.: Addison-Wesley, 1954, Pp. 13–14).

Stereotypes In this discussion, we have been concerned primarily with *negative* prejudices, those prejudgments that are unfavorable. But preconceptions are not necessarily malicious, and some are even *positive*, predisposing us to attribute favorable qualities to a person who may not in fact possess them. Whether positive or negative, such beliefs or expectations about individual members of a group are known as *stereotypes*. We all hold stereotypes of one sort or another. For example, what image comes to mind when you picture each of the following?

1. An Italian barber?

2. A French chef?

3 A Jewish tailor?

4. An author and scholar?

5. A professional football player?

6. A racketeer?

Most of us probably have a fairly clear idea of what an "Italian barber" should look like, a stereotype perhaps influenced by actual encounters and possibly influenced by the caricatures in movies or television skits. If the occupations were not included in the first three items, we might choose a different set of adjectives to describe the "typical" Italian, Frenchman, or Jew. The term *national character* has been used to refer to personality configurations that are usually applied to adult members of a particular society. However, research on the personality characteristics of ethnic groups has revealed no important differences from nationality to nationality, provided that the comparisons are made between members having approximately the same social status and amount of education.

Some interesting work has been done on American stereotypes of various national and ethnic groups.

In such studies, opinions are solicited by presenting to subjects a list of groups and asking them to select from a large list of traits those characteristics that best match their image of each group. Early studies of this nature showed that Americans considered themselves "industrious, intelligent, and materialistic"; Germans "scientifically minded, industrious, and stolid"; Negroes "superstitious, lazy, and happy-go-lucky"; Italians "artistic, impulsive, and passionate"; Turks "cruel, very religious, and treacherous"; and so on. In the original study, conducted in the 1930s and 1940s, Princeton undergraduates were the subjects. Later studies on the views of different student populations supported the original findings, indicating that American students with varying cultural backgrounds and personal experiences shared common stereotyped conceptions of ethnic groups. Some popular movie stereotypes are shown in Figure 22.3.

G. M. Gilbert conducted a later study (in 1951) also on Princeton subjects. It is interesting that he found that the students were much less willing to make generalizations about ethnic groups. Many of the students thought it was unreasonable to be asked to make such generalizations, particularly since they had had very little experience with members of those groups—an interesting variation from the original study, in which most students had been willing to characterize Turks as "cruel and treacherous," even though many of them had never met a Turk! The Gilbert study also pointed out certain changes in prevailing stereotypes. For example, in the wake of World War II, American stereotypes of the Japanese and Germans had been considerably more negative. Since that time, however, the stereotypes themselves have altered as have the tendencies to form them.

These changes probably reflect the powerful and pervasive influence of cultural factors upon our beliefs, for since World War II social scientists, edu-

cators, and legislators have begun to combat effectively a number of widely held prejudices. As a result, ethnic and racial stereotypes have come to be viewed, at least by increasing numbers of the educated, as unfounded generalizations. In large measure, no matter what one's view of a "Turk" or a "black" or a "white" may be, it is usually based on what has been learned from hearsay, rather than on direct experience. But, if we are taught that no important differences exist between ethnic groups, we are less likely to interpret our initial experiences with members of other groups from a prejudiced point of view. Nonetheless, the shift in attitude has been one of degree, and prejudice remains quite prevalent in modern society. It is still difficult for one to grow up truly open-minded and unprejudiced.

Stereotypes of course need not be of an ethnic nature. Other common preconceptions are those we form about people engaged in various occupations. Recall, for example, the final three items on the foregoing list: "an author and scholar," "a professional football player," "a racketeer." When you look at the first item, the author-scholar, is the initial image that comes to mind female? Probably not. Indeed, had the item been "a respected author and scholar" the tendency to think of a woman might

have been even lower. The existence of such a pervasive influence of cultural stereotypes is supported by studies showing that women themselves will think less of a given work if they think it has been written by a woman rather than a man (as we mentioned in the introduction to this unit). Your image of the professional football player is probably one of a rather substantially built man. This too is predictable, and reasonably accurate, since most professional football players are indeed large, though, like any generalization, it has its exceptions. Finally, what is your image of the racketeer? Chances are the person in mind was not particularly attractive, sensitive, or well-spoken.

Whatever images you yourself may have formed of the six ethnic and professional stereotypes, you probably agree that, although some may be based partly on personal experience, others are founded entirely on hearsay, the source of which may be unknown. But such a tendency to use second-hand information is neither surprising nor completely undesirable. We would be limited indeed if all of our knowledge and beliefs were based on direct, personal experience. Indeed, knowlege obtained by hearsay may in fact be essential. What can be most destructive is to retain preconceptions that are largely inaccurate, and to apply them uncritically to individual members of the stereotyped group.

In summary, probably the two most unfortunate consequences of prejudice are the following. (1) We may erroneously attribute an individual's actions or fate to motives and causes that are consistent with our prejudices: this means that, in our minds, a person about whom we hold a negative stereotype probably "can't win" no matter what his behavior, and furthermore an unbecoming action or an unlucky occurrence only strengthens our stereotyped point of view. (2) When a stereotype is staunchly maintained in a society, members of the stereotyped group may come to believe in the stereotype themselves.

Figure 22.3
Hollywood's films sometimes reflect racial *stereotypes*. *Top:* Humorous, musically gifted Negroes have given way to virile and violent blacks. *Bottom:* The cunning and sinister Oriental man and the quiet and alluring Oriental woman have been portrayed in many Hollywood films—often by non-Asians. The square-jawed, straight-nosed Caucasian hero fulfills still another stereotype. [Upper left: "Boogie Woogie Dream," Hollywood Pictures Corporation. Upper right: "Shaft in Africa," Copyright © 1973 Metro-Goldwyn-Mayer, Inc.]

The Causes of Prejudice   Elliot Aronson, in 1972, suggested that the primary causes of prejudice are four. One is economic competition, occurring especially if people are afraid of losing their jobs to members of a minority group. Thus, those who feel deprived, but are not as deprived as others, tend to be the most prejudiced, especially when their fortunes seem to be evaporating even further. Indeed, recent opinion polls have shown that groups just one rung above blacks on the socioeconomic ladder tend to exhibit the most prejudice against them.

The second cause of prejudice suggested by Aronson, *displaced aggression,* has already been discussed. Its significance was demonstrated further by an experiment by Neal Miller and Richard Bugelski in 1948 in which subjects who had already expressed negative attitudes toward minority groups were then put through a series of difficult and frustrating tasks. After this frustrating experience, their attitudes toward minority groups were reassessed; virtually all subjects showed an increase in prejudice.

The third cause of prejudice suggested by Aronson is individual *personality.* Some people have personalities that seem to predispose them toward disliking members of minority groups. In other words, according to Aronson, some of us are predisposed to be prejudiced. Such personalities, apparently rooted in childhood experiences, are termed *authoritarian personalities,* manifested by tendencies not only toward prejudice, but also toward conformity, dislike of change, and antidemocratic sentiment. The authoritarian personality exhibits a normal amount of outward respect for authority, but his basic fear and insecurity prompt him to strike out against defenseless minority groups. The prejudice of this personality type differs from the preconceptions maintained by most other people, in that it tends to be universal, embracing *all* minority groups, rather than a selected few. We will return to the authoritarian personality

when we consider attitudes in Chapter 23 and the measurement of individual traits in Chapter 26.

The fourth cause of prejudice suggested by Aronson is simple *conformity,* which we discussed in Chapter 21. According to Thomas Pettigrew, most prejudice results simply from *efforts to conform* to social norms. For example, among several socioeconomic groups in certain areas of the South, one is *expected* to be prejudiced against blacks. A white Southerner who merely supports equal political and economic rights for black Southerners may find himself labeled a "nigger lover." Pettigrew's argument is strengthened by the example of the West Virginia coal miners who are integrated below the ground— where no social norms dictate otherwise—but continue in many ways to observe segregation above ground.

That social conformity may be the main cause of prejudice seems even more plausible if we examine the other possible reasons for racial prejudice in the South. Economic competition cannot be the main reason for southern prejudice, for example, because blacks compete with whites more effectively in the North, where measurements consistently indicate antiblack sentiment is lower in general than in the South. Nor does the Southerner tend to be more of an authoritarian personality. Pettigrew checked this possibility by administering F tests (a measure of the authoritarian personality, discussed in Chapter 26). The scores revealed no difference between Southerners and Northerners on the authoritarian scale.

Remedies   If Pettigrew is correct, and the primary cause of prejudice is conformity to social norms, then prejudice should disappear when the norms are changed. Evidence suggests that prejudice does diminish as norms shift, although changes are not as rapid as we might hope. Apparently, once the norms

Figure 22.4
In the film based on William Golding's novel *Lord of the Flies*, most of the English schoolboys who survive a plane crash on a tropical island turn into savage killers when they are free of the controls of civilization. [Copyright © 1963, Continental Distributing, Inc., Filmersa Prod.]

for behavior are altered, attitude change often follows, especially if economic competition does not exist. Thus, as the laws are changed, effectively eliminating *de facto* segregation, many overt behaviors are forced by law to change. To date, the results of enforced changes suggest that if individuals are obliged to interact as individuals of equal status— even if that interaction has been dictated by law— their attitudes toward one another will improve. As a consequence of such continued contact, the prejudiced person encounters experiences that contradict his attitude. Of course, some prejudiced people may cling to their preconceptions, but the large majority of prejudiced people, especially those who have been prejudiced simply because of social pressure, begin to see that their stereotypes have been misleading and incorrect, and gradually shed them. Although this description is admittedly somewhat oversimplified, it is a reasonably accurate one. However, two qualifications should be stressed. (1) As noted previously, if economic competition is a factor, prejudice will be far more difficult to eliminate merely by increased contact. (2) If both groups are not granted equal status, increased contact between them will probably be ineffective in eliminating prejudice.

WARFARE AND VIOLENCE

We turn now to violent interactions among groups. Indeed, warfare and violence between groups pervade human history. Though violence itself is usually condemned by civilized societies, organized violence occurring in war is not subject to the same restrictions as are individual acts of violence.

THEORIES OF AGGRESSION

The Biological Instincts One explanation of organized national aggression is that it is a man-

ifestation of man's inherently aggressive nature. According to this "biological" explanation, it is man's innate "aggressive instinct" that makes warfare an unavoidable aspect of human existence. The source of this instinct has been variously designated as "a lust for killing," a "death instinct," a "need for aggression," or a reflection of "innate pugnacity." If we accept the aggressive instinct as fact, the implications are inevitable: man should accept and adapt to his own basically violent nature, and warfare must be accepted as natural and inevitable.

William Golding's novel *Lord of the Flies* is essentially a presentation of this biological explanation of aggression. A group of British school boys are marooned by themselves on a jungle island. As the boys pass more and more time without the strictures of civilization, they become increasingly disposed toward brutality and aggression. Eventually their inherent aggressive instincts toward destruction and savagery come to rule their behavior; they begin to resemble a pack of wolves more than a group of school boys (Figure 22.4). Golding seems to be saying that, when left to their natural instincts, even the innocents of the human species resort to their heritage of aggression. It is only because civilization is subsequently reimposed on the boys that they are prevented from destroying one another.

The Social Incentive   The explanation of war as an inevitable outcome of man's biological instincts is, however, incomplete without a consideration of the characteristics of modern society and organized institutional aggression. Modern war is not a phenomenon occurring between two individuals. Rather, it is a highly publicized, impersonal, and well-organized social effort. Indeed, organized warfare as we know it could not even exist without an extremely advanced technological society. An alternative view, contradicting the biological approach, maintains that we are *taught* to engage in warfare and aggression and that these teachings are supported and fostered by economic and political forces that benefit from organized aggression. The rewards for lessons well learned are readily evident. Wars are ostensibly waged for the most noble of reasons. The soldiers on both sides are led to believe that if they are victorious, they will be rewarded by freedom, riches, divine salvation, and so on, and that humanity in general will benefit. Successful warriors are lauded and made into national heroes, and the qualities that are presumed to have enabled them to excel—such as bravery and strength—are held up as ideals toward which to strive. In short, numerous incentives are provided by society in an effort to channel man's energies toward war. This fact itself makes the biological explanation of war questionable. If war were a natural proclivity of man, why would society need to go to such lengths to induce him to engage in it? Why, for example, would nations ever have to draft citizens into military service?

A second argument against the biological explanation of war is that warfare is unique to humans. If it were a part of man's biological heritage, some suggestion of warlike tendencies should be evident in the behavior of man's biological ancestors. However, nothing resembling organized warfare occurs among the other primates or lower mammals. Even between individual animals, fights to the death are rare, and what fighting does occur is usually an effort either to defend territory from intruders or to obtain food. The evolution of appeasement postures—the submissive gestures frequently observed in many social species in response to threat or attack from another of the same species—suggests that natural selection has proceeded in a way that has in fact inhibited aggressive tendencies in lower animals. Moreover, a closer look at our own species may even reveal that warfare is not as universal among humans as is usually assumed. For example, Margaret Mead has pointed out that, even today, primitive human societies exist that apparently have never known warfare. The lack of evidence for organized aggression in lower animals and in some primitive human societies, then, does indeed suggest that war may well be a product of "advanced" societies and not of man's biological instincts.

Social Methods of Desensitization   What then are the social factors than induce man to engage in warfare? We have already mentioned various social and personal rewards of warfare—such as freedom, material rewards, and national acclaim—but evidently these inducements may not be the fundamental causes, for several psychologists have suggested that war and physical violence in general are actually repugnant to humans. Therefore, the most important determining factors are the ways in which society *desensitizes* people to war, making it more acceptable and justifiable to the people taught to engage in it.

One frequently cited method of making international violence more acceptable is the *dehumanization*

Figure 22.5
An American bomber pilot's view of the war in South Vietnam. [United Press International Photo by David Kennerly]

Figure 22.6
An American soldier's view of the war in South Vietnam. [United Press International Photo]

of the enemy. The enemy is coldly portrayed as something less than human, and unworthy of the treatment normally afforded other human beings: killing other humans comes to be seen as little if anything more than stepping on destructive insects. Advanced technology has also made the atrocities of war more tolerable by removing the people that commit them from the scene of the action. The long-distance weapons, the remote-control buttons, and the strategic decisions arrived at far from the actual battlefield make the deeds of modern warfare seem somehow less objectionable. The pilot who drops the bomb is removed from its devastating consequences and may therefore be able to detach himself from the death and destruction that ensues. Roger Johnson has written that many of the American pilots who bombed North and South Vietnam were sent to either Hong Kong or Japan on leave rather than allowed to stay in South Vietnam, where they might have seen casualties of their bombing. By removing the individual from the suffering that is caused, and from his own responsibility for it, violence is made to seem less repugnant (Figures 22.5 and 22.6).

A final means by which individuals can be gradually desensitized to the realities of war is that of organized military and social training. Redundant drills in military camps provide individuals with the skills required for war and enable them to adapt to the consequences of using those skills. Firing a gun for the first time can induce mild feelings of fear in many individuals. These feelings, however, soon wane upon repeated practice. Similarly, apprehension at firing a gun at a target shaped like a human eventually dissipates, as does firing the gun at a real human being. It has been suggested that news films of battlefield atrocities may have similar desensitizing effects on the citizens at home who condone warfare—after repeated viewings of extreme violence, one's emotional reaction may become nothing more than that engendered by just another episode of a popular police-detective series. Indeed our language itself is a densensitizing agent, for as Albert Bandura has pointed out, modern English is replete with moderately inoffensive terms that are used to refer to acts of violence. The use of such terms presumably deemphasizes for the individual his natural emotional reaction to the deed: for example, in Vietnam, the act of killing was commonly referred to as "wasting."

NATIONAL AGGRESSION

Most psychological studies of aggression are concerned with factors that impel the individual to aggress. However, as we have suggested, war is not a phenomenon occurring between individuals, but rather it is more appropriately described as the behavior of a subculture or of a nation. The most profitable approach to the study of warfare may therefore be one which focuses not on the aggressive behavior of the individual, but on the aggressive behavior of nations as integrated units. This is the approach adopted by Rosalind and Ivo Feierabend in the 1960s in their investigations of the factors that give rise to political aggression among nations.

Internal Aggression The Feierabends and their co-workers have developed a composite measure of political stability based on the aggressive behavior occurring within nations. In the Feierabend's view, strongly aggressive events, such as assassinations, indicate a high degree of internal instability, whereas the absence of aggressive acts—or the occurrence of only very minor ones—is evidence of internal stability. Statistical data, collected in the course of several years, indicates that technologically underdeveloped nations exhibit far less stability, and therefore far more aggression, than do modernized

nations. However, among the underdeveloped nations, *transitional societies*—those in the process of developing from a primitive stage to a more modern stage—have been shown to be less stable than the traditional primitive societies that were not developing. The Feierabends maintain that the aggression in the developing nations arises because the process of modernization engenders new hopes and aspirations in a people. These hopes and wants may eventually be satisfied, but their satisfaction necessarily takes a period of time. During this period, the discrepancy between new aspirations and existing social conditions creates severe frustrations among the people. These frustrations are presumably greater than those experienced by a more deprived and more primitive, but less transitional, society that has developed no such aspirations. Indices of frustration, therefore, appear to be negatively correlated with stability. The more frustrated a nation—that is, the more unfulfilled its hopes and aspirations—the less stable the society and therefore the greater the internal aggression exhibited by that nation. The nation that is highly stable and less aggressive than others exhibits low frustration. In such nations, literacy is widespread, as are medical care, adequate nutrition, and technological conveniences. One source of internal national aggression (assassinations, riots, mass arrests, coups, and so forth) therefore, seems to be frustration, that is, the discrepancy existing between a people's modern aspirations and its primitive levels of satisfaction. Needless to say, not all highly developed nations exhibit stability, for, within even the most technologically advanced, large numbers of the population may not share in the benefits, and large-scale frustration and internal aggression can ensue.

A second factor that may give rise to internal aggression is a moderate degree of governmental *coercion*. Political coercion is essentially a national form of punishment. Mild punishment of individuals is known to facilitate aggression, perhaps simply because it produces greater frustration. The Feierabends' data indicate that the punishment of nations, too, actually results in more aggression. Countries in which only *moderate* coercion is present are those with the greatest aggressive instability, whereas libertarian governments and totalitarian governments are clearly more stable. Presumably the reason that stability prevails under totalitarianism is that aggressive acts indicative of instability are not allowed to occur at all.

International Aggression   What do these data on internal national aggression tell us about war, that is, about international aggression, the external aggression directed toward other nations? The Feierabends have examined instances of international hostility committed by seventy-five nations in the years from 1955 to 1960, and rated them by the degree of violence associated with each act. Finland was found to be the least aggressive of the nations ranked; the Soviet Union and the United States were found to be the most aggressive. These results suggest that social frustration may not be the only factor contributing to international hostility. It is possible that a nation's prominence as a world power also inclines it to participate in extensive international aggression.

But what of the nations that cannot be considered great powers? For them, social frustration does seem to be the primary factor influencing international aggression. Thus, in the Feierabend study, most of the countries that had been rated as frustrated were shown to be not only internally aggressive but externally aggressive as well. In contrast, 75 percent of the stable countries were peaceful. The Feierabends have concluded that a knowledge of the degree of frustration and internal instability existing within a country enables one to make a more accu-

rate prediction of that country's international behavior.

In sum, psychological research on the causes of war suggests that, to some extent, frustration facilitates aggression. More importantly, warfare is not the inevitable result of an aggressive instinct but rather something that is socially induced. Before humans kill their fellow humans in warfare, their revulsion to bloodshed must be overcome, and they must be taught how to kill.

Suggested Readings

Allport, G. *The nature of prejudice*. (1954) Cambridge, Mass: Addison-Wesley. [A classic.]

Aronson, E. *The social animal*. (1972) San Francisco: W. H. Freeman and Co. [Contains an excellent treatment of prejudice.]

Brown, R. *Social psychology*. (1965) New York: The Free Press. [Contains important treatments of roles and stereotypes (in Chapter 3) and the authoritarian personality (in Chapter 10).]

Pettigrew, T. (1961) "Social psychology and desegregation research." *American psychologist, 16*, 105–112. [An interesting analysis.]

CHAPTER TWENTY-THREE

Attitudes

An *attitude* is a person's organized tendency to think, feel, and act in a certain general way in response to some aspect of his social environment or in response to a given class of objects. Attitudes are broad viewpoints that can be identified, at least to some extent, by the consistencies displayed in thoughts, feelings, and overt behavior. For example, if we are told that one person is a conservative and another a liberal, we attribute certain distinguishable and consistent attitudes to each. We expect differences between the two in their political and economic thinking, in their appearance, in their activities, and in the people they seek out as friends, as well as in what they say and do. Attitudes, then, are a complex collection of predispositions to think, respond, and behave in certain ways. They are an extremely important area of study for the social psychologist because of their influence in shaping an individual's perceptions, expectations, beliefs, feelings, and behaviors—that is, in shaping all of his responses to the various events, objects, people, and issues in his world.

Attitudes vary greatly in comprehensiveness, or the degree to which they influence the individual and others. Some, such as staunch conservatism, can be quite general, affecting almost every aspect of the individual's life. Others—prejudice against a minority group, for example—affect the individual primarily in his specific relations with identifiable groups of other individuals. Still others, such as sexual attitudes, may influence the individual in only very circumscribed and specific situations.

ATTITUDE PATTERNS

Since attitudes often occur in sets, if we know a person's attitude with regard to one subject, we may be able to predict what attitudes he will have toward others. For example one such set of attitudes is found in *authoritarianism,* which received extensive investigation immediately after World War II, because researchers had witnessed the effects of fascism in Germany and Italy and were concerned about the growing racism in America. This is the picture that emerged from their investigation: a highly authoritarian person takes a cold and hard view of the world and assumes a power-conscious personal stance in it. For example, authoritarians tend to see the world as divided into the weak and the strong. They believe that society depends on the strict enforcement of rules and laws. They believe that punishment for breaking the law should be swift and severe—many believe that prison is too good for most criminals. They are not tolerant of ambiguity, preferring that objects and situations be definite—yes or no, black or white. They believe strong leaders and obedient followers are needed to maintain their society. They are usually ethnocentric, firmly believing that differences exist between their own race and other distinguishable groups of people and that those differences should be upheld. Extremely authoritarian persons display hostility toward nearly all minorities, racial, religious, and ethnic. (Indeed, in one study, authoritarian subjects even downgraded fictitious groups!)

Authoritarianism, then, is a pattern of attitudes, and if we recognize someone as an authoritarian, we can predict what many of his attitudes will be. However, it is important to realize that we should not be too quick to attribute this or any other pattern of attitudes to people. Someone might strongly maintain a certain point of view that often occurs in conjunction with certain others and yet not himself subscribe to those other attitudes. For example, social pressures in the southern United States might compel a white person to speak disparagingly of black people, but this does not by itself indicate that the speaker is necessarily an authoritarian personality whose other attitudes can then be predicted. Only if we find evidence of negative attitudes toward other "out-groups" or other attitudes in the set can we begin to infer authoritarianism. Similarly, a person can be in favor of extreme punishment for criminals, perhaps as the result of a painful personal experience, without sharing the extremely rigid attitude toward obedience to authority that is upheld by the rabid authoritarian.

MEASURING ATTITUDES AND OPINIONS

American politics furnishes numerous examples of the accuracy with which opinions—specific expressions of an attitude—can be measured. In the Nixon–McGovern election in 1972, for example, some 83,000,000 people voted—65 percent for Nixon, 34 percent for McGovern. Two public-opinion organizations that make a business of predicting the outcomes of elections predicted the results of the 1972 election to within one percentage point. This means that they estimated the vote, in advance, to within a margin of less than 800,000 voters. The national television networks predicted the final outcome of the vote to the same accuracy only one-half hour after the polling places had closed in New York City, after only a seemingly negligible percentage of the vote had been reported, and a full two-and-a-half hours before the polls closed in California. This informed millions of people of the outcome—and accurately predicted their vote—before they had even gone to the polls. How is such accuracy possible?

One possibility can be discounted at once: nobody asks *all voters* to describe their political attitudes and how they will vote before the election itself. Many people cannot even tell you how they will eventually decide to vote. The estimate of the way in which 83,000,000 people will vote is made by asking the right people the right question at the right time or times. The task of selecting the right people is called *sampling*. Asking the right questions requires adjusting one's questions so that they have exactly the right degree of *bias* or specificity for a particular type of respondent. Finally, determining the right time or times requires that one analyze *trends*.

Remember that we are attempting to predict how 83,000,000 people will vote by talking with only a very small fraction of that number. Although we cannot provide the exact details of the way in which such predictions are made—these being closely guarded secrets of corporations that charge large sums of money for the information that their practical expertise can make available—we are able to outline the fundamentals of the general procedure.

Sampling Suppose that we want to know the average height of a group of a hundred people, but can only measure the actual heights of twenty of them. Which twenty do we want? Obviously, we will select the twenty who are closest to the average, so that the average of their heights will be very close to the average of all one hundred. But since we do not know the average height—we are supposed to estimate it—we might elect to choose our twenty people unsystematically—or at *random*—and then apply certain statistical procedures to estimate how far off we are likely to be.

But random selection does not guarantee that we will obtain the best possible sample—that closest to the average. Suppose, for example, that we learn that half of our group of one hundred are midgets, who vary in height but whose average height is three feet shorter than that of the others; or that our hundred are composed of families, with half the people being children between four and six years of age. It is obvious that a random selection could yield, at least occasionally, samples consisting entirely of midgets or children, as well as an alarmingly large proportion of unrepresentative samples, including too many midgets or children for our purpose. Thus, it would be better to take a sample of the short persons and a separate sample of the tall, and base our estimate of the overall average on both samples. To be sure, an intermediate step of this nature takes time and is feasible only when the composition of each subgroup is

known. But pollsters, who earn their living from their accurate assessments of public opinion, know that any time they can spend in dividing their hundred people into logical and relevant subgroups is worth more in accuracy than the amount of time saved by relying only on random sampling. The rule is this: find out as much as you can about the people you are surveying, and then use random sampling only when there is nothing surer. The process of separating people into categories is called *stratification*, and the random sampling of each stratum separately is called *stratified sampling*.

In trying to predict voting behavior, stratification is very important. Indeed, enough is known about the factors determining people's decisions on a presidential candidate that even multidimensional stratification (divisions according to several different variables) is possible. Some variables that have proved to be important in predicting how an individual will vote are age, sex, religion, years of formal education, income and general wealth, residence (whether urban or rural), region of the country, and, of course, political allegiance. In a properly stratified sample, each of these variables is properly represented.

Within a stratum, random selection must prevail. If a pollster is sent out to survey the intended vote of fifty Roman Catholic women between thirty and thirty-five years of age, with no more than a high-school education, with no inherited wealth, with family incomes of between $10,000 and $15,000 per year, and from small towns in the Midwest, the pollster must be sure to obtain a broad sample, which random selection facilitates. If the pollster finds all of his subjects in front of a school to which they have just brought their children, an obvious distortion could be introduced because those with children may not be representative of the whole group.

Years of polling experience have shown that certain groups can be used to predict the behavior of the general population more accurately than others. The old saying, "As Maine goes, so goes the nation," is no longer applicable, but national polling–survey organizations do rely on their own select key groups that they have found to be highly accurate predictors. These groups, of course, are not revealed, if for no other reason than that their vote must not be influenced by public announcement of their significance.

It is because of such groups that television and other surveys can accurately predict the vote in a whole state on the basis of returns from a small number of voting precincts that report early, that have habitually voted the way the whole state did in previous elections of the same type, and whose voters have not radically changed since those earlier elections. It is a safe assumption that, before election day, the residents of these precincts are heavily beset by poll-takers who are aware of their representativeness.

The reactions of some groups may be misleading and could disrupt the prediction of an election. For example, before the 1972 election, pollsters carefully monitored the political sentiments of voters between eighteen and twenty-one years of age, who had the right to vote for the first time. The pollsters suspected that they might vote for McGovern so disproportionately as to throw off predictions based on the solicited opinions of older voters whose voting habits were better known from previous elections. They did not, and the poll-takers had learned in advance that they would not.

Some parts of a stratified sample are more important than others, because they represent more people than other parts or because they contain voters who are known to be more changeable and harder to predict. When this is expected or known,

a proportionally larger number of people are included from those parts of the sample.

Bias   Notice the variations in the following questions:

1. Can we count on your vote for the President this year?
2. Are you voting for the team of the President and Mr. Agnew, or for McGovern?
3. Will you vote for President Nixon or Senator McGovern?
4. Do you expect to vote for Mr. McGovern or Mr. Nixon in November?
5. Which candidate will get your vote for President in November?

Each question reflects a different kind and degree of *bias*: that is, each uses subtle hints to induce the respondent to answer in a certain way. From Question 1 through Question 5, the bias in favor of Nixon decreases. The successful poll-taker must take great care to ask his questions in such a way that the respondent will answer honestly, without distorting his replies in some way. (See Figure 23.1–23.3.)

Other forms of bias may also occur in a public opinion survey. Responses can vary significantly with the race, sex, appearance, or manner of the poll-taker. On some issues, for example, blacks may express different opinions to black poll-takers than to white. Similarly, a male pollster of extremely conservative appearance would probably come away with different expressed opinions on free love and birth control from a group of female college students than would a young female pollster dressed like a college student. If polling is to be effective, then, both questioner and question must be carefully selected with the intention of encouraging the respondents to tell what they really think.

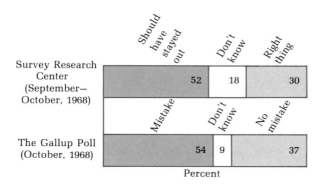

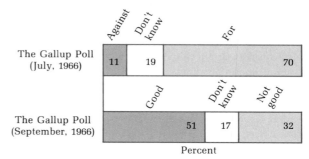

Figure 23.1
Similar opinion-poll questions asked at the same time should produce similar results. The Survey Research Center asked: "Do you think we did the right thing in getting into the fighting in Vietnam, or should we have stayed out?" The Gallup Poll asked: "In view of the developments since we entered the fighting do you think the U.S. made a mistake in sending troops to fight in Vietnam?" [Figures 23.1, 23.2, 23.3, 23.4 are from Philip E. Converse and Howard Schuman, " 'Silent Majorities' and the Vietnam War," *Scientific American*, June 1970, 17–25. Copyright © 1970 by Scientific American, Inc. All rights reserved.]

Figure 23.2
Different questions on the same broad issue can create the impression of shifts in public opinion, whether or not such shifts have actually occurred. In July 1966, the Gallup Poll asked people whether they were for or against the U.S. bombing of oil storage dumps in Haiphong and Hanoi. In September 1966, the Gallup Poll asked people whether it would be a good idea for the United States to submit the problem of what to do about Vietnam to the United Nations and agree to accept the U.N.'s decision. These poll results could be interpreted to mean that many hawks turned into doves in a short time. However, another interpretation is that many people simply favored decisive action to end the war and would support either peaceful or violent measures. [Copyright © 1970 by Scientific American, Inc. All rights reserved.]

Trends   One way of assessing the results of a current poll is to determine the way in which it fits in with the trend established by previous, similar polls. The graph (Figure 23.4) shows the trend established in the course of three years of polling American voters' opinion of the way President Lyndon Johnson was "handling the situation in Vietnam." By the end of the period, the number of voters approving his performance was low, and though such diminished support of a President is unusual, this decline is not surprising if one considers the inexorable downward trend that preceded it. Johnson decided not to run again, and

it is possible that his decision was based partly on the results of the surveys as well as on the disappointing results of the New Hampshire primary contest against the antiwar spokesman Senator Eugene McCarthy. The election confirmed what the polls showed: Johnson's utter lack of success in raising his popularity more than temporarily by anything he tried. As the curve in Figure 23.4 shows, whether he stopped the bombing of North Vietnam or resumed it, the trend continued, interrupted by

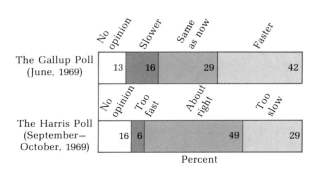

Figure 23.3
The method of presentation of a poll question can greatly influence the results. Both polls asked about the rate of troop withdrawal from Vietnam. The Gallup Poll offered as alternatives only "Faster" and "Slower" but interviewers accepted "Same as now" if it was volunteered. The Harris poll offered all three alternatives, thereby making it easier for people to go along with the then-current rate of withdrawal. [Copyright © 1970 by Scientific American, Inc. All rights reserved.]

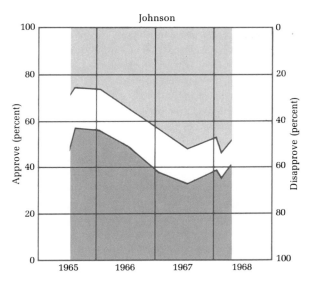

Figure 23.4
This graph shows support for the Johnson administration's handling of the war shrinking and opposition gaining ground. [Copyright © 1970 by Scientific American, Inc. All rights reserved.]

only slight and temporary indications of increased support.

Trend analysis is important in predicting elections not only because of changes in voters who have already formed an opinion but also because substantial proportions of the voters do not make up their minds until quite near the election. The undecided vote can often determine the outcome in a close election. Studies have shown that it is hard to predict the behavior of those who decide late, but once the polls begin to show a trend, the trend tends to continue.

The Influence of Opinion Polls Few people like to back a loser. Thus, when polls show a substantial advantage for one or another political

candidate, a *bandwagon effect* can occur, as more and more people join in supporting the apparent winner. This effect increases the candidate's lead, establishing a *vicious circle* (at least from the other candidate's point of view) that further enhances the bandwagon effect. But the bandwagon effect is somewhat balanced by a traditional tendency among some segments of American society to support the *underdog*. Now that public-opinion surveys have demonstrated such incredible accuracy in their predictions, we can expect serious study to be undertaken in the near future on the significance of the bandwagon effect and sympathy for the underdog.

Runaway election victories—such as Johnson's over Goldwater in 1964 and Nixon's over McGovern in 1972—have stimulated speculation about the influence on voters who may be affected by early predictions of the national winner (such as those made on television in 1964 and 1972 before some people had voted). Early predictions are not as important in close elections—such as the Kennedy–Nixon election in 1960 and the Nixon–Humphrey election in 1968—in which the issue remains in doubt until after the polls have closed throughout the nation. However, it is likely that they add to the bandwagon effect in one-sided contests, if only because they discourage the opponent's supporters from going out to vote. To date, however, apparently no studies have been made of this potential determinant of voter attitudes.

Unobtrusive Measures of Attitudes   Polls ask explicit questions, but attitudes can also be studied unobtrusively. We can, for example, obtain considerable information about the attitudes of art lovers toward art just by noticing how they move through an art gallery, what they look at, and how long they look.

Individual Attitude Scales   Not only is it useful to learn which way a person is leaning on an election issue, but it can also be extremely valuable to determine how strongly he holds his attitudes. We shall consider only two from the many, and often very complex, methods of assessing the strength of an attitude. One method is the use of simple rating scales. For example, a person might be asked, "Do you favor or oppose the legalization of marijuana? Do you hold your opinion very strongly, strongly, weakly, or very weakly?" Or he might be asked to indicate the strength of his attitude by placing an

X along a line that extends from the labels "Strongly in favor" to "Strongly opposed." The second scale seems to be the more sensitive, since the distance of his mark from the two labels allows for much finer distinctions in the expression of the intensity of his attitude.

A second method of assessing attitude strength is by means of an empirically selected set of questions that reflect gradations in the strength of an attitude on a given topic. Someone whose attitude is not strong may answer "yes" only to Questions A, B, and perhaps C; someone with a strong attitude will answer "yes" not only to A, B, and C but also to D, E, F, G, H, and so on. This method, called *Guttman scaling* after its originator, is a highly satisfactory way of assessing attitude strength, since the order of the questions can be scrambled, making successful deception nearly impossible. For example, in a well-constructed questionnaire, we know something is amiss if someone says "no" to Questions D, E, F, and G but switches to "yes" on H and J.

MODIFYING AND CHANGING ATTITUDES

Consider how much time and energy is spent by a broad range of organizations and people in efforts to modify other people's attitudes. What the advertiser, politician, businessman, parent, writer, teacher, minister, propagandist, and seducer all have in common is their tireless effort to change someone else's attitude about something. It is no wonder that attitude change has been one of the most popular topics in recent social psychology.

What is the difference between a change of "attitude" and a change of "opinion"? The terms themselves are often used interchangeably, but there is a substantial difference between them. An attitude is more comprehensive and general than an opinion:

it is the predisposition to react a certain way to an object or type of object, and therefore to form certain opinions about that object. Opinions are the manifestation of an underlying attitude. It is probable that a number of opinions about a given subject would have to be changed before any significant alteration of the more general attitude occurred—and a single changed attitude should, therefore, result in a vast array of changed opinions.

THEORIES OF ATTITUDE CHANGE

Three major theories have been devised to explain how and why attitudes develop and change: (1) one stresses the importance of *learning*, (2) one stresses the effects of *incentives*, and (3) one stresses the importance of *consistency*.

The Learning Theory   The late Carl Hovland and his associates popularized the view that attitudes are learned, that these tendencies to react in a certain way to various groups, people, events, or things are the results of our previous experience with them or with similar items. Changes in attitude are brought about by new experiences. The learning theory is the basis for many techniques of advertising, such as the displays showing attractive people in a particular make of car, or virile outdoorsmen smoking a certain brand of cigarette in attractive surroundings. The idea is that people tend automatically to respond positively to the attractive people and surroundings, and it is hoped that the positive reactions aroused by these items will be associated with the cars, cigarettes, and other products. Presumably, if the car then evokes positive feelings, people are more likely to buy it. Other ads show people who are extremely happy after a medication has relieved their headache or constipation. These ads are based on an assumption that the viewer will derive such vicarious

pleasure from the actors' joy that the next time he himself is afflicted with the same malady, he will respond by taking a dose of the advertised product. If it actually works for him, his attitude toward it should become even more positive.

Incentive Theory   According to this theory, a person adopts that attitude which he thinks will award him the maximum gain in a particular situation, after having calculated both what he may gain and what he may lose. A high-income professional person might, for example, have a negative attitude—and a long list of low opinions—toward minority groups because it is in accord with the attitudes maintained by his circle of friends. But suppose that the individual's professional practice, which produces the income for his comfortable lifestyle, begins to draw a great deal of business from minority clients. Even though a more positive attitude toward these minorities might alienate him somewhat from his social group, it will boost his practice so much that he may adopt this attitude as the one that maximizes his gain.

The Consistency Theories   According to this group of theories, when an individual is faced with disagreement or *inconsistency* between two of his attitudes or between an attitude and his actual behavior, he *modifies* either his behavior or his attitude to make them consistent. It is held to be more common to change attitudes than actions.

These theories vary somewhat in their specificity, their applicability, and their style. The first of them, the *balance theory*, from which other *consistency theories* have descended, was devised by the gestalt psychologist, Fritz Heider (b. 1896). Heider believed that we try to keep our attitudes toward people and events in balance, and that our attitudes should be congruous. Thus, if someone whom we like, admire, or respect teams up with someone we dislike, incongruity occurs and our attitudinal system is out of balance. The mechanism for restoring balance is attitude change. Therefore, we either lower our opinion of the person we like, or raise our opinion of the disliked person, or both. A similar type of incongruity arises when someone we dislike advocates a course of action that we have believed to be good for a long time. As a quite automatic response, either we begin to believe that the person cannot be all that bad if he agrees with us, or we begin to wonder if the course of action in question is all that good an idea.

Imbalance between two of a person's attitudes can occur in other ways as well. We are continually absorbing new information—quite frequently, some new information prompts us to modify almost spontaneously one or another of our attitudes. But a change in one attitude alone is usually impossible, because such a change results in imbalance. This discrepancy is itself either a cause for further change or a force that resists the original change in attitude. For example, suppose a person becomes convinced that pollution is a dangerous and undesirable condition. If he is sincerely committed to this position, he will have to modify other attitudes as well, and many of them are fundamental to his day-to-day existence. He probably drives a car, which produces polluting exhaust fumes; his clothes may be washed with polluting detergents; he may own stock and derive income from a business whose factories pollute the atmosphere; if he watches television or reads in the evenings, he probably uses electricity from a plant that spews smoke into the air. If he is truly convinced that pollution is a major menace, he must, to achieve balance among his attitudes, change a great many of them. To achieve balance between

attitudes and action, he must make corresponding changes in many of his daily habits. The difficulties in making these changes may induce him to modify his antipollution stance. Perhaps he will develop the attitude that although pollution is a hazard, it is one to be concerned about but not yet acted against.

The *congruity theory,* derived from the balance theory, is an attempt to confront some practical and quantitative aspects of attitude change. This theory proposes that balance is regained by an *averaging* of the scale values of the conflicting attitudes. For example, suppose a reasonably close friend—who has for you a positive value that might be expressed as $+2$—expresses an opinion with which you strongly disagree—say, a value of -3. Congruity theory suggests that your attitude toward your friend and your attitude toward the opinion are compromised into an average. Your friend becomes less attractive to you, and the opinion more attractive.

Dissonance Theory   One other descendant of balance theory—*dissonance theory*—continues to be one of the most influential, and flamboyant, theories in contemporary psychology. When two attitudes or an attitude and an action come into conflict, *cognitive dissonance* is said to result within the individual, who then strives to reduce it. Generally, the greater the disparity between the dissonant items, the greater the degree of cognitive dissonance that is generated, and the stronger the effort to reduce it.

Dissonance can be reduced either by outright rejection of one of the dissonant items, by modification of an attitude or an action, or by other means that enhance consonance, such as by acquiring socially supportive, consonant friends. If a smoker becomes aware of the statistics supporting the relationship between smoking and disease, substantial dissonance develops between his smoking habits and his newly awakened suspicion that he may be inviting illness every time he smokes. He can reduce the dissonance by not smoking; by discounting the Surgeon General's conclusions and embracing instead the alternative theories proposed by the tobacco companies; by adopting an optimistic belief in the imminent discovery of miracle cures for cancer and heart disease; or by acquiring consonant support in the form of new friends, all of whom are very old, healthy, and have smoked all their lives. Any one of these alternatives reduces dissonance—and causes changes in attitudes or behavior.

Dissonance increases correspondingly with the effort that one invests in adopting a new attitude or action pattern, and it also increases if the rewards, or payoffs, for adopting the new attitude or action diminish. For example, jokes that take a long time to tell (or listen to) may receive a better response than shorter jokes that are equally humorous. The reason is that dissonance is created between a conclusion that is not particularly funny and the amount of effort the listener has put into following the lengthy preamble to the punch line. People may reduce this kind of dissonance between invested effort and a low "pay-off" by finding the joke funnier than it really is.

Similarly, dissonance theory allows one to make certain predictions about the way in which someone will resolve attitudinal conflicts, given the particular payoff he has received for changing the attitude, or for pretending that he has changed it. Let us suppose, for example, that a well-informed biology student is paid to deliver a speech before a civic group affirming the biological inequality between two races—a position with which he does not concur. Dissonance theory predicts that if he reads it for

five dollars he will undergo a more positive change in attitude toward the content of the speech than he will if he reads it for a thousand dollars. The reasoning is as follows: someone with as little money as the average student would do almost anything for a thousand dollars, and he can justify his action to himself by maintaining that he did it for the money alone. But if he has done it for very little money, serious dissonance arises between the opinion he expresses on the evening he gives the speech and his inner attitude, and a change in his own attitude is therefore necessary to reduce that dissonance.

As persuasive as these various consistency theories are, they are subject to dispute simply because the fact remains that two *inconsistent attitudes* can both be held tenaciously by an individual. Political attitudes are a good example. Many people who hold liberal views on national political issues may be staunchly conservative on some local community issues. For example, a large number of liberals exhibited this kind of inconsistency when they were confronted with court orders that required the busing of their own children to integrated schools in the late 1960s and early 1970s.

FACTORS IN ATTITUDE CHANGE

Having discussed the *theory* of attitude change, we must now look at the net results of the large number of experiments on such change. Findings have not been particularly definitive—but the substance of the research suggests which factors seem to be most important in changing attitudes.

The basic procedures for an experiment on changing attitudes are deceptively simple: (1) measure the attitude of a person or the average attitude of a group; (2) then expose subjects to an experience devised to change that attitude—a speech, reading matter, a model scene to look at, even punishment,

| Change group | Measure attitude → Persuasion → Remeasure attitude |
| Control group | Measure attitude → No persuasion → Remeasure attitude |

Figure 23.5
A procedure for studying attitude change.

and (3) finally, measure the same attitude again in order to find out if it has been changed. (See Figure 23.5).

Studies of this nature have been many indeed, and have been concerned with nearly every imaginable variable. We shall discuss first those factors that induce change in attitudes, and then those that enhance stability, selecting the more interesting and important in each category.

The factors that appear to promote attitude change include the following: the status of the currently held attitude, the source of the persuasive (or unpersuasive) message, the medium through which the message is conveyed, the nature of the message or experience, the characteristics of the person holding the attitude, social and interpersonal factors, and the personal consequences of changing the attitude (Figure 23.6). Let us examine each of these factors briefly.

A prime factor affecting attitude change is the nature and strength of the person's original attitude. It is difficult to change attitudes that are strongly held, that have been held for a long time, and that are well integrated into the person's general attitudinal structure. Conversely, it is relatively easy to change attitudes that are almost indifferent, rather new, and peripheral to the central organizing structure of the personality. Consequently, those conducting experimental studies of attitude change have usually avoided major issues, since attitudes on these subjects are more firmly ingrained and tend not to yield, at least not in the course of an experiment. Instead, most studies center on minor issues. For example, if the subjects are college students, one might attempt to influence their attitudes toward the ingestion of fluoride for the prevention of dental decay. Consequently, there is not much reason to believe that methods that have produced attitude change in these studies will necessarily work on more important issues. However, that is an empirical question—and ready for experimental investigation.

Attitude change often occurs because a message or communication has persuaded the person to change his mind. That message has a communicator, or source, and the subject's view of the source is important in determining the effect of the message. The chances for change are greater if the source is perceived as credible, prestigious, and expert in the area under study. Such judgments are not easy to predict, and will vary with both subject and source. On any given issue, one man's expert may be another man's fool.

What the subject perceives as the *motives* of the communicator can be a significant influence. The communicator who has no apparent self-interest is more effective than one who seems to have an ulterior motive. If one is to undergo a change in attitude, then, it is important that he trust the motives of the communicator. Experiments have shown, for example, that someone who is represented to subjects as a convicted criminal is much more effective in changing attitudes toward criminal punishment if he advocates harsher punishment for criminals than he is if he advocates more leniency. In advocating the first alternative, he seems to have nothing to gain personally, and his opinions are hence more persuasive.

SOURCE OF MESSAGE — Prestige? Expertise? Credible motives? — Medium and message — PERSON — Strength of attitude / Personality variables / Consequences of change — Social variables — Other people

Figure 23.6
Factors influencing attitude change.

Messages come to people by means of various *media*, both oral and written: books, magazines, records, radio, television, social conversation. To be successful, the medium must suggest reality to the person. Many attitude-change studies have been criticized on the ground that the medium—often a mimeographed booklet consisting of argumentative reading matter, directions for reading it, and various attitude-measuring questionnaires to be answered— fails to suggest reality. Indeed, the printed word, once man's primary medium of communication, has been widely replaced by other media, such as television. Certain advertisers believe that television is an effective medium for changing attitudes, but scientific verification of its effectiveness is difficult to attain. Considerable evidence, however, indicates that television provides realistic models, which some people imitate. Such evidence suggests that TV violence and mayhem will influence some children to experiment with violent behavior, just as a cooking show will affect some people's cooking. However, it is important to recognize the existence of counteracting effects as well. Some children may copy the violence, but others may be upset by it and decrease their violent behavior. Furthermore, experimenting

with cooking-show tips has caused more than one person to create some incredible disasters. To date, the amount of reliable scientific evidence is not sufficient to yield more conclusive generalizations on the effects of the television medium.

Studies make it clear that the *nature* of the message is an important determinant of attitude change. Thus a reasonable argument, substantiated by fact, is essential for changing some attitudes, such as scientific ones. However, if other kinds of attitudes are to be changed, such as those springing from personal experience, the message must probably be based on another's personal experience. The appropriate technique varies with the people to be persuaded and the situation. Research in this particular area is just beginning, but some interesting ideas have emerged already. For example, appeals to fear seem to be especially effective in changing attitudes about certain types of activity, such as smoking, that may be dangerous to the health and hence lend themselves to the realistic arousal of fear.

Much of attitude change is related to *characteristics of the person who holds the attitudes.* Some personalities are more subject to persuasion, suggestion, and inducements to imitate someone else than are others. Perhaps more interesting, and more generally applicable, are the changes in attitude that seem to be a natural part of growing up—and of growing old. Older people are generally more conservative than younger people, for the obvious reasons that many of them have more to lose if things change, and are less capable of defending what they have against loss.

Different *social and interpersonal variables* influence the changes that occur in attitudes. As we indicated earlier, studies have shown that mere interpersonal contact on a basis of equality between members of different races having equal status can produce sub-

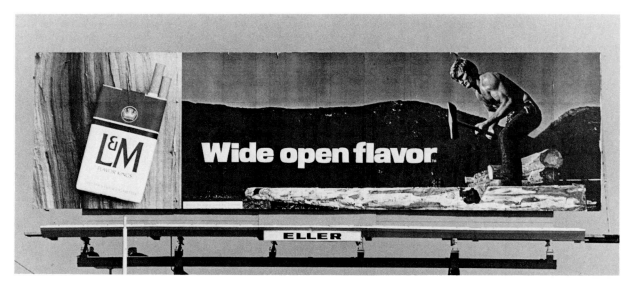

Figure 23.7
These billboard advertisements present milk and
cigarettes and semi-nude models. [David Powers]

stantial attitude change. During World War II,
marked shifts in racial attitudes occurred among
members of the military. Other studies have shown
that personal interaction between blacks and whites
of equal status seems to produce more positive
reciprocal attitudes toward each other.

Another factor is the *consequence* of the attitude
change. An attitude is strengthened if it is followed
by explicit and realistic confirmation of its value—
the more immediate and meaningful the confirmation, the better. On the other hand, attitude
change can be weakened if it is followed by some
negative result.

FACTORS IN ATTITUDE STABILITY

Stable attitudes are those that are especially resistant
to change. For the most part, the factors that induce
stability are, as one might infer, the opposites of
those factors inducing change. An interesting and
novel dimension to the area of attitude stability has
been added by recent studies on *immunization* against
attitude change. For example, suppose that a person
has always driven a Ford car, but for one reason or
another his local Ford agency suspects that he may
be susceptible to the new Chevrolet commercial.
The immunization technique that Ford representa-
tives might employ is analogous to the procedure of

medical immunization. The idea is simple: introduce a bit of the Chevrolet sales pitch (like bacteria) and then present fair counterarguments to the person (like antibodies). Shrewd application of this idea has, in experiments, provided immunization against some subsequent arguments that might otherwise have been fairly persuasive. Experiments on this kind of immunization have shown that merely mentioning the alien attitude is effective in preventing attitude change, just as is the presentation of the alien attitude followed by an explicit refutation of it. Each method provides better immunization than does the presentation of arguments supportive of the attitude that the person currently holds. Immunization can also be produced simply by forewarning the subject that he may encounter arguments against his present attitudes; in the maintenance of one's established attitudes, to be forewarned is to be forearmed.

EXAMPLES OF ATTITUDE CHANGE

Advertising The foregoing theories of attitude change, and the various factors influencing attitude change and resistance to change, are well understood by people in the advertising profession, a field based on the art of persuasion. These theories and factors are utilized in a wide variety of different techniques, to which all of us are exposed continually (Figure 23.7). Some ads are primarily designed to attract the viewers' attention—with a device that might be anything from attractive to startling—and then to present the product quickly before attention wanes. Apparently, associations between a bizarre attention-getting device and the product do not worry advertisers who assume that exposure of the product to the audience—by almost any means—is what is important.

We have already mentioned the application of learning and conditioning procedures. Some advertisers try to transfer the viewer's feelings about a quiet day in a beautiful countryside to a mentholated cigarette, or his positive response to the face of a celebrity to an automobile, an underarm spray, or a razor blade. Such advertisements emphasize the importance of the communicator by appealing to the inclination of some people to imitate a well-known or admired figure.

In a few advertisements, the nature of the message is one of authenticity. For example, automobile tires are shown to withstand being driven over a surface of sharp nails or tin cans and glass. And occasionally, we are asked to support underdogs—thus we might be told that we should buy a less popular product because, since it is only second in popularity, more of an effort is made to make it better.

Brainwashing   A much less commonplace technique of persuasion is that known as *brainwashing*. In brainwashing (intensive involuntary indoctrination), the message is communicated to the person by subjecting him involuntarily to a new and raw personal experience. Although much of our knowledge of this subject is limited to literary and anecdotal descriptions, it seems clear that brainwashing is accomplished in three phases.

The first phase is the establishment of an individual's total dependence on those who wish to brainwash him; thus, he relies completely on his captors for food and water, facilities for elimination and hence for basic cleanliness, the freedom to indulge in such activities as scratching or spontaneous movement, and finally the right to sleep.

Once the basic dependence has been established, the person is ready for the second phase, in which he is taught to believe his previous attitudes are absurd, and brought to the point at which he asks himself, "How can my own views possibly be correc when they have brought me to this helpless dependence on others?"

Phase three is the construction of an entirely new set of attitudes, so that the final product is a drastically changed person, who automatically thinks and voices newly acquired attitudes.

To date, no scientific studies of brainwashing are available, but studies of sensory deprivation lend credence to the possibility that this procedure is a powerful technique for radical attitude change—although as we saw in Chapter 21 such change is usually quickly reversible when the brainwashed individual returns to his normal environment.

Suggested Readings

Brown, R. (1965) *Social psychology*. New York: Free Press. [A careful summary of much of the work on attitudes and attitude change.]

Festinger, L. (1957) *A theory of cognitive dissonance.* Stanford: Stanford University Press. [One of the few major statements in contemporary psychology. Well done, interesting, and significant.]

Hovland, C. I., & Weiss, W. (1951) "The influence of source credibility on communication effectiveness." *Public opinion quarterly, 15,* 636–650. [An example of Carl Hovland's work.]

Lindzey, G., & Aronson, E., eds. (1969) *Handbook of social psychology.* (2nd ed.) Reading, Mass.: Addison-Wesley. [In particular, see the article by W. J. McGuire in Volume 3. An excellent set for reference. Academic in tone, but readable.]

McGuire, W. J. (1970) "A vaccine for brainwash." *Psychology today, 3,* 36–39. [A popular account of attitude immunization.]

Zimbardo, P. G., & Ebbesen, E. B. (1969) *Influencing attitudes and changing behavior.* Reading, Mass.: Addison-Wesley. [A highly interesting work on attitude change.]

UNIT EIGHT

The Study of Personality

The study of personality must be as old as the human race itself. Certainly the earliest of recorded writings have characterizations of people—their strong and weak points, their personal assets and liabilities; and the ancients devised elaborate and often modern-sounding systems for describing and categorizing individual personalities. It is hard to believe that prehistoric man, and perhaps even prehumanoid primates, failed to measure the capacities and note the habitual practices of both friends and enemies, if only to divine their reliability as partners or their vulnerability as enemies. People have always taken the measure of others; it is natural for a person to recognize the uniqueness of others, as well as the uniqueness of himself.

The modern era of personality theory began with the writings of Sigmund Freud, the Viennese physician and psychiatrist whose dog stares quizzically out at us in the photo on the facing page. An old man, still at work in an office lined with bound notes and hundreds of statuettes, Freud posed for this picture in London in 1939 after fleeing the Nazi persecution of Jews in his native Austria. Behind him were forty years of writings on human motivation, personality and its development, abnormal personality, psychotherapy, and sociology and anthropology.

Freud began his career in medicine, and held a chair at the University of Vienna. His interest in the human mind led him to accept as patients people who could not find psychiatric help elsewhere because of the apparently incurable nature of their afflictions: there were hysterics, each of whom had a paralysis that was medically "impossible"; and obsessives, who could not stop thinking about the same scenes over and over again, also for no apparent medical reason. His work with such "incurable" patients led him into the study of hypnosis, because he found that hypnotized subjects could often be temporarily relieved of their symptoms. More importantly, hypnotized subjects would talk about delicate matters, usually sexual experiences, which seemed to Freud to give plausible psychological reasons for their paralysis. For example, a patient who described under hypnosis a terror of touching things had a paralysis of the hands. With patients who resisted hypnotic trances, Freud found that hypnosis was not necessary for the discussion of their experiences. Relaxation, psychological support, and daily persistence of the patient and the doctor were sufficient.

Patients often described dreams, in which Freud thought that he saw their problems symbolized. He developed a system for decoding the symbols so that he could explain to the patients what was causing their problems. This work resulted, on January 1, 1900, in the publication of his first statement of his theory of human personality, *The Interpretation of Dreams*. Freud subsequently elaborated his methods and theories. We shall treat the former in Unit X, the latter in this unit, in Chapter 24.

Nearly all later theorists of personality, whose work we discuss in Chapter 25, took account of Freud's ideas: some elaborating on them, others reacting against them. Cultural changes had their impact on theorists: those who worked in less sexually secret and repressive eras than did Freud tended to place less emphasis on sexual factors in personality and personality disorders. But few have successfully challenged Freud's most basic idea: much of adult behavior consists of continued, usually unconscious, attempts to attain pleasure and gratification in a way that repeats, at least symbolically, modes of gratification employed very early in life, during infancy or childhood.

The contemporary study of personality, discussed in Chapter 26, is concerned with two very distinct but closely related points of view. First, students of personality are interested in what it is that makes each person unique. At the same time, they are interested in what it is that characterizes human personality in general. In the first instance, the goal is to find the best way to describe how Tom is different from Dick, and Dick is different from Harry. In the second instance, the concern is with what Tom, Dick, and Harry all share in common. These two concerns are closely interrelated, since whatever we discover about human beings in general will apply to each individual human being, and whatever we discover about an individual will tell us something about what it means to be human.

The distinction between personality in general and the essence of individuality can be clarified with a few examples. All of us, as human beings, experience emotions of joy and of anxiety; we all experience accomplishments and suffer frustrations; we all have social interactions and spend some time in solitude. Part of what it means to be human, then, has to do with the emotions we feel as we interact with our worlds. At the same time, individuals differ in each of these three aspects of personality, as well as in a wide variety of others. And these differences are what make each person a unique individual. Each of us experiences a different balance between pleasant and unpleasant emotions, and each deals with emotions in a different way. Some of us are totally engaged in social interactions most of the time, while others are primarily reclusive; and there are many gradations in between these extremes. All of us differ in the degree to which our actions lead to satisfying accomplishments or to discouraging frustrations.

After first considering Freud and other personality theorists, we shall discuss some of the ways that have been devised over the years for measuring various important aspects of individual personalities: interests, aptitudes, traits, and other characteristics. Finally, we shall be forced to ask the question that pervades much recent work in the area of personality: Does the concept of personality make any sense—does "a personality" really exist?

CHAPTER TWENTY-FOUR

Freud's Contribution to Personality Theory

Sigmund Freud (1856–1939) created the first modern theory of personality out of his broad experience in the practice of psychotherapy. It is a shame that Freud's theory is rarely granted its due in introductory psychology texts, because this theory has had an incalculable influence on modern psychology, and on modern thought in general.

THE IDEAL PERSONALITY THEORY

Theories of personality must accomplish several tasks. They must deal with human motivation and emotion, explaining why people behave and feel as they do. In the process, they must attempt to identify the agencies, or parts of the personality, that govern the various personality functions. Personality dynamics—the interplay of forces and conflicts within the personality—are important because they tell us how and why people react as they do to psychological events within themselves, as well as to events in their environments. A good theory explains how personalities develop, taking into account overall human development and perhaps even human evolution. Such a theory should also describe man's hopes and fears—how they arise, and how he goes about coping with them in order to attain adjustment. The individual's social roles must also be con-

sidered, because man is so thoroughly a social creature. The ideal theory of personality will explain the abnormal as well as the normal and, by explaining, point the way to psychotherapies that should prove to be effective. Finally, the complete theory should offer its students insight into the essence of what it means to be human—it should offer a deep understanding of human nature. We shall see that Freud's personality theory approached the ideal on most of these counts.

THE BASIC IDEAS OF FREUD'S THEORY

There are two basic concepts that underlie Freud's theory of personality: (1) the concept of *multiple determination*, or *overdetermination*, and (2) the concept of the *unconscious*. In Freud's view, there is a cause for everything, and often there are multiple causes of a single event. Usually, the causes are not even known to the person involved; but they exist, nonetheless, in his unconscious mind. One bit of evidence for this is that once the underlying psychological causes of a puzzling event are uncovered, the person often recognizes them.

Freud believed that even chance remarks, failures to remember words, and slips of the tongue are strictly determined. He discussed many examples in *The Psychopathology of Everyday Life*, from which we have selected the following three. One day Freud could not recall the country, then ruled by Prince Albert, in which Monte Carlo was located. The names he thought of were "Piedmont," "Albania," "Montevideo," "Colico," and "Montenegro." Why? "Albania" was probably a distortion of the name of the Prince, "Albert." "Pied*mont*," "*Mon*tevideo," and "*Mon*tenegro" all share the syllable "*mon*" with the forgotten name, "*Mon*aco." "Colico" has a similar syllabic and rhythmic structure. The names that came to his conscious mind were clearly all the result of associations with the unconscious answer, "Monaco." They were determined by the unconscious material. (We saw similar examples in Chapter 2, when discussing the tip-of-the-tongue phenomenon.) In another example, one of Freud's patients reported that she told a friend that she would be "back in a movement," instead of "a moment," when she was going out to buy a laxative—a clear but unconscious influence from "bowel movement." Freud acknowledged that his own behavior could also be unconsciously determined. At one point, he had two patients who each traveled all the way from Trieste to consult him in Vienna. He habitually confused them, calling Mr. Peloni, "Mr. Askoli," and vice versa. After some thoughtful analysis, he realized that he was unconsciously telling each man that he had not just one but two foreign patients who traveled such a long distance to see him. In each of these three examples, unconscious events determine behavior. Indeed, Freud's most important contribution was his conception of the unconscious.

THE THREE PARTS OF A PERSONALITY

Freud believed that human behavior could be explained by assuming that every personality has three hypothetical parts: the *ego* and the *superego*, both of which are partially conscious and partially unconscious, and the *id*, which is totally unconscious. An individual's personality—all that the individual does, thinks, and feels—is determined by the interplay of these three dynamic agencies.

The *id* is the primitive part of the personality, oriented toward immediate gratification of needs, drives, and wishes. If the id had its way, the person would continually be engaging in an orgy of pleasure, and mindlessly destroying anything or anyone that got in its way. The id is biologically oriented and seeks primarily physical pleasures: sexual stimulation, elimination, eating, drinking, and anything else that is biologically satisfying. Freud called the id's mode of thinking the *primary process*; gratification is its only aim, and it should be complete and immediate. Since the id is unconscious, we are never directly aware of it, but it is always there, wishing for, and actively pushing us toward, raw pleasure.

The *ego* is the executive part of the personality, facing the real world and managing the insistent demands of the id. The ego is you as you appear to yourself and others. The ego tests reality instead of dreaming, and engages in what Freud called the *secondary process*, in contrast to the id's primary process. The secondary process is more reality-oriented, and tries to work out ways of delaying the gratification of the id's wishes in order to avoid punishment, social rejection, and guilt.

Guilt, according to Freud's theory, comes primarily from self-punishment by the third part of the personality, the *superego*, roughly the equivalent of conscience. The superego is the socially determined part of the personality formed by the *introjection*, or internalizing, of parental and societal values through *identification* (Figure 24.1). The superego opposes the id's sexual and aggressive drives and promotes conformity to society's values and moral precepts. Part of the superego is the *ego ideal*, which represents what the individual ideally would like

Figure 24.1
Children often imitate adults and thereby learn various overt behaviors. Freud stressed the point that children internalize parental and societal values as well. [David Powers]

to be. The ego-ideal grows out of the child's identification with a person he admires—usually a parent—and his incorporation of certain of the other person's values and ways of behaving into his own personality.

In summary, (1) the id seeks pleasure, (2) the superego seeks to limit pleasure, in the interest of socialization, (3) the ego seeks to reconcile their conflicting demands. If the ego denies the id, frustration results. If the ego denies the superego,

guilt results. How the ego solves this problem determines what kind of personality an individual possesses and how well adjusted he is.

THE DYNAMICS OF PERSONALITY

Freud believed that two groups of instincts are of primary importance in the development of personality: (1) the *sexual* instincts (defined very broadly), and (2) the *aggressive instincts*. He focused particularly on the sexual instincts, whose driving energy he called *libido*. According to Freud, much of personality development and functioning depends on a process called _cathexis_, in which the ego consciously or unconsciously distributes the id's libido to objects, people, and actions in order to attain the goal of pleasure. Libido, then, has both an aim and an object. For example, adult libido usually seeks genital sexual pleasure (*aim*) through sexual intercourse with someone of the opposite sex (*object*). But both the object and the aim may be changed for some of an individual's libido. If the object is changed, as in homosexuality, Freud said that the energy (libido) has been *displaced* from one object (an opposite-sex person) to another (a same-sex person). If the aim is changed, as in a person's deriving pleasure from creating a work of art, Freud said that the libido has been *sublimated*; its basically sexual nature remains unchanged, but its aim is different. _Displacement_ and _sublimation_ are two key mechanisms in a person's development. Together they determine the objects and aims of the libido.

To account for the diversion of psychic energy from its primary goals, Freud explained that the id's urging for discharge of energy in sexual pleasure is often opposed by the demands of the outside world (reality) or the superego. (One's conscience may permit only certain kinds and amounts of sexual activity without unpleasant feelings of guilt). But since the ego must somehow discharge the libidinal energy, it seeks other outlets in displacement and sublimation. The exact nature of the displacement and sublimation depend on the individual's stage of development at the time—and so, too, does the adult personality that they determine. (We shall discuss the stages of psychosexual development in the next section.)

An important element in Freud's theory is the concept of *ambivalence*—the coexistence of contradictory emotions. Freud suggested that pure emotions are rare, mixtures more common. We are ambivalent toward persons when we both love and hate them at the same time, or toward objects when they give us feelings of both joy and sorrow. One or the other of the feelings may be partially or wholly *unconscious*, but they coexist in one person at the same time and are directed toward the same object. It is, in fact, unusual for anyone who is truly close to us to escape ambivalence. Parents love their children, but are confined and limited by having to care for them. Children love their parents, but are frustrated by their prohibitions. Siblings are ambivalent toward each other, hating the competition for parental affection, but loving the mutual affection. It is important to recognize ambivalence, since both of the emotions involved participate in determining personality.

PSYCHOSEXUAL DEVELOPMENT

Freud's theory is a powerful array of psychological ideas, not only because they are so provocative but also because he took pains to cover everything, including how a personality develops. Development is especially important because, as we pointed out earlier, the exact nature of a personality characteristic depends upon the stage of development in which the libido that determines it was transformed from strictly sexual expression.

For Freud, psychological development was fundamentally a psychosexual process, involving distinct *psychosexual stages*. These stages differ from each other in terms of the source of sexual pleasure, the central developmental problem of the stage, and the effects on the eventual adult personality of various outcomes at each stage. The sources of sexual pleasure identified by Freud were the *erogenous zones*: the genital organs, but also the lips and mouth, and the anus, depending on the developmental stage in question. It is a very physical theory—Freud believed that stimulation of these zones is the principal source of pleasure for a child at different stages. As a child moves from stage to stage, a portion of his libido is transferred from zone to zone. But some libido is left behind—or *fixated*—at each stage. The libido remains associated with the erogenous zone of that stage, and the individual continues to attain pleasure in ways that are appropriate to that early stage of development. How much the adult personality is influenced by ideas and how much behavior is drawn from each stage of psychosexual development is determined by how much libido is fixated at that stage. This is the doctrine of *infantile determinism*—the theory that the adult personality is formed in infancy and childhood.

There are three main ways in which libido from an early stage of development survives to influence adult personality. In one, it is essentially unchanged and results in anomalous sexual behaviors. In another, the libido is *sublimated*—that is, changed in its aim. And in the third, the ego uses *reaction formation* in order to deal with the libido; in other words, some characteristic of the libido is *directly reversed*. We shall see how these mechanisms work as we discuss the various psychosexual stages.

Broadly speaking, Freud divided development into three stages: the *pregenital stage* (from birth to about five or six years), the *latency stage* (up to adolescence), and the *genital stage* (from adolescence on). The pre-genital period is itself subdivided into the *oral*, the *anal*, and the *phallic* stages. Freud thought that the fate of libido in these stages is what determines adult personality.

In the *oral* stage of psychosexual development, pleasure is derived primarily from the oral erogenous zone, the lips and mouth. Nutritive needs combine with this orally placed libido to make sucking and nursing the important activities of this stage. When teeth develop, biting becomes possible. Oral libido occasionally survives to adulthood unchanged, and the result, according to Freud, is oral sexual perversions. But the more interesting effects are produced by sublimated oral libido.

Freud distinguished two very general types of adult personalities that owe their characteristics to sublimated oral libido: the *oral-receptive* personality and the *oral-aggressive* personality. The *oral-receptive* derives from the earliest, sucking stage of infancy. An adult with this type of personality is said to be friendly, generous, optimistic, and expects everyone to mother him. Since he expects good things from the world, for very little effort on his part, he typically responds poorly to frustration, overreacting and often feeling deeply betrayed by those who have frustrated him.

The second personality that owes its characteristics to sublimated oral libido—this time from the biting stage—is the oral-aggressive. Ambitious and envious, the oral-aggressive is said to continue symbolically to bite and aggressively to tear off from the world what he wants. Typically the oral-aggressive is talkative, persuasively argumentative, and orally abusive when thwarted.

When Freud encountered patients who exhibited the personality traits characteristic of an oral-receptive or an oral-aggressive, he theorized that libido had been fixated at that earliest stage of psy-

chosexual development. This led him to examine the patient's earliest nursing experiences in order to find out why libido had been left there. In the case of the oral-aggressive, for example, it may have been that the mother abruptly stopped breast-feeding when painfully bitten by the newly-toothed infant. Such an abrupt withdrawal of such an important part of the infant's world—the breast—might account for the fixation of the libido and hence for the personality characteristics of the adult patient.

Freud held that the second, anal, stage of development is the source of several general personality types. When anal libido remains into adulthood without changes, there is a continued childlike interest in elimination and in the feces themselves and a fascination with anal stimulation. Freud suspected a great deal of anally fixated libido in cases of passive homosexuality.

The classic *anal* personality, one of Freud's most carefully studied personality types, originates from reaction formation—the ego handles the id's anal libido by turning it into its exact opposite. The individual unconsciously still seeks anal pleasure through elimination, as he did in the anal stage as a child. But, after reaction formation, the anal personality is marked by just the opposite: orderliness and neatness. He is parsimonious and obstinate, and often has a fear of wasting time. He typically keeps everything, being unable to throw away or eliminate anything. He is extremely reliable, but tends to be petty.

Freud often left the evidence for his assertions to the aptness of the analogy, but in the case of the anal personality he noted that these characteristics first begin to appear at just about the time that toilet habits become controllable and regular. The libido that was formerly invested in taking pleasure from uncontrolled elimination is at that point taken over by the ego to power its reaction formation.

Figure 24.2
Freud held that during the *phallic period*, a child becomes aware of pleasurable genital feelings and forms the wish for an exclusive (sexual) relationship with its opposite-sex parent. The idea of a rivalry with the same-sex parent thus arises and presents the child with a dilemma.

Sublimation of anal libido produces additional types of anal personalities. For example, Freud believed that the pleasure a child experiences with his feces often sublimates into an adult craving for, and an interest in, money for its own sake. The miser is a pronounced example of this type. The sense of power, once derived from controlling elimination, is derived in adulthood, after sublimation, from the control and manipulation of money, which also has connotations of power.

Freud saw the origins of sculpture and other manual arts in a sublimation of the child's early pleasure in manipulating feces. The adult continues to manipulate and to derive pleasure from it, but in socially acceptable ways. Of course, the connection is totally unconscious and hence not known at all to the sculptor.

Sooner or later, both boys and girls discover that genital stimulation of the penis or clitoris is pleasurable. As we shall see, Freud felt that this discovery was utilized psychologically for a while

during the *phallic period*. If libido is sublimated at this stage, instead of passing on to the more tender and mature genital period of sexuality, the individual will be insolent, aggressive, and domineering, with difficulties in achieving mutual, as opposed to personal, social and sexual satisfactions.

Freud felt that genital sexuality becomes latent, save for occasional self-stimulation, during a *latency period*, only to be awakened again when libido increases greatly at puberty. We now realize that the latency period is more eventful, but it is the reasons for its occurrence that are central to Freud's theory.

Freud thought that during the phallic period the child experiences an *Oedipal conflict*—named for Oedipus, the ancient Greek who came to grief after unwittingly killing his father and having sexual intercourse with his mother. (Although Freud did propose a female counterpart fo the Oedipal conflict, called the *Electra conflict* (Figure 24.2), his descriptions are primarily of the male's experience, as in the following discussion.) In the Oedipal stage, the little boy develops a deep affection for his mother, wishing to possess her sexually and thus to displace his father. However, the boy fears retaliation by the father. This fear may take the form of *castration anxiety*, especially if he imagines that little girls lack a penis because the parents cut it off as a punishment. (Corresponding to castration anxiety is the notion of "penis envy," which supposedly develops in the girl when she realizes she lacks a penis.) The boy's wish to get rid of his father so that he can have mother all to himself occasions guilt, since small children find it difficult to distinguish fantasy from reality, and thus feel that they could actually kill a person with a wish. This idea is derived from a combination of the apparent *omniscience* of the parents, who seem to the child to know exactly what the child is thinking all the time, and from chance correlations between thinking of something and then seeing it happen—what Freud called the *omnipotence of thought.* It is the combined pressures of guilt, fear of castration, and the presumed relative inadequacy of the pleasure derived from genital stimulation at this age that lead to the relatively asexual *latency period.* For the little boy, a healthy resolution of the Oedipal complex involves renouncing claims on the mother and at the same time identifying with the father and striving to be like him.

At puberty, Freud thought, sexual feelings for the parents return, but only briefly because normal development allows many more possible sources of sexual pleasure for the normal adolescent to pursue, at least in fantasy.

In summary, then, here are Freud's views. Normal adult personality is composed in part of the traits we have described as originating in sublimation or reaction formation at earlier stages of development. Most individuals have a dominant focus from one era of personality development; that is, they are primarily *fixated* at the oral, anal, phallic, or genital stages. But there are characteristics from other stages too. Thus a primarily oral person may have many genital characteristics, and it is not unusual for phallic and oral-aggressive traits to go together, with very few genital traits at all. To the characteristics derived from fixation at earlier stages of development are added further sublimations of libido in the adult years. And there is some libido left over for discharge in regular and normal sexual gratification. Freud summarized adult maturity in the phrase *"lieben und arbeiten"*—love and work. Love, of course, is the direct expression of libido; work, like other behaviors not explicitly sexual, represents the sublimation of libido.

ANXIETY AND DEFENSES AGAINST IT

Freud recognized that a large part of any personality is determined by the mechanisms an individual adopts in order to alleviate or at least control *anxiety*. (Freud theorized that anxiety originated in the *trauma of birth*, the total helplessness of the infant thrust unwillingly into a new extra-uterine environment and drawing its first painful breath of air. But Freud failed to develop or place emphasis on his ideas of the birth trauma.)

Freud distinguished three kinds of anxiety, on the basis of their causes. *Reality anxiety* is simply normal and adaptive fear of real dangers in the real world. *Moral anxiety* expresses the ego's fear of the superego, which may punish the ego with guilt feelings because it disapproves of what the ego is planning. *Neurotic anxiety*, the most serious kind, represents the ego's fear of the id's natural impulses or of other unconscious urges that have their origins in past experience. The ego's reaction to any form of anxiety is to try to get rid of it. In cases of reality anxiety, the ego can try to see to it that the particular dangers are removed or avoided; in moral anxiety, the ego's course can be altered to avoid the superego's censure and still satisfy the id. But in neurotic anxiety, the ego must mobilize one of its *defense mechanisms,* which, though it may control anxiety, can do so only inadequately and temporarily. Defenses also use up psychic energy, which is then unavailable for normal pursuits and development. They also set up *symptoms* that have their own effects. All too often, these symptoms cause more trouble and anxiety than they were originally set up to avoid. Another complication is that symptoms enjoy a *secondary gain*—advantages of their own—which can keep them going long after the original, anxiety-avoiding purpose has passed. For example, people who develop feelings of illness in order to avoid sexual encounters (because of fears of inadequacy) may keep their symptoms long after their sexual opportunities have disappeared. (We shall also discuss defense mechanisms in Chapter 28.)

Figure 24.3
Reaction formation.

Figure 24.4
Displacement.

We have already taken note of one of the primary defense mechanisms in our discussions of *reaction formation* (Figure 24.3). With this mechanism, the ego allows the libidinous wishes of the id to become conscious, but *only in the reverse*. People who are afraid of sexual failure, for example, are often publicly the most rabid pursuers of the opposite sex, at least in their own accounts. The ego has chosen to deal with the fear of failure—probably itself the result of the superego's prohibitions against sex—by converting it into its opposite. Like all defense mechanisms, this one is at once unconscious and unrealistic. Psychic energy is used up in an elaborate misrepresentation.

We have also considered *displacement* (Figure 24.4), which serves in the ego's war against anxiety. In displacement, the object of a wish or need is changed by the ego in order to make the wish more acceptable to the superego. In a sense, a boy's transfer of libido from the mother to girls of his own age is a displacement (certainly it involves an avoidance of anxiety); however, Freud preferred to deal

with the resolution of the Oedipus situation as a part of normal development rather than as a defense. Displacement is a very common phenomenon. We should probably examine attitudes toward authority from this point of view, because the unconscious attitudes we once had toward our parents may have been displaced, often in modified form and intensity, to persons in authority.

In the preceding section on psychosexual development we discussed *fixation* at early stages of development, which occurs when libido is sublimated or reversed at these stages. This produces personality characteristics that remain a part of the person even after he has grown to adulthood. Fixations are motivated by developmental anxiety, and they may be considered defense mechanisms.

Regression (Figure 24.5) is another mechanism that relies on earlier modes of gratification to avoid anxiety. The mature ego doggedly pursues goals

Figure 24.5
Regression.

Figure 24.6
Repression.

and tries to work out a successful compromise between the id's demands, the standards of the superego, and its own aims. But when frustrated and anxious it may regress to an early mode of satisfaction. For example, in regression to an oral mode of functioning, the person exhibits either full confidence that others will work it all out for him (oral-receptive), or lapses into useless verbal abuse of the problems confronting him (oral-aggressive). Anal regression, by contrast, often takes the form of anal retention—the inability actively to continue to participate, as if the person is a child again, saying, "If you will not admire my gift (feces then, but now arguments, solutions, courses of action), I shall stop giving them to you." This is of course all unconscious, and like all defense mechanisms, basically unrealistic.

Fundamental to an understanding of anxiety is an awareness of the dynamics of the most primitive of defense mechanisms, *repression* (Figure 24.6). In repression, the ego simply refuses to admit to consciousness any hint of the anxiety-arousing thoughts or urges. This takes a considerable and continual

investment of psychic energy because the thoughts and urges are continually pressing to become conscious. The anxiety is there too, even though repressed. Thus such an individual usually displays a great deal of *free-floating anxiety*, or vague uneasiness not attached to specific objects. If the repression is complete, however, the person may appear to be entirely free from anxiety—a condition pathological in itself, since a certain amount of reality and moral anxiety is normal. Although he may show no positive symptoms of anxiety, such an individual will have little psychic energy available for healthy pursuits.

The classic defense mechanism, *projection* (Figure 24.7), is yet another masterpiece of the ego's psychological gymnastics. In projection, the ego attributes to other people characteristics that are really applicable to itself. For example, X's feeling that Y is trying to cheat him may in fact be a statement that X is too ashamed to admit that he is trying to cheat Y. Once again, all of this is unconscious.

Defense mechanisms often come in tandem, two working together to protect the ego from anxiety. A common combination is reaction formation and pro-

Figure 24.7
Projection.

jection. The ego accepts anxiety-provoking notions from the id but only after reversing them, and then for good measure projecting them outside onto other people. The statement, "People do not seem to take pleasure from my company," may actually represent the feeling "I really wish to take pleasure from myself (autoerotically)," which has first been reversed and then projected onto other people. Or, a statement to the effect that there are important people who are working hard to help me may actually reflect self-hatred, probably originating in an overly stringent and powerful superego. In these cases, the feelings of self-love or self-hate have provoked anxiety, necessitating elaborate defenses to protect the ego.

A final, instructive example is the correlation that Freud noted between paranoia and homosexuality. Although not all paranoids are overtly or consciously homosexual, Freud believed that most homosexuals are paranoid. In Freud's view homosexuality is an aberration in which the aim of the libido is intact, but the object has become people of the same, rather than the opposite, sex. Without trying to evaluate here the various theories of this phenomenon, we shall merely indicate how a combination of reaction formation and projection could produce paranoid feelings in the homosexual. Suppose I really want to love a person of the same sex, but my superego says no—hence anxiety. So I unconsciously reverse my attitude, by reaction formation, to a dislike of persons of my sex; then I project those feelings into other people. The result is that I feel, consciously, that they are against me. In truth, I am attracted to them. Individual cases differ, of course. Although what we have just discussed is plausible, it might not always be the correct interpretation. For example, paranoia could be the primary phenomenon and homosexuality the defense mechanism; in other words, neurotic fear of others of the same sex *could* be reduced by exaggerated love of some cooperative members of that sex. It is complex, but so are the human mind and human emotions.

THE INTERPRETATION OF DREAMS

Dreams are meaningful and open to interpretation, said Freud at the start of the twentieth century, and many advanced thinkers received this view with skepticism. Freud backed up his bold contention with a 450-page book on what dreams mean, how they originate, and how they can be interpreted. The book was called *The Interpretation of Dreams*, and it worked a psychological revolution.

The thesis was simple: dreams are an expression of an individual's personality as much as waking behavior and feelings, although special understanding and interpretation are needed to make sense of dreams. Freud thought that dreams helped to keep us asleep by dealing with thoughts and urges from the unconscious in ways that make them innocuous and protect us from their potentially anxiety-arousing messages. Freud's key concepts were the *censor*, which monitors dream material to select out threatening bits or themes for alteration, and the *dream work*, which does the altering. In the dream work, unconscious thoughts and urges are *condensed* into a shorter time span and story line, objects are *displaced*, and acts and ideas are *symbolized*. Interpreting a dream requires reversing these processes: attaching meaning to symbols, identifying the true objects from the displaced ones, and expanding the condensations. According to Freudian theorists, the interpretation of a particular dream of a given individual is a difficult and unique problem for only specialists to undertake. We shall, nevertheless, discuss a few dreams in Chapter 30, when we consider Freud's practical contribution to modern psychology: psychoanalysis.

FREUD TODAY

Freud's intellectual influence on contemporary thinking remains, as does his historical importance, but his day-to-day impact on the practice of psychology has diminished. Freud's theory of personality is less relevant today than it was during the period of active suppression of sexual behavior in which he developed it. As a guide for psychotherapy, Freudian analysis takes too long (many years) and requires too much training of the therapist (an MD degree, personal analysis, more years of training) to be practical in a mass society. As an approach to life, Freud's emphasis is on inevitability and pessimism, while the optimism of behaviorism and humanism are currently more appealing. As a guide for experimental research, Freud's ideas have proved too difficult to define exactly and measure convincingly. And as an intellectual endeavor, a

thorough working knowledge of Freud's theory, its history, and its application is an extremely demanding study.

Nevertheless, we must admit that (1) Freud's ideas about personality still ring true in many areas, (2) psychoanalysis still helps many people, (3) his philosphy of determinism is still accepted by most psychological scientists, (4) his theory has influenced experimental work to some degree and other personality theories greatly, and (5) two thoroughly informed students of Freud can succinctly communicate about personality at a level of sophisticated mutual understanding that cannot be attained in many other schools of psychology.

Suggested Readings

Freud, S. (1915) *Psychopathology of everyday life*. (Translated by A. A. Brill.) New York: Macmillan. [Describes the exact determination of seemingly trivial everyday occurrences, such as slips of the tongue and failures to remember. Compelling.]

Freud, S. (1933) *New introductory lectures on psychoanalysis*. New York: Norton. [Clear exposition and description of all of Freud's basic ideas. Can be followed up by other works by Freud from the library.]

Hall, C. S. (1954) *A primer of Freudian psychology*. Cleveland: World. [Fine condensation of the basic ideas.]

CHAPTER TWENTY-FIVE

Other Theories of Personality

Freud evolved the first modern theory of personality, which inspired a whole generation of personality theorists. His work was so influential that later theorists felt compelled to react to it—and often to formulate their own theories in terms of their agreement or disagreement with Freud. The dissenters from his views provided psychology with one of the most interesting, productive, and provocative eras in its history. Theorist after theorist vied with Freud to capture the essence of human personality. As prolific as the era was, however, it produced few intellectual descendants, and today it is rare to find a theorist attempting to describe the whole personality. However, the ideas of the Freudians, post-Freudians, and later theorists are still provocative and useful.

FREUD'S INTELLECTUAL DESCENDANTS

As we have already suggested, every personality theorist is a descendant of Freud to some degree, because each was forced to establish his or her own position on the many issues Freud raised—notably the matters of unconscious motivation and the sexual

origins of personality. In this section we shall limit ourselves to a few of Freud's most representative followers, who span the era from 1900 to the present day (see Figure 25.1).

C. G. JUNG

Carl Gustav Jung (1875–1961) was drawn to Freud's original inner circle of practicing psychoanalysts around 1900 when he discovered in his own analytical studies confirmations of psychological phenomena that Freud was then describing in his writings. Jung was probably the most intellectual and most widely informed of all of Freud's colleagues. Agreeing with the general outline of Freud's theory, Jung differed with Freud on several points—particularly the nature of libido and of the unconscious. Although he founded and was the first president of the International Psychoanalytical Association—the Freudian society—Jung soon broke with Freud over various intellectual issues, and the relationship between the two was never close after about 1911.

It was Jung who invented three of the most widely known concepts of modern psychology: *introversion, extroversion,* and the _complex_. Introverts and extroverts are *psychological types* of personalities. As the names

Figure 25.1
Sigmund Freud and some of his associates in 1909.
Seated: Freud, Stanley Hall, C. G. Jung. *Standing*: A. A.
Brill, Ernest Jones, Sandor Ferenczi. [Historical Pictures
Service, Chicago]

Figure 25.2
These designs are inspired by mandalas, which are
graphic symbols of the universe that are used chiefly
in Asian religions as meditation objects. Often, representations of deities are arranged symmetrically within
the mandalas (which take their name from the sanskrit
word for "circle"). Jung noted that identical mandala-
like designs occur in widely separated cultures and held
them to be universal symbols.

imply, introverts habitually face inward and are
more pensive and self-centered, whereas extroverts
habitually face outward and are more gregarious,
aggressive, and oriented toward mastering the world.
The pure introvert and pure extrovert, of course, are
extreme types: most personalities are blends of the
two. These psychological types also represent *complexes,* that is, organized ways of thinking and acting
that tend to dominate the individual's behavior and
to attract and color any new information that the
individual acquires about the world. Another
example of a complex is the inferiority complex—a
set of ideas and reactions all centering around an
unconscious inferiority feeling and tinged with
anxiety. According to Jung, complexes are intricately
interwoven and overlapped to form a personality.

Jung believed in the libido, as did Freud, but he
interpreted it as a more general force than sexual
desire. For Jung, the essence of the libido lay in the
dynamics of oscillation between opposite psychological states. Noting that rage is often followed by
periods of calm and that extreme hatred often turns
into liking, Jung theorized that an oscillation between
progression into the world and *regression* into the self
was the natural psychological dynamism. The ego's
task is to come to grips with both the world (pro-

gressive) and with the self (regressive). Thus, it is
normal for an individual to return to a dreamy state
of self-reflection following extreme concentration
on mastering the world, much as it is normal for
an individual to regress to earlier developmental
stages following a period of real adult growth. Jung
saw the libido as flowing between the conscious,
progressive mode and the often largely unconscious,
regressive mode. Psychopathology arises when the
libido is blocked, for whatever reason, from again
becoming progressive. Wishes and urges are then
stuck in the unconscious, and become manifest only
in fantasy, dreams, or neurotic symptoms, sometimes
even bursting loose in overwhelming force as
psychosis. This theory does not differ greatly from
Freud's, except for its acceptance of regressive
oscillations as a normal part of personality.

Figure 25.3
Alfred Adler delivers an address at the Berlin-Schöneberg Rathaus in 1930. [Historical Pictures Service, Chicago, Erich Salomon]

Jung's view of sublimation, whereby energy is taken away from instinctual pursuits and diverted to cultural pursuits, was also similar to Freud's. Jung saw the transition as akin to the idea of "transubstantiation" (in the religious sense) and referred to this process as the _transcendent function_. From his studies of primitive peoples and myths, Jung developed a theory of _symbols_ (Figure 25.2), which he felt were effective in helping the will to bring about the redirection of instinctual energy. He interpreted such practices as fertility dances and war dances among primitive peoples as symbols that actively aid in transmuting psychological energy from instinct to culture—from sex to farming, and from hate and fear to warfare.

The _collective unconscious_ was Jung's most original contribution. He acknowledged the personal unconscious, which was strictly an individual's own and contained repressed infantile wishes and countless long-forgotten experiences. But he also felt that man's ideas as well as his brain had been shaped by the centuries of evolution. The remotest experience of modern man's ancestors, even from the time when they were merely animals, still have effects, according to Jung, in the form of unconscious ideas. These ideas are common to everyone: the collective unconscious is shared by any person with his fellow human beings. The collective unconscious is populated with _archetypes_, or primordial images rep-

resenting basic human experiences. Jung held that these archetypes emerge (1) in myths, which are similar from culture to culture, (2) in dreams, which can be amazingly similar from individual to individual, and (3) in common human reactions to crucial life experiences, such as the sudden death of a friend or the birth of a child. Jung drew his evidence for the collective unconscious from different cultures around the world and also from different periods in history. He also wrote of a patient who spoke of particularly interesting but eccentric images in his dreams. Several years later, archaeologists unearthed an ancient scroll, which, in translation, spoke of the same images! Jung concluded that the images were a part of the unconscious of both the modern patient and the ancient scribe.

ALFRED ADLER

Alfred Adler (1870–1937) deserves mention not because his contribution was either fundamental or particularly challenging, but because it has become so familiar to the general public. It was Adler who coined the term _inferiority complex_. He theorized that there is a very important complex that clusters

Figure 25.4
Karen Horney in 1944. [Historical Pictures Service, Chicago]

around what a person considers to be his inferiorities. The purpose of this complex, which is part of every adult's personality, is to avoid the anxiety associated with inferiority feelings by generating strong efforts to *compensate* for it. Examples are numerous, since people generally do try to compensate for their shortcomings. Freud thought that Adler overemphasized this idea; to him, inferiority compensation was a simple matter of reaction formation.

THE NEO-FREUDIANS

Freud and his inner circle were active in the years from 1890 to 1939, the year of Freud's death. Later, there arose a group of theorists who became known as the neo-Freudians because their writings, although based substantially on Freud's theory, attempted to incorporate new social and psychological insights. The neo-Freudians stressed, particularly, the problems of ego function and the importance of the social environment as a determinant of personality.

In this group, we find Karen Horney (1885–1952), Erich Fromm (b. 1900), and Erik Erikson (b. 1902). Karen Horney, in her writings on the psychology of women, challenged Freud's notion of penis envy, explaining how inferiority feelings in women could be produced by society's attitudes toward the sexes. Erich Fromm attempted to apply Freudian ideas to national political attitudes in such books as *Escape from Freedom*. Erik Erikson expanded Freud's theory of psychosexual development to include social factors. (We discussed Erikson's views in Chapter 18.)

POST-FREUDIAN THEORIES

We were tempted to use the heading "non-Freudian theories," but that label is true for only some of the theories we shall discuss. Others have a distinctly Freudian cast, regardless of how much their authors have tried to break new ground by going beyond Freud or going off in new directions.

Gordon W. Allport   G. W. Allport (1897–1967), one of the most original and influential of the modern personality theorists, conceived of personality in terms of each individual's own, particular characteristics. According to Allport, an individual develops a unique set of organized tendencies, or traits; generally, these traits are organized around a few *cardinal* (primary) *traits*. Allport's theory thus rejects the notion of a relatively limited number of personality types in favor of descriptions of highly *individual* personalities made up of a large number of traits.

Allport emphasized the contemporaneous nature of motivation. Abandoning Freud's theory of infantile determinism, he declared, "Drives drive now!" To explain the persistence of behavior after its original purpose has ceased to exist, he invented the concept of the *functional autonomy of motives* (which we discussed in Chapter 6.) One of his favorite examples of

Figure 25.5
Gordon W. Allport. [Courtesy of Beacon Press]

functional autonomy was the sailor who has come to love the sea so much that he retires within sight of it. Whether or not sexual or other organic motives were involved in the sailor's original attraction to the sea, to imagine that retiring near it was motivated by anything other than genuine love of the sea was, for Allport, totally absurd. Rather, the affection for the sea was functionally autonomous—independent of any other earlier motive.

The variety of Allport's interests is evident in his pioneer discussion of maturity (Chapter 18) and his discussion of prejudice (Chapter 22). Late in his life, he turned to the consideration of developmental processes and the essence of being and becoming a human being. All in all, he constructed an original and wide ranging personality theory. However, Allport did not provide detailed accounts of sex, fear, abnormality, and psychotherapy. One suspects that these topics were omitted as not being central, in his view, to the study of normal adult personality.

Henry A. Murray Henry Murray (b. 1893), working out of his broad experience in medicine, bio-

chemistry, and psychoanalysis, constructed an account of personality that had several original elements—notably, a forceful presentation of the role of the environment in determining behavior. Murray is best known for inventing the Thematic Apperception Test (TAT), an unusual and reliable personality test, which is described in the discussion of his measurement procedures in next chapter. Probably his most admired work, though, was in the field of human motivation. Struck by the multiplicity of human motives, he attempted to catalog and later measure them.

Robert W. White A trend toward the preeminence of the ego in personality theory, which started with Jung, culminated in R. W. White's (b. 1904) championing of the concept of ego *competence*. The notion of competence is deceptively simple, like so many other ideas in personality theory. Basically, competence is directed both inward, toward mastery of feelings and wishes, and outward, toward a sure control over the environment, both inanimate and social. White points out that the whole of development can be understood in terms of the individual's feeling his own increasing competence and the actual attainment of competence in an ever-enlarging number of areas. White's views brought the ego to its ultimate position in personality theory. The ego became truly and actively in charge of things, rather than being just a passive administrator of the personality's affairs.

CONSTITUTIONAL THEORIES OF PERSONALITY

Constitutional theories of personality point out the substantial correlation between body physique and personality. There have been many such theories, from the dawn of recorded history. William H. Sheldon put together the modern version. He

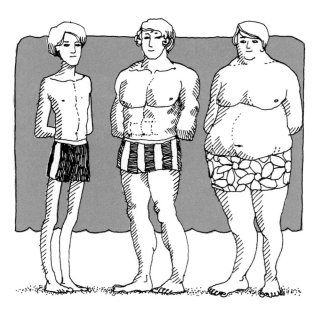

Figure 25.6
William H. Sheldon developed a theory of personality
based on body type. His three main categories are
represented here.

classified human physiques according to three *body-type dimensions*: *ectomorphy*, *endomorphy*, and *mesomorphy*. According to Sheldon, these body types are correlated with basic personality, or *temperament*. Tall, slim ectomorphs will have personalities dominated by *cerebrotonia* ("cerebro" refers to the brain), a temperament characterized by reflection. Muscular and compact mesomorphs will have personalities dominated by *somatotonia* ("soma" refers to body), characterized by power and aggressiveness. The rounded endomorphs will have personalities dominated by *viscerotonia* ("viscero" refers to the gut), characterized by relaxation and passive pleasure. Bodies with various proportions of these three physiques will have personalities with roughly corresponding proportions of the three temperaments.

Sheldon and his group of co-workers (which included S. S. Stevens, whose sensory work appears in Unit IV) showed that physiques and temperaments can be reliably judged and that there is a correlation between them. What is arguable is whether the physique *causes* the temperament. We certainly react differently to people with different physiques, and it may be that temperament is influenced by others' reactions, rather than by the physique itself (Figure 25.6).

There have been many attempts to develop more extensive numerical descriptions of personality, sometimes with very highly sophisticated mathematical and statistical techniques. We shall discuss some of them in the next chapter.

THE GESTALT SCHOOL

As we saw earlier (Chapter 14), *gestalt* psychologists made great contributions to the theory of perception, but they failed to influence other areas of psychology substantially. The gestaltists made only short forays into personality theory. Some ideas of *Kurt Lewin* (1890–1947) are representative, and they also illustrate a rare use in psychology of analogies with physical science. Lewin saw the person as pushed and pulled in a *field of forces*. The resultant effect of the forces in the field determines the person's behavior, much as the behavior of a falling leaf is determined both by gravity and by the various gusts of wind that strike it, or the behavior of a bit of iron by the magnetic forces around it. Lewin was most at home in discussing conflicts. His basic idea was that a person gravitates to different positions in his *life-space* (a field of forces) as the forces vary. The rules are relatively simple: stay close to the positive forces and remote from the negative forces, and in a group of all negatives or all positives, stay *relatively* close to the least negative or the most positive. Lewin felt that a person tried to *restructure* fields

Figure 25.7
A graphic representation of Kurt Lewin's "fields of forces." The large solid dot represents a personality. Pluses and minuses represent forces acting on the personality.

that were uncomfortable. For example, in an all-positive field a person may move the parts around in order to be as near as possible to all of them. In an all-negative situation, though, restructuring may fail. In that case, the person may *leave the field* for an entirely new set of forces with which he hopes to be better able to deal, as in Figure 25.7D. Lewin is best known in the personality field for this concept of *leaving the field*. It is reminiscent of Freud's ideas of denial and repression.

HARRY STACK SULLIVAN

Harry Stack Sullivan (1892–1949), an influential American psychiatrist, felt that Freud and other personality theorists dangerously neglected man's social interactions. So important did Sullivan consider these interactions that he constructed his entire theory and mode of psychotherapy around them. Indeed, he felt that personality did not exist outside of social relationships with other people. This implies that personality is very changeable. For example, Sullivan thought that if a man walked from a roomful of children into a roomful of college presidents, his personality—not just its outward expression—would change. Personality *is* social relationships with others.

Not suprisingly, Sullivan saw personality development as a matter of acquiring relationships with others. This begins with the mother and the nursing relationship in infancy; expands to the family, where discipline of the self becomes necessary; and

Figure 25.8
Harry Stack Sullivan. [Courtesy of W. W. Norton & Co.]

expands still further as the individual matures. All along the way, social relationships are formed in order to avoid anxiety and gratify needs.

Sullivan will probably be best remembered for his conception of the *malevolent transformation*, his name for the disruptive changes in social life. One of these changes occurs when the happy and secure child, fresh from a successful nursing experience, finds that the world is full of uncooperative people—parents, siblings, and even parts of himself—who cannot be manipulated and controlled. This is a malevolent tranformation because these people seem to be enemies, relative to the normal mother during nursing. This transformation is useful, however, in development; it provides not only the anxiety but also the persons with whom to form new social bonds that reduce the anxiety. Other transformations occur whenever the social environment again changes, and they are of various degrees of "malevolence."

BEHAVIORISM

The behaviorists, when they have dealt with something as apparently mentalistic as personality, have been as radical as Sullivan in rejecting theorizing about internal psychodynamics as a useless exercise. They prefer to observe *how a person behaves*, both in social and in nonsocial situations. Personality for them is nothing more than the sum total of a person's habitual behavior; for behaviorists, development consists simply of maturation and learning, with the emphasis on learning (after motor skills have matured beyond their barest rudiments). We shall note some experimental attempts to study personality-relevant behavior when we discuss behavior modification in Chapter 32. Most of what the behaviorist says about personality, however, is a purely theoretical extension to interpretations of human behavior of the principles that seem to govern animal learning in the laboratory. These are the concepts of discriminative stimulus, response, and reinforcement for operant behavior (Chapter 4), and conditioned stimulus and conditioned response for respondent behavior (Chapter 3). B. F. Skinner's book, *Verbal Behavior*, discussed in Chapters 8 and 9, is the best available example of such an *interpretive extension* of the behaviorist viewpoint.

CARL ROGERS AND ABRAHAM MASLOW

In contrast to the behaviorists' emphasis on objective observations, two contemporary personality theorists—Carl Rogers (b. 1902) and Abraham Maslow (1908–1972) have both emphasized the individual's own *self-concept*. Rogers' *self-theory*, which grew out of his method of psychotherapy (which we shall discuss in Chapter 31), stresses the theme of *psychological growth*. According to Rogers, a person normally pos-

sesses a great capacity for growth and realization of his individual potential. Development runs into trouble only when the self fails for some reason to incorporate and learn to live with its own new thoughts, feelings, or behaviors. Development continues when the self discovers that it does have certain thoughts and feelings and that—far from there being anything wrong with the thoughts and feelings—*accepting* them leads to feelings of self-integrity, self-fulfillment, and satisfying psychological growth. It is normal for growth to continue; abnormal for growth ever to stop.

To describe optimal personality development, Abraham Maslow introduced the concept of *self-actualization*. We looked at this idea in Chapter 18, in our discussion of maturity, but here we want to see it in the context of a theory of personality. In terms from Freudian thought, self-actualization can be understood as continuing sublimation and displacement: an individual continues to expand his interests and his contribution to society. It is really just a matter of continuing to grow psychologically. Maslow spiced his writings with analyses of public figures who seemed to typify self-actualization— for example, Eleanor Roosevelt and Albert Einstein. These two people had little but their self-actualizing tendency in common. Throughout their lives, they both continued to be active and productive; perhaps that is the best way to describe Maslow's idea.

Self-actualization has, perhaps incidentally, been linked with humanistic psychology, a movement that has as its avowed purpose the bringing back— some would say, introducing for the first time—the essence of being human into psychology. Humanists point to *alienation* as the villain in modern life and to *relatedness* as the savior. They emphasize human experience and its betterment: the experience of ectasy should not be so rare in our lives; there should be more deep conviction and less phoniness,

Figure 25.9
Albert Einstein in 1946, thirty years after his best contribution to physics, and one year after opposing the use of the atomic bomb on Japan. [United Press International Photo]

Figure 25.10
Eleanor Roosevelt in 1961, seventeen years after the death of her famous husband, President Franklin D. Roosevelt, and while she was a delegate to the United Nations. [Courtesy of the United Nations]

less pretense, and less inhibition; there should be more development and much more emphasis in formal psychology on the individual person.

THE NEWER VIEWS OF PERSONALITY

No one has seriously attempted in recent years to formulate a complete theory of personality. The newer approaches set out either to categorize what has been said before by other theorists, or to raise what appear to be more basic, molar questions about personality.

An example of the first approach is the schematic division of personality into *core* and *peripheral* personality—a distinction that can be ferreted out of any personality theory. The idea is that a personality has a central focus, called the core, which directs the fundamental approach of the person to the world and determines his or her most important personality characteristics. The core is very difficult to

change. The periphery is populated with characteristics that are either expressions of the core, individual traits resulting from accidents of personal experience, or particular and personal interests that further make for individuality. Peripheral aspects of personality are more publicly available and are also easier to change. Although the core–periphery view is interesting and applicable across the board as a unifying idea in personality theory, it has yet to inspire theorists to produce any really new thinking about the human personality.

An example of the second approach is the discussion of *consistency* versus *situationality* in the individual personality. As Walter Mischel has pointed out, the question here is not whether a person can be induced to behave in inconsistent ways in different situations, although this is the theme of much of the research spawned by this approach. There is adequate evidence, for at least superficial traits, of glaring inconsistencies; we can easily dream up situations that will induce a person to behave in seemingly inconsistent ways. But people *are* consistent over a wide variety of situations. It appears that any attempt to theorize that situation-produced inconsistency is the key to understanding personality characteristics seems surely to be an uphill fight. The basic issue is the circumstances and situations under which consistency or inconsistency prevails; in this area, the situational approach to personality has yet to make much headway.

WHICH PERSONALITY THEORY IS BEST?

As natural as it is to ask which personality theory is best, there is no answer. The theories we have introduced here all have their strengths and weaknesses. And too little is known about personality to permit the selection or elimination of any theory on scientific grounds. For the student just beginning his study of human personality, it is certainly less important to adopt one theory than to understand the basic principles of several of them—their fundamental concepts, approaches to psychological problems, and modes of thinking. In fact, we urge the interested student to try not to make a final choice. Breadth and tolerance are valuable traits for the study of a new field. Our advice is to concentrate on the methods that are used to study personality; we shall discuss some of the more important methods in the next chapter. Were there a reliable method that produced real, large, and long-lasting *changes* in human personality, there would at least be fresh data for the personality theorist. In the absence of such data, some contemporary psychologists of personality feel that the very concept of personality adds little or nothing to our understanding of human beings.

Suggested Readings

Allport, G. W. (1937) *Personality: A psychological interpretation.* New York: Holt, Rinehart, Winston. [An original interpretation of personality by a close student of the normal person.]

Fordham, F. (1953) *An introduction to Jung's psychology.* London: Penguin Books. [An authoritative introduction to Jung's complex and often mystical ideas.]

Hall, C. S. & Lindzey, G. (1970) *Theories of personality.* (2nd ed.) New York: Wiley. [Excellent survey of the most important and influential theories of personality.]

Mischel, W. (1971) *Introduction to personality.* New York: Holt, Rinehart, Winston. [An informative example of the newer views of personality.]

Sheldon, W. H., Stevens, S. S., & Tucker, W. B. (1940) *The varieties of human physique.* New York: Harper. [Constitutional psychology at its best.]

CHAPTER TWENTY-SIX

Measuring Human Characteristics

Each of us is a unique person with a unique life history and a unique set of characteristics. The psychological study of individual differences attempts to describe in *quantitative* terms not only our interests and aptitudes but also our whole personalities—in themselves and in comparison with those of other people. In this chapter, we shall consider the types of measuring instruments psychologists employ, how they are constructed, and how successful they are in assessing and predicting our characteristics.

Individuals differ in many physical and psychological dimensions. Psychologists have been primarily concerned with differences in (1) individual interests and aptitudes and (2) personalities. These differences are important for predicting job success, marital happiness, and recovery from personality disorders. Before we consider how personal characteristics are measured, it is necessary to clarify what we mean by "interests," "aptitudes," and "personality." Then we can see how assessments of these characteristics have been used by schools, employment services, computer-dating services, and clinical psychologists to influence—to a large or small extent—our daily lives, our access to opportunities, and our futures.

Probably the most straightforward of the assessments of individual differences are the interest inventories. For the most part, people can be quite frank and objective about the kinds of things they like to do and the kinds of things they wish they were capable of doing. We can readily and honestly answer whether or not we like to watch football, read historical novels, or listen to sermons. Similarly, we can usually say whether or not we would like to be a shoe salesman, clergyman, judge, college professor, or mortician. Interest inventories can even enable testers to assess the likelihood that a particular set of interests will be enduring. Such tests are particularly useful in vocational counseling.

There is a wide variety of aptitude tests measuring almost every imaginable behavioral and mental skill. The best-known aptitude tests are the IQ tests, which we have already encountered in Chapters 8 and 16. There are also aptitude tests for specific job-related skills, for more general skills, and even for creativity.

Personality characteristics are harder to specify than either interests or aptitudes. Part of the problem is described in Chapters 24 and 25: no two people necessarily agree on what is meant by personality or

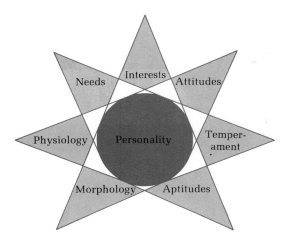

Figure 26.1
J. P. Guilford's personality classification. Personality
is seen as the integrated whole that may be viewed
from each of the seven perspectives shown. [Adapted
from J. P. Guilford, *Personality*. New York: McGraw-
Hill, 1959.]

how it may best be characterized. Thus, there is an
unusually large number of tests that aim to measure
some aspect of personality. One of the more popular
classifications is J. P. Guilford's, which describes
personality as an integrated whole that may be
viewed from each of seven different perspectives, as
shown in Figure 26.1. For Guilford, personality is
composed of temperament, interests, attitudes,
aptitudes, morphology, physiology, and needs. He
recognizes the contribution to personality of physical
characteristics (physiology and morphology), motivational considerations (needs and interests), emotional
components (attitudes and temperament), and
abilities (aptitudes). According to Guilford's scheme,
personality encompasses many of the psychological
processes that we have been considering throughout
this book. It is no wonder then that there are

hundreds—if not thousands—of personality tests, many
of which are extremely ingenious and revealing.
We shall discuss some of the more important ones in
this chapter. Unfortunately, we shall also see that
most personality tests fail to meet the minimum
criteria for a good psychological test. Before we go
on to the tests themselves, we should look at these
criteria.

THE CRITERIA FOR A GOOD TEST

If a test is to be successful in measuring individual
differences in a meaningful way it should satisfy
four criteria: it should be objective, standardized,
valid, and reliable. (1) An *objective test* is one that
can be administered and scored by any qualified
person, with the same result in every case. Many
personality tests fail to satisfy this criterion. (2) A
standardized test is one that has been administered to
a large and representative sample of the population
so that the individual's score can be meaningfully
compared with the scores of other individuals. (3) A
valid test is one that actually measures what it was
intended to measure, as shown by comparing scores
on the test with some appropriate *criterion* measure.
For example, when we say that the law school
aptitude test (LSAT) is valid, we mean that
individuals who score high on this test tend to do
better in law school than those who score low on it.
Lack of validity is a serious drawback shared by
several commonly used tests. (4) Finally, a test
is *reliable* if it is self-consistent—that is, if the same
person makes similar scores when tested on different
occasions. One common method for checking a
test's reliability is the *split-halves technique*: a
subject's score on half of the test items is compared
with his score on the other half. The more consistent
the scores on the two halves, the more reliable
the test.

It is important to note that a test may be very reliable and still not be valid. For example, the items on the test might be so clearly constructed and the scoring of the test so objective that the same individual will make virtually identical scores when taking the test over and over again. This tells us that the test is reliable, but it says nothing at all about whether or not the individual's score validly measures what the test is supposed to measure. For example, a person's height, his immediate memory span, and his feelings about President Ford may all exhibit high reliability—in the sense that the same individual will make pretty much the same score on successive measures—but a test based on items such as these three might not validly predict anything at all. Reliability simply does not imply validity. On the other hand, validity implies a fair measure of reliability; results from a test that is hopelessly unreliable cannot be valid.

THE USE OF PSYCHOLOGICAL TESTS

Psychological tests assess and predict characteristics of the individual and his potential for learning and performing any of a wide variety of skills. There are two main methods of prediction and assessment: the *statistical method* and the *clinical* (or "intuitive") *method*. The statistical approach measures how the individual rates on some particular test in comparison with other individuals who have taken the test in the past and for whom the relation between test scores and later performance is known. Clinical assessments, on the other hand, rely less on empirical validation and more on the judgment and intuition of a clinician. In other words, clinical expertise is substituted for statistical evidence. Both types of tests are commonly used to describe and compare individual characteristics and to predict

future performance, but clinical prediction has fared rather badly when compared with statistical prediction in studies of predictive validity. Nevertheless, a talented, sensitive, and experienced clinician can occasionally learn more about a human personality in ten minutes of conversation than an objective tester may learn in several hours of testing.

THE CONSTRUCTION OF TESTS

The principal methods of test construction are based on (1) some *a priori* theory; (2) the statistical technique of factor analysis; or (3) purely empirical considerations. In the latter, items are chosen not because of their apparent *content* but rather because they effectively differentiate between individuals rated high and those rated low on the characteristic being measured.

Tests Constructed on the Basis of Theory
Psychological tests may be designed according to particular theories, in which case the theories prescribe the test items that should distinguish between individuals with respect to an interest, an aptitude, or a personality trait. For example, the *Eysenck Personality Inventory* (*EPI*) was constructed on the basis of Hans Eysenck's theory of personality (discussed later in this chapter). If a test is to have validity, however, it must have virtues other than a mere consonance with the theoretical assumptions of its author. This is true for relatively straightforward tests of interest; it is even more crucial when general aptitudes are being measured; it is nowhere more important than in the realm of personality theory, where there is little agreement among different investigators as to just what personality is. Thus, tests that are designed according to a theory must be validated experimentally, as was the EPI. For example, test scores on the EPI were used to

predict performance in a variety of laboratory learning studies in which both anxiety and cognitive complexity were manipulated. A more concrete example of experimental validation will be discussed later in this chapter.

What are the advantages and disadvantages of tests designed according to a theory? One practical advantage is that a theory provides a rationale and guidelines for selecting test items. A second advantage relates to the theory rather than to the test: to the extent that the theory permits the construction of tests that usefully predict behavior, the theory gains support. One disadvantage is that the items selected for the test by the theory may be less useful in differentiating between individuals scoring high and low on a particular trait than are items selected and tested without regard to content—that is to say, items that are selected empirically. But the ultimate criterion for a successful test must be its validity, and whatever methods produce the most valid scores are to be preferred.

Factor Analytical Methods of Test Construction *Factor analysis* is a statistical technique that facilitates the measurement of complex characteristics, such as intelligence and personality, by breaking them down into more readily measurable components, or factors. The tester first obtains a large sample of scores from a variety of tests, each of which presumably measures some factor of a complex characteristic—say, intelligence. He then computes the intercorrelations of the scores of the various individuals on every possible pair of tests, to determine how well the tests correlate with each other. (We discussed statistical correlation in Chapter 1.) Suppose that individuals who make high scores on tests of mathematical reasoning also make high scores on tests of logic; we can conclude that the mathematical and logical tests are highly cor-

related. On the other hand, if scores on one test do not bear any systematic relation to scores on another test (for example, a vocabulary test and a test for dominance), then we say the tests are uncorrelated. Computing the correlations between each and every pair of tests is a tedious task. For example, in order to compute all of the intercorrelations in a battery of fifty tests, one would have to perform 1,225 statistical computations. Fortunately, electronic computers reduce computation time considerably.

Once the correlations have been obtained, the method of factor analysis, whose details need not concern us here, is applied in order to arrange the various tests into groups of factors, each of which is composed of highly intercorrelated tests. The number of factors is thus invariably smaller than the number of tests. For example, a battery of eleven tests might yield only three factors, consisting perhaps of clusters of six, three, and two intercorrelated tests. On the basis of this result, we would say that these three factors underlie the complex characteristic the test battery is measuring. We used eleven tests where three would have given the same information. Factor analytical methods have been widely used in the study of intelligence (for example, in the Thurstone Primary Mental Abilities Test), and in the study of personality (for example, in the EPI, discussed above, and Cattell's questionnaire, which discriminates among sixteen personality factors).

Empirical Methods of Test Construction
Some tests are constructed exclusively by empirical methods. For example, the developers of the Strong Vocational Aptitude Blank (discussed in the next section) and the Minnesota Multiphasic Personality Inventory sought test items that were generally answered differently by those known to rate high and those known to rate low on a particular trait. If

institutionalized paranoiacs tend to respond to a particular item (such as "Sometimes I feel they are after me") differently from normal people, that item may be incorporated into tests for paranoia. It should be noted, however, that the nature of the test question need not bear any obvious relation to the underlying trait. Thus, if paranoiacs respond differently from normals to the item "I enjoy raking leaves," that item would also be included in the test for paranoia. Items that are included in empirically constructed tests may or may not be intuitively suggestive of the trait being measured, and they need not be related to a theory about that trait. The rationale is strictly correlational: individuals are scored on the basis of how similar their answers are to those of people known to rate high or low on the trait.

INTEREST INVENTORIES

The three most widely used tests of interest are the *Strong Vocational Interest Blank*, the *Kuder Preference Record*, and the *Allport-Vernon Study of Values*. The first two have been used extensively to determine what occupations different people are likely to find congenial, and how similar their interest profiles are to those of people who have successfully pursued particular occupations. The Allport-Vernon Study of Values, on the other hand, gauges the individual's preferences and interests in broad areas such as the "economic" and the "religious." Because of its emphasis on values, it is often considered a personality test rather than an interest inventory.

The Strong Vocational Interest Blank The Strong test was constructed empirically and consists of items selected to differentiate between people who have been successful in a particular occupation and the rest of the general population. A male subject's answers to the questions comprising the Strong test

may be compared to those made by men in some fifty different occupations, including artists, veterinarians, math and science teachers, army officers, YMCA physical directors, city school superintendents, and morticians. (Strong also developed a comparable test for women subjects, whose answers are compared to those made by women in a number of occupations.) The Strong test has been extensively revised and updated over the years; in addition, it is well standardized and validated. Development and validation of the Strong test have revealed that not only do people in different occupations differ in terms of interests related directly to job activities, but that they also differ in terms of interests related to almost every other aspect of everyday life, including hobbies, sports, artistic enjoyments, and interpersonal relations. Thus, a person who knows very little about what is required of a city school superintendent, a forest service employee, an osteopath, or a vocational counselor can nonetheless be meaningfully tested by asking about his or her interests in many familiar activities. If the answers resemble those of successful architects, for example, then it is likely that the person being tested could easily develop an interest in architecture.

The present version of the Strong test consists of eight parts and contains a total of four hundred items. In each of the first five parts the subject indicates whether he or she likes, is indifferent to, or dislikes, activities from each of the following five categories: occupations, school subjects, amusements, miscellaneous activities, and human characteristics. In the final three parts of the test the subject ranks listed activities in order of preference, answers questions comparing his interest for given pairs of items, and responds to items requiring him to rate his own characteristics, including his perceived abilities. These answers yield a profile (pattern) of

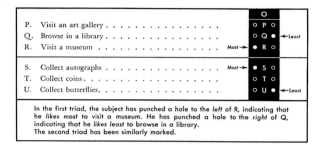

Figure 26.2
Sample items from the Kuder Preference Record–Vocational. [Reproduced by permission of Science Research Associates. © 1948, G. Frederic Kuder.]

scores, which may be compared with the typical profiles for each occupation.

The Strong test is used by vocational counselors in guiding young men and women toward potential careers, by graduate and professional schools in assessing applicants' interest in a particular field of study, and by personnel managers in assessing the interests of prospective employees.

The Kuder Preference Record   The Kuder Preference Record–Occupational, a recently developed interest inventory has been validated empirically in roughly the same manner as the Strong test. It provides scores for thirty-eight occupations, including such specific occupations as radio station manager and county agricultural agent. An older but more popular member of the Kuder family of interest inventories is the Kuder Preference Record–Vocational, which scores a subject's relative interest in a limited number of broad areas rather than in specific occupational activities. Sample items from the test are shown in Figure 26.2. Note that the subject is required to indicate which of three activities he or she likes best and which he or she

likes least. The test is then scored according to ten interest scales: mechanical, computational, scientific, artistic, literary, musical, persuasive, social service, clerical, and outdoor. An individual subject thus obtains scores on each of the ten interest scales. His scores may then be compared with those made by the general population. The manual accompanying the Kuder Preference Record–Vocational classifies occupations according to their one or two major interest areas. Thus, a landscape architect is classified under "outdoor–artistic." A person scoring higher than the general population on these scales, therefore, would have interests similar to those of successful landscape architects.

The Allport-Vernon-Lindzey Study of Values
The Allport-Vernon-Lindzey scale measures the relative importance to the subject of six areas of interest or value: theoretical, economic, aesthetic, social, political, and religious. The subject answers questions, such as those shown in Figure 26.3, each of which seeks to discover which of two or more interest areas predominates in the subject's personality. The subject's scores for the six interest areas may be plotted in terms of a graphic "profile," as shown in Figure 26.4. The profile shows at a glance the subject's predominant values or interest areas. Since it would be impossible to obtain all high or all low scores, scores on this test say nothing about how one person's interest in one value-area compares with that of another. As the figure shows, the average male profile has higher peaks in the theoretical, economic, and political values, whereas the average female profile peaks in the aesthetic, social, and religious values. Profiles of people in various occupations show characteristic shapes: engineering and medical students peak in the theoretical value, whereas the typical clergyman's profile shows a peak in the religious value and a dip in the economic value.

PART I. In the boxes to the right, rate the two alternative answers 3 and 0 if you agree with one and disagree with the other; if you have only a slight preference for one over the other, rate them 2 and 1, respectively.

EXAMPLE
If you should see the following news items with headlines of equal size in your morning paper, which would you read more attentively? (a) PROTESTANT LEADERS TO CONSULT ON RECONCILIATION; (b) GREAT IMPROVEMENTS IN MARKET CONDITIONS.

a   b
☐   ☐

PART II. In the boxes to the right, rate the answers 4, 3, 2, and 1 in order of personal preference, giving 4 to the most attractive and 1 to the least attractive alternative.

EXAMPLE
In your opinion, can a man who works in business all the week best spend Sunday in—

a. trying to educate himself by reading serious books
b. trying to win at golf, or racing
c. going to an orchestral concert
d. hearing a really good sermon

b   c   d   a
☐   ☐   ☐   ☐

Figure 26.3
Sample items from the Allport-Vernon-Lindzey Study of Values. [Reproduced by permission of Houghton Mifflin Company.]

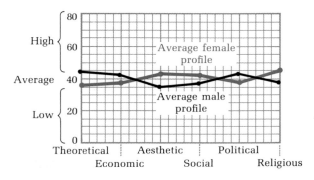

Figure 26.4
Mean scores of men and women on the Allport-Vernon-Lindzey Study of Values. [Reproduced by permission of Houghton Mifflin Company.]

APTITUDE TESTS

Aptitude tests are intended to evaluate the subject's potential for future performance in a particular area. Such tests range from general tests of intellectual aptitude to very specific tests of motor dexterity, artistic judgment, and clerical aptitude. After continuing our discussion of intelligence (begun in Chapters 8 and 16), we shall present a brief survey of some of the other important aptitude tests in current use.

INTELLIGENCE TESTS

In Chapter 8 we noted that the commonly employed intelligence quotient (IQ) is described by the equation:

$$IQ = \frac{Mental\ age}{Chronological\ age} \times 100$$

We also noted that IQ tests, like other aptitude tests, are designed to predict future success from current achievement; that is, IQ tests utilize present evidence of past intellectual achievement to predict future intellectual growth. IQ, like most other human test scores, seems to be influenced by both hereditary and environmental factors, as suggested by some studies of identical twins and foster children (see Chapter 16). There is clear evidence that children raised in intellectually challenging environments tend to score higher on IQ tests than those raised in impoverished environments, where opportunities to learn and practice the intellectual skills measured by these tests are fewer. Thus, children raised on the farm tend to score lower than children raised in the city, and children from economically well-to-do homes tend to produce better scores than the economically disadvantaged. In a very real sense, IQ measures the ability to profit from prior experience—to transfer verbal, arithmetical, and reasoning skills successfully learned in the school or home environment to similar tasks presented on IQ tests.

OTHER APTITUDE TESTS

Although scores on intelligence tests may be useful predictors of academic success, they may be of no value in ascertaining whether an individual is suited

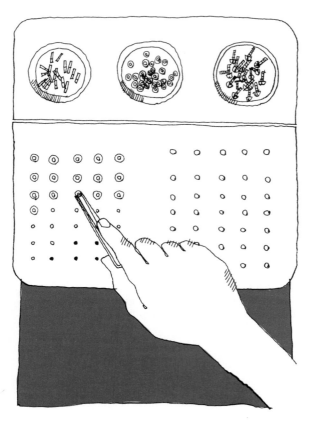

Figure 26.5
Crawford Small-Parts Dexterity Test. [Based on a photograph from the Psychological Corporation.]

for a particular job. Assuming that a person is of at least normal intelligence, his suitability for a particular job may depend mainly on his interests and his specific abilities. As noted earlier, the Strong and Kuder inventories assess interests; specialized aptitude tests assess whether or not, given the interest, a person is likely to have the specific skills required for a particular job.

Motor Functions   Many jobs require a certain degree of motor coordination or manual dexterity. One of the most popular tests designed to measure these abilities is the *Crawford Small-Parts Dexterity Test* (Figure 26.5), which assesses a variety of manipulative skills. In the illustration, the subject must insert pins into tiny holes with a small pair of tweezers and afterward cover each pin with a small collar. In the second part of the test, the subject

inserts small screws into threaded holes. In each part, a subject's score is the time required to finish. Another test of dexterity is the *Bennett Hand-Tool Dexterity Test*, illustrated in Figure 26.6. In this test the subject removes all of the nuts and bolts from the left upright shown in the figure and mounts them on the right upright according to a predetermined sequence. Again the subject's score is the time taken to complete the task. Other motor tests include those requiring coordination of hand and foot movements in conjunction with visual stimuli (such as the *Complex Coordination Test* used in Air Force programs), tests assessing simple hand and finger movements required on the assembly line (such as the *Tweezer Dexterity Test*), and tests assessing manual dexterity for movements that require activity of the arms as well as the hands and fingers (such as the *Purdue Pegboard Test*, which requires no tools). Although performance of these tasks requires very little knowledge of ordinary mechanics, it is obvious that the subject's past experience with tools is likely to affect his score.

Mechanical Aptitude   Factor-analytical methods have indicated that mechanical aptitude comprises three main factors: perceptual abilities, spatial abilities, and manual dexterity. Aptitude tests for manual dexterity have already been discussed. One of the many tests assessing spatial and perceptual abilities is the *Minnesota Spatial Relations Test*, consisting of four form-boards, each of which contains fifty-eight differently shaped cutouts. The subject fits a set of blocks into the various cutouts and is scored both for the number of errors and the time taken to complete the task.

Clerical Aptitude   The *Minnesota Clerical Test*, like most tests constructed to assess clerical aptitude, emphasizes the speed with which a subject can utilize perceptual information. For example, in the number-comparison subtest of the Minnesota Clerical Test, the subject is given two hundred pairs of numbers, each of which consists of from three to twelve digits; for each pair, the subject ascertains whether or not the two numbers are identical. The less time the subject takes, the greater his clerical aptitude.

Artistic Aptitude Most tests of artistic appreciation require the subject to choose between two slightly different art objects. Items are chosen so that art experts have no difficulty agreeing on which of the two is the more artistically accomplished and which involves a distortion of one or more artistic principles. The subject's artistic aptitude is assessed by the extent to which his choices agree with those of the experts.

Creative Ability Creative ability is measured in much the same way as is problem-solving, discussed in Chapter 8. Tests of creative ability include both *fluency tests* and *originality tests*. In the *word-fluency test* the subject is required to list words containing a particular letter and is scored in terms of the raw number of appropriate responses listed within the allotted time. In tests of *associational fluency*, the subject must write words similar in meaning to a given word. In each case, the test measures the subject's command of vocabulary as well as his ability to emit verbal responses quickly and appropriately.

Originality tests may also cover vocabulary skills, but they put a premium on unconventional responses. For example, in one test, the subject must say the first word that comes to mind in response to a stimulus word. The less common the response, the higher the originality score obtained. Subjects in creative professions such as the sciences and arts tend to score higher on these tests than do salesmen, business executives, and politicians.

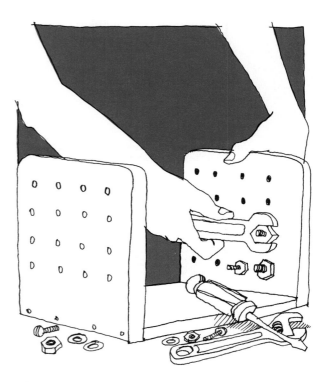

Figure 26.6
Bennett Hand-Tool Dexterity Test. [Based on a photograph from the Psychological Corporation.]

General Aptitude Tests Tests utilizing the factor-analytic approach to measuring ability include multiple-aptitude test batteries such as the *Differential Aptitude Tests* (*DAT*) and the *General Aptitude Test Battery* (*GATB*). The DAT, used primarily for vocational and educational counseling of secondary school children, yields scores on verbal reasoning, abstract reasoning, mechanical reasoning, spatial relations, clerical speed and accuracy, language usage, and numerical abilities. Sample items are shown in Figures 26.7 and 26.8. The DAT has had reasonable success in predicting college achievement. The GATB, developed by the U.S. Employment Service for use by its employment officers, utilizes twelve tests, which rate the following nine aptitude factors: intelligence, verbal aptitude, numerical aptitude, spatial aptitude, form perception,

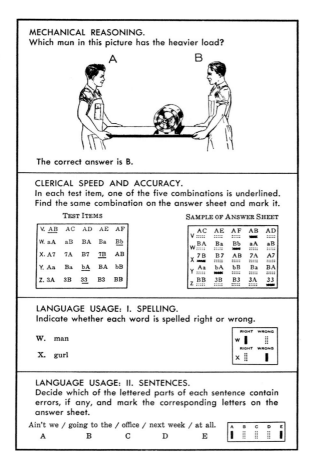

Figure 26.7
Sample items from the Differential Aptitude Tests (DAT).
[Reproduced by permission. Copyright 1947, 1961, 1962
Psychological Corporation.]

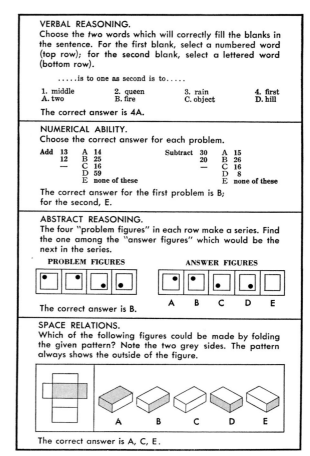

Figure 26.8
More DAT items. [Reproduced by permission. Copyright
1947, 1961, 1962 Psychological Corporation.]

clerical perception, motor coordination, finger dexterity, and manual dexterity. The GATB has proven to be one of the most successful multiple-aptitude batteries. Whereas the DAT has been used to predict academic success, the GATB has been used for purposes of job classification and has been validated against occupational criteria.

PERSONALITY TESTS

Personality tests, whether designed to assess personality traits or to diagnose personality disorders, have met with less success than interest inventories and aptitude tests. Part of the problem is the complexity

of the human personality. As we saw earlier, there are many different personality theories. Since there is much less agreement about what personality is than about what aptitudes or interests are, it is not surprising that efforts to test personality have produced more mixed results. At the same time, however, personality tests are in widespread use, and for that reason alone we should know something about them. In addition, some of the tests are modestly successful, particularly in diagnosing serious personality disorders. We shall examine some of the most useful and the most popular types of personality tests and try to gain an appreciation of their strengths and weaknesses.

Typical items on personality questionnaires might include the following: (a) "I often have unpleasant dreams," (b) "I sometimes drink alone," (c) "I rarely do anything dangerous just for the thrill of it." Subjects are usually instructed to answer "true" or "false" to such questions. But what is meant by "often" or by "unpleasant" in a, by "sometimes" in b, or by "rarely," "dangerous," and "thrill" in c? Since the questions are ambiguous, individuals taking the test are bound to interpret them differently. Moreover, it is not always clear what is being measured. For example, does a measure despondency, unfulfilled desires, or adjustment? Does b measure alcoholism, loneliness, or independence? Inventories based on such questions have been shown to have little predictive validity. This is particularly true when the items are chosen in accordance with the particular theory of personality to which the tester happens to subscribe or simply because they make sense to the tester. Tests such as the MMPI (Minnesota Multiphasic Personality Inventory) have at least some empirical validity because of the way in which they are constructed.

There are several types of personality tests, including questionnaires (such as the MMPI), observational or situational tests (such as interviews and rating scales in which the tester judges behavior samples), and tests of production or interpretation (in which the subject completes or interprets some incomplete or ambiguous test materials and his responses in turn are interpreted by the tester).

Questionnaires Perhaps the most widely used personality questionnaire is the _Minnesota Multiphasic Personality Inventory (MMPI)_. It consists of 550 items to which the subject must respond "true" or "false." The items include such statements as these: "I am happy most of the time"; "I find it hard to keep my mind on a task or job"; "I daydream very little"; "Often I cross the street in order not to meet

someone I see"; "I have never indulged in any unusual sex practices"; "I believe I am being plotted against." Responses are interpreted according to traditional clinical scales, including the following:

1. _hypochondriasis_, indicating undue concern or anxiety about one's health;

2. _depression_, marked by pessimism and passivity;

3. _hysteria_, or a tendency toward psychosomatic disturbances;

4. _psychopathic deviancy_, showing a lack of social and moral responsibility;

5. _masculinity/femininity_, a high score indicating, for males, a high degree of "feminine" (or sensitive) behavior, and for females, a high degree of "masculine" (or aggressive) behavior;

6. _paranoia_, or a tendency to believe you are being persecuted;

7. _psychasthenia_, suggesting obsessive worry and phobias or compulsions;

8. _schizophrenia_, suggesting bizarre thought and action;

9. _hypomania_, suggesting excitability and manic moods; and

10. four _validity scales_ or sets of "lie items," representing checks on cheating, carelessness, and miscomprehension. (If a score on any of these scales is sufficiently high, the entire questionnaire is considered invalid.)

Scoring of the MMPI produces an MMPI profile, which can be compared with that produced by a normal adult. Although the individual scales are based on a psychiatric classification system that is no longer taken very seriously and that is difficult to interpret, the profile obtained by looking at scores on all nine scales has demonstrated some utility in depicting personalities of psychotics (high scores on scales 6–9), neurotics (high scores on scales 1–3), and delinquents (a peak at 4).

Despite the fact that the MMPI is probably used more by clinicians than any other device in the diagnosis of personality disorders, it is at best only marginally effective. The problem is that although group data based on several hundred patients with severe personality disorders indeed differ significantly from the group data of hundreds of normal subjects, these group differences are not very useful when it comes to the diagnosis and prediction of an *individual case*. The most effective use of the MMPI is for the separation of people suffering from mild disorders (the neuroses), who score high on scales 1–3, from people suffering from serious personality disorders (the psychoses), who tend to score high on scales 6–9. Even here, however, nearly one out of every three patients would be misclassified on the basis of MMPI scores! The classification is, fortunately, never made on the basis of the test alone, which is supplemented by interviews.

The *Manifest Hostility Scale* (MHS) was constructed, in part, from items contained in the MMPI. The test consists of such items as "I like to poke fun at people" and "I have very few quarrels with members of my family." A "yes" answer to the first question and a "no" answer to the second question are scored as hostile.

The *California F-Scale* is a measure of *authoritarianism*, a set of attitudes characterized by prejudice, political conservatism, conformity, and antidemocratic sentiment. Aroused by Hitler's rise in Germany and his persecution and mass murder of Jews, a group of psychologists attempted to identify the personality characteristics of the *potential* fascist. Out of this work came measurement of authoritarianism by items such as the following: "Obedience and respect for authority are the most important virtues children should learn," "Homosexuals are hardly better than criminals and ought to be severely punished," "No

weakness or difficulty can hold us back if we have enough willpower," and "The businessman and the manufacturer are much more important to society than the artist and the professor."

Scores on the F-Scale are correlated with scores on other scales, such as the MHS, and are also correlated with conservative political and economic beliefs, as several studies of attitudes have shown. For example, the higher a person's F-score, the more likely he is to be opposed to "socialized medicine." In the 1960 presidential campaign, supporters of Orville Faubus, a champion of segregation, were found to have higher F-Scale scores, on the average, than supporters of liberals such as Adlai Stevenson and Hubert Humphrey. It should be stressed, however, that there is no sure guarantee that the F-scores correlate with actual behavior (rather than with attitudes).

Other Questionnaires   There are hundreds of different personality questionnaires, many of which attempt to measure very specific traits. The Air Force has a *Military Ideology Scale* (MIS) constructed to measure the acceptance of military ideology in airmen undergoing basic training. Scores on the MIS can, to some extent, be predicted by scores on the F-Scale; to some degree, authoritarianism and acceptance of military ideology are correlated.

Cattell's 16 PF Questionnaire uses factor analysis to attempt a description of the entire personality as reflected by sixteen scales, including emotional stability, dominance, and radicalism. The test has thus far not proved useful, however, in describing the personality of individual subjects.

The Eysenck Personality Inventory (EPI) is based on Eysenck's theory of personality, which rests on the assumption that there are two primary personality dimensions: introversion-extroversion and normal-neurotic. In Eysenck's usage, *introversion* refers to a tendency to withdraw into one's self, especially when under stress, whereas *extroversion* is characterized by sociability and a need for companionship in times of stress. The extremes of the normal–neurotic dimension are characterized by stability, even-temperedness, and calm at one end of the scale, and instability, moodiness, and anxiety at the other. As indicated in our discussion of test construction, the EPI was validated by determining a correspondence between test scores and actual behavior in laboratory studies.

Finally, the *California Psychological Inventory* (*CPI*) is similar to the MMPI—from which half of its items have been drawn—except that it stresses more favorable and normal personality traits than does the MMPI, which was developed for the diagnosis of psychological disorders. The CPI, often called "the sane man's MMPI," includes scales that measure the following three aspects of personality: (1) poise and self-assurance; (2) sociability and maturity; and (3) achievement and aptitude.

Observational Ratings The most popular type of observational rating test is the *interview*, which has long been used in the assessment of applicants for employment or for admission to many professional schools. Interviews are often supplemented by *rating scales*; the interviewer records his impressions according to a set of predetermined characteristics. Both interviews and rating scales may be subject to the *halo effect*, a phenomenon that occurs when the interviewer's later impressions are biased by his first impression, or when all of his impressions are biased by prior knowledge about the applicant. Thus, if the interviewer has information that a person scored high on an intelligence test or on a schizo-phrenia scale, he is likely to rate the person high on the trait in question regardless of how the person actually behaves during the interview.

Behavior can also be observed in situations in which the tester does not interact directly with the subject. For example, the tester may merely observe the subject behaving in a particular (perhaps contrived) situation. Observation of children's doll play is a case in point. Sometimes the tester does not even see the subject. For example, he may simply be given a sample of the subject's expressive behavior, such as his handwriting. Although for many years *graphology* (the study of handwriting) was thought to be in the same nonscientific category as astrology, very recent evidence collected by Daryl Bem of Stanford University suggests that handwriting samples may provide important clues to aspects of personality. In particular, Bem has had remarkable success correlating handwriting and suicide. If two suicide notes are given to a handwriting expert, one of them a real suicide note, and the other a fake, the handwriting expert will generally be able to choose the true suicide note on the basis of a fairly rapid analysis of the handwriting.

Tests of Production Tests such as the Draw-a-Person Test, the Sentence Completion Test, and the Word Association Test all require the subject to produce a sample of behavior, which is expected to give a clue to some aspect of his personality. In the *Sentence-Completion Test*, the subject is given only the first few words of a sentence and is then asked to complete it. For example, the subject might be asked to complete the following sentences: "I am afraid of . . .," "My mother closed . . . ," "I very much like to . . . ." In the *Draw-a-Person Test*, the subject draws a male and a female figure. The tester observes which is drawn first, whether or not the figures are clothed, and what activities are portrayed. In the *Word Association Test*, the subject is presented with a word and instructed to answer with the first word that comes to his mind. The stimulus list includes words that are related to potential psycho-logical problems (such as "sex," "father," and "guilt"). Unfortunately, most of these production tests have little validity as diagnostic instruments. In the first place, little empirical validation has been attempted; in the second place, interpretation of the test results varies widely from tester to tester.

Tests of Interpretation   The basic idea behind *interpretive*, or *projective, tests* is that the subject's motivations, needs, and personality are likely to affect his responses to an unstructured stimulus situation. On the basis of what the subject *projects* into his response, the clinician interprets some aspect of the subject's personality. The two most important and commonly used projective tests require the subject to interpret or describe a grossly unstructured stimulus (often, an ink blot or a vague and ambiguous picture).

The Thematic Apperception Test   Perhaps the most important and innovative projective test is the *Thematic Apperception Test (TAT)*, which consists of thirty pictures of drawings and paintings and one blank card. A given subject is presented with twenty of these stimulus cards (including the blank) and is asked to make up stories about them. (A picture like those in the TAT is shown in Figure 6.3.) The test thus involves the presentation of a standard stimulus administered in a fairly constant and objective manner, and the assessment of the subject's response to it. Interpretation of the test may be made subjectively by the tester, in which case scoring varies widely from tester to tester, or it may proceed according to a very specific scoring system, which has been experimentally validated. In either case, the tester generally asks first who the hero is in the story; then he analyzes the content of the story in terms of a particular personality theory—originally that of Henry Murray, who developed the TAT. Many clinicians, however, rely on their own subjective judgments to score the TAT. Some base their

subjective interpretations on the whole response, whereas others analyze item by item and then base their final impressions on all of the overall scores.

When used with a specific scoring system, the TAT has proven to be an important clinical tool for personality assessment. The original scoring system was developed *a priori* on the basis of Murray's theory of personality and with the kind of experimental validation discussed earlier. For example, Murray constructed a scale of the need for affiliation, which, on intuitive grounds, appears to measure the extent to which people need the companionship, affection, and friendship of others. Murray then performed an experimental manipulation that was designed to increase the need for affiliation in one group relative to a control group. Afterward, he retained only those response categories from his original scale that clearly distinguished between the responses of the experimental and control groups to the TAT cards. Other examples of the use of the TAT to measure human motivation are given in Chapter 6.

The Blacky Test   The *Blacky Pictures* include ten cartoon-like drawings involving a dog named Blacky, who generally appears with his mother, father, or a sibling. The subject tells a story about each picture, just as in the TAT. This test, however, has more structure than the TAT, since the tester usually makes some preliminary remarks before showing each cartoon. The Blacky Pictures have been utilized more frequently with children than with adults, as an aid to clinical diagnosis.

Inkblot Tests   The *inkblot test* was developed by the Swiss psychiatrist Hermann Rorschach in the 1920s. The test consists of a series of inkblots, similar to the one shown in Figure 26.9, which are much less structured stimuli than the cards of the TAT and the Blacky Pictures. Another difference is that

Figure 26.9
An inkblot of the type used in the Rorschach Inkblot Test.

Rorschach used the *intuitive* approach in constructing the test. Rorschach defined certain responses to his items as indicative of some variable, such as "hostility." For example, responses such as "an angry face," "a rifle," or even "teeth" and "gossiping" might be considered indicative of hostility. Intuitive construction serves as a beginning in the development of a useful clinical test; however, empirical validation is needed if the test is to have practical value. The Rorschach Test became the most widely used clinical measure in the United States during the late 1940s and the 1950s, and so it received extensive clinical validation.

A test that is an outgrowth of the Rorschach and that has often proved more reliable and more useful in the prediction of behavior is the *Holtzman Inkblot Test*. A subject taking the Holtzman Test is asked to make a single response to each of forty-five inkblots. Responses have been standardized for a number of different criterion groups. Thus, the scores of a suspected schizophrenic may be compared with those of a group of known schizophrenics and with those of more normal people, such as college students.

Projective tests do have some advantages: subjects find them interesting and are likely to cooperate in their administration. To some extent the Holtzman Inkblot Test and certain portions of the TAT—particularly those associated with the need for affiliation and the need for achievement—have also proven useful in personality assessment. As a group, however, the projective tests are regrettably weak in reliability and validity. This is not surprising, since projective tests require the therapist to interpret the subject's response to an already ambiguous stimulus, leaving much room for error along the way.

CRITICISMS OF PSYCHOLOGICAL TESTING

The criticisms of psychological testing fall into two main categories: *ethical* and *empirical*. The ethical objections center on claims that psychological tests either discriminate against certain socioeconomic groups (particularly aptitude tests), constitute invasions of privacy (particularly personality tests), or discriminate against individualism, initiative, and creativity (particularly interest inventories). The empirical criticisms revolve around the criteria for good tests. Is a given test sufficiently objective, standardized, valid, and reliable? Many tests, particularly personality tests, fail to meet one or more of these criteria. Probably the most important criterion for a test is validity, and the evidence suggests that many personality tests and other tests involving subjective judgments on the part of the tester do not meet that criterion. We shall conclude this chapter by discussing these important criticisms.

Ethical and Social Objections One objection to psychological tests is that they are an invasion of privacy, that they probe into matters that are nobody's business—nobody but the person being tested, that is. This objection has been leveled most forcefully at personality tests, since most people are happy to reveal their interests, and most also realize the practical value of aptitude tests.

More serious than the privacy objection is the claim that tests contribute to a current trend in our society towards the perpetuation of the *status quo* and the supression of initiative, creativity, and individuality. This objection is aimed particularly at interest inventories used in vocational guidance and in the selection of employees. If employees are selected on the basis of whether or not their interest profiles are similar to those of people already in the field, the field might perpetuate itself as it is, shutting out potential creativity and positive change.

Certain tests have been criticized because they are discriminatory. This is a particularly serious problem when it comes to aptitude tests, which are used to predict school success and which may subtly influence such success. For example, if teachers are given completely false IQ scores for students, the teachers still tend to report that the students with the higher scores perform better. Thus, it is possible that the IQ score itself may help to fulfill its own prediction. Furthermore, the evidence suggests that IQ tests generated by, in, and for a predominantly white middle-class society are largely inappropriate, if not meaningless, when applied to subgroups like poor blacks or poor people in general.

Lack of Validity An impressive array of evidence suggests that for most purposes personality tests have such low validity that they are useless for predicting behavior. L. R. Goldberg and his colleagues, in 1967, determined that people's self-ratings are better predictors of the personality ratings given them by their peers than are the ratings of several personality inventory scales. Even when the predictions made by the personality tests are combined in various ways, and the best combination taken,

the tests' predictions continue to be inferior to the self-ratings. In other words, personality inventories, even those based on such sophisticated statistical techniques as factor analysis, cannot describe the individual's behavior as well as simple self-ratings, judging by comparisons of the two sets of ratings with external criteria, such as the ratings by peers. This particular result suggests that you have at present a better idea of what people think of you than you would have if you believed the interpretation of your scores on a personality test. The discrepancy could be even greater if projective tests were used, since those tests involve a compounding of subjective interpretations—both in your response to an ambiguous stimulus and in the clinician's interpretation of the response.

In a more striking study, Goldberg showed that a group of clinical psychologists using a highly developed, validated, and popular test, was no better at detecting organic brain damage than a group of secretaries. (The brain damage had been independently diagnosed by a team of neurologists.) This result did not arise because the secretaries did a surprisingly good job of diagnosis; instead, neither group did well. Other studies have supported Goldberg's conclusion and have shown that nonprofessionals, such as secretaries and college students, do as well as psychologists and psychiatrists when their predictions are evaluated against empirical criteria.

Perhaps more surprising, the judgment of a psychiatric patient may be as good as that of his psychiatrist. In one study—by J. J. Lasky and his colleagues—patients were equal to psychiatrists in predicting the behavior of other patients with respect to health, career, family adjustment, and future rehospitalization. In a recent study, D. L. Rosenhan in 1973, showed that sane people who successfully infiltrated a psychiatric hospital were not detected by the physicians or nurses even though their behavior in the hospital was normal! These pseudopatients faked schizophrenia to gain entry into the institution but behaved normally as soon as they were admitted, claiming that their symptoms had gone away and that they now felt fine. The staff treated them as cooperative but insane, but many of their fellow patients successfully detected their sanity.

If professional judges can do no better statistically than nonprofessionals—or even their own patients—it should therefore follow that a nonprofessional would not improve his predictive ability after extensive clinical training. In one study—by W. J. Crow in 1957—with senior medical students, half received extensive training on interpersonal (physician–patient) relationships while the other half did not. Students receiving this training (including extensive experience with patients) actually became progressively *less* accurate than did the control students in predicting patients' self-ratings and profiles on the MMPI.

A study with the TAT—by Gardner Lindzey and Charlotte Tejessey—shows that this test is often less effective than self-ratings in predicting aggressive behavior, as measured by a battery of situational and observational tests. Furthermore, J. J. Sherwood showed in 1966 that self-reports are as good as projective tests in indicating need for affiliation and need for achievement—two characteristics whose TAT scales have been clinically validated. One returns to G. W. Allport's dictum: if you wish to know what a person is, thinks, or feels, ask him!

The evidence indicates that self-reports tend to be as good or better than judgments based on personality tests. Two further studies, both reported in 1965 by Walter Mischel and his colleagues, illustrate this point. In one study, volunteers for the Peace Corps made better predictions about whether or not they would be accepted after training than did any of the three categories of personality tests that we have considered: indirect inventories, observational tests (interviews), and projective tests. In a second study, students were better at predicting their own grades (as determined by both essay and objective-type tests) than were several measures of achievement, aptitude, and personality.

Taken together, what do these results mean? It may be that we have yet to develop and validate the appropriate tests to measure personality, or that our training of clinicians is faulty. On the other hand, it is becoming increasingly likely that the reason personality assessment is so difficult is not because our measuring techniques are at fault but because there is no "underlying personality" to be measured. The further away we get from behavioral evidence and direct verbal reports, the less valid measurements of personality become—their validity approached unacceptable levels in even the most probing of personality tests, the projective tests. There is increasing agreement that the notion of personality as made up of "traits" or "clusters" has outlived its usefulness, and that we should restrict our attention to observed behaviors and their correlated stimuli. Whether the notion of "personality" itself will become obsolete is an interesting question that faces psychology in the next decade.

Suggested Readings

Anastasi, A. (1961). *Psychological testing.* (2nd ed.) New York: Macmillan. [A comprehensive treatment of testing.]

Cronbach, L. J. (1970) *Essentials of psychological testing.* (3rd ed.) New York: Harper and Row. [Also a comprehensive treatment of testing.]

Mischel, Walter (1968) *Personality and assessment.* New York: Wiley. [An excellent evaluative overview.]

Rosenhan, D. L. (1973), On being sane in insane places. *Science, 179,* 250–257. [An interesting and disturbing report.]

UNIT NINE

The Study of Abnormal Personality

The study of abnormal personality is the branch of psychology that deals primarily with behavioral disorders. The difficulty of defining abnormality has led psychologists to explore a variety of ways of drawing the line between the normal and the abnormal. Historically, the line has been drawn differently by different groups of psychologists. (1) The *statistical* definition states that an individual's behavior is abnormal if it deviates more than a certain amount from the average of a group of individuals. (2) The *clinical* decision that someone is "mentally incompetent" relies on an evaluation of a person's responses to psychological tests and interview questions. The clinical approach has the advantage of taking into account the way in which the person interacts directly with another person, the therapist or interviewer. (3) The *social* definition emphasizes adjustment—the degree to which one can function happily and productively in one's current situation. (4) The *behavioral* definition dwells on the overt actions of the person and how rewarding or punishing feedback from his environment has shaped current behavior. (5) In the *humanistic* view, continuing psychological growth is the index of normality; a person who is normal on all other counts may still be abnormal if he does not continue to grow.

None of the above approaches is entirely satisfactory—for example, what is good adjustment in a prison camp? and who evaluates the clinical evaluator?—but each touches on an important aspect of the issue.

Just as there are several approaches to defining abnormality, there is also a diversity of opinion about the causes of abnormality. In this unit we shall mainly discuss the *psychoanalytical*, or Freudian, perspective and the *physiological* perspective; we shall mention the *behavioristic* perspective but shall leave full consideration of this position to Chapter 32.

In the course of our discussion, we shall describe a variety of types of abnormal individuals. In accord with tradition, these types have been divided into three categories, according to their apparent severity: (1) *Personality disorders* are, by and large, the least severe disorders. (2) *Neurosis* comprises disorders that range in severity from mildly troublesome to relatively incapacitating. (3) *Psychosis* is nearly always a very serious, mind-distorting disease.

We have formulated the following working definition of abnormality, which we think is compatible with the main points of view in contemporary psychology, and which covers the entire range of the traditional three-fold classification of abnormal personality types: a person's behavior, emotional response, or mode of thought is abnormal if changes in it would result (1) in a happier or more productive person or (2) in an increase in the happiness and productivity of those close to the person, without harming the person himself.

CHAPTER TWENTY-SEVEN

Personality Disorders

We have taken the following as our working definition of psychological abnormality: *any behavior, thought, or feeling that, if changed, would make a person's life generally happier or more productive without making anyone else's life less happy or less productive.* Thus, psychological normality is basically a matter of human happiness and individual productivity; psychological abnormality is whatever limits these qualities.

THE IMPORTANCE OF TIME, PLACE, AND CONTEXT

What constitutes normal behavior necessarily depends on the time and place and context in which it occurs. For example, behavior that is normal for a person who is alone may be abnormal in the presence of other people; likewise, what is normal social behavior with others may be abnormal if one is alone (Figure 27.2).

The nature of the social context is also important. Behavior that is acceptable among friends may not be appropriate for family or working situations. Usually, people are flexible enough so that they can change their behavior to suit the occasion. In fact, this is one of the most important things a child learns in the course of its social development (see Chapter 18).

Figure 27.1
Saul Steinberg's view of someone who seems somewhat less than well adjusted. [Copyright © 1960 by Saul Steinberg. From *The Labyrinth*, Harper & Row.]

Figure 27.2
The importance of context: what is normal in one setting may seem out of place elsewhere.

The person's age and degree of social development may also be a factor in evaluating the appropriateness of his behavior. Basically what happens is that what is abnormal at one age becomes normal at a later age: exactly the same personality characteristics are abnormal at one time and normal at another because the social context changes. Manipulative and undisciplined behavior that is not permitted for a child may become effective in certain competitive social environments later in its life. Likewise, teenagers whose behavior does not conform to the cultural stereotype of adolescents may become normal simply by growing older.

This chapter will primarily discuss circumstances in which an individual's behavior is inappropriate to the social occasion, or in some other way does not conform to the standards of the society in which he lives. Because they are, generally speaking, socially unacceptable, personality disorders are often called *sociopathic disorders.*

THE MEASUREMENT OF ADJUSTMENT

Our definition of psychological abnormality implies that happiness and productivity are the measures of personal adjustment. It is impossible to evaluate either of these qualities by exact or consistent quantitative measurement. Other, equally subjective, measures of adjustment are (1) the degree of *strain*

the person exhibits in his daily life, (2) the *freedom* with which he expresses himself, and (3) whether his personality continues to grow.

Strain is a general term that refers to the energy and effort a person must put out each day in order to hold his life together. Some individuals go about their daily business calmly and effectively. Others are agitated, tense, and only marginally effective. They often skip jobs or leave them unfinished, and they are easily rattled. We have to suspect that the latter are less well adjusted to their situations than the former.

Freedom of expression is almost a natural consequence of good adjustment. People who have psychological and physical energy left over for use in personal expression and amusements after fulfilling the requirements of their daily life are generally considered to be well adjusted. Even if the person spends his free time and energy on his work, the mere fact that it is a free and deliberate choice is indicative of adjustment.

Well-adjusted people continue to grow in *personal abilities* (in the sense we have already discussed toward the end of Chapter 18). But in the context of adjustment, growth means not so much *increasing* as it does *deepening*: there is greater commitment to individual values, and human relationships become closer, more intimate, and more meaningful.

PRESSURES ON ADJUSTMENT

Every person must make daily adjustments in his environment. The environment includes physical and social conditions such as health, physical surroundings, social and sexual relationships, and work. Any of these may be the source of frustrations and anxieties that may affect the individual's happiness, productivity, freedom to express himself, and so forth.

Dealing with Anxiety   Over-all, *anxiety* in its many forms and from its various sources is the most widespread problem of adjustment. Most people adopt straightforward means of meeting anxiety; if they are worried about their health, they go to a doctor; for spiritual problems, to a minister or counselor; if they have interpersonal troubles, they discuss them and come to some agreement; for financial anxiety, they save and work hard; for anxieties arising from self-doubt, they realistically try hard and rationally accept their own limitations. But some people work out the kind of roundabout and unrealistic approach to managing anxieties that Freud described as *defense mechanisms* (Chapter 24). We shall return to these in their more extreme forms in Chapter 28.

An often neglected aspect of anxiety is that a certain amount of it is normal. Every day brings its own concerns, which when we take care of them, give us a sense of accomplishment. A particularly healthy form of anxiety is concern for the well-being of others, because it shows a personal adjustment that is secure enough to allow time and energy to be invested in compassionate and humanitarian actions.

Sexual Behavior   Regardless of the ethics, morals, or practices of the day, it seems that *sexual adjustment* often poses problems. Nevertheless, most people do work out an adequate sexual adjustment that is appropriate for their age level. However,

a person may well *underrate* his or her own personal sexual adjustment. Romantic novels and stories, popular books and magazines, elaborate psychological and physiological analyses of orgasm, manuals of sexual techniques, and even the often-exaggerated stories of friends—all these may lead a person to suspect that his or her sexual experiences are not as satisfying as they should be. Sexual adjustment is such an important topic that we shall return to it in a separate section at the end of this chapter.

Accepting Personal Limitations   Frustration has traditionally been identified as a cause of aggression. People differ in the amount of frustration that they can sustain in their daily lives. Some can endure petty annoyances and heavy disappointments with apparent calmness. Others become increasingly irritable and may begin to attack others for seemingly insignificant faults.

A well-adjusted person handles frustration, the inevitable result of limitations imposed on his actions, fairly easily, since it motivates him to increase his attempts to overcome the obstacle. By placing realistic limits on his expectations, he is able to reduce the number of frustrating experiences he must encounter. This means that he sets reasonable goals that he is likely to achieve without meeting insurmountable obstacles or undergoing uncomfortably large amounts of frustration. Thus, adjustment also requires a realistic perception and acceptance of one's own capabilities in relation to the surrounding circumstances.

Success itself may require considerable adjustment. The old saying "Pride goeth . . . before a fall" can be applied to the letdown that sometimes follows success. Achieving a goal may leave a person with a depressing lack of new goals. For example, a successful forty-year-old businessman may reflect on his career and find that he has nothing left to achieve. He may find it more taxing to maintain his career at its present level than he did to achieve that level in the first place. He is like a momentarily successful child in a game of "king of the mountain." He may make the mistake of concentrating on one transient achievement in his career, rather than gaining satisfaction from each attainable goal and each accomplishment as they come along.

Dealing with Authority and Responsibility

Everyone lives in a world with other people who exert a certain amount of control over one's life. Freud states that our attitudes toward *figures of authority* are derived from our conscious and unconscious attitudes towards our parents. Whether or not this is so, the person must learn to live with authority figures without being either in permanent submission to them or in permanent rebellion against them. Probably the best adjustment to authority combines cooperation for the sake of achieving mutual goals and resistance to unreasonable demands.

Assuming responsibility for others can be taxing for some personalities. Making conscientious decisions that bear intimately on the well-being of others requires judgment and courage—qualities that a poorly adjusted person finds hard to sustain.

THE PSYCHOPATHIC PERSONALITY

Most people are sensitive to what they do to others, they feel guilty when others are hurt or they get something for nothing, and they try to be consistent, to tell the truth (most of the time), and to be a fair and decent person. Not so the *psychopath*. Not that psychopaths are necessarily hostile or openly aggressive; quite the contrary, many psychopaths are very, very nice—frustratingly so, as we shall see.

A psychopath is out for himself alone—he is indifferent to how others are hurt by what he does.

He has a goal in mind—usually getting something for nothing—and getting there is all that matters regardless of laws, customs, or regulations. The psychopath's actions usually fall short of outright violence, but not always. He lies very well and cheats whenever it serves his purposes. He is inconsistent, telling a different story to each person he talks to in order to persuade them individually, or changing his arguments to fit the requirements of the moment rather than painting a consistent picture.

So far, the reader may not be able to distinguish the character we are describing from some very successful people they have known. Although some successful people may indeed be psychopaths, the outstanding psychological characteristic of the true psychopath is that he has no guilt or shame over what he does. Even more frightening, he does not even seem to realize that he does things which other people consider to be very wrong. It seems that he just does not care. But he must care, in some sense, because he so carefully orchestrates his daily symphony of lies and genial dissemblance that he rarely if ever gets caught. True psychopaths are so ingratiating, and appear so vulnerable or pitiable, that the people they manipulate refuse at first to believe the magnitude of the sham they are seeing and, when they must accept it, sometimes conclude that the psychopath has not done anything that is really bad enough to deserve punishment!

The following case study of a psychopath highlights the salient symptoms that we have just discussed: (1) a lack of shame or guilt and (2) lack of attention to the consequences of one's behavior. In addition, it shows what bad effects psychopathic personalities may have on others under adverse circumstances.

The patient was treated when he was in his late thirties and early forties. His life seemed irretrievably on the skids. He was the son of prosperous parents and came from a

good neighborhood. During his childhood, he was well-
adjusted in school and was popular with his classmates.
In high school, however, he became arrogant and irritable,
and less and less popular. Within his family at home, he
exhibited deliberate dishonesty; and he ran away from home
a few times.

His family was loving and supportive throughout, giving
him money and attempting to find him work. But he became
unable to hold a job, took up residence in a poor section
of town, came to prefer the company of prostitutes, and
began drinking. Typical of his psychopathic symptoms was
a tendency to bother family friends at odd hours request-
ing money from them. On one occasion, he moved a pros-
titute into the house of family friends, while they were
on vacation, and made a shambles of the place before their
return.

In the therapeutic setting, he was very nice and contrite,
leaving each time with promises to reform. However, he
showed no realization that he was ruining his life and
hurting others. He offered a seemingly innocent and plausible
reason for even the most outrageous of his actions. He
spoke of other people and of emotional attachments in a
clear and intelligent way, but the impression was that he
neither really cared for the people nor really felt the
emotions.*

Theories Explaining the Psychopath   Not
surprisingly, the behaviorist feels that the answer
to correcting psychopathic behavior lies in learning.
It is a little more complicated than that, however,
because several types of learning may be significant
in any individual case. The key characteristic of the
psychopath is his skill in winning at interpersonal
games. It might seem at first glance that he is noted
for his insensitivity to *punishment*—the behaviorist's
equivalent to the Freudian superego. But that is
a superficial view, because the psychopath is rarely,
if ever, punished; he is too clever at maneuvering

*The case is condensed from H. Cleckley's *The Mask of
Sanity* (Saint Louis: C. V. Mosby Company, 1950).

himself around people until he accomplishes his
objective. The psychopath has learned to be the art-
ful interpersonal dodger—rarely getting caught or
cornered and, somehow, never taking "no" for a
final answer. What he has learned can be summarized in a set of rules: (1) be exposed to others only
as little as is necessary and then only on your own
terms, (2) always maintain an uncriticizable appearance which is either not noticed or too good to draw
comment, (3) always be pleasant with just the correct
proportion of authority and reticence, (4) ignore
anything that is even vaguely negative, (5) use only
unimpeachable excuses for wrongdoing, such as
illness, and (6) leave—in order to come back another
day—before your requests are refused.

In contrast, the Freudian, or psychodynamic, view
of the psychopath centers on two ideas: (1) the
superego and (2) the orally receptive personality.
Psychopaths certainly do display orally receptive
characteristics (see Chapter 24). In particular, they
willingly accept what is good, leaving the bad. More
apparent, though, is the orally oriented view that
the world owes them a free living.

Of course, not all orally receptive personalities
are psychopaths. Freudians theorize that psychopathic
individuals have, in addition, an extremely weak or
nonexistent superego. They have failed to incorporate
into themselves the rules and regulations of parents
and society that usually make up the superego. The
result is that psychopaths literally cannot feel guilt
when they break rules. With no feelings of guilt,
there is no reason to refrain from their unconscion-
able but often successful and rewarding behavior.

DRUG ABUSE

It has been said that every culture that has ever
existed has discovered or invented psychologically
active drugs. True or not, man's continuing attrac-

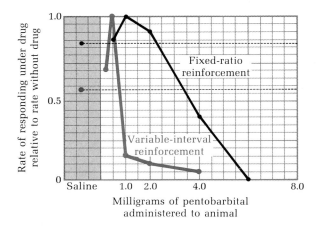

Figure 27.3
The complex effects on an animal's behavior of a depressant, the barbiturate pentobarbital. The horizontal axis is the dose of the drug (in milligrams) that was administered. The vertical axis measures the drug's effect on behavior: points above the *horizontal lines* (which represent the effects of behaviorally inactive saline injections) indicate an increase in behavior as a result of the drug: points below that line represent a decrease of behavior. One curve shows data on behavior maintained by a variable-interval schedule of reinforcement; the other curve shows data on behavior maintained by a fixed-interval schedule. Note two important effects: (1) some doses of the depressant actually increase behavior, and (2) it takes well over twice as large a dose of the drug to depress behavior maintained by the ratio schedule. [Adapted from P. B. Dews, "Studies on Behavior: I. Differential Sensitivity to Pentobarbital of Pecking Performance in Pigeons depending on the Schedule of Reward." *Journal of Pharmacology and Experimental Therapeutics*, *113*, 1955, 393–401.]

tion to the alterations of consciousness and feeling produced by such drugs is undeniable, as are their widespread therapeutic and religious uses. In the context of abnormal behavior, our concern is with drug abuse—that is, drug use that interferes with the human potential for happiness and productivity.

If an appropriate dose of a pure drug is administered in a prescribed manner to a normal individual, the effects may be predictable. Some effects appear to be desirable and can be classified as positive—sometimes as therapeutic—effects; other effects are undesirable and can be classified as negative effects. Many drugs, even those with positive effects at appropriate dosages, pose great hazards at other doses.

One factor that can make the predictability of a drug's effect uncertain is the nature of a drug's *dose-effect curve*, the relationship between increasing amounts of the drug and its effects on us. Figure 27.3 shows two examples of the effect on an animal's learned behavior of a sedative, the barbiturate pentobarbital. Notice that moderate doses of the drug have an effect that is opposite to the effect of high doses: at moderate doses the sedative actually stimulates behavior. Next, note that the effects of the drug vary with the behavioral situation in which it is taken (in the example, a variable-interval versus a fixed-ratio schedule of reinforcement). Both of these factors must be taken into account in attempting to determine a drug dosage for a person. Furthermore, experimental data cannot be relied on with certainty, since they are the results of studies in which only pure drugs of precisely calculated doses are employed, and in which the controlling variables of behavior have been quite thoroughly studied. The uncertainties are even greater if we attempt to predict the effects of drug abuse, because drugs purchased illicitly are often adulterated and misidentified, and are taken by people about whom

we know very little, and about whose behavior and feelings we know even less.

Additional variables are drug tolerance, drug dependence, and drug addiction, which accompany the taking of psychologically active drugs in varying degrees. *Tolerance* refers to the body's need for larger and larger doses of the drug to attain the same effect with repeated administrations; in other words, to a decrease in the effect of a given dose as it is administered more and more often. Long-time users of some drugs ingest very large doses to obtain only minimal effects. *Dependence* is a psychological concept referring to a psychological need for the drug under certain circumstances, whereas *addiction* refers to a physiological need for a drug. The individual who is "dependent" on alcohol, for example, may habitually drink alcohol before social interactions or to induce sleep. Deprived of alcohol, the dependent person will feel some additional anxiety in a social situation, or lose a few hours sleep. In contrast, a person who is addicted to, say, heroin literally requires regular doses of the drug to function physically and mentally. Deprived of the drug, he exhibits *withdrawal symptoms*, such as excruciating physical pain and mental anguish, that typically last for days and weeks. There is no question that any drug that affects moods and behavior, if used habitually for a particular reason, produces some degree of dependence (and possibly addiction), even if the effect is merely that it is missed when not available.

There are dozens of psychologically active drugs, and still more are constantly being discovered or invented, tested, and evaluated by drug manufacturing companies. The reason for such research is partly economic, since there is a large market for drugs (for example, for a safe anorexic—an appetite reducer for the obese). The research is also partly humanitarian—a safe and effective anti-anxiety drug would benefit a large number of people.

The motivation for taking any psychologically active drug is to alter in some way a person's state of awareness, and therefore his mood, feelings, and perceptions. Sometimes, the motive is to turn on, get high (euphoric), pick oneself up, or feel generally stimulated. At other times, it is a wish to relax, to escape, or become stuporous and unaware. On still other occasions, simple curiosity is the motive, at least initially.

We shall now discuss in some detail the effects of some of the psychologically active drugs in Table 27.1.

Alcohol The drinker experiences some relaxation, a loss of inhibitions, and, sometimes, euphoria. Negative effects of alcohol include impaired judgment and coordination, decreased emotional control, slowed reaction time, and, in some, a tendency toward aggressiveness. Of all the drugs used in our society, alcohol is the most common, and it is clearly the most abused. American alcoholics (or alcohol addicts) may number as many as 6,000,000, and the hours that are diverted from personal and business pursuits for the purpose of compulsive drinking number in the billions. If consumed frequently in large doses, alcohol has serious negative effects; for example, it can damage the liver, brain, and other organs, and its cessation can produce withdrawal symptoms. One reason for its abuse is that the negative effects are slow in appearing, at least in the habitual drinker, whereas the consumption of a couple of drinks seems to improve a person's mood rapidly, and to make him feel more sociable. Besides, it is one of the few legal intoxicants that is readily available in stores at relatively low prices.

An *alcohol-dependent* person is psychologically, and sometimes even physiologically, dependent on alcohol; he finds it difficult or impossible to conduct his daily life without it. An *alcohol addict* cannot function either physically or psychologically without drinking.

Cultural and group pressures play a large part in initiating drinking. The proportions of alcohol consumption in the United States are almost incredible: in some places it is actually somewhat uncommon to meet an individual over thirty years of age who does not drink. Many people never become more than social drinkers, imbibing because everyone else does and because social interactions seem to become a little more fun after a drink or so. For many others, drinking becomes a habit; at a certain time of day, cocktails are served as a matter

Table 27.1
Some Effects of Commonly Used Drugs

Drug	Desired Effects	Some Other Potential Effects	
		Short-Term	Long-Term
POPULAR DRUGS			
Alcohol	Reduction of anxiety; relaxation; sociability; euphoria; sedation; etc.	Impaired coordination, emotional control, judgment, and reaction time; aggressive behavior; hangover	Physiological dependence; brain damage; liver damage; obesity; painful withdrawal
Caffeine (in coffee and Coca-Cola)	Mild stimulation	Insomnia, nervousness	
Cannabis (in marijuana)	Reduction of anxiety; relaxation; euphoria; heightened sexual response; etc.	Anxiety and fear from overdose; impaired judgment; irritation of respiratory passages (when inhaled in smoke)	Possible physical damage
Nicotine (in tobacco)	Stimulation; relaxation; distraction; sociability	Irritation of respiratory passages	Cancer; heart disease
Sedatives	Relief from insomnia; relaxation	Impaired coordination, emotional control, judgment, and reaction time	Dependence
Stimulants	Relief from mild depression; stimulation; reduction of appetite; euphoria	Nervousness, irritability	Dependence
Tranquilizers	Reduction of anxiety	Drowsiness; blurred vision	Dependence
NARCOTICS			
Opium, heroin, morphine	Relaxation; relief from pain; euphoria; escape; etc.	Impaired judgment and coordination; constipation; loss of appetite; impotence; sterility; infection from dirty needles;	Physiological dependence (addiction); painful withdrawal; serious health problems
HALLUCINOGENS			
LSD, DMT, mescaline, psilocybin (in peyote)	Visual imagery; increased sensory awareness; consciousness expansion; etc.	Nausea; anxiety; fear; chills; sweating; headache; impaired coordination, emotional control, judgment	Intensification of existing psychosis
MISCELLANEOUS			
Glue and gasoline vapors, myristicin (in nutmeg)	Euphoria	Impaired coordination and judgment; vomiting; nausea, tremors; suffocation	Some vapors cause anemia; brain, liver, and kidney damage
Mixtures of drugs	Various	Almost any combination of the above effects; sometimes fatal	Uncertain; sometimes very harmful or fatal

Figure 27.4

of course. Of those who have a serious problem with drinking, it is estimated that about 500,000 are or will become derelicts of sorts, lacking the ability to make a productive contribution to their own welfare and to society (Figure 27.4).

What effects of alcohol could sustain such persistent self-destructive behavior? Studies have shown that there is considerable regularity in the stages that lead from a problem with drinking to a total dependence on alcohol. (1) *Casual drinking.* An ounce or so of alcohol provides relaxation and temporary euphoria that gives the drinker relief from anxiety. The disadvantageous effects of alcohol take longer to develop than the pleasant ones: the latter occur within minutes, while the former may not appear for an hour or so. The most unpleasant effect, hangover, does not appear for several hours. As we have seen in Chapter 4, immediate rewards are more effective than delayed punishment, so that the person who takes a drink in order to reduce tension and anxiety

tends to repeat the drink, if he finds it works, and to apply the remedy to other problems as well. (2) *The development of tolerance.* A physical tolerance to alcohol is rapidly established; that is, the body adjusts itself to the effects of the dose, so that it soon takes two or three drinks to achieve the same relaxation formerly achieved from one. As the amount of alcohol consumed increases, so does the tolerance, until the drinker is unable to function physically or psychologically without a certain amount of alcohol. (3) *Loss of productivity.* The needed amount of alcohol becomes so great that the alcoholic is unable to function either with or without the drug.

Withdrawal from severe alcohol addiction is marked by *delirium tremens*, a condition characterized by tremor, hallucination, psychological and physical pain, and general unpleasantness—including a nearly unquenchable thirst for a drink. We shall discuss what can be done for alcoholics and what they can do for themselves in Chapters 31 and 32.

Cannabis   As a popular drug, *marijuana* (also called "grass" and "pot") is second only to alcohol in the United States, although barbiturates (in the form of sleeping pills) are probably almost as widely consumed. Marijuana is illegal, but still widely taken—thus perhaps paralleling in quality the illegal and often inferior alcoholic beverages consumed during Prohibition. It is difficult to establish what quantity of the active chemical (tetrahydrocannabinol) is an effective dose, since the potency of the chemical varies in each batch of plants. The drug is usually smoked, and, hence, taken in the small amounts afforded by each puff. The effects of five minutes of communal smoking of one cigarette typically last about three or four hours. Marijuana can also be eaten in a variety of foods.

Although not everyone responds to marijuana, particularly the first time they try it, the desired effects are euphoria and a variety of other agreeable sensations, such as increased sexual feelings and changes in temperature sensations on the skin, distortions of time and space perception that are not unpleasant, and an enhancement of appetite. Marijuana thus rivals caviar as an hors d'oeuvre, as well as rivaling alcohol as an intoxicant. Its advocates point out that it produces no noticeable hangover. The negative effects of marijuana are impaired perception and coordination, excessive bravery (which can lead to accidents), a loss of emotional control, spells of giggling, and a loss of memory. Hostility rarely occurs. Unlike alcohol, marijuana seems to bring out the foolish, rather than the aggressive, aspects of human nature. Overdoses can produce anxiety and fear. Although there has been a concerted research effort to determine whether the long-term results of continued marijuana use are harmful, none has been definitely established as such. The suspicion that indulgence in this drug leads to the use of narcotics has been discounted by many as unfounded, but the possibility remains that, since marijuana is illegal and thus sometimes difficult to obtain, some habitual users may seek another illegal source of stimulation if their first-choice drug is unavailable. Also, it may be that some of the long-term psychological effects of detachment and euphoria that marijuana produces in a person are debilitating, and perhaps the drug causes physical damage.

Sedatives *Barbiturates* (for example, "yellow jackets") are a type of sedative that is, unfortunately, much too readily available. An oral dose of about 75 milligrams in a capsule gives about three hours of effect. The results are drowsiness and sleep, relief from low-grade anxieties, some noticeable reduction in tension, and, only occasionally, euphoria. These symptoms are accompanied by such negative side-effects as impairment of one's perception and

judgment and a decline in the ability to react rapidly to events. Also, should the dose or situation be unsuitable enough, the subject assumes the additional risk of losing emotional control and becoming either gloomy, quarrelsome, stuporous, or any combination of these moods. Long-term dependence on large quantities of sedatives can lead to addiction; consequently, if they are abruptly discontinued, withdrawal symptoms similar to the alcoholic's *delirium tremens*, psychosis, or, occasionally, suicidal acts may ensue.

Although death can be caused by an intentional overdose of barbiturates, a more common cause is an accidental overdose, occurring when a sedative is taken in combination with another drug, such as alcohol. It is dangerous to mix barbiturates and alcohol: a long evening of moderate alcohol consumption followed by the ingestion of a barbiturate can result in severe respiratory depression and death.

Stimulants The amphetamines are classified as stimulants. An oral dose of about 3 milligrams of one of these drugs produces effects for three or four hours. The effects are increased alertness, a loss of appetite (sometimes desired), and often euphoria—a feeling of happy well-being, sometimes accompanied by spells of giggling. The user should expect to put up with insomnia, a dry mouth, dilated pupils that may cause bright light to be uncomfortable, rapid and perhaps slurred speech, and possible aggressiveness. It is worthwhile to reiterate that the occurrence and magnitude of these effects depend on the person, his environment at the time of ingesting the drug, and factors related to the dose of the drug. Long-term use of stimulants can lead to excessive restlessness, irritability, and an inability to sleep without the aid of sedatives. The end result may be the transformation of the person into a veritable drug-controlled automaton, requiring stimulants during the day and sedatives at night.

Amphetamines are dangerous because they increase heart rate and can cause heart damage; overdoses can cause fibrillation of the heart muscles resulting in inadequate blood circulation and death. In addition, habitual users of stimulants face the same hazard in giving them up abruptly as are faced by habitual users of sedatives: there may be a severe withdrawal backlash that produces depression, paranoia (fears of persecution by other people), and even suicidal tendencies.

Narcotics *Narcotics*, such as *opium* and *heroin*, are smoked or injected to produce effects lasting for about four hours. The user obtains sedation, relief from pain, and euphoria, at a cost of impaired thinking and coordination, a diminished ability to focus attention, constricted pupils that do not respond to light, decreased rates of pulse and respiration, and chronic constipation. Apparently, the feelings of detachment, relief, and well-being easily counteract these negative effects, but drugs that are taken by injection pose the added danger of infection from dirty needles. And, finally, the gravest danger is addiction.

The narcotics addict must continue taking the drug to avoid painful withdrawal symptoms. Since narcotics are illegal, they are extremely expensive and difficult to obtain. An addict can spend more than a hundred dollars a day for the drugs he craves: thus, even an affluent addict can be driven to crime in order to raise the money to pay those who provide the drug.

Hallucinogens *Lysergic acid diethylamide* (LSD) is one of the *hallucinogens*, a class of drugs that produce the most striking alterations in one's perceptions. The effects of an oral dose of only 150 *micrograms* can last twelve hours. Under the influence of LSD, people see varied visual images of a surreal nature if they let their minds idle. Some advocates have claimed that LSD produces heightened awareness in all sensory domains, but particularly in those which the taker habitually relies on the most; sometimes, LSD-inspired experiences are described as "consciousness expanding," although the discoverer of LSD compared his own first—accidental—experience merely to drunkeness.

The visual images produced by LSD are said to resemble those experienced by psychotics. One danger of this particular drug is that persons with psychotic tendencies may find that their previously mild disturbances are intensified by the LSD experience. Another danger is a "bad trip" on LSD: unless thoroughly prepared beforehand, as well as socially supported during the experience, a person is likely to find that the highly unusual experience provokes anxiety, itself intensified by LSD, which turns the experience into a terrible twelve-hour waking nightmare instead of a beautiful dream. Furthermore, the memory of the "bad trip" itself may be so linked to anxiety that the person may have the momentary impression that he is "flashing back" to the nightmare when he is reminded of it or recalls it vividly after a period of time.

Once again, the effects of LSD, like those of any drug, depend on the individual's personality, his expectations, and his immediate situation as well as on the drug itself and the dose. In addition to being a very interesting drug, LSD is a very dangerous one.

Toxic Vapors Glue sniffing sounds like a joke. Unfortunately, it is not. For the first moment or so, the inhaled vapors cause the user to experience a dizzy euphoria and a feeling of being in a different state of consciousness. The penalties for these effects, however, are potentially violent behavior, poor muscular control, and a runny nose and tear-filled eyes. In large and recurring doses, glue sniffing can produce anemia and damage to the brain, lungs, and liver within a short time. There is also some danger of suffocation.

Conclusion We should not take alterations in our bodies and minds lightly. Even though objective examination of the currently available evidence does not suggest that legal alcohol is any safer than illegal marijuana, a person's dependence on *any* drug for comfort, amusement, or pleasure is to be regretted. Certainly, it should not be necessary to take a pill or to have a drink or to smoke a joint in order to feel good. Perhaps drugs would be used less if more people became more aware of normal bodily and sensory processes. It might also help if people learned meditative and other techniques of relaxation and self-control. And perhaps it is time to examine the cultural values that drive so many people to drink—and to other drugs.

Figure 27.5
The "workaholic" is unable to relax or play or loaf.

WORK ADDICTS

Most people enjoy moderate periods of rest—just being by oneself without anything to do. They treat such periods as opportunities for reflection and find such periods extremely rewarding.

There are people, though, who cannot rest. "Workaholics" must work; they become quite upset if they are prevented from working. Such people lead hectic lives, claiming that they often wish to stop working—but they become so agitated and restless away from work that they cannot even take a vacation, let alone retire. If asked why they do not cut down, they say that they would but that there is always so much to do that they never have the chance. For them, not getting something finished causes an irresistible urge to go to work. Work-

aholics feel that it is accomplishment that they want, but the evidence is that what they really want is simply busyness. Denied the chance to work, they may create projects with no apparent purpose: busy-work.

SEXUAL DISORDERS

There are a host of common difficulties in sexual adjustment. Although the people who have these difficulties are thus deprived of fully enjoying life's pleasures, they are rarely considered abnormal personalities unless they begin to worry about the problem so much that the worry interferes with other areas of life.

PROBLEMS RELATED TO APPETITE AND DESIRE

Appetite refers to the frequency of sexual intercourse, a measure of the strength of sexual urges; *desire* refers to sexual preference, and technique. We shall briefly discuss difficulties in adjustment in each of these areas.

Two partners may differ in the frequency with which they seek sexual relations. When this difference is pronounced, it may lead the unsatisfied partner to seek additional sexual outlets, which may threaten sexual adjustment with the other partner. It is fundamental to sexual adjustment that the frequency of sexual contacts become mutually agreeable and satisfying.

Sexual desire also shows considerable and important variations. People differ not only in what arouses them sexually but also in the sexual acts and techniques they prefer. Recent studies have shown that these individual differences are not necessarily related to gender: masculine and feminine sexual preferences are often culturally, rather than biologically, determined. (For example, it has been shown that women can be aroused by looking at pictures of nude men just as men are aroused by looking at pictures of nude women. Research has also established that men can enjoy sexual foreplay as much as women.)

Difficulties in adjustment arise most commonly when heterosexual partners are mismatched in appetite or desire. Such difficulties are not infrequent and are harmful only to the extent that they lead to anxiety, embarrassment, or shame for one or both of the partners in the relationship.

ANOMALOUS SEXUAL BEHAVIOR

Once again, we have to recall the definition of abnormality given at the beginning of the chapter. In considering the normality of sexual behavior, cultural influence is extremely important. This is especially true of fairly common sexual anomalies like homosexuality. In ancient Greece and in some modern countries, for example, homosexuality was, and is, considered to be a normal part of male sexuality. Older married men took young boys as lovers as a matter of course; those who did not were con-

sidered to be abnormal. Western culture at present maintains the opposite opinion. The range of human sexual behaviors is extremely wide; for various reasons, each society selects some that are to be considered normal and rejects others.

Anomalous sexual behaviors can be conveniently divided into two types: those of aim and those of object. The former are deviations in the source of sexual pleasure; the latter, deviations in the object of sexual desire. It is important to bear in mind that people in each of these categories derive genuine sexual pleasure from practices that are usually held to be deviant or perverse. Nor are all of the deviations that are described in what follows necessarily abnormal by our definition, although they do represent sexual behavior that is different from that of most people.

Anomalies of Aim The main anomalies of aim are voyeurism, exhibitionism, sadism, and masochism. In *voyeurism*, sexual pleasure is derived from seeing sexual activity or sexual organs. Freud traced this deviation to what he called the *primal scene*, the child's either witnessing or imagining parents in the midst of sexual intercourse. That experience, particularly if it took place during the Oedipal period (see Chapter 24), was at once so sexually exciting and so provocative of anxiety (the opposite-sex parent seemed to be betraying the child's love) that a portion of the person's libido became fixated on *viewing* rather than *doing*. Be that as it may, almost everyone is strongly affected by seeing sexual intercourse, and most people are interested in the appearance of sexual organs, whether they admit it or not.

Exhibitionism is a deviation in which pleasure is derived from *being seen*, rather than from seeing. Sexual exhibitionism is manifested either in performing sexual acts or displaying one's sexual organs in public. Rarely is this deviation based on pride; more often it is a plea for help derived from deep insecurity about sexual adequacy. Its basis differs at different stages of development, and its acceptability varies with the social context. For example, there is a great difference between the guest at a private swimming party or at a nudist colony and the infamous "dirty old man in a raincoat" exposing himself in doorways.

The voyeur and the exhibitionist have in common a participation in only a small part of sexuality. There may be a bit of each tendency in everyone, but most people achieve a richer sex life. (Exhibitionism is further discussed in Chapter 32.)

Sadism owes its name to the Marquis de Sade (1740–1814), a Frenchman who wrote extensively of the sexual joys of inflicting pain on others. *Masochism* is named for Leopold Sacher von Masoch (1836–1895), an Austrian novelist from Lemberg in Galicia, who described the sexual joys of having pain inflicted on oneself.

Sadism and masochism have a great deal in common, although superficially they seem to be opposites. Both achieve sexual pleasure through aggression, and both confuse pain and sexual pleasure. Again, there may be a bit of sadist and masochist in everyone. Love and hate, joy and sorrow, physical pleasure and physical pain—all are strong feelings and, as such, are perhaps closer together physiologically—and psychologically—than we normally realize. Public executions have been known to draw incredibly large crowds, and a fair proportion of the people at the scene of an automobile race seem to relish spectacular crashes. The Spanish ritual of the bullfight is probably the frankest expression of the union of pleasure and pain.

Anomalies of Object   There are nearly as many anomalies of sexual *object* as there are objects in the world. The sexual *philias* (from a Greek word for "attraction") include just about everything one can imagine: pedophilia (children), parthenophilia (virgins), acrophilia (tall people), and even necrophilia (dead partners). Philias may include animals, particular physical characteristics of people, and any number of objects. The most common anomaly of object is *homosexuality*, attraction toward people of the same sex.

What causes sexual anomalies? Any sort of sexual activity, once initiated, tends to continue if it is pleasurable. (Some counterforce such as internal anxiety, external social pressure, or punishment is required to stop it. If this counterforce is not present, however, the activity is not abnormal from the point of view we have adopted in this chapter.) The harder question, then, is not what keeps sexual anomalies going, but how they start.

More than any other area, this one has been dominated by Freudian theory (Chapter 24). Freud saw the sexual anomalies as rather simple developmental phenomena. The primal scene of witnessing parental intercourse is important because it appears so violent to the child, and because it seems so clearly to represent a betrayal by one or the other parent. A desire to give sexual pleasure to young individuals (pedophilia) is said to be a holdover from frustrated childhood desires for sexual fulfillment. The attachment of sexual pleasure, desire, or arousal to peculiar objects was seen by Freud as just a matter of cathexis. And, finally, according to Freud, pure libido may still be left at oral, anal, and phallic stages of development with the result that the individual continues to desire and derive a part of sexual pleasure from those erogenous modes. In all these examples, the abnormality comes from anxiety and individual deprivation, not from the particular form of the behavior itself.

Only recently have behaviorists entered the field of sexual anomaly. They have had relatively little to say, however, except that unusual sexual behavior (1) occasionally occurs for some reason, (2) is found to be pleasurable, and (3) then tends to be repeated. They do place emphasis on the fact that *any* stimulus or situation, no matter how inappropriate, can become conditioned to sexual arousal when sexual arousal occurs in that situation. Behaviorists feel that such relationships can be modified—if recent attempts to modify unusual behavior by *reconditioning* are as successful as early results suggest.

Suggested Readings

Aldrich, C. K. (1966) *An introduction to dynamic psychiatry.* New York: McGraw Hill. [The psychiatric view of disordered personalities.]

Coleman, J. C. (1972) *Abnormal psychology and modern life.* (4th ed.) Glenview, Illinois: Scott, Foresman. [A very readable textbook on abnormal behavior, with a thorough treatment of the major personality disorders.]

Ullmann, L. P., & Krasner, L. (1969) *A psychological approach to abnormal behavior.* Englewood Cliffs, N.J.: Prentice-Hall. [The behavioristic perspective on abnormality.]

White, R. W. (1964) *The abnormal personality.* (3rd ed.) New York: Ronald. [An excellent overview of personality disorders.]

CHAPTER TWENTY-EIGHT

Neurosis

A _neurotic personality_ can be likened to an onion. At the core, there is an unresolved problem—either an actual frightening experience, or the possibility of one. Around the core are arranged layer upon layer of protective coverings, or _defenses_, that hide it from consciousness. The first layer covers up the original problem; the next layer covers up the cover-up, and so on.

As an example of the way this process works, let us examine the case of a young boy who feels threatened with the loss of his father's love and esteem if he does not become an outstanding athlete. This threat is too much for the boy to handle; it terrifies him and also makes him feel intense hostility toward the father. As the boy grows up, he represses his feelings into his unconscious. To keep them hidden there, he adopts many defensive thoughts and behaviors.

As an adult, he cannot recall either the fear or the hostility, but it permeates his entire personality. He is still unconsciously afraid of and hostile toward older men, but he protects himself against these feelings by going out of his way to appear friendly towards males older than himself. He dresses and acts like a person older than his actual age. Unconsciously, he still fears failure, but he strives to appear successful and invulnerable in business and in all that he undertakes. He also manages to appear and act proficient in a variety of sports, but he never competes in any of them, unconsciously still fearing failure. He cultivates older, nonathletic friends, which helps him to avoid active athletic competition. He is also extremely sensitive to comments on his physique, lest he appear unacceptably unathletic. However, he does enjoy telling stories about his physical prowess, making it seem greater than it is. Feeling himself to be actually unathletic, he must constantly guard against situations in which he might have to test his strength, stamina, or coordination—because he might fail.

Note that there is interaction among the layers of this, or any, neurotic personality. There is a bundle of behaviors that interlock to support each other and serve not only to repress old fears, whose original causes no longer exist, but also to compensate for the disadvantages and restrictions caused by the successive layers of methods of avoiding the fears.

Figure 28.1
Anxiety. William Steig's view of the experience.
[Copyright 1950 by William Steig]

THE NATURE OF ANXIETY

This chapter is based on the views of Sigmund Freud and those who have followed him. Although other theories have been advanced to explain the mechanisms of neurosis, as we shall see in the unit on psychotherapy (particularly in Chapter 32, Behavior Modification), Freud's view is, historically, the most fully developed. Furthermore, the Freudian framework will allow us to discuss the wide variety of clinical phenomena that any discussion of neurosis must face and explain.

Anxiety is the anticipation of a frightening or painful experience (Figure 28.1). It is generally agreed that the neurotic behaves the way he does in order to avoid anxiety. Freud's theories about the sources of anxiety—realistic, moral, and neurotic—have been outlined in Chapter 24.

Freud suggested that any kind of anxiety acts as a warning signal of conflict between the different parts of the personality—the id, the ego, and the superego—from which the ego must protect itself. This process of protection takes the form of *defense mechanisms* that promote ways of thinking and acting that serve to alleviate anxiety or to avoid it altogether. If the anxiety is very strong, the defense mechanisms are overused until they absorb most of the person's time and energy, usually creating problems and anxieties of their own. The resulting behavior is called a *neurotic symptom*. (It is interesting to recall from Chapters 3 and 4 that neurosis-like states can be experimentally induced in animals by presenting them with inescapable conflicts.)

The infant or young child, who is, of course, smaller and weaker than those around him, and who has not yet acquired a sense of proportion about things, often feels his ego threatened with annihilation, either from the external world (experiences of pain, discomfort, hunger, loneliness, or rejection by parents) or from his internal world (his developing superego, which conflicts with the often threatening impulses of the id). The ego reacts drastically to the conflict that seems to threaten its very survival. If the threatening situation is not resolved, it continues to be frightening. The original danger may pass away, but the memory of it still arouses anxiety. As the child grows up, his ego becomes stronger and more resilient, but it still reacts drastically to the anxiety that has become a signal of the old threat that has been buried in the unconscious and still retains much of its power. The anxiety signal provokes defenses that keep the threatening material—and sometimes even the anxiety itself—unconscious. Thus, the individual normally does not consciously know what he is really afraid of; his defenses may work so well that he may not even be aware that he is afraid. Much of psychoanalysis and therapy, as we shall see in Chapter 30, is aimed at bringing the old anxiety-provoking threats and fears into consciousness, so that the individual can see that they are no longer frightening.

The defenses against anxiety have their own effects, which can be either beneficial or anxiety-provoking in themselves. Primarily, defenses *avoid* anxiety, which is a desirable short-term effect. In addition, the symptoms produced by the defense mechanisms often enjoy a *secondary gain*; that is to say, they are advantageous in their own right. Working hard, for example, can be extremely rewarding financially, even though it may really be an expression of anally fixated libido or a sublimation of repressed sexual desires. What originates as a symptom may become the individual's greatest social asset, the one that most contributes to his success.

The opposite effect is more common, however; most symptoms arouse their own anxiety at the same time as they avoid the original anxiety. For one thing, an individual who employs neurotic defenses is more vulnerable in social relationships than a person who does not. Like our pseudo-athlete at the start of the chapter, he must constantly be on the alert lest his unrealistic symptoms be exposed. Karen Horney, a neo-Freudian, has used the example of the individual who reacts against fears of inferiority by pretending to know everything. In the course of his day, he lies a lot, claiming to know things that he really does not know. But he must be constantly on the alert for real experts who could expose his ignorance. His vulnerability requires that he expend a great deal of energy in constant vigilance and ingenuity.

Another source of defense-generated anxiety is seen in cases of defenses that conflict with each other. Consider the plight of the man with whom we started the chapter. He still really wants to win his father's respect with an athletic success, but in defending himself against his fears and hostility, he has worked out a set of contradictory defenses that not only take a lot of energy to maintain but also effectively block the athletic success that could represent a therapeutic experience.

Anxiety, then, provokes defenses that are in turn expressed behaviorally as symptoms and personality characteristics. Superimposed on all this complex apparatus are variations in the strength of anxiety and corresponding variations in the intensity and salience of the neurotic symptoms. The variations in anxiety have two sources: the outside world and the person himself. It is not unusual for a person to go along quite well for many years, but then to display severe neurotic symptoms when he runs into an anxiety-provoking experience. For example, an individual may cope with the comparatively structured life of college perfectly well but begin to employ many defenses when faced with getting a job or finding a career in the relatively less structured business world. Or, internal anxieties may manifest themselves in defensive behavior when a person's first child is born—the person becomes a parent. The exact source of the anxiety, the kind of defense, and the particular symptoms that occur will depend on the individual, his history, and his present situation. Freud has told us that only two things are certain: the ego will defend itself against anxiety, and the ego's childhood experiences will inevitably determine what course the defenses and symptoms will take.

DEFENSE MECHANISMS

In general, the individual's reaction to the stress of anxiety or to the unacceptable feelings that anxiety causes is to find a way (1) of making it acceptable (by rationalizing, for example), or (2) of ignoring it altogether (by repression or denial). Some of these defense mechanisms have already been discussed in Chapter 24. As we have said, the

interaction of defense mechanisms can become quite
complex, since they may be used in combination
to support each other. The behavior that results from
the defense mechanisms ranges from being apparently normal and socially acceptable—even praise-
worthy (as in some types of sublimation)—to being
conspicuously unusual or personally destructive
(phobias and compulsions).

One of the ego's methods of defending itself
against anxiety-provoking material is *repression*. The
ego refuses to accept either the desires that originate
in the id or the ideas that represent them, and
pushes them back into the unconscious so that the
individual is never aware of them. Repression is
often combined with other defense mechanisms, so
that the anxiety, while never conscious, may still be
expressed in behavior.

In *regression*, a person meets his fears with immature reactions that are thinly disguised adult analogies to the ways in which he met his fears at an
earlier stage of development. During a particularly
stressful period, an adult who usually handles frustrations calmly may throw the equivalent of a temper
tantrum over some unexpected setback. At that
moment, the tantrum may represent an earlier, successful way of meeting a crisis.

For regression to occur, the person must have
some libido still engaged at an earlier stage of
development. For example, suppose that a person
is unconsciously afraid of sexual advances by an
older person, feels anxiety, and still has not resolved
the Oedipal relationship with the opposite-sex
parent. The person resorts to particularly childish
behavior, treating the other adult as the opposite-sex
parent, not as a seducer.

As we have mentioned in Chapter 24, *sublimation*
is Freud's idea of the healthy resolution of sexual
conflicts in which libidinal energy is invested in
socially approved activities.

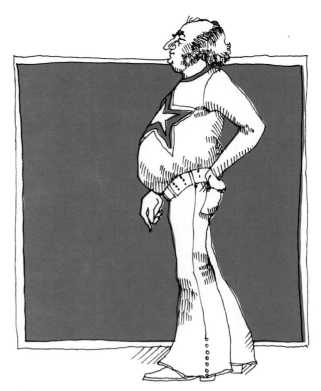

Figure 28.2
Denial: clothes cannot subtract years.

Other defense mechanisms are denial, rationalization, displacement, projection, and reaction formation. *Denial* resembles repression in that the person
simply denies that the uncomfortable thought or
situation exists or is true. Unlike repression, it does
not push the material into the unconscious; the
person knows it is there, but he just continually
denies its existence. For example, portly people often
deny that they are fat; to make their point, they
wear clothes designed for thin people. This only
gives them an appearance of literally overflowing
their clothes—a ludicrous result. Similarly, older
people often deny their age by dressing and behaving like much younger people (Figure 28.2).
Artificial devices—girdles, hair pieces, padded
shoulders, elevator shoes—have long been used to
deny the facts of one's appearance.

Rationalization means drawing up apparently
reasonable explanations to justify one's behavior
or attitude in a certain situation in order to preserve
one's self-respect and avoid anxiety. The child who
concludes that he really did not want the candy his

sister ate because it is bad for his teeth and the child who snatches the candy from his sister because it would be bad for *her* teeth are both rationalizing. So is the businessman who concludes that being president of the company would only have aggravated his ulcer.

In *displacement,* anger or fear towards a dangerous object is redirected towards a substitute object that is less threatening. As we have mentioned in Chapter 24, displacement is often used in dealing with authority figures. A person who has been scolded by his employer may not dare to retaliate for fear of being fired, so he relieves his frustration by taking it out on another employee or a friend. If he does not want to anger them, he may pound a desk or kick a wastebasket. Displacement is a common and often useful mechanism; it provides a safe way of letting off steam in a frustrating situation. It is interesting that animals also seem to react this way to stressful situations when two desires are in conflict; in ethology, the phenomenon is called displacement activity (see Chapter 15).

In *projection*, the individual not only denies his own feelings but attributes them to others. Thus, a person who is actually afraid of people may project his timidity onto others, saying that *they* are afraid of him—*he* controls *them* instead of vice versa. There is another type of projection that is even more common among neurotics. This is the projection onto others of your feelings—not about them or about yourself—but about third parties. Typically, you then condemn them for such feelings. So Alfred says that Bill chases girls and is consequently a bad person, if Alfred unconsciously wishes to chase girls but finds it impossible. In any case, a person protects himself from anxiety by pretending, totally unconsciously, that his own feelings are really not his at all but those of another person. The real feelings of a neurotic may thus, according to Freud, be those he attributes to others.

Some have felt that Freud's greatest single insight into the ways the ego defends itself is the affinity of opposite emotions. In *reaction formation*, unacceptable emotions are admitted to consciousness in reversed form. Thus, a mother who actually feels some hostility towards her child may become extremely affectionate and overprotective. It is as if she wants to prove to herself, to the child, and to the rest of the world that she is far from hostile.

The following case involves a double reaction formation. A forty-year-old man comes to a therapist's office distraught because his aged mother is ill and must come to live with his family. He dislikes her, but cannot see any way around the inevitable and impossible living situation. Under analysis (which we shall discuss in Chapter 30), it comes out that as a young child, he pitied his mother because his father failed to provide her with what she wanted. She frequently expressed this to the child in an apparently innocuous way, enlisting his sympathy and support. This intensified his Oedipal conflict with his father, giving him reason to doubt, even to hate, the father. The father died while the son was still a child, at a stage when the son still felt hatred and guilt. The child unconsciously felt that his hate had killed his parent and that he was now doubly responsible, both for his father's death and for fulfillment of his mother's wishes. As an adult, he has come to hate his mother because of anxiety over her dependence and his helplessness, so much so that her imminent appearance throws him into a state of anxiety for which he seeks professional help.

NEUROTIC SYMPTOMS

We now have to consider how defense reactions can lead to neurotic behavior. Remember that what we mean by neurotic behavior is human activity that severely limits the happiness and productivity of an individual and those around him.

One symptom of neurosis is *free-floating* anxiety, a general feeling of uneasiness that is not accompanied by specific defense reactions or behaviors. In this case, the person is aware of anxiety, but not of its cause. The only symptom of free-floating anxiety may be a "nervous day" or days. The individual may later be able to recognize the cause of his uneasiness but only because it goes away when he has taken care of some particular task. But he may never realize its unconscious sources.

Free-floating anxiety itself is basically a feeling of helpless fear, dread, and foreboding. The novelist Robert Louis Stevenson described it well: "Punishment coming . . . long after memory has forgotten and self-love condoned the fault." The helplessness is magnified by our being conscious only of the signal of danger (anxiety) and not the danger (the unacceptable desire or thought) itself. This may be likened to hearing a sound in a darkened room. Since we cannot see what made the sound, we may imagine the most horrible and ghastly sources. Moreover, the neurotic never finds out what made the sound; his efficient defenses prevent him from turning on the lights.

An extreme form of such generalized anxiety is the *acute anxiety attack*, which may indicate that the ego's defense system has begun to break down. Some psychologists believe acute attacks to be among the forerunners of psychoses (which we shall discuss in Chapter 29).

Conversion Reaction   It was the observation of a form of conversion reaction, *hysteria*, that first led Freud into the serious study of psychopathology, which in turn so altered psychological thinking. In a conversion, the person's wish to repress certain ideas or to avoid certain actions is converted into an apparent organic disability that prevents him from encountering fearful material or carrying out those actions. Individuals who have seen or heard something unbearably fearful—or simply dread doing so—may become unable to see or hear. Deep anxieties may often be expressed in the inability to move an offending part of the body. Many cases of impotence would be classified as conversion hysterias.

Conversion hysterias present two contradictions: first, the patient is physiologically normal, and second, his symptoms may be inconsistent with what is known to be true of the nervous system. Hysterically blind people cannot see, but their visual systems are entirely normal physiologically. Hysterically paralyzed people may exhibit symptoms that are neurologically impossible: they may be unable to move the arm, but they can manipulate the fingers at the end of it perfectly well.

The symptoms seem to be a direct physical expression of the anxiety-preventing mechanism. The blind cannot see frightening experiences, and the deaf cannot hear them; the impotent cannot carry out sexual intercourse, and the paralyzed cannot express their anger.

Obsessions and Compulsions   "If in worry, fear, or doubt, run in circles, scream and shout." This is exactly how both the obsessive and the compulsive neurotic handle anxiety—with ritual behavior.

Obsessive neurotics handle unconscious anxiety by repeating the same thought over and over whenever anxiety threatens to intrude upon their consciousness. The thought, which is in itself innocuous, may be directly related to the original anxiety-provoking material, or it may be only a symbol of it. The obsession may accomplish two purposes. It distracts the ego from the source of anxiety, so that it becomes a kind of magic formula for warding off pain. It also proves to the ego that thinking the thought does not cause pain, so that the underlying anxiety is unnecessary. For example, the obsessive observation that everyone you pass on the street ignores you may perhaps be based on a fear that some undesirable characteristic of yours will be noted and criticized. In many cases, the obsessive thought may have to be repeated at regular intervals, such as every evening, or before every meal, or before speaking. In extreme cases, the individual can think of little else.

Compulsive neurotics ward off anxiety with actions that they repeat whenever there is any threat from the unconscious. They perform innocuous rituals, such as repeatedly looking into a mirror when they feel in doubt about something. The compulsive behavior may be as ordinary as the habit of making checklists or checking every burner on the stove before leaving the house.

Sometimes the association between the compulsive pattern and the underlying anxiety is easily uncovered. In one case study, a compulsion to add up the numbers on automobile license plates was traced to a dread of failing high school mathematics. In another, ritualistic attempts at seduction combined with compulsive masturbation were traced to a fear of impotence that arose during an unsatisfactory resolution of the Oedipal conflict.

Obsessive and compulsive symptoms often go together. For example, one who is obsessed with the idea that his hands carry germs is also likely to exhibit a compulsion to wash his hands frequently. Obsessions and compulsions may prove to be effective defenses if they succeed in distracting the ego from anxiety, and if they make use of ideas or rituals that do not themselves generate additional anxiety or make the person conspicuous. It is only when they begin to absorb most of the person's time and energy, thereby seriously interfering with his daily life, that these symptoms may attract attention and so immobilize the individual psychologically as to indicate the need for therapy.

R. W. White in _The Abnormal Personality_* has provided an extensive case of obsessive-compulsive neurosis from which the following partial case history has been drawn.

As a child of ten or eleven, Peter Oberman came to depend on his grandfather rather than on his overbearing and abusive father or timid mother for parental love and affection. This situation gave rise to feelings of anxiety and ambivalence: Peter loved his grandfather and was afraid he might die, but he also chafed under the rather boring philosophy lectures that the old man insisted on giving him. He was periodically overcome with thoughts of accidents that might take the grandfather away from him. When these thoughts came, he found that he was able to cancel their negativity with stylized gestures and peculiar rituals. For example, when it occurred to him that his grandfather's house might catch fire, he found that he had to touch the ground to prevent the fire and to reassure himself.

As more hostile thoughts emerged, more stylized gestures evolved to take care of them. People noticed his peculiar behavior, and so, to avoid being conspicuous, he developed a system for taking care of all of the bad thoughts of the day before going to sleep in the evening. This involved pointing a certain lucky number of times in a certain lucky direction. Soon the number reached as high as 256. At this point, Peter was a prisoner of his obsessive thoughts and compulsive behavior. The ritual to exorcise the bad thoughts of the day took up to an hour at night.

The Phobias   There are persons who experience instantaneous and overwhelming, emotional and grossly physical anxiety in the presence of certain specific objects, situations, or symbols. Among the common _phobias_ are: fear of cats or other animals (zoophobia), fear of crowds or enclosed spaces (claustrophobia), and fear of heights (acrophobia). Whatever the stimulus, the anxiety it arouses is intense

*Third edition. New York: Ronald, 1964.

Figure 28.3
Some people experience acute anxiety in the presence of
harmless spiders.

Figure 28.4
Some people experience acute anxiety in crowded
elevators.

Figure 28.5
Some people experience acute anxiety if they look down
from a height.

(Figures 28.3 through 28.5). In the extreme form of
the reaction, there is a cold sweat, followed by an
urgent desire to escape; escape itself, in the form
of flight or loss of consciousness, may follow.

Freud's special insight was that phobias are the
result of a displacement and a projection, both
defenses against anxiety. The real object of fear
arouses so much anxiety that it never becomes conscious; the fear is displaced to an external object
(often not really dangerous) and projected into the
outside world where it can be avoided. The individual may be aware that his phobia is unreasonable,
but he is unable to discover the unconscious source
of his fear without help. In a therapy situation, the

association between the phobic object and the original source of anxiety may be uncovered fairly easily. For example, one man's fear of the number thirteen was traced to a childhood fear of becoming sexually involved with a nursemaid who had frequently expressed a dread of the same number.

Phobias are not very successful defenses against anxiety. Although the person may find it possible to avoid the phobic object or situation for long periods of time, when by chance he does encounter it, his reaction is much stronger than that of people with other types of neurotic symptoms. Even imagining the presence of the object may cause strong anxiety reactions. This, of course, means that the person must arrange his life so that he is not likely to encounter the phobic object or situation unexpectedly. In addition, he may have to employ other defense mechanisms to counteract the effect of the phobia. For example, a person who develops acrophobia must be constantly on guard to avoid high places, especially if he does not wish his phobia to become known. He must expend much energy in finding valid excuses for not walking over high bridges, looking down stairwells, riding on unenclosed elevators, reserving tenth-floor hotel rooms, or even driving along mountain roads. His symptoms may seriously interfere with his living and working habits.

Probably no personality is totally unneurotic, at least in Freud's sense, since the same developmental mechanisms control the formation of every personality, neurotic or not. To be neurotic to some degree is clearly not to be abnormal. Only when exaggerated neurotic symptoms so displace ordinary and balanced personality traits that the individual is deprived of some usually available source of human happiness and productivity is normality impaired, and therapy perhaps indicated.

Suggested Readings

Aldrich, C. K. (1966) *An introduction to dynamic psychiatry.* New York: McGraw-Hill. [A modified psychoanalytical, psychiatric view of neurosis and anxiety.]

Freud, S. (1933) *New introductory lectures on psychoanalysis.* (Translated by J. H. Sprott.) New York: Norton. [Freud's view of neurosis in the context of his therapy for it.]

Krafft-Ebing, R. von (1965) *Psychopathia sexualis.* (Translated by F. S. Klaf.) New York: Stein and Day. [The classic account of clinical and theoretical findings bearing on the sexual origin of neurosis.]

Ullmann, L. P., & Krasner, L. (1969) *A psychological approach to abnormal behavior.* Englewood Cliffs, N.J.: Prentice-Hall. [The behaviorist's approach. Illuminating.]

White, R. W. (1964) *The abnormal personality.* (3rd ed.) New York: Ronald. [Excellent account of neurosis, especially its roots in the normal course of the development of personality.]

CHAPTER TWENTY-NINE

Psychosis

Psychosis is traditionally distinguished from neurosis in terms of the psychotic's lack of contact with reality. The neurotic person may do peculiar things and express peculiar thoughts, but he has an awareness of the real world. By contrast, the psychotic exhibits serious interference with his capacity to recognize, think about, and test reality. His actions and language are bizarre and apparently meaningless, indicating an inability to relate to his environment in anything that even vaguely resembles a normal way.

SCHIZOPHRENIA

Schizophrenia literally means "split personality," but that is an archaic and incomplete description of a small minority of the cases. Formerly, this group of diseases was referred to as *dementia praecox*, a name that suggested that it was primarily an affliction of the young, but this, too, is incomplete and largely inaccurate. Today, schizophrenia is a diagnosis applied to a wide range of symptoms. All cases exhibit symptoms of impaired contact with reality, particularly interpersonal reality, but the range and variety of particular symptoms is great.

It is possible to divide the mass of schizophrenics into four large groups: simple, hebephrenic, catatonic, and paranoid schizophrenics. We shall discuss the typical or modal disorder in each category. But, as with most systems of neat categories, there is considerable variation among the individuals in each category. There is also some difficulty in classifying many individual cases of people who are clearly sick but do not fit any one category. There are cases that simply defy classification. Another danger of using categories is that the process of putting a label on a disease tends to make the patient lose his individuality. It also encourages a tendency for the therapist to read into the case symptoms and complications that are present in the typical textbook example. Neither of these is at all conducive to effective treatment or accurate research on any type of mental illness.

Simple Schizophrenia *Simple schizophrenia* is marked by extreme apathy and withdrawal from activity and from other people. A typical early symptom, particularly with teenage schizophrenics, is a simple failure to get out of bed in the morning, remaining there in apathy until physically moved. It has been said that the person seems to revert to infancy, but that is only a description by analogy of the apathy that may involve loss of all ordinary adult abilities. The person will not talk, moves only to obtain pleasure, such as masturbation and nourishment, or may not move at all, even for elimination. He seems simply to give up, becoming totally helpless and dependent on others. In addition, he is apparently unable to express his emotions; he neither laughs nor cries.

Gradual onsets of simple schizophrenia also occur. A person may gradually cease to communicate with other people and then drift into inactive dependence. Fortunately, the prognosis is good for the first attack: with skillful encouragement and help or with the behavioral techniques described in Chapter 32, many simple schizophrenics regain contact with reality.

Catatonic Schizophrenia *Catatonic schizophrenia* is distinguished in part by frozen poses maintained for hours on end (Figure 29.1). These may alternate with phases of frenzied activity. The poses remind one of inactive compulsions—instead of repeating an act or an oath over and over, the catatonic does everything in a highly stylized way. The onset is typically gradual but progressive, with intermittent lucid periods. The periods of inactivity become longer and the postural posing more pronounced and usually more bizarre as the days and weeks go by. The prognosis is fair to good, depending on the severity of the symptoms and the age of the patient.

Hebephrenic Schizophrenia This is not a continuing disorder as are the previous two forms of the disease. *Hebephrenic schizophrenia* waxes and wanes; sometimes, the victim seems almost rational and normal, but at other times he certainly is not. The main symptoms are inappropriate emotional

Figure 29.1
Catatonic schizophrenia is distinguished by postures held for hours.

reactions, such as laughing and giggling, bizarre actions, and distorted language (Figure 29.2). Speech is usually rapid and emotional, but the distortion of language is more important. Classically, it has been referred to as a *word salad*, since the words appear to be all jumbled up and tossed about.

Recent studies have shown that there is a definite structure not only in the grammatical but also in the semantic aspects of hebephrenic speech. Simply put, the hebephrenic describes a world that belongs only to him, has associations and flights of ideas that are logical and consistent to him but meaningless to others, and has his own personal linguistic peculiarities that continually break in on the flow of his speech (much as we might say, "You know").

Figure 29.2
Hebephrenic schizophrenia is distinguished by inappropriate emotional behavior and distortions of language.

He may coin words (neologisms) that have a consistent but strictly private meaning. It seems that the problem is not in the language itself but in the associations of a mind that sees the world in a peculiar and deeply abnormal way.

We can get some of the flavor of the hebephrenic disorder from the following two excerpts provided by R. W. White in his book *The Abnormal Personality*.* The first recounts an interview with a male hebephrenic in which the answers are surprising and the thinking fleeting and disorganized.

*Third edition. New York: Ronald, 1964.

Q. How old are you?
A. Why, I am centuries old, sir.
Q. How long have you been here?
A. I have been now on this property on and off for a long time. I cannot say the exact time because we are absorbed by the air at night, and they bring back people. They kill up everything; they can make you lie; they can talk through your throat.
Q. Who is this?
A. Why, the air.
Q. What is the name of this place?
A. This place is called a star.
Q. Who is the doctor in charge of your ward?
A. A body just like yours, sir. They can make you black and white. I say good morning, but he just comes through there. At first it was a colony. They said it was heaven. These buildings were not solid at the time, and I am positive this is the same place. They have others just like it. People die, and all the microbes talk over there, and prestigitis you know is sending you from here to another world. . . . I was sent by the government to the United States to Washington to some star, and they had a pretty nice country there. Now you have a body like a young man who says he is of the prestigitis.
Q. Who was this prestigitis?
A. Why, you are yourself. You can be a prestigitis. They make you say bad things; they can read you; they bring back Negroes from the dead.

The second example is a written piece by another hebephrenic with a suggestion of paranoid thinking. It is important to note that the patient took it very seriously and that it had exact meaning for her, although not for other readers.

This creation in which we live began with a Dominant Nature as an Identification Body of a completed evolutionary Strong Material creation in a Major Body Resistance Force. And is fulfilling the Nature Identification in a like Weaker Material Identification creation in which Two Major Bodies have already fulfilled radio body balances, and embodying a Third Material Identification Embodiment of both; which is now in the evolutionary process of fulfillment but fulfills without the Two Parents' Identification Resistances, therefore shall draw the resistances and perpetuate the motion interchanging of the whole interrelationship; thus completing this Creation in an interchanging Four in Three Bodies in One functioning self contained, self-controlled and self-restrained comprising the Dominant Moral Nature and consummating a ratio balanced Major Body of maximum resistance, in a separated second like Weaker Material Major Body Functioning Counter Resistance Force to the Strong Material Major Body Resistance Force, the beginning of this creation; and the Dual Force Resistances then as a Major Body and Major Body Functioning completes a Universe in material balance functioning the preservation of all things.

The overt onset of the disease is relatively rapid; it is as if the individual rather suddenly figures out a private interpretation of what the world is all about and what his problems are. The prognosis is poor: hebephrenics are too certain that they are right to be able easily to change their private language and view of the world for another. The completeness of their world system suggests that years of partially unconscious effort may have gone into its construction before it made its appearance.

Paranoid Schizophrenia *Paranoid schizophrenia* is the type of psychosis that provides material for the comedies and cartoons about people who believe themselves to be Napoleon or Teddy Roosevelt or some other famous person. Such comic portrayals

Figure 29.3
Paranoid schizophrenia is distinguished by well-developed delusions.

do not come close to the tragic reality of paranoid schizophrenia.

There is somewhat of a paranoid cast to many types of neurosis, as we have seen in Chapter 28. In its schizophrenic manifestation, however, the behavior is bizarre, uncontrollable, and totally out of contact with reality. Rather than defending himself against anxiety, as a neurotic does, the paranoid psychotic seems to be at the mercy of his anxiety. The delusions of persecution and of grandeur seem to be bizarre attempts to personify the individual's fears and make him seem more important so that he is equal to his imagined enemies (Figure 29.3). The delusions are typically well developed, coherent systems, involving highly elaborate enemies who are after the patient for highly elaborate reasons.

The onset in these cases is typically precipitated by a personal crisis, often a sexual one. According to Freud's theory, the primary cause is an unconscious recognition of homosexual attraction that is so frightening that it leaves the ego no other defense than a psychotic breakdown. The prognosis in sudden breakdown is generally good. But more gradual onsets, in which the normal psychological fabric of the individual comes to collaborate with the abnormal symptoms, have a poor prognosis.

What Causes Schizophrenia   There can be no simple answer because there is no simple disease, as we have just seen. There are many theories that attempt to account for it, but theories of disease are not generally accepted unless they generate successful therapies. Unfortunately, that has yet to occur in any thoroughly convincing way in the study of schizophrenia. There are a number of camps, each endorsing a different theory, and at least one group of therapists backs a combination of other theories.

One of the several leading current approaches to the problem of schizophrenia is chemical therapy. It attempts to find a biochemical basis for schizophrenia and, concurrently, a pharmacological cure through drugs. We shall discuss the chemical approach later in this chapter.

The other theories can be put into three classes: (1) constitutional, (2) environmental-behavioral, and (3) psychodynamic.

Constitutional theories put great weight on genetic factors. It is true that heredity can be implicated in schizophrenia, as we saw in Chapter 16. There may be a hereditary *predisposition* to become schizophrenic. But it is as yet hard to imagine how such a complex body of symptoms could be inherited and lie dormant for years before it is expressed in a person's behavior. Researchers will need to learn more about genetics and human psychological development before they can draw such a pessimistic conclusion.

A more optimistic approach is to focus research on environmental factors influencing the disorder. Even if theorists were to conclude that the disease is genetically determined, it would still be possible to search for a cure but somewhat more difficult to find a means of prevention.

When behaviorists look at the apathy that is characteristic of some forms of schizophrenia, they think of punishment and extinction (Chapters 3 and 4). When they consider the bizarre actions and speech patterns, they think of contingencies of reinforcement, both emotional and material, that might possibly sustain such a lack of contact with the reality that most of us experience. Behaviorists, of course, see all psychological functions in terms of behavior, and they see behavior as actions shaped and maintained according to the basic learning principles.

The behaviorist, more than any other psychologist, deals with individual cases. He cannot, therefore, make general pronouncements about the nature of the disease, since they can only be proved by actually trying out therapy methods based on his recommendations to see if they do successfully alter the behavior of *individual* schizophrenics. His guesses as to the behavioral principles that could be involved in the causes of individual cases of schizophrenia would include extinction (since the schizophrenic has no effect on the world, he ceases to respond to it); punishment and avoidance (life has become so painful that it is no longer worth the effort); and reinforcement (the schizophrenic has discovered a mode of behavior that for some reason is genuinely reinforcing for him, although it seems markedly odd to us. For example, he may receive special attention, care, and expressions of concern from others). Therapeutic methods derived from the behavioristic approach have had some success, especially in the treatment of severely withdrawn and inactive children (as we shall see in Chapter 32).

Psychodynamic theories of schizophrenia are not numerous. Many symptoms suggest a regression to the earliest, oral stages of development, but that is a stage at which the basically intellectual techniques of psychoanalysis are least useful. Whether for this reason or not, psychoanalysts have generally not taken schizophrenics into analysis. It is difficult to psychoanalyze someone who will not talk or who speaks a different and incomprehensible language. There have been some efforts in this direction, though. Frieda Fromm-Reichman achieved an analytically based treatment in which she literally attempted to bring schizophrenics up again, treating them as if they were babies, complete with bottles, and advancing them through life's stages as rapidly as she felt they were ready. Her success was mixed, and the therapy was very time-consuming.

Some theorists have described _schizophrenogenic environments_, particular combinations of circumstances and events that they feel contribute to the disease. These have in common unusual combinations of tight control and extreme permissiveness—under certain conditions. Such an environment often includes what has been called a _schizophrenogenic mother_. The mother tends to dwell heavily and intellectually on everything the child does, dividing it into two or more distinct districts: the highly controlled district where she is in command and where with her permission the child can feel in charge as her lieutenant, and all other districts. which are implicitly, but clearly, set off and sometimes explicitly rejected ("Let's put those ideas in our closet, dearest.") as things that are separate from dear mother and dearest child. Schizophrenia appears if the individual, as a child or as an adult, has reason to go into the closet. He will likely stay there, for that is where he and his mother put a lot of things he really wanted, ideas that are quite different from those he has been living with.

MANIA AND DEPRESSION

In addition to schizophrenia, the _manic-depressive psychoses_ account for large numbers of the occupants of mental hospitals and institutions. How many sepa-

rate diseases this designation covers is uncertain. _Depression_ seems to exist as a separate entity outside of the _cyclic_ manic-depressive disease, but _mania_ may not.

The feelings of woe and grim foreboding that are natural for everyone in their low periods are greatly enhanced in a depressive psychosis. Depressives experience apathy, nonspecific fear, feelings of worthlessness and ineffectiveness, and deep, all-pervading sadness (Figure 29.4). This contrasts with the super happiness of mania—agitation, boundless energy, consciousness of unlimited ability and potential, and a wonderful aura of well-being. But the optimistic energy of mania is usually as objectless as the fear in depression. Although they are poles apart emotionally, individuals in either state are unrealistic in terms of their view of the environment and their inability to act effectively on it.

Swings of mood are normal, of course—everyone has emotional ups and downs, but usually people's moods are based on reasonably realistic appraisals of how things are really going. It is as much their lack of contact with reality as it is the intensity of their moods that distinguish the psychotic.

We are fortunate in having an inside description of a depression from the autobiography of Clifford W. Beers, _A Mind that Found Itself_.* Beers suffered a depression but later recovered sufficiently to describe it. From his description, it is clear that depression feeds on itself. The depressed individual gives a sad and self-hostile interpretation to whatever he encounters in the world, and this only serves to maintain or deepen the depression.

Beers was hospitalized after attempting to kill himself by jumping out of his bedroom window. He felt that this was a crime, that he would certainly be brought to trial, that everyone in town knew of his crime and thought very badly of him for it.

*Garden City, New York: Doubleday, 1931.

Figure 29.4
Depression is marked by extreme apathy and extreme sadness.

Everyone he saw was out to get him for it. When traveling, he felt that the landscape and the rows of homes that he passed were deliberately sad, indicating the low opinion everyone had of him. He gave distorted interpretations to whatever he heard. When told by a supporter that they would get him "straightened out," he saw himself literally straightened out at the end of a hangman's rope or in a coffin. As he recovered from his injuries, he had fantasies that the hospital staff were fattening him up to slaughter him. Every event imaginable was construed in terms of his own death.

Psychiatrists have recently had considerable success in controlling these extreme swings of mood with drugs, to the point that it seems plausible to look for biochemical causes for the symptoms. We shall examine this possibility in the next section. However, there are traditional theories as well. One places the cause on an inherited predisposition to emotional instability. Another reads the moods as manifestations of a very strong superego, which is either very pleased or very upset with its ego. And the behaviorists emphasize the effect of the intensity of one mood on the intensity of the next: for example, the deeper the depression, the higher the mania that follows. It is fortunate that there are antidepressant drugs as well as tranquilizers, because none of these theories is especially helpful in treatment.

PHYSIOLOGICAL APPROACHES TO PSYCHOSIS

The medical psychologist Ward Halstead emphasized that there are several different brains: the *physical* brain of the anatomist, the *electrical* brain of the neurologist, and the *chemical* brain of the pharmacologist.

Physical alteration of the brain by surgery was once thought to hold great promise for psychological treatment, but this procedure has lately become controversial. Apparently beneficial changes in personality resulted from _prefrontal lobotomy_, a surgical procedure in which the front part of the brain was disconnected with a knife from the rest of the brain. Patients reported that they emerged from the surgery with a happier, more peaceful view of themselves and their lives. But the long-term effects were not always good—some people tended to become vegetative and apathetic, and there have been cases of deterioration. Although psychosurgery has not fulfilled its earlier apparent promise, it is still practiced by some.

Electroconvulsive shock continues in use for some kinds of depressions, because it sometimes relieves the symptoms. For a few seconds an electric current is passed through electrodes attached to the patient's head. The patient undergoes convulsions and unconsciousness. Sometimes the process is repeated several times over the course of a couple of weeks. Patients sometimes report relief of their symptoms, which is the goal of the treatment. Why this apparently primitive treatment works is not known. Some behavioristic theorists have suggested that it is highly aversive and that the patient unconsciously refrains from a relapse into depression in order to avoid undergoing the treatment again.

518

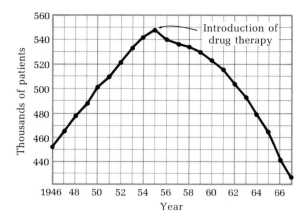

Figure 29.5
The number of patients in government mental hospitals declined rapidly after the introduction of drug therapy. [Data from D. H. Efron, ed., *Psychopharmacology: A Review of Progress*. Washington, D.C.: U.S. Dept. of Health, Education, and Welfare, 1968, p. 2.]

Modern psychiatry is deeply involved in psychopharmacology; it is common to find pharmacologists and even biochemists affiliated with faculties of psychiatry. Drugs that have psychological effects have worked so well that they have ushered in a whole new era in the treatment of mental illness. This is still an empirical method of treatment— nobody knows exactly *why* a particular drug works.

LSD (lysergic acid) played a major role in directing attention to this area. A synthetic compound first discovered in a Swiss laboratory in 1943, LSD produces effects that are likened by some to a psychosis: detachment, hallucinations, and bizarre mental states. If mental illness can be simulated chemically, maybe chemical therapy can abate it, reasoned the pharmacologists. They may or may not prove to be correct.

Drug therapy for depressive and manic psychosis seems possible because the moods might remain more in line with reality if their intensity can be reduced. But drug therapy for schizophrenia, where there is *abnormal content* in the person's bizarre thoughts and actions, seems harder to achieve.

Chemical therapy for depression was discovered by accident: it was noted that tubercular patients were happier when taking an experimental drug called iproniazid. This drug was then tried out with success on depressives, and was followed by others that had similarly beneficial clinical effects, but without damaging side-effects.

The use of drug therapy for mania came from observations that the chemical lithium produced calming effects on animals. It is more successful with manic patients than are simple sedatives.

Chemicals that are effective against anxiety have become household words—Valium (diazepam), Miltown (meprobamate), Librium (chlordiazepoxide). These drugs have a mild sedative effect, but they also seem to have some specific effects against

anxious feelings. They typically have little effect on severe psychotic symptoms, however.

Fortunately, stronger agents are available for use with schizophrenics and manic patients. The phenothiazines are examples. Briefly, these drugs are believed to work by inhibiting the action of a normal chemical system in the brain whose overactivity is thought by some theorists to produce schizophrenia. Psychologically, phenothiazines calm the patient, making the padded cell and straitjacket largely devices of the past. They also reduce the hallucinations and delirium that often mark schizophrenic attacks.

Each of these drugs has the usual spectrum of side effects, and continued use can lead to often dangerous withdrawal difficulties. But they do their main antipsychotic job so well that they have torn the bars from the windows of mental institutions and freed time that therapists formerly had to spend in protecting the patient's physical well-being for use in trying to improve his mental well-being.

ORGANIC PSYCHOSIS

Every psychological event is "organic" in the sense that it must involve some correlated organic (physiological) events. The term *organic psychosis* is reserved technically for a group of fairly similar mental deteriorations that result from known conditions of the body. For example, extreme fatigue or high fever that might occur in an illness often produce symptoms that indicate so little contact with reality that the patient could temporarily be qualified as psychotic. They are of short duration, however, disappearing after a night's sleep or when the fever subsides.

More serious and long-lasting are psychosislike states of detachment produced by old age, brain-affecting diseases such as advanced syphilis, and extreme alcoholism, which has profound deteriorative effects physically as well as psychologically.

MENTAL-HEALTH STATISTICS

The number of institutionalized individuals who are considered victims of serious mental illness seems to have declined in the last twenty-five years. Drugs are largely responsible (see Figure 29.5). The modern tendency is not to put people into mental hospitals if they can be kept functioning on the outside. This means that they are not exposed to the further deterioration that afflicts those who are incarcerated—living with other abnormal people is not usually good therapy. Also, many of the younger persons who had been institutionalized have been released since they can maintain themselves on the outside with the help of antipsychotic drugs. The seriously disturbed, the dangerous, the hard-core chronic cases, and the legally insane still remain in mental hospitals (Figure 29.6). Some cases who have been institutionalized for years have grown so accustomed to the life and viewpoint of the mental hospital that they could not exist without it, regardless of whether or not they might ever achieve a miraculous recovery. Besides, they often have no place to go—in most cases, no resources or property and no job skills.

Figure 29.6
The largest mental hospital in the United States, Pilgrim State Hospital in New York, has housed fourteen thousand patients at one time. [Fairchild Aerial Surveys, Inc.]

They may be burdened with friends and family who *know* they are crazy, or they may have no outside contacts at all. For these patients, there is no help available, nor is there likely to be any in the foreseeable future.

Suggested Readings

Bettelheim, B. (1955) *Truants from life.* New York: Free Press. [The author's experiences in treating schizophrenic children.]

Buss, A. H., & Buss, E. H., eds. (1969) *Theories of schizophrenia.* New York: Lieber-Atherton. [A collection of various approaches to the phenomenon of psychosis.]

Coleman, J. C. (1972) *Abnormal psychology and modern life.* (4th ed.) Glenview, Illinois: Scott, Foresman. [Highly readable account of the major forms of psychosis.]

Ullmann, L. P., & Krasner, L. (1969) *A psychological approach to abnormal behavior.* Englewood Cliffs, N.J.: Prentice-Hall. [The behaviorist's view.]

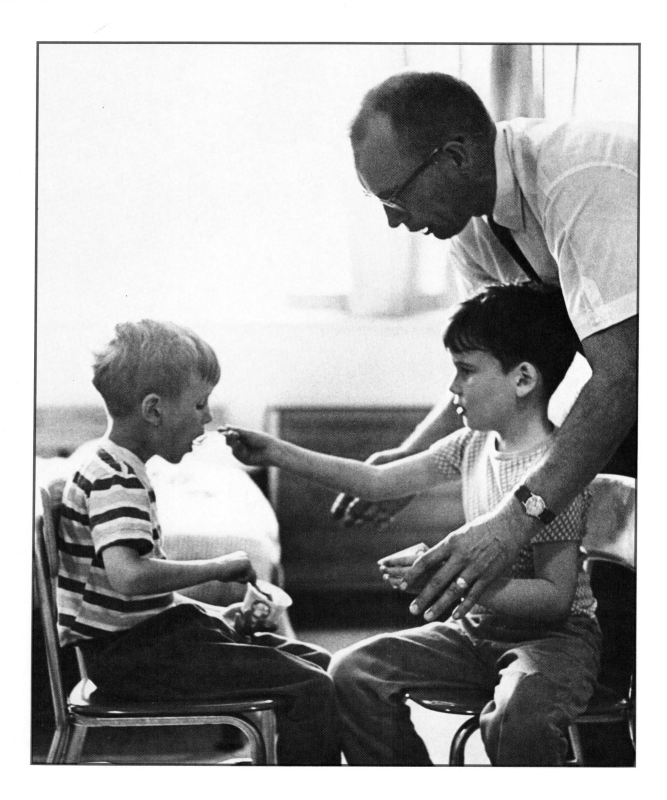

UNIT TEN

Psychotherapy

The forms of psychotherapy are many and varied. We will examine several, beginning with (1) psychoanalysis, which is based on Freudian theory, then taking up (2) the various types of humanistic therapy, which emphasize the importance of the self, (3) the different forms of group therapy, ranging from the group rehabilitation of drug addicts to weekend encounter groups, and finally (4) behavior modification, in which the therapist employs the principles of learning, withholding reinforcement of maladaptive behavior while providing reinforcement for adaptive behavior.

A well-known therapist and psychologist, Paul Meehl, once observed that as a therapist he was "utterly incapable" of believing that his therapy did not benefit his patients. As a psychologist, however, he also recognized that his own personal conviction could not be taken at face value. He therefore stressed that experiments should be performed in order to ascertain whether or not psychotherapy is effective and whether or not it justifies the great expenditure in terms of money, time, and energy on the part of its patients.

A central question to be confronted in any study of psychotherapy is its effectiveness. How effective is psychotherapy in curing psychological disorders? Is any one form more effective than another? To answer these questions, we must decide what we mean by "cure." Is it a partial change in behavior or a complete transformation of one's personality? And what criteria do we employ to determine whether or not cure has been achieved? Finally, how much time should elapse before we decide whether or not a treatment has been successful? Do we look for effects while therapy is still in progress, at its conclusion, six months later, or ten years later?

All of these complexities do not make it easy to decide whether therapy has benefited a particular patient. Controlled studies are needed, studies in which subjects who have undergone a particular therapy are compared with those who have received another form of therapy and with still others who have received none at all. Objective criteria should be employed to determine whether subjects in each group have improved, and to what degree. A few studies of this type have in fact been performed.

In one set of studies, people who were afflicted by a severe neurosis (one severe enough to keep the patient unemployed for at least three months) were observed for periods of several years. Findings showed that in a large proportion of subjects, the disturbance "cured itself"— technically, it underwent _spontaneous remission_—without the aid of therapy. Within one year, 45 percent were reported as cured—meaning they returned to work, expressed no further complaints, and enjoyed reasonably successful social adjustment; within two years, 72 percent were cured; and within five, 91 percent. Furthermore, improvements were shown to endure for at least five years. Similar types of investigations, based on data from insurance files and hospital records, on a variety of subjects—children, low-income adults, middle-income adults—also showed that large numbers of disturbed people underwent significant improvement, enabling them to function with reasonable competence in their day-to-day lives, on their own. The combined results of all such studies are most encouraging for the neurotic, because they indicate that his chances of being cured within two years are better than two to one, even if he is _not_ treated.

These results are less encouraging for the efficacy of psychotherapy, since Hans Eysenck and others have shown that about the same proportion of patients improve in the same amount of time with the aid of traditional psychotherapy. In other words, on the basis of these statistics there is no support for the claim that psychotherapy assists patients more than the mere passage of time. Of course, there may be benefits of psychotherapy that are not reflected in the statistics.

Another well-controlled study was the Cambridge-Somerville Youth Study, in which experimenters observed the progress of 650 children (six to ten years old) who had been labeled as "potential juvenile delinquents" by welfare workers. Having enlisted the cooperation of numerous therapists, they attempted to answer the following question: will children who receive therapy be less likely to develop into juvenile delinquents than those who do not? Subjects were divided into groups in which they were evenly matched for age, IQ, education level, and other relevant criteria, and were then randomly assigned (by a coin toss) into either an experimental group or a control group. One-half of the subjects received extended therapy for two to eight years, whereas the control subjects received none. Ten years after the onset of the study, workers examined court records to determine whether the therapy group had a lower incidence of delinquency, as measured by appearances before court-prevention boards or in the courts themselves. No significant difference was found between the two groups, although the control group had a slightly lower record of court appearances. Thus, the Cambridge-Somerville Youth Study fails to provide evidence supporting the efficacy of preventive psychotherapy.

Other studies purport to show that, for all forms of psychotherapy, the statistical average result is zero—that is, one-third of those who enter therapy improve, a second one-third do not change, and a discouraging one-third leave therapy in worse condition than before. But in response to these studies, some psychologists have argued that averages, even if accurate, are meaningless if a substantial number of people are really helped, even temporarily.

Other studies suggest that behavior modification—which differs significantly from other forms of therapy in that it is concerned with the treatment of the symptom (or maladaptive behavior) alone and not with the underlying cause—has been much more effective for larger numbers of people. For example, one therapist, Albert Ellis, was concerned with the issue of the effectiveness of therapy. Using analytic therapy, he had succeeded in curing approximately 67 percent of his patients (a proportion designated by some studies as standard). In the late 1950s, he decided to experiment with a new kind of treatment that he called *rational psychotherapy*, in which he ignored the origin of the symptom and tried to show the patient that his feelings of depression or anxiety were caused by current stimulus situations. With the new treatment, he raised his proportion of cures to 90 percent. Although the methods of behavior modification (which we shall discuss) had not yet been fully developed, Ellis was certainly applying the behavior therapist's approach—and successfully—in his efforts to treat symptoms rather than inner causes.

In a more recent study, Gordon Paul utilized three different types of treatment in an attempt to help students overcome feelings of extreme anxiety at the prospect of speaking in public. The subjects were divided into four groups: (1) a control group, in which no treatment was administered; (2) a group whose members met regularly with a therapist but were not actually treated, although they may have benefited from the attention they received from the therapist; (3) a psychotherapy group whose members underwent a form of client-centered psychotherapy; (4) a behavior-modification group. The same therapists were used in each of the three experimental groups; that is, each therapist saw a few of the students in each group. The student's task was to deliver a public speech at the conclusion of the treatment. Independent judges (who did not know which groups the speakers had been in) judged whether the speaker was reasonably relaxed. The proportion of relaxed speakers among the untreated subjects was very low (around 20 percent); the proportions of relaxed speakers in the second and third groups were identical (47 percent); finally, all of the subjects in the behavior modification group were judged to be relaxed (100 percent).

But despite its apparent success, behavior modification has received its share of criticism. For example, some critics have argued that any kind of "behavior control" is dehumanizing. Of course, this objection can be leveled against any enterprise in which some kind of control over an individual is exercised by another person or agency (be it doctor, employer, therapist, or government). These issues have been discussed in detail by B. F. Skinner in his controversial books *Walden Two, Beyond Freedom and Dignity,* and *About Behaviorism,* as well as by his critics.

The issue of the ultimate value of the different psychotherapies is yet to be resolved to everyone's satisfaction. In the chapters that follow we will examine in more detail some of the more important of these various therapies.

CHAPTER THIRTY

Psychoanalysis

Psychoanalysis is the form of psychotherapy that is based on Sigmund Freud's theory of personality. A fundamental understanding of analysis and its effects can probably be obtained only after many years of study and self-analysis at a minimum, and some people require in addition a period of actual psychoanalysis by a trained and compatible analyst. But an intellectual grasp of this method is not beyond anyone who can think in analogies and comprehend some of the fundamental elements of his own emotional life. Freudian thought—along with that of Piaget, the gestaltists, and the behaviorists—is a cornerstone of psychology.

THE BASIC PROCEDURES OF PSYCHOANALYSIS

Let us begin with a brief description of the basic procedures of the therapeutic technique known as psychoanalysis. A psychoanalyst is a practicing physician, with a medical degree, who has completed his internship, a psychiatric residency, specialized training in a psychoanalytical institute including his own psychoanalysis, and an extensive period of apprenticeship to a practiced analyst. For the sake of

our discussion, let us assume that you are a prospective patient of a psychoanalyst. By the time you reach him, he will probably have performed many other analyses, most taking several years to complete. You will have been oppressed by symptoms of neurosis for years, and may have consulted a variety of doctors and psychotherapists before deciding that psychoanalysis is for you. You may even have embarked on analysis previously, perhaps with several different analysts, and elected not to continue for one reason or another. What is in store for you?

If you are undergoing a typical analysis, you will have at least three appointments with the analyst every week, each lasting slightly less than an hour. For these sessions you will agree to pay perhaps $50 or more an hour (or $600 a month), whether or not you keep appointments. This provision provides very strong motivation to keep on coming. You will have been told that your analysis will require more than a year (and cost at least $8,000). Before the analyst agrees to accept you as a patient, he will, in one or more preliminary sessions, have found out enough about you, your background, your intelligence and imagination, and your ability to co-

operate with him to ascertain that he has a good
chance of being able to help you—to perform a
successful analysis of you. You, in turn, will have
made comparable assessments, insofar as you are
able, of your prospective analyst—with his encouragement and guidance. The reason for establishing these
initial terms is simply that enough emotional
problems can be expected to arise in the course of
your analysis that your energies should not be diverted, by financial, scheduling, or other extraneous
matters. If your analysis is successful, you will come
to trust this stranger as much as a parent or close
friend, if not more. You will reveal to him your most
intimate hopes and fears, past and current, and,
indeed, with his help, you will probably discover
others that you were unaware of. The stakes are,
therefore, high and important.

All that you and your analyst will ever do together
is talk—if he is a conventional analyst. You will
describe yourself, your dreams, and your fears. A
key technique is *free association*: that is, the analyst
will explicitly direct you to say the first thing that
comes into your mind. The general aim of free
association and its modifications is to induce you to
relax various psychological controls that everyone has
been socialized to impose on himself to some degree,
so that you become increasingly aware of those
thoughts, fears, emotions, and other underlying
sources of behavior that you had previously discounted as unimportant, or had not even realized
were there. At the proper points in your treatment,
the analyst will also explain and interpret your daily
behavior and your accounts of your feelings, and
help you to make your own interpretations.

Psychoanalysis has been called the *talking therapy*.
This label, though basically accurate, fails to suggest
the number of hours that the analyst will spend,
for every hour in the consulting room, just reflecting
on your case; or the self-analytical hours you must

Figure 30.1
Free association.

devote to careful observation of yourself and to
interpretation of your own behavior, although spon-
taneity in free association will continue to be very
important.

An analyst can treat only a few patients at any one
time. That is one reason why analysis is so

expensive. Furthermore, only some of those who can afford it can undergo psychoanalysis. Therefore, for purely numerical reasons, psychoanalysis is hardly the cure for everyone's problems, but it is nevertheless one of the most intriguing of psychological creations and a potential source of penetrating insight into why people behave the way they do.

THE ORIGINS OF PSYCHOANALYSIS

Although the credit for developing the technique of psychoanalysis and the impressive structure of theory that underlies it belongs to Freud, he borrowed the fundamental idea from two colleagues, both hypnotists, with whom he took what would today be called his postdoctoral training. (His principal method, free association, was discovered by one of his patients!) His two mentors were the Frenchman J. M. Charcot, under whom Freud studied, and the German Joseph Breuer, with whom he collaborated.

Freud was attracted by Breuer's success in treating cases of female hysteria with the use of hypnosis. Apparently, the therapist was better able to contact the real person—unhampered by inhibitions and defenses—if she was under hypnosis and he could talk her out of her hysterical symptoms; the therapy functioned somewhat as a posthypnotic suggestion, and the symptoms disappeared when the person awoke from the trance. Working together, Freud and Breuer noticed that, when under light hypnosis, many patients talked of their pasts, revealing memories of experiences that had a bearing on their affliction. A person who felt hysterical pain and disgust upon being touched on the arm might recall, under hypnosis, that an unpleasant sexual advance had begun with the pressure on her arm as her molester helped her across a puddle in the street.

Freud was soon convinced that symptoms of hysteria were caused by one or more forgotten or repressed experiences. Often the symptom was symbolic; for example, a forgotten experience that had evoked extreme disgust might be expressed as nausea. Moreover, Freud believed that the memories would invariably be found to be sexual, if sufficiently pursued beyond their surface manifestations to their true source. In this conviction, he diverged from Breuer who did not believe that the causes were necessarily sexual. The divergence increased when one of Freud's patients discovered that she was aided in recalling past events—whose recall often relieved a patient's symptoms—by free and undirected, relaxed thinking, *without* being hypnotized. Thus began the method of *wide-awake* free association, in which the patient thought about whatever came to mind, and described it to the therapist. Freud discarded hypnosis, and proceeded to put his own theories into practice.

He theorized that the symptoms were the symbolic expressions of a forgotten experience; that free association was a method for enabling the person to remember the experience; and that recall of the experience and the sexual emotion that went with it was the therapeutic event that resulted in the disappearance of the symptom and eventually the cure of the patient. He termed this re-experiencing and purging of the recalled emotion a *catharsis*. Before we discuss the ways in which free association and catharsis are used by the analyst to bring about insight, and eventual cure, let us examine the importance of dreams in Freudian treatment.

THE MEANING OF DREAMS

Freud believed that additional clues to the nature of the forgotten (repressed) experiences could be obtained from dreams and the patient's free associations to their contents. Dreams were meaningful because they reflected the person's thoughts and feelings, though in disguised form. In fact, since they occurred during sleep, when the normal waking defenses might not be so strong, successful analysis of them should yield extremely rich material about the real unconscious person. Freud described his theories on dreams in 1900 in his book *The Interpretation of Dreams*.

He felt that "genuine" dreams always represented wish-fulfillment, from some earlier period, usually infancy or childhood. A "genuine" dream in this context refers to one which evokes in the dreamer an emotional reaction that usually carries over to the waking state. In particular, those dreams that give rise to emotions of shame, anxiety, or exhilaration fulfill the wishes of the unconscious in some way, no matter how well they may be disguised. In Freudian theory, it is maintained that a major contribution of dreams to psychoanalysis is the insight they provide into what the "real" person really wants—if the dreams can be untangled, and accurately translated, or interpreted.

This real meaning of a dream, then, is not clearly stated. Rather, this *latent content* is expressed by the *manifest content*, which consists of symbolic transformations of one's thoughts and feelings. As we mentioned in Chapter 24, the transformations that occur—called the *dream work*—were considered by Freud to be the means by which one's subconscious copes with various potentially disturbing thoughts, emotions, and messages, thereby disguising them so that they will not arouse the anxieties of the dreamer and thus disturb his sleep. The part of the personality that selects which impulses should be disguised is called the *censor*. Thus, if threatening messages emerge from the subconscious, the censor modifies the material into a form that is not unduly disturbing to the individual. One mechanism of dream work is *condensation*, in which several different events or feelings can be combined into one dreamed event,

which might itself be only a *symbol* of the condensation itself. Such a symbol of condensation is what is sometimes called a "Freudian symbol."

The task of interpreting a dream involves working backward from the manifest content to the latent thoughts and feelings. Meaning must be attached to the symbols, condensations must be expanded, and transformations must be unraveled—all in the context of the personality that has done the dreaming. The first step is to evoke free association from the patient. The analyst's interpretation is based on the patient's associations and what they reveal about the dream work that has taken place, as well as on his knowledge of the usual patterns of symbolization and condensation and of the patient's individual mental and emotional processes.

The interpretation of symbols and the expansion of condensations require a great deal of knowledge about the personality of the dreamer. It is true that certain Freudian symbols seem to represent certain objects consistently: thus caves often represent the human female body; the people in a dream, and especially their number, usually correspond to those in one's own immediate social environment; riding into a tunnel is usually a symbolic expression of sexual intercourse; and boxes generally represent female sexual organs, whereas pencils and telephone poles often reduce under analysis to the penis. Nevertheless, every symbol, at least as it occurs in a particular dream, is unique, and its interpretation is neither simple nor automatic. Rather, it is a subtle, intricate, and long-term process in which the analyst continually modifies his interpretative hypotheses of various symbols by testing them against other parts of the same dream, as well as against other dreams and the varied material revealed in the course of the ongoing psychoanalysis.

A few dreams are exceptional in that they are common to virtually everyone, and Freud believed

Figure 30.2
Almost everyone has dreamed of going naked in public.

that their nearly universal occurrence indicated a universal meaning. One such dream is that of finding oneself naked in public (Figure 30.2); another is that of the death of a loved one.

The Nakedness Dream The *typical* nakedness dream (as opposed to other nakedness dreams that might be experienced by various individuals) has the following identifying features. In the dream, the person feels naked, or lacking some important item of dress—for example, without a necktie at a formal affair, without pants in public, or without a sanitary device during menstruation. The dreamer experiences definite feelings of shame, and an overwhelming urge to run and hide. However, this urge is inhibited by the inability to move. Usually, on awakening, the dreamer has difficulty recalling exactly what his feelings about his state of undress were, and the

people who have witnessed it are always ill-defined, indifferent, and unnoticing—or, as Freud described the observers in one of his own dreams, of "solemn and stiff expressions of face." Thus a *contradiction* exists between the shame the dreamer feels and the indifference of the onlookers. Freud maintained that this contradiction was important.

In *The Interpretation of Dreams*, Freud introduces his analysis of this universal type of dream with a reference to the biblical Garden of Eden, and reminds us that in the beginning it was natural to be unclothed. It was only after Eve had taken a bite of the apple that the concept of shame of the body and of sexual relations between a man and a woman arose. Similarly, little children—before they acquire "knowledge"—love to be naked (Figure 30.3), and to exhibit their genitals to others; to do so is to fulfill a natural human impulse. Thus, to dream of being naked before others is actually the fulfillment of a wish to do what is only natural, but, in modern societies, forbidden.

Upon awakening, why does the dreamer feel doubt about how naked he was? Freud admits his own uncertainty about this issue, suggesting that it may be caused by the work of the dream *censor*, or it may be just the result of a vague condensation of numerous remembered instances of nakedness from infancy, childhood, and even adulthood. He explains that the shame occurs because the exhibitionism in the dream is an expression of the unconscious, which has been strongly repressed. Consequently, the temporary release of that repression is terrifying, but shame rather than fear is experienced. Freud explains the inhibition of movement as a common expression of the conflict between the unconscious, which says, "Exhibit!" and the dream censor, which says that the exhibition should stop.

Freud next relates this dream to the Hans Christian Andersen story, "The Emperor's New Clothes",

"Put something on!"

Figure 30.3
Steig's view of a child nudist. [Copyright 1935 by
William Steig]

wherein the Emperor is convinced that his tailors
have produced clothes that can be seen only by
special people. He wears them, although he himself
cannot see them, and so appears on the streets of
his kingdom totally naked. His subjects, all wanting
to be special people, do not admit that they cannot
see his clothes. Freud obviously enjoyed relating that
it is a *child* who first speaks up to announce that the
Emperor is naked.

Then comes the usual Freudian rush of additional
evidence: Freud draws upon legend—the Homeric
legend of the Odyssey—to elaborate his theory of
the universal dream of nakedness. Ulysses's dream
seems tailormade for Freud's point, but of course
that is why Freud chose it. Ulysses has been traveling for a long time and now dreams the classical
dream of the wanderer. In the dream, he yearns to

return home but suddenly recognizes that he is
ragged and tattered (forms of symbolic nakedness),
dirty, and thoroughly unpresentable. On waking, the
dreamer is soaking wet with perspiration. The dream
is clearly wish-fulfillment when it deals with desires
to go home, but the unpresentable condition represents a condensed version of all the unconscious
anxieties caused by, and causing, being away from
home. The unconscious threatens to break through in
the aftermath of this recognition and that accounts
for the heavy sweat, characteristic of anxiety dreams.

The Death Dream   The second typical universal
dream concerns the death of someone, usually a
parent or sibling. The dreamer sees the dead person
being carried from the home, or attends the funeral.
Grief is the essential emotional ingredient—without it,
the dream is not typical, and the interpretation will
be a highly personal rather than the universal one.
(For example, one patient dreamed of seeing her
young nephew dead in his coffin, but did not
experience grief in the dream. Freud traced this
personal dream to a wish to see again a friend whom
she had last seen at a funeral of another nephew
years before.)

The universal death dream originates from a wish
to see the subject of the dream dead. The wish is
usually not current, but rather one that has occurred
during childhood and has been repressed. The
objects of the wish are most commonly siblings
or parents of the same sex. The dreams are thus
expressions of repressed childhood wishes to be rid
of a sibling or parent who had rivaled the dreamer
for the love of the opposite-sex parent. Sibling
rivalry and the Oedipus or Electra complex (the
repressed desire for sexual possession of the
opposite-sex parent), though suppressed by us in
our conscious lives, persist and are manifested in our
dreams.

Freud's examples are particularly convincing here. He cites recalled memories of a patient who as a little child had his "autocratic rule . . . upset, after lasting for fifteen months, by the appearance of a female rival." He traces a dream of frolicking with siblings and cousins in a field and seeing them all sprout wings and fly away to a childhood wish to see all the rivals dead. The patient *then* recalled, specifically and with certainty, that she had been told by an aunt that dead people went to heaven as angels, hence the wings. And again, a woman dreamed that a lynx was walking on the roof of her house, something—or maybe she herself—then fell down, and she saw her mother being carried dead from the house, to her horror. Freud interpreted this dream as a childhood death-wish directed against the mother. When the patient accepted this interpretation, both intellectually and emotionally, she then recalled that she had once been called lynx-eyed by a child she feared and that she had once seen a tile fall from the roof and cut her mother who was then covered with blood.

Recall that Freud could offer these interpretations before a lengthy analysis because the dreams were typical and had, in his clinical experience, always represented the same thing. Other, nonuniversal dreams are specific to the individual dreamer. They therefore require much more analytical work by the analyst and a great deal of free association to dream elements by the dreamer before their meaning can be understood. Such gradual long-term interpretation, however, is often well worthwhile because of the clear insights dreams can provide into an individual's unconscious mind.

THE CONCEPTS OF PSYCHOANALYSIS

Psychoanalysis generally begins with the assumption that a patient's neurotic behavior is caused by one or more repressed experiences from childhood. The goal is to cure the neurosis by enabling the patient to recall the repressed experience from his subconscious, and to recall also the emotional effects of that experience. The patient then recognizes the real basis of his neurotic behavior—the repressed memory—as well as its irrationality. He is thus able to free the psychic energy that has been trapped by unconscious memories of the past, and to use it more productively for normal and adaptive pursuits in his current life. Some of the important phenomena that occur in the course of analysis are *resistance, transference, insight,* and *cure.*

Resistance   Freud noted that *resistance* occurs in a wide variety of forms. His patients were continually instructed to indulge in really free association—to report everything that occurred to them. But, every patient sooner or later withheld some thoughts or feelings, either because of shame, fear of the analyst's disapproval, or a rationalization that certain items were too trivial to matter. Some patients even claimed that nothing came to mind! Freud called such behavior *resistance*, because patients resisted progress in uncovering unconscious material, the goal of psychoanalysis.

You can observe resistance in yourself if you try to analyze one of your own dreams. Do not expect to be totally successful, for it takes a certain amount of self-knowledge as well as immense skill, both of which are beyond the abilities of most of us. However, as you dwell on the possible significance of a certain dream, you will eventually find yourself resisting meaningful interpretation in some way. For example, you may experience a vague feeling of uneasiness, as if reminded of something extremely discomforting, or you may decide that your line of reasoning and remembering is too absurd to pursue. If you come really close to repressed material, you may even feel slightly dizzy and have a strong urge to do something else, which seems for the moment to be of extreme importance—but, when you run off to do it, it seems unimportant, or you cannot even recall what you ran off to do. Such feelings can be appreciated only by trying to interpret one of your own dreams.

Another form of resistance to analysis is an *acting out* of previous behavior, toward the analyst or another person in the outside world, instead of toward the original object of the behavior—a parent, sibling, or childhood peer. Freud felt that acting out was resistance to the actual recall of what had happened—in other words, one made use of the behavioral action as a protection against thinking and feeling. We shall return to this form of defense when we discuss transference. Other forms of resistance are more ordinary and transparent, such as being late for appointments or skipping them altogether.

Resistance can be conscious or unconscious. The resistance that a patient consciously, or knowingly, offers to analysis is a useful indication of those areas of the personality that are vulnerable and therefore need further analysis. The unconscious resistance is even more revealing, but greater skills are required of the analyst if the guarded areas are to be probed and eventually understood. The various manifestations of unconscious resistance are subtle: for example, a patient is late for a trivial but valid reason, which is subsequently revealed to have significant bearing on a piece of the problem. Another form of unconscious resistance is the inability to produce free association at a particular time or under particular circumstances which, analysis usually subsequently reveals, are of fundamental significance.

Freud suggested that the major causes of resistance are two. First, the person's defenses are inevitably

threatened, and the ego—that part of the personality confronting the external world (see Chapter 24)—offers resistance to the challenge. We have just mentioned some of the many forms that this resistance can take; most of them are as irrational and inappropriate as the defenses they are raised to protect. They can be difficult to combat, however, because they conform to the personality and can appear to be genuinely owing to other causes. The second motivation for resistance is that certain symptoms of repression actually yield secondary advantages that the person does not want to give up. For example, the person who is driven by neurotic motivation to work eighty hours a week may, from a pragmatic point of view, not wish to lose the ability to work long hours, and thereby reduce his income. In the course of an analysis, resistance has to be patiently but strongly opposed and overcome.

Transference   The crux of psychoanalysis is *transference*, a phenomenon in which the patient's past behavior and emotions toward another person (from the earlier Oedipal period) are shifted to the analyst. Thus, patients react to opposite-sex analysts in much the same way as they once interacted with the opposite-sex parent—with ideas of sexual seduction; and to same-sex analysts as they did to the same-sex parent—with feelings of rivalry and competition. Freud found this tendency so widespread and inevitable that he coined the phrase *repetition compulsion* to describe it. People, he felt, *must* repeat the Oedipal involvement, if not with the analyst who can understand and correct or improve it, then abnormally and neurotically with people in everyday adult life.

Later analysts broadened the concept of transference to include the transference of behaviors and emotions that occur habitually in other interactions, and that are not necessarily Oedipal or sexual in origin. Harry Stack Sullivan was the foremost spokesman of this point of view. He referred to the whole of transference as the *parataxic distortion.* The patient tries out on the analyst not only his earliest, and infantile, interpersonal coping skills but also his current everyday adult interpersonal styles of behavior. If the patient is deeply neurotic, his mode of interaction will be infantile; if he is not seriously disturbed, his manner of behaving may be only what he has acquired as an adult.

It is important to distinguish between patients who are truly neurotic and those who enter analysis for other reasons such as mild anxiety, desire for more freedom or richer personal development, or merely strong curiosity. Some analysts will take only certain kinds of patients. Those who are truly conservative still feel, as Freud did for years, that only hysteria, obsessional–compulsive conditions, and phobias are suitable for psychoanalysis. Others will undertake analysis with receptive but generally normal people if they are intelligent and sufficiently motivated. Of course, the nature of the transference differs with the type and degree of the difficulties present in each individual. It will be more infantile the greater the amount of libido remaining at infantile stages of development; and less so the more truly sexually mature the personality.

In order to preserve the purity of the transference, Freud insisted that his patients know next to nothing about him. He never saw his patients outside of the analytical hour, insisted that they lie down (relaxation also facilitates free association), sat himself in a chair behind their head and out of view, and furnished his consulting room with ancient carvings that he himself loved but that probably had little if any meaning for his patients and revealed little at all about Freud himself. Not knowing him, they could not react to him objectively but rather totally *projectively*—that is, they could only project their early

impulses toward their father or mother onto him, and thus relive and rework the Oedipal relationship without any of the social constraints of reality.

This establishment of distance also keeps the analyst from becoming emotionally aroused—such conduct is what Freud called *countertransference,* in which the therapist's reactions and responses to the patient are determined by his personal emotions rather than by his medical and psychoanalytical training. In order that his students would be less likely to practice countertransference, Freud insisted that each of them undergo their own psychoanalysis so that they would have a minimum of residual irrational impulses and affects to project onto their patients. The analyst's own rationality and objectivity is of maximum importance because transference is a *very highly* emotional experience. The patient's defenses are down, the anxiety is potentially overwhelming, and a grown man or woman is intimately relating to the essentially unknown analyst as he or she once related to the parent in childhood. Transference is the crucial phenomenon in analysis, and its interpretation and resolution provide the key to success.

R. W. White, in *The Abnormal Personality,** has provided us with a very simple but nevertheless instructive example of transference:

> *Mr. Phillips entered analysis as his marriage was breaking up because of his arrogant and hostile need to control everyone and everything around him. He had been divorced once before for the same reason, but had subsequently remarried the same woman. He was a very successful businessman, having taken over his father's concern and enlarged it even beyond what his father had been able to do.*
>
> *The father had been an overbearing, arrogant, and ruthless man who had continually dominated and intimidated his son. The son reacted by striving to outdo the*

---

*Third edition. New York: Ronald, 1964.

father in each of these personality characteristics, as well as in business. It appeared that he had been quite successful.

Very early in the therapy Phillips continually baited the analyst and attempted to draw him into his habitual hostile mode of interacting with other human beings. The analyst instead reacted with such mildness and realistic but low-keyed friendliness that it was immediately apparent to the patient how bizarre, unrealistic, and unnecessary his hostile approach and his baiting had been. Here, the transference worked ideally although simply. Faced early with the realization of the irrationality of his behavior, Phillips was able, in the course of three or four months, to evolve a more normal social relationship with the therapist as an intellectual and human equal. Having found out that such a reciprocal relationship was possible, Phillips was able to establish similar, more meaningful relationships within his family, replacing the dictatorial atmosphere that had prevailed, and his marriage was saved.

The Phillips case is an exceptional one in that the neurotic symptoms, generated originally in interaction with the father, were easily transferred to the therapist because they were continuing as open modes of social functioning for the adult Phillips. In most analyst-patient relationships, however, transference is not achieved as readily, nor is the impact on the patient as immediate and obvious.

Insight   Psychoanalysis is as much a process of education as it is one of self-revelation and self-discovery. Throughout the treatment, the analyst points out the infantile roots of the patient's oral and anal traits (see the section "Psychosexual Development" in Chapter 24) and of his ways of dealing with the world. Both patient and analyst are constantly concentrating on the repressed material that is at the root of the patient's symptoms. In his interpretations, the analyst guides the patient toward the nature of the infantile amnesia and of his unconscious tendencies. If analysis is successful, the

patient at some point experiences *insight*—a sudden recognition that the ways in which he copes with the world have a common cause and that the cause is real, though infantile and unconscious. Insight does not occur in the initial stages of analysis: in the long process leading up to it, the analyst continues to point out the consistencies in the patient's problems, and the patient reflects on the interpretations that are offered, and even agonizes over them. Then suddenly the patient's entire outlook on himself and his world gels somehow—it is as if the missing piece to a puzzle appears—and the patient perceives a new opportunity for effective and productive interaction with the world around him. Insight is typified by a surging sense of well-being, usually followed by recall of a previously repressed infantile experience that confirms the recently fused picture. In this way, psychoanalytical progress is made.

Transference is important in facilitating insight, because the patient sees the analyst as he has always imagined his own parents to have been, and he behaves accordingly. When this behavior becomes so patently ridiculous that even the patient can recognize its irrationality (aided by the analyst's interpretations of that behavior), insight comes more easily, recall of repressed experience is facilitated, and eventual cure is more imminent.

Cure   A cure is a substantial increase in productivity in the patient's life after analysis. An adult is not unhappy simply because he had an unhappy childhood, but rather because he still employs childhood means of gratification. Analysis enables the person to realize the inadequacy of such gratification, and so opens the way for new and more effective ways of behaving. If the neurosis is simple, as is a phobia, then the loss of it alone can produce a cure. But most neuroses are much more complex, and the ways that a neurotic has been interacting with the world must be replaced with new ones. Whether or not the new ways are productive largely determines whether or not cure is permanent.

During analysis, the defenses are gradually dropped and material rises from the unconscious. The ego discovers that this previously suppressed material does not arouse anxiety, and so concludes that the defenses are not needed. The ego therefore discards the defenses and goes on with life. Freer than before, the person has an enhanced *potential* for happiness rather than ready-made and automatic happiness.

Viewed from another perspective, analysis leads to conflicts between the patient's habitual ways of behaving, feeling, and thinking and what is realistic and appropriate in his interaction with the analyst. It is the job of the analyst to point out these conflicts and to interpret them. It is up to the patient to struggle for the insight into his own functioning that facilitates the recovery of repressed material and the accompanying emotions that constitute catharsis. His goal is to *work through* the material successfully, that is, to confront the same conflicts again and again under the analyst's supervision until he can confront and resolve them independently in real life. If he does so, the symptoms that caused him to seek the analyst in the first place should disappear.

At this point, it is time to end the relationship between analyst and patient. The process of termination is the final trying period in the therapeutic relationship, which has been an extremely close and emotional one. In this concluding stage, the analyst assists the patient in a *reintegration* of the elements of the analyzed personality, helping him to develop new ways of behaving to replace the earlier and limiting ones, which analysis has taught the patient to relinquish. Again, productivity, success, and happiness are not automatically guaranteed. Consequently, the analyst must anticipate and take steps to avert the phenomena of *relapse* and *symptom substitution*, both of which indicate that analysis is incomplete and should be continued.

Relapse Relapse often occurs as a reaction to the *separation anxiety* evoked by the prospects of ending the analytical relationship. Some of this is normal anxiety—based on the patient's genuine doubts that he can live his own life without the triweekly visits to the analyst. Often, though, neurotic anxiety, consisting of irrational fears of separation itself, appears at this stage. This type of reaction is an indication that analysis has been incomplete, and that additional significant material is still repressed, making it impossible for the ego to cease depending on the therapist. Whether this is a result of an incomplete working through of the transference—the patient still behaves like a child who fears a parent's departure—or whether it arises from not yet analyzed infantile modes of functioning must be determined by further analysis.

Symptom Substitution According to Freud, symptom substitution is another indication that a patient's neurotic anxiety is not yet completely discharged. In symptom substitution, the original symptom has disappeared, but another has appeared to take its place. For example, suppose a patient's obsession with clean hands disappears after analysis has traced it to a repressed experience that had occurred during the anal period; if it is then replaced with an obsessive interest in an orderly hair style, this substitution means that the libidinal energy that was fixated at the anal stage has not yet been fully discharged. Sometimes such substitution occurs because more than one experience has been repressed; the accomplished analyst knows when to keep digging for more material. Sometimes the cause is a failure to experience the emotional content of the recalled material; but again, if the analyst is an accomplished one, he will have already prepared the way for the emotional catharsis by the time the repressed material is brought to the surface. Indeed, to recall traumatic and frightening events from childhood without undergoing emotion is itself quite abnormal and requires its own special analysis. More recently, the actuality of symptom substitution has been challenged by the school of behavior therapists, whose ideas we shall examine in Chapter 32.

Freud published individual case studies of several analyses that he himself had performed. These stage-by-stage summaries of select cases, emphasizing the high points of each, are excellent supplementary readings on the intricacies of Freudian theory and analysis. For specific suggestions, read Freud's own works listed in the Suggested Readings.

Suggested Readings

Ford, D. N., & Urban, H. B. (1963) *Systems of psychotherapy*. New York: Wiley. [Decent and sympathetic treatment of Freudians, and all others.]

Freud, S. (1965) *New introductory lectures on psychoanalysis*. (2nd ed.) (Translated and edited by J. Strachey.) New York: Norton. [An excellent reference.]

Freud, S. (1938) *A general introduction to psychoanalysis*. (2nd ed.) (Translated by J. Rivière.) New York: Liveright. [The master's own description, for a general audience and in his own marvelous prose, which survives translation. A classic, do not miss.]

Thompson, C. (1950) *Psychoanalysis, evolution, and development*. New York: Hermitage House. [Spare and lean but pointed and ultrareadable prose. A fine account of its subject.]

Wolman, B. B., ed. (1967) *Psychoanalytic techniques*. New York: Basic Books. [A collection of essays on analysis, intended for the practicing therapist, but useful to the serious student.]

CHAPTER THIRTY-ONE

Humanistic Therapy and Group Therapy

In this chapter we shall examine two kinds of psychotherapy: the humanistic and various group therapies. The humanistic approach places emphasis on the importance of the human being and on the subjective human experience: indeed, it is one of the few therapies that an individual can perform, to a limited extent, on himself, with the aid of a good book on the subject. Its purpose is to make the subject aware of that which is naturally human in everyone. In the various forms of group therapy, participants derive help and support from one another as well as from the psychologist or therapist who is leading the group. Certainly, groups do not necessarily endorse the humanistic approach, nor does humanistic therapy require a group. However, we shall see that the two have much in common—in theory, practical application, goals, and even historical precursors.

SELF-THEORIES

Underlying humanistic therapy is *self-theory*, the culmination of the development of ego theory (Chapter 25). In the therapeutic literature of the 1940s, self-theory was described and developed

chiefly by Carl Rogers. The Rogerian concept of self is more comprehensive than the Freudian ego because it comprises portions of the id and the superego as well. Rogers added to the motivational structure of Freudian theory by introducing the ideas of the innate goodness of the self, its natural potential, and its desire for knowledge and healthy growth. The crux of his theory is that everyone tends to grow and expand as a natural matter of course, but what is of vital importance to an individual is that he become aware of his own potential for growth. Such awareness is as important to the self as is awareness of the various aspects of its current external situation.

It is the nature of the self to be whole and integrated. However, for various reasons—ignorance, anxiety, fear of other people's disapproval, fear of its own disapproval—the self may reject part of itself. What is most important, then, according to Rogers, is an uncritical recognition by the self of its own dissociated thoughts or feelings. Once these elements are uncritically recognized, the normal self accepts and incorporates them as a natural process, and grows as a consequence. The ideal state of normal self-awareness is that in which the entire self is perceived by the self and integrated into its favorable and balanced opinion of itself. In comparison to the Freudian concentration on the obscure depths of the unconscious, or to the behaviorist emphasis on the necessity of repeated learning experiences for personality formation and development, self theory is founded on the assumption that a human being is undergoing the healthy and natural process of increasing his understanding of himself and developing his personality and potentialities as much as possible. Consequently it has been welcomed by many in the field of psychology as a fresh and productive approach.

THE ROGERIAN THERAPIST

Rogers developed his therapeutic technique concurrently with his theory of human nature and functioning. He called it _client-centered therapy_, emphasizing that it was the patient who did the work of discovering and accepting previously dissociated parts of himself. This technique can be described as "nondirective," since the client is not told what to do or what to believe by the therapist but rather is permitted to uncover his own thoughts and feelings in his own time (Figure 31.1).

In the sessions with the therapist, the patient talks about himself. He begins to make important discoveries about himself—to become aware of his real feelings and thoughts, rather than what he tells himself he feels or thinks. Once he sees that there is really nothing wrong about those thoughts and feelings that he had previously concealed or ignored, he accepts them and can integrate them into his view of himself, growing as a result.

The Rogerian therapist's function is markedly different from that in other forms of therapy: his primary task is to reflect the client's own content and feelings without supplementing or interpreting them. If the client says, "I am anxious around people," the

Figure 31.1
Rogerian therapy.

therapist will not deny it or offer an interpretation, but reflect it, and perhaps seek further clarification from the client: "You feel that people make you anxious. All people?" In his reply—for example, "No, only certain kinds of people, I guess"—the client begins to probe himself, to disclose his real feelings so that he can see for himself what they truly are. The therapist acts as a mirror in which the client sees what he is describing about himself and by means of which he can correct the image if it is not accurate. The therapist continues to encourage the client, responding in an affirmative but noncommittal way in order to make it as easy as possible for him to keep on describing himself. In short, the therapist adopts an attitude of _unconditional positive regard_, accepting whatever the client presents without question or reservation, while continuing to reflect it. The theory is that the dissociated elements of the self have been cast off because of either social or self disapproval, and that this can be corrected by letting them surface and be accepted in the unconditionally positive atmosphere established during the therapy sessions.

Thus, the therapist does not allow himself to be drawn into the superficial content of the material the client presents. For example, if the client says, "I feel very different from everyone else on campus," it would be inappropriate to reply, "I'm surprised. You seem like the typical college student to me." Rather, the therapist must reflect the feeling, perhaps responding, "You feel that you should be more like others in some way?", so that the patient can clarify his own feelings. Similarly, Rogers has cited the example of the student who complained to his therapist about the bad grades he had received, protesting that they were not indicative of his true ability. Again, the therapist would have to avoid responding to the *verbal* content, for example, by asking what grades the individual had received; rather he would attempt to reflect the *emotional* content of the remark, so that the person could clarify for himself his reactions to his grades.

The Rogerian technique is particularly suitable for maladies that are due to inaccurate and self-negating interpretations of current daily experiences, the interpretations arising out of an insufficient awareness of one's own personality. Perhaps the most common example is the person who represents himself in the way others, such as his parents, always wanted him to be, but who in fact is personally quite different. Thus the treatment of many disturbed individuals comes down to a resolution of the conflict between false egos and the real ego— between what I think I am, what others want me to be, and what I really am. Sooner or later, almost everyone is confronted by this kind of identity crisis, but individuals differ greatly in their ways of meeting it: some assert themselves as they really are without regard to conflicting socializing influences, some deny their own feelings entirely and allow their behavior

to be governed by the wishes (real or imagined) of other people, and some confront the conflict anew daily. The Rogerian therapist encourages the client to express each part of his self, the real and the socially derived. By reflecting what the client says and appears to feel, he facilitates the person's identification of his true self and his acceptance of that self.

CONTRIBUTING THEORISTS

Although Rogers has been the primary spokesman for this point of view, others in psychology have also contributed to this movement, and we shall discuss a few of them briefly. Even though their therapeutic techniques depart from the nondirective mold, their concepts of man's basic nature and the possibilities for human growth are akin to the Rogerian ideas.

Self-Actualization Abraham Maslow contributed heavily to the theory of human growth with two notions—*nested motivation* and *self-actualization*. He believed that human motives are *nested* in a hierarchical order; thus a person is always motivated, but by higher-order motives as the lower-order motives are satisfied. The basics of survival are motives of the lowest order and receive one's primary attention if they are not satisfied. But once one has food, water, warmth, and shelter, attention moves on to sex, affiliation, achievement, and competition. Having successfully achieved in these areas, the person becomes motivated to make contributions that will benefit others. At the top of the hierarchy is the need to grow—to actualize, or make real, the breadth and depth of one's human potentialities. Such *self-actualization*, Maslow maintained, is the highest and most noble of all motives. He never developed his own therapy, but he influenced others who, in their own therapies, applied the belief that people should be freed from lower-order motives so that they can work toward self-actualization.

Gestalt Therapy　Fritz Perls developed a holistic theory, based on the gestalt school of thought (see Chapter 14). He believed that the integration of the whole person is primary, and that abnormality consists not of certain kinds of actions or thoughts but rather of not committing the whole self to the action or thought. The goal of his therapy, too, was enhanced self-awareness, and the basic underlying idea is the following: what you want to do is good, because you are you; therefore accept yourself and do what you want, but with total commitment. For example, if a person was faced with anxiety over masturbation, he might be advised not to cease masturbating but rather to put his total self into it, so that he derived maximum enjoyment from the orgasm. Perls was among the first of the humanistic psychologists.

Logotherapy　Another important contributor to the humanistic influence on modern psychology is Viktor Frankl, the originator of *logotherapy*. Frankl wrote that *logos* is the search for meaning that rules a person's life. Mental illness occurs when the search for meaning is thwarted or unsuccessful. Logotherapy, like most other humanistic therapies, stresses the *present* existence of the patient. The only past experiences that are drawn upon are those that the patient decides are relevant enough to mention as he tries, with the therapist, to understand and find meaning in his present life. It is interesting that Frankl developed his ideas while interred in the concentration camp at Auschwitz by the German government during World War II. In these surroundings, he searched within himself for a meaning to life that would justify continuing to live under such miserable circumstances.

Other theorists have been concerned with the necessity for a compassionate relationship between the therapist and the patient. Still others were in-terested in the balance between freedom and responsibility, emphasizing that freedom was the essence of mental health. But, they recognized, if one is to be truly free, he must be able to accept responsibility, and responsibility creates anxiety, which in turn limits the individual's ability to take advantage of freedom. In all of these approaches mental health turns out to require a controlled but uncontrived balance.

Conclusion　The foregoing ideas on growth, self-actualization, holistic participation, and meaning have all been substantial contributions to the area of psychotherapy. The problems of identity, commitment, and continued motivation to live and work beset the young, the middle-aged, and the old alike. The concepts of humanistic psychology can be applied therapeutically to aid a wide variety of people in their efforts to adjust themselves to their surroundings or to those changes that are an affliction of life itself: thus the client might be a child trying to make a meaningful place for himself in the family, an adolescent searching for adult identity, a youth avoiding commitment and the accompanying risk of failure, a successful forty-year-old businessman wondering what to do with his life next, or an old person anticipating nothing but death.

Rogerian thought emphasizes that the prerequisite to effective adjustment to the current reality is the recognition that the situation does exist and, more important, that the self has real and acceptable feelings about it. The late American socialist, Norman Thomas, at the age of eighty, revealed his self-awareness and self-acceptance when he remarked, in the breaking voice of the very aged, "I'm a horrible old wreck, and I *hate* it! But I can still *think* and *enjoy* it." Maslow would have admired Thomas as a self-actualizing person, just as he would have admired a successful middle-aged corporation

Figure 31.2
Group therapy.

executive who proceeded to expand his knowledge and potential and to work toward the betterment of his community. Perls would have emphasized the need for total immersion in any new activity: thus, both the adolescent, who plays hard, and the middle-aged employee, who begins again to work as hard as he can at doing his job as best he can, derive renewed energy for the real purposes of living. And meaning, though often hard to find, can in reality be found anywhere.

GROUP THERAPY

Throughout the history of man, people have joined together in groups for a mutually beneficial purpose. In many of these groups the motive has been basically psychological—perhaps merely to change the attitudes of the members toward something or someone. But the formation of groups of people for the express purposes of mutual psychotherapy is a quite recent development (Figure 31.2).

THE ORIGINS OF GROUPS

The origins of group therapy can be traced to the followers of Kurt Lewin, whose major ideas about personality we reviewed very briefly in Chapter 25. They established a Psychological Training Center in Maine for the purpose of exposing groups of business executives to the principles of social psychology (as formulated by Lewin) and to the practical applications of these principles in real groups. The hope was that such training would make the executives better managers by providing them with a

Figure 31.3
Group training for business executives.

deeper understanding of people and of interpersonal relationships and conflicts (Figure 31.3). Apparently, large corporations have found such training highly productive, if the persistence with which they continue to pay the large enrollment fees for many of their key personnel is any indication.

The formation of groups as we know them today, for therapeutic reasons alone, received a great boost in Chicago in the late 1940s, just after World War II. Thousands of returning veterans were in need of counseling, and it was necessary to train large numbers of counselors to meet the demand. Carl Rogers experimented with training them in groups, a primary purpose being to enhance the trainees' own self-awareness and sensitivity to others. His efforts were so successful that he extended his method to psychotherapy itself. Group therapy was

especially appropriate for returning veterans, Rogers thought, since they all had just come from similar dehumanizing experiences, all shared common problems and misgivings, and all faced a major behavioral shift from a destructive role to one of productivity, personal enjoyment, and fulfillment.

The group trend peaked in the late 1960s. Serious therapeutic groups continue to be used, but much of the popular experimentation with small groups has been abandoned.

TYPES OF THERAPEUTIC GROUPS

The purposes for which a therapeutic group is formed differs from group to group. Some of the most well-publicized groups have been those created to rehabilitate drug addicts, such as the groups conducted by Synanon. Two other groups that, like Synanon, exist for the purpose of helping their members overcome common problems of adjustment

Figure 31.4
An Alcoholics Anonymous meeting. [Courtesy of
Alcoholics Anonymous]

are Alcoholics Anonymous, organized to help its
members combat alcoholism (Figure 31.4), and
Weight Watchers, organized to conquer compulsive
overeating. In all three groups, the general principles
of operation are the same: members share established goals; social support is derived from other
members; a strong group spirit of competition
motivates members to observe the rules and attain
the goals; and alternative activities are provided.
We can conclude that in order for such groups to
succeed in solving common problems, they must
provide their members with common goals, support,
motivation, and replacement activities. Apathy,
aimlessness, and loneliness are drawbacks that such
groups are well equipped to counteract.

Some groups are composed of the mentally
retarded or the mentally ill, who may benefit from

structured communal association under the expert
supervision of a psychologist skilled not only in their
special problems but also in the special intricacies of
group behavior and interaction. The majority of
groups, however, consist of normal people who have
sought group therapy for various reasons. For
example, some are families who benefit from
discussion of mutual problems under the guidance
of a specialist in family matters. Many other groups
consist of diverse individuals, strangers at the start,
who enroll in the psychologist's group because they
feel that the developing experience of the group
will help them to lead more normal and productive
lives.

The various types of therapy groups differ in
numerous ways. The *size* of the group may vary from
the members of a family plus a therapist to groups
of twenty or thirty. *Duration* varies as well, although
most groups in general are of shorter duration than
other forms of therapeutic relationships. Some
groups—the *ongoing* groups—meet regularly for a year
or more, but many more are formed only for a short
period of social self-exploration. Among the ongoing
groups, it is common for the membership to fluctuate
from time to time: some members drop out, new
ones join the group, and members skip meetings for
one reason or another. The most common type of
group is not ongoing. It consists of half a dozen
people, plus one therapist, and it meets for a few
days, usually a long weekend.

Groups differ in their *procedural flexibility*. Some
therapists have a fixed routine that all members of
the group observe: they begin by introducing themselves in turn, and then relate their impressions of
themselves or others, reveal their fears, and analyze
their own and others' expressions. Other groups are
totally unstructured, having no set procedure whatsoever, and the members merely interact with each
other and with the therapist, who participates as

Figure 31.5
Some therapists encourage a degree of physical intimacy among the members of a group.

a somewhat more experienced and enlightened but coequal member of the group. Most groups are in between the two extremes, with the therapist unobtrusively leading the members toward their goal by the channels that happen to present themselves as the group's dynamics—the various individual behaviors and resulting interactions—unfold.

The therapist always acts as the group's *leader*, if only because the majority of the members will *ascribe* a *leadership role* to him whether or not he wishes it. Within the group, other leaders emerge unless the therapist strongly discourages this tendency. Some are *natural* leaders, in that the group willingly follows their lead; others are *bully* leaders who wrest power from others and try to compel obedience by issuing orders, badgering, persuading, or ridiculing. In well-conducted groups, such leaders are allowed to emerge so that all the members of the group can see and analyze what is taking place and why. In fact, this kind of takeover is one area of interpersonal relations in which a member's individual social style can emerge most clearly.

Groups differ greatly in the degree of *intimacy* that is allowed or encouraged among its members. Naturally some intimacy is necessary, since therapy cannot proceed without some self-revelation. In some task-oriented groups—for example, a group of

executives striving for human sensitivity—intimacy may be limited to discussions of common problems occurring in business, personal problems, and perhaps family relationships. In other groups, deep psychological intimacy is encouraged, and each member describes his own deepest feelings and worries, as he views them, in great detail. Still other leaders encourage social intimacy. Members, after becoming initially acquainted with one another, dissect each other's interpersonal styles, often mercilessly, and thereby unconsciously reveal aspects of themselves. Some leaders believe that physical intimacy encourages the awareness that will promote therapeutic developments. Members are therefore encouraged to touch and hug each other (Figure 31.5), to rely on each other to lead them around blindfolded or support them in a swimming pool, to reveal themselves physically by taking off as much of their clothing as they comfortably can. In some of these groups, nudity is a preliminary goal: the therapist does not allow members to discuss problems or express criticism of others in the group until they all feel comfortable among themselves totally naked (Figure 31.6).

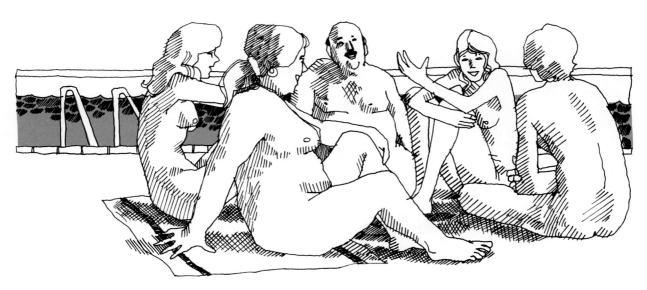

Figure 31.6
Some therapists employ nudity to establish a feeling of mutual acceptance in a group.

A final difference between types of groups is the extent to which *participation* is required—the degree to which the therapist himself personally digs for material from the members, or structures the sessions to force the revelation of material. Indeed, in some of the highly structured groups, the therapist actively encourages all members to participate as deeply and intimately as they can, often more than is really comfortable. In the unstructured groups, the degree of participation by individual members varies: some members are judged by the other members as too quiet or withdrawn, and others are inevitably regarded as too outgoing, personally expressive, or outright bossy. Many groups seem naturally to find direct and indirect ways to bring out the withdrawn members and to silence the overbearing ones.

The Marathon Group Certain groups differ from the others in that they have a specific orientation not common to most therapeutic groups. Such is the *marathon group*, whose members seem to undergo therapy by exhausting themselves socially and physically. They are in constant social contact with each other for as long as forty-eight hours, taking only periodic cat naps to sustain themselves. The theory is that the exhaustion and continued contact will cause a person's true feelings about others and about himself to become evident, both to himself and to others. In addition, one's original anxiety about the prospects of solitude changes to a sense of relief after prolonged social exposure.

The Psychodrama Group One of the most interesting types of groups is that formed specifically for the purpose of enacting plays and dramas of therapeutic significance. Originated by Moreno, *psychodrama groups* have proved very successful, especially with children. It has been found that people often gain insights into their own behavior and motivation if they *act out* their roles or the roles of

Figure 31.7
In psychodrama groups, members act out situations in their lives.

others close to them (Figure 31.7). Thus a worker obtains a more realistic impression of the conflicts experienced by the boss if he acts out the role for half an hour or so, just as the boss experiences, however transiently, the dependence and uncertainty of a subordinate by adopting his role. Also, significant insight into the problems of a troubled child has come from watching him play-act as another sibling, and from listening to his own reactions to what he himself does in the play.

The members of a psychodrama group can also gain insight into themselves by watching someone else imitate them. In the course of an innocent psychodramatic production, they learn how they are seen by others. In family therapy, for example, it is interesting and usually very informative to assign the parts of the mother and father to the daughter and son, and vice versa. If the members of the family are encouraged to reverse roles in this way "just for fun," parents and children reveal with a minimum of constraint what they think and feel are the attitudes and motives of the others. Additional information is obtained by direct questioning of the actors. For example, a son may be asked why he did a certain thing when playing his father. His answer may reveal what he thinks his father's motives to be.

THE THERAPEUTIC PROCEDURE IN GROUPS

If group therapy is to be effective, a standard procedure or sequence of events must necessarily take place, even among widely variant groups. A group is founded on the basic assumption that a participant wants to change himself or his life in some way for the better. The initial event is the exposure of the person to an unfamiliar and somewhat alien social situation. Even if the group consists of the members of a family, the presence of the therapist adds an element of unfamiliarity, since the usual family relations must now be enacted in the presence of a stranger. The unfamiliarity makes it easier for the person to examine his social relationships and his feelings about people, because new relationships are necessarily formed in a group.

Although most of these new relationships are not as intense as that between analyst and patient, the interactions that can occur are similar to some aspects of the psychoanalytic transference in that they make it possible for the individual to recognize what is unrealistic in his relationships to members of the group and thus to his world in general. The tendency to examine social feelings and styles is enhanced by the person's desire for change in his life. This wish motivates the member to follow the therapist's instructions in the hope that the group experience will enable him to uncover the formula for a happier and more sensitive existence.

In the group, each member reveals aspects of the self, including those aspects that have been molded by social contact with other people. With the help of the therapist and other members of the group, the member examines these aspects, trying to understand them and reincorporate them into a new, more aware, and effective self. The assumption is that people have become so accustomed to concealing and ignoring their own feelings in their efforts to conform to the approved and appropriate behavior for various social situations, that they have forgotten how to respond to their own emotions or the emotions of others. Thus the reawakening of emotional sensations is of fundamental importance. Members are encouraged to develop genuine feelings toward the others: indeed, such emotional reactions need not be positive, for recognizing and understanding negative feelings toward another is also thought to be part of the growth process. They are also encouraged to develop reciprocal caring relationships with others in the group, to be genuinely concerned about *their* feelings and problems. It is believed that if members can learn to be aware of their own feelings again and to feel and express genuine concern for others, attaining a deeper self-understanding in the process, then the group will have been a success.

THE STAGES OF GROUP INTERACTION

Let us now examine the separate stages of group dynamics, many of which occur not only in the course of group therapy but in almost every other type of group interaction as well. These stages are the initial arrival and meeting, the "icebreaking," the acquisition of new information, the challenge, justification, reconciliation, and departure.

The first stage in the group's existence is the initial meeting. The members see each other for the first time, when mutual expectations are either fulfilled or disappointed, and learn each other's names. Society has neatly provided us with the institution of the *introduction* to cope with the initiation of an intragroup relationship. In fact, one of the primary functions of a therapy group is to make the member aware of just how much of his life is controlled by what society has provided, and how little of it is directed by what he really wants and feels. Such awareness is the first step in the development of a more meaningful personal existence.

"Icebreaking" is an all-encompassing term for the various ways that groups have for putting members at ease and initiating group rapport. In those groups that have come together for strictly social reasons, icebreaking is done in a variety of ways, such as a reference to a mutual friend or a topic of common public interest. In most therapeutic groups, however, one of the aims is to avoid the prescribed formulas of behavior that dominate typical social situations. In many groups, therefore, the icebreaker is the leader's initial instructions to the members. For example, the members may be required to give specified factual information about themselves plus a brief description of what they think are their best and worst personality traits. Or the leader may attempt to establish a degree of interpersonal intimacy by instructing members to hug each other: this device is commonly employed by those therapists who emphasize the use of physical contact to express feelings of caring.

The *acquisition of new information* is a natural outcome of observation and experience, whereas the *challenge* is a reaction to the new information that is available for incorporation into the self. What the person acquires is information about the feelings and reactions of other members of the group toward him and, as a result, new knowledge about himself. It is the revelations about the self, and others' feelings toward the self, that is challenged: if the news is welcome, the self asks whether it is valid; if it is disappointing or frustrating, it attempts to change or evade it; if the reaction is meaningless, the challenge is to find out what it means. The leader helps members to answer another's challenges by aiding and encouraging everyone to communicate effectively with each other on these issues.

Justification is the response to a challenge that provides added information and supporting reasons. From the interplay of learning, challenging, justifying, and additional learning comes *reconciliation*, the process whereby the new recognitions are incorporated into the member's revised view of himself and his world. The clever therapist facilitates this process by arranging and designing his own questions and actions in such a way that the members encounter situations within the group that reveal the consistencies between their previous and newly acquired knowledge of themselves.

Departure is the final, but nevertheless important, phase of group activity. In groups that meet only once, such as for a weekend, it is obviously important that a therapeutic reconciliation take place within each member before he departs. One potential danger of group therapy, particularly short-term therapy, is that one's inadequacies will be revealed or pointed out (perhaps even erroneously) and not be reconciled, leaving the departing member with more uncertainties about himself and his competence than he had upon arrival. In groups that will meet again or regularly, the therapist wants each member to depart with a therapeutic goal to work on by himself in his day-to-day living between group meetings. Any therapeutic effects of the group on the individual are minor indeed if limited only to his functioning and interactions within *that* group alone.

PERMANENCE OF GROUP EFFECTS

Groups obviously provide the member with novel experiences, and many of them offer chances for engaging in new modes of behavior: they can be trying, dull, anxious, stimulating, relaxing, or fun. But do they have any permanent effects on an individual member after he leaves the group? The answer depends on both the group itself and the individual.

Groups can bring about change in two fundamental ways: either by enhancing such qualities as self-awareness or sensitivity within the individual; or by providing the member with a social skill, such as the ability to feel and manifest concern for the needs and feelings of others. These new qualities or skills can permanently influence the individual in his day-to-day living if he can transfer them from the unique atmosphere of the group to his normal environment. Such transferral is not simple, though, because groups do not change the environment to which a member returns. If the conditions that produced the member's original ways of behaving are strong enough, the original behavior may be rapidly reinstated. (For example, the spouse who returns home from a group with a greater sensitivity to the needs and feelings of the opposite sex may be confronted by the same behavior from the mate that produced the decline in sensitivity in the first place.)

Similarly, an acquired social skill that proved quite adequate, competent, and satisfying within the structured confines of the group can seem affected, insincere, too intense, or needlessly self-revealing in conventional social interaction, and therefore it fails to help the person at all. For these as well as other reasons, some group therapists concentrate only on trying to increase self-awareness and sensitivity. Others insist that group therapy can be successful only for previously established units, such as the family, because only then does the necessary continuity exist between the supportive atmosphere established in the group and the real-life situation to which the individual will be exposed again after therapy is terminated.

People come to need therapy for a variety of reasons—lack of experience, unfortunate past experiences, or failure to develop personally or socially. The potential effectiveness of groups lies in the possibilities they offer for providing useful experiences that teach, allow development, and undo the effects of an unhappy past by replacing it with a fulfilling and meaningful present.

Suggested Readings

Frankl, V. E. (1962) *Man's search for meaning: an introduction to logotherapy.* (Translated by R. Lasch) Boston: Beacon Press. [The American debut of Frankl's provocative therapeutic ideas.]

Perls, F., Hefferline, R. F., & Goodman, P. (1951) *Gestalt therapy.* New York: Julian Press. [Regrettably overlooked statement of the gestalt approach, with many surprisingly useful ideas about everyday problems.]

Reisman, J. M. (1966) *The development of clinical psychology.* New York: Appleton, Century, Crofts. [A survey, but good on the background and current status of the schools of therapy.]

Rogers, C. R. (1961) *On becoming a person: a therapist's view of psychotherapy.* Boston: Houghton Mifflin. [The client-centered therapist's best statement of his beliefs.]

Schutz, W. (1967) *Joy: expanding human awareness.* New York: Grove Press. [The door-opener to the enjoyment-of-life therapies. Mildly scandalous when it appeared, it has survived our tests of readability and significance.]

Yalom, I. D. (1970) *The theory and practice of group psychotherapy.* New York: Basic Books. [Authoritative account of the serious side of grouping for therapy.]

CHAPTER THIRTY-TWO

Behavior Therapy

A thirty-seven-year-old woman resisted eating to such an extent that her weight had plummeted from 120 to 47 pounds in the course of several years. By the time psychotherapeutic treatment was sought, she was in imminent danger of dying from malnutrition. Since there was no time for the kind of extended treatment that most forms of psychotherapy require, a new kind of therapy was tried in which a team of therapists concentrated on treating the symptom—refusing to eat—rather than trying to uncover and treat any underlying problem. The therapists did not attempt to determine the source of her behavior, nor did they make any inferences or interpretations about her condition. They decided to apply the principles of operant conditioning (Chapter 4) in an attempt to alter the woman's eating behavior before it was too late.

The first step was to induce a response (eating) by selecting appropriate reinforcers (other than food, which would obviously be unsatisfactory). Among the pastimes that the woman enjoyed were conversing with people, listening to music, reading, and watching television. Therefore, the therapist made these reinforcers dependent upon eating behavior:

when the patient did not eat, she was kept in a fairly barren room and did not have any of the reinforcers available. For example, nurses who had to come into the room to perform essential duties were instructed not to speak or otherwise pay attention to the patient. At meal times, a therapist came in with a tray of food and sat silently with her, rewarding her by talking to her if she merely touched her fork (Figure 32.1). Applying the method of successive approximations, or "shaping" (Chapter 4), the therapist reinforced responses that progressively approximated the desired behavior (eating). The behavioral requirement was successively raised from (1) touching her fork, to (2) lifting it, and finally to (3) inserting food into her mouth. That is, the requirement for obtaining social reinforcement was gradually stiffened until the patient had to eat in order to obtain reinforcement. In addition to providing the patient with companionship, other acts of reinforcement were wheeling in the television set and turning on the phonograph. Later she was given permission to go outside, to receive special visitors, and to eat socially with other patients. Since all these reinforcers depended on the patient's eating, she

Figure 32.1
When the patient touched her fork, the therapist
rewarded her by speaking (see the text).

began to gain weight. But after a period of time,
her weight gain suddenly stopped. It was discovered
that after eating, she was intentionally vomiting.
For this reason, the behavioral requirement was
changed again, and in order for her to receive continued reinforcement, some gain in weight had to
be registered periodically on the scale. As a result,
her weight began to increase once more. She was
soon released in good health, weighing a reasonable
83 pounds. Follow-up studies indicated that she
continued to maintain her weight gain. Her family
was given some advice on operant-conditioning techniques so that meal time continued to be a reinforcing occasion for the patient in her home
environment.

Notice that the woman was cured without reference to her past history. In fact, the therapists
avoided any talk about her background so that the
effects of reinforcement would not be confounded
by any potential effects of "working through" the
problem. Later they did learn something of the

history and the causes of the woman's problem. The
patient had been extremely overweight as a child,
and attempts to lose weight had been reinforced
by her family and friends. As a result she adjusted
her eating habits so much that she became thin. In
time she married, but the marriage was a deeply
unhappy one. She continued to curtail her eating
until a doctor finally told her that she was much
too thin and that if she lost any more weight, he
would recommend that she return home to her
parents. Her weight dropped at once, and she went
back home. Although she surely would have denied
it, her weight loss and her continued resistance to
eating seemed to be her means of escape from the
unhappy marriage. Furthermore, whereas the weight
loss had previously been reinforced by social
appreciation of her trim figure, it was now reinforced
by the concern manifested by family, friends, and
doctors because of her refusal to eat. Thus, although
the patient's history had surely been the source of
her problem, the therapist's success in curing the
disorder without delving into that history demonstrates that "working through" is not essential for
cure.

This treatment was one of the pioneer applications of *behavior therapy*. How successful, in general,
can we expect a therapist to be if he relies only
on general laws of conditioning to eliminate symptoms without attempting to uncover the underlying
sources that have presumably caused the symptoms?
In this chapter we shall see that, since the late 1950s,
behavior therapy has burgeoned to become the most
effective therapy now available for the cure of many
types of disorders. Before discussing its principles,
applications, and therapeutic value, however, let
us point out some basic distinctions between
behavior therapy and the more conventional psychotherapies, such as psychoanalysis and client-centered
therapy.

THE ORIENTATION
OF BEHAVIOR THERAPY

First of all, behavior therapy and the conventional therapies differ significantly in underlying theory. The conventional therapist bases his clinical technique on the particular personality theory to which he subscribes. For examples, a psychoanalyst would probably embrace the Freudian theory of personality and a client-centered therapist, the Rogerian theory of self. The behavior therapist contends that personality theories simply are not necessary.

Another vitally important difference between the two is in foundation. The base of conventional therapies could be said to be philosophical, so that these forms focus on abstract concepts, such as "personality" and "will." In contrast, behavior therapy is founded on the study of behavior, and emphasizes observable and measurable phenomena—for example, the responses of a patient's muscles or the secretion of his glands.

As a consequence of these two basic differences in orientation, it follows that conventional psychotherapies emphasize the inner causes of behavior, whereas behavior therapy is concerned with the external environmental events controlling that behavior. Furthermore, the conventional therapies, particularly psychoanalysis, are concerned with the interpretation of behavior, whereas behavior therapy stresses the behavior itself and the adoption of other, more desirable responses. Finally, in the conventional psychotherapies—particularly client-centered therapy—the uniqueness of the individual is emphasized; but in behavior therapy the patient is approached as an organism governed by general laws of behavior.

In practice, much of the difference between conventional psychotherapy and behavior therapy can be reduced to a difference in strategy: the con-ventional psychotherapist tries to alter the underlying causes of the symptoms, whereas the behavior therapist treats the symptom itself. In this chapter, we shall describe some efforts of behavior therapists to remedy behavior disorders by the empirical treatment of the symptoms. We shall also discuss the concept of *symptom substitution,* the assertion that if symptoms are removed without effective treatment of their underlying cause, other symptoms may appear to replace them. Conventional psychotherapists uphold this theory, whereas behavior therapists reject it. The conventional psychotherapist believes that the symptom is the manifestation of an underlying disorder, whereas the behavior therapist believes the symptom *is* the disorder and that its removal constitutes a cure. The issue of symptom substitution is crucial to this distinction.

THE CONCEPTS OF BEHAVIOR THERAPY

Behavior therapy is the application of the principles of learning—those of Pavlovian and operant conditioning—to the modification of a patient's behavior. The techniques of behavior modification are many and varied: some are based on just one type of conditioning, others on both. (To review the basic concepts of Pavlovian and operant conditioning, see Chapters 3 and 4.)

Recall that in *Pavlovian conditioning* the unconditioned stimulus (that which normally elicits the subject's reflex, or unconditioned response) is paired with another stimulus, the conditioned stimulus. As conditioning progresses, the conditioned stimulus eventually elicits a response (the conditioned response) that is similar to the subject's unconditioned response to the unconditioned stimulus. For example, in behavior modification, Pavlovian conditioning has been applied to create conditioned but negative, or aversive, responses to stimuli that presently elicit maladaptive behaviors from the patient. Thus a technique called aversion therapy has been administered—with some success—to alcoholics by pairing the stimulus alcohol with a stimulus that is naturally aversive to the patient, such as electric shock or a nausea-inducing drug. In time, alcohol becomes so strongly associated with the painful sensation of an electric shock or with feelings of nausea that it elicits a negative response when presented alone. Pavlovian conditioning is also employed to eliminate certain undesirable responses, such as phobias (unnatural fears); in such cases, the unconditioned fear-arousing stimulus is paired with a state of deep relaxation (the relaxation can be induced in the patient by the therapist in a variety of ways). The stimulus is then presented to the subject while he is relaxed, and he becomes progressively "densensitized" to it, until he finally fears it no longer.

The therapeutic application of operant principles is exemplified by the case history of the woman who refused to eat, cited at the beginning of this chapter. Recall that in operant conditioning we are not concerned with reflex responses but with responses that are shaped and maintained with reinforcement. It is believed that if a response is reinforced, the probability of its recurrence is increased, and if it is followed by punishment the probability of its recurrence is decreased.

One of the early and dramatic applications of operant conditioning to a behavioral disorder was an attempt in the late 1950s to reinstate verbal behavior in two mute schizophrenics with the use of reinforcement. One of these patients had been mute for fourteen years, the other for nineteen. Several attempts to restore the speech of these patients by means of conventional methods had been totally unsuccessful.

The behavior therapists first had to choose a reinforcer for the desired behavior (speech), since the mute patients could not communicate their own preferences. The accidental dropping of a pencil by one of the therapists—who was treating the patient who had not spoken for nineteen years—led to an unexpected solution to this problem. As the therapist stooped to pick up the pencil, a piece of gum fell from his pocket. When the patient's eyes moved toward the gum the therapist decided to use the gum as a reinforcer. At first the subject was reinforced simply for consistently moving his eyes toward the gum. Later he was given gum only for progressive approximations to speech, such as movement of the lips and then vocalization (the patient could croak). The next approximation was the emission of recognizable words: after the therapist had vainly entreated the patient to "say gum—gum" for five sessions, the patient looked quizzically up at him and said "gum, please." He then proceeded to answer questions about his name and age. Subsequently, the subject answered other questions posed by the therapist; eventually he talked with others if they ceased their attempts to interpret his nonverbal behavior (he did not bother speaking to those who continued to reinforce the nonverbal behavior).

Treatment of the other patient was only partially successful. Again using gum as the reinforcer, therapists succeeded in teaching him to answer direct questions in certain situations, but unlike the other patient, he showed little tendency to generalize to other situations. Nonetheless, in view of the fact that he had not spoken for fourteen years, even this partial (and rapid) success was remarkable. In short, the application of simple shaping procedures was sufficient to reinstate verbal responses in both patients. Other applications of behavior therapy are more complex.

THE TECHNIQUES
OF BEHAVIOR THERAPY

The behavior therapist applies various principles of Pavlovian and operant conditioning in order to alter a patient's responses or behavior in some way— to increase adaptive behavior while decreasing or eliminating maladaptive or neurotic behavior— without attempting to interpret the behavior itself or the emotional structure of the patient. Let us now examine the most important and illuminating of his techniques.

Extinction   Behavior extinguishes when it is no longer reinforced. One of the early series of extinction treatments was conducted by Ted Ayllon and his co-workers in the psychiatric wards of a hospital in Saskatchewan, Canada. Like most of the early behavior-modification studies, these conditioning techniques were utilized only because all other efforts had failed, and the patients were therefore considered untreatable. The experimenters observed that nurses were often responsible for their patients' abnormal behaviors, because they reinforced the behaviors with attention. The experimenters successfully demonstrated that by eliminating the reinforcing attention, a wide variety of ingrained bizarre behaviors could be eliminated.

For example, one group of subjects consisted of several men known as the "rubbish collectors" because they habitually hoarded newspapers and magazines by stuffing them into their clothing. The experimenters reasoned that the hoarding was being reinforced by the attention given the subjects when they were routinely "dejunked" by the nurses several times a day. This hypothesis was confirmed when the hoarding behavior disappeared after the nurses discontinued dejunking. The hoarding behavior underwent extinction because it was no longer being reinforced by the nurses' attention. Had the nurses realized the effects of their previous behavior? In fact, they protested the efforts to disrupt the hoarding behavior. They felt that it was providing the hoarders with a needed "sense of security," and that to abolish it might cause more bizarre and less adaptive symptoms to emerge. What actually happened, however, was that once hoarding was no longer reinforced with attention, the rubbish collectors stopped hoarding newspapers and magazines and instead sat in the lounge and read them!

Stimulus Satiation   Another technique successfully employed by Ayllon's Saskatchewan group to eliminate hoarding behavior was *stimulus satiation*. The patient was a woman who had hoarded towels during nine years of hospitalization. The nurses had long since stopped trying to alter her behavior. Although they continually removed towels from the patient, the average number in her room at any given time remained between nineteen and twenty-nine. Because the removal of the towels occasioned only a slight amount of interest from the patient, the experimenters concluded that extinction (by the withholding of the nurses' attention) would not be effective; it was decided instead to utilize a program of stimulus satiation. Throughout the day, the nurses presented towels to the patient whenever she was in her room, and when she was absent they would count the number that had accumulated. The towel count rose steadily within the next several weeks until it reached 625. Then, a new behavior emerged: the patient began taking some of the towels out of the room. At this point, no more towels were delivered. In the course of the next twelve months, the average towel count stabilized at an acceptable one to five per week, with no effort at removal by the nurses. Interesting changes in the patient's verbal behavior accompanied the treatment. For example, early in the treatment the patient would be grateful when towels were brought to her and would thank the nurse. Later, however, she protested that she had enough of these "dirty towels" (a possible symptom substitution, since the towels were in fact clean).

Again, the psychiatric nurses distrusted the treatment despite its success. Like that of the rubbish collectors, this hoarding behavior was regarded as a reflection of some deeply rooted need for security. The nurses feared that elimination of the hoarding behavior could only result in other maladaptive behavior, probably of a more serious nature. Nonetheless, a twelve-month follow-up study revealed that the hoarding did not recur, nor was it replaced by other maladaptive behavior.

Counterconditioning In *counterconditioning*, as its name implies, abnormal behavior is diminished or eliminated by conditioning a more desirable response to replace it. For example, in another series of studies, Ayllon's Saskatchewan group used positive reinforcement of one behavior to eliminate an opposing or incompatible behavior. One patient was a woman who wore an excessive amount of clothing. Her basic dress at any one time consisted of several sweaters, dresses, and undergarments, in addition to a large bundle of clothing that she carried around in her arms. The prescribed program of treatment was to reinforce the response of removing some clothing (one obviously incompatible with the irregular behavior of dressing excessively). In their procedure, the patient was weighed in all her clothing before each meal, and her actual body weight was then subtracted from her recorded weight in order to determine the weight of the clothing. She was then obliged to register a total weight that was increasingly less than her usual total weight before she could obtain her meals. At the first weighing

she was given an allowance of twenty-three pounds in excess of her current body weight. Each time she emitted the desired response (the removal of some clothing), thereby obtaining a meal, the maximum weight requirement was lowered. Dramatic results were rapidly obtained: since food reinforcement continued to depend upon the removal of clothing, the frequency of the desired response increased. The weight of the patient's clothing, which had been approximately twenty-five pounds before treatment declined steadily until it stabilized at a reasonably normal three pounds. In addition, the patient's behavior outside the experimental setting, as well as the behavior of others toward her, also changed in a beneficial direction. In this treatment, then, the desired response, the removal of excess clothing, was successfully maintained by food reinforcement.

Perhaps the most intriguing of the counterconditioning techniques is Halmuth Schaefer's approach to alcoholism. Instead of reinforcing abstention as does Alcoholics Anonymous, Schaefer has tried to replace the pattern of obsessive drinking behavior with a pattern of behavior practiced by the so-called "social drinkers." To do this, Schaefer first meticulously observed the nature of drinking by both social drinkers and alcoholics. He found several reliable differences, including the type of drink (alcoholics rarely chose "mixed" drinks) and the variability of the inter-sip interval (the drinking of alcoholics was more stereotyped, and was characterized by a regular inter-sip interval; social drinkers' inter-sip intervals were more variable). Schaefer next utilized aversion therapy—discussed in detail later— to change the alcoholics' drinking pattern into a social drinking pattern. Initial results based on this program show that Schaefer's technique has more success in dealing with alcoholics than any other tried to date. His patients learn to control their drinking and have almost without exception become

556

successful in remaining responsibly employed,
temperate in their drinking, and better able to cope
with life's stresses.

Systematic Desensitization   Systematic desensitization is one of the most important and highly
regarded techniques of behavior modification. The
patient is conditioned to relax in the presence of a
series of anxiety-arousing stimuli, presented in order
of increasing intensity. Stimuli may be physically
presented, projected on a screen (Figure 32.2), or
merely imagined. For example, a person with an
extreme fear of flying may be trained to relax while
he imagines himself in a variety of anxiety-arousing
situations: for example, he might imagine himself
at the airport, then in a plane that is on the ground,
and finally in one that is in the air. Indeed, the final
session might take place in an airliner itself. This
arrangement of stimuli, in order of anxiety-provoking
potential, is called a *stimulus hierarchy*. The assumption, then, in systematic desensitization, is that since
relaxation and anxiety are mutually incompatible,
the patient who learns to relax will not be anxious.

Systematic desensitization has also been successfully applied to the treatment of *impotence*. For example, the man is instructed to engage in sex play but
not to attempt intercourse. Failure is thereby pre-
cluded, and the subject learns to relax at sex play,
becoming more responsive sexually. Only when the
patient has both a very strong erection and an
uncontrollable desire to have intercourse is he
allowed to do so. Systematic desensitization has
proven highly successful in treating frigidity as well.

An instructive example of systematic desensitization that was unsuccessful was the attempted
treatment of an exhibitionist. The subject was a
twenty-five-year-old married man. He tended to
exhibit in department stores and on the street. He
had served nine prison sentences and had been

Figure 32.2
In systematic desensitization, slides of anxiety-arousing
objects or situations may be presented.

through psychotherapy without success. The first
step in the treatment was to insure that the patient
was relaxed. When he indicated that he was, he was
asked to think about various stimuli that were not
anxiety-arousing—perhaps his wife, for example.
While the patient was still relaxed, the therapists
gradually and progressively introduced other stimuli
that were increasingly more anxiety-arousing, eventually presenting those that had tended to produce
exhibitionism—namely, the sight of plump female
legs in the department store or in the street. The
therapists did not proceed to a stimulus of higher
anxiety until the patient had claimed that he was
completely relaxed. The patient reported rapid
improvement after a few sessions. In addition, for
the first time in a long while, the patient had good
sexual relations with his wife. After about forty-
five sessions, the subject was apparently cured. More

than thirteen months passed without his manifesting any sign of symptoms. During this period, he continued to have a satisfactory sexual relationship with his wife, and he was employed. Unfortunately, he then suddenly lost his job because his employer learned of his previous activities and fired him. Finding himself jobless and without welfare, the patient reverted to exhibiting and was caught within a couple of months. This incident of exhibition was different from the others, however; it had occurred in a ladies' washroom, a location in which he had never exhibited before and to which the systematic desensitization had not been extended. In addition, the incident had occurred when the patient reported "feelings of inadequacy" prompted by the loss of his job. Although the therapists had known that the patient tended to exhibit more often when he was unemployed, they had made no attempt to induce the patient to relax while imagining himself jobless. It was noteworthy that the patient reported no desire to exhibit in the surroundings that he had previously selected—department stores or the street. The treatment was thus partially successful. Indeed, it was entirely successful in eliminating the exhibition response to all those stimuli that had been included in the stimulus hierarchy; apparently the treatment had failed only because the hierarchy was incomplete.

In summary, systematic desensitization is an excellent technique for the cure of anxiety. It is a simple technique and is especially appropriate for those patients having vivid imaginations and the ability to relax. People with less vivid imaginations can be shown slides of the anxiety-arousing stimuli or the stimulus items themselves. People who have difficulty relaxing, may be induced to relax by hypnosis or tranquilizing drugs. Finally, systematic desensitization can be self-applied with some success: if you have anxiety reactions and are gifted with a reasonably good imagination and the ability to relax, you may want to try this technique yourself. Although the success rate of systematic desensitization varies with the type of anxiety, it has been generally successful in treating approximately 90 percent of the disorders to which it has been applied.

Aversion Therapy As its name implies, aversion therapy is the attempt to eliminate undesirable behaviors by the use of aversive consequences, such as electric shock or nausea. In one study, a patient went to a therapist because he was impotent and because he had a *fetish* for women's panties. (A fetish is a habitual tendency to become sexually aroused by a certain type of inanimate object.) The therapist realized that fetishes are rarely cured by traditional therapies. Indeed, psychoanalytic therapies have warned against trying to cure a fetish, claiming that symptom substitution is likely to occur, causing other, still more undesirable symptoms—such as homosexuality, sadism, or impotence—to emerge. Nonetheless, the therapist decided to treat the fetish by utilizing electric shock, taking care not to allow the effects of shock to generalize to legitimate sex objects. The therapist paired a variety of stimuli related to panties (including thinking of panties) with shock. By the second session, the patient's evaluation of the "attractiveness of panties" was undergoing a change. After about forty sessions (about three per week) had taken place, he reported a complete cure. The patient remained cured over a two-year follow-up period. The therapist also successfully treated the patient's impotence with systematic desensitization.

Aversion therapy has been less successful in the modification of the behavior of alcoholics and homosexuals. One reason is that most alcoholics and homosexuals return to the same environment in which they first acquired their habits. In general, behavior-modification techniques will be effective only insofar as the environment does not continue to provide reinforcement for the reacquisition and maintenance of the behavior that has been eliminated. However, it should be added that aversion therapy has been much more successful in the treatment of both alcoholics and homosexuals than have the traditional methods of psychotherapy. When aversion therapy is combined with counterconditioning in the treatment of alcoholics, remarkable results have been obtained, as we indicated earlier in the description of Schaefer's technique.

Discriminative Therapy   Discriminative therapies are those in which the patient's behavior is brought under stimulus control—so that undesirable behavior can be arrested and replaced by more appropriate responses. For example, alarm systems have been employed by Nathan Azrin in the successful treatment of bed-wetters. When the child begins to urinate, the first drops of urine trigger an alarm that wakes him. Eventually, the associated internal sensation of a full bladder wakes the child before the alarm goes off so that he is able to use the toilet in time. A posture-training device, consisting of a vest and buzzer, operates in the same way to shape appropriate posture in severely retarded subjects who tend otherwise to stoop. Whenever the patient stoops, the vest activates the buzzer, which continues to sound until he straightens himself again.

Azrin has successfully extended this sort of technique to bowel movements. Retarded children who cannot control their bowels are fitted with an alarm system which sounds if they defecate without using the toilet. When the retardee successfully uses the toilet, he achieves a battery of reinforcers, including social approval. Gradually, the retardee's behavior becomes controlled by the internal sensation associated with the incipient bowel movements; eventually,

he goes to use the toilet instead of triggering the aversive alarm.

Discriminative therapies have also been used to restrain subjects from smoking. For example, Azrin developed a cigarette box which unlocks only after a specified interval has elapsed. The smoker hears a click, which tells him that the box is unlocked and that a cigarette may be obtained. The interval between clicks is progressively increased until the smoking behavior is significantly reduced, and eventually eliminated. In this procedure, the intention is to bring the smoker's behavior under the control of the click so that the click designates the occasion for smoking. Once smoking behavior is indeed determined by the clicks alone, it can be decreased by progressively decreasing the frequency of clicks.

Modeling Therapy and Imitation   *Modeling,* a form of imitation training developed by Albert Bandura at Stanford University, has been applied to a variety of behaviors, such as snake phobias. Bandura divided people with snake phobias into four groups: (1) a control group that received no treatment; (2) a group that received systematic desensitization treatment to the extent of "imagining" snakes but without receiving any actual contact with snakes; (3) a group that was shown films of people handling snakes; and (4) a modeling group, whose members first watched the experimenter playing with the snake through a one-way mirror, and then were required to approach the snake slowly, touch it, and gradually handle it more and more, until they were copying the behavior displayed by the model. The ultimate criterion for cure was the ability to sit in a chair for thirty seconds without showing any obvious signs of fear while the snake crawled on an arm of the chair. All subjects in the modeling (fourth) group met this criterion. The systematic desensitization and the film-watching groups showed more progress than the control group, but decidedly less than the modeling group. Bandura then successfully employed modeling to cure *all* of the subjects from the three other groups.

Studies show that modeling is a powerful tool for shaping other types of desired behavior as well. It has been used to induce imitation in a variety of situations and has even been successfully employed to teach language to severely retarded children. What happens, however, if a subject does not imitate? Donald Baer and his group worked with several severely retarded children who had been observed for a number of days and found *never* to imitate the behavior of others. Baer and his co-workers shaped an imitative tendency in these children in the following manner: (1) One experimenter would make a motor movement, such as lifting his arm, while saying "do this." (2) The second experimenter would lift the child's arm in response and also provide him with reinforcement. Eventually, the manual assistance was phased out until the child was imitating on his own. Once an imitative tendency had been successfully established, modeling was used to shape desirable behaviors, including speech.

The Token Economy   One of the most important and widely used techniques of behavior modification is the *token economy*, which has been employed successfully with school children and with mental patients. The economy is based on the awarding of tokens, which can then be turned in for one of a variety of different reinforcers of the subject's choosing. Since these *conditioned reinforcers* have been paired with not one but several different reinforcers, they have become powerful *generalized reinforcers* with which a subject does not become satiated, as he would with, say, candy or cigarettes. For example, in a classroom setting, school children work to obtain tokens that may later be traded in (at the end of the hour or day) for any one of a number of reinforcers, such as candy, toys, play privileges, and so forth. Tokens are convenient to work with, since dispensing the tokens (or points) does not interfere with ongoing activity. At the same time, praise is paired with the tokens, so that ultimately the praise itself becomes reinforcing and tokens are no longer required.

Similarly, tokens are awarded to severely retarded patients in hospital settings in order to institute such behaviors as walking around, grooming, and taking part in social activities. The hope is that the activities themselves will ultimately take on reinforcing value or naturally lead to reinforcing events. The theory of a token economy, then, is that if the tokens are effective in instituting normal, productive behavior, the productivity itself will be reinforcing and tokens will be less and less necessary to maintain the behavior.

One of the most successful applications of the token economy has been a juvenile-delinquent rehabilitation system developed by Harold Cohen. Cohen's CASE (Contingencies Applicable to Special Education) project successfully rehabilitated youthful inmates at one institution in Washington, D. C. The inmates acquired points (the equivalent of tokens) for engaging in specified educational behaviors. For example, points were awarded for correctly answering academic test questions. At any time the subject could turn in the points for such reinforcers as lounge privileges, soft drinks, or material from the outside world chosen from mail-order catalogs. Each point was worth a penny. The program was voluntary, and no inmate received points if he did not learn. Not only was the program remarkably successful in demonstrably teaching the inmates verbal, arithmetic, and other skills, but it had unexpected side effects. Within six to eight months, the average inmate's measured IQ increased by about sixteen points. Furthermore, as learning progressed, it became its own reward: one of the most highly valued items came to be a private office where the inmate could better pursue his studies.

THE TREATMENT OF AUTISM

Behavior therapy has proven applicable in the treatment of autistic children, who are marked by a profound lack of orientation to reality. The autistic child seems totally concerned with his own private world and his own sources of stimulation to the exclusion of social interactions and stimulation from the external environment. In many children, autism is accompanied by self-destructive behavior. Some must even be maintained in straitjackets to prevent them from blinding or killing themselves by repeatedly clawing at their eyes or banging their heads against the wall; as soon as the straitjacket is removed, however, the child's pattern of self-mutilative behavior returns. What maintains this behavior, and how can it be eliminated? Conventional psychotherapeutic treatment has been ineffective, because it is obviously impossible to work through a patient's problems if that patient is a child who will not interact with others or even talk.

The behavior therapist Ivar Lovaas of the University of California, Los Angeles, has had unprecedented success in treating self-destructive children. Indeed, Lovaas has remarked that the treatment of an autistic child resembles an attempt to build a person from scratch. Combining the techniques of extinction, punishment, positive reinforcement, modeling, and other methods of behavior modification, he and his associates have managed to eliminate the self-destructive behavior and replace it with various social skills, such as the use of language.

In one study, Lovaas reasoned that the child's self-destructive behavior was maintained by the attention

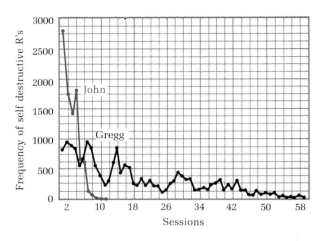

Figure 32.3
Extinction of the self-destructive behavior of two autistic boys. [Adapted from O. Ivar Lovaas and James Q. Simmons, "Manipulation of Self-Destruction in Three Retarded Children." *Journal of Applied Behavior Analysis*, 2, 143–157, 1969.]

given to it by loving parents and nurses through their natural tendency to comfort a child who is mauling himself. Lovaas suggested that the reinforcement from the attention given the child was more disadvantageous than the pain incurred by the behavior, and that it should be possible to extinguish the behavior as had been done with the "rubbish collectors." The results shown in Figure 32.3 indicate that extinction was effective in eliminating self-destructive behavior. Unfortunately, the amount of time required for extinction to be successful has been so great that it is not advisable as a normal procedure: in severe cases, the child could seriously harm itself before extinction is complete.

In another study, Lovaas further showed that it was possible to intensify the behavior by communicating sympathy or understanding whenever the child emitted self-destructive responses. This finding suggests that approaches in which one attempts to "understand" why the child is self-destructing, and to give him attention or other social reinforcement when he is self-destructing, may constitute very dangerous treatment indeed. Thus the traditional standard practice in the treatment of autistic children, in which nurses and parents have responded to self-destructive behavior with reassurance, warmth, and understanding, apparently maintains the destructive behavior in the child.

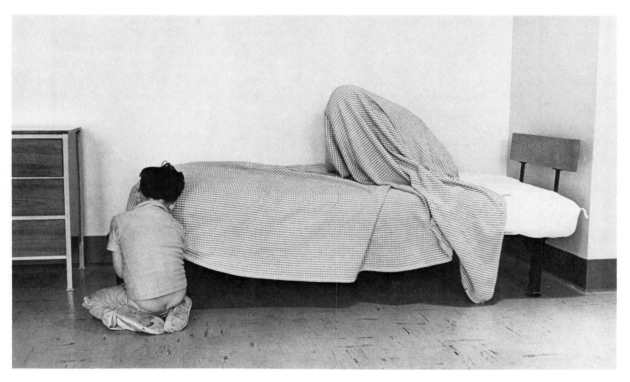

Figure 32.4
Two autistic boys in typical postures. One is hidden
beneath the bedspread. Compare this photograph with
the one on page 520, which shows Ivar Lovaas with two
autistic boys who are being exposed to conditioning
procedures. [Photo by Allan Grant]

Since extinction proved too slow to be a safe
method for eliminating self-destructive behavior,
Lovaas initiated punishment in the form of painful
electric shock. The punishment had an immediate
suppressing effect. But when punishment no longer
followed the emission of self-destructive behavior,
the behavior increased.

If punishment is to be a really effective treatment
for self-destructive behavior, its applicability must
extend to other situations. However, even if a child
has stopped emitting self-destructive behavior in
the presence of one experimenter and in a particular
room where shocks have been administered, once he
is exposed to different adults in different situations,
he may resume his self-destructive behavior. If
the suppression of such behavior is to persist in
new situations, then, it is desirable that at least two
and preferably more, experimenters administer the
shock, and in more than one situation.

When the child has stopped hurting himself, does his behavior change in any other way? Do undesirable effects (or substitute symptoms) occur? On the contrary, quite desirable side effects, such as a decrease in the tendency to avoid others and a decrease in whining, as well as other desirable changes, have been observed. Indeed, the newly trained children seem to be more receptive to schooling in both social and intellectual skills, and they generally show sharp gains in measured intelligence and in other aptitude and achievement scores.

Follow-Up-Studies   Given that some progress has been made in rehabilitative treatment, what is the future for a self-destructive child? Follow-up studies show that his chances for a normal life are fair, particularly if he is treated at a young age and, more importantly, if the parents have been trained in the principles and techniques of operant conditioning. Parents who are successful in raising their autistic children, then, must first be willing to respond negatively as well as positively—with appropriate anger and acts of punishment as well as with affection and reinforcement. They must at all times reject the temptation to regard a child's self-destructive behavior as a normal reflection of a need "to express himself." Finally, they must be willing to devote themselves almost completely to their autistic children—a time-consuming job indeed.

Given the appropriate training and an appropriate home environment, autistic children may acquire abilities that have previously been considered impossible. Studies show that if such children can remain in an environment that reinforces their newly acquired behavior, they continue to improve and some have even become normal (manifesting an average IQ, average achievement in school, and typical everyday behavior). But if a child is returned to an institution in which the policy is implicitly

to reinforce autism, behaviors acquired during treatment tend to disappear. But the child has not forgotten the acquired behavior, he has merely reverted to the type of behavior expected of him by the institution: if he is again taken from the institution to a setting in which he receives the Lovaas treatment, he exhibits *within hours* all that he had previously learned.

SYMPTOM SUBSTITUTION

The concept of *symptom substitution* maintains that the removal of the maladaptive behavior is not enough unless the underlying cause has also been eliminated, because, if the source has not been removed, it will produce other symptoms to replace, or substitute for, the original symptom. This principle—accepted as valid in many cases by conventional therapists and rejected out of hand by behavior therapists—is one of the major issues of disagreement between the two schools. Indeed, conventional therapists fear that the substitute symptom may well be more abnormal than the original symptom that the patient has utilized in the attempt to resolve his inner conflicts. In other words, they believe that removal of the symptom without treatment of its cause may have very serious consequences. In contrast, the behavior therapist maintains that the symptom *is* the problem and that eliminating the symptom eliminates the problem. He does not believe that a substitute symptom will replace it. The issue of symptom substitution remains a subject of considerable debate, because the amount of conclusive information is still very small. Numerous clinical case-studies and anecdotes suggest that symptom substitution may occur in some people, but behavior modifiers have yet to uncover any evidence that convinces them that it occurs.

Recently, concentrated efforts have been made to examine the question of symptom substitution. One study was a follow-up of children who had been cured of bed-wetting by techniques of behavior therapy. The purpose was to determine if the subjects would adopt, in place of bed-wetting, another behavior that was equally if not more maladaptive. The experimenters sought reports on student behavior in both home and school: parents were asked to comment on the success of the treatment and on the child's general behavior and teachers were requested to note any adverse changes in behavior that might arise to replace the bed wetting. The teachers could be objective observers of their pupils' behavior because they did not know which ones were receiving the treatment. The results revealed no symptom substitution in two years of follow-up study. Instead, the teachers reported no demonstrable change in the pupils' behavior. The parents reported that their children seemed happier and better adjusted emotionally and mentally. Of course we should accept the parents' conclusions with reservations, since their view of the improved health of the child may have been influenced by their own delight at no longer having wet sheets to launder every morning. Nevertheless, symptom substitutions were not verified, and the findings strongly suggested that the elimination of the symptom, at least in these cases, constituted a total cure.

CONCLUSION

Therapists who practice behavior modification believe that this form of therapy has four advantages over conventional psychotherapy: (1) it is effective for larger numbers of people; (2) it is cheaper, (3) it is quicker, and (4) failures can be identified sooner.

If this is so, and we hope that it is, then psychology may have found in behavior modification a therapeutic equivalent to the physicists' nuclear reactor—a practical application of its findings that can neither be denied nor ignored. False starts like alchemy—and *perhaps* psychoanalysis—exclude themselves from practical consideration when experience proves that another approach is realistically and empirically correct and effective. But they continue to be intellectually and historically important, and to merit our attention, study, and appreciation.

Suggested Readings

Ayllon, T., & Azrin, N. (1968) *The token economy.* New York: Appleton-Century-Crofts. [One of the pioneer token economy programs.]

Bandura, A. (1969) *Principles of behavior modification.* New York: Holt, Rinehart and Winston. [A more detailed treatment, surveying much of the literature.]

Becker, W. C. (1971) *Parents are teachers.* Champaign, Illinois: Research Press. [Shows how behavior modification may be successfully applied to behavior problems in the home.]

Cohen, H. L., & Filipczak, J. (1971) *A new learning environment.* San Francisco: Jossey-Bass. [Describes a remarkable program of rehabilitation and instruction.]

Schaefer, H. H., & Martin, P. L. (1969) *Behavioral therapy.* New York: McGraw Hill. [Fine, very readable overview.]

Ulrich, R., Stachnik, T., & Mabry, J. (1966–74) *Control of human behavior.* Glenview, Illinois: Scott, Foresman. [Three volumes of readings, mostly from journals reporting original research, on a wide variety of activities in behavior modification.]

GLOSSARY

Glossary items are indicated by brown underscores where they first appear in the text.

absolute threshold   The minimum amount of physical stimulus that is needed to produce a sensation 50 percent of the time. (In hearing, a pressure of as little as .0002 dynes/cm^2 can be heard.)

accommodation   According to Piaget, the developmental process by which mental schemata change in order to incorporate new information about the world.

accommodation, visual   Changes in the shape of the lens that permit the eye to focus on objects at different distances.

activation theory of emotion   A theory that states that emotion is a state of increased activation reflected in increased electrical activity of the brain and, like other levels of activation, mediated by the brainstem reticular formation.

adaptation   In general, adjustment to environmental conditions.

adaptation level   Helson's term for a person's current perception of the average of some characteristic, against which new instances are judged larger or smaller.

adipsia   Lack of drinking.

afterimages, visual   An image that persists after the termination of stimulation. Positive afterimages retain the brightness and hue of the stimulus; negative afterimages reverse brightness and take on the complementary hue.

algorithm   A set of problem-solving rules that take into account all possible outcomes of each step in the solution.

allele   One gene of a pair of genes.

ambivalence   In psychoanalytic theory, the simultaneous and often-unconscious holding of opposite emotions, such as love and hate, toward one person.

androgens   Male sex hormones.

anomie A sociological concept referring to the disruption of personal and social values during periods of major social upheaval. The term can also refer to the sense of rootlessness that people experience during such periods.

antidiuretic hormone (ADH) A hormone from the pituitary gland that stimulates the absorption of water by the kidneys, thereby concentrating and reducing the volume of the urine.

anxiety A feeling of painful or apprehensive uneasiness accompanied by various forms of physiological arousal.

aphagia Lack of eating.

apperceptive mass The totality of a person's associations to a stimulus or an event. (Considered in some theories to be equivalent to the meaning the stimulus has for the person.)

assimilation According to Piaget, the process of taking in new information about the world during intellectual development.

attitude A person's organized tendency to think, feel, and act in a certain general way in response to some aspect of the social environment or to a given class of objects.

attribute A psychological dimension of sensation. (A sound, for example, has attributes of pitch, loudness, volume, and density.)

attribution theory A theory in social psychology that holds that people (1) attribute their own behaviors and the behaviors of others to internal or external causes and (2) react to behaviors on the basis of the causes to which the behaviors have been attributed.

authoritarianism According to some psychologists, a personality constellation marked by extreme rigidity, consciousness of power, pronounced prejudice, and narrowmindedness.

authoritarian personality See *authoritarianism*.

autoclitic According to Skinner, a verbal expression (like "please") that is under the stimulus control of other verbal behavior (like "start" or "stop"). Also includes syntactic responses whose effect is to order other verbal expressions gramatically.

autokinetic effect The apparent movement of a stationary object, such as a point of light in a dark room, which often occurs as a result of suggestion.

autoshaping A technique for teaching a pigeon to peck a response-key. Brief periods of key-illumination are accompanied by presentations of grain. Initially, the bird pecks at the grain (to eat it), then it begins to peck on the illuminated key also.

avoidance A learning procedure in which the occurrence of the designated response results in the postponement or omission of an aversive stimulus.

babbling A continuous stream of apparently meaningless sounds, such as the babbling of young children that approximates the rhythms and intonations of adult speech.

backward conditioning An ineffective respondent-conditioning procedure in which the conditioned stimulus (CS) is presented after the unconditioned stimulus (US).

balance theory Heider's theory of attitudes and attitude change, which stresses that people tend to keep their attitudes toward other people and events consistent and in balance, altering one or another attitude to accomplish that end.

bandwagon effect In public-opinion polling, a developing trend that becomes larger and larger as more and more people "climb on the bandwagon."

behavioral contrast   An increase in reinforced responding in the presence of one discriminative stimulus brought about by presenting that stimulus in alternation with periods of extinction or less reinforcement.

behaviorists   Psychologists who hold that overt, observable behavior is the only worthwhile subject matter for psychological study.

behavior therapy   The application of conditioning techniques (primarily operant conditioning) to changing or eliminating abnormal behavior. (See also rational psychotherapy.)

bias   In public-opinion polling, any factor that tends to distort the answers to questions.

binaural cues   Cues for the distance and location of sounds requiring two ears.

binaural intensity difference   The difference in the intensity of a sound at the two ears, owing to their different distances from the source of the sound; a cue to the location of the sound.

binaural time difference   The difference in the time of arrival of a sound at the two ears, owing to their different distances from the sound; a cue to the location of the sound.

binocular cues   Cues for depth perception requiring two eyes.

binocular disparity   The difference between the retinal images of the two eyes that arises because each eye sees an object from a slightly different location.

binocular parallax   The difference in optic angle of the two eyes. (Since our two eyes are about 2¼ inches apart, they each see an object from a slightly different angle.)

biofeedback   The use of instrumentation to enhance awareness and control of our own physiological processes. (When we observe a meter on an instrument that measures our brainwaves, galvanic skin response, or muscular tension, we are apt to discover that we can "move the needle" on the meter, thereby demonstrating a degree of voluntary control over the physiological process.)

Blacky test   A projective test using a series of cartoons of dogs who engage in behavior that the subject describes in a story.

brainstem reticular formation   The region of the brain located between the spinal cord and the forebrain and cerebrum; stimulation of the reticular formation results in general arousal of the brain.

brainstorming   A problem-solving technique in which the members of a group offer any ideas or solutions that occur to them without regard to their practicality. Members of the group may be stimulated by the ideas of others to reach a practical solution of the problem.

cardinal numbers   The ordinary numbers used in counting and referring to how many objects there are in a group of objects.

caretaker   General term for the one who cares for an infant or child. Often, but not always, the mother.

catatonic schizophrenia   The variety of the disease marked by rigid postures held for prolonged periods.

catharsis   The therapeutic event involving the re-experiencing and purging of recalled emotional experiences, during psychoanalysis.

cathexis   A Freudian term referring to the attachment of libidinal energy to a person or object by the ego.

cellular dehydration   A condition of less than an optimal amount of water in the cells of the body; one of the instigators of thirst.

censor   Freud's term for the agency of the personality that monitors dream material and selects threatening or anxiety-arousing themes for alteration.

chromosomes   Minute rodlike structures that carry the genes. Human cells normally carry twenty-three pairs of chromosomes.

chunking   The technique of organizing material to be remembered into large meaningful units (chunks) that are more easily recalled than isolated and meaningless small units.

circular reaction   During early childhood, repeated sensorimotor interaction with the environment, as when a child repeatedly shakes a rattle or caresses a doll.

classical conditioning   See respondent conditioning.

client-centered therapy   A form of psychotherapy designed by Rogers, in which the client—rather than the therapist's interpretation of the client's feelings and actions—is the focus of attention. (The client discusses a problem; the therapist accepts what the client says and mirrors the client's feelings in an effort to bring the client to a fuller understanding of his true feelings concerning the problem.)

clinical method of prediction or assessment   The use of a trained clinician's intuition and judgment rather than standardized, objective tests in the assessment of personality, personality disorders, and therapy.

closedness   One of the gestaltists' criteria for a good figure, referring roughly to the completeness of the figure.

closure   The gestaltists' term for a person's perceptual tendency to "close up" figures. (For example, people tend to ignore small gaps in circles.)

cognitive dissonance   A state that is generated by conflict between two attitudes or between an attitude and a behavior. Dissonance can be reduced by an attitude change that makes the two attitudes or the attitude and the behavior agree (become consonant).

collective unconscious   Jung's term for the part of each person's unconscious mind that is identical with a corresponding part of the unconscious mind of every other human being who has ever lived.

color anomalies   Defects of color vision in which the colors of some wavelengths are abnormally perceived.

color mixing   The mixing together of pigments or lights of different colors to form new colors. When lights are mixed by shining them on the same surface, the resulting color is determined by the *addition* of the lights. When pigments are mixed, the resulting color is determined by *subtraction* (by absorption) of some wavelengths of light by each pigment.

competence   In personality theory, White's term for a person's developing and continuing sense of being able to deal effectively with the world and with himself.

competence in a language   A linguistic term for the ability of a person to know and speak a language in the sense that he can generate and recognize grammatical sentences.

complex   Jung's term for any of the several central focuses of a personality: the organized ways of thinking and acting that dominate a person's behavior. (After Adler coined the term "inferiority complex," the word "complex" came, improperly, to be used to describe only abnormal tendencies.)

compulsive neurotic   A neurotic personality dominated by repetitive stylized behaviors that seem designed to protect the person from attacks of anxiety. (For example, an unconscious fear of germs and disease may be expressed in extremely frequent hand-washing.)

concepts   Higher-order mental representations or ideas.

concordance   A simple measure of the resemblance between pairs of individuals or objects. Two objects are concordant in a characteristic if they both exhibit it.

concrete operations   One of Piaget's stages of intellectual development. Marked by concrete mental operations, rather than abstract thinking, this period extends from the development of symbols (around two years of age) to the appearance of truly abstract conceptualizations (around eleven).

concurrent schedules   In operant conditioning, the existence of two or more schedules of reinforcement during the same period of time, usually for different responses.

conditioned reflex   A reflex that owes its existence to the organism's previous experience rather than to the organism's inherited structure. (See also respondent conditioning.)

conditioned reinforcement   A reinforcer that has gained its reinforcing power through the organism's experience with it rather than from the organism's inherited structure.

conditioned response (CR)   The elicited response in respondent (Pavlovian) conditioning. Also used to refer to any operant behavior that has been learned or modified by reinforcement.

conditioned stimulus (CS)   In Pavlovian conditioning, the previously ineffective stimulus that comes to elicit the conditioned response after being paired several times with an unconditioned stimulus that elicited the response. (See also respondent conditioning.)

conditioned suppression   The rate of positively reinforced behavior is lowered (suppressed) during a stimulus that has typically come before the occurrence of an aversive stimulus. (The behaviorists' model of anxiety, since we feel anxious as we wait for the aversive event to occur.)

conditioning   See respondent conditioning and operant conditioning.

cones   Color receptors; one of two kinds of photoreceptors in the retina of the eye. (See also rods.)

connected discourse   Written or spoken grammatical utterances; normal language.

connotative meaning   As opposed to denotative meaning, the emotional tone of a word or sentence. "Denotative meaning" refers to dictionary-like meaning; "connotative meaning" refers to the other meanings that are conveyed from speaker to listener.

conscience   (1) In general psychological usage, a person's internalized sense of the rightness or wrongness of his actions, which results in guilt if wrong actions occur. (2) In Freudian theory, the superego.

conservation   The idea that the physical characteristics of an object, such as its length, quantity, area, or weight, need not change with changes in the appearance of the object. (A child has developed conservation when it realizes, for example, that the volume of a fixed amount of water does not change when the water is poured into differently shaped containers.)

continuous reinforcement   A schedule of reinforcement in which each occurrence of a response is reinforced.

control groups   Groups exposed to all experimental conditions except the independent variable in order to demonstrate that extraneous factors are not operating in the experiment.

convergence, visual   The concurrent inward swing of the two eyes as they focus on nearer and nearer objects. The muscular sensation of convergence is one cue to the depth of objects.

counterconditioning   The teaching of new behavior that is incompatible with current, undesirable behavior. (For example, learning to relax on airplanes can replace fear of flying with relaxation; one cannot be relaxed and fearful at the same time.)

countertransference   During psychoanalysis, the tendency of the analyst to treat the patient as if the patient were one of the members of the analyst's intimate childhood family. (See transference.)

culture-fair test   A test whose items do not require knowledge that is specific to a given culture or ethnic group. In theory, a test that requires only pure ability or intelligence, as opposed to culturally influenced prior learning.

cure   In psychotherapy, the more-or-less permanent disappearance of the patient's abnormality.

cycles per second   The number of recurrences of a periodic vibration or other wave form in one second. Now replaced by the term "Hertz," which is abbreviated "Hz."

dark adaptation   The process whereby the eye adapts to conditions of low illumination. The rods, which are more sensitive than the cones, become active after a period of time in the dark allows the regeneration of their photopigments.

decay theory of forgetting   The theory that memorized material gradually fades from memory over time. (See also interference theory of forgetting.)

decibel (dB)   The unit of sound intensity. The decibel scale is logarithmic, that is, every increase of one decibel represents the same multiplicative increase in the physical intensity of the sound.

deep structure   A linguistic term for the underlying grammatical form of a sentence, as distinct from the surface structure. (Sentences such as "they are playing cards" are ambiguous because they could result from either of two deep structures, depending upon whether "are playing" or "playing cards" is a unit.)

defense mechanisms   In Freudian theory, the ways in which the ego behaves in order to avoid anxiety. (See specific mechanisms such as displacement, projection, reaction formation.)

delayed conditioning   A form of respondent conditioning in which the interval between the start of CS and the onset of the US exceeds 0.5 seconds.

delta movement   A form of apparent (illusionary) movement.

denial   In psychoanalytic theory, a defense mechanism in which the ego simply denies the existence of anxiety-arousing material.

denotative meaning   In contrast to connotative meaning, the objective, dictionary-like meaning of a word or other utterance.

dependent variable   The variable whose value changes as a result of the experimenter's changes in another variable, the independent variable.

depression   A psychological state marked by lowered activity, gloomy thoughts, anxiety, feelings of worthlessness, and an inability to deal effectively with life.

deprivation paradigm   An experimental method for determining the effects of experience on behavior. The organism is deprived of the opportunity to practice or exhibit the behavior until beyond the age at which the behavior normally occurs. Then, given the opportunity to perform the behavior, the organism demonstrates how much the lost practice hinders its current ability.

detection   The correct perception of the presence of something, usually a stimulus or sensation of very small magnitude.

developmental stages   The successive levels of development through which all individuals pass. According to Piaget, each stage incorporates and goes beyond the abilities of the stage before.

difference threshold   The smallest change in a physical variable that is detected by an observer on 50 percent of the trials. With physical intensities, Weber's law applies—the difference threshold is proportional to the magnitude of the stimulus. (See also absolute threshold.)

discrimination   (1) recognizing the difference between two or more stimuli; (2) the indication of a perceived difference between two stimuli, usually as evidenced by different kinds or amounts of behavior in response to each stimulus.

discriminative stimulus (S^D)   In operant conditioning, the stimulus in the presence of which a response is reinforced. The stimulus is said to "set the occasion" for the reinforcement of the behavior, and to *control* the behavior that has been reinforced in its presence, in the sense that that behavior has a high probability of occurrence in the presence of the discriminative stimulus.

dishabituation   The reappearance of an elicited response after repeated presentations of a stimulus has habituated it, usually caused by a change in the stimulus. (See also habituation.)

displacement   In Freudian theory, a mechanism (often for defense against anxiety) in which the object of libidinal energy is changed.

displacement activity   When instinctive behaviors conflict, animals often engage in other (displacement) behavior, as if the energies from the conflicting instincts have been displaced to the new behavior.

dissonance theory   Festinger's theory that conflicting attitudes (or attitudes and behavior) generate cognitive dissonance, which the individual seeks to reduce by changing either his attitudes or his actions.

distal stimulus   The stimulus "out there" in the real world, as distinct from the retinal image of it or the person's perception of it.

distinctive features, linguistic   The characteristics of speech sounds that a hearer uses in distinguishing them.

distributed practice   A method of memorization in which periods of practice are spread out over time with rest periods in between, rather than being massed and continuous.

dizygotes   Twins resulting from the fertilization of two different ova; fraternal twins.

DNA macromolecules   Large and highly complex molecules that compose genes and carry the hereditary code of an individual.

dominant allele   One of a pair of genes that influences the phenotype at the expense of the other member of the pair. The other allele is present in the person but recessive (that is, not expressed in the phenotype). It may nevertheless be passed along to progeny.

Down's syndrome   A hereditary chromosomal abnormality; children with Down's syndrome have a shortened life expectancy, a low IQ, reduced behavioral capabilities, and a general psychological lassitude; they tend to be short and typically to have a modified and folded eyelid. Formerly known as mongolism.

dream work   Freud's term for the process of condensing and transforming dream material to avoid anxiety.

drive reduction A theory of motivation that states that reinforcing or rewarding events are those that reduce an organism's drives (such as those for food, water, sexual contact, etc.); a broader and later version of the theory includes a curiosity drive, an activity drive, and so forth.

echoic Skinner's term for a verbal expression that is an exact copy of another verbal expression, as in precise imitation.

echolocation Location of objects by bouncing sounds off them and noting the characteristics of the returning signals; used by bats in flight to detect objects.

ego In Freud's theory of personality, the executive part of the personality, charged with reconciling the demands of the id and the superego and with dealing with reality.

egocentric Generally, the belief that one's own view of the world is the only one. During intellectual development, before the development of perspectivism, the child's view is egocentric, that is, the child does not realize that others see (or feel or know, etc.) things from a different perspective than his.

ego ideal In Freudian theory, what the superego would most like the individual to be.

eidetic imagery A photographic memory for scenes. An eidetic image can be "viewed" by its possessor long after the actual scene has disappeared.

electroconvulsive shock A therapy for some kinds of mental illness, notably depression, in which convulsions and coma are produced by passing an electrical current through the brain.

electroencephalogram (EEG) A record of the electrical activity of the brain recorded from electrodes attached to the scalp.

electromagnetic waves Waves having frequencies within the electromagnetic spectrum, which includes visible wavelengths—light—as well as waves used for radio and television transmission and X-rays.

elicited aggression Aggressive behavior that is elicited by a stimulus (usually painful), as distinct from aggressive behavior that persists because of its reinforcing consequences.

eliciting stimulus The conditioned or unconditioned stimulus that elicits a reflex, as distinct from a discriminative stimulus that sets the occasion for behavior rather than eliciting it.

Emmert's law The geometrical fact that, for a given size of retinal image, the farther away an object is, the larger it must be. Often demonstrated by projecting afterimages against more distant sufaces, on which they appear proportionally larger.

empiricists The group of perceptual psychologists who emphasize the importance of experience, rather than inheritance, in the development and determination of our perceptual world. (See also nativists.)

equilibrium In Piaget's theory of development, the point at which the person's schemata are consonant with what he experiences in the world. (According to Piaget, the assimilation of new information and the accommodation of schemata work together during development to formulate ever more comprehensive equilibria.)

erogenous zones In Freud's theory of personality, those areas of the body that provide pleasure when stimulated during various stages of development, such as the lips, the anus, and the genitals.

estrogens Female sex hormones.

ethnocentrism   A belief in the reality of psychological differences between the races coupled
with a belief in the importance of such
differences.

ethology   The study of animal behavior with special
emphasis on species-specific behavior, usually
conducted in the natural habitat of the animal
but sometimes in laboratory settings as well.

exhibitionism   The deriving of pleasure from—or
the compulsive repetition of—public displays
of naked parts of the body, usually the
genitals.

experimental neurosis   Abnormal behavior exhibited
by an animal after experiencing (1) an increasingly difficult discrimination or (2) punishment
when reward was expected.

extensional meaning   The nondictionary types of
meaning conveyed by a speaker without
necessarily intending to do so.

extinction   (1) In respondent conditioning, the
decrease in the response elicited by a conditioned stimulus when it is repeatedly
presented without the unconditioned stimulus.
(2) In operant conditioning, the decrease in
the rate of occurrence of a response when it
is no longer followed by reinforcement.

factor analysis   A statistical technique for determining clusters of co-varying measuring
instruments. For example, out of thirty personality tests, only three may contribute
significantly to our knowledge of the personality because each of the other twenty-seven
merely duplicates the information of (co-
varies with) one of the three.

Fechner's law   The psychological magnitude of a
sensation is proportional to the logarithm of
the physical intensity of the stimulus.

feedback   Knowledge of the results of an action;
perception of a state of the body or of the
environment.

fetish   Strong attraction (usually sexual) for an
object that is not usually found to be strongly
attractive.

figure-ground reversal   Referring to the gestaltists'
observation that the figure and background of
certain figures may change places—the background suddenly standing out as the figure.

fixation   In Freudian theory, an object or way of
behaving to which libido (psychic energy) is
attached at an early stage; fixations survive in
the adult personality as immature or neurotic
characteristics.

fixed-interval (FI) schedule of reinforcement   A
schedule that arranges for the reinforcement of
the first response occurring after a fixed period
of time has elapsed since the previous
reinforcement.

fixed-ratio (FR) schedule of reinforcement   A schedule that arranges for the reinforcement of the
nth response emitted since the previous reinforcement. (The number of responses per
reinforcement, n, is constant.)

formal operation   In Piaget's theory of intellectual
development, formal operations refer to the
complex and abstract modes of thinking that
dominate adult thinking.

free association   A technique of psychoanalysis (with
other applications) in which the person says
the first thing that comes into his mind. Sometimes the person freely associates to a word
provided by the analyst or experimenter.
Presumably, some unconscious material may
be revealed in such free associations.

frustration-aggression hypothesis   The idea that frustration is the cause of aggression and aggression the usual consequence of frustration.

functional autonomy of motives Allport's statement that adult motives are independent (autonomous) of the earlier experiences that may have played a role in establishing the motives. For example, likes or dislikes learned on the basis of sexual (or other) pleasure become independent of sex and function as pure motives in their own right. "Drives drive now!"

functional fixedness A kind of mental rigidity in which the subject cannot perceive that a familiar object with a familiar use can in fact be put to novel uses in order to solve a current problem.

galvanic skin response (GSR) A change in the electrical conductivity of the skin; GSR readings are high when someone is aroused or anxious, lower when someone is relaxed.

gametes Male or female germ cells—sperm and ova—containing only twenty-three unpaired chromosomes. At fertilization, the male and female gametes merge together.

general adaptation syndrome Selye's description of an organism's reactions to prolonged stress: first alarm, then resistance, and finally exhaustion.

generalization After the establishment of a conditioned stimulus or of a discriminative stimulus, the organism tends to respond similarly to other stimuli that are in some way like the conditioned or discriminative stimulus; a failure to discriminate perfectly between the stimuli. (See also generalization gradient.)

generalization gradient A graphical description of generalization showing that the tendency to respond declines as the stimulus becomes more and more different from the original conditioned or discriminative stimulus.

genes The carriers of heredity.

genotype An organism's genetic constitution—that is, the sum of all of the genetic traits it displays or carries. (See also phenotype.)

gestalt German for "whole"; refers to a school of perceptual psychologists who were concerned primarily with object perception and the psychological laws of organization that govern object perception.

gestalt psychologists Perceptual psychologists concerned with the laws of perceptual organization that govern our perception of objects and the structure of our perceptual world. The best-known gestalt psychologists were Max Wertheimer, Wolfgang Köhler, and Kurt Koffka.

gestalt therapy A psychotherapy advocated by Perls and others which places emphasis on the participation of the whole person in life's activities. This was a forerunner of modern humanistic therapies.

glucostatic theory A theory of the initiation of hunger that attributes it to low artery–vein glucose differences (which indicate that little glucose is being utilized by the body).

grammar A set of linguistic rules for constructing and recognizing proper and well-formed sentences in a language. A person who can generate and recognize grammatical sentences is said to know the grammar of his language.

groupthink A phenomenon of group decision-making in which the group arrives at a risky or ill-advised proposal even though each of the individual members of the group may have reservations, which they are reluctant to express primarily because the group appears to be unanimous and invulnerable. (See also risky-shift.)

habituation The decrease in the magnitude of an unconditioned reflex with repeated elicitation. (In common psychological usage, such a reflex is said to "habituate.")

hair cells A part of the organ of Corti that participates in the transduction of mechanical energy (set up by sound waves) into electrical discharges of the auditory nerve.

halo effect The tendency to overvalue information because of earlier positive information. (For example, if we are told that a person is very intelligent, we are likely to judge his future actions as more intelligent than they really are.)

hebephrenic schizophrenia The variety of the disorder marked by severe disturbance of language, which has been described as a "word salad."

Hering shadows The shadow cast by an object in colored illumination appears to have a hue that is complementary to the color of the illumination.

heritability index Expresses the proportion of the phenotypic variation in a group of individuals that is a result of genotypic variation.

hermaphrodites People with some or all of the physical characteristics of both sexes.

Hertz (Hz) The unit of periodic vibration; one Hz is equal to one cycle per second. Formerly abbreviated *cps*.

heuristic strategies General methods of approach to the solution of problems. For example, we may (1) try to work backwards from the required solution or (2) attempt solution by evaluating the difference between the current and the required state of affairs or (3) examine the solution of similar problems for hints about solving the current problem.

hippocampus A structure in the brain believed to play a role in the regulation of emotional states, and in the transfer of material from short-term memory to long-term memory.

homeostasis A state of physiological equilibrium that is maintained by innate and automatic regulatory mechanisms.

homeostatic drives Those drives whose satisfaction is necessary for the survival of the individual organism.

hue Psychological term for the color of light or surfaces.

human dyad A group of two people.

hyperphagia Overeating.

hypnotic trance A state that a hypnotist induces in a subject, who then is extremely responsive to the hypnotist's instructions.

hypothalamus Area of the brain believed to play a role in motivation and emotion.

hysteria An abnormal condition in which psychological problems take on physical expression, usually either paralysis or anaesthesia of some part of the body.

id According to Freud, the most primitive, unconscious part of the personality. The id is oriented toward immediate gratification of needs, drives, and wishes.

identification Freud's term for the phenomenon in which a child becomes so like an admired adult that it seems to incorporate the adult's ways. The child is said to identify with the adult.

identity A person's sense of who he is and of his purpose in life.

imitation Doing the same as someone else.

immediate memory The process by which we can recall something for a half-second after having perceived it. Some items in immediate memory are encoded into short-term memory; others are forgotten.

immunization In the field of attitude change, the process of protecting a person from attempts to change his attitude by "inoculating" him with counterarguments beforehand.

imprinting   The rapid and more-or-less permanent acquisition of a stimulus–response relationship at a very early stage of development. (Certain species of birds, soon after hatching, will follow the first moving object that they encounter and thereafter tend to follow that object and not others. The birds are said to become imprinted on the object. Later in life, they may attempt to mate with that object, however inappropriate it may be.)

independent variable   In an experiment, the variable independently manipulated by the experimenter; changes in the independent variable bring about changes in the dependent variable.

induced movement   The apparent movement of stationary objects, as when the eyeball is gently pressed with the finger.

infantile determinism   Freud's notion that the adult personality is determined by events and experiences during infancy.

inferiority complex   In personality theory, a "complex" is a grouping of elements. According to Adler, one of the central complexes of a personality is organized around what the person feels to be his inferiorities, in an attempt to compensate for them. An inferiority complex is not necessarily abnormal, although the term has become pejorative in general usage.

information processing   In psychology, the general name for an approach to psychology as the science of how people process information in thinking, memory, and problem solving.

ingratiation   Term used in social psychology to indicate the process whereby a person influences another to like him so that the other will benefit him in some way.

inkblot test   A projective personality test in which a person is asked to describe what he sees in an ink-blot because his responses may reveal something about his personality, his unconscious thoughts, or his abnormalities.

insight   The sudden occurrence of the solution to a problem or of a novel idea.

instinctive drift   The tendency of a trained animal to substitute instinctive behavior for learned behavior. (For example, animals taught to exchange tokens for food may later attempt to eat the tokens.)

instincts   Complex behaviors that appear to be unlearned, uniform within a species, and adaptive.

instrumental conditioning   (See operant conditioning.)

intelligence quotient (IQ)   A measure of intelligence. IQ is equal to a person's mental age divided by his chronological age and multiplied by 100.

intensity   General term for the magnitude of the physical stimulus

intentional meaning   As opposed to extensional meaning, what a speaker really intends to convey with his message.

interference theory of forgetting   The hypothesis that forgetting is caused by interference from previously or subsequently learned material with the material to be remembered, rather than by the mere passage of time. (See also decay theory of forgetting.)

interposition   A cue to depth; if one object appears to be interposed between the observer and another object, the interposed object is judged to be closer to the observer.

interval scale   A scale of measurement with an arbitrary zero point but with equal intervals. The numerical distances on such a scale have meaning but ratios do not. (For example, Fahrenheit temperature is an interval scale: it is meaningful to say that 70° is as much warmer than 60° as 60° is warmer than 50°. But, it is meaningless to say that 60° is *twice* as hot as 30°.)

intervening variable   A state or mechanism that comes between a cause and its effects. (If we deprive an animal of water and note that he drinks when water is made available, we may say that a state of thirst, caused by the deprivation and causing the drinking, intervenes between the two.)

intraverbal   Skinner's term for a verbal response to a verbal stimulus when there is no formal correspondence between them. For example, the response "1492" to the stimulus "Columbus" is an intraverbal.

introspection   The psychological technique of observing oneself, especially one's thoughts, feelings, and sensations, in an effort to discover psychological laws.

isophonic contour   The locus of intensity-frequency pairs that sound the same with respect to some attribute such as loudness or pitch.

just noticeable difference (jnd)   Same as the difference threshold.

language   (1) A form of behavior, (2) a mental acitivty, (3) a medium of communication.

latency   In conditioning, the time elapsed between a stimulus and a response.

latent content   Freud's term for the real meaning of the symbols in dreams, as distinct from the manifest content (what the dream appears to mean on the surface).

latent learning   Learning, as in a maze, without obvious reward; latent learning is demonstrated by the relatively *rapid* improvement of performance when a reward is introduced.

lateral hypothalamic recovery syndrome   The constellation of events that occur when an animal recovers from the aphagia produced by lesions in the lateral area of the hypothalamus.

lateral hypothalamus   A portion of the hypothalamus; lesions there produce aphagia, and stimulation induces eating, even in satiated animals.

law of Prägnanz   See *Prägnanz, law of.*

laws of probability   See *probability, laws of.*

learning   In general, the gaining of knowledge, understanding, or skill through study, instruction, experience, insight, or reinforcement.

learning curve   A graph of the changes in behavior that occur during learning, usually showing increased speed or decreased errors during a series of practice trials.

level of significance   Statistical term indicating the degree of confidence we can have that the result was not caused by chance alone. The level of significance is expressed as the number of times in 100 that the given result could be expected to occur by chance alone. Thus a level of "5 percent" means that the result would be expected by chance alone only 5 times in 100.

lie-detector test   A test in which various physiological accompaniments (heart rate, breathing, GSR, etc.) of verbal answers to questions are compared with previously recorded physiological accompaniments of truthful answers and intentional lies in order to try to detect other lies.

linear perspective   Referring to the fact that parallel lines (such as railroad tracks) seem to come closer together as they become more distant, and that lines that come closer together as they approach the top of a drawing or painting tend to give depth to a scene.

localization of function   The doctrine that particular psychological functions are located in particular parts of the brain.

logotherapy   Frankl's therapy, which emphasizes the meaning of life and existence.

long-delay learning   Respondent conditioning in which there is a long interval between the CS and the US and UR. (For example, if an animal eats a distinctively flavored mild poison but becomes ill only several hours later, it may nevertheless shun eating that flavor in the future.)

long-term memory (LTM)   As distinct from short-term memory, ordinary memory for events that occurred thirty seconds and longer ago.

magnitude estimation   A method for the direct measurement of sensory magnitudes. The subject is told that a given stimulus has a psychological magnitude of an arbitrary value of 10 and that he is to rate the magnitude of other stimuli proportionally to the magnitude of 10. (If another stimulus is half as loud, call it 5, if twice as loud, call it 20, etc.) From the results, a power function, relating the physical intensity to the psychological magnitude, can be constructed.

magnitude production   Similar in theory to magnitude estimation but different in that the subject adjusts the physical magnitude of the stimulus to produce given ratios of psychological magnitude with reference to a standard magnitude.

mand   Skinner's term (from "command") for verbal responses that specify their own reinforcer. (For example, "Pass the butter." is a mand, since it specifies its reinforcer, the butter.)

manic-depressive psychosis   A severe mental illness characterized by loss of contact with reality and extreme and uncontrollable swings of mood from the deepest depression to wildly elated mania.

manifest content   Freud's term for what dreams appear to mean, as distinct from their real, latent meaning.

marathon group   A therapy group meeting for an extremely long and continuous period of time.

masking   Interference with the perception of a stimulus caused by the simultaneous occurrence of another stimulus. In hearing, for example, a tone becomes harder to hear if it is accompanied by white noise. The noise is said to "mask" the tone.

masochism   The deriving of (usually sexual) pleasure from pain inflicted on the self by others.

massed practice   As distinct from distributed practice, the continuous study of material to be memorized without rest periods.

maturation   The emergence of personal characteristics and behavioral phemonena through growth processes.

mature personality   A concept defined differently in different theories of, or approaches to, human personality. Usually the definition contains the criteria of reasonable adjustment, contribution to community and society, and secure satisfaction with one's accomplishments.

McCulloch effect   A visual afterimage in which the direction of viewed colored lines has an effect. (Best defined by seeing it, so see Color Plate VI.)

measurement   The assigning of numbers to things according to a set of rules.

meditation   A contemplative exercise by which a person produces a state of relaxation by focusing attention on a picture, a repeated sound or phrase or question, a mental image, etc.

meiosis   The process of forming gametes. A sequence of complex changes in a cell resulting in the formation of four cells (gametes) each with twenty-three unpaired chromosomes.

memory drum   A device for repetitively presenting verbal material to be memorized to a subject one item at a time.

memory span   The amount of material that can be retained in immediate memory, usually seven items plus or minus two.

menopause   The female "change of life" brought about by the cessation of ovarian functioning and the consequent lack of female hormones in the body.

mentalist   One who is concerned with the workings of the human mind.

method of constant stimuli   A method for determining thresholds of sensation. Several stimuli, from above and below the threshold, are presented, and the subject indicates which he can perceive. From the results, the stimulus that can just be perceived 50 percent of the time can be estimated.

method of forced choice   A psychophysical method for determining the threshold of sensation in which the observer is forced to choose one alternative on each trial.

method of limits   A psychophysical method for determining thresholds of sensation. The intensity of the stimulus is raised or lowered until the subject can just detect it or just not detect it.

mitosis   Normal cell division during growth, in which a complete duplicate set of chromosomes is transferred to each newly created cell.

mnemonics   Aids to memory, strategies for remembering.

modeling   A type of imitation in which one individual does what he sees another (the model) doing.

monaural cues   The parameters of sounds, such as their apparent intensity, that allow an individual to infer the distance of the sound using only one ear.

monocular cues   The parameters of visual stimuli that allow an individual to infer the distance of objects using only one eye.

monozygotes   Twins resulting from the fertilization of one ova; identical twins.

morphemes   Linguistic term for the units of a language that carry meaning (words, endings that indicate tenses or plurality, etc.).

motion parallax   Referring to the different directions of apparent movement of near and far objects as the head is moved.

motivated forgetting   Loss of memory for material because of a conscious or unconscious wish or reason not to remember, for example, painful memories.

Müller-Lyer illusion   An illusion of length in which two lines of equal length appear unequal because of the angles of the lines attached to their ends.

multiple determination   The doctrine that there may be several causes of a given occurrence.

nanometer (nm)   A measure of physical distance used to specify the wavelength of light. One nanometer is equal to one millimicron, or one-billionth of a meter.

national character   The characteristics that citizens of a nation are alleged to share. (For example, "All Scots are thrifty.")

nativists   A group of perceptual psychologists who place emphasis on the inherited factors determining perception rather than on experience. (See also empiricists.)

necessary cause Causes that must be present before an effect can occur. A necessary cause need not be sufficient, in and of itself, to cause the effect.

negative afterimage A visual afterimage in which the brightness relationships in the original image are reversed and in which the hues in the afterimage are complementary to the hues of the original image.

negative reinforcement Reinforcement of a response by the postponement, withdrawal, or termination of an aversive stimulus.

nerve deafness A condition in which hearing is normal if the stimulus is above a certain intensity but severely hindered if the stimulus is below that intensity. Characterized by the phenomenon of recruitment—that is, the relatively rapid gain in the perceived loudness of a tone that is increasing gradually in intensity.

nervous system The brain, spinal cord, autonomic nervous system, nerves, ganglia, and some sense organs. The nervous system receives electrical impulses from the sensory receptors, interprets them, and transmits electrical impulses to effector organs, which produce overt behavior. It also produces consciousness.

neurotic personality A personality in which the means taken to avoid anxiety interferes with or limits normal human functioning.

night blindness A condition in which vision is normal in daylight but absent in low levels of illumination, as at night.

nominal scale A scale in which the numbers attached to things serve only as names, without any meaning attached to the number itself. (For example, the numbers on the uniforms of baseball players.)

nonregulatory drives Drives such as sex, curiosity, activity, etc., which are not absolutely necessary for the survival of the individual organism.

nonsense syllable A syllable, usually of three letters (consonant–vowel–consonant), which has no meaning. (Sometimes considered useful in eliminating the influence of meaning on memorizing, but the evidence is that people memorize nonsense by giving it a meaning of their own.)

normal distribution A statistical, standard distribution; a bell-shaped curve.

norms The habitual standards of a group to which the individual members of the group tend to conform.

object constancy Knowledge that objects remain the same even when our view of them changes.

objective test A test that can be administered, scored, and evaluated by anyone who can read and follow the directions and read and recognize the correct answers.

object permanence Knowledge that objects continue to exist when out of sight. Very young children appear to believe that objects do not exist when they are out of sight.

obsessive neurosis A neurosis characterized by repetitive and unavoidable thoughts or rituals that recur in order to avoid anxiety; an obsessive neurotic must habitually, for no apparent reason, engage in some act or thought at regular intervals or on certain occasions.

Ohm's acoustic law States that we are able to perceive the individual tones in a combination of tones.

ontogeny of behavior   The process of developing behavior during the life of an organism through growth and experience, as distinct from the phylogeny of behavior, which refers to evolutionary changes in behavior over many generations of individuals.

operant aggression   Aggressive behavior that persists because of its reinforcing consquences, as distinct from aggression that is elicited by (usually painful) stimuli.

operant conditioning   Generally, the modification of behavior by its consequences. Positive reinforcement of a given behavior increases its frequency; punishment decreases its frequency. Positive reinforcement also brings the behavior under the control of the discriminative stimuli in whose presence the behavior is reinforced.

operations   In Piaget's theory, internalized actions that are reversible and that can be integrated with other actions. Roughly equivalent to way or mode of thinking.

opponent-process theory   A theory of color vision that postulates three opponent processes: one between black and white, one between red and green, and one between yellow and blue. All wavelengths of light stimulate the black-white process, which is responsible for sensations of brightness. If two complementaries, such as yellow and blue or red and green are present simultaneously, their effects counteract each other within the appropriate opponent process, and only their effects on the black-white process are seen, that is, gray.

ordinal scale   A scale in which the numbers refer only to the order of the magnitude of the things numbered without implying that there are equal intervals between the things. (For example, the rank orders of the heights of the students in a class.)

organic psychosis   A psychosis for which there is a known and clearly identifiable physiological cause, such as brain deterioration or systemic poisoning (as by lead).

orienting reaction   Reaction of attentiveness (but not startle) to novel or new stimuli. The reaction can be observed directly (as when a dog pricks up his ears), or detected by monitoring physiological processes, such as changes in certain blood vessels that change consistently when the reaction occurs.

overdetermination   Freud's notion that there may be many causes of a single event (or many meanings of a symbol), even though fewer causes (or meanings) would be sufficient. There is *over*determination in the sense that there are more causes (or meanings) than are necessary and sufficient.

overlearning   Practice that is continued beyond initial mastery of the memorized material or the skill.

paired-associate list   A list of paired items. The subject is asked to learn to respond with the second of the pair when presented with the first of the pair.

paranoid schizophrenia   The variety of the disease characterized by fears of persecution and often by delusions of grandeur.

parataxic distortion   Sullivan's term, which is applied to the behavior of a psychoanalytical patient who treats the analyst in ways that the patient once treated parents and in ways that the patient currently uses in social interactions. Similar to Freud's transference.

partial-reinforcement effect   Responses that are reinforced only on some occurrences show greater resistance to extinction than do responses that are reinforced on all occurrences.

part method   In memorizing lengthy material, the method of breaking it into parts, memorizing the parts separately, and then their order. Distinct from the whole method, in which the whole of the material is memorized from beginning to end in one piece.

Pavlovian conditioning   See respondent conditioning.

payoff matrix   A matrix whose cells display the profit or loss (reward or punishment) consequent on the outcomes defined by the rows and columns of the matrix.

periodic wave   Regularly repeating energy fluctuations such as those found in sound waves, light waves, brainwaves, etc.

phase   The degree to which two or more periodic waves are in synchrony with each other.

phenotype   (1) The characteristics that are manfested by an organism. (2) An organism or organisms manifesting a particular phenotype. (See also genotype.)

phi movement   A form of apparent movement in which two or more successively illuminated lights create the illusion of movement.

phobia   Intense and irrational fear of some specific object or situation.

phonemes   Linguistic term for the smallest units of speech (basic sounds) of a language.

phonological rules   The rules governing the actual sound system of a language. (For example, the rule specifying when the final "s" in a plural English word is pronounced as "s" or "z.")

phonology   The study of the sounds of a spoken language.

photopigment   The substance in a photoreceptor (rod or cone) that absorbs light energy and, by changing chemically, stimulates electrical activity in the optic nerve.

photoreceptors   The rods and cones of the retina, which are sensitive to light.

phylogeny of behavior   The evolutionary development of behavior patterns in a species over the course of several generations; the Darwinian natural selection of behavior patterns.

place theory of pitch perception   The physical frequency of a sound wave is coded by the place of stimulation along the organ of Corti to produce sensations that differ in pitch. Different frequencies maximally stimulate different places; stimulation in different places leads us to hear different pitches.

plasticity   Modifiability.

positive afterimage   A short-term (about 0.5 second) visual afterimage in which the brightnesses and hues of the original image are maintained.

Prägnanz, law of   A gestalt law of perceptual organization emphasizing the wholeness and meaningfulness of percepts.

prefrontal lobotomy   A surgical separation of the prefrontal lobes of the brain from the rest of the brain. Performed in certain cases of psychosis; it is much less used than formerly because of undesirable side effects.

prejudice   The usually incorrect prejudgment of an individual's characteristics because of his membership in some race or group.

Premack principle A principle of motivation stating that an animal will emit a response of low probability in order to gain the opportunity to engage in behavior that is currently of a high probability. (For example, a food-deprived rat will run in a wheel to obtain food; food is a reinforcer for wheel running: an activity-deprived rat will eat in order to gain the opportunity to run in a wheel; running is a reinforcer for eating.) In general, what behavior will be reinforced by the opportunity to engage in what other behavior depends on the relative frequency with which the animal would engage in the two behaviors at the moment.

primacy effect The initial items in a list tend to be memorized more easily than middle items in the list. (See also recency effect.)

principle of proximity See *proximity, principle of*.

principle of similarity See *similarity, principle of*.

prisoners' dilemma game A social psychological game in which the best outcome for each player comes from cooperation, but in which cooperation does not occur for lack of trust of the other player.

probability, laws of Given randomness, as in the throw of an unbiased set of dice, a set of rules for specifying the average number of times that a given outcome would be expected to occur solely by chance in a sequence of, say, one hundred trials.

projection A Freudian defense mechanism in which the unconscious feelings of an individual are attributed to other people (projected onto them).

projective tests Psychological tests in which the subject tells a story about such ambiguous material as an ink-blot, a cartoon, or an ill-defined photograph. The subject is presumed in his story to project some of his own personality onto the characters or the ambiguous material. (See also thematic apperception test).

proximal stimulus The image of an object that we actually see, as distinct from what is "really out there." (See also distal stimulus.)

proximity, principle of One of the gestalt laws of perceptual organization, which states that objects that are close together tend to be perceived as belonging together.

pseudoconditioning Apparent respondent conditioning that is in fact owing to causes other than the pairing of the CS with the US.

psychodrama A technique originated by Moreno in which people play-act at being other people for purposes of psychological diagnosis or psychotherapy. Especially useful in family therapy, where children play the parents, and vice versa, and reveal in their acts what they think the thinking of the other generation to be.

psychological tests Any of a wide variety of tests, questionnaires, inventories, activities, etc., devised for measuring or judging a person's psychological characteristics.

psychopath A personality who appears not to distinguish right from wrong and who feels no guilt over wrong behavior.

psychophysics The science of the relationship between parameters of physical stimuli and our qualitative and quantitative sensations evoked by them.

psychosexual stages In Freud's theory of personality, the stages of psychological development: the oral, anal, Oedipal, latency, and genital.

punishment In conditioning, the delivery (after a response) of an aversive stimulus that has the effect of reducing the probability of that response.

Purkinje effect The shift in relative visibility from long to shorter wavelengths of light under conditions of reduced illumination, as during the evening hours, first described by Purkinje.

quanta The basic, irreducible units of light energy.

ratio estimation A technique of psychophysical scaling in which the observer is asked to estimate the ratio between two psychological magnitudes, such as the loudness caused by two different levels of sound intensity.

ratio production A method of psychophysical scaling in which the observer is asked to adjust the intensity of one stimulus so that the psychological sensation caused by it is in a certain ratio to the sensation caused by a different physical intensity.

ratio scale A scale with a nonarbitrary zero point on which there are not only equal intervals but also equal ratios.

rational psychotherapy Originated by A. Ellis, who decided to try to treat the symptoms of disturbed patients without bothering with the root, psychodynamic causes. This was a forerunner of behavior therapy, which takes largely the same approach.

rationalization In Freudian theory, the defense mechanism of making up rational reasons for behavior that is in fact motivated (usually unconsciously) by other reasons.

reaction formation In Freudian theory, the defense mechanism against anxiety in which the exact opposite of the true, but unconscious, wish or feeling is actually experienced.

recall Remembering without explicit assistance.

recency effect The last few items in a list are memorized first, before the first and middle items, apparently because they are the most recent after reading through the list. (See also primacy effect.)

recessive allele The one of the pair of genes that does not find phenotypic expression, but which may nevertheless be passed on to offspring.

recognition Remembering that an encountered item has been encountered before.

reconstruction Bartlett proposed that much of memory is reconstruction—the describing, in terms of how they must have been, of past events that are really not completely recalled. The reconstruction is based on what little can actually be clearly remembered and on our expectations, past experiences, and prejudices.

recovery of function The return of a capacity following its elimination by brain damage. For example, strokes in the frontal region of the brain often severely disturb speech, but speech may largely recover in the course of time.

regression In Freudian theory, returning under stress to modes of functioning appropriate to infancy or early childhood.

reinforcement The process of following a response with a reinforcing stimulus with the result that the frequency of occurrence of the response increases.

reinforcement hierarchy See Premack principle.

releaser See sign stimulus

reliable test A test that gives the same answer on each administration.

repetition compulsion Freud's term for a patient's need to repeat with his analyst the emotional essence of his childhood Oedipal relationship with his parents.

repression In Freud's theory, a defense mechanism in which the ego refuses to admit to consciousness any hint of anxiety-arousing wishes or feelings.

resistance   Freud's term for the reluctance, often unconscious, of the patient to provide information during therapy.

resistance to extinction   In operant conditioning, the persistence of behavior after the discontinuation of reinforcement; in respondent conditioning, the persistence of the CR after the US is no longer presented with the CS.

respondent   The response in an innate or conditioned reflex; the UR or CR.

respondent conditioning   The process in which a previously ineffective stimulus (the conditioned stimulus, CS) comes to elicit a response after having been paired with an unconditioned stimulus that innately elicits the response. (For example, food in the mouth naturally elicits salivation. If a tone is paired with food in the mouth many times, the tone will come to elicit salivation.)

retention   The remembering of memorized material.

retinal stimulus   The pattern of light energy reaching the eye.

rigidity   The tendency to persist in a belief or course of action without being open to change.

risky-shift   The social psychological phenomenon in which a group of people agrees on a more risky course of action than did any of the members of the group privately. After the group decision, the individual members continue to select somewhat riskier alternatives individually. (See also groupthink.)

rods   Photoreceptors in the retina of the eye that respond to very low levels of illumination but which do not produce the perception of color.

role   The behaviors that one is supposed and is expected to exhibit because of his position in a group or groups.

sadism   The achievement of (usually sexual) pleasure from inflicting pain on someone else, or from seeing pain inflicted on someone.

sampling   The selection of a group that is representative of the whole population so that their answers to questions will represent those of the population.

saturation   The concentration of color; the degree to which a hue differs from gray.

scaling   Determining exactly the changes in sensation that occur with changes in the physical stimulus.

schedule of reinforcement   A rule for determining which among many occurrences of a response will be reinforced. (See also fixed-interval, variable-interval, fixed-ratio, and variable-ratio.)

schemata   Piaget's term for the mental structures that make up our understanding of the world.

schizophrenia   A variety of serious psychoses having in common a lack of contact with reality. (See also simple, hebephrenic, catatonic, and paranoid schizophrenia.)

schizophrenogenic environments   Environments that facilitate the development of schizophrenia.

schizophrenogenic mother   The type of mother (or caretaker) having personality characteristics that facilitate the development of schizophrenia.

secondary gain   Ways of acting that are originally designed to avoid anxiety may have beneficial consequences in their own right, that is, they provide a secondary gain for the individual.

secondary sex characteristics   Bodily changes that occur during puberty specific to the sexes but not necessary for reproduction; for example, differential growth of body hair, change in the male voice, etc.

selection gain   In selective-breeding experiments, the amount of difference between (a) the average on some characteristic of the offspring of parents selected as being high in their group on that characteristic and (b) the average of the whole group of parents.

self-actualization   Maslow's term for the highest of motives, which comes into play only when all the other motives are satisfied. Self-actualization leads a person to serve humanity as well as to develop his own potentialities to their fullest possible extent.

self-theory   A theory of personality developed by Rogers and others that puts emphasis on complete self-knowledge and self-acceptance.

semantic differential   Osgood's technique for quantifying the dimensions of meaning. After subjects rated the meaning of a variety of words on a number of adjective pairs, factor analysis showed that only three dimensions accounted for most of the variation in their ratings. The dimensions are: potency, evaluation, and activity. Osgood proposed these as the dimensions of meaning.

semantic rules   Rules determining which words can be used meaningfully in a particular syntactical position in a sentence.

semantics   The study of meaning.

sensation   An organism's subjective response to stimulation.

sensorimotor stage   Piaget's term for the first stage of intellectual development, in which the infant has only sensorimotor interactions with his world.

sensory contrast   The alteration of the appearance of one visual stimulus by the simultaneous or successive presentation of a second visual stimulus.

sensory transduction   The process whereby a receptor turns physical energy from the environment into electrical energy in the nervous system.

separation anxiety   (1) In general, anxiety generated by the imminent departure of the self or others. (2) In particular, anxiety aroused by the approaching end of psychoanalysis.

serial lists   Any lists that are to be memorized in order.

set   A predisposition to proceed in a certain way or according to a certain plan.

shape constancy   The phenomenon that causes objects to seem to maintain their shape despite changes in the angle at which we look at them.

shaping   A technique in operant conditioning in which reinforcement is used to mold desired behavior by reinforcing successively closer approximations to it.

short-term memory (STM)   The ability of an individual to hold several items of information in his memory for about twenty seconds or so even if he is not allowed to rehearse or repeat them.

signal-detection theory   A mathematical theory of the relationship between "misses" and "false alarms" in detection tasks. It is especially applicable to the measurement of the absolute and differential thresholds.

sign language   Language in which visible signs replace words.

sign stimulus   An aspect of the environment that innately elicits complex instinctive behavior patterns from the members of a given species. Also called a "releaser," the sign stimulus is said to "release" a given behavior.

similarity, principle of   A gestalt law of perceptual organization: similar items in a group are seen as belonging together.

simple schizophrenia   The variety of the disease in which the simple lack of contact with reality, infantile behavior, and inactivity are the chief symptoms.

simultaneous conditioning   Respondent conditioning in which the US follows the onset of the CS within 0.5 seconds.

simultaneous contrast   Alteration of the appearance of a visual stimulus by the simultaneous presentation of another visual stimulus.

size constancy   The phenomenon that individuals and other familiar objects appear to be of about the same size regardless of their distance from the observer and hence a difference in the size of the retinal image (within limits).

social comparison theory   The theory that many judgments about ourselves, especially under stressful conditions, cannot be made without comparing ourselves with others.

sociopathic disorders   Another name for the psychopathic disorders.

species-specific behavior   Behavior that is characteristic of all normal members of a given species.

species-specific defense reaction   The response to threat or pain that is characteristic of a species. In avoidance conditioning, it is easier to reinforce negatively such natural responses than to reinforce responses with which the natural ones may interfere.

specific hungers   An organism's tendency to select foods that are rich in needed nutrients. Now believed to be at least partly determined by an aversion to habitually deficient foods.

split-halves technique   A technique for assessing the reliability of a test. The test is so constructed that when the performance of a group of subjects on each half of the test is compared, a reliable test produces the same score for each subject on each half.

spontaneous recovery   A phenomenon occurring in both respondent and operant conditioning in which the tendency to respond during extinction temporarily increases after a pause in the procedure or at the start of the next daily session of extinction.

spontaneous remission   Recovery from mental illness without any specific therapeutic intervention.

standardized test   A test for which the distribution of scores in the general population is known with reasonable accuracy.

statistical analysis   In general, a set of techniques for estimating how many times out of one hundred the obtained result would be expected on the basis of chance alone.

statistical inference   A set of techniques that allows us to judge how confident we may be that a given difference between two groups (or a correlation between two sets of scores) has occurred because of nonchance factors. (See also statistical analysis.)

statistical method of prediction or assessment   As distinct from the clinical or intuitive method, prediction or assessment based on the numerical results of statistical analysis.

status   An individual's position in society in relation to others.

stereotype   A fixed and rigid (usually incorrect) idea of what a person will be like based on what is believed to be true of the members of a group to which the person belongs.

stimulus   In general, an occurrence that has some effect on some organism. There are many different specific meanings. (See specific types of stimuli: for example, sign stimulus, discriminative stimulus, etc.)

stimulus object   The distal stimulus.

stimulus satiation   A technique for lowering the value of a stimulus for a subject by providing the subject with an overabundance of such stimuli.

structuralism   The school of psychology that searches introspectively for the components of sensation and their combinations in the structure of conscious experience.

sublimation   In Freud's theory, a mechanism in which the aim of the libido is altered. (For example, Freud felt that an interest in sculpting could be traced to sublimation of the anal libido which was, in infancy, invested in playing with feces.)

successive contrast   Alteration of the appearance of a visual stimulus by the presentation of another stimulus either before or after it.

sufficient cause   An event that is sufficient to cause another event. Sufficient causes may not be necessary causes, since other causes may work equally well.

superego   A main sector of the personality that is only partially conscious and that shapes the personality by representing parental values and the rules of society; conscience.

supernormal stimulus   A sign stimulus that is of greater magnitude in the sign-related property than a normal stimulus and so evokes an even stronger instinctive reaction than that evoked by a normally occurring sign stimulus.

surface structure   Linguistic term for the arrangement of words in an utterance, as distinct from deep structure, which is a description of the grammatical structure underlying the utterance. (See also deep structure.)

symptom substitution   The psychoanalytic notion that if a neurotic symptom ceases to occur without the resolution of its underlying and unconscious causes, a new, substitute symptom may arise to take its place. (Strongly challenged by behavior modifiers who treat only symptoms and report no symptom substitution.)

syntactic rules   Rules governing the permissible ordering and placement of words in a grammatical sentence.

syntax   (1) The way in which words are assembled into phrases and sentences. (2) The study of the rules of grammar.

systematic desensitization   A technique of behavior therapy in which a patient is gradually introduced to increasingly fear-arousing stimuli in such a way that his fear of them all gradually extinguishes.

tact   Skinner's name (from "contact") for verbal responses that are the names of things.

telegraphic speech   The simple, brief sentences of children, which do not have the grammatical embellishments of educated adult speech. Children's sentences can, however, be said to have a grammar of their own.

temporal conditioning   Respondent conditioning in which the regular temporal interval between US presentations becomes a CS, without any environmental CS being presented.

textual   Skinner's term for verbal behavior that is a response to other verbal behavior in another medium. Examples are reading words aloud from a printed page and playing the piano from sheet music.

textural-density gradients   A cue to visual depth described by Gibson. The basic idea is that the density of a scene increases with distance from the observer because objects become apparently smaller and closer together.

thematic apperception test (TAT)   A test developed by Murray and his associates in which the subject writes stories about a dozen ambiguous photographs. The stories are scored, by complex but objective and reliable procedures, for the degree to which they reflect the subject's motives, such as his need for achievement or for power. The idea is that the subject will reveal something of his deeper motives in the stories he tells about the ambiguous pictures.

thought   The activity that goes on in our heads when we think. Thought itself is not describable in words, but any thought can usually be expressed in words, or in symbols.

three-term contingency   An interrelationship among three factors: a response that is followed by reinforcement in the presence of a discriminative stimulus tends to recur in the presence of that discriminative stimulus.

token economy   A minieconomy in a school or mental hospital in which tokens, which can be exchanged for valued rewards such as candy, private living quarters, or radios, are used as conditioned reinforcers of desirable behavior.

trace conditioning   Respondent conditioning in which the US follows the termination of the CS by more than 5 seconds.

transcendent function   Jung's concept of a person's rising above strictly instinctual pursuits to higher levels of motivation. He saw the instinctual energy (libido) as transubstantiated, whereas Freud saw the nearly equivalent mechanism of sublimation as not changing the basically sexual nature of the libidinal energy.

transference   The goal of psychoanalysis, in which the patient transfers to the therapist his earlier modes of emotional involvement with parents and then works through them, thereby alleviating his neurotic tendencies.

transfer of training   The process by which the learning of one thing facilitates or inhibits future learning or facilitates or inhibits the recall of previously learned material.

transformational generative grammar   A set of rules for generating only (but all) grammatical sentences of a language. The rules specify ever finer transformations of underlying grammatical structures. (See also deep structure.)

traveling wave   The disturbance set up on the basilar membrane by a sound wave transmitted across the oval window and into the inner ear. This wave stimulates the auditory receptors within the organ of Corti, which are the actual sensory cells of audition.

unconditioned response (UR)   The response that is innately elicited by the unconditioned stimulus; a respondent.

unconditioned stimulus (US)   The stimulus that innately elicits a reflexive response.

unconscious   That part of any person's mind that, though real and effective in directing behavior, is not directly known to the person.

vacuum activity   Instinctive behavior patterns that occur under conditions of high drive in the absence of the sign stimuli that usually are necessary for their release.

valid test   A test that measures what it is supposed to measure.

variable-interval (VI) schedule of reinforcement   A schedule (1) that specifies that the first response occurring after a period of time has elapsed since the last reinforced response will be reinforced, and (2) that varies the interval between reinforcements. The schedule is usually summarized by the average length of the interval.

variable-ratio (VR) schedule of reinforcement   A schedule that specifies (1) that the first response occurring after a number of responses have occurred since the last reinforced response will be reinforced, and (2) that varies the number of responses between reinforcements. The schedule can be summarized by the average of the numbers.

ventral noradrenergic bundle   A tract of nerve fibers that runs by the ventral hypothalamus in the brain and is believed to play a role in the regulation of hunger.

verbal behavior   (1) The use of words. (2) Term used by Skinner to refer to any behavior that requires the intervention of another organism for its reinforcement, such as speech, writing, facial expressions, etc.

vicious circle   Interlinking of causal variables such that the negative outcome of an event produces the cause for another negative outcome, etc. (Interpersonal aggression is often a vicious circle: attack leads to reprisal which leads to further attack and further reprisal.)

volley theory of pitch perception   The theory that the frequency of vibration of the physical stimulus is encoded as the frequency of nervous discharge in the auditory nerve. Because no single nerve can fire frequently enough to duplicate the higher frequencies that we can hear, it is proposed that (1) several nerves take turns in firing volleys to the brain, and (2) the brain then adds together the volleys from the different nerves in determining the total frequency.

voyeurism   The taking of pleasure (usually sexual) from observing the activities (usually sexual) or bodies of others.

wave patterns   Used to describe the general appearance of graphical recordings of periodic waves. (In the EEG, the relaxed person's alpha-wave pattern is described as "slow with high amplitude," and the beta waves of the alert person are described as "fast with low amplitude.")

Weber-Fechner law   Same as Fechner's law.

Weber's law   The amount of increment in physical stimulus needed to produce a "just noticeable difference" is proportional to the magnitude of the initial stimulus.

white noise   An acoustical stimulus composed of all audible frequencies at the same intensity with random phase relations between them; it sounds like "shhhhhhhhhhhhh."

whole method   The method of memorizing material as a whole, without breaking it into parts to be memorized separately.

Whorf's theory   The notion that perception is limited by language in that differences for which the individual does not have a name or other linguistic category may not ordinarily be perceived. That is, they can be sensed, but they are not perceived because they do not, and never have, made a difference for the individual.

Young-Helmholtz theory (of color vision)   This theory postulates that there are three types of color receptors—one for each of the three primary colors, red, green, and blue—and that various combinations of excitation of these receptors result in the perception of the color that mixtures of the three primary colors produce.

zygote   The single cell from which the entire organism develops; formed by the merger of a sperm and an ovum at conception.

INDEX OF NAMES

TOPICAL INDEX